Man, State, and Society in Contemporary Southeast Asia

MAN, STATE, AND SOCIETY

Other books in the series include:

Man, State, and Society in East European History (1970)
Stephen Fischer-Galati, Ed.

Man, State, and Society in the Contemporary Middle East (1970)
Jacob M. Landau, Ed.

Man, State, and Society in the Soviet Union (1970)
Joseph L. Nogee, Ed.

Man, State, and Society in Contemporary North Africa (1970)
I. William Zartman, Ed.

Man, State, and Society in Communist China (1971)
Allan B. Cole, Ed.

Man, State, and Society in Contemporary Tropical Africa (1971)
Robert A. Lystad, Ed.

Man, State, and Society in Southeast Asian History (1971)
John K. Whitmore and Michael Vickery, Eds.

Man, State, and Society in Contemporary Southeast Asia

EDITED BY

Robert O. Tilman

PRAEGER PUBLISHERS

New York • Washington • London

PRAEGER PUBLISHERS
111 Fourth Avenue, New York, N.Y. 10003, U.S.A.
5, Cromwell Place, London S.W.7, England

Published in the United States of America in 1969
by Praeger Publishers, Inc.

© 1969 by Praeger Publishers, Inc.

Library of Congress Catalog Card Number: 68–16095

Printed in the United States of America

CONTENTS

PREFACE   xiii

ACKNOWLEDGMENTS   xvii

1. Introduction   3

PART ONE: THE SETTING

2. The Structure of Southeast Asian History: Some Preliminary
   Observations   *Harry J. Benda*   23
3. Cultural Continuities and Discontinuities in Southeast Asia
                                                       Lauriston Sharp   45
4. Southeast Asia: The Balkans of the Orient? A Study in Continuity and Change   *Charles A. Fisher*   55
5. The "Million City" in Southeast Asia   *D. W. Fryer*   72
6. The Countryside and the Jungle   *W. R. Geddes*   88

PART TWO: TRADITION, MODERNITY, AND SOCIAL CHANGE

The Interaction of Tradition and Modernity

7. Burmese Buddhism in Everyday Life   *Manning Nash*   103
8. Islam and Politics in Indonesia   *Rosihan Anwar*   115
9. Modern Medicine and Traditional Culture: Confrontation on
   the Malay Peninsula   *Robert J. Wolff* 132
10. Western Culture and the Thai Way of Life
                                                      Michael Moerman   145
11. Problems of Management and Authority in a Transitional So-
    ciety: A Case Study of a Javanese Factory
                                                     Ann Ruth Willner   162
12. Mysticism in Indonesian Politics   *Mochtar Lubis*   179

Education and Social Change

13. The University Student in South and Southeast Asia
                                    Joseph Fischer   187
14. Modernization in a Muslim Society: The Indonesian Case
                                    Clifford Geertz   201
15. The "Clerk Mentality" in Burmese Education
                                    James F. Guyot   212
16. Education and Political Development in Malaysia
                                    Robert O. Tilman 228

PART THREE: POLITICS: IDEOLOGY, IDENTITY, AND
POLITICAL ORGANIZATION

The Meaning of Nationhood and National Identity

17. Paradoxes of Asian Nationalism   *Rupert Emerson*   247
18. Reflections on Asian Communism   *Harry J. Benda*   259
19. The Birth of *Pantja Sila*   *Sukarno*   270
20. A Nationalist Awakening   *A Young Lao Official*   277

The Structures and Organizations of Politics

21. The Political Role of the Army in Indonesia
                                    Daniel S. Lev   287
22. GESTAPU in Indonesia   *Justus M. Van der Kroef*   303
23. The Military in Thai Politics   *David A. Wilson*   326
24. The Role of the Military in Development Planning: Burma
                                    Louis J. Walinsky 340
25. Religion and Politics in Malaya   *K. J. Ratnam*   351
26. Politics in the Philippines   *Carl H. Landé*   362
27. North Vietnam: A Profile   *Bernard B. Fall*   382

Leaders

28. Prince Norodom Sihanouk of Cambodia
                                    Roger M. Smith   393
29. Sukarno and History   *Bernhard Dahm*   403
30. Ho Chi Minh, Like It or Not   *Bernard B. Fall*   412

PART FOUR: INTERNAL AND INTERNATIONAL INTEGRATION

Internal: The Problem of Ethnic Diversity

31. The Chinese in Southeast Asia: A Longer View
                                    Maurice Freedman 431

32. The Overseas Indian in Southeast Asia: Burma, Malaysia, and
    Singapore   *R. Hatley*   450

Internal: The Problem of Geographic Diversity

33. The End of the Indonesian Rebellion
                               Herbert Feith and Daniel S. Lev   467
34. Development and Mobility Among the Phu Thai of Northeast
    Thailand   *A. Thomas Kirsch*   481
35. Malaysia and Singapore: The Failure of a Federation
                                         Robert O. Tilman   490

International Relations and Organization

36. Regionalism in Southeast Asia   *Bernard K. Gordon*   506

PART FIVE: THE QUEST FOR ECONOMIC PROGRESS

37. Cultural Value and Economic Change in Burma
                                            Mya Maung   527
38. Value Systems and Economic Development in Japan and Thai-
    land   *Eliezer B. Ayal*   535
39. Kinship and Commerce in a Thai-Lue Village
                                       Michael Moerman   550
40. Economic Progress in Southeast Asia   *Douglas S. Paauw*   556

APPENDIX A: A Statistical Summary of Contemporary Southeast
    Asia   585

APPENDIX B: Maps   592

CONTEMPORARY SOUTHEAST ASIA: AN INTRODUCTORY BIBLIOGRAPHI-
    CAL GUIDE   599

INDEX   619

CONTRIBUTORS   633

TABLES

1. Government and Government-aided Schools, FMS, 1896–1936   230
2. Channels of Recruitment, MCS Officers, 1962 (by percentages)   233
3. Cabinet Members and Alliance Party Officers: Major Language of Education, 1962   234
4. Government Schools, Government-aided Schools, and Enrollments, FMS, 1921   234
5. Literacy Rates, Ten Years of Age and Older, Among Males, 1957   242
6. Estimated Dates of Restoring Prewar Output Levels   560
7. Southeast Asia: Estimated Annual Rates of Growth of Real Product   561
8. ECAFE Estimates of Average Annual Rates of Growth in Real Aggregate and Per Capita Product, 1950–59: ECAFE Countries   562
9. Ratio of New Growth to Rehabilitation, 1946–60   564
10. Estimated Average Rates of Gross Fixed Capital Formation, 1950 Decade   566
11. Ratio of Exports to Gross Domestic Product, 1938 and 1957–59   569
12. Indexes of Export Volumes (1953 = 100)   571
13. Southeast Asia: Area and Population, 1966   586
14. Asia: Rank Ordering by Ten Indexes of Development   587
15. Southeast Asia: Summary of Economic Data, 1966–67   588
16. Southeast Asia: Education Summary   589–90
17. Overseas Chinese in Southeast Asia   591

FIGURES

1. Structures   219
2. Motivation and Performance   225
3. Total Import-Export Trade, Singapore–Federation of Malaya, 1961–65   492
4. Malaysian Airways Operations, 1960–65   495
5. Singapore Airport Passengers: Departures to, and Arrivals from, Points in Malaya, 1961–65   496
6. Malayan Mail Received and Dispatched, Singapore Airport, 1961–65   497
7. Growth and Export Volumes   571
8. Sectoral Shares, 1950–52 to 1958–60   576

PREFACE

With the world in the midst of an information explosion, perhaps it is old-fashioned to begin by trying to justify any kind of new publication. I am, however, burdened by the personal conviction that any compilation composed largely of previously published essays should, in principle, be viewed with some suspicion and that the one-author, one-book formula is the best, other things being equal. Thus, as the editor of another collection of readings, I feel that my first task must be to convince my readers that this particular volume has its *raison d'être*. Happily, this task is easier for modern Southeast Asia than for most areas of the world, as any professor is aware who has tried to collect a set of background readings for a course on the subject. For Southeast Asia, a considerable amount of monographic literature is available—less than for East and South Asia but, nevertheless, more than might be expected—but there are few good general studies giving at least minimal attention to a survey of issues and problems concerning man and his relation to his political and social environment in more than a single country.

This gap in our scholarship is not accidental. The fact is that in Southeast Asia "other things" are not equal, which was the one caveat I added earlier. Given the diversity of Southeast Asia (which is the theme of Part One of this volume and is apparent throughout), there are few, if any, Southeast Asia scholars today who are qualified, willing, or able to generalize about the area as a whole. In part this is so because Southeast Asia, by its very nature, does not easily lend itself to meaningful generalizations, and in part it is true because the task of becoming familiar with all nine countries of the area is so formidable that, to the present time, few scholars have accomplished it. Until such time as we have the really broad-gauge scholar of modern Southeast Asia, the best substitute may be a structured collection of contributions by many authors, each dealing with his own specialty in the country with which he is most familiar. Most of the essays in this volume have been published elsewhere, and, thus, the reader could have drawn most of this material together on his own. However, in first scanning the available writings, selecting and editing the most relevant, and presenting this material in a structured and convenient format, I hope that the finished product will prove to justify its existence.

I should warn the reader at this point that, while every state receives attention in at least one essay, I have made no conscious attempt in the selection of articles to achieve a national balance. The first two priorities were quality and relevance; distribution ran a very poor third. It will also be apparent that some of the essays reprinted here are out of date in terms of terminology, political boundaries, etc. These were included, however, because the analysis is still relevant, even if the information is not entirely current.

In a volume such as this, I am most indebted to the individual authors, for without their contributions this collection could not exist. I was also totally dependent on the various publishers for permission to reprint these essays, and I have acknowledged my appreciation to them in a special section as well as in a footnote appended to each essay.

For three consecutive years, students of my graduate seminar on modern Southeast Asian politics at Yale willingly served as guinea pigs by reading and discussing essays in this collection (and many more besides). Their critical comments, as well as their helpful suggestions for additions and deletions, were earnestly solicited and gratefully received. Happily, Yale graduate students are both able and responsible, and thus their opinions must always be weighed carefully. In this case, their criticisms often created more work for the editor, but, in the end, it also made my task easier. Finally, I am indebted to my many colleagues and friends throughout the world who supplied me with suggestions, as well as citations and reprints. All of these I consulted carefully, but in the end many could not be used in this collection. Publishers and readers being what they are, many excellent articles had to be cut from my syllabus at various stages, but the more serious student will find most of these cited in one of the two appended lists of "Suggestions for Further Reading."

With apologies to my many friends who are accomplished in Southeast Asian linguistics, I must point out that I have tried to achieve consistency in foreign-language spellings, sometimes at the expense of linguistic accuracy. Where various authors chose different spellings for the same terms, I have somewhat arbitrarily selected one style and retained it throughout the volume. The single exception occurs in the case of Bahasa Indonesia and Bahasa Melayu. Although the terms or names may be the same, where the context requires it, I have used differing Malay or Indonesian spellings. Chiefly this involves the "dj" (Indonesian) and the "j" (Malay), the "j" (Indonesian) and the "y" (Malay), and, less consistently, the "oe" (Indonesian) and the "u" (Malay).

ACKNOWLEDGMENTS

Although an appropriate acknowledgment has been given in each essay, I should like to emphasize my indebtedness and appreciation to the following publishers for granting me permission to reprint copyrighted material:

American Anthropology, Asia, Asian Survey, China Society (London), *Esquire, Ethnology,* The Free Press (a Division of The Macmillan Company), *Geographical Review, Geography* (Sheffield, England), *Human Organization,* International Textbook Company, *The Journal of Asian Studies* (formerly the *Far Eastern Quarterly*), *Journal of Social Issues, Journal of Southeast Asian History* (University of Singapore), *Minerva* (London), *Orbis,* Oxford University Press, *Pacific Affairs* (Vancouver), *The Philippine Economic Journal* (University of the Philippines), Princeton University Press, *Problems of Communism, Quest,* The RAND Corporation, the Research Analysis Corporation, The Republic of Indonesia, *Solidarity* (Manila), l'Université Libre de Bruxelles (Brussels), *World Politics, Yale Review,* and the Yale University Southeast Asia Studies.

In addition to these previously published essays, five substantive chapters of this volume appear here for the first time in print. I am indebted to their authors (Rosihan Anwar, Bernhard Dahm, Bernard K. Gordon, R. Hatley, and K. J. Ratnam) for permission to use this material. The papers by Anwar and Ratnam were first presented at the Twenty-seventh International Congress of Orientalists (University of Michigan, August, 1967). Dahm's paper was prepared for the 1968 Annual Meeting of the Association for Asian Studies (Philadelphia, March, 1968). Gordon's essay is a much abbreviated and edited version of an unpublished report prepared for a research project at the School of Advanced International Studies, The Johns Hopkins University. Hatley's paper was originally prepared for a seminar on the political and social problems of modern Southeast Asia held at Yale University in the spring of 1967.

Man, State,
and Society
in Contemporary
Southeast Asia

1

INTRODUCTION

THE AREA AND ITS PEOPLE

Despite its currency today, "Southeast Asia" is a term of rather recent origin. In the past, it was occasionally employed by scholars, merchants, or travelers (sometimes as two words; sometimes hyphenated), but it did not gain general acceptance until World War II.[1] Even at the present time, not all specialists agree on the area's exact borders, though almost all now accept at least a common core of countries as part of Southeast Asia. In American usage, Southeast Asia is usually taken to include the nine mainland and insular countries of the south-central-Asiatic crescent (which stretches from Japan to Suez), beginning with the Philippines in the northeast and Western New Guinea (Indonesia) in the southeast and extending arclike through Burma at the extreme northwest of the area. Thus, the nine

[1] "Southeastern Asia" first appeared as a subheading under "Asia" in the *International Index* in volume VII (1934–37) but did not gain a place in the *Readers' Guide to Periodical Literature* until volume XIII (1941–43). It seems likely that the real impetus for the popular acceptance of "Southeast Asia" as a geographical entity came with the creation of the Allied Powers' South-East Asia Command (SEAC) in 1943.

3

countries with which we are concerned in this volume are the Philippines
and Indonesia (both insular), Singapore (insular but linked to the mainland by a man-made causeway), Malaysia (both insular and mainland),
and Thailand, Laos, Cambodia, Vietnam, and Burma (all mainland). Europeans will sometimes add Ceylon and possibly Taiwan to this group and
occasionally even India, Pakistan, and the Himalayan kingdoms. (In American usage, this latter combination of South and Southeast Asian states is
often referred to as "Southern Asia"—a useful shorthand term but one that
makes little geographical sense.)

Southeast Asia may seem to be a residual category of miscellaneous
countries left over after scholars and politicians had staked out East Asia
(dominated by China and Japan) and South Asia (dominated by India),
and, indeed, Southeast Asia specialists have expended much energy merely
trying to defend the integrity of the area. The fact is that the area is not
self-evidently a natural unit, and it did come into existence more by default than by design. Thus, it is not surprising that it is characterized more
by its diversity than by its homogeneity. This is not to say that there are
no problems, issues, or practices common to the area as a whole, for indeed
there are; however, few of these are unique to Southeast Asia. Moreover,
while most social, geographical, economic, and political characteristics are
shared by several states, few are common to all, and, finally, within each
state and throughout the area as a whole, it is usually easier and often
more meaningful to point out dissimilarities than similarities. This heterogeneity is so crucial in contemporary Southeast Asia that policy-makers and
scholars alike can ignore it only at great risk.

Geography and Demography

With numerous exceptions, Southeast Asia is characterized by forests,
hills, relatively long but narrow rivers, and low population densities.[2] About
60 per cent of the total land area of 1.75 million square miles is covered
with forests of various kinds, ranging from the scarce but difficult-to-extract
hardwoods of the tropical rain forests to the commercially more exploitable
monsoon forests of Burma, Thailand, and Indochina.[3] Although the terrain
can only be described as mountainous, there are few ranges, except in West
Irian, that are high by Asiatic standards, and there are few soaring peaks
to break the hilly relief of the countryside. One of the highest mountains
of Southeast Asia, Mount Kinabalu in Sabah (13,452 feet), is uncharacteristic and stands out almost as much as does Fuji-san in Japan.[4] The river
valleys, which tend to be numerous but narrow, are separated by forbid-

[2] Several useful geographies of Southeast Asia are available. For a statistical summary
of important data, from which many of the figures used here have been derived, see
the Appendix.

[3] A convenient shorthand term for the present states of Cambodia, Laos, North Vietnam, and South Vietnam.

[4] Mount Kinabalu is not the highest mountain in Southeast Asia. It is exceeded by
several peaks in West Irian, but the mountains of New Guinea form a high range and,
thus, do not stand out as dramatically.

ding terrain that makes lateral surface communications difficult and often impossible to achieve.

Population densities vary greatly throughout Southeast Asia. The island of Java averages about 950 people per square mile, with considerably higher rates in certain areas. Even higher densities are to be found in Singapore (about 8,500 per square mile for the island as a whole), though the unique city-state nature of Singapore diminishes the value of any comparisons. In contrast to these high densities, Sarawak and Sabah average only 18 people per square mile, and, in one-third of the state, the density is less than 3 per square mile. Throughout Southeast Asia, the average population density in 1958 was about 125 people per square mile, a figure that compares favorably to Fisher's figures of 305 for India, 350 for China, and 610 for Japan.[5]

The major population problem facing Southeast Asia today is not density but annual growth. During the colonial period, measures of modern hygiene and disease control were introduced, together with rudimentary improvements in prenatal and postnatal medical care, and these innovations have been accepted and expanded by most of the indigenous governments since independence. As a result, infant mortality rates declined perceptibly. and life expectancy increased. There was no corresponding decline in the birth rate, however, with the result that the population of almost every state of Southeast Asia (Singapore is the major exception) now grows at an annual adjusted rate of at least 3 per cent. This fact has two major implications. First, the total Gross National Product (GNP) must grow by at least 3 per cent annually merely to maintain the per-capita GNP. Second, an annual population growth of 3 per cent produces far more spectacular totals in a relatively short time than might at first be suspected, for, according to compound-interest rates, such a population will double every twenty-four years. Some states of Southeast Asia are undertaking birth-control programs, but, thus far, only Singapore has attacked the problem methodically and achieved noticeable results.

Although[6] every state of Southeast Asia has at least one impressive city[6] and much of the population in each country tends to be clustered about the cities and towns, the fact remains that Southeast Asia is still primarily agrarian. Despite concerted attempts to encourage industrialization—particularly in the Philippines, Malaysia, and Thailand—the economic base throughout the area continues to be agriculture. In each state, however, there are really two agricultural bases, one export-oriented and one subsistence-oriented, and it is the differing mix of these two sectors that is most useful in differentiating the various states on an economic basis. Malaysia's grip on the world rubber market (some two-thirds of the world's natural-rubber supply comes from the Malay Peninsula) makes it an outstanding example of an export-oriented agricultural economy. The almost total absence of any kind of exports marks Laos as a subsistence-oriented

[5] C. A. Fisher, "Southeast Asia: Balkans of the Orient?" n. 1, p. 55, below.
[6] See D. W. Fryer, "The 'Million City' in Southeast Asia," in this volume.

agricultural economy.[7] Between these two extremes lie the other states of Southeast Asia, again with the exception of Singapore, which is unique in the area and perhaps in the world.

Race, Language, and Religion

The ethnic and cultural diversity of Southeast Asia is even more marked than its geographic and demographic heterogeneity, and, again, this diversity is almost as apparent within the various states as within the region as a whole. Ethnologists have divided mainland Southeast Asia into four general ethnolinguistic groups (Thai-Kadai, Sino-Tibetan, Austroasiatic and Malayo-Polynesian), three of which may also be found in insular Southeast Asia, but even this useful fourfold classification does not sufficiently convey the ethnolinguistic diversity of the area.[8] In fact, almost every major racial group in the world is to be found somewhere in Southeast Asia, and the area as a whole is a veritable Tower of Babel. Although a subsequent section of readings will give more attention to the contemporary political implications of this diversity, for our purposes here, it will be sufficient to note that few countries escape the internal problems created by this diversity. Perhaps the most extreme case is Malaysia. If a Malaysian politician really wants to get to know his constituents personally, he may have to be fluent in two South Indian languages (Telugu and Tamil), from one to five Chinese dialects (depending on the ages and origins of his Chinese constituents), Malay, and English. If his constituency happens to be in Sabah or Sarawak, he probably can forget about Telugu and Tamil, but he does have to know at least one or two tribal languages and would do well to know several others in many areas.

If the task of the politician seems formidable, that of the genuine Southeast Asia specialist is impossible. Even if he wishes to communicate only with the top elite, he should be fluent in English, Dutch, French, Indonesian, Malay, Tagalog, Thai, Cambodian, Vietnamese, Burmese, and Chinese (preferably several of the major dialects, but certainly Mandarin at a minimum), and if his interests are more anthropological in nature, his linguistic talents must be even greater. Although it would be difficult to tabulate, it is apparent that a scholar wishing to prepare himself fully for comparative work throughout Southeast Asia would have to add at least another twenty-five to thirty languages and dialects to this already impressive repertoire!

Almost every major religion of the world is found in Southeast Asia— Buddhism in its two major variations (Theravada in Burma, Thailand, Laos, and Cambodia; Mahayana in Vietnam), Islam (in Malaysia and

[7] Opium reportedly accounts for almost half of Laotian exports. The opium trade is illegal, however, and, although it is conducted relatively openly by senior military officers, statistics on the industry are not recorded.

[8] The best treatment of the ethnolinguistic diversity of Southeast Asia available is Frank M. LeBar, Gerald C. Hickey, and John K. Musgrave, eds., *Ethnic Groups of Mainland Southeast Asia* (New Haven: Yale University Press, 1964). The ethnolinguistic map contained in a pocket on the inside back cover of that volume is basic to an understanding of contemporary politics in mainland Southeast Asia.

Indonesia), and Christianity (in the Philippines). Despite the convenience of the preceding examples, however, no state in Southeast Asia can claim to be solidly within the fold of a single religion. The closest to religious homogeneity is probably the Philippines, which is about 90 per cent Christian, but even here there are diverse Protestant and Catholic sects (notably the Anglopayans and Iglesia-ni-Kristo) and other significant religions (the most important of which are represented by the Muslims of Mindanao and the Sulu Archipelago). Indonesia claims to be overwhelmingly Muslim (also about 90 per cent), but this figure obscures the very real cleavages that separate Indonesians into at least three distinguishable and often hostile groups that are identifiable by their varying degrees of Islamization. Thailand is predominantly Buddhist but has an important Muslim minority bordering on Malaya; Laos and Cambodia are predominantly Buddhist but have primitive hill tribesmen (on the borders in the case of Cambodia; scattered throughout in the case of Laos), whose rituals bear little resemblance to Buddhism in any form. Vietnam is some 85 per cent ethnic Vietnamese, and the vast majority of these are Buddhist. However, to group all Buddhists of Vietnam together is a gross oversimplification; moreover, the 10–15 per cent Roman Catholic minority has been far more important politically than its small numbers might suggest. Finally, as a later essay will reveal, every state of Southeast Asia has some ethnic Chinese, and these overseas Chinese practice various religions, varying from none to a highly eclectic combination that incorporates most of the major beliefs of the world.

Boundaries: Traditional and Modern

Given the diversity of Southeast Asia, it is little wonder that there seem to be so many opportunities for political instability in the area. The fact is that few, if any, "nation-states" in the accepted sense exist in Southeast Asia. Southeast Asian national boundaries are more the doodlings on maps in colonial capitals than they are "natural" borders. Borders encapsulate social groups with highly diverse "primordial sentiments" (to borrow the apt term of Clifford Geertz),[9] and, in almost random fashion in many cases, these borders also cut across groups with common social ties. With only rare exceptions, it was really the colonial period that was responsible for the creation of the "nations" of contemporary Southeast Asia. This is not to say, however, that the present boundaries are destined to last only until the process of decolonization has set history back on its natural track. On the contrary, all political boundaries must have a beginning at some point in history, and the nineteenth and twentieth centuries are probably as good as any. The longer the political boundaries remain intact, the more they will be accepted as the proper political boundaries.

Nevertheless, given the short history of these boundaries and the resulting low level of legitimacy they have attained, one should not be surprised

---

[9] Geertz, one of the best anthropologists currently working on Southeast Asia, uses this term in his essay "The Integrative Revolution," in Geertz, ed., *Old Societies and New States* (New York: The Free Press, 1963), pp. 103–57.

that they do not have the same sanctity for Southeast Asians that political borders have for Americans and Europeans. Moreover, in an area where the idea of a clearly delineated border did not exist until it was introduced by the Europeans, there are still many foggy marchlands where contending spheres of influence meet, and, in each of these, there are many opportunities for disputes—disputes that in the context of today's world will become "international." Finally, there are numerous animosities of a primordial nature, which antedate the arrival of European influence, and their lingering effects are likely to cause considerable unrest in Southeast Asia for many years to come. It is only within the context of these observations that one can begin to understand the various flirtations between Malaysia and Indonesia,[10] the fear of central authority on the part of almost all hill tribes,[11] the lingering mutual distrust shared by northerners and southerners in Vietnam,[12] and the troubled relations among present-day Vietnam, Cambodia, and Thailand.[13]

Given all of the diversity and the internal stresses and strains just described, is one justified in treating Southeast Asia as a single unit? Were it not for several significant reservations, I would be tempted to reply in the negative.

First, any grouping is really a matter of convenience. Geographical proximity alone suggests that there has been at least a minimum of social and political interchanges among the various units, and each of these interchanges provides at least an entree into the fabric of another country. It is true that one might set up far more logical categories of countries, but the logic of this categorization can be of little comfort to the field researcher, who must find the most effective and efficient means of coming to terms with his environment. In the end, of course, we shall have to have at least two sets of classificatory systems—one stemming from our disciplinary needs and one drawing from the realities of geography, with all of its social and linguistic implications. The latter classificatory system will probably continue to be based on the present "areas," at least as far as Asia is concerned.

My second reservation stems from the realization that many Southeast

10 Despite poor relations between Indonesia and Malaysia throughout much of the postwar period, there are several Malay factions on the peninsula that would welcome closer political ties between the two major Malay states. On this subject, see my *Malaysian Foreign Policy* (McLean, Va.: RAC Monograph Series), chapter 1.

11 The highland-lowland split seems to be a common element of society everywhere in the world, as even the younger readers of "Snuffy Smith" in the American comics should be aware. For discussions of this problem in numerous settings in Southeast Asia, see Peter Kunstadter, ed., *Southeast Asian Tribes, Minorities, and Nations* (Princeton, N.J.: Princeton University Press, 1967), 2 vols.

12 North Vietnam, the heartland of Vietnamese nationalism throughout history, has always regarded southerners as people of a lower civilization who need to be guided along the path of enlightenment. Southerners, in turn, have tended to distrust the traditional nationalist ambitions of the north and have generally regarded northerners as too clever to be very trustworthy.

13 See Bernard K. Gordon, *The Dimensions of Conflict in Southeast Asia* (Englewood Cliffs, N.J.: Prentice-Hall, 1966), chapter 2.

Asian leaders are beginning to think of themselves as "Southeast Asian." This is not to say that a Southeast Asian "system" is about to emerge in full bloom, but it does highlight the fact that many Southeast Asians are now conversing among themselves, rather than talking through European intermediaries. Moreover, while there are still no really effective Southeast Asian international organizations, the continued existence of the Association for Southeast Asia (ASA—Malaysia, Thailand, and the Philippines) and the creation of the Association of Southeast Asian Nations (ASEAN— the ASA states, plus Singapore and Indonesia), together with a sudden rash of Southeast Asian conferences and more specific functional organizations (for example, the Conference of Southeast Asian Ministers of Education), all lend credence to the view that there may be greater reason in the future for lumping nine highly diverse states from the Philippines to Burma into a single entity with the convenient label "Southeast Asia."[14]

THE POLITICAL SYSTEMS OF SOUTHEAST ASIA

The Colonial Experience

With the exception of Thailand, all of the states of Southeast Asia have experienced Western colonialism in some form, beginning with the capture of Malacca by the Portuguese in 1511. By the time the Anglo-Dutch treaty of 1824 delineated the spheres of influence of these two states, a patchwork of colonialism was established in Southeast Asia, which was to remain until the Japanese invasion of the area during World War II. The British were ensconced in Burma, Malaya, Singapore, and the three territories of the northern and western coast of Borneo; the Dutch controlled all of what is today Indonesia (including western New Guinea); the Spanish held the Philippines (until relieved of their responsibilities by America's first adventure in overseas imperialism, during the Spanish-American War, in 1898); the French were still at the missionary stage in 1824, but they made up for lost time by a series of rapid expansionist moves that brought the entire Indochinese Peninsula under their control by the end of the nineteenth century; the Portuguese—the original colonial power in Southeast Asia—were squeezed into a small pocket on the island of Timor, where they remain today, apparently oblivious of the natural historical laws of decolonization. The one Southeast Asian state to escape this expanding Western imperialism did so because of colonial jealousies: Thailand found itself locked between the British in Burma and Malaya and the French in Indochina, but colonial rivalries served to buttress its sovereignty, which was given its first legal recognition in the Anglo-French agreement of 1896.

During the colonial period, the groundwork was laid for much of the politics of contemporary Southeast Asia. In many cases, nationalist animosities to colonial powers served to create within the various countries a façade of national unity. At the same time, the colonial powers contributed

---

[14] For a much more optimistic view of the emergence of a political "Southeast Asia," see Bernard K. Gordon and Ann Crown Cyr, "Progress towards Southeast Asian Solidarity," *Solidarity*, II (July–August, 1967), 54–64.

much to the creation of the political and economic infrastructure that made independence in the modern world both possible and desirable, although this was not, of course, the goal of any colonial power when it introduced such things as a rational bureaucracy, railways, roads, modern sanitation, and Western education. The "gifts" of colonialism were usually designed to benefit the colonial regimes themselves, and, while some members of the various colonized societies might enjoy important side benefits in the end, there were few periods in the history of colonialism when European motives could be described as purely altruistic. Accepting this hard fact of history, however, it is still possible to point out that the style of politics and the very social and economic foundations of the states owe much to the impact of the colonial period. It is true that this is changing, and perhaps, in the future, more indigenous forces will set the dominant tone for politics in Southeast Asia, but this is not yet the case.

The Coming of Independence

The catalyst of independence movements in Southeast Asia was the Japanese occupation of most of the area during World War II. What had been a European sphere of influence, parceled out among the various administering powers, fell quickly and easily before the onslaught of a small Asian state that had itself emerged as a significant power only about the time that the more developed European states were consolidating their imperialist positions in Southeast Asia. Japan demonstrated forcefully that, despite claims and past performances, the white colonialists were not invincible—a lesson that was better learned by the Southeast Asians than by some of the Europeans themselves. When the colonial powers returned, in 1945, it was to a different Southeast Asia, for colonialism in any form was no longer legitimate in the eyes of the elites, and, more important, overt opposition to it no longer seemed hopeless.

For Indonesia and Vietnam, the road to independence involved bloody revolutions against their colonial masters, which have left scars (for Indonesia) and open wounds (for Vietnam). The Dutch and French governments in exile received British assistance in reoccupying their lost territories, and, in both cases, the anticolonial revolution began almost as soon as it became apparent that anti-Japanese resistance forces (in the case of Vietnam) or Japanese-encouraged leaders (in the case of Indonesia) would not be permitted to realize the dreams of independence that emerged in the Japanese interregnum. Although Indonesia proclaimed its independence on August 17, 1945, it did not become effective until the Dutch finally withdrew completely after four years of intermittent fighting and bargaining. In Vietnam, territory south of the 16th parallel was reoccupied by British forces, according to the Potsdam agreement, but the commanding British general (Douglas Gracey) encouraged a "coup" by the interned French military, despite orders from London to refrain from becoming involved in Franco-Vietnamese politics. In the north, Chiang Kai-shek's Nationalist Chinese (temporarily occupying Vietnam north of the 16th parallel, also pursuant to the Potsdam agreement) faced the *fait accompli* of the Democratic Republic of Vietnam, which had been proclaimed by Ho Chi Minh on September 2, 1945. Two months later, fighting broke out between Vietminh and French forces, and there followed a bloody and brutal struggle, which ended only with the complete defeat of French forces at Dien Bien Phu on May 7, 1954. The Geneva Conference, marking the end of one era and the beginning of another, convened just one day later.

In marked contrast to this revolutionary pattern stand the Philippines and Malaya. It had been the announced plan of the United States, in the Tydings-McDuffie Act (1934), to cut its colonial ties with the Philippines after a ten-year transitional period, and the Japanese occupation only slightly disrupted the timetable for independence. While this decision had been provoked as much by domestic economic pressures in the United States as by Filipino nationalist demands or any altruistic motives on the American part, it is, nevertheless, true that it altered the nature of the Japanese impact and had a continuing influence on Philippine-American relations. Despite occasional backsliding in American policy, it was apparent to the Filipinos that they were moving toward independence even before the war, and this goal was realized only two years late, on July 4, 1946.

Although Britain had to fight a twelve-year guerrilla war in Malaya against a Malayan-Chinese, Communist-influenced insurrection (the "Emergency" of 1948–60), the leaders who stood in Merdeka Stadium at a few seconds past midnight on the morning of August 31, 1957, to witness the raising of the new Malayan flag were not revolutionaries. They were, in fact, the very leaders who aided the British in putting down the revolt, and the British, on their part, had yielded to their demands for a new federation in 1948, granted municipal elections in 1952, and given Malaya virtual internal autonomy after the general elections of 1955. Without these adjustments, Malaya's postwar history might have more closely resembled that of Vietnam and Indonesia.

In Malaya and the Philippines, Britain and the United States made a graceful exit from colonialism, and, although barbs have sometimes been exchanged between parents and offspring, their generally amicable relations have demonstrated the wisdom of bending with the prevailing wind of change.

The remaining colonies of Southeast Asia achieved independence almost as side effects of a larger drama being played out elsewhere. Burma's nationalist movement, which culminated in independence on January 4, 1948, vacillated between cooperation and conflict with the British but was continually overshadowed by the more spectacular events occurring on the Indian subcontinent, where independence, partition, and the Hindu-Muslim war kept British policy-makers occupied for years. Similarly, in Indochina, the main feature was playing in Vietnam. The shrewd maneuverings of Prince (then King) Norodom Sihanouk of Cambodia were mostly calculated to embarrass the embattled French by taking advantage of their troubles in Vietnam, and, in Laos, intrafamily squabbles among the traditional elite were acted out without massive French involvement, largely because of France's preoccupation with the worsening situation in Vietnam. Both states were given varying degrees of autonomy, but independence was "perfected" (to use the French description) only after the inevitability of a French defeat in Vietnam had become painfully obvious in Paris. Sabah (formerly British North Borneo), Sawarak, and Singapore were freed from colonial control by absorption into the larger Federation of Malaysia on September 16, 1963, but Singapore had enjoyed considerable internal autonomy since 1959, and it went on to become a fully independent state after separating from Malaysia on August 9, 1965.

Politics and Political Styles

Governments in Southeast Asia cover the full spectrum of political types. British-protected Brunei is a throwback to the old days of omnipotent Oriental potentates, who were, however, more legend than fact. One colony remains (Portuguese Timor), seemingly out of place in the midst of anticolonialist Indonesia but apparently more secure than its geographical position suggests. In addition to these two anomalies, there are three military regimes (Burma, Thailand, and Indonesia), three practicing democracies (the Philippines, Singapore, and, at least prior to the suspension of its constitution in May, 1969, Malaysia), three states that are dominated by one or two strong leaders who head differing structures of government (North Vietnam, South Vietnam, and Cambodia), and one state that could probably best be described as a "no-party nonstate" (Laos).

Burma's military rule can be characterized as a paternalistic but stern military dictatorship. General Ne Win, who twice relieved the elected U Nu from his premiership, has followed Burmese tradition by turning inward, attempting to resolve Burma's problems by shutting out all foreign influence—Russian, Chinese, American, and British. Ne Win cut off all U.S. AID programs, expelled the Asia and Ford Foundations, and, most recently, turned on mainland China and the overseas Chinese in Burma with equal vigor.

Thailand has a benevolent military dictatorship that shows few if any serious signs of a desire to reintroduce the democratic process. In a country where coups and countercoups were so numerous that merely tallying them becomes a major research task, the present military regime has provided an element of uncharacteristic stability. Despite the revolution of 1932 against the monarchy (which was retained as a symbol of Thai sovereignty) and several periods of liberal democracy accompanied, to the chagrin of many, by almost unrestrained political activity, Thailand's ruling elite is, in fact, even more closed today than it was at any time since the 1932 revolution.[15] A new constitution was in the making, from 1959 to 1968, but there was little reason to believe that it would inaugurate a new era of liberal democracy. Despite some liberal democratic trappings, the constitution provided considerable insulation for the executive from outside influence and guar-

[15] For support of this assertion, see the excellent essay by Hans-Dieter Evers, "The Formation of a Social Class Structure: Urbanization, Bureaucratization, and Social Mobility in Thailand," *American Sociological Review*, XXXI (August, 1966), 480–88.

anteed that political power would remain in the hands of the military leadership. Thai government has been relatively effective, but how long it can remain both closed and legitimate in the face of a growing awareness of its past shortcomings is questionable.

Indonesia's present military regime emerged as a reaction to the excesses of Sukarno's "Guided Democracy" (1959–65), which was devoted to solving crises connected with political integration more through symbol-manipulation than through the establishment of effective government, as several essays in this volume demonstrate. General Suharto and his followers have, indeed, attacked some of the major problems facing Indonesia, and the fact that prices rose only about 120 per cent in 1967 (650 per cent in 1966; 1200 per cent in 1965) reveals that this has been done with some success. However, Indonesia is still restive, and, even among the most rational leaders, power itself can become a not unpleasant perquisite of high office.

Of the three practicing democracies in Southeast Asia, the most unrestrained variety is to be found in the Philippines. Although Philippine politics is based on a two-party system, the Philippines is more like a political bazaar where there are no fixed-price goods and every item brings the price the traffic will bear. Each of the two parties is supported by a small hard core of party activists and party voters, but most followers (and many leaders) shift back and forth between the Liberals and the Nacionalistas, almost at will. The rule is alternation, not continuation, of parties, and, in fact, no Philippine president has ever been re-elected for a second full term. In such a bargaining environment, a vote has intrinsic value, for it will "buy" a share in the winning party, and, thus, the democratic process works, though not in precisely the manner the American tutors had in mind when they introduced the trappings of their own system. In a system like that in the Philippines, however, corruption runs rampant, although, in fairness to the Filipinos, it must be admitted that "corruption" is, like beauty, in the eyes of the beholder.

The democratic systems of Malaysia and Singapore are far more restrained than is that of the Philippines. After a bitter struggle within the party itself, as well as with other parties, the People's Action Party of Cambridge-educated Lee Kuan Yew emerged from the general elections of 1963 as the dominant voice of Singapore politics, and, since the general elections of 1968, it has ruled virtually unchallenged in the democratically elected parliament. Before the upheavals that began on May 13, 1969, the Malaysian Alliance—a confederation of three communally based parties of the peninsula plus the Alliance parties of Sabah and Sarawak—dominated the Malaysian Parliament in Kuala Lumpur. Since the party, following British tradition, was well disciplined, and its leadership had subtly but effectively defined the limits of democratic dissent, it was possible for the Alliance to govern Malaysia with almost no outside help whatever. In so doing, Alliance leaders reserved their more disruptive debates for the closed sessions of the Alliance executive committee and tended to bring into the Parliament only the policies on which they had already reached agreement. The situation after the postelection riots of May, 1969, is still fluid, but it now seems apparent that the rules of the political game have been changed substantially. Both Singapore and Malaysia (at least as of May, 1969), like the Philippines, are practicing democracies, but the styles of politics are so different among all three that it almost seems inappropriate to group them under a single category.

In the turmoil of postwar Indochina, Cambodia has been a remarkably placid island under the leadership of a royal figure who has employed both traditional and modern techniques to gain and hold support. As a subsequent essay will show, Prince Norodom Sihanouk has maintained a strict neutrality in foreign policy while pursuing domestic policies apparently well suited to the needs of his small country. Sihanouk, in many ways, has been the most fortunate of all Southeast Asian rulers, for he is descended from a line of accepted and respected royalty and rules over one of the most homogeneous populations in all of Southeast Asia. The Khmer people have a long common history, and, thanks to the contraction of their empire under the pressure of the Vietnamese, Thais, and Europeans, they came to be relatively well concentrated within the boundaries of present-day Cambodia. Yet, one should not permit these facts to detract from the solid accomplishments of Sihanouk. While ruling in a highly personalistic manner, he has, nevertheless, maintained peacefully the existence of Cambodia, and, in Indochina today, this is no small accomplishment.

The crisis militarism that has characterized South Vietnamese politics stands in contrast to the more deft and effective leadership of the personable Ho Chi Minh in the north. While generals have come and gone in the south, with few personalities after the fall of Ngo Dinh Diem in 1963 making a serious impression on events, Ho, as the late Bernard Fall points out in an essay in this volume, could probably have gone down as a genuine American folk hero in another set of circumstances. Regardless of one's interpretation of events in Vietnam, it is impossible not to appreciate Ho's impact on politics in that divided and troubled land. His government, which could be labeled as "democratic" only in the sense in which the Communists use the term, does seem to rest on a fairly impressive consensual base. For most of the period since World War II, Ho has definitely been the leader, and others have had to content themselves with the role of followers. On the basis of admittedly conflicting evidence, however, it does not seem correct to equate this to a police-state dictatorship in which acquiescence is obtained by the use of selective or mass terror.

THE PROBLEMS AHEAD

National Integration

With only a few exceptions, each of the states of Southeast Asia faces a monumental task in creating a nation from among the many diverse elements of its plural society. If, in the final analysis, as Emerson has conceded in his *From Empire to Nation*, a nation is a group of individuals who distinguish the "we" from the "they,"[16] a nation-state must be such a

---

[16] Rupert Emerson, *From Empire to Nation* (Cambridge, Mass.: Harvard University Press, 1960), part II.

collection of individuals enclosed within a set of fairly well-defined political borders. To elaborate further (and still to some extent following Emerson), ideally, a nation-state should have a common language, common cultural heritage, a shared history, and a set of common symbols. Of these, the last named (common symbols) is probably the crucial element. For, in a sense, the others (language, culture, history) are more descriptive of the processes whereby common symbols emerge. There are, however, other ways in which common symbols might arise, at least in theory. As Lipset has suggested, longevity itself may generate legitimacy and consensus,[17] and any government effective and efficient enough to maintain itself over a long period of time will produce citizens who share a common history and perhaps even participate in a common culture and speak a common language. In such circumstances, common symbols will undoubtedly emerge. On the other hand, a competent and capable leader may seek a short cut through history by attempting to generate the national symbols *sui generis*.

As the Nigerian experience has painfully shown, even the most promising new state can fail completely in the challenge of nation-building, and success in any given case will probably stem from a combination of effective government, conscious symbol-building, and gambler's luck. Thus far, only one state in Southeast Asia has actually lost a constituent part of its territory during its period of independence, and this, curiously enough, happened to one of the better-governed states of the area—Malaysia. One of the poorest-governed (Indonesia) was threatened by disintegration in 1958 but successfully overcame the crisis by a combination of force and symbol manipulation under the charismatic Sukarno. Yet, in Sukarno's case, symbol-wielding alone could not sustain his government when it was found so utterly lacking in effectiveness and efficiency. Together, the two cases should warn us how difficult nation-building is with the raw material available to most Southeast Asian political leaders.

Economic Development

Despite all the attempts of the developed countries to prime pumps in the underdeveloped world, the sobering fact is that the gap separating haves from have-nots grows larger every year. This is not to say that no underdeveloped state is enjoying some improvement in its standard of living on an absolute scale, for many, indeed, are. But, given the staggering growth potential built into the developed economies, an underdeveloped country must actually out-perform a developed one in terms of efficiency. The plight of the underdeveloped world is something like that of Alice in Lewis Carroll's *Through the Looking Glass*. In the other world, in the Garden of Live Roses, Alice, after running at top speed until she is exhausted, discovers that she is resting under the tree where her journey began. Turning to the Queen, Alice remarks quizzically:

"Why, I do believe we've been under this tree the whole time! Everything's just as it was!"
"Of course it is," said the Queen. "What would you have it?"

[17] Seymour Martin Lipset, *Political Man* (Garden City, N.Y.: Doubleday, 1960), pp. 77–83.

"Well, in our country," said Alice, still panting a little, "you'd generally get to somewhere else—if you ran very fast for a long time, as we've been doing."

"A slow sort of country!" said the Queen. "Now here you see it takes all the running you can do to keep in the same place. If you want to get somewhere else you must run at least twice as fast as that!"

The states of the underdeveloped world have been running very fast, but the gap between them and their point of comparison—the developed world—has grown. Moreover, there is evidence that the *real* gap is less significant than the *perceived* gap—that is, the gap that is recognized and vaguely measured by the politically relevant citizens of an underdeveloped state. The perceived gap is a function of technology (the possibility of communicating the existence or extent of the gap) and empathy (Lerner's concept of the ability of a person to imagine himself in the shoes of another, more fortunate person),[18] and persons become politically relevant when they begin to believe that their own actions can in some way alter their environment for the better. In such situations, the somewhat dated concept of "rising expectations" may take on a new and revolutionary meaning. This, at least, should be a major concern of present-day governments in Southeast Asia.

Political Viability in a Predatory World

Stated briefly, no state today can reasonably expect to be left alone to muddle through history entirely on its own. Given the communications revolution and the insecurity felt by the major powers, it is unlikely that there will be many cases of naked aggression, for there always seem to be concerned powers with a vested interest in maintaining the status quo against such traumatic changes. Nevertheless, in more subtle ways, each of the major powers persistently applies pressure to less powerful states in an effort to mold them into patterns more supportive of the national interests of the major power. These pressures, while sometimes propping up faltering regimes, in turn impose additional demands on the governments of the lesser states and make it impossible for them to take a random walk through history without interference.

In Southeast Asia, four of the larger powers (Britain, the U.S.S.R., China, and the United States) have at some time tinkered with history. France withdrew from the area in defeat in 1954, and the Netherlands finally completed its not-so-graceful exit with the cession in 1962 of West Irian to Indonesia, via the United Nations. Britain has now indicated an intention to withdraw east of Suez within the next five to ten years, and the United States seems to be moving in cautiously in ever-increasing measure. In American eyes, the major threats seem to be China and Communism (in that order, it would seem), and China seems to reciprocate by regarding as the major threats America and anti-Communist indigenous governments (in that order).

[18] Daniel Lerner, *The Passing of Traditional Society* (Glencoe, Ill.: The Free Press, 1958), pp. 49–54.

Regardless of the stand one takes in this unfortunately polarized world of supporters and dissenters, it is apparent that in the highly charged setting of pressures and counterpressures, survival itself becomes one of the major goals of any Southeast Asian government. And, in varying degrees, each of the governments of the area has been faced with some very real problems of survival. Moreover, it is apparent that the worst is not yet over, and the ability to survive in this predatory world may in the end constitute the ultimate test of all Southeast Asian governments.

ONE

The Setting

Is there a Southeast Asia? Where is it? Who are the Southeast Asians? Despite their simplicity, these questions are not easily answered. We can, of course, circle a part of the globe with a heavy line and label the vast enclosed area "Southeast Asia," but what have we caught in our net? What are the common characteristics of the lands and the peoples of this area? What sets them apart from the lands and peoples of South Asia? Or East Asia?

In this introductory section, we are concerned with answering some of these questions as best we can, while at the same time providing the reader with a feeling of life as it is lived in Southeast Asia. Harry J. Benda, in the first essay, attacks our questions with the tools of the historian and emerges with some tentative answers. Historically, Professor Benda tells us, there is a Southeast Asia, but it is an entity that has three distinct cultural fault lines (separating Sinicized, Indianized, and Hispanized Southeast Asia), upon which are superimposed some six historical periods (classical, postclassical, early colonial, modern colonial, the Japanese interregnum, and independence). Historically, then, we are justified in speaking of "Southeast Asia," but we must be careful to retain some realistic flexibility in searching out parallels, common characteristics, and the like.

In chapter three, Lauriston Sharp views the area from the perspective of the anthropologist, and, while admitting the existence of discontinuities and unconformities in Southeast Asia, he sees these more as evidence of the inadequacy of the accepted "cookie-cutter concept of culture." All over the world, the " 'cake of custom' has blown up," and though Southeast Asia contains cultural contradictions, this is not adequate reason for rejecting the concept of a "Southeast Asia" in a cultural sense.

In chapter four, Charles Fisher, a geographer, retraces some of the paths taken by the historian and anthropologist and adds a new political-administrative dimension. Although there are striking parallels between post-World War II Southeast Asia and post-World War I southeastern Europe, the political results have been different. International boundaries in Southeast Asia may be illogical, as even a hasty perusal of the ethno-linguistic map will demonstrate, and "Southeast Asia" itself may be illogical, but the fact remains that few states have made serious efforts to change these boundaries or to change the image of their geographical location on the globe. Thus, it would seem that Southeast Asia is, at least, not the "Balkans of the Orient."

In this entity known as Southeast Asia—which by the end of chapter four should have demonstrated its right to exist—there is admittedly almost as much diversity as homogeneity, and chapters five and six are intended to give the reader some appreciation of the extent of this diversity. The intellectual, political, and commercial life of each of the states of Southeast Asia is big-city oriented, and D. W. Fryer's essay takes us on a brief but informative tour of five of these focal points for the modern segment of Southeast Asian life. Manila, Bangkok, Singapore, Djakarta, and Saigon-Cholon—the "million cities" of Southeast Asia—together with Kuala Lumpur, Pnom Penh, and Hanoi, are the places where change is most evident and where modern Southeast Asia meets the West day-to-day.

While the cities may be the political and economic centers of Southeast Asia, they are still atypical examples of life in Southeast Asia. Southeast Asia is more than 85 per cent agrarian, and some 60 per cent of the land is covered by forest. In the final essay in this section, W. R. Geddes, an anthropologist by way of philosophy and psychology, gives us a fascinating glimpse of life in one countryside and one jungle in Southeast Asia. Although no one would dare assert that life among the Land Dayaks of Sarawak is the same as that of the peasants in the Mekong Delta or, for that matter, of peasants or highlanders anywhere else in Southeast Asia, chapter six shows us the other side of the coin and serves as a useful reminder that most of our contact with Southeast Asia is limited to a minute part of the total area.

2

THE STRUCTURE OF SOUTHEAST ASIAN HISTORY: SOME PRELIMINARY OBSERVATIONS*

HARRY J. BENDA

THE CLASSICAL ERA

The "classical" era in Southeast Asian history roughly spans the millennium between the fourth century B.C. and the fourteenth century A.D.[1] This delineation is meaningful for two important segments of the area: for what Coedès has called the "Hinduized" (I actually think that Harrison's[2] "Indianized" is far more appropriate) polities of mainland and island Southeast Asia, and for the "Sinicized" parts of the Indochinese Peninsula (even though Chinese influence only commenced in the first century A.D.). As far as modern scholarship can reliably ascertain, the

* Abridged by the editor and reprinted by permission of the author and the publisher from *Journal of Southeast Asian History*, III (March, 1962), 103–38.

[1] What Southeast Asia was in prehistoric times, and whether it possessed characteristics common yet unique to the area, we so far do not know. The starting point for history, and many centuries beyond, are thus left in the darkness and at best open to conjecture. . . . For the time being at least, we . . . cannot expect meaningful historical research in what for want of a better word we may call the "preclassical era." . . .

[2] Brian Harrison, *Southeast Asia: A Short History* (London: Macmillan Co., 1954). "Hinduization" appears too restrictive a term, especially with regard to Buddhism.

Philippines were only peripherally touched by Indianization, so that they seemingly constitute a distinct, third part of what we usually call Southeast Asia today.[3]

[The] quest for a meaningful entity [with the label "Southeast Asia"] is . . . partly answered by a threefold basic division in terms of major cultural and social orbits. Whether these criteria should not lead us to include Ceylon within the orbit of Indianization remains an open question. A major problem for further research is the feasibility of discerning a common Southeast Asian element bridging these basic divisions. One possible way of looking for answers to this problem may be to see whether the modifications in transplanted Indian and Chinese patterns, respectively, can be traced to common, or at least similar, indigenous factors. This, for sure, [is a precarious approach and] is therefore suggested with tentative temerity. Still, the comparative study of indigenous customary law,[4] and perhaps also of religious patterns antedating the introduction of world faiths,[5] may one day yield significant data for such an approach. . . .

The structural, generic approach to Southeast Asian history should commence with the endeavor to discover, or reconstruct, a set of social, economic, and political relationships during the classical era. Periodization will logically coincide with major structural changes affecting these relationships, and thus need not necessarily correspond to mere shifts in the political fortunes of this or that dynasty or ethnic group. I shall select two major such sets for detailed discussion. My selection is, of course, arbitrary, tentative, and by no means exhaustive.

As the first criterion, I shall suggest the social and political structures prevalent in Southeast Asian realms in the classical era. I think that four basic types are discernible within the three major cultural areas, the Indianized, the Sinicized, and the Philippine. To start with the last of these, until the arrival of the Muslims and Spaniards, Philippine social and political life apparently revolved around the barangays, small fragmented territorial units headed by *datu's*, and as yet unintegrated into larger principalities. Such principalities, and far more complex social stratifications, did exist elsewhere in Southeast Asia. In Annam and Tonkin, a Chinese social pattern of landed gentry and a political system based on the Confucian bureaucracy were superimposed on indigenous molds. In the Indianized parts of Southeast Asia, finally, two basic types of politics seem to have

[3] For a recent treatment, see John L. Phelan, *The Hispanization of the Philippines: Spanish Aims and Filipino Responses, 1565–1700* (Madison, Wis.: University of Wisconsin Press, 1959).

[4] See, for example, Robert Lingat, "Les régimes matrimoniaux du Sud-Est de l'Asie," *Publications de l'École Française d'Extrême Orient*, Vol. 34 (1952) and 34-bis (1955). Lingat speaks of a common parentage which united the Burmese and Siamese customary matrimonial law with the primitive (that is, pre-Chinese) law of Vietnam (Part I, pp. 165–66). On the differences between Southeast Asia and China and India, respectively, see *ibid.*, pp. 75–76, 111–12, 165–66.

[5] See Jeanne Cuisinier, *Sumangat: L'âme et son culte en Indochine et en Indonesie* (Paris: Gallimard, 1951). See also the systematic study by Robert B. Textor, *An Inventory of Non-Buddhist Supernatural Objects in a Central Thai Village* (Ph.D. dissertation, Cornell University, 1960).

evolved: the inland-agrarian "hydraulic" prototype of which Angkor and the early Mataram are good examples, on one hand, and the riparian or coastal, commercial prototype of which Srivijaya may have been the most important and most highly developed. The former, perhaps the most prevalent polity in mainland Southeast Asia, seems to fit Wittfogel's "Oriental despotism" rather well—far better, I should think, than does China, or, for that matter, Annam. It displayed the typical division into court and peasantry, with virtually complete royal control over the agrarian economy, the absence of a substantial landowning class, and political power channeled through an appointive, quasi-bureaucratic nobility.[6] The other prototype deviated sharply from such "Oriental despotism" since it contained a more cosmopolitan population composed of traders and merchants of various, including indigenous, races, an urban, trading bourgeoisie with substantial financial resources and, consequently, very likely possessing some degree at least of "countervailing" political power.[7] Admittedly, we still know far too little about these latter polities, but I think it stands to reason that they must have profoundly differed from the inland-looking, self-sufficient despotisms of Cambodia, Central or East Java, and the like.

Obviously, a wide range of specific questions concerning social and political structures will have to be asked to bring out the similarities and differences between the four Southeast Asian polities briefly outlined above. Only a few will be suggested here, notably the administrative apparatus, the system of political and fiscal control, the problem of political stability at the center, patterns of landownership and its relation to political power, and the whole fascinating, if much neglected, complex of the connecting tissue between ruler(s) and ruled—the connection, in other words, between what the late Robert Redfield has so happily termed "the Great Tradition" of urban court society and "the Little Tradition" of the peasantry.[8] I shall presently return to this theme under the next heading of religion.

There is still another aspect of this structural comparison worth considering. I am wondering whether the existence, side by side, of such different social and political structures could not help explain some of the inner dynamics of Southeast Asian inter-principality relations and rivalries. In the case of Java, we seem to have ample proof that it was the struggle

[6] Karl A. Wittfogel, *Oriental Despotism: A Comparative Study of Total Power* (New Haven, Conn.: Yale University Press, 1957). In several respects, Wittfogel seems to have exaggerated the extent of political control exercised by his "Oriental despots." Max Weber's "patrimonialism" often provides a more accurate analysis. See Max Weber, *Wirtschaft und Gesellschaft* (Tübingen: J. C. B. Mohr [Paul Siebeck], 1947, Part II, esp. pp. 702–5. See also the suggestive article by S. N. Eisenstadt, "Internal Contradictions in Bureaucratic Politics," *Comparative Studies in Society and History*, I (1958–59), 58–75. I gladly acknowledge my indebtedness to Professor W. F. Wertheim, who has discussed these problems with me.

[7] This polarization is brilliantly developed by J. C. van Leur, *Indonesian Trade and Society: Essays in Asian Social and Economic History* (The Hague/Bandung: W. van Hoeve, 1955).

[8] Robert Redfield, *Peasant Society and Culture* (Chicago: University of Chicago Press, 1956), pp. 70 ff.

between inland and coastal polities that accounts for part of the history of both Majapahit and the later Mataram. Could the constant clash between Vietnamese, Chams, and Khmers, for example, be similarly analyzed in terms of a basic polarization between different, if not hostile, social and political systems?[9] To venture one general proposition, it would seem that Southeast Asia did not share the European pattern in which the centers of commercial civilization superseded and ultimately replaced agrarian polities. Could the cosmopolitan composition of the trading class—or the absence of a viable native trading class—account for the difference?

The second criterion concerns religion, and in particular the relationship between ecclesiastic and secular authority. Filipino religion up to the end of the fifteenth century—that is, before contact with either Islam or Hispanic Catholicism—seems to have been structurally rather simple, with neither an elaborate clerical establishment nor a sophisticated creed exceeding animism and nature and ancestor worship. Again, both Indianized and Sinicized orbits had, by contrast, experienced profound contact with highly sophisticated religious systems. In the Sinicized realms, Taoism, Mahayana Buddhism, and Confucianism had been introduced from China. More important, the shifting balance of power between the Buddhist clergy and the Confucian mandarinate (the latter representatives of a civic, religious-political cult) that occupies such a fascinating and complex place in Chinese history[10] had apparently likewise been transmitted to the recipient Southeast Asian regions. Buddhism in Vietnam should, then, in the first place be examined in a Chinese, and only secondarily in a comparative Southeast Asian, context. Indianized Southeast Asia was, of course, Buddhist, too, during the classical era, but its Buddhism—of either Vehicle— was a direct importation from India which had not passed through the sieve of Chinese Mahayanism. Buddhism in the Indianized regions is in fact often hyphenated with Hinduism, or Brahmanism, and is sometimes —as in the Javanese context—referred to as "Siva-Buddhism."

The crucial structural difference between the Buddhist establishments in these two realms may well have been that in Sinicized Annam and Tonkin the Buddhist monkhood, after several vicissitudes in its position, ceased to form an integral part of the politico-religious elite. From the mid-thirteenth century onward, it thus came to play a more or less peripheral role at the scholar-gentry-dominated center (though not necessarily at the village level, as we shall presently see).[11] In the Indianized principalities, on the other hand, Buddhism had seemingly adapted itself [to], if it had not actually merged with, the Brahmanic court order to such an extent that Brahmans and Buddhist monks reinforced each other, or in other words, came to form one elite group at courts revolving around deified kings who presented themselves now as Hindu gods, then as reincarnations of the

[9] This polarization may, it seems to me, some day also throw additional light on the relationship between Srivijaya and the Javanese Sailendra dynasty. Could one and the same dynasty successfully and simultaneously rule over both kinds of polity?

[10] See Arthur F. Wright, *Buddhism in Chinese History* (Stanford, Calif.: Stanford University Press, 1959).

[11] See Le Thanh Khoi, *Le Viet-Nam: Histoire et Civilisation* (Paris: Les Editions de Minuit, 1955), pp. 174 ff.

Buddha, if not of both simultaneously. This, in any case, is the way in which the religious, syncretic amalgam of Indianized Southeast Asia in classical times has usually been presented to us. I have, indeed, sometimes wondered whether these descriptions apply only to the late classical era, and whether they therefore obscure—largely for want of proper documentation—an earlier period in which Brahmanism and Buddhism in Southeast Asia may have been in conflict. The history of Java in the eighth and ninth centuries, to mention one possible example, would make it appear that dynastic rivalries may have coincided with religious divisions. In India, as is well known, Buddhism was in the end completely displaced by Brahmanism, and it is difficult to believe that this polarization between the two systems was not to some extent at least reflected in our area.[12]

Another comparison of religion in the two orbits of Indianization and Sinification deserves attention. Both Brahmanism and Buddhism in the Indianized realms were court religions, or more properly, ecclesiastic establishments undergirding, and intermeshing with, political authority. While Tantric Buddhism here and there may have spread downward to the peasantry, the "official" religion seems to have been a court affair pure and simple, once again corresponding to Wittfogel's concept of the role of religion under total, despotic power. The peasantry was probably forced to participate in the religious rites centering on the god-kings, but such participation was very likely passive, and the state religion did not as such cater to the villagers through its teachings or—more important from a structural point of view—by providing a rural clergy for them. The peasantry, then, presumably continued to live in a spiritual, largely animistic, world of its own. This, however, may have been the prevalent picture in the "hydraulic" inland principalities only. Whether Buddhism in a thriving trading and maritime community like Srivijaya, a major center of Mahayana Buddhist learning, did not play a somewhat different role for greater numbers of the population outside the court circle would certainly deserve closest study if the records permit it.[13]

In the Sinicized orbits, the "separation of state and church" (that is, the

[12] The paucity of historical materials has always made it extremely difficult to ascertain the causes of the disappearance of Buddhism in India, but a powerful Brahmanic reaction to Buddhism may well have been one of the major determinants. See Helmuth von Glasenapp, *Brahma und Buddha: Die Religionen Indiens in ihrer geschichtlichen Entwicklung* (Berlin: Deutsche Buch-Gemeinschaft, 1926), pp. 252–53. R. C. Mitra, in his more recent *The Decline of Buddhism in India* (*Visva-Bharati Studies No. 20* [Calcutta, 1954]) opposes such an interpretation, largely in terms of doctrine, and stresses the Hindu acceptance of the Buddha as a reincarnation of Vishnu (pp. 139 and 159, respectively). I am indebted to Professor Ludo Rocher for drawing my attention to this important book. I believe that the key to the problem does not lie in the study of syncretic beliefs, but in the realization that Brahmans and Buddhists represented socially, economically, and politically distinct and potentially hostile interests. Thus the "acceptance" of Buddhism may well have taken place after the decline—or destruction—of the Buddhist organizational establishment had become a fact.

[13] Max Weber has stressed the urban origin of Buddhism, and its attractions to urban dwellers. See his *The Religion of India: The Sociology of Hinduism and Buddhism,* trans. by H. H. Gerth and D. Martindale (Glencoe, Ill.: The Free Press, 1958), p. 226.

ultimate supremacy of the Confucian mandarinate over the Buddhist monks) at times seems to have brought the monks closer to the peasantry, without, however, endowing Vietnamese peasant religion with a lasting, let alone profound, Buddhist element. Occasionally Buddhist monks apparently placed themselves at the helm of peasant unrest,[14] but they seemingly did not occupy a central place in the structure of the Vietnamese village. Comparative study of Chinese Mahayana Buddhism and its social role in the countryside may perhaps provide the clue for this state of affairs. It is possible that the scholar-gentry's quarrel with, and ultimate victory over, the Buddhist clergy was caused by the very dangers inherent in the alliance between Buddhism and what Wittfogel has deprecatingly termed the "beggars' democracy" of the peasant village.[15] Buddhism in Vietnam was allowed to continue as a private faith, but it could no longer be nourished from peasant roots.[16] At the same time, Chinese and, later on, indigenous, Confucian control insulated Vietnam from the intrusion of other world faiths whose penetration and ultimate consolidation marked the beginning of the postclassical epoch in other parts of Southeast Asia. Interestingly enough, rural Vietnam thus came to exhibit a religious vacuum which, in subsequent centuries and well into modern times, allowed the mushrooming of a plethora of religious beliefs and practices and, with them, of a wide range of ecclesiastic personnel.

The relationship between urban, court-centered and rural, village-centered religious establishments is, then, another crucially important factor in the comparative study of Southeast Asian history. In particular, the connection between peasant religion and agrarian unrest straddles the religious and socio-political realms, and runs like a continuing thread through the area's history. . . .

Postclassical Southeast Asia

With the exception of Vietnam, Southeast Asia experienced significant changes in the period between the fourteenth and sixteenth centuries. In the Philippines, two world religions appeared, and, with them, new social and political patterns were being established. Muslims and Spaniards introduced both highly sophisticated faiths and consolidated principalities. Although Islam was pushed back from Luzon, it maintained itself in the southeast Philippines—as in other Islamized parts of Southeast Asia—for centuries to come.

Elsewhere in the Philippine Islands, Hispanization proceeded to such

[14] See Jean Chesneaux, *Contribution à l'histoire de la nation Vietnamienne* (Paris: Editions Sociales, 1955), p. 33.

[15] The weaknesses of Wittfogel's analysis of religion in *Oriental Despotism* have been pointed out in S. N. Eisenstadt's review in *The Journal of Asian Studies*, XVII (1957–58), 435–46.

[16] See Leopold Cadière, *Croyances et pratiques religieuses des Annamites*, 2d. ed. (Saigon: Société d'Études Indochinoises, 1958) Vol. I, 6 and 31, respectively. See also Le Thanh Khoi, *op. cit.*, pp. 281–82, and Mai Tho Truyen, "Le Bouddhisme au Viet-Nam," in René de Berval (ed.), *Présence du Bouddhisme* (Saigon: France-Asie, 1959), pp. 808–9.

an extent that the very texture of Filipino society was lastingly affected. While it is true that Spanish Catholicism and feudal colonialism were adjusted to, and tempered by, the recipient ˙culture,[17] Philippine social and economic structure from the sixteenth century onward perhaps more closely approximates those of the Hispanic domains in the Americas than those of any other country in island Southeast Asia. . . .

Though at first sight less far-reaching, the changes wrought in the Indianized orbit after the thirteenth century nonetheless constituted a distinct watershed. The Brahmanic-Mahayana Buddhist court civilizations of the classical era gave way to Theravada-dominated principalities on the mainland, and to Islamized sultanates in the islands. The quantitative and qualitative aspects of these changes are by no means clear yet, but modern scholarship has often tended to minimize their significance. Obviously, the new era did not start with a *tabula rasa*, and it has therefore become customary to stress, once again, the theme of continuity. To all intents and purposes, significant traces of Mahayana Buddhism and Brahmanism did not altogether disappear from either religious beliefs or social institutions; it has often been said that Islam in most parts of Indonesia, for example, only formed a thin veneer on *kratons* (courts) still dominated by the spirit and practices of the classical era. Equal importance has been attached to the hypothesis that the domestication of Islam in Indianized Southeast Asia was facilitated by the garb of Indian Sufism in which it appeared in the archipelago.

I have no quarrel with these assertions, which appear both valid and important at this stage of our knowledge. All I would like to do is to add another dimension to the discussion of the introduction of the new religions in Southeast Asia. First of all, let us note how quickly they spread and how deeply entrenched they became. This could only happen because the old order was either religiously deficient or declining, if not both. We do not know whether there was initial resistance to the intrusion of these new religions, but we do know that wherever Theravada Buddhism or Islam struck proper roots, they proved immune to displacements by other faiths. More important, we should try to ask ourselves whether the decline of the *ancien régimes* and their ultimate displacement by the new religions were historically haphazard phenomena. Externally, the advance of these religions into Southeast Asia can be explained by the missionary zeal of Singhalese Buddhism under King Parākramabāhu,[18] on the one hand, and the world-wide resurgence of Islamic Sufism,[19] on the other. But what, specifically, aided them in the area itself?

In the case of Angkor, the old order had seemingly fallen into disrepute

[17] See Phelan, *op. cit.*, chapter 6.

[18] See D. T. Devendra, "Buddhism in Ceylon," in *Présence du Bouddhisme, op. cit.*, p. 866. See also "Introduction du Bouddhisme au Laos" by Pierre-Bernard Lafont, *ibid.*, p. 892, and Karuna Kusalasaya, "Buddhism in Siam," *ibid.*, p. 910.

[19] On this point, see the illuminating essay by Anthony Johns, "Sufism as a Category in Indonesian History and Literature," *Journal of Southeast Asia History*, II, 2 (1961), 10–23. Johns' thesis offers a truly significant explanation of the spread of Islam in Southeast Asia.

and become the object of fear and hatred on account of hardships impressed on the population by the building mania and other excesses of the god-kings. What has been termed the "anarchic spirit of Singhalese Buddhism" has been credited with the role of a revolutionary new faith subverting the status quo.[20] (Needless to say, it was by no means the only cause of Angkor's decline.) Von Heine-Geldern has alluded to the significant difference between the two kinds of Buddhism with regard to their conceptions of kingship.[21] It may be well worth investigating whether Ceylonese Hinayana Buddhism, by denying the attributes of deity to kings and by transferring sanctity from the monarch to the palace, contributed to the endemic royal instability in Indianized mainland Southeast Asia in subsequent centuries.

The innovations introduced by Theravada Buddhism were threefold. In the first place, it created a quasi-egalitarian religious community of which even the monarchs themselves became, albeit for short times and mainly symbolically, members.[22] Secondly, it is conceivable that by virtue of their example and teachings the monks could exercise a measure of restraint on . . . monarchical power. And, finally, the sociologically most important innovation of the new faith lay in the new monkhood which practiced the principles of otherworldly simplicity and frugality, in sharp contrast to the Mahayana monks of the classical era. In spite of the close liaison between the upper ranks of the *sangha* and the courts, the mass of the new monks became village "priests," permeating all aspects of peasant life and forming the undisputed center of rural education and social activities. This, I think, amounted to a revolutionary change in the religious landscape of mainland Southeast Asia, or more precisely, in the traditional balance between secular and ecclesiastical authority. The two were still, it is true, intimately connected, but they no longer represented the twin aspects of court culture only. Indeed, the new religious order had an obvious bearing on rural unrest in Theravada lands. For, as often as not, it came over the centuries to be led by monks, the only spiritual and organizational leaders of the peasantry. In other words, the "beggars' democracy" was no longer leaderless or ideologically confined to its world of local spirits and traditions. Theravada Buddhism had forged a link—an ambiguous link, for sure—between the

[20] See George Coedès, *Pour mieux comprendre Angkor* (Paris: Librairie d'Amérique et d'Orient, 1947), pp. 65–66; Lawrence Palmer Briggs, "The Ancient Khmer Empire," *Transactions of the American Philosophical Society*, N.S. XLI (1951), 253–54; Bernard Groslier and Jacques Arthaud, *Angkor: Art and Civilization*, trans. by E. S. Smith, rev. ed. (New York: Frederick A. Praeger, 1966), p. 196.

[21] Robert von Heine-Geldern, *Conceptions of State and Kingship in Southeast Asia* (Data Paper No. 18, Cornell University, Southeast Asia Program, 1960), pp. 7–8. Professor D. G. E. Hall has also drawn attention to the significance of Singhalese Buddhism for periodization. See his articles, "Looking at Southeast Asian History," *The Journal of Asian Studies*, XIX (1959/60), 247–48, and "On the Study of Southeast Asian History," *Pacific Affairs*, XXXIII (1960), 272.

[22] These "innovations" were, indeed, originally introduced into Buddhism in the third century B.C. by King Asoka. See Weber, *The Religions of India, op. cit.*, pp. 237–42. But it was apparently only with the spread of Singhalese Buddhism that this, and other, aspects permeated Southeast Asian Buddhism.

Great Tradition and the Little Tradition, and therein surely lies its major significance in terms of structural change.[23]

Close parallels, as well as interesting contrasts, exist in the Islamized parts of the former Indianized realms. The extent and depth of the consolidation of the two religions obviously differed to a marked degree, depending on internal social factors. Thus, in the agrarian principalities of the mainland, where the new faith was not associated with any particular social and economic class, "conversions" apparently proceeded smoothly and without encountering concerted opposition from defenders of the old order. As for Islam, while we have no direct evidence that this intrinsically egalitarian creed owed its spread to innate peasant opposition to the Malaysian *anciens régimes*, its expansion was by no means unopposed by some of the powers that were. We must not ignore the sociologically important fact that Islamization proceeded from the coastal, mercantile principalities or dependencies—such as Malacca, Achin, and Banten—to such inland, agrarian polities as Mataram. The dynamics of Islamization is thus clearly bound up with the age-old rivalry between two kinds of societies, now sharpened by an increasingly wealthy and independent trading and commercial class (and its administrative allies in some instances). This is the context in which the history of Islam must be understood. Mataram on Java offers the clearest example.

The sultans of Mataram won a temporary victory over Islam through the stratagem of *pro forma* adopting the new faith themselves. Having taken the wind out of the enemy's sails, so to speak, they proceeded to attack him on the two fronts that most seriously threatened the status quo. The prime religious-political targets were, of course, the rebellious commercial port districts. Their systematic destruction by Mataram was, I believe, greatly facilitated by the ceaseless and ultimately successful persecution of Indonesian traders at the hands of the Dutch East India Company. Mataram's second target was those overzealous propounders of the new faith, the ulama. In spite of the far-reaching theological differences between Theravada Buddhism and Islam, the ulama in fact occupy a position and perform some social functions not too dissimilar to those of the *pongyi*. Both can arrogate to themselves the duty to check secular power, and both act as leaders of the peasantry. From the point of view of secular authority, the ulama are, however, potentially far more dangerous clerics. While some ulama attach themselves to courts as religious officials, the vast majority remain fiercely independent and individualistic. In the absence of a religious hierarchy in Islam, the ulama are thus difficult to discipline and control. Moreover, since the Muslim concept of the *ummah* allows of no Gelasian division into separate secular and ecclesiastical realms, the ulama can, and often do, more freely interfere in politics than do Buddhist monks. These qualities—however much they may have been tempered by

[23] These structural changes are of far more crucial significance than any alleged geographical differences between an "aggressive" northern Mahayanism and a "peaceful" southern Hinayanism. For a trenchant critique of this controversy, see Paul Mus's Introduction to *Présence du Bouddhisme, op. cit.*, pp. 190–92.

Sufism in Indonesia—apparently rendered the ulama formidable obstacles to the royal absolutism of the newly-converted Mataramese sultans on Java. (In passing it should also be noted that, unlike the rulers of declining Angkor, those of Mataram represented a new and vigorous dynasty.) In a crushing blow, Mangakurat I reportedly had 2,000 recalcitrant ulama slaughtered in the late seventeenth century.[24]

Its dynamic coastal bases destroyed, its lines of communication with overseas Muslim centers cut by joint action of Mataram and the V.O.C.,* and its most voluble propagators annihilated—thus was Javanese Islam forced into domestication and its long, syncretic slumber. Temporarily, then, the continuity of Javanese history was assured, and with a vengeance. But to assert, as Schrieke[25] has done, that the Java of A.D. 1700 was essentially identical with the Java of A.D. 700 is to fall victim to the very Javanese pseudo-"historiography" that Schrieke himself has so brilliantly dissected. It is to ignore that continuity was purchased at high cost, and that, even then, it was not simply a matter of returning to the status quo ante. Just as the "refeudalization" of parts of Western Europe in the fourteenth and fifteenth centuries only retarded, without ultimately halting, the development of a new social order, the victory of Mataram (and of the V.O.C.) could not forever contain Javanese Islam. Outside Java, especially in parts of Sumatra, the social and political significance of the new faith had in fact already become apparent at a very early date. (The social and political significance of Islam in the Malayan principalities in the early centuries still requires inquiry.)

Our attention has only too often been diverted from the social and political ramifications of Islamization by studies devoted either to the syncretic content matter of Muslim, especially Sufi, teachings in Indonesia, or to the manifest deviations of the Malaysian adat from Islamic law. Such scholarship, it is true, has rendered invaluable service to our understanding of customary law, and, more specifically, of such problems as the Javanese *abangan*[26] complex. But the dichotomy between Islam and adat needs to be studied sociologically as well as juridically: In the ulama, Islam had introduced into island Southeast Asia an ecclesiastical elite group, competing with, or even challenging (albeit often unsuccessfully), the traditional holders of secular power. As soon as contact with the outer world of Islam was re-established on a more or less regular basis, this new elite came to play an increasingly aggressive social and political role. The Padri War and the Java War—and a long chain of ulama-led rural unrest—would suggest that the reinvigoration of Islam commenced in the early nineteenth cen-

[24] See B. J. O. Schrieke, *Indonesian Sociological Studies: Selected Writings of B. Schrieke*, Part I (The Hague/Bandung: W. van Hoeve, 1955), p. 77.

* Verenigde Oost Indische Compagnie (United East India Company).

[25] *Ibid.*, Part II, pp. 4 and 100, respectively. In a paper on "Reconstruction of Malaysian History," presented to the First International Conference of Southeast Asian Historians at Singapore (January, 1961), Dr. Syed Hussein Alatas developed a similar critique.

[26] For a discussion of the *abangan* complex, see Rosihan Anwar, "Islam and Politics in Indonesia," below.

tury under the impetus of Wahhabism, rather than as a result of reformism and modernism only at the turn of the twentieth century, as is commonly claimed.[27] The Achin War, too, was perhaps ignited by Wahhabi
puritanism. Thus, in spite of temporary suppression in parts of island
Southeast Asia, Islam had come to stay, and lastingly to affect the fabric
of society. It provided leadership to the peasantry and linked—in an even
more tenuous fashion than did Theravada Buddhism on the mainland—the
Great Tradition of the *kraton* with the Little Tradition of the *tani*.

THE ERA OF EARLY EUROPEAN INVOLVEMENT

While Vietnam survived the end of the classical era virtually unchanged,
the Philippines and Indianized Southeast Asia had, as we saw, experienced
varying degrees of religious, social, and political innovation. . . . The beginnings of the postclassical era are, however, more easily delineated than
its end, the more so since the threefold division of the area which has so far
adequately served our purposes obviously breaks down from the seventeenth
(if not already from the sixteenth) century onward. Let me suggest that
for the next period in Southeast Asian history we superimpose yet another,
geographical, division: Only in Malaya and Indonesia, where Portuguese
and above all Dutch influences directly and more or less importantly impinged on society, does the postclassical "settlement" undergo additional
changes. Elsewhere, Southeast Asian history moves, both internally and externally, within the broad confines established in earlier times. We have to
wait until the middle of the nineteenth century before ever wider parts of
the area come to share intrinsically similar and profound economic, social,
and political upheavals caused by modern Western imperialism and colonialism. It is only then that the constituent parts of Southeast Asia, without necessarily shedding their individuality and historical legacies, are
welded together to a previously well-nigh unprecedented extent.

As so often before in this essay, we find ourselves face to face with the
problem of continuity and change in assessing the effect of early Western
contacts on Southeast Asia. The brilliant labors of Van Leur have seemingly
inflicted a shattering blow to the traditional "V.O.C.-centered" approach
to the area's history in the sixteenth, seventeenth, and even eighteenth
centuries. Once again we are exhorted to respect the majesty of the Malaysian (especially, of course, the Javanese) infrastructure, and to view the
Dutch, let alone their Portuguese predecessors and competitors, as mere
tangential influences on the course of Southeast Asian history. Arresting
and welcome as Van Leur's corrective is, he, too, may have been guilty
of overstatement and exaggeration, as is so often the case with pioneers.[28] It is

[27] On the penetration of Islamic orthodoxy into Java in the early nineteenth century,
see G. W. J. Drewes, "Indonesia: Mysticism and Activism," in G. E. von Grunebaum
(ed.), *Unity and Variety in Muslim Civilization* (Chicago: University of Chicago Press,
1955), p. 298. Professor J. M. van der Kroef has drawn my attention to the importance
of Wahhabism to Indonesian Islam.

[28] See J. M. van der Kroef, "On the Writing of Indonesian History," *Pacific Affairs*,
XXXI (1958), 352–71.

easy to disparage, and dismiss, the notion that somehow Southeast Asian history entered its "Vasco da Gama" phase with d'Albuquerque's conquest of Malacca in 1511.[29] And obviously we are well advised by Van Leur to forego the Dutch merchantmen as observation posts of history, and to focus, instead, on internal Southeast Asian developments.

At the outset, the V.O.C. may indeed not have constituted more than an additional factor in the age-old pattern of Southeast Asian trade, forced to trade and move cautiously in an essentially Asian matrix; but quite soon the Company undeniably became a *primus inter pares*, to say the least. While its monopolistic control over Indonesian and Asian trade has recently been seriously questioned,[30] it did profoundly affect the economy, and the social structure, of those parts of Indonesia in which it exercised quasi-sovereign political control. The V.O.C.'s part in the destruction of the Islamic trading class has already been mentioned; it is legitimate to speculate on the fate of this class and its role in Southeast Asian history, had it been allowed to develop and grow in the context of an Asia free from Western intrusions. Though expelled from Java by Mataram, might not this nascent bourgeoisie have exerted increasing economic and political pressure on the "Oriental despotisms" in the islands? Or, to look upon it from another angle, can it not be argued that the V.O.C., by its avowedly reluctant interference in politics, arrested historical development by "freezing" into a new-old rigidity those parts of Indonesia in which its control became firmly established? It seems to me rather spurious to claim that it was the infrastructure, as symbolized by the re-established *ancien régime* of Mataram, that could have deflected or canceled out the organizational, military, and economic supremacy that the Company had come to wield, and that allowed it to act as well-nigh supreme arbiter in internal Javanese politics. Indeed, we may go even further and ask ourselves whether its support to the aristocracy—which before long, but certainly under the later system of forced produce deliveries, obtained a vested interest in the new status quo—did not significantly impinge on the relationship between court and peasantry. Nor should we ignore the continuous and apparently justified awe in which Company officials held the "Mohammedan popes and priests," the ulama. The gulf between secular and ecclesiastical elites must very likely have grown during the seventeenth and eighteenth centuries, and very largely as a result of the aristocracy's alliance with the Dutch overlord—an alliance which deprived it of real sovereignty and yet strengthened its autocratic hold over the *tani*. At the same time, the ulama's stat-

[29] The term was coined by the Indian historian, K. M. Pannikkar, in his *Asia and Western Dominance: A Survey of the Vasco da Gama Epoch in Asian History, 1498–1945* (London: G. Allen & Unwin, 1953). His book has often been attacked for its extreme "Europocentrism." See D. G. E. Hall, *East Asian History Today* (Hong Kong: Hong Kong University Press, 1959).

[30] See Kristof Glamann, *Dutch-Asiatic Trade 1620–1740* (Copenhagen: Danish Science Press; The Hague: Martinus Nijhoff, 1958). See also John Bastin, *The Changing Balance of the Early Southeast Asian Pepper Trade* (Kuala Lumpur: Department of History, University of Malaya, 1960).

ure probably increased in the eyes of the harassed peasantry during those centuries.

Fortunately, the vast archival resources covering the Company's activities are mostly accessible and still largely unexplored. Thus, while hypotheses concerning Southeast Asian, especially Indonesian, history before the coming of the Europeans will at best continue to depend on limited evidence supplemented by a great deal of scholarly ingenuity, the records of the seventeenth and eighteenth centuries should in the years to come yield increasingly solid source materials for a properly documented balance sheet of the impact of the V.O.C., and of Western trade in general, on island Southeast Asia. Van Leur was on solid ground when he warned us against supplying the categories of European historiography to Asia, but this must not bar us from examining these centuries as a possibly distinct, if only transitional, period in Southeast Asian—or at least Malaysian—history.

THE ERA OF MODERN COLONIALISM

Between the middle and the end of the nineteenth century, Southeast Asian history enters a new epoch. This new era is characterized by increasing, and ultimately decisive, Western influences upon Southeast Asian societies. In at least three significant aspects, these influences differed from those of earlier times. In the first place, they originated in industrialized nation-states of the Atlantic community rather than in either feudal monarchies and missionary enterprises on one hand, or in chartered trading companies on the other. Second, and no less important, they came to envelop virtually all of mainland and island Southeast Asia with the exception of Siam (Thailand), which has retained its political independence throughout modern history. Finally, while the consolidation of Western control brought law and order to wide areas and, with it, a virtual cessation of dynastic and inter-principality rivalry and martial "interaction," the era of modern colonialism nonetheless introduced, or vastly accelerated, internal structural changes—many of them in the realm of the Little Tradition—in most Southeast Asian societies.

It is true that the mode, range, and intensity of Western influences varied, and that they are differently refracted through the accumulated layers of preceding social, economic, political, and religious experiences of each individual region. However, the collision between external pressures and indigenous traditions in the late nineteenth and twentieth centuries has very likely resulted in more or less similar structural changes, and probably more pervasive ones than Southeast Asian societies had experienced in earlier centuries, if not millennia. It is true that the frontiers of the new colonies came to be sharply delineated and jealously maintained, and that as a result "Southeast Asia" as an entity became more ephemeral than ever before in the area's history. Westernization has nonetheless provided a kind of intrinsic unity which has tended to de-emphasize some of the major historical differences between the Indianized, Sinicized, and Philippine segments of Southeast Asia.

The danger does exist that the importance of these Western influences, especially of those impinging on the peasantry, can be exaggerated and interpreted from an overly "Europocentric" point of view. The fact that the most readily available source materials are of Western origin must therefore be constantly borne in mind. This, however, seems to me a *caveat* that can be fairly easily heeded by responsible historians primarily concerned with internal, structural problems. Other difficulties may not prove quite so manageable, in particular the "colonial versus anticolonial" controversy that is bedeviling the study of the modern era. National pride seems to dictate the desirability of stressing the grandeur of the "infrastructure" at the expense of alien influences, thus rendering the study of Western colonialism increasingly difficult. At the same time, however, the same national pride paradoxically insists that all the ills of Southeast Asian societies be traced to the evil influences of Machiavellian colonialists. These condemnations run the gamut from anguish at the destruction of traditional serenity to the accusation of colonialism's support to degenerate, "reactionary" ruling classes. On the other end of the scale, we encounter the diehard colonialist historians, with an at times spiteful cleaving to the White Man's Burden and the alleged benefits that Western rule generously and selflessly bestowed on Southeast Asia.

It is probably too early to expect that colonialism, like other historical phenomena, be a priori neither praised nor condemned, nor for that matter exorcised. Let us at least endeavor to analyze it in the context of its own—however recent—times, rather than with the wisdom of apologetic or accusing hindsight. Much of what is ascribed to colonialism or imperialism was, in fact, due to the sheer historical confrontation of different civilizations and societies—unplanned, unpremeditated, and on a virtually world-wide scale. But above all else, let us realize that, in the heat of controversy, we have tended to lose sight of the rather perturbing fact that modern colonialism, as a historical category, is only too often taken for granted, instead of being subjected to searching analysis.

As such, it should offer a wide range of fascinating problems. To select a few at random, modern colonial regimes were really unique in substituting nonpolitical, or apolitical, administrations by civil service "experts" for political structures proper. The relationship between these administrative experts and political forces in the metropolitan countries, and with Western economic interests in the colonial domains, would deserve close attention. More fundamental questions could be asked. Was not the colonialism of the last century in many respects a contradiction in terms? Was it not expected to square the circle, especially when it attempted to serve both the interests of Western entrepreneurship and the welfare of the indigenous peasantry in the twentieth century? How could concern for the "common man" be effectively translated into economic improvement, while new economic opportunities and modern sanitation jointly produced a menacing population explosion? Again, could economic modernization proceed without bringing far-reaching social, and ultimately political, changes in its wake? How, then, could the impressive but nonpolitical symmetry of "law and order" be adapted to dynamic growth? And finally, did not colonialism dig its moral grave when it helped rear its own potential gravediggers, the new intelligentsias, whom it then denied the social and political rewards of Western education?

To avoid misunderstanding, I am merely suggesting these questions for a closer study of the generic nature of modern colonialism. I am not asserting that colonialism in Southeast Asia was in even remote danger of collapsing under the weight of these quasi-Hegelian contradictions. On the contrary, I believe that it could in spite of them have lasted for quite a long time, since the forces actively opposing it were in most cases far too weak to subvert the colonial status quo. What destroyed colonialism in Southeast Asia was the Japanese invasion, not internal revolt.

Returning to the more limited, "Asiacentric" frame of reference of this exploratory essay, I shall concentrate on some of the most important structural changes that modern colonialism has wrought in Southeast Asia. I shall begin with the effects of colonial rule—and particularly also of Western education—on the political elite structures. The oft-used distinction between "direct" and "indirect" rule, though less precise than we might wish for, is nonetheless useful in dividing the colonial domains into two general categories.[31] In the "indirectly" ruled parts of Southeast Asia—as, for example, in Annam, Malaya, and in many of the "Outer Islands" of the Dutch East Indies—the indigenous social and political structure was in part maintained, here and there perhaps even artificially buttressed. At the same time, however, the traditional ruling classes were shorn of the instrumentalities of sovereignty, especially of the power to wage war, one of their principal *raisons d'être*.[32] "Indirect" rule often provided the younger members of the aristocracy with a virtual monopoly on access to Western education and was thus instrumental in rearing an intrinsically conservative yet modernized sub-elite group.

The "Oriental despotisms" in "directly" ruled areas—as in Burma, Java, and Cochinchina, for example—were almost invariably replaced by Western-style administrations manned by Europeans. Education in such areas benefited a sociologically far more heterogeneous—if numerically no less restricted—clientele, with the result that the nascent modernizing elites in "directly" administered regions tended to be less tied to the precolonial social and political status quo, and hence less conservative. The Philippines do not fit the twofold division at first sight. But Spanish rule, we must not forget, not only antedated the era of modern colonialism, it also differed from it profoundly in that it had Hispanized, and actually "feudalized," the entire social structure. Hence, while Spanish rule was by our definition "direct," it created a local landowning gentry which, in turn, became the

[31] The classic study is still Rupert Emerson's *Malaysia: A Study in Direct and Indirect Rule* (New York: Macmillan Co., 1937).

[32] The case of Thailand demonstrates the structural importance of continued political independence. While the native officer class was by definition absent in colonial areas, in this noncolonial Southeast Asian country, the traditional elite produced its modernizers from among the military. See my essay, "Non-Western Intelligentsias as Political Elites," *The Australian Journal of Politics and History*, VI (1960), 205–18.

sole beneficiary of Spanish, and in the twentieth century of American, educational, economic, and political privileges.

Western dominance had, then, upset the Southeast Asian elite pattern to a remarkable extent. Though the traditional ruling class(es) in "indirectly" ruled areas retained the outward paraphernalia of their erstwhile prestige and authority, they were nonetheless becoming political, if not also social, anachronisms. Ideologically far more radical and organizationally far more modern, the new intelligentsia elites in "directly" ruled territories, on the other hand, lacked not only the sanctions of the traditional past, but also organic links with Southeast Asia's Little Tradition. They thus did not possess a viable "electorate" that could have endowed them with political bargaining power vis-à-vis the intrinsically nonpolitical colonial order. Indeed, both traditional and modern elites could by and large only function overtly in a social and economic setting that narrowly circumscribed their effectiveness. Without delving too deeply into the history of the modern nationalist movements in the various countries of Southeast Asia, we may note that they all were inhibited by the colonial environment— and by inherent weaknesses of their leadership caused by that environment —to an extent that rendered them, with some very few exceptions only, negligible political threats to colonial regimes. The "rectilinear" interpretation that pictures Southeast Asian nationalism as a strongly-based movement irresistibly sweeping toward victory by forcing concessions from reluctant colonial governments is a doubtless pleasing, but very likely untrue, historical myth. This is not to deny the great significance of Southeast Asian nationalism, but only to urge that it, too, be studied carefully rather than on a priori grounds. But it may be suggested that political liberalization in the twentieth century was, as a rule, the result of complex domestic pressures in metropolitan countries rather than a response to challenges from the colonies.

By comparison with nationalism, religious developments during the colonial era have received comparatively scanty attention, or rather, they have only too often, and without qualifications, been subsumed under the general heading of nationalism. Ideological cleavages between nationalist and religious movements, while they have here and there been extremely important, are not nearly as significant dividing lines as are the social roots nourishing them. At the risk of oversimplifying, we may say that national movements proper were born during the late colonial era; they were led by, and primarily addressed themselves to, urban, Western-trained intelligentsias. Only very rarely had these modern movements deep roots in the countryside. Intellectually and temperamentally, urban intelligentsias were in general unable to strike such roots; in the few instances where they sought to establish them, governmental repression inhibited their efforts effectively. Religious movements, by contrast, drew their major sources of strength from the peasantry; as we have seen, both *pongyi* and ulama had already become foci of peasant life and often leaders of agrarian unrest in the postclassical era. It is, indeed, very likely that the erosion of the traditional elites' political authority in the modern colonial period increased the prestige and social status of religious leaders. For several decades, these leaders in fact constituted the only traditional native elite group that more or less remained intact under alien domination. Their importance is clearly demonstrated in the incessant waves of agrarian unrest that punctuated the colonial era; every now and then, they erupted into large-scale rebellions against colonial rule, fomented and led by religious leaders. It is by no means certain whether these rebellions—such as, for example, the Saya San revolt in Burma—should be invested with nationalistic overtones, for even cursory examination will show that, ideologically at least, agrarian unrest, even in the twentieth century, represented continuity rather than change: It was antigovernment (in a sense anarchic) rather than nationalist; it extolled a return to the alleged golden past common to millennial movements in many agrarian societies, rather than progress conceived in terms of modern nationhood.[33]

Yet, though religious movements continued to draw sustenance from the perennial protests of the Little Tradition, they had nonetheless undergone significant changes. A religious renaissance affected both Theravada Buddhism and Islam during the nineteenth and twentieth centuries, and in the colonial environment, it was bound to be partly deflected into social and political avenues. These new currents—especially Wahhabism and reformism in Islam—found expression through a new, primarily urban but also rural, leadership, which took upon itself the dual task of strengthening religious discipline and of opposing some facets of foreign overlordship (including, of course, the work of Christian missions).[34] Equally important was the fact that these new manifestations of religious life appealed to a new audience, especially to the small indigenous middle class among both peasantry and urban inhabitants, which was here and there slowly emerging as beneficiaries of the new economic frontiers opened up by Western capitalism.[35] Some of the best-known religious-political movements in modern Southeast Asia—for example, the *Sarekat Islam* in Indonesia and the Young Men's Buddhist Association of Burma—thus represented ideologically, socially, and organizationally, an interesting mélange of old and new. They are worthy of careful scrutiny because of this very blending of tradi-

[33] In Erich H. Jacoby's *Agrarian Unrest in Southeast Asia* (New York: Columbia University Press, 1949) we find a rather uncritical approach to such problems as the connection between urban-centered nationalism and agrarian unrest. See especially chapter 8. Jacoby's treatment of these questions is by no means unique: In fact, it is rather typical of recent works on Southeast Asia.

[34] I have dealt with these aspects of Indonesian Islam in my *The Crescent and the Rising Sun: Indonesian Islam under the Japanese Occupation, 1942–1945* (Bandung/The Hague: W. van Hoeve, 1958), pp. 1–100, *passim*. See also William R. Roff, "Kaum Tua—Kaum Muda: Innovation and Reaction in the Malay Community of British Malaya, 1900–1941," a paper presented at the First International Conference of Southeast Asian Historians in Singapore, January, 1961. Published in *Papers on Malayan History* (Singapore, 1962).

[35] See Clifford Geertz, *The Religion of Java* (Glencoe, Ill.: The Free Press, 1960), chapters 10–14, *passim*, and W. F. Wertheim, *Indonesian Society in Transition: A Study of Social Change*, 2d rev. ed. (The Hague/Bandung: W. van Hoeve, 1959), chapter 8.

tional and modern factors which endowed them, for a long time, with greater potential strength than was at the command of the predominantly urban, secular, and Western-oriented nationalist movements of the late 1920's and 1930's.[36] Indeed, the tensions between religious and "secular" elites form a most significant—but usually neglected—part of Southeast Asian history in colonial times. . . .[37]

THE JAPANESE INTERREGNUM

It can be convincingly argued that the demise of Western colonialism in the early 1940's should form the terminal point for the study of Southeast Asian history, since the destruction of the colonial status quo directly led to the subsequent, and still contemporary, era of revolution, liberation, and modern nationhood. I would, instead, plead that the Japanese interregnum be provisionally accorded the status of a distinct historical epoch in Southeast Asian history. I disagree with the almost generally prevailing notion that that interregnum was no more than a superficial (because brief) episode which can be conveniently and adequately relegated to a preface to present-day Southeast Asia. Whatever its significance for postwar developments, the Japanese occupation differed from them in the one, but crucial, respect that Southeast Asian history during those short but eventful years was to a large extent still made, or at least decisively influenced, by aliens. Only after 1945 do Southeast Asians, to varying degrees, once again determine their own fate, in part at least by continuing, or conversely by reacting against, the twin legacies of Western and Japanese overlordship. It is, indeed, no exaggeration to say that, without the Japanese interlude, the balance between continuity and change in contemporary Southeast Asia might conceivably still be weighted in favor of continuity, or, at best, of more gradual, evolutionary change. Japanese rule, moreover, was not merely a period of military occupation. In many ways, the Japanese wittingly or unwittingly interfered in virtually all aspects of Southeast Asian life, albeit to different extents in the various countries, and to different degrees in areas occupied by army and navy, respectively. If only as a catalyst, then, the last stage of foreign domination fully deserves—in spite of great gaps in available documentation—careful attention as a significant stage in the history of Southeast Asia.

A full understanding of the effects of Japanese rule has to commence with the observation that its short-run *raison d'être* differed profoundly

[36] See Harry J. Benda and Ruth T. McVey (eds. and trans.), *The Communist Uprisings of 1926–1927 in Indonesia: Key Documents* (Ithaca, N.Y.: Cornell University, Southeast Asia Program, Modern Indonesia Project, 1960), Introduction.

[37] It is regrettable that, in the brilliant work on the evolution of Javanese social structure by Dutch sociologist D. H. Burger, this aspect is neglected. Only some of Burger's articles, "Structuurveranderingen in de Javaansche Samenleving," published in several installments of *Indonesie* during 1949–50, have so far been translated into English. A similar lacuna concerning Islamic elites mars the otherwise highly useful work by J. M. Gullick, *Indigenous Political Systems of Western Malaya* (London: The Athlone Press, 1958).

from the purposes of modern Western colonial rule. (The contours of peacetime colonial rule by a victorious Japan can, of course, only be the subject of conjecture). The exigencies and demands of the war seemingly dictated a twin policy of ensuring, by whatever means, internal peace and order while extracting the maximum benefits in terms of material and human resources from the occupied territories. In the process of enforcing these policies, the occupying power for better or worse rode roughshod over much that Western colonialism had created, whether in the Westernized sector of the economy, the precarious advances in social welfare and social engineering in general, and, last but not least, in political liberalization. To a large extent, that is to say, Japanese rule constituted a calculated or unintentional reversal, and often a destruction, of the colonial order, here and there accompanied by perhaps equally important endeavors at Japanizing the occupied countries. The careful administration by trained colonial experts suddenly gave way to often crude improvisation by military personnel or militarized bureaucrats without adequate academic or administrative training. While—particularly in the early stages of the occupation—concern for internal, indigenous problems occupied a secondary place in Japanese plans, Japanese actions almost from the outset affected Southeast Asian societies to a marked degree, and often far beyond the intentions of Japan's policy-makers at home and in the occupied regions. In several respects, the occupation era was thus, not unlike modern Western colonialism, subject to internal contradictions.

My greatest concern here is, of course, with the most important structural changes that Nipponese domination effected within the framework of earlier social relationships, particularly those created in the modern colonial period discussed in the preceding section of this essay. These were on the whole more conspicuous in formerly "directly" administered areas where the demise of Western colonialism had led to a partial socio-political vacuum that the Japanese proceeded to fill by various indigenous elite groups. The areas formerly under "indirect" rule did not, of course, remain unaffected by Japanese policies either, and here and there—notably, for example, in Achin[38]—the interregnum did produce significant changes. Since the traditional ruling classes had been among the main beneficiaries of Western colonial rule, the Japanese seem to have distrusted them en bloc and to have more heavily relied on competing, notably religious, elites. But whatever their early misgivings, the Japanese ultimately came to respect the social status quo wherever it was represented by more or less entrenched, traditional political or economic elites; the *présence Japonique* thus left the fabric of the Malay,[39] Filipino, and, of course, of the Thai

[38] See the excellent study by A. J. Piekaar, *Atjèh en de oorlog met Japan* (The Hague/Bandung: W. van Hoeve, 1940).

[39] Professor Yoichi Itagaki presented an interesting analysis of "Some Aspects of the Japanese Policy for Malaya Under the Occupation, with Special Reference to Nationalism" at the aforementioned Singapore conference. (Published in *Papers on Malayan History*, Singapore, 1962.)

ruling classes relatively intact. The exceptional case of Vietnam, where nominal French control continued until early 1945, deserves additional study.[40]

In Burma and Java, particularly, where no such significant vested indigenous classes existed, the Japanese from the very outset sought the cooperation of other elite groups, and in fact very considerably aided in their consolidation. The relative strengthening of these groups—notably of the Western-trained, nationalist intelligentsias—should, however, not be misread as a concerted Japanese move to make more than spurious and carefully guarded concessions. The "rectilinear" interpretation of Southeast Asian nationalism has led to the rather naïve view that through lack of numbers and ignorance, if not because of intrinsic weakness, Japanese administrators were forced to allow free play to nationalist sorcerors' apprentices, either as quasi-collaborators or as anti-Japanese resistance fighters. The record would seem to indicate that until almost the end of the occupation (in the case of Burma and the Philippines, until the Allied re-invasion), the Japanese were in undisputed control of internal events; it was they who held the keys to all power, and it was they who rigorously maintained the limits within which urban elites, especially, were allowed to move. Whether nominally exercising the authority of "independent" governments or whether playing less elevated roles as leaders of as-yet dependent peoples, the scope of nationalist elites was pitifully restricted, their activities narrowly circumscribed, and their bargaining power vis-à-vis the occupying power virtually nonexistent. Much of their weakness was doubtless due to Japanese unwillingness to devolve real co-determination, much less power, on anyone, let alone on partners whose radical ideological orientations they had good reason to suspect; far more significantly, the intelligentsias, moreover, lacked both internal cohesion as elite groups proper and, as yet, widespread popular support. Yet, if in terms of actual power the representatives of Southeast Asian nationalism demonstrably gained little while Japanese overlordship lasted, they nonetheless owe to the occupation an immense increase in their social and political stature and prestige and a great deal of improved organizational techniques. They had come close enough to the fulcrum of politics so that when the war abruptly ended they almost inevitably emerged as the best-qualified group to grasp control in the vacuum created by the Japanese surrender, and prolonged (as in Indonesia) by tardy reoccupation and attempted recolonization by the former metropolitan powers.

If the interregnum had brought the urban intelligentsias from the periphery to the center of public life, it wrought no less important changes in the status of religious elites in Southeast Asia. With the exception of Indonesia,[41] this aspect of Japanese policies has so far unfortunately remained relatively neglected. But since the peasantry's acquiescence in, if not sup-

[40] The best discussion is still Philippe Devillers, *Histoire du Viet-Nam de 1940 à 1952* (Paris: Editions du Seuil, 1952), Part I.

[41] See *The Crescent and the Rising Sun, op. cit.,* pp. 103–94, and Pickaar, *op. cit., passim.*

port for, wartime policies was doubtless one of the most crucial Japanese targets, their efforts to win allies among religious leaders flowed logically from a realistic understanding of the key role of *pongyi* and ulama (and perhaps also of the lower Catholic clergy) in peasant life. Rightly or wrongly, the Japanese may, moreover, have felt that religious leaders were politically less sophisticated and hence ideologically more reliable than Western-educated intellectuals. In stark contrast to the colonial powers' aloofness vis-à-vis Southeast Asian religions, the Japanese apparently fostered religious organizations, often bringing rural and urban religious leaders together in mass movements under military or naval control. Their concern for these leaders did not, it is true, altogether obviate the recurrence of agrarian unrest under religious, sometimes even anti-Japanese, banners. Yet, on the whole, the Japanese apparently utilized, revolutionized, and consolidated the religious elites and thus endowed them with potential strength—vis-à-vis both traditional and nationalist elites—without precedence in modern Southeast Asian history.

The occupation regimes did not only exert decisive influence on the position of already existing social groups, they were also instrumental in creating entirely new ones, which soon started to compete for influence, prestige, and—in postwar years—for power with other elites. The most important of these were without doubt the new Southeast Asian military leaders reared by the Japanese army commands in many parts of the area. While colonial armies had, as a rule, been drawn from ethnic minorities and officered by Westerners, the Japanese recruited and trained entire armies and officers corps from among the major ethnic groups in Southeast Asia. Enthusiastic young men of common birth, but without either religious or Western training—hitherto the exclusive prerequisites for nonaristocratic elite status—eagerly responded to the opportunities to gain social status and prestige thus opened up to them. Side by side with the military proper, we find other new leaders emerging from the plethora of youth and other organizations brought into being by the occupying power. Prestigious—if in terms of actual significance perhaps hollow—positions awaited them as auxiliary police, as scout leaders, as aides in the distribution of food and clothing—and as spies for the New Order in villages and towns. These emerging elite groups are of more than only sociological interest, for they represent a veritable revaluation of traditional social values in Southeast Asia, a concomitant of the revolutionary tide generated by the occupation policies and propaganda. Politicized and often militarized during the war years, these young people rapidly developed into a clientele for political, nationalist appeals, into transmission belts between city and countryside, but also into new potential leadership groups challenging older-generation political and religious elites.

For purposes of a thorough analysis of the Japanese interregnum, the above brief sketch of structural changes among Southeast Asian elites would have to be supplemented by studies concerning the often equally significant innovations introduced by Japanese rule in other segments of urban and rural societies. Ruthless recruitment of labor battalions and auxiliary soldiers caused displacement of manpower throughout the area without regard to racial or national affiliations. Increasingly heavy pressure on food supplies by the occupation authorities brought untold hardship to many peasants, but it also led to widespread squatting on former estate lands in some parts of Southeast Asia. Indigenous societies were, then, subjected to outside pressures of unprecedented vehemence, while at the same time Japanese-sponsored propaganda sought to imprint many new values on broad layers of the population. Add to all this the sudden removal and public humiliation of the former Western overlords, and political and economic encroachments on other segments of the "plural societies," and the distinct, and truly revolutionary, character of the occupation era will stand out in bold relief. Perhaps the relief is too boldly drawn and should be carefully sieved through the eyes, and the written accounts, of Southeast Asians themselves, to attain a more balanced appraisal of this stage of Southeast Asian history.

The Era of Independence

The emergence into internal independence and world politics constitutes the most recent chapter in Southeast Asian history. For obvious reasons, these developments have so far been more intensively studied by social scientists than by historians, but there is reason to hope that before long this imbalance may be at least partly repaired. For, though postwar history has been extremely turbulent and eventful, the historian may be able to approach it with a somewhat longer view and less concern for the immediate destiny of Southeast Asia. I will, however, reserve for another occasion an analysis of this most recent period. Suffice it to say that I hope that the cumulative structural changes charted in these pages may provide a tentative basis for the generic understanding of later historical developments. Thus, the origins and orientations of the various elite groups and their relative positions vis-à-vis each other should emerge rather clearly from the history of earlier eras. The significance of religious establishments for postwar developments may likewise be deduced from their historical antecedents. Yet there can be little doubt that significant quantitative and qualitative changes have taken place since 1945 that will require the most careful study. One of the most fascinating and rewarding tasks awaiting the historian surely is the perennial problem of continuity and change in postwar Southeast Asia: While to varying degrees the actors in modern history are the products of change, their style of making history may well increasingly revert to earlier, indigenous, molds.

3

CULTURAL CONTINUITIES AND DISCONTINUITIES IN SOUTHEAST ASIA*

LAURISTON SHARP

In 1961, our Association President, Norman Brown, discussed with us the problem of the content of cultural continuity in India.[1] He pointed out that in spite of many variations in time and local differentiations in space, the highly developed civilization of India from the third millennium B.C. to the present offers to the student a picture of a continuing entity, a kind of moving picture in which the successive events of a plot seem to be informed and given a special character and vitality by some pervasive element running through the story, an element which might be sought, it was concluded, in the particular perdurable values basic to many Indian behavior patterns.

In China, too, there has been cultural continuity over a period of millennia, ways of life which through long episodes of expansion and change have nevertheless retained a characteristic identity. "While China most certainly

* Reprinted by permission of the author and the publisher from *The Journal of Asian Studies*, XXII (November, 1962), 3–11.

[1] W. Norman Brown, "The Content of Cultural Continuity in India," *The Journal of Asian Studies*, XX (August, 1961), 427–34.

has not been 'unchanging,' it has shown strong cultural continuity and Chinese history has been characterized by 'change within tradition,' " is the conclusion of two other past Presidents of our Association.[2] Even scholars who emphasize the heterogeneity of Chinese behavior in time and space are willing to admit that some common cultural binder has existed; thus Eberhard has recognized "the concept of 'Chinese' culture only as an ideal, as a cultural idea, which, however, in the course of history, has been more and more imbued with reality."[3]

Scholars studying Indian and Chinese behavior have thus found regularly repeated and identifiable behavior patterns extended in time and space and bound together, at least in an empirical or statistical sense, in clusters: temporal cultural continua or cultural traditions, located within spatial cultural continua or culture areas. Combined, and elevated to a somewhat more abstract level, these continua of behavior in space and time give us Indian or Chinese culture, beginning at such and such a period—Harappa, Maurya, Gupta, or Shang, Han, T'ang—and extending to such and such geographical limits as they move down through the centuries of Indian and Chinese history. These cultures are conceived of as singular entities, maintaining in this continuity a kind of cultural character, a distinctiveness, which would clearly be lost if they were fragmented or broken up into discontinuous parts.

This view of two great behavioral continuities existing through the centuries and the provinces of the Indian and Chinese cultural traditions and areas sees innovations, whether originating within or outside these civilizations, as becoming transformed to fit within the peculiar Indian or Chinese cultural configuration or personality. This conception of history is one easy enough to adopt; for without the continuity, without the plot, without the entity culture (or civilization) that seems "to do things," we are left with only a welter of particular events, a chaos of behavior items, when our whole symmetrical, rhythmic, and continuing animal being cries out for cosmos, for ordered structure, and for perdurability. If they stand apart from a continuing story, the items of history appear of little value to us except as unrelated oddments of interest, even though they may well constitute, as a Chinese student of mine once happily expressed it, "exciting tids and bits" for the scholar's swelling pack of notes. Much better to cling to a view— which indeed can be justified—in which the great cultural streams flow on sluggishly but steadily between known banks through time, clearly recognizable still as Ganges or Hwang.

This conception of civilizations as recognizable objects in the landscapes of time and space coincides nicely with the conventional view of culture which the anthropologists have so thoroughly and, in my opinion, too successfully promulgated during the past thirty years, and which is by now so widely accepted that most of us use the term, it would be my claim, with-

[2] Edwin O. Reischauer and John K. Fairbank, *East Asia: The Great Tradition* (Boston: Houghton Mifflin, 1958), p. 23.

[3] Wolfram Eberhard, "Kultur und Siedlung der Randvölker Chinas," *T'oung Pao,* XXXVI (1942), Supplement 4.

out thinking sufficiently about what its referents might be. There is, they tell us, the totality of mankind's past and present and (we sincerely trust) future learned and patterned behavior which is usually referred to as "human culture." But all of us also recognize the use of the term for the patterned learned behavior of the personnel of a society, and this is commonly called "a culture." If we ask what a society is, it turns out conveniently to be any group or category which has a culture, a circular conception often leading to grave difficulties of analysis. One escape is to go on to the more refined conception of the "sub-culture," a cluster of similar behaviors which identifies some segment of a larger group; or we may move in the other direction, following Toynbee or Northrop, putting similar cultures together until we have a "super-culture." . . . In any case, and however we turn, we are still confronted with the problem of cultural boundaries in space and time.

With such simple conceptual equipment as this, as I have pointed out elsewhere, "many anthropologists have been persuaded under the pressure of international events after the war to pursue their cultural studies within a framework of academic area or regional programs. Many of us, attempting to move from our preparation for tribal studies, from our field experiences in circumscribed camps, islands, pueblos, street corners, Middletowns, or Wisslerian culture areas into the wide expanse of national or subcontinental regions of millions of people, have found ourselves indeed ill-equipped for expeditions of such scope, our baggage of empirical data, tools, and theory in sore need of reorganization and improvement. Too frequently we have brought with us little more than this old cookie-cutter concept of culture, with which we have tried to stamp out neatly edged goodies in various fancy but flat designs from a ready-mixed, nonrising batter of behavior as sticky and indigestible as that from which Bagehot's 'cake of custom' was half baked."[4]

Equipped only with the conventional cookie-cutter concept of culture, we find ourselves in grave analytical difficulties when we turn to Southeast Asia, lying between the great creative but self-producing civilizations of India and China. In this Austro-oriental corner of Eurasia, now set off so clearly from India on the west by a cultural oil-and-water border between the Bengal plain and the hills of Assam, and from China on the north much less distinctly, and shading off vaguely eastward to Irian and the Pacific islands, we look in vain for any general major cultural stream flowing steadily out of a distant past. We do find the river that is Vietnam, oozing south from an overflowing Chinese source these two millennia. Though we know all too little about it, Vietnam in itself may perhaps be seen as a cultural continuum in time in the Brown, Reischauer, and Fairbank sense, a suborder within Southeast Asia; or, with more emphasis on space, simply as a branch of the great Chinese civilization extending southward as an intrusion into an adjacent region. Still, the Indochinese mainland as a geographical entity is real enough, and the border created by

---

[4] Lauriston Sharp, "The Overseas Program, the Professor and the Potential Ph.D." (unpublished paper, 1961).

Vietnam between chopsticks to the east and spoons or hands to the west simply serves to emphasize the lateral unconformities currently found in this area.

Discontinuities, cultural fault lines, borders between ways of behaving confront us everywhere as we move across Southeast Asia, the one part of the globe where we find represented in small space all four of the only great surviving human traditions which singly or in combination may influence and inform our behavior for generations to come: the Sinic, Indic, Islamic, and North Atlantic. But these, too, are cross-cut by complex and intricate divisions: Buddhists and Catholics, Muslims and Kafirs; traditionalist and modernist; Communist and capitalist; urban elites Westernized in varying degrees and still illiterate rural masses; industrial sectors and agricultural sectors. And if we move vertically rather than horizontally, we encounter in the divisions between hill and valley peoples an ethnic stratification such as is rarely found elsewhere, the despair of cultural cartographers.

What can we make of this confusion? How do we proceed? Is Southeast Asia simply a residual category which should be abandoned—with appropriate bows toward Paris, London, New Haven, Ithaca, Berkeley, Tokyo, and Kyoto—as a useless unit for cultural and historical analysis? This is, of course, an old question, as old as the nineteenth-century early use of the term "Southeast Asia." In returning to it, let us try to ignore the culture carrot dangled before us these many years by the anthropologists and proceed to sort out some of the continuities and discontinuities of human experience in Southeast Asia as they actually appear to exist in time and space.

In this search we should first work back from the present and up the little streams, the short runs of Southeast Asian history and prehistory. If we push back far enough we come eventually to a vast spatial and temporal continuity, the relatively homogeneous remains of an Oriental Lower and Middle Palaeolithic, or Old Stone Age. From Java and across the Sunda shelf through Malaya, Siam, and Burma, north to Chou-k'ou-tien near Peking, and west to the Pamirs in a great triangle is the area of the chopper tools or, perhaps more indicative, an area lacking the first axes typical of Europe, Africa, the Near East, and most of India during much of the Pleistocene, or glacial, period. The New World being uninhabited by man for most of this period, we have all human behavior—or all we know of it —divided into an Oriental and an Occidental sphere. More finds within the Oriental triangle may blur this distinction, but at present the two technological traditions seem adequately documented. Southeast Asia, at times extending far north of its present geographical boundaries, was definitely a part, and a conforming part, of the Palaeolithic Oriental sphere, with its cultural borders toward northeast India already quite clearly delineated. During the late Pleistocene in the East, some local industries appear which differ from each other; but perhaps a further evidence of early homogeneity in the East is that the development of different technological traditions was slower and much less exuberant than in the West. Some late

Palaeolithic remains, or Mesolithic, such as the Hoabinhian, even seem to carry on the chopper-tool tradition.

The geologically "Recent" period witnessed the development of a major east-west cultural fault or unconformity in the Orient. This line, dividing the early and north Chinese Neolithic from the early New Stone Age of Southeast Asia, ran its wandering course north of the Yangtze River, for tropical Southeast Asia has only quite recently shrunk south to its present geographical borders in southern political China. Sometime between about 8000 B.C. and the third millennium in the area south of this Yangtze line, there developed quite independently of specific influences from any other part of the world the wholly distinctive Early Southeast Asian Neolithic.

The indigenous development of this tropical Early Neolithic complex in Southeast Asia was a major creative achievement by the people of the area. It clearly set these Austroasiatic and Austronesian speakers apart not only from the Dravidians and later Aryans of India but also from the Chinese who would expand outward from the Hwang Ho. It has been largely neglected, in part because the evidence for it is still mainly circumstantial, and in part because it chiefly affected . . . historic peoples of Oceania and Africa who have only recently become of interest to most of us.

As reconstructed, this cultural complex was marked most notably by a unique cluster of food plants and by the later addition of a variety of pig and the chicken to the already domesticated dog. The tropical vegetable and fruit crops first cultivated in Southeast Asia—yams, taro, breadfruit, bananas, pandanus, perhaps coconuts, and others—were limited in their northern spread by ecological conditions, so that in North China the way was left open for cereal crops to be developed or borrowed. However, the prerice Southeast Asian food complex, together with other Early Neolithic cultural elements originating in Southeast Asia, could be extended east and west through the tropical zone, and was to a remarkable degree. Austronesian speakers carried practically the entire complex eastward through the previously empty reaches of the Pacific to Easter Island, and perhaps even beyond. By migration or diffusion, elements spread westward into India and on into tropical Africa, with important effects on the native economy and distribution of populations in both areas. Some elements not linked with environment spread beyond the tropics, moving at different rates; the chicken, which reached China early, is not mentioned in Homer, Hesiod, or the Old Testament, and Plato, with Socrates' sacrificial cock, was one of the first to document its eventual appearance in the Mediterranean world.

We know little of the specifics of the rise of this original contribution of Southeast Asia to the stream of mankind's total history. Indeed, the preceding statements are largely based on inferences and extrapolations from recent data provided by botany, ethnology, linguistics, and other disciplines, for the archaeological record is weak and incomplete. But, as we look at the margins of the palimpsest which is Southeast Asian history, we find, I believe, good evidence of a widespread lateral cultural continuity, a rather uniform spread of distinctive behaviors distributed throughout the mainland and island regions of the area by energetic and mobile people of the Early Neolithic, some of whom were even ready to go beyond their own cultural borders. In this horticultural Neolithic phase, the gardening and fishing communities scattered thinly across all of Southeast Asia, from the Assam Range to Taiwan and from South China to the Arafura Sea exhibited, like their Palaeolithic predecessors, an impressive degree of cultural similarity, and their common traits are evidence that cultural discontinuity is not an historical imperative for this area.

The agricultural Late Neolithic period of Southeast Asia, with its dry and wet rice cultivation by digging-stick, hoe, or later plow, apparently developed in direct interaction with the Neolithic phases of northern China, and the China coast. These diverse and as yet little understood interrelationships certainly were occurring by the early half of the second millennium B.C., when the first archaeological hint of rice appears in Honan; its second known appearance is in the Ganges-Jumna Doab at the other end of the monsoon rice zone 500 to 1,000 years later. It is clear that from this period on down to the present, the experience of most of the Southeast Asian region has been dynamically related to Kroeber's great Eurasian "oikoumenê," an intriguing concept providing a Eurasia-centric view of interwoven events in the larger area which were reflected on the peripheries, whether the southeastern extremities or the far western peninsula of Europe.[5]

Differential geographical factors and conditions of diffusion created local variations in the Southeast Asian Late Neolithic as compared with the relative homogeneity of the earlier horticultural period. Indeed, the earlier cultural phase persisted in southern and eastern parts of the region which were never reached by rice agriculture, in spite of extensive maritime trade which spread many common traits around the inner coasts of the mediterranean South China Sea. Elsewhere, dry and wet rice technologies in themselves created somewhat differing ways of life adjacent to each other, one in the hills, one in the valleys. The latter expanded by apparently slow processes of change involving less substitution than addition, and perhaps lagging behind more stressful developments in China and India. Centuries before our era, irrigated rice production had advanced in the great river valleys, the alluvial marshes, and the terraced slopes of Southeast Asia where this cereal, yielding twenty times as much food per land unit as wheat under wet tropical conditions, was simply added to the already ample subsistence which gardens, orchards, fish ponds, scavenging pigs, dogs, and domestic fowl provided for earlier villagers. The modern, still uncrowded Southeast Asian peasant, with an archaic rice technology, little improved in millennia and not including night soil but in a stable and wonderfully appropriate climate, need retain for his own use only one-third of the rice crop his average family produces.[6] There is no evidence that such excess production led to an indigenous development of civilization, in the technical sense of urban centers and their dependent

[5] A. L. Kroeber, *The Nature of Culture* (Chicago: University of Chicago Press, 1952), pp. 379–95.
[6] Lauriston Sharp and others, *Siamese Rice Village* (Bangkok, 1953), p. 173.

peasantries, but the ground was laid for the support of this type of culture when it entered Southeast Asia from the outside.[7] In the meantime, increasing cultural diversity, while establishing lateral or geographical discontinuities, seems to mark no major break with the past of the Early Neolithic, so we assume that many features of the earlier period continued on into the still distinctively Southeast Asian Late Neolithic traditions of the area, which were to confront the civilizations advancing from the north and west.

The character of this confrontation, when Chinese, Indian, and later Indo-Islamic cultural elements poured into the region, has aroused considerable debate in recent years. Our very language ("advancing," "poured into") reflects the long-standing bias of its own and foreign scholars who have viewed this simply as a receiving area into which have come contributions from other regions, a dead sea whose brackish waters, like those of the Tonle Sap, have been freshened only by tributaries flowing into it from the great hydraulic river systems found elsewhere in the world. Were representatives of other cultures pressing in near the turn of our era, or were Southeast Asians reaching out to select for importation those traits congenial to their own traditions? And who were these representatives, and how did they move? Did Vietnam become indeed a "Little China," and Java simply a cultural colony within a "Greater India"? Did influences from outside affect only special groups of the population, or were they widespread? Are we dealing here with cultural continuities or discontinuities, and if the latter, were they massive or minor?

Beginning with the Dongson period a few centuries B.C., we find indeed a great cultural influx from India on one quarter and from China on the other, the latter extending influences not only to the coastal southeast and into northern Vietnam but also to the southwest where, in Yunnan, as documented by recent excavations, Western Han and Scythian elements mixed with basic Southeast Asian cultural traits.[8] Except in the northeast, where a more thorough acculturation was imposed, the major importations, and especially those from India, were mainly derived from what have

---

[7] In an earlier day, the rice farmer's export surplus could contribute directly to the support of towns and cities. This is made explicit in an account of rice technology southward from Yunnan written (with hints of modernity) in A.D. 863 by a Chinese official from Hanoi: "The irrigated fields have one ripening [of nonglutinous rice] each year. . . . Cultivation is . . . everywhere . . . supervised . . . by *Man* ["Southern Barbarian"] officials sent by the *Man* generals of the cities and garrison-towns . . . drought does them no harm. When the harvest is over the *Man* official gives the advance of grain or rice according to the number of mouths in the cultivator's family. The rest all goes in taxes to the government." Fan Ch'o, *Man Shu*, translated by G. H. Luce, edited by G. P. Oey (Ithaca, N.Y.: Cornell University Press, 1961), p. 67.

[8] Yün-nan shêng po wu kuan, *Yün-nam Chin-ning Shih-chai Shan ku mu hsiang fa chüeh pao kao* (Peking, 1959), 2 vols. Some of the swords found at this Rock Fortress Mountain site, dated after about 100 B.C., are near replicas of swords from earlier Iron Age sites of the Danube area. Such far western influences in the Dongson period had been anticipated by Heine-Geldern. For a brief statement of his views, see Robert Heine-Geldern, "Die kulturgeschichtliche Bedeutung Südostasiens," *Geographische Rundschau* IX (Braunschweig, 1957), 121–27.

been called the "Great Traditions" as opposed to the peasant "Little Traditions," indicating the probably elite character of the selective contacts through which artifacts and behavior patterns were transferred, notably in the fields of religion and mythical cosmography and related aspects of the magico-religious state, city planning, warfare, metallurgy and other arts, literary materials, and forms of writing. There were also suggestive rejections of cultural complexes presumably available for transfer through upper social strata, such as the rigidities of caste, the subordination of women to men in practice (the theory being accepted), forms of kinship organization, eroticism, some domestic rituals, and the use of dairy products.

Given the traditional role of Southeast Asian chiefs or other high status holders as commercial and ritual entrepreneurs, the early-developed navigational skills of Southeast Asians, the fact that monsoons did blow in both directions and always required some layover between outward and inward voyages, the role of Southeast Asians in early interregional link trade as seen in such entrepôt ports as grew up at the mouths of the Chao Phraya and Mekong, and the evidence for northward- and westward-moving inland trade, there seems no good reason to deny Southeast Asians their active part in these early cultural relations. Except for Han Chinese pressing southeastward, no *Völkerwanderung* or population movement need be invoked to explain routes of transfer, but simply a lively system of communication networks such as in fact existed. Besides transportation and trade facilities and surplus food and materials production, with the consequent technological unemployment often found in such an "overdeveloped" economy, there are other aspects of the wet rice Late Neolithic cultures of Southeast Asia which would help explain and, in my opinion, require us to accept the extended and rapid spread of innovations imported from the Eurasian oikoumenê as overlays to be subsequently absorbed as integrated cultural inlays.[9] We need only contrast what we know of early

9 In the precivilized village or tribal cultural systems of the area, there was not only geographical mobility by land and sea but also social mobility—the widespread three-class system of lords, commoners, and slaves was an open system, so that foreign ideas and behaviors could percolate up or down and around or across a cultural system without being confined to any one compartment of society except through sumptuary rules; the small, short-lived nuclear family and bilineal kin group, as opposed to the more inflexible unilineal kin group of the Tibeto-Burmans and Chinese, was presumably prevalent at this period except in parts of Sumatra, the Lesser Sundas, Celebes, and Taiwan, and permitted, when community and family interests conflicted, a primary loyalty to the agents of extra-family units (a responsible lord or *devaraja*) such as could hardly exist in India or China, except among eunuchs; sexual egalitarianism permitted men to play many feminine roles, and women masculine roles, this flexible arrangement incidentally doubling the labor force when need arose; cooperative service owed to a chief became the local variety of the ritually organized *corvee*, in which laborers might work with fellow "nationals" from a wide area, and soldiers might feel they were supporting their king and cosmos in marching with strange but fellow Viets (or Chams or Khmers) against the cursed Chinese (Viets or Chams); village or tribal rituals and beliefs were nonexclusive and tolerant of variation, but there were no structured supra-village religious systems; cultural roles in general were improvised and non-rigid, so that behavioral change was acceptable as a variation or supplement to usual behavior rather than as a substitute for it.

tribal or village communities of Late Neolithic type, many of which cannot have been too unlike those discovered in the Philippines in the sixteenth century, with a settlement such as the Dongson Rock Fortress Mountain in Yunnan during the first century B.C. or A.D., or with a Funan village as we might reconstruct it a few centuries later looking up to its "king of the mountain," to realize that for the common wet rice farmer a cultural revolution had occurred. In the areas of civilization, the wet rice valley and coastal communities of mainland Southeast Asia and the western islands during the early centuries of our era, the new importations led not only to the rapid formation of urban aggregates and states but to a general massive discontinuity with the past for all participants in these systems. The innovations, and particularly supra-village ideologies, penetrated from the new mediating mandarin, Brahmanic, or later Buddhist elites down into large masses of the people, changing them into a peasantry and attaching them to the urban centers in a process comparable to the one requiring a much longer time span, in which the contemporary far west of Eurasia, during the first millennium A.D., absorbed the heritage of Mediterranean civilizations.[10]

This urban revolution, with its rapid acquisition from outside of already developed aspects of civilization, is not the only example of sudden and thorough shifts of cultural behavior available from Southeast Asia. We find in this area also, unaccompanied by mass migrations, the large-scale replacement of Indonesian, Khmer, and Mon dialects on the mainland by Vietnamese, Thai, and Burmese from the north; the wildfire spread of Islam after the establishment of Malacca, but only to Austronesian speakers, including some Chams; the crescendo of revolutionary changes in behaviors, including ideas and sentiments, beginning with the intensification of the colonial experience in the 1880's. It is such rapid and extensive developments as these and others which produced the previously noted cultural discontinuities that currently characterize this region. If we heed the warning of more recent scholars from van Leur to Smail against defining these discontinuities and breaks by culture-bound standards based solely on European experience (which too easily provides such readymade concepts as "feudal," "medieval," "nobility," even "village," and so on), then these fragmentations of the experience of a region in time and

---

10 Continuities which actually exist should, of course, not be underemphasized. The contributions of India (including Ceylon) and China to the Southeast Asian civilizations were certainly restyled by them, and quickly, into a total configuration, a character different from that of either source. Traditional interests and values continuing from earlier periods doubtless informed this development of their own styles by the local civilizations, so that the processes of creative transformation, like those of selection, must be studied in relation to the past. Also, within these new civilizations, there developed internal social structural discontinuities between upper classes and commoners and slaves, in which the behaviors of the latter as compared with the former may be judged less discontinuous with the past. Nevertheless, while we can say that Chinese civilization was characteristically Chinese 3,000 years ago, we cannot say the same of Southeast Asia, for here, in the areas of civilization after the turn of our era, many behavior patterns of all classes were thoroughly transformed from those obtaining previously. Discontinuities need not imply hodgepodge or badly integrated cultural systems.

space raise basic questions regarding the nature of culture and of cultural change.[11] And these questions are more forcefully thrust upon us by the broken histories of Southeast Asia than by the historical continuities of India or China. They may also more forcefully be thrust upon us by disciplines other than history or anthropology, subjects which conventionally have sought and all too frequently tended to find the continua within the neatly bounded cookie-cutter shape.

The fundamental questions concerning cultural behavior we are in no position to ask or to answer intelligently until we explicitly look for and emphasize the cultural discontinuities and unconformities, the fault lines of history and of current cultural organization and social interaction. For a more honest understanding of the realities of culture we should lay less stress on a search for traditional and passive continuities and instead seek out differences, dissonances, conflicts within actual behavior clusters bound by time or space, and not bound by our imposed, locality-dominated conceptions of "a tradition" and "a culture." In an area such as modern Southeast Asia, and I suppose elsewhere as well, we can no longer escape the generational discontinuities, the dual roles of the old man who overtly rejects change for himself but covertly demands it for his son, the stressed differences between social strata whose members may suffer a malaise of frustrated hopes and guilt, the dichotomies between ethnic majorities and deprived or ignored minorities, the sudden changes in family structure, all the horizontal and lineal breaks which clearly exist in these complex societies today. In the humanities and social sciences, so long concerned with the past and present, we now ignore these realities only with peril to the future. Complacently unattended and overheated, "the cake of custom" has blown up.

[11] J. C. van Leur, *Indonesian Trade and Society: Essays in Asian Social and Economic History* (The Hague/Bandung: W. van Hoeve, 1955), pp. 3–43; John R. W. Smail, "On the Possibility of an Autonomous History of Modern Southeast Asia," *The Journal of Southeast Asian History*, II (1961), 72–102.

4

SOUTHEAST ASIA:
THE BALKANS OF THE ORIENT?
A STUDY IN CONTINUITY AND CHANGE*

CHARLES A. FISHER

Southeast Asia, which comprises the peninsular countries from Burma to
Malaya and Vietnam, and the island realms of Indonesia, British Borneo,
and the Philippines, is often compared with the Balkans, and in many
respects this is a very useful geographical analogy. Thus, in the first place,
as the Balkans—or southeastern Europe—forms part of the great march-
land between what has historically been German-dominated central
Europe and the Russian lands to the east, so Southeast Asia forms part of
a similar border region, between the predominantly Indian cultural realm
of southern Asia and the preponderantly Chinese cultural realm of eastern
Asia. Both the Balkans and Southeast Asia are thus areas of transition and
instability—cultural and political fault zones, to use a somewhat highly
colored but nonetheless expressive metaphor—between two greater entities.
And this is only partly a matter of geographical position; it is also in part a
reflection of their intrinsic physical character, which in turn presents a
second aspect of this analogy.

* Reprinted by permission of the author and the publisher, the Geographical Association, from *Geography*, XLVII (November, 1962), 347–67.

Southeast Asia, like the Balkans, is an area of geographical fragmentation, an area broken up into peninsulas and islands, a characteristically mountainous region, where lowlands are the exception rather than the rule. Although mainland Southeast Asia contains some of the world's greatest rivers, their valleys are markedly constricted and disproportionately narrow, as may be seen by comparing the Irrawaddy with the Ganges, or the Salween with the Yangtze, and these Southeast Asian river valleys are separated one from another by exceedingly difficult upland country. Thus, although locally the fertility of the alluvial soils may be considerable, areas capable of nurturing a dense population are widely scattered, and this dispersal has worked against any political unification of the area as a whole.

A further factor militating against unification, which again finds an obvious parallel in the Balkans, is the character of the region as a great crossing place of land and sea routes. Thus, just as the Balkans forms a bridge from Asia Minor into the heart of Europe, and at the same time flanks the critical seaway from the Black Sea to the Mediterranean, so Southeast Asia forms a land bridge between Asia and Australasia, and is broken by the great sea route linking the Indian and Pacific Oceans.

In its turn, this nodality of geographical position lies at the root of the ethnic, cultural, and political history of both regions. For both have experienced a succession of migrations of peoples, with new and stronger ones repeatedly seizing the precious patches of lowlands and driving the earlier inhabitants to take refuge in the hills or remote cul-de-sacs of the Indonesian and Philippine archipelagos elsewhere. And both regions have similarly been subjected to alien cultural influences and foreign conquest, primarily because of the focal position which they occupy in the world at large.

It is to this that we owe the extreme and baffling complexity of the ethnic and linguistic geography of both regions, in which varying-sized clusters of plainsmen constitute the dominant groups, though these differ one from another in language and often in religious persuasion, while a whole series of lesser hill peoples occupy the geographical divides and blur the political rivalries between them.

And, in like fashion, we may attribute to the similarity of geographical position the presence of world-famous but in origin essentially exotic and cosmopolitan cities at the focal crossing points of both regions. Indeed, the parallel between Constantinople and Singapore is remarkably close, both of them forming the meeting places for traders engaged in long-distance rather than local traffic, and both, in their respective eras of predominance, symbolizing the ambitions of external powers to hold the key to the vital crossroads, namely the Straits of Marmora and Malacca respectively, and the relative ease with which this could be achieved, thanks to the geographical fragmentation and political weakness of the larger region of which both formed part.

Yet, of all the parallels which might be drawn between these two regions, the one which springs most readily to mind at the present time is surely that of the political tremors which have activated these two great fault zones, as alien overlords have withdrawn and new national states have come into being in their place. After centuries of subjection to the Turk, the Balkans, to everyone's surprise, united to expel him in the First Balkan War of 1912, only to fall victims to their own internecine conflicts immediately after their struggle had been crowned with success. And today it is still an open question whether the ending of European rule over Southeast Asia has brought lasting stability to that region or merely prepared the way for renewed Balkanization. But before attempting to consider the implications of this particular aspect of the analogy, it is necessary briefly to consider certain relevant aspects of the history and geography of Southeast Asia.

Owing to its position between India and China, its physical compartmentalism, and its lower population density,[1] Southeast Asia has tended at all times to be overshadowed by these larger neighbors. In detail, however, geography has ordained that its relationships with these two neighbors should be very different in nature. So far as the former is concerned, Southeast Asia is separated from India by one of the most definitive natural boundaries in the world, namely the series of parallel longitudinal ridges, of which the Arakan Yoma forms part, that make a right-angled bend with the eastern end of the Himalayas, and in so doing mark the critical divide, in Lyde's phraseology, between "the typical Atlantic east-and-west trend of the feature lines" to the west, and "the typical Pacific north-and-south trend"[2] over the eastern margins of the continent, including, of course, Southeast Asia itself.

Because of the extremely forbidding nature of this western mountain wall, with its succession of serrated ranges, forested to their crests and intensely malarious, practically no direct overland contact has existed between India and Southeast Asia, and the links that have developed have been more tenuous ones by sea. It was by such means that Indian explorers and traders, pioneering the seaways to China, first paved the way for the great Indian acculturation of Southeast Asia in the early centuries A.D., a process which, contrary to recently held belief, we now know to have involved no great movement of settlers, though it certainly involved an immense and fructifying flow of ideas. And, in one form or another, trading contact with India has continued by sea from that time to this.

With China, on the other hand, or at least with what is politically China today, overland contact has existed for thousands of years. For while the characteristic north-south grain of the country, again so strikingly reminiscent of the Balkans, bars the way from India, the great valleys gouged out of the massive plateaus of the Yunnan-Tibetan borderland have determined the direction of migration routes here since time immemorial. Whether the earliest Negrito and other dark-skinned people, remnants of

[1] Notwithstanding some high densities locally, notably in Java, the Song Ca Delta, and parts of the Philippines, the average density for Southeast Asia as a whole was only 126 to the square mile in 1958. This may be compared with 305 in the Indian subcontinent, 350 in China proper, and 610 in Japan.

[2] L. W. Lyde, *The Continent of Asia* (London, 1933), p. 35.

whom still survive in a few remote parts of Southeast Asia, came in by such routes we do not know, but undoubtedly all the more recent arrivals did so prior to the sixteenth century, including both the Proto-Malays, today represented by the hill peoples in many parts of Southeast Asia, and the later Deutero-Malays and other still more recent and closely related Mongoloids who now form the dominant groups in nearly all the main lowlands of that region.

Except for some of the most recent of these migrations from the north, of which the last major one was that of the final wave of Thais in the thirteenth century, the peoples involved had not advanced beyond the tribal level of organization, for it was not until relatively late in the day that the Tibeto-Yunnan border came under direct Chinese influence. Accordingly, it was as a result of the Indian acculturation to which they were subjected in Southeast Asia that they first acquired the higher attributes of civilization, such as the arts of writing, the acceptance of one of the higher religions, namely Hinduism or Buddhism, and the concepts of urban life and state organization. Over the greater part of lowland Southeast Asia, therefore, the indigenous state pattern, and indeed the traditional ways of life as a whole, arose out of this meeting and interaction of peoples coming down from the north and ideas flowing in from across the Indian Ocean.

In view of the manner in which Indian cultural diffusion followed the sea routes, it is not surprising that the earliest of the Indianized states to emerge in Southeast Asia were all situated along the coast itself, bordering one or other variants of the through sea route to China, with their individual nuclei at convenient river mouths, which provided routes into the interior. Such, for example, were Funan and Champa on the coast of Indochina, the Mon kingdoms of lower Burma and nearby Siam, Langkasuka in peninsular Siam, and several states in western Indonesia, of which the greatest was Palembang, the precursor of the extensive trading empire of Srivijaya.

However, as time went on, all of these came to be eclipsed by other, and mostly larger and more highly organized states, centered not on the coast but in interior river basins, in some cases several hundred miles from the coast. In part, at least on the mainland, this very important shift in the location of the political centers of gravity in medieval Southeast Asia resulted from fresh invasions, perhaps of initially more vigorous peoples from the north, who succeeded in subordinating the earlier coastal peoples, while yet acquiring from them the attributes of Indianized civilization. But that is only part of the reason for the shift into the interior and at least equally important, it would appear, was the nature of the land itself. Although river mouths are obviously attractive points to the passing trader, the terrains in their immediate vicinity, if they lie as these did in the humid tropics, would not be easy to control by small groups of men with no very elaborate technical equipment, in particular because of the extreme profusion of the natural vegetation, and the severity of the seasonal floods of such great rivers as the Irrawaddy, Menam, and Mekong, which regularly inundate vast areas to depths of as much as 10 to 20 feet.

On the contrary, we might reasonably expect much greater progress to be made by peoples living further inland, in the rain-shadow areas, whose thinner vegetation could more readily be cleared for cultivation, and where the rivers, especially the tributaries of the main streams themselves, are much more easily controlled. And it is in fact precisely in such areas, to wit in the dry zones of the middle Irrawaddy in Burma, the middle Menam in Siam, and the Tonle Sap river and lake basin in Cambodia, and also in the seasonally dry riverine lands of east-central Java, that this second series of states developed and rose to predominance after the initial stage of Indianization had come to an end.

Whereas in the coastal nuclei of the earlier states the main problem of the cultivator lay in the excess of water, a problem which was never fully solved until European times, in all the drier inland nuclei, successful cultivation of rice depended on irrigation, and it was around a network of irrigation canals that these later states grew up. Under such conditions, moreover, a denser population could be supported than heretofore, with the result that the peoples inhabiting these particular river valleys came to outnumber their neighbors, and were ultimately able to extend their hegemony over them into the bordering uplands. For all these key regions were also focal places within major river basins, and the waterways in question provided the necessary transport network round which the states expanded.

For this reason, and also because of the very great difficulties of movement across the grain of the country, it is not difficult to understand why the pattern of states which emerged should have corresponded so closely with the major drainage units. This is most obviously true of mainland Southeast Asia, where historic Burma corresponds to the Irrawaddy Basin, and Siam to the Menam, both of which are easily navigable and have relatively broad lowlands, whereas the Shans and Karens, whose main river valley is the spectacular but narrow trough of the unnavigable Salween, have never developed comparable numerical or political strength, and the similar and only slightly less acute navigational problems of the upper and middle Mekong have likewise been reflected in the political divisions of Laos and the separation of the latter from Cambodia, whose own nucleus lay not in the Mekong Valley but in the basin of Tonle Sap which drains into it. Here again there are many points of resemblance with the Balkans.

Be that as it may, all the mainland states considered above, as also the great state of Majapahit in east-central Java,[3] were essentially inland riverine states in origin, governed from large and impressive capital cities,

---

[3] Until recently, it was believed that this kingdom, which reached its zenith in the fourteenth century, ruled over the greater part of what is now Indonesia. Modern historians, however, think that its effective rule was limited primarily to the eastern two-thirds of Java, though it seems also to have exerted some measure of hegemony over various outlying parts of the archipelago.

which in turn were nurtured by considerable areas of irrigated riceland. But it is very misleading to generalize from what we know of these few focal areas, notably Angkor in Cambodia, about which so much has been written, for beyond these inner cores much the greater part of these states' territories almost certainly supported an altogether sparser population living by shifting cultivation.

Moreover, by the time the first Europeans visited these lands, something of a decline had apparently set in almost everywhere. Certainly none of the surviving cities on the mainland or in the islands approached the size and grandeur of the earlier Angkor or Majapahit respectively, and while this decline was partly due to the seemingly endless succession of internecine wars which plagued these states (and not least the supposedly pacifist Buddhist ones), this may itself have been merely a symptom rather than the cause of the trouble. Indeed it is tempting to see in this decline, and in the perhaps related rather easy-going character of most Southeast Asian peoples today, yet another example of the gradual but inexorable running down of human vigor after centuries of exposure to the exhausting climate and endemic disease, from which even these less humid parts of Southeast Asia have suffered throughout their history.

In the foregoing discussion, we have been concerned with that part of the region, and it is much the greater part, in which the main nonindigenous elements in the civilization were predominantly Indian in origin, a situation which was not fundamentally changed by the coming of Islam, likewise through the principal intermediary of Indian traders, after the thirteenth century. In the event, however, the Islamic tide did not engulf the mainland, north of Malaya, which thus remained Buddhist, but it did spread beyond Indonesia into the Philippines, thereby bringing that relatively remote archipelago for the first time fully within the Southeast Asian cultural realm. Likewise, the predominance of Indian cultural influence over the greater part of Southeast Asia was not vitiated by the fact that during the 1,000 years or so before the coming of the Europeans, most of these countries entered into sporadic trading and diplomatic relations with China, which the latter, in its own majestic way, chose to regard as indicative of their subordinate or tributary status towards itself.

But in one part of Southeast Asia, namely the Annamite homeland, Chinese influence was of altogether greater significance. For here it was China, and not India, that constituted the primary civilizing force. This again appears to be largely a matter of geography, for if the Arakan wall marks the physical limit of Southeast Asia in the west, the corresponding boundary to the east is surely the Annamite Cordillera, which reaches down to the coast near the 18th parallel, leaving the lands to the north (which incidentally have a much more pronounced cool season than any other part of Southeast Asia) open to easy access overland from China.

Thus it was that in the second century B.C. the Annamite homeland of Nan Yüeh, to the north of the Cordillera, became absorbed into Imperial China, and from then until they reasserted their independence in A.D. 939, the Annamites were made to adopt the Chinese pattern of religion, the

Chinese ideographic writing, the system of administration by mandarins, and, not least, the distinctively Chinese agronomy and advanced methods of diking and water control. In this way, the Song Ca Delta became the first of the great Southeast Asian deltas to be effectively controlled by the hydraulic engineer, and this made possible the support of a much higher density of population than that even in the other irrigated parts of the region. It was as a result of these advantages that, after gaining their independence in the tenth century A.D., the Annamites gradually advanced southward, eventually snuffing out the former state of Champa, and wresting the mouth of the Mekong from Cambodia. And at the time when the French took over Indochina, the northern Annamite lands were apparently still the most densely populated part of Southeast Asia, and their inhabitants significantly seemed to lack the easygoing attitude which has been so widely commented upon in other parts of the region.

Concerning the era of European rule in Southeast Asia, it is not necessary to write at length, for here the story is more familiar, or at least more accessible, than that of either earlier or more recent times. The following comments, however, may usefully be made.

Like the Arabs and Indians before them, the Europeans came as traders by sea, and for over 300 years, from the sixteenth to the mid-nineteenth century, their influence was mainly limited to a few scattered areas within at most about 50 miles of the coast. But thereafter, in the space of half a century, they pressed inland, the several Western powers staking out claims to every square inch of the region, except for the residual buffer state of Siam, which lay well off the main sea route to China.

Yet though acquired in bits and pieces, the subsequently consolidated holdings of the Europeans, as they appeared on the twentieth-century map, bore a recognizable outward resemblance to the pre-existing indigenous units. This state of affairs, which differs so profoundly from the situation resulting from the contemporary scramble for Africa, was the outcome not of any particular desire to preserve the older units, but reflects rather the controlling influence exerted in this area of extremely accidented relief by the great riverine and sea routes, which had likewise molded the earlier patterns.

Nevertheless, this apparent continuity in political patterns was thoroughly deceptive. For, in effect, the old units had been turned inside out. Almost inevitably, development by external powers favored the choice of the main ports of entry as capitals, from which new railway and road systems were devised, ultimately to penetrate deep into the interiors and bring even the traditional no man's lands of the higher interfluves within the effective sphere of one or other Western administrative machine. But except for a few important mining areas inland, the coastal fringe was everywhere the principal scene of Western economic activity, thanks to the immense advantage it possessed for export production, by virtue of its very proximity to tidewater. Thus, with the help of the hydraulic engineer, the vast deltas of the Irrawaddy and the Mekong (and also incidentally of the Menam) were turned into major rice exporters, and likewise in the coastal margins of western Malaya and northeastern Sumatra, as also earlier in much of Java, large areas of natural forest were turned into the artificial but much more productive forests which we call plantations.

In all these areas, therefore, and most particularly in the series of new giant port cities which lie within them, the economic and social effect of the last century or so of Western rule was truly revolutionary. Not merely did the local population increase rapidly in number, as a result of the cessation of internecine war, the creation of new economic opportunities, and the introduction of better health and sanitation, but there occurred also a massive influx of alien Asians still further to swell the total. Like the German miners, artisans, and small traders who had penetrated into the less developed lands of eastern and southeastern Europe since the Middle Ages, Chinese pioneers had already been settling, for similar reasons, in various parts of Southeast Asia for some hundreds of years. But the scale of this migration, as also of Indians to Burma and Malaya, increased out of all recognition as the European economic advance created new openings for manual and clerical workers, and small traders, which the more easygoing indigenous population were often characteristically reluctant to fill.

This transformation of the traditional Southeast Asian way of life certainly had its bad and its ugly sides, which it would be foolish to deny. But if, in my earlier analogy, I have appeared to bracket it with the dismal story of the Turkish occupation of the Balkans, of which it was said that where the Turk trod the grass never grew again, that has assuredly not been my intention. A sixfold increase in the indigenous population in little more than 100 years is but one indication of the vast growth in wealth associated with the expansion of export production. By the 1930's, Southeast Asia produced 93 per cent of the world's rubber, 75 per cent of its copra, 55 per cent of its palm oil, 90 per cent of its cinchona, 60 per cent of its tin, 91 per cent of the rice entering overseas trade, and vast quantities of many other commodities besides.

Nevertheless, man does not live by rice alone. In the developing political climate of the twentieth century, it was only to be expected that the demand would be raised for independence, a demand which at bottom is simply the desire every one of us feels for the right to run his own life in his own way. Nor is it surprising that the political leaders of the Indianized parts of Southeast Asia should have modeled their tactics mainly on those of the Indian Swaraj Movement, though down to the outbreak of World War II their progress in this respect lagged far behind that of their mentors.

Inevitably, however, the Japanese occupation, with its various offers of independence within the Co-Prosperity Sphere, greatly accelerated the growth of nationalist sentiments. Moreover, once the British had decided to grant India its independence after the war (as the Americans had already promised theirs to the Philippines by 1946), it would have been politically impossible to refuse it to Burma or Malaya, and so, by a chain reaction, the Dutch also had to adopt similar policies in Indonesia and the

French to follow suit in Indochina. And all of this regardless of the facts that, outside the Philippines, none of the Western governments in Southeast Asia had previously reached the final stages of preparation for such transfers—some indeed having scarcely begun to think in such terms at all —and that the war had caused appalling damage and disruption to the economic and social life of every one of the territories in question.

Nevertheless, the Philippines became independent in 1946, Burma in 1947, and Indonesia followed in 1949, though not before the Dutch had twice resorted to "police action" against the self-styled Republican Government, and had insisted on retaining control, at least for the time being, over Western New Guinea. However, in August, 1962, it was agreed between the Netherlands and Indonesia that, after an interim period under the United Nations from October, 1962, until May, 1963, the administration of West New Guinea would be handed over to Indonesia.

There remained the two special cases of British Malaysia and French Indochina, which call for a little more comment. Owing to the fact that Malaya, which lies at the very heart of Southeast Asia, had a population in which alien Chinese and Indians together outnumbered the indigenous Malays, communal rivalries had retarded the growth of any all-embracing national sentiment there, and the British were thus reduced to the curious task of creating a nation to whom to hand over power. In so doing, they treated the overwhelmingly Chinese city of Singapore separately from the rest of the country, the new Federation of Malaya, in which the Malays were left numerically as the largest single group, though not an absolute majority over the other two peoples combined. Thereafter, the Federation of Malaya obtained its independence within the Commonwealth in 1957, and the state of Singapore was granted internal self-government in 1959.*

In French Indochina, a very different situation existed. To begin with, the unity of the old Federation of Indochina had already been undermined by the Japanese policy of treating Laotians, Cambodians, and Annamites (or Vietnamese, as these last now came to be known) as separate nations. Moreover, by the time the French were able to take over from the Chinese occupation forces north of the 16th parallel, the Vietnamese Republican Government of Ho Chi Minh had established itself firmly in that region, and it soon became clear that these revolutionary nationalists were exceptionally hard bargainers and hard fighters, and as such they proved in the end to be more than a match for the French.

In its nationalism, as in so many other respects, Vietnam has constituted an exception to the general Southeast Asian pattern. Notwithstanding a deep sense of historic enmity toward China, Vietnamese political evolution seems to have had more in common with that in China than with the corresponding movement in India, not only because of the much closer affinities with China in ways of thought, but also because of greater geo-

* The Federation of Malaya was expanded on September 16, 1963, to include Singapore, Sarawak, and Sabah, and was renamed the Federation of Malaysia, a name it retained after Singapore withdrew from the Federation on August 9, 1965.

graphical similarities in the problems to be solved. Thus, in the 1920's, Sun Yat-sen's proposals to give "the land to the tiller" aroused great interest among Vietnamese nationalists, and later, after Chiang Kai-shek had succeeded Sun Yat-sen and begun to modify his policies so that the Chinese Communists could begin to claim that they were the true inheritors of Sun's land-reform policy, a similar divergence of sentiment likewise developed among the Vietnamese nationalists. In this context, Ho Chi Minh's Vietminh movement represented the left wing, and undoubtedly he drew much of his support from the peasantry on account of what were believed to be his proposals for land redistribution, even though in fact, both in China and in North Vietnam, the plans eventually put into effect differed radically from those originally advanced by Sun Yat-sen.

Already from the outset, this extreme left-wing character of the Vietminh placed it in a different category from the nationalist movements in most other parts of Southeast Asia, but when in 1949 China itself became Communist, the Vietminh had an ally immediately behind it, and the French struggle against the Vietminh thus came to represent an active sector of the global frontier between the Communist and the Western worlds. Yet despite the immense financial assistance which the French thereafter obtained from the United States, they were unable to reverse the tide, and after the fall of Dien Bien Phu, the Geneva settlement, which partitioned Vietnam near the 17th parallel, was negotiated in the summer of 1954.

Since the signing of the Geneva agreement, the Vietminh-controlled area to the north has become an integral part of the Communist bloc, while the rest of the country to the south has been consistently and lavishly supported by American aid in order to strengthen its resistance to Communism. Meanwhile, it was intended that Laos and Cambodia should become independent neutral buffer states between the Communist world and the rest of Southeast Asia, but the exposed position and grave internal divisions of Laos seriously weakened its capacity for sustaining such a role, which in any case was anathema to United States foreign policy during the Dulles era.

In these circumstances, Laos has since proved to be a focus of recurrent crisis ever since 1954, and although the United Kingdom, the United States, and the U.S.S.R. have made a renewed attempt effectively to neutralize this tormented little kingdom, it requires considerable optimism to believe that its troubles are now at an end. For, owing to its geographical position flanking the divide between North and South Vietnam, and so providing, via its almost uninhabited eastern mountain regions, a surreptitious means of passage from one to the other, Laos can hardly escape involvement in any future conflict between the two.

In this connection, moreover, it is relevant to note the words uttered as long ago as 1897 by the future Marshal Lyautey of the French Army. "Tonkin" (the present North Vietnam), he said, "is a doorway; this door must be kept bolted."[4] Unfortunately, this provides cold comfort today,

---

[4] Quoted in Roger Lévy, "Indochina: A Keystone in Asia—A French View," *Indian Quarterly*, VIII (1952), 36.

when we remember that, whether or not the door is bolted now, the Trojan horse is already inside the stable. Meanwhile, it is surely significant that the 1954 partition line, which extends the boundary of the Communist world south to the 17th parallel, corresponds almost exactly with the southern limit of China for more than 1,000 years, from 111 B.C. to A.D. 939. It remains to be seen whether the present boundary will be as lasting.

With these few but important exceptions, in Indochina and Malaya, the new states of Southeast Asia are all coextensive with the former colonial units, and it remains now to consider their prospects for survival in their present form. This question of viability may profitably be examined from the two distinct but complementary viewpoints of economic and political geography.

With the exception of the minute city state of Singapore, which has been left like a head without a body and so must perforce live by its wits, which are fortunately considerable, none of the new states, on the whole, is badly off in respect of the ratio of its natural resources to the size of its population. And if they had achieved their independence without having first been ravaged by war, most of them could have looked forward to a relatively bright future in this respect. But the severity of the damage caused by the war, and also in most cases by the postwar disturbances, whether of disaffected minorities or Communists, or both, set the clocks a long way back. Indeed, it is only during the last few years that the export production of the region as a whole has regained its prewar level, though population has gone on increasing rapidly in the meantime, and in fact the exports of some states, notably Burma and South Vietnam, are still well below their prewar level, though others, particularly Malaya and Thailand, have substantially improved their positions. Indonesia presents a marginal case, in that setbacks in Java have been offset by gains in Sumatra, but that only serves to aggravate the already serious economic imbalance between the overcrowded and agriculturally overdeveloped metropolitan island, and the still underdeveloped but more promising outer territories. Even before the war, the social and other consequences of this imbalance were causing the Dutch serious disquiet, and it is clear that only a massive transmigration of people, and a related opening up of new ricelands in the outer islands, as well as further, but more carefully planned, industrialization in Java, can now save the situation. And of this there seems to be little immediate prospect.

Elsewhere, however, given only reasonable political stability and the wisdom not to proceed too quickly in changing the patterns of the economies which they have inherited, all these states should be capable of earning much more than a mere subsistence livelihood. However, all the new states are in fact extremely anxious to reduce their dependence on a few specialized lines of primary produce, whose market prices are apt to fluctuate wildly, and all of them wish to increase their at present relatively limited amount of manufacturing industry. All of this, of course, represents an attempt to move away from a "colonial" to a more independent type of economy, but in order to pay for factories, transport, and other services, it is necessary to develop primary production still further or to obtain still more loans from abroad, and both of these courses are apt to be regarded as themselves perpetuating the very colonial economic status from which they wish to break away. Nevertheless, this is not an insoluble problem, and indeed is a far less serious matter than the task of achieving political viability, at which, therefore, it is necessary to look in greater detail.

In seeking to understand why the particular "portions of land and portions of humanity"[5] which constitute the present states of Southeast Asia continue to hold together as they do, instead of either disintegrating or recombining in other patterns, it is helpful to make use of Professor Hartshorne's concept of the state-idea or *raison d'être*.[6] And in this respect, quite apart from the intrinsic interest and drama which it presents, Southeast Asia today provides a veritable laboratory for politico-geographical analysis, though there are times when one could wish that a few more safety precautions were taken when some of the experiments were being carried out.

Clearly, under the colonial system the *raison d'être* of all these rival territories was self-evident, and the degree of human variety which they contained, ethnic, linguistic, and religious, was irrelevant to this, so long as the colonial power was capable of holding the ring. But now that colonial rule has ended, ostensibly because it violates the basic principle of self-determination, the question inevitably arises: what are the selves that are going to do the determining? Or, in other words, have the old units which, apart from the exceptions noted above, still exist any real meaning in present circumstances?

In fact, virtually all the new units contain a much greater diversity of population than people in the West usually associate with the concept of a nation-state. More specifically, each contains at least three different kinds of component peoples, which may be categorized as follows. First, in all cases there is at least one advanced indigenous group, ethnically Deutero-Malay or other similar Mongoloid, with its own literate culture and adhering to one of the higher religions, be it Buddhism, Hinduism, Islam, or Christianity. Commonly, a group of this kind forms the largest single element in the population, and very often occupies the geographical core of the state, as in the case of the Cambodians, Burmans, Vietnamese, and Javanese. But such a group is not everywhere in an absolute majority, the Javanese being a case in point, and in many of the states there are other more or less similarly advanced but numerically smaller groups as well. Such include the Shans and Mons in Burma, and numerous linguistic subgroups in both Indonesia and the Philippines.

Secondly, all of the new states contain one or more traditionally less advanced indigenous groups. These are mostly, but not entirely, hill peo-

5 "Jeder Staat ist ein Stück Menschheit und ein Stück Boden." F. Ratzel, *Politische Geographie*, 3d ed., Berlin and Munich (1925), p. 2.

6 Richard Hartshrone, "The Functional Approach in Political Geography," *Annals of the Association of Geographers*, XL (1950), 95–130.

ples, predominantly either Proto-Malay or still earlier Negrito or Papuan. At least until recently, these were animists and had no literate culture, but since Christian missions have been particularly active among such peoples, many of them are now both Christian and literate. Accordingly, Christianized groups of this kind are found among the Karens in Burma, the Sumatran Bataks, and the Ambonese of the Moluccas, while various other hill peoples exist in their more or less traditional state in every country within the region.

Finally, in addition to the two indigenous categories noted above, there is characteristically also a third element, consisting of one or more nonindigenous groups. Of these, the most ubiquitous is the Chinese, but in Burma and Malaya, Indians and, notably in Indonesia, at least until recently, Eurasians are also important. All told, there are some 12 million Chinese, and they are found in every single state, though the proportion they form of the total varies from less than 1 per cent in the Philippines, 2 per cent in Burma (where Indians form 4 per cent), 3 per cent in Indonesia, and 6 per cent in South Vietnam, to 14 per cent in Thailand, 38 per cent in the Federation of Malaya (where Indians account for a further 10 per cent). In all cases, however, these aliens include within their numbers a disproportionately large percentage of the local clerical, trading, commercial, and industrial classes, and of such professions as medicine, engineering, law, and education.

Altogether, therefore, the population patterns of all these countries are extremely complex, being at the same time both multilingual and plural. In no case does a single language or one particular religion at present provide a common denominator for the whole population, though the degree of approximation toward such a situation varies a good deal from state to state. Nor, with the exception of Thailand, which is not really a new state at all, and also of its small neighbor Cambodia, has any of these states a sufficient historic continuity in its present form with the precolonial past for monarchical or dynastic traditions to provide an adequate *raison d'être* in the contemporary world.

Indeed, what appears to be holding all the remaining states together at the present time is a combination of three forces, which may be summarized as follows. First, there is a kind of politico-geographical inertia or momentum (though it is not always clear which) associated with the established patterns of administration, transport, and communication taken over from the former colonial regimes. Secondly, there is the sense of recent history, associated particularly with the demand, and in some cases the struggle, for independence, against one specific colonial power. While probably only a minority of the population ever actively participated in these events, the experience was certainly shared vicariously by much larger numbers, who derive a real sense of solidarity from it. But this rarely extends to all the indigenous groups within the state and, except in the Federation of Malaya and Singapore, certainly does not extend to the bulk of the nonindigenous groups. Thirdly, and arising out of the second, is the desire, particularly among a small educated elite, to demonstrate that they, no less than the Europeans, are capable of running a modern state. Many members of these national elites habitually think in the language of the former metropolitan power, and in so doing have acquired many of its habits of thought. This, accordingly, makes for significant mental barriers, beyond the purely linguistic, between the political leaders of the several states, and these contribute substantially to the preservation of the present political units.

In practice, the governments of most, if not all, of the states have been taken over by members of these small elites, drawn mainly from the one or more advanced indigenous groups and put or confirmed in office by the latter's majority vote. But while this arrangement may be democratic enough, it has not everywhere proved acceptable to minority groups, and in the case of the Karens in Burma, the largely Christian inhabitants of the South Moluccas, and some of the more extreme Muslims in other parts of Indonesia, it has led to attempts at secession, which have involved long-drawn-out guerrilla fighting. But whether this has happened or not, the new regimes have normally realized the need to take steps to prevent such disintegration by fostering a sense of common nationhood among as many as possible of the peoples within their particular territory.

To the indigenous minority peoples, who are normally neither feared nor envied, the dominant peoples have mostly tried hard to be conciliatory. Indeed, they have generally made every effort to emphasize and strengthen whatever ties are available to bind all the indigenous peoples more closely together, and here popular history and myth have often proved particularly useful. Thus, Indonesia has adopted the *Garuda* bird as its national emblem, and the phrase *Bhinneka tunggal ika* ("unity in diversity") as its motto, both of them derived from medieval Majapahit, which, according to Indonesian folklore, if not to modern historiography, once ruled over the whole archipelago.

In Burma, again, the Buddhist religion, though a stumbling block to the Karens, is a strong and growing bond between Burmans, Shans, and Mons, and it is also being disseminated among many of the lesser hill peoples. Whether or not this proselytization is related to a conscious desire to make use of Buddhism as a nation-building force, it will almost certainly contribute to that end in Burma today. But in Indonesia, although some 80 per cent of the population profess Islam, the religious as well as the many other differences between the Javanese and the non-Javanese Muslims, together with the survival of Hinduism in Bali, and in the presence of large numbers of both Protestant and Roman Catholic Christians elsewhere, made Sukarno reject the concept of an Islamic state, on the grounds that it would be more likely to promote division than unity.

In the long run, the most effective way of promoting national unity will be by the spread of common languages and associated programs of national education. In this respect, considerable progress has been made, for example, with the use of Malay in both the Federation of Malaya and in Singapore, and simultaneously with the propagation of Bahasa Indonesia (not Javanese but a form of modernized Malay, closely akin to that used in Malaya) in Indonesia, while Burmese is also becoming more and more a lingua franca in Burma.

Nevertheless, complete unity will not be achieved by these means in the immediate future, and for the present the hard fact must be faced that none of the accepted Western criteria of nationhood extend in a meaningful sense to the whole population of any of the new states. In these circumstances, it is therefore all too easy to make use of the only force which is widespread among the mass of all the indigenous peoples in the several states, namely the sense of difference between themselves and the truly alien groups, whether the former colonial rulers or the alien Asians in their midst. While it is gratifying to note that some governments have done their utmost to bridge these communal barriers—and in this respect none has done more than the Federation of Malaya, where, on purely numerical grounds, the problem would at first sight appear to be the most acute of all —it is not perhaps surprising that Indonesia, which has the widest range of diversity among its indigenous population, and the further complication that the outer territories are becoming increasingly resentful of Java's attempts to live off their earnings, should provide the most extreme examples of xenophobia directed against the nonindigenous elements.

Thus, Indonesian restrictions against Chinese tradesmen in the rural districts of western Java have led in recent years to an actual mass repatriation of established Chinese settlers. But several other countries, notably South Vietnam, the Philippines, and Thailand, have likewise been attempting to curb the activities of the local Chinese communities, and while all these measures may be primarily aimed against the economic power of the local Chinese, the practice of turning the alien into a whipping boy can also serve to solidify national feelings among the rest of the population.

This remark has an obvious application also to the succession of measures directed by the Indonesian Government since 1949 against the Dutch. In this connection, the Dutch retention of Western New Guinea provided a convenient focus, and indeed proved as valuable a gift to Indonesian nationalism as the British maintenance of the Ulster connection did to the Irish republicans. Thus, in both cases, it came to be fashionable to continue fighting for independence long after it had been won, and although this picturesque custom has its lighter side, it also can yield useful political dividends.

Yet, in a deeper sense, the practice of railing against the former overlord is really only one facet of what the psychologist calls a "love/hate relationship," and this is apparent not only in the Indonesian attitude toward the Dutch, but also, in some measure at least, in that of most Southeast Asian nations vis-à-vis the erstwhile metropolitan powers. Thus, while their leaders are often given to extolling their countries' glorious past and the superiority of Asian spiritual values over the materialism of the West, they seem in general to be much more concerned to preserve the appearance and reality of the Western-style states which they have inherited than to revert to their own indigenous political patterns.

One aspect of this situation is particularly interesting to the geographer, though its symbolism is perhaps of deeper significance than is usually realized. After the Russian Revolution of 1917, the Westernized capital of St. Petersburg was rejected in favor of the more truly indigenous Moscow; in like fashion, the Turkish nationalists later replaced Constantinople by Ankara; and, more recently still, the Chinese Communists forsook Nanking for Peking. In all these cases, the shift in capital represented not administrative convenience, but rather a deliberate break with supposedly harmful external influences, and a turning-in on historic traditions and indigenous spiritual resources.

But in Southeast Asia since 1945, there has been no shift from Rangoon to the Dry Zone, nor from Batavia to Surakarta, though the Dutch name of the former has been changed back to the Javanese Djakarta. On the contrary, both in these and in the other Southeast Asian states, the great alien port cities are now the fastest growing points of all. Only in one case do we find an apparent parallel with the examples quoted above, namely in Singapore, the Southeast Asian Constantinople, which was rejected as unsuitable to be the Malayan capital, and its place taken by Kuala Lumpur. But Kuala Lumpur, the former mining camp of the nineteenth century, with its predominantly Chinese population even today, is no indigenous Ankara. And in any case, this particular decision was initially taken not by the Malays, but by Whitehall.

Thus, whereas during the colonial era, the Europeans turned the indigenous units inside out, the reversion to indigenous rule has involved no corresponding reversal of this particular process, and the new rulers have retained the European-style entities as going concerns. This applies not only to the capital cities, but also in many cases very largely to the internal administrative patterns, and in every instance to the over-all territorial limits of the state. Indeed, the words officially used by the Indonesians with reference to their claim to West New Guinea: "the territory which the Indonesian people claim as their own is exactly the same territory, not more and not less, as the territory which formerly . . . was called the Netherlands-Indies territory,"[7] could be echoed, *mutatis mutandis*, by every other state in the region.

When we look at the linguistic and religious maps of Southeast Asia, and compare this situation with that of the nationalist redrawing of the map of Europe during the present century, this may seem rather surprising. Indeed, there is hardly a single international boundary in the whole of Southeast Asia which would not have called for "rectification" by the Versailles treaty makers. Cambodians overlap into Vietnam, and Vietnamese into Cambodia; Malays extend into southern Thailand, while both Shans and Lao peoples beyond the latter's borders are the closest kinsfolk of the Thais. And in the archipelago, the inhabitants alike of Malaya, British Borneo, Portuguese Timor, and some of the southern parts of the Philippines enjoy no less close linguistic and religious affinities with their nearest

[7] *Report of the Committee New Guinea (Irian)*, 1950, Part III, p. 30. Published by the Secretariat of the Netherlands-Indonesian Union.

neighbors in Indonesia. Yet, amid all the confusion and unrest in South-east Asia since World War II, not a single attempt has been made to redraw international boundaries on linguistic or related lines. How different, it seems, from the events which brought the Second Balkan War so swiftly on the heels of the First.

To what should we attribute this difference? One possible explanation might be that individual nationalisms, in both regions, resulted primarily from reaction against a single specific alien power. In the Balkans, this power was everywhere the same, namely Turkey. But in Southeast Asia, there were several such alien powers, so that Indonesian nationalism represented a reaction against the Dutch, Burmese nationalism a reaction against the British, and so on. Moreover, *within* each of the new Southeast Asian states, it is true, Balkanization has been a very real threat, though it has not extended *across* the international borders where there has been no common reaction against the colonial power on the other side.

But there may also be a more important and if so a more encouraging explanation. In short, may it not be that the respect hitherto shown by all the new states for the boundaries which they have inherited reflects a real sense of responsibility on the part of their statesmen, who realize just how much the very survival of the new order depends on what remains, in the twentieth-century world, of the sanctity of treaties and loyalty to the principles of the United Nations, to which they already owe so much? For the sake of Southeast Asia and of all its neighbors, it is to be hoped that this is indeed so.

5

THE "MILLION CITY" IN SOUTHEAST ASIA*

D. W. FRYER

In a world survey of cities with a population of 1 million or more, made in 1931, Mark Jefferson[1] could not include a single representative from Southeast Asia. Since 1945, five cities in this area have attained the million status—Djakarta, Manila, Saigon, Bangkok, and Singapore. Of all the major political units in this part of Asia, only Burma has failed to produce a "million city." In Malaya, the most highly urbanized country, 35 per cent of the population live in towns of 5,000 or more, and towns of more than 10,000 increased their population by 52.6 per cent in the last inter-censal period, 1931–47. But the concept of Southeast Asia as an area of rural peoples with a rhythm of life determined by rice cultivation is still largely correct. The proportion of urban dwellers is about the average for the Asian continent, and, except possibly in Java, there are far fewer cities, in relation to the level of population, than in either South or East Asia.

* Reprinted by permission of the author and the publisher from *Geographical Review*, XLIII (October, 1953), 474–94.
[1] Mark Jefferson, "Distribution of the World's City Folks," *Geographical Review*, XXI (1931), 446–65.

By Western standards, the countries of Southeast Asia had only one city apiece until very recently. Most of the other settlements of any size were overgrown villages, and in some degree they still retain aspects of their village origin. In Southeast Asia the evolution of indigenous cities on the Chinese or Indian scale was not possible. Chesneaux[2] suggests that many of the large indigenous Asian cities grew up within "the traditional framework of the great agricultural empires," but in both peninsular and archipelagic Southeast Asia physical fragmentation, reinforced by a great diversity of peoples, hindered the development of large states. Though occasionally established, they were highly unstable and of short duration. The princely houses of the petty native states were insufficient stimuli to city growth, and commerce was equally inadequate. The only effective impulse, as Credner[3] points out, was a favorable combination of trade foci with administrative, military, and religious functions of the highest order. Dependence on changeable watercourses for irrigated rice culture and transportation, and the personal whim of the ruler, produced a marked arbitrariness in city location, and the small extent of states ensured that cities could only be of moderate size, grouped around the *kraton*, or palace.

Thus, the integration of several small territorial units into a political state was a necessary preliminary to the appearance of the large city. But even the extensive colonial possessions created by the European powers could not, with their comparatively simple economies, support more than one large city each. This was inevitably located at the point of entry. Singapore, however, is anomalous: Its external lines of communication have more than compensated for its earlier lack of direct access into the Malay Peninsula.

The large city, then, is a foreign innovation, possessing a high proportion of nonindigenous inhabitants, serving mainly foreign interests, and tacked onto a rural background. The achievement of independence in much of Southeast Asia, and its approach elsewhere, must bring many changes in the relations of the large city with the rest of the country.

Fulfilling similar functions as administrative, judicial, and above all commercial centers, and providing other specialized services mainly for their own inhabitants and the outside world rather than for the country as a whole, the "million" cities thus present many similar features of morphology and development, despite variations in their historical and cultural backgrounds. It is not surprising that the two oldest cities, Manila (1571) and Djakarta (1619), founded in the era of mercantilism, possess the greatest similarities and are apparently to continue comparable development as the capitals of new states. On the other hand, the two nineteenth-century cities, Singapore (1819) and Saigon (1859), are strikingly different. Bangkok (1782) is the only indigenous city in Southeast Asia that has attained first

[2] J. E. Spencer, "Changing Asiatic Cities," *Geographical Review*, XLI (1951), 336–37, discussing Jean Chesneaux, "Notes sur l'évolution récente de l'habitat urbain en Asie," *L'Information Géographique*, XIII (1949), 169–75, and XIV (1950), 1–8.

[3] Wilhelm Credner, *Siam, das Land der Tai* (Stuttgart, 1935), p. 366.

rank, but until comparatively recently it functioned rather as the focus of what has often been described as an economic appendage of the British Empire than as the capital of an independent state. Though the smallest of the five cities in numbers, Singapore is the most important, both economically and strategically. More than any of the others it serves the whole of Southeast Asia, and its future is perhaps the most obscure.

The Foundation of the Cities

The sites of the great cities were places of little importance, selected by foreigners on technical considerations that had no validity for the indigenous inhabitants. The aim of the Europeans was to create economic bases at tidewater, and only later did the administrative function become equally significant. Singapore was virtually uninhabited, though a flourishing commercial center had existed on approximately the same site some centuries before. Manila and Djakarta, though located in populous countrysides, arose from minor settlements, and Saigon was nothing more than a village surrounding an Annamese imperial fortress. Bangkok illustrates the arbitrariness of city location dependent on the personal decision of the ruler; for though founded on the site of an earlier settlement, this possessed no particular geographical significance and was unoccupied by indigenous peoples at the time.

With the exception of Saigon, all the great cities were founded in the days of sail, but, despite the unexacting requirements of sailing vessels, good harbors with safe anchorages, facilities for careening, and easy access into the interior were not readily found in Southeast Asia, where the modest tides of the shallow seas on the Sunda Shelf only occasionally bring deep water close inshore. It cannot be said that the sites selected by the Europeans were always the best. Silting has been a problem, and technological changes have necessitated almost everywhere the creation of virtually new ports close to the old towns to cope with the increasing size and draft of vessels, and to expedite the handling of new export commodities. It is not surprising, therefore, that the indigenous Bangkok has tended to lag behind.

Manila, the oldest of the five cities, is perhaps also the most interesting. It did not begin primarily as a port and commercial base, nor did its early start confer the usual advantages, in spite of the possession of what is probably the best natural harbor in the whole of Southeast Asia. Manila Bay, protected by the mountainous Bataan Peninsula, and with a relatively narrow entrance, gives shelter from the prevailing winds and the occasional typhoons that cross Luzon. Its north shore is formed by the swamps of the delta of the Pasig and Pampanga rivers, but on the east a narrow strip of plain lies between it and the southern Sierra Madre. Part of this plain is occupied by the extensive but shallow Laguna de Bay, whose outlet is the short and meandering Pasig River. At its mouth were two stockaded Muslim settlements, from the southerly of which the present city takes its name. The potentialities of Manila as a fortress and administrative center were at once recognized, and its splendid harbor and nodality in relation to the productive plains gave it an ascendancy over the earlier Cebu City (1565). But in a colony that was itself a dependency of another colony, and separated from the homeland by two oceans, economic development was retarded.

The objective of Jan Pieterszoon Coen, the founder of Batavia, was the establishment of an economic base[4] that would free the Dutch East India Company from English and Chinese competition and be strong enough to deter native princes from interfering in the Company's activities. Essentially, commerce was of greater importance than administration in old Batavia, though the Company could hardly avoid participation in politics; the recent change of the city's name to Djakarta, the name of the native settlement on whose site the city arose, is indicative of a change of function as well as of political control. The city began its life as a storehouse, which was secretly fortified and, after a successful defense against the English and the local ruler, was made the nucleus of a new town. Expediency seems to have been the principal reason for the selection of the site. Certainly the harbor had little to commend it, and, early in the eighteenth century, silting was already a problem.

Bangkok is the only indigenous city of Southeast Asia to attain a population of 1 million, at least in modern times, though Jogjakarta is estimated to have reached this level during the postwar Indonesian movement for independence. The geographical focus of Thailand is clearly in the lower Menam plain, but for four centuries the capital was Ayuthia, some sixty miles upstream (1350–1767). After the destruction of Ayuthia by the Burmese, Thonburi, a fort on the west bank of the Menam Chao Phraya, was selected as the new national capital, but in 1782 a further dynastic change led to the establishment of a new administrative capital on the opposite bank, then unoccupied save for a small community of Chinese traders. Situated on a bend in the river some twenty miles from the sea and surrounded by marshland, the site of Bangkok possessed the sole but great advantage of being easily defended.

Saigon, like Bangkok, is a riverine city and tidal port set in a broad alluvial lowland, but it is more than twice as far removed from the sea. When captured by the French in 1859, it was the main political center of the newly colonized Annamese land of Cochinchina and consisted of an agglomeration of native huts around the imperial fortress, with virtually no permanent buildings. The French immediately began its reconstruction as a modern city, so that, unlike the other four cities, Saigon has no old core. Nothing is left at present of the native town. Cholon, the "great market" some three miles to the west along the Arroyo Chinois, is an entirely separate Chinese foundation dating from about 1778. Though the cities have now coalesced, each retains its own distinctive character and functions, and the "Région de Saigon-Cholon" is thus a true twin city, unique in Southeast Asia.

[4] B. H. M. Vlekke, *Nusantara: A History of the East Indian Archipelago* (Cambridge, Mass., 1943), pp. 122–23.

Singapore is anomalous in being situated on an island, and, like Bangkok, it did not arise on a previous settlement. The modern development of the Malay Peninsula could not have been imagined by Raffles in 1819; he intended that his city should achieve pre-eminence by its policy of free trade, which would attract the Chinese entrepôt trade from Batavia. The site selected lay on the south coast of Singapore Island, where the mangrove-lined Singapore River discharged into the sea. Here was situated what was probably the best anchorage in the days of sail; for the roads between Tanjong Rhu and Tanjong Pagar gave good protection from all but south-east winds, and the force of these was broken by islands to the south.

The Old Towns

The great cities were developed on plans, rather than allowed to grow haphazardly, but it is hardly surprising that technological and sociological changes have defeated the aims of the early planners. The old towns represented the transplanting of the city forms of contemporary Europe to Southeast Asia. The walled city of Intramuros, the older section of Manila, was a replica of the fortified town of sixteenth-century Europe, as was the earlier Portuguese Malacca. Batavia was likewise a fortified city, but the low terrain and abundant water encouraged the Dutch to copy the characteristic features of the cities of Holland. Thus, old Batavia, the Benedenstad, was constructed on both sides of the Tjiliwong, and canals on a rectangular pattern were excavated.

Nearness to water, yet with freedom from flooding, was the essential requirement of all the cities, but seasonal variations in precipitation and periodic torrential downpours continue from time to time to defeat even modern techniques of civil engineering. The Batavian canals were only partly successful: In the wet seasons they flooded, and in dry periods they degenerated into a "dismal succession of filthy bogs and stagnant pools."[5] Pollution of the canals and the extension of the coastal swamps due to sedimentation gave old Batavia an evil reputation for disease.

Bangkok and Saigon, on low alluvial plains, with great seasonal fluctuations in river levels, were confronted with difficult problems. Official buildings commanded the little higher ground that was available, and the great bulk of the population lived in wooden houses built on stilts or on pontoons. Early Bangkok had no street pattern. The Royal City, or "Grand Palace," was a self-contained walled city, about a square mile in area, with palaces, temples, and administrative buildings. A canal across the neck of the bend in the Chao Phraya converted the old city into an island, outside which permanent buildings and roads did not exist and all communication was by boat along the canals, or klongs.

Singapore possessed the advantage of greater topographic variety. Eminences of granite formed good sites for public buildings, and the city spread out over the land above flood level on both sides of the swampy Singapore River.

[5] J. J. Stockdale, *Sketches of the Island of Java* (London, 1811), p. 129.

All the old towns, with the exception of the architecturally exotic Bangkok, have a gridiron layout, which has meant the maximum of congestion in modern times. Racial zonation, well marked in the old towns, has tended to persist. Europeans have long since abandoned their old quarters, but the Chinese have remained in strength; indigenous peoples, however, are significantly absent. In Manila and Bangkok, the old cores have been retained intact and new business and financial quarters have been created away from the old cities. Though Intramuros has lost its military functions and most of its administrative ones, it still keeps, in part, those of a judicial and religious nature. Old Bangkok, however, has lost little of its earlier importance and is one of the greatest tourist attractions in Southeast Asia. In Singapore and Djakarta, the old core has been reconstructed as the business district, but since this took place before the advent of the motor vehicle, congestion is still acute. Saigon, having no old core and therefore able to plan its development without encumbrances, nevertheless also adopted a gridiron layout, but it is not easy to suggest an alternative that would have made better use of the environment.

THE EXPANSION OF THE CITIES

The rapid growth of the cities in the late nineteenth and the twentieth centuries has been due to the investment of capital, largely from the mother country, in production for export; the consequent improvement of the ports and the creation of a communications network focusing on them; a considerable increase in the scope of administrative activities; and, more recently, the establishment of secondary industries. Though these have provided the impetus, expansion has been possible only through the application of new techniques of engineering (particularly in drainage and water supply) and preventive medicine, making the cities as healthy as those of the West.

The three centuries of stagnation in Manila are a remarkable historical record. Expansion beyond the walls of Intramuros began almost a century later than the growth of old Batavia, which too had suffered a period of stagnation in the seventeenth century. Even the short British occupation (1762–64) and the revolt of the American colonies failed to arouse Spanish interest in the distant possession, and the growth of Manila in the latter half of the nineteenth century was a reflection of the investment of foreign capital in the archipelago, stimulated by the opening of the Suez Canal. In 1863, relocation of the administrative area began, with the move of the Governor to the Malacañan Palace, north of the river, and in the last three decades of Spanish rule, development on the north bank of the Pasig was rapid. After the American occupation, Manila grew quickly. A modern harbor was constructed on reclaimed land on the seaward side of Intramuros (1903), and the main development of the city was shifted south of the Pasig, where new administrative and residential districts were created. Since World War II, the city has again expanded, owing partly to an influx of population from the country and partly to the use of reconstruction funds for development. The built-up area is now practically continuous from the swamps of the Bitas River mouth in the north to Parañaque in the south, a distance of about ten miles. Northeast and south-east of the urban fringe, rice fields still cover the plain, and parts of the city itself are regularly flooded in the rainy season (April-October). Develop-ment has proceeded farthest inland on the higher ground between the coastal plain and the Marikina River, which drains southward to the Pasig. Here are the newer districts of Mandaluyong, San Juan del Monte, and Quezon City, the last virtually a satellite town, which is the new adminis-trative center of the Republic.

As a result of its long history and changing administration, Manila has a greater variety of architectural styles and street patterns than the other four cities. Old buildings of wood and adobe in the colonial style were found in Intramuros (which was largely destroyed in 1945) and occasion-ally outside, but in the main business district in Binondo and in the admin-istrative quarter of Ermita, modern steel-framed concrete buildings now predominate. Manila is not a city of skyscrapers. Good foundations are im-possible in the alluvial sediments, and deep piling to reach the underlying granite or "floating" on enormous cellular rafts of concrete is necessary for large buildings in all the great cities. In the districts of earliest expansion, radiating plazas and boulevards are to be seen; elsewhere the gridiron lay-out of the typical American city has been adhered to, except in the newer areas to the east, where attempts have been made to relate development to topography. Racial zonation is well marked. The Chinese community in-habits the narrow streets north of the Escolta in the business quarter, and the principal indigenous residential areas lie north of the city in the crowded districts of Tondo, Sampaloc, and Santa Cruz. Europeans, Ameri-cans, and wealthy Filipinos reside on the higher ground in the districts of Ermita and Malate, south of the river.

Modern Batavia, the immediate forebear of Djakarta, dated from the reconstruction of the old city in the early nineteenth century. The expan-sion of trade and growth of population in the eighteenth century had made necessary the redevelopment of the town, still closely confined around the old fort. In 1808, Governor General Daendels moved the ad-ministrative headquarters to Buitenzorg (now Bogor), pulled down the old fort, and used the material for the construction of a new residential district some three miles south of the old town, on the higher ground of Weltevre-den. Three miles south of the new district the military camp of Meester Cornelis was established, and thus the axis of future development was aligned north–south, avoiding the low rice-growing plains on each side.

Weltevreden, like the old town, was laid out on a rectangular pattern around large open squares, the Koningsplein and the Waterlooplein. Later in the nineteenth century, the old city itself was largely rebuilt, and many of the canals were filled in, but the Town Hall and the buildings of the East India Company still remain. The old town is now the main business and financial district. Weltevreden has experienced several changes in the present century. The northern part between the Koningsplein and the

Molenvliet, one of the surviving canals, has become a secondary business district, and its residential character is tending to disappear. The main European residential districts were in south Weltevreden and the newer Gondangdia and Menteng, where the street pattern is not so uniformly rectilinear. These new districts eventually linked up with the development around the military base of Meester Cornelis, and in 1935, the three old foci, Batavia, Weltevreden, and Meester Cornelis, were united in the Municipality of Batavia. As in Manila, racial segregation was pronounced; the Chinese lived in the old town, and in the lacunae between the developments along the roads, the indigenous peoples lived in kampongs, a veritable *rus in urbe*. Since the establishment of the Republic, the city, renamed Djakarta, has changed considerably. The kampong area has been greatly enlarged, and old Dutch street and district names have been discarded. Weltevreden has ceased to have a separate identity, and Meester Cornelis has become Djatinagara.

Bangkok owes its transformation from an overgrown floating village into a modern metropolis to the activities of King Chulalongkorn (1868–1910), the creator of modern Siam, whose reign marked the beginning of commercial rice cultivation in the Menam plain and the teak industry in the north. The development of Bangkok was closely bound up with the exporting and processing of both commodities. The Klong Ong Ang marks the first stage in the expansion of the city, to the east of the Grand Palace; development on the right bank was retarded by the absence of bridges over the Chao Phraya, and even now there has been little expansion in that direction. At the end of the nineteenth century the filling in of the klongs and their replacement by roads were begun. The main axis of development was to the southeast, along the "New Road," as well as along the river. The expansion of commerce necessitated a business district, which was created in the Bangrak area, south of the Chinese quarter of Sampeng, and the increase in government functions led to an expansion of administration into Samsen and Dusit, to the north, while new European residential districts arose in the southeast. The west bank of the river, however, where the high tower of Wat Arun forms the most conspicuous landmark in the city, long remained an indigenous area, with a large population living in boats. The port has lagged behind in adaptation to changed technologies, and improved facilities are long overdue.

Saigon is virtually a twentieth-century city, though the construction of a business quarter and a modern port was begun shortly after the French occupation, and, as in the case of Bangkok, growth has been linked with the rice export trade. However, administration has been relatively more important than in any of the other cities. Before the creation of Vietnam, Cochinchina was a French colony, governed from Saigon by French officials exclusively, and the city alternated with Hanoi as the residence of the Governor General of Indochina. With the loss of effective control over most of Tonkin, Saigon has become the main French base and center of power in Indochina.

The direction of expansion of the city has been westward toward Cholon, but Saigon is much more compact than any of the other great cities. The main business district lies in the southern part, close to the Arroyo Chinois, which links the Saigon River with Cholon. The shopping and administrative areas, characterized by wide boulevards, are a little to the northwest, and the European residential area lies on the "Plateau" to the north, a few feet above sea level. Cholon is a complete contrast, and until the war it had a much larger population. Unlike Saigon, which has a rectangular pattern of broad streets, Cholon has grown haphazardly along its many waterways. In 1932, the two cities were combined in a special administrative area, but they have remained largely independent of each other. Saigon is mainly concerned with administration and port activities, whereas Cholon has developed as the principal industrial area of Indochina. As in Djakarta, the enormous postwar increase in population has resulted in a great expansion in the area occupied by temporary dwellings, around the city margins.

The founder of Singapore did not omit to provide his city with a plan for development.[6] The early mercantile and financial quarter was on the right bank of the Singapore River, where it has remained ever since. Raffles planned a racial residential zonation, the Chinese to be confined to the right bank above the business district, the Europeans to inhabit the opposite bank. Though this was eventually abandoned, Singapore's "Chinatown," with the highest population density in the city, still marks the old Chinese area. The early gridiron pattern was continued in the development to the east, the first direction of expansion. In the ninetenth century, the city began to expand onto the somewhat higher land to the north, and here the new European residential district of Tanglin arose; but commercial interests are steadily invading the older part of the better residential areas to the north. With the reclamation in the last fifty years of the numerous swamps that set limits to expansion, the lacunae in development have been filled in, and the city sprawls along the south coast of the island for more than ten miles. Indeed, at no great date in the future, the whole island will be effectively urbanized. The armed services occupy large areas, and their establishments constitute, in effect, separate towns. Room for expansion is becoming increasingly difficult to find, but the city's public-housing achievements, particularly the new development at Tiong Bahru, on the west side, are worthy of note as being among the best in Asia.

In appearance the five cities are not greatly dissimilar to cities of the West, but there is a more clearly defined zonation of commercial, industrial, and residential development, the last showing a racial differentiation, which, though everywhere tending to break down, is nevertheless still conspicuous. Differences are also discernible in the suburbs, with their two-story "shop-houses," and above all in the outer margins, where "temporary" houses of wood thatched with nipa palm cluster together in overgrown kampongs or barrios, engulfed by the outward sprawl of the cities. Here, large numbers of indigenous people live in an environment that is neither urban nor rural.

[6] For a full account, see E. H. G. Dobby, "Singapore: Town and Country," *Geographical Review*, XXX (1940), 84–109.

The central business and "downtown" districts are entirely nonindigenous. International banks, commodity exchanges, and great mercantile houses reproduce all the features of the business quarter of the Western city, though there is a steady infiltration by Indian and Chinese financial and mercantile interests. The main shopping areas are also predominantly European, though here again Chinese and Indian establishments are numerous. Congestion is proportionately as great as in the Western city, and none suffers worse in this respect than Manila. Binondo, the main business district, lies on the north bank of the Pasig, and circulation is impeded by the bridges over the river; approach from the north is slowed by bottlenecks where narrow bridges span the many small canals, or *esteros*, which make the district virtually an island.

Administration is a main function of the five cities. So far as Djakarta and Singapore are concerned, it is highly likely that the gradual growth of a parliamentary democracy in the mother country, which necessitated an increase in the size of the colonial administration,[7] was a dominant factor in city growth; similar tendencies have been observed in other cities, though the degree varies considerably. The administrative areas are distinct, but the enormous growth in official business in the last twenty-five years and the expansion of the cities have necessitated some decentralization of administrative functions. Only Singapore is not an official capital, but despite the creation of an administrative capital for the Federation of Malaya at Kuala Lumpur, Singapore is unlikely to suffer from this apparent loss of government business.[8]

THE PORTS AND THEIR FUNCTIONS

In the cities of Southeast Asia, lacking the heavy industrialization that has accompanied the development of ports in the West, port functions are relatively more important. Nevertheless, in any great port a certain amount of industrialization is inevitable, and the cities already possess a considerable industrial variety.

Unlike the smaller ports of their respective territories, which serve mainly local needs, the five cities are international ports, with a commerce that is becoming more widespread as the ties of former colonies with the homeland are loosened. The ports handle a large proportion of the export trade of their territories, but an even larger proportion of the import trade; distribution is thus a principal function in the economic life of the cities.

The modern ports, constructed on reclaimed land, are entirely artificial,

[7] Amry Vandenbosch, *The Dutch East Indies* (3d ed.; Berkeley and Los Angeles: University of California Press, 1942), p. 75.

[8] Nevertheless, Singapore still is, as it always was, an administrative center of the first importance. The Colony has its own government offices, and also those of the Commissioner-General for the United Kingdom in Southeast Asia. It contains the headquarters of the Far Eastern Naval, Military, and Air Forces of the British Commonwealth, and many Commonwealth and foreign consular and diplomatic offices. Finally, the City of Singapore has its own Municipal Council, which is responsible for the administration of many public utilities.

but nowhere, even in the tidal ports of Bangkok and Saigon, are enclosed basins necessary. The modern ports, however, have not completely succeeded in displacing the old harbors; the Pasig and Singapore rivers continue to carry a heavy traffic of lighters from the Roads, with a great saving in port dues.

Manila is unusual in possessing two harbors, one north of the Pasig, which handles the large interisland traffic, and the main harbor for transoceanic vessels, south of the entrance to the river. The Pasig itself is dredged to a depth of eighteen feet as far as Jones Bridge, and is lined with quays. Native craft carry a considerable traffic upstream and along the many *esteros*. Manila normally handles about 30 per cent of the total export trade of the Philippine Republic, and more than 90 per cent of the imports.

With some 30 million tons of shipping entering and clearing annually, Singapore is one of the world's great ports. The functional pattern is similar to that of Manila. The modern port of Keppel Harbor handles most of the trade with the more distant parts of Asia and the rest of the world, and much of the entrepôt trade with South China and the rest of Southeast Asia is handled in the Roads. The political separation of Singapore from the Federation of Malaya complicates assessment of the trade of the port, since official statistics now exclude trade with the Federation; though it is not quite clear what proportion of Singapore's trade is conducted with the Federation, in 1951 the port handled 74 per cent of Malaya's imports and 67 per cent of the exports. Singapore shares with Bangkok the distinction of exporting more by value than it imports; the other ports all have an "unfavorable" trade balance. The great naval base, considerably enlarged since the war, is well removed from the commercial port; it lies on Johore Strait, some seventeen miles from the city, almost as far distant as the Cavite base is from Manila.

Tandjung Priok, the port of Djakarta, is of all the modern ports the farthest from the city center. Its construction some six miles northeast of the city was necessitated by the silting of the Tjiliwong, which has built up an expanse of mud flats along the coast more than a mile in width; the flats have, however, been put to productive use through the excavation of fishponds. The old harbor, connected with the modern port by the Antjol Canal, does not compare in importance with the Singapore River or the Pasig, nor does the rather large coastal and interisland trade have an independent harbor, as in Manila, though one of the Tandjung Priok basins is used almost exclusively for this purpose. In the unrest that preceded the formation of the Indonesian Republic, the trade of Tandjung Priok decreased greatly, but since 1950, recovery has been rapid. Some ground, however, has been lost to other ports: In 1951, Tandjung Priok handled only 10 per cent of the exports of Indonesia, though its share of the imports was better maintained, with some 52 per cent of the national total.

Saigon is both a commercial and a naval port, though as a naval base it cannot rival Singapore or Cavite. It is approached by way of the Saigon River, which, though possessing adequate depth for vessels up to 30 feet in draft, has a sinuous channel, which prevents ships longer than 550 feet from ascending to the port. The strong scour of the semidiurnal tides reduces the necessity for dredging. The port occupies about three miles of the right bank of the river and is divided into three sections. Overseas trade is handled by the quays between the Arroyo Chinois and the Canal de Dérivation, in the Khan Hoi district; smaller vessels use the quays nearer the city; and the naval port lies farthest upstream, close to the Arroyo de l'Avalanche. Lighters convey cargoes from ships anchored in the river below the city to wharves along the Arroyo Chinois and the Canal de Dérivation, the twin waterways that link Saigon with Cholon. Before 1939, Saigon handled about 40 per cent of the total foreign trade of Indochina; rice formed about 50 per cent by weight of the exports. At the present time, the military operations taking place in the country have greatly reduced the trade of Saigon, and the rice export is only some 100,000 tons a year.

Bangkok alone of all the ports is still inaccessible to large ocean-going vessels. A bar at the mouth of the Menam Chao Phraya prevents entry, and the terminal for large vessels has long been Gaw Si Kang, an island in the Gulf of Siam east of the river mouth. From Gaw Si Kang, strings of lighters are drawn by tugs to the wharves of Bangkok, which extend for about six miles along the left bank below the Grand Palace. The dredging of the bar to allow ocean-going vessels to reach the port would have presented no great difficulties, but opposition from the lightering interests prevented anything from being done until shortly before the war, when work was begun on a new port at Klong Toi, about five miles below the city. It is now proposed, as part of a plan to expand rice cultivation in Thailand, to deepen the channel so that vessels of 26-foot draft can ascend to the port. Bangkok has an almost complete monopoly of the foreign trade of Thailand, and in a real sense, it is the only port of the country.

INDUSTRIAL DEVELOPMENT

The five cities contain a large proportion of the total industrial capacity of their respective territories. Industry is well represented, though much of it is better described as processing than as manufacturing, and its range of activities is continually increasing. The primary processing of foodstuffs and raw materials is dominant; rice milling is particularly important, except in Singapore, but rubber, copra, sago, tapioca, hemp, sugar, and tobacco all assume considerable local significance. A beginning has been made with the higher stages of manufacturing, such as rubber products and even foam rubber, in Singapore; other manufactures are furniture, boats, footwear, glass, bricks and tiles, oils and soaps, electric batteries, and certain chemical products. Manufacturing industries proper use relatively little machinery and power and produce for the home market, in which there is a considerable element of local protection. Food and drink industries are well developed (including brewing and distilling); textiles are poorly developed. Heavy industry is confined to the repair and refitting of vessels. All the ports have forges and foundries for making minor repairs; Singapore and

Djakarta, which have dry-dock facilities, can undertake more extensive work. Repair shops for maintenance of railway equipment are located in all the cities except Singapore; the assembly of imported motor vehicles is carried on in Manila, Djakarta, and Singapore. Industry relies largely on electric power, which is expensive because of the paucity of local coal supplies.

Small-scale industry is almost entirely in the hands of the Chinese; the larger undertakings are overwhelmingly European-owned, though there are some large Chinese industrial establishments. Only a small proportion of the inhabitants of the cities are engaged in industry: In Singapore, where industry is expanding rapidly, only 11 per cent of the adult working population were employed in industrial establishments, according to the census of 1947. This unduly low figure does not take account of the large employment in the establishments of the armed services, much of which was industrial.

The industrial areas lie close to the ports or along the rivers and canals. They are surrounded by areas of high population density; for the relatively high cost and limited availability of public transport operate to retard the divorce of place of work and residence, which is so conspicuous a feature of the Western city. Newer industrial areas, however, are appearing on the margins of the cities, and as the range of industrial activity grows, industry is likely to become more widely dispersed.

POPULATION

All the five cities would have probably reached the 1-million level in a comparatively short period if the war had not intervened. During the Japanese occupation, population decreased in the cities because of the shortage of food, and the wartime dislocation that elsewhere in Asia resulted in a large influx of rural dwellers into the cities did not operate here. With the end of the war, the tide set strongly in the opposite direction. The breakdown of effective administration in many parts of Southeast Asia following the Japanese surrender, armed insurrections against the central governments, the struggle for independence, the depredations of extreme factions, and the difficulty of protecting disliked minorities, particularly the Chinese, all combined to attract many rural dwellers to the comparative safety of the cities. This immigration of refugees was perhaps greatest in Saigon-Cholon: From a population of about 300,000 at the time of the Japanese occupation, the twin cities have increased to an estimated 1.4 million. Djakarta has grown almost as spectacularly. At the census of 1930, the city of Batavia had a population of a little more than half a million; by 1950, the Indonesian government estimated Djakarta's population to be not less than 2 million; and at present, the city may well contain nearer 3 million. Even on the most conservative estimate, it is by far the most populous city in the whole of Southeast Asia.

In the census of 1948, Greater Manila had a population of 1.18 million; however, several separately recorded districts of Rizal Province are integral parts of the built-up area, and their inclusion raises the total to more than a million and a quarter. The fourteen districts of the City of Manila proper showed a 58 per cent increase over the 1939 census figures. Singapore and Bangkok have been relatively unaffected by postwar immigration from the country. In the intercensal period 1931–47, the population of the island of Singapore grew by some 68 per cent, owing to the gradual establishment of an equality in the sex composition of the Chinese population, together with a steady decline in the death rate; allowing for natural increase since the census, the population of Singapore Colony at present is about 1.1 million, of whom about 70 per cent reside in the municipal area. Before the war, Bangkok was approaching 900,000, but in the census of 1947, the population was only 1,116,600;[9] hence the war may have somewhat retarded the city's growth.

The present rate of growth due to natural increase seems to be about 3 per cent a year in all the cities, which is much higher than the rate in their respective national territories. This will present many difficult problems of development. As might be expected, the already overcrowded districts have experienced the greatest increases; in Manila, for example, the districts of Tondo, Sampaloc, and Santa Cruz have increased their populations by 80 per cent or more since 1939. As compared with Western cities, densities in the poorest areas are extremely high; 1,500 persons to an acre would not be excessive for the net density of the worst blocks.[10] On the other hand, density development in the best residential districts is very low, frequently one or two houses to an acre, so that the cities sprawl widely.

From the beginning, Chinese immigrants have constituted an important element of the cities. At first encouraged, and later feared, by the authorities, the Chinese were confined to special quarters, such as the famous Parián of Manila, where they have tended to remain. Dislike of them has been a universal rallying point of numerous indigenous politicians, and the murder of many Chinese in the period following the Japanese collapse recalls the massacres of the early history of Manila and Batavia. Where immigration has been comparatively free, at least until fairly recent times, the Chinese have become a majority: Singapore is more than 77 per cent Chinese—the largest Chinese community outside China—and in Bangkok, more than 60 per cent of the population are Chinese or of mixed Chinese-Thai ancestry. The lower proportions of Chinese in the other three cities are due to the earlier restrictions on immigration, together with an influx of indigenous peoples from rural areas in the postwar period. Events in China, however, have everywhere increased illegal Chinese immigration. The removal of many Chinese from rural Cochinchina to the Saigon-Cholon area has raised the percentage of Chinese in Cholon to about 60, and it is probably not less than 30 in the combined cities. In Manila and

[9] With Thonburi. According to the *Statistical Year Book of Thailand*, N.S., Vol. 1, 1952, recently received, the total for the two is 1,178,881.

[10] Net density is the average density of the population of a given residential area, which consists solely of the dwellings and one-half of the width of streets giving access thereto. The figure quoted here is an estimate by the Singapore Improvement Trust of the situation in the most overcrowded part of the city.

Djakarta, it is much lower, and the total number of Chinese is not easy to estimate; both cities contain more than 50,000, and the number of persons of mixed Chinese and indigenous blood is undoubtedly much larger. Despite many vicissitudes, the Chinese have proved indispensable, and their importance in the economic life of the cities can hardly be overstated.

Europeans constitute only a very small proportion of the population of the cities. Only in prewar Batavia did they amount to as much as 5 per cent of the total, and this was in part due to the inclusion of Eurasians as Europeans in the Dutch statistics. Of the other immigrant groups, the most numerous are Indians and Pakistanis, who in Singapore made up 7 per cent of the population in 1947. Djakarta has a small community of Arabs, engaged in shopkeeping or moneylending.

The indigenous peoples have a higher birth rate than the immigrant peoples, but also a higher death rate, so that the relative proportions of the two groups have tended to remain the same. Lately, the migration of indigenous peoples to the cities, especially in the new independent states, has altered the balance somewhat, and the partly alien character of the cities may tend to decline. Simultaneously, restrictions have been placed on the economic activities of the Chinese in the Philippines and Thailand, but the outcome of these measures is unlikely to be that intended.

THE FUTURE OF THE CITIES

The future of the great cities remains problematic. They have attained their present size and pre-eminence through their role as intermediaries in the interchange of foodstuffs and raw materials with the manufactured products of the West, but this activity has been carried on entirely by aliens. So long as this economic pattern persists, the great port cities will continue to occupy a leading position in the life of Southeast Asia. But the pattern may not persist, and it is clear that the economic development of Southeast Asia will include an increasing attention to home production of both foodstuffs and manufactures. Southeast Asia may return to the political instability of precolonial times; it may become part of the Communist sphere; or it may succeed in maintaining neutrality between the Communist and non-Communist worlds. In any event, the great cities cannot escape some readjustment, and they may well lose ground to other centers. Already there is opposition to the dominant position of the great city in national affairs. If extremist elements prevail, it appears likely that other cities may come to the fore; just as Shanghai has been supplanted by a revived Peking, so the victory of the Vietminh would be likely to confer supremacy on Tonkin. The future of Singapore is particularly difficult to forecast, since it is the only city that is not an administrative capital of a state. Its integration into the Federation of Malaya would give the immigrant Chinese numerical superiority and would be strongly resisted by the Malays of the peninsula. Political changes in China and Southeast Asia itself may make the entrepôt trade difficult to maintain, and as a center of world communications, Singapore has already lost ground to Bangkok, which is better placed for tans-Asian and trans-Pacific air routes. Moreover, its utter dependence on outside sources for food,[11] and to some extent for water, must greatly limit its usefulness as a strategic base—problems that have already given rise to some concern. Of all the cities, only Bangkok appears to be without a potential rival, despite an attempt in 1945 to relocate the administrative capital.[12] It may well be that the great cities' brightest future lies in an increase in the range and pace of industrialization.

[11] "Food Supplies for Singapore," Singapore, 1951.

[12] Bangkok's central position in Southeast Asia, equidistant from South and East Asia, is reflected in its selection as the headquarters of the United Nations Economic Commission for Asia and the Far East.

6

THE COUNTRYSIDE AND THE JUNGLE*

W. R. GEDDES

A hundred years ago, old jungle covered most of the rolling land around the site where Mentu Tapuh now stands. Three miles upstream, the village of Mentu, of which Mentu Tapuh was to be an offshoot, must already have been inhabited for a long time, for today no tradition survives of an earlier ancestral home, the people believing that their ancestors emerged naked from a cave nearby and built Mentu as their first village. But until a century ago or less, the inhabitants of the village were never more than a small group of frontiersmen on the edge of a far-spreading forest. In the following years, they were joined by migrants from the denser Land Dayak populations lying to their west and south. Their numbers also probably grew through natural increase when the White Rajah's peace robbed dis-

---

* Reprinted by permission of the author and the publisher from W. R. Geddes, *Nine Dayak Nights* (Melbourne: Oxford University Press, 1957), chapter 2. This is part of an eight-chapter introduction to a lengthy story told to the author by several Land Dayaks in Kampong Mentu Tapuh, Sarawak. The story ran on for nine nights and is recorded by Geddes in a somewhat abridged form in this book. The characters mentioned in this chapter were mostly participants in the sessions, though the major story-teller was Raseh, the leading spirit-medium of the Kampong.

ease of its ally in war. More and more land was cleared. Mentu Tapuh was established, and today much of the old forest in its neighborhood has given way to a tangle of secondary growth, denser on the ground but more open to the sky. This is the "countryside," where the farms are made. It is very different from the jungle. The sun smiles on it. It is not very frightening. But it is lonely.

The countryside is not quite all dense with the tangle of secondary growth. Some of it is green with paddy. Some of the rest, which was green with paddy last year, is now covered only with grass, waist-high. But beneath the grass, the bamboo, shrubs, and vines will be rising, soon to make these old fields like most of the countryside all the time, for only a little of it is cultivated at once, and that little changes in place from year to year. Every June, each village family will clear one or two new fields, covering together an area of from two to four acres. The tangled growth on the chosen area is cut down, and burnt when it is dry. The seed is put in, the plants tended, and the harvest gathered. Thereafter, a few fields, or parts of fields, may be used for a year or two longer as sugar-cane or cassava gardens, but most of the clearings will be given up, for ten years or so, to the lush, wild, overwhelming weeds. The farmer is glad to see these weeds take possession quickly, for if they do not, and only choking *lalang* grass springs up instead, he knows that he can never farm in that place again.

Yet the sight touches the soul. For a whole season, all one's interests have centered in the field. One has walked there in the dawn, and home again in the late afternoon. One has worked there in the sun, gossiping with helpers, blackened the girls in the working-party with charcoal on the day of the burning, laughed with gaily dressed companions on the happy planting day, feasted with the gods there, worried over the paddy's health—fearing rats, or grubs, or blight, or storm, or flood—and gathered the harvest, despondently or with gratification. And now one must turn away from the field to face another year in quite another place.

I say it touches the soul. But the Dayaks say it may separate the soul from the body. Therefore, at the yearly festival after the harvest is stored, they summon back souls that may still be wandering in fields now given up. They call them back home—back to the village, crowded, noisy with cocks and pigs and children, contrasting so comfortingly with the quiet, overgrown countryside.

The primary jungle—we would call it primeval had the word not become spoiled with too much use, because it conveys well the feeling the jungle gives rise to—has been pushed back, but still not very far. From the north, it sends out a broad tongue along a high limestone ridge right into the village sky, and from the base of this tongue, a mile or two away, it widens out into a forest extending hundreds of square miles, the last great area of jungle in this part of Borneo and now declared a reserve by the government, which is anxious about the watershed of the Sadong River.

The jungle is very different from the countryside. Everyone is deeply aware of it, perhaps most of all those who keep away from it. To try to understand the attitudes of the Land Dayaks, I believe that one must do more than study their economy, their politics, their mating and breeding habits. One should go into the jungle, quite often and sometimes alone. It is fascinating to wander in it, and a relief to come out. It is well, however, not to go so far in as to deny oneself the pleasure of this relief. The jungle is very deceitful, duplicating what seem at first to be singular features in a way so confusing that one may quickly be like the hero of our story "walking on and on, for ever walking uphill and downhill, on hills of a thousand different kinds."

It is true that one is not likely to go on wandering forever. The Dayaks have a clever way of seeking those who have gone astray. Search-parties set out in various directions, beating the big brass festival gongs to guide the wanderer toward them. But they are not silly enough to begin searching until it has become clearly necessary, and, in the meantime, the one or two nights that one may spend in the jungle, sodden and bitten and frightened by hints of inhuman company, may not be worth the vivid impression they will undoubtedly give. To be lost is one of the greatest fears of the Land Dayaks. There are some bold hunters in Mentu Tapuh who range far, but they are only two or three. Most men rarely go far from the tracks or nearer stream-beds, although in parties, which sometimes may be made up mainly of women, they may go further to collect rattan vine. Practically and emotionally, the jungle means much to the Land Dayaks, and a great part of its emotional meaning is fear.

The jungle has, of course, many delights, which differ according to time, place, and person. Anyone, Dayak or European, is probably elated by the early morning valleys, with a whole day of light ahead, when the birds and the gibbons are calling. The woman gathering rattan may be gladdened by finding a length with the sections five hand-spans apart, the Dayak equivalent of a four-leaf clover, but more useful since it can make an elegant staff for an old man. The pig-hunter may be excited by fresh tracks. For myself at least, there were many lovely glades where the butterflies, or *teribomban* as the Dayaks called them, not recognizing the killing-bottle, played, some of them small, and some fit to be classed as birds, their miraculously colored wings perfect or so tattered by life as to make their agile flying another miracle.

But delight is not the most constant feeling in the denser jungle. There is a heightened sensibility and a wariness. Exuberance is out of place in the presence of much that is bigger, and so much that is other, than man. In the silent and ancient shade, the fallen trunks, the moist, rough carpet of decay; the endless limited vegetable views, growth upon growth, of trees and vines and ferns glossy on top but hooked barbarously beneath; the animal manifestations, there and gone or heard or only suspected—all of these convey a sense of a life-force or life-forces, apart from man, greater than him, inconsiderate of him, and amid which he upholds himself by his will and skill. The sense is a subtle one. No one takes the trees to be anything more than trees. A vine is but a vine, to be slashed if it is in the way. An animal is only an animal, to be killed if it is worth it. What counts is the total effect—and the sense of something more. For a European, city-coddled, the experience of the jungle is sobering, enlightening, and vaguely threatening. The Dayaks are already enlightened. They know that their place in total nature is small, however distinctive. Therefore they feel the threat more.

But can we say that they do feel this way about the jungle? Unless we are psychoanalysts, with a ready-made formula that explains everything but the content of people's thoughts, we can never be quite sure how anyone else thinks. But we do know that the Dayaks have fears of the jungle, and that these fears are irrational. They are irrational because they go far beyond proven facts.

There are, of course, some dangers in the jungle that are real. The spirit of an English wood is different from the spirit of the forest in Borneo, and the difference is partly due to the worse things in the latter. There are more poisonous snakes. One may not see them often, but there are stories about them. A man walking near Mentu Tapuh was sprung at by a large king cobra. Its teeth caught in the long trousers he luckily was wearing. He seized it by its throat and strangled it. I do not know whether this is true, but everyone in the village says it is. One morning, a woman came to me saying that she had been bitten by a snake. Her arm was swollen enormously. She said that on the previous evening, when she had been walking home in the dusk from her paddy field, she saw the snake—of a kind easily seen because of its scarlet head and the scarlet tip to its tail. She cut off its head with her bush-knife. Knowing the snake was poisonous, she carried the head carefully to the side of the track to bury it. She returned to pick up the body of the snake to take it home to roast for supper. As she lifted it, she was bitten. Of course she did not stay to investigate, but the explanation on which everyone agreed was that, when she had first come upon the scene, one snake had been swallowing another. The head she cut off was the head of the snake that was being swallowed, and in the dusk she did not notice that another lay behind. While she was burying the severed head, the second head completed its swallowing and so was free to punish the hand that had robbed it of the upper part of its meal. . . .

Snakes, then, there certainly are. But although they add a little to the mistrust of the jungle, they do not explain it. The Dayaks know that the likelihood of harm from them is small. All except a mating king cobra, and apparently also an occasional malicious one, will harm man only when he is in the way of their flight. During the lifetime of the oldest man in Mentu Tapuh, only three villagers have been killed by snakes. It is at nighttime that the greatest fear of the jungle is felt, and then the danger from snakes is at its least, although we must note one widely believed tale of a man who woke up to find himself inside a python. Fortunately he was wearing his knife in its sheath at his side, so he cut his way out. The slime on his body when he returned home proved the truth of his story. Snakes do figure in our story, but not as creatures of fear. The dreaded reptile is not a snake. It is a dragon. And there are no dragons in the jungle, although Lutong, the father of Raseh, swears that he saw one in the river when he was fishing. It was twenty-four feet long, and glowed.

From other animals in the jungle there is even less danger. A bear may panic dangerously when cornered, but bears are rare, and a fearful person can refrain from cornering them. Clouded leopards, which are still rarer, have never, as far as I know, hurt anyone. The animal mentioned most in our story is the orangutan. It, too, is a victim of man, not a menace to him. Or rather, we had better say it could be a victim under different circumstances, for the orangutan now enjoys privileged status in the jungle. Because the southwestern part of Borneo and a small area in Sumatra are the only places in the world where this great ape is found, it has been placed under government protection. The present generation of Land Dayaks, fully understanding the high importance of the species to overseas scientists, appreciate the need for this measure. Although their fathers and grandfathers regarded the animal as a legitimate prize of the hunt, and although they know it to be in such numbers that their occasional killings, as distinct from the depredations of European collectors, could not threaten it with extinction, they never now harm a hair on its back. They would swear to this fact, and I am prepared to swear with them. In any case, despite the formidable look of a large specimen, the orangutan is harmless, and what Dayak would harm a harmless animal?

There is another ape in the jungle—the gibbon. It is fairly numerous and is not an uncommon item on Mentu Tapuh menus. The Dayaks recognize the likeness of both of these apes to man, but from this likeness they draw a conclusion contrary to that of Darwin. The contrast in view shows how two authorities considering the same facts can deduce from them exactly opposite theories. The evolutionists say that man is an ascended ape; the Land Dayaks say that the ape is a descended man. The orangutan, they say, sprang from a man who, becoming ashamed at some misdeed in the village, ran away into the jungle. He stayed there so long that he took on the form of an orangutan, and his children were like him. The wife, on this theory, is the missing link.

The gibbons had a different founder. He was a villager who differed from most men in that he was very fond of cooking, which meant that he spent a great deal of time bending over a smoky fire. One night he visited his beloved in her bed. When dawn came, he was horrified to see that she was black. He rushed to get a looking glass and was overcome with shame to realize that the black had come from his own body, which was irremediably encrusted with soot. He ran away into the jungle, where he clung to a branch in shame. He clung there so long that his arms stretched. He became the progenitor of the gibbons, which are black in color and long-armed like himself. This theory is superior to that of Darwin in that it leaves no debate about the origin of differences of pigmentation among the primates.

This catalogue of animals is relevant to our story, but none of them is dangerous enough to explain the anxiety felt in the jungle. The anxiety is about other things—about nature itself, and about supernatural beings. Neither ground of fear would we admit as reasonable. Therefore, the Dayaks, by differing from us, prove themselves irrational.

The peculiar and the great in nature are suspect, because they suggest a force, either perverted or exceedingly strong, that may act wantonly. A vine writhed fantastically may ensnare the soul of a person who crosses over it, or under it, or through its coils. Large trees may fall, or big rocks roll, to crush the passer-by. We, too, can accept the fact of such things happening. Why they should happen at one moment rather than another, or to one thing rather than another, we rarely know, but we are sure there is a cause, although we might be thoughtless enough to speak of an "accident." The Dayak view is rather different. A possibility of autonomy is allowed to the trees and the rocks. The risk from them is therefore greater than we might consider it.

There is a virtue in the Dayak view for one who wanders much in the jungle. We said that anyone might feel the jungle as vaguely threatening. The European, allowing nature no right of surprise, may have to move with his anxiety through the somber, entangled shadow, trying not to recognize his company. The Dayaks, by giving substance to their fears, can take action against them in advance.

The action that they do take is ritual, and this often means fun as well. At the times of the biggest festivals, an especially twisted vine is brought from the jungle to the long-house verandah. Maidens dance around it with fighting-knives, leap over it, and finally sever it, thus robbing such vines of their power to ensnare souls. This is psychological reassurance. It counteracts the formation of concepts of danger when one is in the jungle. More regularly, morale is boosted on most of the many occasions when invocations are made to the ancestral spirits. Among other evil influences against which the priest prays are listed "the cry of the vine, the twisted and knobbly vine; the thunder clap; the falling of the dead tree; the big rocks turning over; the stones tumbling down." Trouble is not to be expected from them after they have been spoken to in this fashion.

But direct anxiety about nature is always a vague worry, hardly crossing the threshold of consciousness, except at prayer-time, or when an excuse is needed for a festival episode, or when blame is to be laid for a happening already over, or perhaps when one is deep in the far jungle. Much more vivid is the fear of demons, demons who may be met with anywhere in the jungle, but whose most common dwelling places are the banks of streams, the swampy places where the growth is stunted and the ground thick with roots, and on hilltops.

The story regarding these beings, whom we are calling "demons" for want of a better name, states that once upon a time there were two kinds of people, both created by the supreme god, or "origin-spirit." They were constantly quarreling with each other, so the supreme god decided that they should live apart and that one kind should be invisible to the other. The invisible group, which by 1951 had separated into many different tribes, each with its own peculiar characteristics, are the demons. As if to compensate for the advantage that their invisibility gave them over ordinary men, the god decreed that demons troubling man must call off their attacks if they were fed and feted.

Therefore, all Dayak festivals are to a large extent parties put on for the demons. For all the days and nights of the festival, the big brass gongs should be kept booming out over the countryside inviting all mischievous, malicious, and resentful beings in the neighborhood to come up onto the long-house verandah to see the dancing, to eat the delicacies, to drink the wine. Then, in a final ceremony when exhaustion has brought the fun to an end, they are sped on their way, quite impolitely, since they are under an obligation to go, but with enough provisions to sustain them on what they are told should be a very distant journey. The village is thus cleansed of harmful influences—until such time as the desire of the villagers, their food supplies, their freedom from pressure of work, or an event of outstanding happiness or unhappiness, suggests a further round of merrymaking.

The festivals and the group of people living together—since a crowd frightens the big demons—cast a kind of *cordon sanitaire* around the village. The demons most to be dreaded are those who dwell beyond this cordon and who have not attended the parties. They are to be met with in the distant countryside and particularly in the deep jungle. They are of many kinds. Those who play a main part in our story are enormous, which is the reason why we have translated the word *antu*—the generic term for demons—as "giant." Other demons may appear as fierce animals. Some are seductresses who lure men into love and then consume the means by which they express it. Lahot in Mentu Tapuh is said to have met such demons. They were three beautiful girls who led him back to their long house. It was a long house that looked exactly like his own, so that had he not been a wary young man he would have been deceived into thinking that he was being entertained safely in his own home. When they were in the house, the girls began to show their fondness for him, but he delayed the introductions by saying—the Dayaks being frank in such matters—that he wished to urinate. Once outside, he hastened beneath the long house, quickly piled rubbish against its supports, and set it alight, cremating his would-be mistresses.

With such demons about, it is no wonder that many persons fear to go far in the jungle. The timid and the children prefer to stay at home altogether. Others of those whose business takes them into the jungle enter with the urge to get out again as soon as possible. But how, may we ask, can even the boldest dare to venture into notorious demon country? The answer lies in the true nature of the demons. We have not yet fully explained it. To give a form to our coming explanation, we may hint now that the country the demons really live in is the country of the mind, and the laws they obey are those of the imagination.

The demons are not spirits—immortal, afterworldly, insubstantial, and invulnerable. They are creatures like man, bound like him to the mortal cycle of birth, marriage, childbearing, and death, and having the same kinds of weaknesses. Thus, they are not inevitably beyond human power. Man can escape them, beat them, cheat them—if he is fast enough, strong enough, or clever enough. Some demons can apparently use their cloak of invisibility, or change their shape, at will. They may display superhuman strength. They seem able to be here, there, and somewhere else the next moment. Yet despite these powers, which should make the demons invincible, men believe that they can protect themselves against them.

Some of the means of defense are reasonable, as, for instance, the use of charms, or spells, or incense, or, most potent of all, a skew-cross set at the mouths of tracks or in the fields. The Dayaks fear or dislike certain things, so it is reasonable that the demons should also have their own fears and dislikes. Other means of defense are ethical, and so we must commend them. Certain tribes of demons are, in effect, policemen. They punish those who break the village code, or punish the associates of the breakers. Laduh, we saw, was struck because of something he should not have done. There is one tribe that punishes idle gossip, although they must be a lax crowd. Another tribe punishes priests who miss parts of their invocations. Grandfather Jon was struck dumb for half an hour for doing this, but his lapse was a particularly foolish one, for it was the names of the demons themselves that he forgot.

Poisonous insects, which if not really demons are much like them, behave in the same way, especially scorpions and centipedes but also hornets. One should not tempt these insects, but one may not expect to get bitten unless one has been bad. An interesting case was that of Tuntong, a young boy from the village of Suhu who was staying with me in Mentu Tapuh. In his village there is an unhygienic prohibition on the washing of mats. I asked him to wash my mat. He said it was wrong. I pointed out that he was in Mentu Tapuh not in Suhu. As he was a very kind boy, he washed it. Unfortunately, when he sat down after his labors, he sat on top of a hornet, which stung him in an embarrassing place. The headman of Mentu Tapuh told him that it was his own fault for breaking the laws of the village to which he belonged. Tuntong could have fined me for egging him on. On another occasion, I was myself stung by two hornets in my bed after the old men had warned me of the danger of allowing children to beat on tins in my house in imitation of gongs when it was not festival time. This was strange, because none of the men had been near my sleeping place! Thereafter I always had my house cleaned along with the others at the times of the festivals.

One insurance against demons, therefore, is to be good. We must note, however, that demons are anywhere likely to be capricious. They are alleged to have given the Catholic missionary dysentery, when by rights they should have left a distinguished visitor alone. And in the jungle they may be terrible individualists, admitting no law but their own evil.

It is the purely physical means of defense that strike us as unreasonable, because they are used against beings who are not constrained by physical laws. People may believe, for instance, that they could fight demons. In truth, they would not try if they met one. They would certainly run as fast as their legs would carry them. But still, they trust that human legs may outrace creatures to whom, in other contexts, they may impute the power of flying. This is not a logical belief. Of course it is not, because the

demons are illogical. That is half the trouble with them. The Dayak defense against them is their own form of what the Christians would call
faith, expressed in terms of direct action or ritual. One of the great benefits
of our story to the villagers is the bolstering their faith gets from it. The
hero outwits or slays every demon, no matter how big.

Now let us touch wood and then assert that the demons, as the Dayaks
conceive them, are not real. We need to do so for the sake of our argument. We suggested that the fears of the jungle arose from its total effect
—and the sense of something more. If the demons are not real but are
simply the particular substances the Dayaks give to their fears, then there
must be this other, more vague awareness, or something like it, enlivening
their imaginations. . . .

There is another class of beings haunting the jungle whom we have not
yet mentioned. They are called *pinyamun.* Their supernatural abilities put
them on the same mental plane as demons, but theoretically they are men.
They are supposed to be head-hunters on the hunt. The Land Dayaks say
they are Sea Dayaks from the Saribas River region. Other groups in the
country will claim that the danger comes from hunters of different origin,
for the belief in the threat is common to all native groups. Every now and
then, some incident will set off an alarm, and then a ripple of fear runs
over a sizable area of Sarawak. The incidents are always slight.

It may be that a stray anthropologist looks too obviously at the cranial
features of his hosts. Twice Mentu Tapuh shivered while I was there, although not from this cause. The first time was when a headless body was
discovered by the police at a place down on the coast several days' journey
away. It turned out afterwards that a villager had shot one of his fellow
villagers accidentally, decapitating him and burying the head elsewhere, in
the hope that the victim would not be identified as the man with whom he
had gone hunting. The second scare arose over a survey for a proposed
bridge across the Sadong River. It was said that the engineer had employed
Sea Dayaks to collect a Land Dayak head with which to appease the
river spirits for the disturbance they would suffer from the building of the
bridge, the Land Dayaks being naïve enough, still, to believe that a survey
is a prelude to action.

Once the fear begins to spread, it infects everyone—not only the Land
Dayaks but the Chinese and Malays as well, while the District Officer
becomes anxious about the anxiety all around him. But it is the Land
Dayaks who suffer most actutely. Rumors fly from ear to ear of apparitions
here, there, and everywhere. The head-hunters are really demons in a new
guise. Why they so readily take on this guise is not hard to understand. It
is not only because of the long tradition of heads truly lost. The head-
hunters are the bogeymen of the Land Dayaks. Little children who wander
far from their mothers' backs are warned that they lie in wait for them. As
these children grow up, any ventures beyond the ordinary continue to take
them mentally into the head-hunters' range.

During a scare, it is believed that one may meet the head-hunters in the open countryside. One should go abroad only with others, and always carry a weapon. But not, of course, for attack. The Land Dayaks prefer to have their fights in fantasy. The hero of our story slays head-hunters as easily as he slays demons. That is why he is a hero. It is far better to leave the task to him.

When there is no scare on, a person can feel reasonably safe in the countryside. But he can never be certain about the jungle. Head-hunters may appear there without warning. The jungle is generally a much worse place than the countryside. In the jungle, the loneliness felt is the loneliness of humankind in an inhuman world of life. The sense of self is heightened by the contrast, and the village is seen as a dear place of alliance against so much. Grown Land Dayaks do not walk in dread in the jungle. It would not be fair to say that they did. The majority of men may feel nothing more than a vague unease, quite dispersed in daylight hours if others are near. But all persons prefer to get back to the village, with its company, sooner rather than later, and think it by far the best place in all the jungle and all the countryside.

TWO

Tradition, Modernity, and Social Change

Although the tradition-modernity dichotomy has been abused and overworked, it continues to be useful in helping us to understand the complex processes of cultural interaction. Admittedly, there is no pure "tradition," just as there cannot be pure "modernity," since both are only ideal abstractions. We have no historical record of unadulterated "tradition," and "modernity" is open-ended. The tradition-modernity model is therefore only a crutch, an heuristic device that aids in understanding reality, the limitations of which must be acknowledged, however, lest it be elevated to dogma.

There is no truly static society, for social values, structures, and status relationships are always in a state of flux. While the Indian caste system has existed for at least 1,000 years, the interpretation of the rights and responsibilities of caste has changed considerably, but, more important for our purposes here, caste has probably changed much more in the last fifty years than it changed during the previous 500. Similarly, in Southeast Asia, social change has accelerated in the past half-century to the point that the process of change itself becomes both interesting and significant.

In this section, we are interested in many aspects of social change. The questions to which the authors address themselves include many of the following: What are some of the "traditional" social values of Southeast Asia? By whom are they being questioned and challenged? What are the "modern" values? From where did they come? How are these modern values transmitted? What kinds of tensions are produced when traditional and modern values conflict? To what extent do old patterns of behavior and belief reassert themselves in a modern setting? To what extent are modern structures and values changed in the process of interaction? What are the most significant arenas of social change in Southeast Asia? What is the contribution of education to social change? What are the tensions produced in the system and in the individual? Can education be used by an elite for the purposes of "social engineering"?

As we can see from the essays in this section, the arenas of change are many and varied. In the following articles, Manning Nash, Rosihan Anwar, and Clifford Geertz describe change in the realm of religion; Robert Wolff sees it in medicine, Ann Ruth Willner, in a factory, Mochtar Lubis and Robert Tilman, in politics; Michael Moerman, in the institution of the peasantry itself; and Joseph Fischer, Clifford Geertz, James Guyot, and Robert Tilman, in the schools. The resiliency of tradition, even in a modern guise, is stressed by Moerman, Willner, Lubis, and Guyot. The vulnerability of traditional values to alteration by modern ideas, even when the intent is to conserve, is well demonstrated by Geertz, while Moerman and Wolff stress the points that accommodation is mutual, acceptance of "modernity" is selective, and mutation takes place in both spheres during the process of change. In the arena of education, Fischer shows us how intent most of the states are to utilize the schools as agents of modernization and then goes on to document some of the resulting tensions and disorientations. Tilman documents one successful case of social engineering, the success of the British in creating a new English-speaking elite from among the traditional Malay aristocracy.

All of our authors in this section are concerned with new values coming in from outside the society and interacting with old values long accepted by the people. With the exception of only one or two essays, these new values are associated chiefly with Western penetration into Southeast Asia, and there is thus the danger that one may equate "modernization" with "Westernization." The contributions of Nash and Geertz are therefore doubly welcome, for they both usefully demonstrate the point made earlier that "tradition" and "modernity" are relative and open-ended.

When Buddhism arrived in Burma, it was "modern," and *nat*-worship was "traditional." Today, Burmese Buddhism (which still includes *nat*-worship) is traditional, and secularism is modern. It is this process of the interaction of the traditional and the modern, together with the reinterpretation of the meaning of modernity and the accompanying social percolation as the structure of values changes, that make the study of social change so difficult—and also so fascinating.

The Interaction of Tradition and Modernity

7

BURMESE BUDDHISM IN EVERYDAY LIFE*

MANNING NASH

Buddhism is a pervading force in Burmese society. Even to the casual eye the hillsides dotted with pagodas, the hosts of saffron-robed monks, and the innumerable monasteries proclaim the strength and depth of Buddhist belief and practice in Burma. What, however, is less accessible, and hence less known, are the meanings and practices of Buddhism in the ordinary villages, and since villagers make up more than 85 per cent of the Burmese population, this is a serious gap both in the understanding of Burmese culture and in the interpretation of a social structure so largely informed by Buddhist belief.

I intend here to portray three aspects of Buddhism as it is currently carried on in the villages of upper Burma,[1] especially around Mandalay. The

* Reproduced by permission of the author and the American Anthropological Association from the *American Anthropologist*, LXV (April, 1963), 285–95.

[1] Field work was carried out in 1960–61. Two villages were worked in intensively for five months each, and thirty-four more villages in upper Burma were surveyed. Information on nine other villages in the region comes from June C. Nash. The research was supported by a grant from the National Science Foundation. This article is a revised

three aspects to be treated are: first, the general knowledge of Buddhist doctrine and lore that a villager commands; next, the specific activities and groupings occasioned by Buddhism; and, finally, the role of Buddhism in shaping and forming the character of village people and their institutions. Through this review, I hope to give some understanding of Burmese Buddhism as a feature of ordinary day-to-day living, as against a body of dogma and precept, and, at the same time, to illuminate some relations, in a general and theoretical way, between religion and society.

The villager's knowledge of Buddhism, that is, the scripture as laid down in the three baskets (*Tripitaka*), tends to be mainly of the practical code of morality and a few of the *thok*,[2] or verses, that recommend and enjoin the virtues of the middle way. Of the *Abidhamma*, the higher learning,[3] the villager is virtually ignorant, even if he has spent years as a monk. Of the book of monastic rules and regulations, he knows little except that monks must be celibate, must beg for a livelihood, must reside in a *kyaung* (monastery), must not own anything beyond the eight necessities, must not eat after midday, and must spend their time in the pursuit of religious studies. It is on these observances that a man is accepted as a *pongyi*. Anyone wearing the saffron robe obeys this minimal code and is accorded respect and deference as the exemplar of the ideal life. But the personal attributes of monks and their learning give them rank, bring them special gifts, and attract villagers to them for advice.

The villager's understanding of Buddhism rests on three chief pieces of knowledge: first, the ideas of *kan* and *kutho*; second, the notions of the precepts and their observance; and, finally, the folk version of the levels of existence and bits of cosmology that entails. Each of these pieces of knowledge is complex, made up of many-stranded assumptions and assertions and deeply involved with philosophical and ontological nicety. But for the villager they are the matters of fact that define and map the nature of religious reality. Kan is the bundle of ideas tied in with destiny, fate, luck, and life chances. No single English word covers the idea, and a full explication of it would require a special work. But it chiefly means to the villager the whole sum of his past deeds—the moral balance of good and evil that goes on from existence to existence, now taking one corporeal form, now another. Along with kan goes the idea of kutho and its opposite, *akutho*. Kutho is, roughly translated, merit, that is, the good accruing to a person in virtue of his good deeds, while akutho is demerit or the evil that accrues because of violations of the religious code. Kan and kutho

version of a paper read at the American Anthropological Meeting, November 19, 1961, in Philadelphia, Pa. Professor Melford E. Spiro (personal communication), on the basis of his field work in upper Burma, differs in his interpretation of the influence of *anatta* on behavior, and maintains that there is more sacred "technology" in Buddhism than I was able to discover.

[2] The author's script is a modified version of the Burmese Baptist phonetic system of transcribing spoken Burmese.

[3] U Bhikkhu Thittila, "The Meaning of Buddhism, Perspective of Burma," *Atlantic Monthly Supplement* (1958), pp. 46–50; Edward Conze, *Buddhist Scriptures* (New York: Penguin Books, 1959).

are not esoteric to a Burman, and expressions like *kan makambu* (not good kan) are used frequently to explain a misfortune or ill luck, and for many outcomes to uncertain ventures the villagers say *kan ami, kanaphi*—kan is the mother and the father of what happens to us. Similarly, kutho is an everyday concept, frequently heard in local parlance, used as the explanation for performing religious duties, for giving, for observing the precepts. Ask a Burman why he gives to a monk, why he performs any religious act, and his reply is for the kutho involved. Different amounts of kutho come from different sorts of religious acts—giving to a highly respected monk gets the giver more kutho than the same thing given to a beggar; or there is more kutho involved in building a pagoda than in digging a well for a monastery, and that is more meritorious than donating a bell to a kyaung.

Kan and kutho, as pieces of knowledge, state for the villager the essential nature of the human condition. His understanding of Buddhism tells him that he has a fate that is the outcome of all of his previous acts and that current conduct adds to the indestructible nucleus of moral balance. These concepts implicate those of metempsychosis, impermanence, and individual responsibility for one's fate. A villager knows, and can articulate, the ideas that he is but one form of embodied kan in a nearly endless chain of lives—that his present position is the result of action performed in previous existences, and that his present existence is an opportunity to change the balance of kutho and akutho, improve his kan, all as prelude to the next existence. He is aware that nothing but his own actions, words, and thoughts have any effect on his future states. The monk is not an intermediary between him and the extra-human. (In fact, for the villager there is scarcely anything extra-empirical or supernatural in Buddhism. The Buddha is but the *Tathagata*, he who has come to show the way, or *shakyamuni*, the sage of the tribe of the shakyas, the historical figure who in fact pointed the way. On this level, urban intellectuals call Buddhism a "systematic spiritual exercise," rather than use the English word "religion.") At the village level, a Buddhist says *Bodha batha*, if you inquire as to what is the meaning of his religion, and that means the path of the Buddha, or "I try, within the limits of my knowledge and temperament, to follow the path of life that the *Shin Hpaya* (Lord Buddha) taught." Every villager then lives in the consciousness that his spiritual state is his own work and his own responsibility.

The five precepts, which everyone knows by rote, are of course linked to the ideas of kan and kutho. These precepts, and an additional three or five taken on *uboneh* (duty day, tied to the phases of the moon, and occurring four or five times in a calendrical month), are the chief guides to proper conduct. Their observance means kutho, and together with the more important fact of giving, especially to the clergy, inch one along the path to *nibban*, as the Burmese call nirvana. The five precepts are the minimum action aspects of the four noble truths, which are also rote knowledge. However, fewer villagers are able to give the full eightfold path, and knowing this verges on specialist information.

Kan and kutho, precept, and the eightfold path are embedded in a complicated cosmology. For the villager, however, knowledge consists of the thirty-one levels of existence, which most people cannot name, level for level; but all know the three major divisions of the *lokas*, or worlds, and the general character of the life there. The idea of the world as divided into four continents, with the sacred mountain, Myinmodaung, at the center, and the lands of *deva, bymmas*, and the hells, is common knowledge (but this competes with the Mercator world). Included in the cosmology are understandings of the connections between kutho, kan, and the level of existence at which a person is reborn, and, of course, the implied view of a world in which unremitting, accurate account is taken of personal, individual merits and demerits.

Within this structure of belief and knowledge are bits of formulaic utterance that form the daily content of devotion. The standard Buddhist devotional is the *Awgatha*. The Awgatha begins every meeting of Buddhists, and appears during every devotion before the Buddha, or at a pagoda, and a person says the Awgatha at least once a day, either before a household altar or in the village *dhammayon* (building of the law). I present here my rather free translation of the commonest version of the Awgatha in the villages round Mandalay. The translation is a tidy way, as is the Awgatha itself, of presenting some of the basic symbols of village Buddhism.

> Awgatha, Awgatha ("wheel of life" or whole world prayer). In words, deeds, thoughts, in these three things I have erred. Let me be rid of all the angers and passions. I take refuge in the Buddha; I take refuge in the monkhood. I take refuge in the teaching. To the Buddha I am offering respect with hands clasped, bowing, adoring, humble, in devotion to the Buddha.
>
> As I have adored, spare me the fourth level (of hell, in which rebirth is in the form of a monster), spare me famine, killing, disease, spare me the eight calamities (being mute, deaf, stammering, blind, mad, crippled, lacking in concentration, and feebleminded); spare me the five evils (flood, fire, kings, thieves, and enemies). Let the four lacks of virtue (failure to carry out precepts, to know the noble truths, to do one's duty, and to spend money foolishly) be behind me. From all these harmful things may I be protected. Rather let me walk on air, believe firmly (that I can work out my salvation with diligence), be free from desire, and reach nibbana (the blowing out of desire). O, may Lord Buddha grant that I avoid evil and seek nibbana.

The triple jewel (I take refuge in the Buddha, I take refuge in the Dhamma, I take refuge in the *sangha*) is equally a part of all Buddhist devotions and spoken in private and in every religious gathering. The omnipresent formula *aneiska, doka, anatta*—change, suffering, not-self—is a shorthand for the noble truths of the middle way. Most villagers have a string of 108 beads (a magic number tied to the 108 marks of the Buddha), which they finger as they repeat these words. The ideas of impermanence, suffering and not-self are the cornerstones of the Buddhist world view, and they are clearly understood by the villager. He can give hosts of analogies illustrating the meanings of these concepts. Beside the *Mingala Thok*, a verse that describes the moral duties, these are virtually all the formulae, set speeches of mixed Pali and Burmese direct from the scripture, that a person knows. These devotional utterances form the content of most religious ceremonies. Sometimes (especially at funerals and *shinbyus*) the water-blessing prayer of merit is added.

One other sort of knowledge needs to be included, and that is the body of tales about the life of the Buddha, the *Jataka* tales, and the numerous analogies, similes, and metaphors derived from Buddhist teachings. These are used in the teaching of Buddhism to explain a point from monk to layman, from adult to child, and from informant to anthropologist.

The Buddhist knowledge of a villager rests only slightly on written materials. It relies chiefly on oral transmission for continuity. These ideas are rooted in the body of scripture that the monks supposedly study and preserve. (Village monks rarely study any scripture other than the 227 monastic rules, and they do practice, sometimes, some of the specialized meditational devices of the higher learning; these are hardly ever communicated to the laity.) In a village household, books are a rarity. If there is a book, it is a popularized version of the essentials of the religion given here, plus one or two of the better known thok, like the heart and the diamond *sutras*. The villager carries on his Buddhism without the consultation of books and with little reference to the written word. Monks do expound the notion of kan and kutho, and they do stress the keeping of the precepts. But most of the sermons of monks have to do with alms-giving and the devotion to the *sangha*. The monk is not related to a community in a simple parish-head sort of relationship. Almost all villages in upper Burma have at least one kyaung, and many have more. The monk or monks in the kyaung have defined territories from which they get their daily alms, and villagers have limits on the number of monks they usually give alms to. But there are two sorts of kyaungs; one belongs to the village, and the other belongs to the monk. The village-owned kyaung has been built either by the community or by a family or individual, and any virtuous monk has been invited to come and live there. When that monk dies, if he has not trained a younger *ubazein* to replace him, the villager will seek to invite a senior or junior monk from some other monastery to come live in their kyaung. The other sort of kyaung is built for a specific monk and is given to him. It is his kyaung, and he can lean against certain beams or go with torso uncovered in certain parts of the kyaung that a monk who is not owner cannot do. Whatever kind of kyaung the villager goes to, he rarely confines his visits to a single kyaung, or even to the one in his village. And the monk is not the shepherd for a territorially defined flock. In fact, he is not any sort of shepherd at all. He is not a director of the spiritual life of the laity, nor is he the embodiment or representative of the sacred. He is just one point on the continuum of layman to Buddha; he is the exemplar of the virtues of the middle way. He is involved in working out his own path to nirvana (as is everybody else in the society). But the monk is to be especially honored because he is closer to the teaching than a layman, and he shows others what they might become if their character and temperament were suitable. The life of the monk is one of glory (*pon* is glory, and *gyi* is great, and a pongyi is the great glory in the estate of man), not of power. His relations with laity keep him alive, help them see more clearly the meaning of the teaching, and give the laity an opportunity to get kutho by giving to the *sangha*, as the brotherhood of monks is called. Monks do not have power in any direct, temporal sense over people in the community, and as a rule they do not try to get it. Their concerns are not of this world, and if Buddhism is sometimes called an other-worldly religion, it is certain that the *sangha*, and not the believing lay Buddhist, is the referent. Monks are not organized into any set pattern or hierarchy. There are *gaings* (groups or parties) and there are districts (*taik*) or groups of monasteries under a chief *sayadaw* (abbot), but each monastery tends to be independent, and the head of each monastery is supreme in the monastery. A monk can be expelled for breaking his vows in a manner specified in the scripture, but in the villages of which I have knowledge this has, in fact, never been done. Monks take two tasks in relation to the laity with great seriousness and concern: the teaching of the young in monastic schools, and the attendance at Buddhist rituals when they are invited. For the rest, they are detached from mundane concerns, and the villagers respect this detachment, so long as they can from time to time ask a monk to do some magical tatooing (for snake bite or other medicine or to ward off calamity), to prepare an *in* (a charm to ward off evil), or to do some astrological calculations or predictions for them.

Thus, transmission of Buddhist knowledge rests on two chief agencies, the family and the monastic school. At present, the government school teaches some of the Jataka tales and other bits of Buddhism as well. In the family, the young learn the formulae from the parents' constant repetition of them at the house altar, and children are taken to the pagodas, to *shinbyus* and ear borings, to *sunjwes*, and to all religious gatherings, so they hear these over and over. And when Buddhism is used as an explanatory device or a disciplinary aid, they also learn. The instruction is rarely formal, but rather a part of the enculturation process, like learning the language or discovering who one's kinsmen are. There is little stress on the interior state or the intensity of attachment, for all the interest is in getting the sayings right and conforming to the definitions of proper conduct. As children aid and see the parents give the monks the daily offering of good, as they see the beads being told, as they hear the proverbs and analogies derived from Buddhism, as they go to *pwes* and see parts of the Jataka enacted, they learn the things they need to know about being a Buddhist in a village society.

Nearly all boys spend some time in the kyaung as *koyin*, or novices. And the high point of a family's religious life comes in the giving of the shinbyu, the induction of the young man into the novitiate. How long a boy spends in the monastery varies considerably, and sometimes is reduced to the bare requirement of a day or two. The older ideal was to spend at least three *wa* in the monastery. (During the rainy season and in the holy time of the year when no marriages are performed and no plays are given, monks are supposed to confine themselves to the kyaung, and pious lay-men go into retreat. Like so many Buddhist phenomena observed by Westerners, it has been mislabeled "Lent" on the Christian analogy. Simi-larly, devotion has been miscalled "prayer," and duty day erroneously called "Sabbath," but there is no need to multiply examples, only to recall that the language of domestic religion is largely inapplicable to Burmese Buddhism.)

In a village where I studied, about forty miles from Mandalay, more than 85 per cent of the men above twenty-five years of age had in fact spent three wa in a kyaung; but in a village seven miles from Mandalay, where I also did intensive work, less than 20 per cent had spent the tradi-tional three wa in the monastery. In the monastic school, reading and writing are taught along with the essentials of Buddhism—that is, the three pieces of knowledge described earlier. Some girls attend monastic schools, but their time is less and their instruction more scanty.

This brings up another feature of Buddhist knowledge in village society; it is sex-linked and age-graded. Men tend to know more than women, both because of greater instruction and because of the favored place of the male in Buddhist doctrine. Men have pon (in this case a sort of glory) just be-cause they are men, and women do not or almost do not. Older people know more about Buddhism than the younger. The age-difference in knowledge arises on two grounds. In any body of knowledge tied to en-culturation, age and experience bring wisdom and expertness, and, at the same time, the rhythm of the life cycle is such that villagers get more and more concerned with Buddhism and with religion as they grow older. Many proverbs and pithy sayings in the villages describe the life cycle in a number of stages, the last parts of which are to be devoted to works of merit, contemplation, and religious activity. It is not uncommon for a man in his forties or fifties virtually to retire from daily life and to spend most of his time in meditation and contemplation with long hours at the monastery.

In this setting, belief is axiomatic and automatic. The knowledge forms a rather coherent whole. If there are problems of meaning or questions, the villager goes to a monk, who explicates scripture for him or provides a number of anecdotes or analogies to resolve them. The village is a united whole in the matter of belief. There are no doubters, no heretics, no theo-logical debate, and no exploration of alternative meanings. This is rooted in the conception that there are great variations in individual abilities to encompass Buddhism. Differences in interpretation, if they exist, are not matters of contention, for they do not necessarily indicate that a doctrine has alternate meanings but only that individuals have varying capacities to understand the import of a particular doctrine. Without an insistence on dogma or creed, Buddhism is a cultural structure that does not lend itself to the underwriting of factional splits. Religion does not become a matter of contest.

Buddhist knowledge and belief leaves great latitude in the specification of day-to-day living. Its prescriptive and proscriptive code is meager indeed.

It does not deal with crisis situations; it does not apply in those situations "where hope can not betray nor desire deceive"; it is austere, dealing chiefly with remote things and final ends. This lacuna in Buddhism is filled by an indigenous system of belief—the propitiation of *nats*. Nats and nat-worship are omnipresent, intertwined with Buddhist ritual and knowledge. Since one cannot appeal to the Buddha for intervention in the affairs of this life, one asks the nats. There are a host of nats, the thirty-seven chief ones, and the nats of the trees, the fields, the winds, the rains, the house-guardian nats, and the harvest nats. Nat-worship as an aspect of indigenous animism is a subject requiring a special work. What is important here is that the structure of Buddhist belief is such that it requires supplementing by a body of belief oriented to the problems, desires, and hopes of men as they go about their mundane business. In Burma, this structural requirement is filled by the nat systems and several other predictive and divinatory systems: astrology, fortune telling, charms and amulets, magical tatooing, and alchemy. It is a misapprehension to see village religion as animism with a "thin veneer of Buddhism," for it is the Buddhist set of beliefs that incorporates and defines the character and province of the nats. Since, as a formal system, Buddhism implicates a supplementary belief system so that men may conduct their affairs in confidence, it requires a technology of the sacred to handle crisis and uncertainty. Buddhism and the nats are not in conflict and nowhere in contradiction, but work mutually to give the villager a constant and rather clear view of the remoter ends of human existence while allowing him to deal with daily problems. If science and modern technology rapidly spread to the Burmese countryside, the various supplementary predictive systems, rather than Buddhism, would be affected, for they would be in competition with these secular techniques of handling crisis and uncertainty. Urban Burma is some guide in this, for there the nats, tatooing, and alchemy are less an integral part of the religious life, and the educated tend to decry them as they make efforts to fit Buddhism and Western science into a harmonious, congruent world view.

Buddhism is responsible for much of the group activity in upper Burma and for many of the groupings that emerge in Burmese village society. The monks go daily from house to house; the duty days are in the four phases of the moon; and the festal round (except for nat festivals) marks sacred days in the life and legend of the Buddha. The major gatherings of people are religious occasions. The shinbyu is the largest and most elaborate affair that a family undertakes. A family saves for this, stretches its means to give it, invites the whole village, friends, relatives, and acquaintances from neighboring villages. The holding of a shinbyu is an organizational task beyond the capacity of any single household. To assist the givers of a shinbyu are organizations of men and women called the *lubyo* (literally bachelors) and the *aphyo* (literally spinsters). They are headed by a man and a woman called respectively the *lubyo gaung* and the *aphyo gaung*. These groups do the tea serving and food serving to the guests. Some villages have in addition a *htamin che gaung,* a cooking head and group who cook for these affairs. At any rate, a shinbyu mobilizes the whole village and especially the lubyo and aphyo groups.

Sunjwe is a ceremony of giving food to the monks. Monks are invited to have the morning meal at a peasant's house, and a few friends or even the whole village may be invited to take tea and hear the monk give a sermon. A sunjwe can be held at any time, whenever the peasant feels like it, but it is obligatory seven days after the death of a relative, before embarking on any large venture, and after the success of any venture.

In the month of November (roughly, since the Burmese lunar calendar does not exactly correspond to the English), after the season of wa, monks receive robes, utensils, and other gifts from the people. Individuals may hold private *katain,* or giving the monk his necessities, but the village usually gets together and has a communal katain, held under the auspices of a Buddhist association, if there be one. Outside of marriages, elections, and pwes (the Burmese open-air drama), the only times during which groups larger than a few families are to be found in congregation is at these Buddhist fetes. These affairs are a compound of the sacred and secular, the gay and the grave, and the sociability aspects are as important as the religious.

These groupings and activities may be summarized under a few simple rubrics. First they are concerned with the fact of giving. Giving is the chief way to earn kutho, to lay up a store of merit for future lives. Worship and devotion tend to be private and individual and need no organization or cooperation. But these ceremonies require an organizational apparatus. It is not Buddhism per se, but the Burmese insistence on publicity and large numbers at the ceremonies that makes for the organizational aspects.

Another feature of these activities and groupings is that beyond the axis of age, which in every aspect of Burmese life rates respect and deference, they are equalitarian. Status distinctions that do exist in village life—between the rich and the poor, between the pious and the impious, between those who have pon or power and those who do not—are irrelevant to group action. Burmese distinctions lie between person and person and are in no way tied in to institutions or corporate groupings. And I suppose that the equalitarian emphasis of life, the easy social mobility, and the virtual absence of authority of one man over another are rooted in this.

The knowledge and practice of Buddhism shapes much of the public character of the Burman and exerts a determinate influence on many aspects of the social structure. The first effect of the villagers' understanding of Buddhism is on the time horizon. Nothing can matter very much in this brief existence, wedged in among countless others. The effect of actions is very remote, so planning and sustained effort are discouraged, and emphasis is placed on living in the here and now. Burmese life has the dual quality of appearing as a series of rather unconnected, immediate instances without much tie to the past, and with little concern for the future, and at the same time, it is filled with beginnings for projects of great energy which fizzle out and leave nothing in their wake. Burmans can and do plan, but the time horizon is always vague, and failure to do anything within a fixed period means nothing and occasions no emotions.

Many observers have noted the even tenor, the cheerfulness, and the optimism of the village Burman. These are in part derived from his Buddhism. Buddhism, where every man does what he can for his movement along the path to nirvana, leaves the individual feeling that any misdeed can be repaired in the future, that acts of merit can overcome acts of demerit, and that there is forever to do so. A person can only be as religious as his temperament allows him to be. He is always doing the best he can, and when he gets older, he will spend more time at kutho-getting works. Such an understanding leaves no room for guilt, anxiety, remorse, or worry. And the villagers are never long sunk in any of these. The village interpretation of kan makes for optimism. Kan is not a fixed, implacable fate beyond the control or influence of the individual. Kan can be added to, its influence can be improved, and the good can be made to outweigh the evil. Besides, kan is not a single steady force always operating in the same direction. Sometimes the good deeds predominate and sometimes the evil predominates, and who knows but that at the next venture the good may override the evil in a man's fate. Also there is always the hope that in the long run a person can accumulate enough merit to better his condition. And getting merit is so easy, so lacking in interior strain, in emotional turmoil, that cheerfulness and optimism are easy results to fix in the character of the Burman.

The obverse of these features is a kind of superficiality of concern, a lack of deep emotional current, and what, from a viewpoint of the Westerner, are remarkable swings in the personality. Burmese life appears on the surface to lack deep involvements, outside of the family, and Burmans are certainly more self-concerned than other-directed. Each Burman appears as a hard, irreducible atom, only lightly tied to other people, only slightly concerned with the state of community beyond his immediate needs. The common village saying that "there is no love like self-love" sums this up very aptly. The idea of *mehta*, universal love, is far from the villager, and the ability to identify himself with persons in the abstract entirely absent.

This individuating effect of Burmese Buddhism, this placing of each single nucleus of kan at the center of its own universe, permits the Burman wide swings in his reactions to the world. He flares up easily, is bad-tempered and violent upon provocation, and does not cultivate interior restraint or self-discipline. If he cannot have his way, he either withdraws or lashes out violently. The art of compromise, the adjustment of interests between parties, is rare, requiring personal habits not strong in the Burmese. Burmans let each other alone very much, if there is no direct conflict between parties. A man who violates morality norms, or an official who is venal, or a monk who breaks his vows, does not get censure directly. After all, he is responsible for his own fate, all will balance out in the end, and why should I get involved and get into trouble by telling him to mend his ways? is the way a villager reasons. Gossip there is, personal rating too, but community public opinion, organized sanctions, or pressures to conform there are not.

Buddhism, for the villager, is a costly business. The expenditure on gift-giving, on ceremonial, on monk feeding, is a large item in every family budget. Furthermore, when wealth is accumulated, it tends to be invested in merit-giving things rather than economic enterprise: the pagoda, the monastery, the well for the monks, a bell for a kyaung, all of these are hopes and ambitions for those without wealth, and plans and projects for those with it. Buddhism thus diverts a good part of the individual and communal wealth into the channels of religious expenditure. It promotes and abets a common feature of Burmese life, display spending. Buddhism, therefore, is a brake on capital formation and tends to turn the local economy into one of monument building.

The extreme emphasis on the individual atomizes the society into family groupings and inhibits the formation of larger, perdurable associations. It also promotes wide areas of individual autonomy and suppresses organizations oriented to other than religious ends. As such, it tends to make leadership and leaders personalistic and charismatic, rather than institutional or structural. Burmese society is marked by coalition around leaders endowed with certain powers or abilities, and these derived from the notions of strong kan which lead to pon (power and glory), *gon* (virtue or piety, character, and learning), and *awsa* (authority, ability to command).

Concomitant with this is the equalitarian nature of the society, as this·in large measure derives from Buddhism. As said earlier, no social class, no status distinction, except those of sex and age, are in the social structure. Buddhism can be seen to have the effect, then, of individuating, of leveling, of social equalizing, and with this, the consequences of charismatic leaders, power coalition, and *ad hoc*, impermanent affiliations.

My object has been to *delineate* a religious system of belief and practices in order, first of all, to suggest the construction of a type of religious system and, secondly, to stipulate how the parts are interconnected. The effort has been to lay the groundwork for some empirical generalizations about the relations of religion and society. Burmese Buddhism, at the village level, may be *characterized* as a system of belief and practice oriented to the condition of the self in future states, with practices designed to further the movement of the self along a continuum of ever more desirable states. It rests on the process of enculturation, and in that sense is a voluntary communion with limited prescriptive and proscriptive canons. It is centered in the individual, nonhierarchical, with frequent movement between laity and clergy, and it lays little emphasis on the interior state or the quality of conviction as against the performance of religious works.

Whatever we call this type of religion, it has some structural and cultural concomitants that may form part of a theory of religion and society. The need for supplementary systems of handling daily affairs seems built into religions of this sort, as does the structural effect of individuation, the tendency to monument building, the rise of episodic and charismatic leadership, and the unavailability of religious slogan for secular faction-alism.

Whether the social and cultural concomitants are systematically tied to Buddhist belief and knowledge or whether the social structure and Buddhist belief grew up together in the particular ecological and historical setting of upper Burma is a question to be resolved only through comparative study with the local traditions of Buddhism as they are found in the Theravada countries of Southeast Asia. The set of formal features selected here to define the religious system and the posited connections between religion and society will provide either a foundation for future construction or a scaffold to be dismantled.

8

ISLAM AND POLITICS IN INDONESIA*

ROSIHAN ANWAR

Of the Indonesian population, 85 per cent (or 93.5 million in 1967) are Muslims, according to the claim of the Islamic Students Association,[1] although not all of these fully practice their faith. Perhaps 60 per cent of the Indonesian population could be described as constituting the Islamic *ummat*, or community of true believers. These Muslims accept the existence of one God, acknowledge Muhammad as his Prophet, fast during the month of Ramadan, attend Friday prayers at the mosque, and observe all the other requirements and prohibitions of their faith. Yet, despite the existence of a Muslim majority in the population, one year after the attempted Communist coup, a Muslim cabinet minister complained that

---

* This paper was presented in slightly different form at the Twenty-seventh International Congress of Orientalists (Ann Arbor, Michigan, August, 1967) and is published here by permission of the author.

[1] Peladjar Islam Indonesia (PII, or Organization of Indonesian Islamic Students), "Leadership Training" (mimeographed paper, 1963).

only 15–20 per cent of the population actually supported the *ummat* and the Islamic political parties that speak for it.[2]

In the government, also, Muslim leaders are in a minority. The five-member Presidium of General Suharto's cabinet (after July, 1966) has only one, the head of the Nahdatul Ulama (NU, or religious scholars), and only three or four of the twenty-four ministerial portfolios are held by members of Islamic political parties or mass organizations.

Historically, Muslims take justifiable pride in the fact that the first modern, national mass movement organized in Indonesia at the turn of the century was spearheaded by the Sarekat Islam, under the leadership of Hadji Oemar Said Tjokroaminoto. This Muslim organization stood in the vanguard of the movement against Dutch colonialism and imperialism and, for a short period, was very successful in rallying the people under the banner of Islam. Yet, for the past fifty years, Muslims have not maintained political unity, and have not exercised the political power they believe they should in terms of their numbers and historical role. They are baffled by the contrast between their numerical strength and their political weakness. Erroneous assumptions about the correlation between numbers and political support have led to their frustration and disappointment, but there are also ideological, political, and historical reasons for Islam's failure to dominate the Indonesian political scene. Why do so many Muslims decline to join the Islamic parties and turn instead to the nationalists or even the Communists?

After Clifford Geertz, Robert Jay, and others conducted surveys in rural central Java, beginning in 1954, it became fashionable to speak of the *santri-abangan* dichotomy of Islam in Java. The *santri* are orthodox Muslims who take their religion seriously; the *abangan* are more influenced by pre-Islamic Javanese or Hindu-Buddhist mysticism. Although the leaders of the Islamic parties took for granted the support of the *abangan*—sometimes called *Islam-statistik* (statistical Muslims)—the general elections of 1955 showed the fallacy of this assumption. The Muslim bloc as a whole obtained only 45 per cent of the vote; the rest was divided among the Nationalist Party (PNI), the Communist Party (PKI), and the other smaller parties. The myth of numbers was completely shattered. The majority of *abangan* preferred to stay in the PNI, which emerged as Indonesia's largest party and which represented, for the Javanese, secular Indonesian nationalism.

The existence of the *abangan* culture, however, is only one of several explanations for the ineffectiveness and defeat of the Islamic parties. More important is the failure of Islam to become a modernizing force in Indonesia and to remain in the forefront of the nationalist movement. The leadership of the nationalist movement was captured by the PNI in the 1920's; since then, the PNI, rather than the Islamic parties, has played the major role in advocating populism, change and progress, social justice,

---

[2] See *Antara*, September 16, 1966. The statement was made by Ir. Sanusi, a leader of the Muhammadiyah (a reformist Islamic movement) and minister of the textile industry, before the Islamic Students Association (HMI) Congress at Solo.

democracy, and socialism. There were some modern, democratic leaders who stood for certain socialist ideas in the Masjumi Party, a broad Islamic political party founded after World War II. But in the 1955 general election campaign, instead of leading the *ummat* toward democracy and modernism, they compromised themselves by catering to the conservatives and fundamentalists in the rank and file. The Masjumi did indeed receive 20 per cent of the vote, but at what price? The opportunity to democratize the party and to adopt the posture of modernizers was lost. And the Masjumi was the only hope; from the NU, a bulwark of conservatism, nothing of the sort could be expected.

The lack of unity among the Islamic parties themselves has been another formidable handicap in the development of Islamic political power. For the past fifty years, the very number of Islamic political parties and mass organizations, and the variety of schools of thought, testify to a proclivity to fragmentation. After the Russian Revolution of October, 1917, the Sarekat Islam leadership split into factions on the issue of socialism versus Islam. The split became irreparable and led to the decline of the party. Many members of Sarekat Islam, believing that the organization was not sufficiently militant and radical in the struggle against imperialism, withdrew to form the Sarekat Islam Merah ("Red" Sarekat Islam), which became the PKI in 1921. The PKI sought to capture the nationalist movement, but it was driven underground after its unsuccessful rebellion against the Dutch colonial administration in 1926–27.

The suppression of the PKI left the Sarekat Islam without competition for the leadership of the nationalist movement and, for a brief period after the abortive revolts of 1926, Sarekat Islam once again regained its position of leadership. Its revitalization was short-lived, however; on June 4, 1927, the Bandung leadership of a federation of nationalist "study clubs," recognizing the significance of the void created by the banning of the PKI, created a new nationalist party, the Partai Nasional Indonesia (PNI), under the leadership of the youthful and dynamic Sukarno. Sarekat Islam lost the leadership of the nationalist movement because of factionalism within the party, because its leaders were willing to recognize the leadership of others, and because the nationalist-secular movement, blessed by the unity of common opposition to Dutch colonialism and the absence of doctrinal disputes, surged ahead under the new leadership.

Sukarno was a persuasive orator and a skillful manipulator of contending factions, which placed Sarekat Islam at a distinct disadvantage, given the quality of its leadership at the time. Sarekat Islam also failed because a new faction had emerged within Islam. In 1926, the conservative *ulamas* (Islamic scholars) of East Java, who disliked the Pan-Islamic orientation and puritanic Wahhabi sympathies of Sarekat Islam, founded their own organization, the NU, which the Dutch, not entirely ingenuously, supported in order to split the Islamic front.

Alarmed by the increasing radicalism of the nationalist movement, in 1930, the Dutch exiled Sukarno and proscribed the PNI, with the result that there was a general decline in the movement in the decade preceding

World War II. Sarekat Islam, weakened by repeated splits, survived until the war as the Indonesian Islamic Association Party (PSII), but was unable to exert a strong influence on politics.

During the occupation (1942–45), the Japanese permitted both the Muslims and the secular nationalists to become more active politically and, despite some limitations on political activities, the Muslims eagerly seized this opportunity. The Japanese, while outlawing the PSII in an early attempt to discourage the wedding of Islam and politics, did encourage, with the enthusiastic cooperation of the Indonesians, the creation of a new, all-embracing Islamic "nonpolitical" organization. In addition, the highest non-Japanese position in the military administration went to Dr. Hoesein Djajadiningrat, who became head of the Religious Affairs Office in 1943. Although Dr. Djajadiningrat was himself outside the mainstream of the Islamic movement, his appointment had great symbolic significance, and, perhaps more important, he brought into his office several outstanding and accepted Muslim scholars, who helped to shape the Muslim response to the new Japanese permissiveness.

It was only after the proclamation of independence in August, 1945, however, that the Muslims emerged from political obscurity to form the Masjumi, a broad political party that encompassed all shades of opinion within the ummat. Unfortunately, the Masjumi did not maintain their initial unity and strength. The first schism took place in 1947, when the PSII reconstituted itself, partly an opportunistic maneuver by some Islamic leaders to gain seats in the Sjarifuddin cabinet. The second came in 1952, when the NU became an overt political party and left the Masjumi. A new situation arose in 1959, with the establishment of Sukarno's Guided Democracy. The Masjumi resisted Sukarno's authoritarian rule and was banned in August, 1960, but the NU adjusted itself to a regime in which the Communists dominated the manipulation of symbols and the making of policy. Although the NU and its affiliated organizations claimed to have at least 10 million supporters, their political stance was that of a minority. After the abortive coup of the PKI of September 30–October 1, 1965, it seemed for a while that the NU and other Islamic parties would regain their prestige. The armed forces solicited their cooperation in the struggle to rout the remnants of the PKI and eliminate Sukarno's power, but when this had been achieved, Muslims once again receded into the background.

For more than half a century, the Muslim majority in Indonesia has been unable to overcome its internal differences and achieve political unity and power. What are some of the divisive factors within the Islamic community itself, and what are the issues between the Islamic parties and the other political parties?

Most Indonesian Muslims are Sunnites and, in terms of Islamic law, subscribe to the Mashab of Sjafi'i, one of the four orthodox schools. Theoretically, they are therefore entitled to be called *Ahlus-sunnah wal jama'ah* (people who follow the customs of the Prophet Muhammad as taught by the majority of the religious teachers); but, in practice, this denomination is exclusively reserved for, and has been appropriated by, the conservative NU, thus distinguishing the NU from more modernist elements within the *ummat*. To add to the confusion, Perti (Islamic Education Party) calls itself the Sjafi'i.

The debate between the conservative Muslims and the reformists centers around the question of the use of individual reason in the interpretation of the Koran. Reformed Indonesian Muslims argue that it is man's right and duty to use his individual reason to apply the principles of the Koran to the problems of his time (*idjtihad*—or reasoning by deduction). To refuse to do so is to commit the error of *jumud* (stagnation) and *taqlid* (imitation). They cite the nineteenth-century reformer Jamaluddin al-Afghani and the Egyptian Muhammad Abduh as their authorities for this position. On the other hand, a conservative legal scholar, Al-Baghawi, argues that a Muslim who does not thoroughly know Arabic, the Koran, the Sunnah of the Prophet, the writings of the scientists, and the *Qiyas* (the science of analogy) is not equipped to make his own interpretations of Islamic law. If one is not a scholar, the guidance and authority of the religious teachers, the *ulama*, are indispensable, and it would be wrong to brand obedience to the *ulama* as *taqlid*. These arguments separate such organizations as the Muhammadiyah, which is *idjtihad*-oriented, and the NU, which is *taqlid*-oriented.

Educational background has been another divisive factor within the Islamic community. Here the difference is between "intellectuals," Muslims who have received a Westernized secular education, and *kijaji*, religious teachers who have gone through the traditional religious school, the *pesantren*, and may even have visited religious schools at Mecca or Cairo. The relationship between Muslim leaders of such different educational backgrounds is an uneasy one. One reason for the split within the Masjumi in 1952 was that the *kijaji* thought the Masjumi leadership was dominated by "intellectuals." To assert themselves, the *kijaji* turned the NU, which until then had been a purely religious organization, into their own political organization and subsequently withdrew from Masjumi.

The manner in which Islamic rituals should be observed has also been an issue between different groups of Indonesian Muslims. These differences arise from various interpretations of the *fikh*, the code of law. Most of the rituals in dispute (the call to Friday prayers, burials, and so on) do not involve the basic faith but are nevertheless significant and may be carried to extremes. In fact, one can usually learn whether a person is associated with NU or Masjumi by the manner in which he observes the rites.

To be sure, most of these differences are psychological, and time has eroded many of them. An intellectual can become a fundamentalist and a staunch supporter of the idea of the Islamic state, or at least of the idea of the Islamic way of life. On the other hand, not a few *kijaji* develop into broad-minded liberals willing to coexist with people who have secular ideas.[3] Also, many of the younger generation no longer subscribe to differ-

---

[3] The parallel with prepartition India is striking. Iqbal, who had had a Western education, ultimately became the father of the idea of Pakistan, while Maulana Kalam Azad, who had had traditional training, became a supporter of the secular state of India, in which he held for many years the post of Minister of Education.

ences in interpretation of the law and detach themselves from the quarrels of the older leaders. But even if these differences are gradually receding into the background, they do occasionally obstruct the development of unity among the Islamic political parties.

Although the Islamic community itself is divided on a number of points, important issues also separate the Islamic parties from other political parties. Moreover, cooperation between the Islamic political parties and other parties or groups for common goals has been somewhat limited by the Muslims' tendency toward exclusivism. Instead of being useful allies and forging alliances to build their power, they tend to distinguish between "pure" Muslims, who are trustworthy, and "partial" Muslims, who are *ipso facto* suspect.

A major political issue, Muslim advocacy of the Islamic state, the *Negara Islam*, has been a divisive factor in Indonesian politics, and partially explains why the Islamic parties have been unable to exert more political power. When the Indonesian constitution was framed in the months before the Japanese surrender in August, 1945, most Muslim leaders wanted a state based on Islamic principles, under the leadership of a Muslim president. The Japanese, however, had appointed Sukarno Chairman of the Independence Preparatory Committee, and he opposed the ideal of an Indonesian state based on Islam, because he could not envisage its unity. Many parts of Indonesia are non-Islamic: Minahasa in northern Celebes, Batak in Tapanuli, with its predominantly Christian population, and Bali with its Balinese Hindus. Instead, Sukarno proposed the *Pantja Sila*, or Five Principles, as the foundation of the state. These are: acknowledgment of one God, humanism, nationalism, democracy, and social justice. The first principle, however, had no specific content, thus creating confusion about and tension between the ideals of an Islamic theocratic state and a nationalist secular state that values religion but gives no preference to a particular religion.

This tension was manifested in the so-called *Piagam Djakarta* (Djakarta Charter), signed on June 22, 1945, by such Nationalist and Islamic leaders as Sukarno, Hatta, Hadji Agus Salim, Sukiman, and Kiaji Wachid Hasjim. The Charter stipulated that the Indonesian state should be based on the first of the five principles, but with the specific obligation for Muslims to live in accordance with the Islamic law, the *Sjari'at*. This "compromise," however, was abandoned when the constitution was finally adopted on August 18, 1945. Vice President Hatta, a true Muslim himself, believed that, for the sake of unity, even the Djakarta Charter should be deleted from the constitution, and he cooperated with Sukarno to bring this about. Other Muslim leaders accepted this position, hoping that by legal democratic procedures the Republic of Indonesia would eventually develop into an Islamic state.

After the proclamation of independence, the Indonesian people engaged in an armed struggle against the Dutch and British occupation forces, and, for the time being, the issue of an Islamic state was irrelevant. The Renville Agreement in February, 1948, provided, among other things, for the retreat of the remaining Indonesian Republican army from pockets in areas supposedly occupied by the Dutch army. At this time, a faction of the Muslims in West Java began to take a new look at the Republican government then residing at Jogjakarta, Central Java. They refused to abide by the agreement, seeing it mainly as a capitulation to the Dutch and as an imperialist instrument to colonize the Indonesian people. Moreover, they regarded the Republican cabinet then under Premier Amir Sjarifuddin as a "red government," and therefore without standing. They naturally then concluded that they were the rightful heirs of the Republic that had been proclaimed on August 17, 1945, and vowed to continue the struggle against imperialism and colonialism. They stubbornly maintained their resistance and regrouped under an organization called *Darul Islam* (DI), which was led by S. M. Kartosuwirjo, a militant leader of the prewar PSII.

The DI, which came into being in May, 1948, drew its political and military strength from Islamic values and outlook and, although many people claimed that the DI worked toward an Islamic state, there were others who were not convinced of this, certainly not insofar as the first years of the movement were concerned. In the initial stage, the DI was essentially a radical, nationalist movement, a point often overlooked in later years when the attempts of the central government to liquidate the DI inflamed opinion against it.[4]

In the 1950's, the DI branched out to other islands as well—to southern Celebes under Kahar Muzakir, and to Atjeh under Daub Beureueh—and it was only during this period that it came out openly for the idea of an Islamic state. This idea was opposed by the central government, and, by branding the DI as reactionary and a danger to the *Pantja Sila* state, the PKI split Islam as a political force. As a result, *Darul Islam's* agitation for an Islamic state did not make much headway. The question was again debated in the Constituent Assembly, which was formed after the 1955 elections for the purpose of drafting a new, definitive constitution, but here the Muslims who clung to Islam as the foundation of the state were opposed by the Nationalist, Communist, Socialist, Christian, and Catholic parties. The Masjumi, NU, PSII, and other Islamic parties could muster 45 per cent of the votes, but, because decision on essential parts of the constitution required a two-thirds majority, the Constituent Assembly was unable to agree on the ideological basis of the state.

Meanwhile, in February, 1958, a regional rebellion against the central government broke out in Central Sumatra and northern Celebes. The leadership of this movement, known as *PRRI-Permesta*, contained elements of the army, as well as politicians and some prominent Masjumi leaders. In February, 1960, this movement transformed itself into the "United Republic of Indonesia" (RPI). Its concept of the Indonesian state was that of a federation, in which each component area would manage its internal matters. Because two areas, Atjeh and southern Celebes, opted for an Islamic organization, the question of an Islamic state again

---

[4] These attempts finally succeeded on June 4, 1962, with the capture of Kartosuwirjo and his subsequent execution.

became acute. However, the PRRI-Permesta/RPI was not a viable political-military organization, and was easily defeated by the central government. At this point, President Sukarno saw his chance to finish off what he termed "liberal democracy," and thus start Indonesia on the road toward his "guided democracy" of personal rule and authoritarianism. The Constituent Assembly was dissolved, and on July 5, 1959, at the suggestion of the army leaders, President Sukarno decreed the return to the 1945 constitution. On August 17, 1960, Sukarno banned the Masjumi party but not the NU, although the NU had also supported the idea of an Islamic state in the Constituent Assembly in 1959.

President Sukarno banned the Masjumi Party on grounds of insubordination, charging that its leaders had participated in the proclamation of the Indonesian Federal Republic (RPI) in February, 1960, or had openly supported the regionalist rebellion of 1958–61.[5] The Masjumi leadership, however, challenged this ban. It claimed it had sought to prevent the proclamation of the PRRI on February 15, 1958, and, at the request of Prime Minister Djuanda, had even sent a mission to Padang to seek a solution to the rebellion, for which the Prime Minister had later expressed appreciation in Parliament. Moreover, the Masjumi Party Council, on January 24, February 13, and February 17, had stated the Masjumi's view that the formation of the PRRI was unconstitutional. Furthermore, the government itself had conceded that although some leaders of political parties were involved in the PRRI, those who violated the law were not acting on behalf of their party, but in their individual capacity.[6] The Masjumi, as a party, disclaimed any responsibility for the rebellion, and charged that, had it not been for some army support, the PRRI movement would never have been proclaimed. Finally, the Masjumi regarded Presidential regulation No. 7/1959 (the juridical basis for banning the party) as unconstitutional and therefore invalid.

By 1960, despite Masjumi protests, the Muslims had been soundly defeated, and for some years they remained paralyzed. Although the decree of July 5, 1959, stated that the 1945 constitution was inspired by the Djakarta Charter, thus offering some consolation to those Muslims willing to cooperate with Sukarno under his Guided Democracy, this really meant very little. *Pantja Sila* was now firmly established as the basis of the state, and Muslims were forced to reconcile themselves to this fact, although the ideal of the Islamic state persisted.

President Sukarno's decision to ban the Masjumi had been predominantly political. He wanted to establish his personal rule and implement his concept of NASAKOM (an Indonesian acronym for cooperation among the Nationalist, religious, and Communist parties), thereby including the Communists in the government. It was therefore necessary to ban Masjumi and the Indonesian Socialist Party (PSI), both opponents of the PKI. Sukarno arrested and imprisoned the Masjumi leaders involved in the

[5] For a discussion of this rebellion, see Herbert Feith and Daniel S. Lev, "The End of the Indonesian Rebellion," below.

[6] *Minutes of Parliament*, February 28, 1958.

PRRI (Mohammed Natsir, Sjafruddin Prawiranegara, Burhanuddin Hara-hap, *et al.*), but a similar fate befell other Masjumi leaders, such as Pra-woto Mangkusamito, Mohammed Roem, and Isa Anshary, and such PSI leaders as Sjahrir, Subadio Sastrosatomo, and Anak Agung Gde Agung, who did not join the PRRI. All were released long after the abortive PKI coup of September 30–October 1, 1965, except Sjahrir, who died in prison.

NASAKOM was meant to be the cornerstone of Sukarno's political edi-fice, but in fact the Communists exploited it to promote their own cause and to strengthen their position in the power structure. The Muslims be-came alarmed, and there was great tension between the Muslims and the Communists under Sukarno's Guided Democracy.

An interesting development was the change in the attitude of the Islamic parties toward *Pantja Sila*. They had been skeptical of it, but when the Communists attacked it, they began to defend it. The first principle, ac-knowledgment of one God, was the very weapon the Muslims needed in their struggle against Communism. It is hard to know whether acceptance of *Pantja Sila* was merely a tactical move, or a real departure from working toward an Islamic state. Although many prominent Muslim leaders pub-licly stated that they now wholeheartedly accepted the *Pantja Sila*, there have been many private expressions to the contrary. For this reason, large segments of the population still suspect the Islamic parties of wanting to establish an Islamic state, and have therefore withheld their support.

In summary, although the vast majority of the Indonesian population is Muslim, and a smaller majority actively practices its faith, this Muslim strength has not been reflected in Indonesian politics or government. Among the reasons for this are the existence of the *abangan*, the failure of Islam to become a modernizing force, its inability to forge unity, its ten-dency toward exclusivism, and the public suspicion that it is working for the formation of an Islamic state.

The disparity between the political goals and achievements of the Indo-nesian *ummat* has produced a crisis that must soon be resolved by the ex-tinction or recognition of Islam as a political force in Indonesian society. It may be of interest to try to identify the ideological and organizational contours of the crisis. The Islamic magazine *Pandji Masjarakat* has this to say:

At present the *ummat* is faced with a double challenge: first the challenge from within in the form of orthodoxy, ignorance and backwardness of the *ummat*; second, the challenge from without in the form of modern culture introduced by Western people with its concomitants of modernism, material-ism, atheism, Communism, and Christianity.

Orthodoxy leads to stagnation in thinking. Whenever one ceases to think, the dynamics of life will disappear. No change is possible, and without change there is no progress. While the world moves, we remain in the same place. Our society becomes backward in all its facets: social, political, eco-nomic, scientific, and technological.

Western culture began to infiltrate our society in the sixteenth century. Around the eighteenth century, that culture became modern as a result of the *Aufklarung* (enlightenment). It had a positive and a negative effect on our society.

Science and modern technology have a positive effect. A small part of our society has freed itself from stagnant thinking and living and has become an advanced minority group, an intelligentsia. Unfortunately, it not only freed itself from orthodoxy but also from the teachings of Islam, so that those who were schooled in modern culture were ignorant of Islam.

The offspring of Western culture, which clearly brought negative effects to the *ummat*, are materialism, atheism, Communist ideology, and Christian leaders who attempt to convert Muslims to Christianity. They think this is their sacred mission.[7]

Indeed, among the *ummat* there is a strong fear of both Communism and Christianity. Fear of Communism is understandable, since Communists have been able to form a mass party and penetrate the structure of Sukarno's Guided Democracy (1959–66). Fear of Christians is somewhat puzzling, for there are only 6 million Protestants and 2 million Catholics—clearly a minority. But Christians' links with international religious organizations, and their ability to raise large sums for building churches, schools, hospitals, and the like, fill the Muslims with awe. Muslims are aware, as a Christian has said, that "many more Muslims have embraced Christianity in the past 20 years of independence than during the 100 years of missionary work in the colonial period."[8]

One of the main activities of the Muslims in the past few years has been the intensification of the *Da'wah Islamiyah* (the "Call of Islam"), a kind of "missionary work" in which the *muballigh,* or "preacher," brings the faith to areas barely touched by Islam. The *Da'wah* also attempts to reach the "statistical Muslims," to deepen their knowledge and consciousness of Islam. There is no central organization to coordinate this activity, but almost every Islamic political party or mass organization has its *Da'wah Islamiyah* program. There are never enough funds to do this job properly. When Muslims see the ample funds Christians can raise for their missionary work, their frustration and fear of the Christians increase.

Apart from this, the Muslims are painfully aware of what they call "lack of concepts" and constantly seek ways to meet the problems that arise in a transitional society. They have argued, first, that there must be a reinterpretation of teachings, the essence, and the problems of the *ummat*, and this rethinking must use all the information of modern science. Second, Islamic education must be intensified in formal educational institutions, as well as in households and in society at large. Third, the teachings of Islam and those of modern science must be integrated.

This sounds desirable in the abstract, but it is difficult to achieve. Implementation demands theorists, and, in the view of at least one writer, Muslim theorists have made little impact on Indonesian life:

Islamic *ummat!* You are not a minority group in Indonesia. But you are being treated or are acting as a minority group. The theorists in our state are

---

[7] "Tantangan Kurun Kita Jang Harus Kita Djawab" ("We Must Answer the Challenge of Our Epoch"), *Pandji Masjarakat*, October 5, 1966.

[8] D. C. Mulder, "De Islam," *Rondom het Woord* (September, 1965), p. 160.

clearly not Muslims: Their concepts influence national life and development. But as theorists they do not represent the Muslim outlook, so that their concepts do not express the Muslim view of life. Is the *ummat* less creative? Or are their ideas too abstract, vague, and difficult to understand and therefore unattractive? Are the ideas of the Islamic *ummat* not directly related to the life of the people and are they therefore strange to the people?[9]

Lack of leadership, quarrels, and personal ambitions, especially among the older generation, also inhibit a steady growth of the *ummat* and militate against the formation of broader organizational units within the *ummat*. The younger Muslims are aware of this, and many of them refuse to become involved in their elders' feuds.

The crisis of Islam in Indonesia reflects both internal and external political and ideological factors. Fear of Communism has at least partially reconciled Muslims to *Pantja Sila* and facilitated their cooperation with other groups, while fear of Christianity has stimulated the development of Muslim "missionary" activities. Nevertheless, if Islam is to survive as a force in Indonesian society, Muslim leaders must develop new concepts on its relevance for modern life.

New concepts, however, will need new organizational structures. One of the major problems confronting the *ummat* in Indonesia today is how to develop a more satisfactory organizational structure—what is commonly called the *wadah politik Islam*, the Islamic "political receptacle."

There is a demand, especially by young Muslims, for fewer political parties. Although the PKI was banned in March, 1966, the eight remaining parties were legally allowed to continue. Three are Islamic (NU, PSII, and Perti), and each has its affiliated organizations among the youth, students, farmers, and city workers. In addition to these political parties, there are numerous Islamic social-educational organizations, of which the Muhammadiyah is the strongest and oldest. These Islamic parties and associations are often politically at odds with each other, and it has been proposed that they consolidate to achieve better coordination and more political power. This consolidation should be stimulated by the current slogan, *Uchuwah Islamiyah* (the brotherhood and unity of Islam).

There are many compelling reasons for a *wadah politik Islam*. The proliferation of political parties leads to political instability, and without stability, economic development is hardly possible. For youth, unemployment has become an increasingly acute problem. The fact that there are 3 million unemployed in the cities and 14 million underemployed in the rural areas out of a labor force of 40 million illustrates the magnitude of the problem. Each year more young people graduate from the universities. In 1967 alone, 9,000 are expected to graduate and will need jobs, but jobs are scarce under the present chaotic economy. An economic program to alleviate the employment problem of the young generation is imperative.

A program containing plans for birth control, restricting admittance at universities, reducing urbanization, banning imports of luxury goods, curtailing

[9] Muljadi Abdullah, "Mana Konseptors Muslim?" ("Where Are the Muslim Theorists?") *Pandji Masjarakat*, January 20, 1967.

non-productive expenses; a program that gives priority to rural economic development, agrarian economy and small-scale industries is a realistic program.[10]

To ensure economic development in this sense, a *wadah politik Islam* should be formed. Only in a united organization could reform-minded Muslim leaders command the support of the Muslim masses that would permit a development program to be carried out. But what does this entail? Does it involve a fusion, or a federation, of parties? Here one encounters the issue of a single Islamic party versus multiple Islamic parties.

A single Islamic party would enable the Muslims to emerge as a single force with a decisive say in political affairs. There is, however, little enthusiasm for the idea. The *ummat* is easily fragmented because of differences in intellectual level, customs, region, and language. Moreover, the memory of the split in the Masjumi, once the single Islamic party in the country, remains fresh in the minds of many people.

In view of the differences within the Islamic community, the existence of a number of Islamic parties seems preferable but could result in the fragmentation and paralysis of Islamic political action. It has therefore been proposed that each Islamic party maintain its own tradition and identity within a united front. This united front would become the *wadah politik Islam*.

The thinking on this matter has not yet fully crystallized. One faction says that the receptacle should have full powers to decide policy matters, on the basis of consensus that itself is based on compromise among member parties. Another faction argues that this approach would lead to new contradictions that would eventually destroy the receptacle. Still another group favors a rotating system of leadership, whereby each member organization would have the opportunity to implement the front's program during a fixed period. However, would a large political party be willing to relinquish its temporary leadership of the front? The problem is obviously not an easy one, and some have despaired of finding a workable solution. To quote *Galanggang* again:

> The Islamic *ummat* and the Islamic parties are at present faced with an impasse; they are in a situation of bewilderment, and there are some who have already lost hope of ever attaining an Islamic political receptacle in Indonesia.[11]

Political weakness, the backwardness of the *ummat*, and the challenge of modern culture have produced an ideological and organizational crisis in Indonesian Islam. The crisis has stimulated cooperation with other groups, Muslim "missionary" activities, and a debate about new Islamic organizational structures. However, if Islam is to play a vital role in modern Indo-

[10] See Salihin Hasan, "Sebuah fikiran tentang wadah politik Islam" ("A Thought about the Islamic Political Receptacle"), *Gelanggang*, No. 2 (Djakarta, 1967), p. 82. *Gelanggang* is a cultural magazine of Lesbumi, which is affiliated with NU.

[11] *Ibid.*, p. 83.

nesian political life, new concepts need to be developed on the relevance of Islam for modern life, and organizational structures must be created to implement the varied goals and programs of the Islamic community.

Islam can be a major force in economic development. The government's strategy of economic development emphasizes agricultural productivity for the coming years. Since the agricultural sector still accounts for about 70 per cent of the economy, peasant acceptance of and participation in economic development is essential. Because most peasants are Muslims, it is far easier to reach them through an Islamic party or organization than through a secular one, but such an Islamic party should also be a modernist one that is committed to economic development. Since the Masjumi Party has been the major reformist element in Indonesian life, it should be rehabilitated and allowed to function politically, or, if that is impossible, a modernist alternative must be developed to take its place.

Once the PKI coup of September 30–October 1, 1965, had been successfully suppressed and Indonesia had started on the road toward the New Order, the Masjumi leaders who had been imprisoned in 1962 were released, raising hopes and expectations that the party itself would soon be restored. In August, 1966, the army held a second seminar in Bandung to discuss political, social, and economic affairs as they related to the needs of the New Order. The seminar report stated, among other things:

> It must be admitted that there are still national potentials, particularly in the field of politics, which have not yet found their natural channel, and if this situation is to be allowed to continue, it will constitute an element that may contribute to the rise of an unstable situation in the future. Therefore, it is but natural that members of the banned parties (PSI, Masjumi, and Murba), who have retained their Indonesian citizenship with similar rights and obligations as other citizens, should participate in political life so that they acquire the same opportunity to vote and be elected.

The Masjumi took this to mean that the rehabilitation of the party was only a matter of time. When the Murba (Proletariat) Party was rehabilitated, hopes rose high, but suddenly the armed forces (ABRI) issued a statement on December 21, 1966, stating that "the Masjumi and PSI and so forth are regarded as deviating from the *Pantja Sila*." There are, indeed, elements in some of the services who dislike the idea of rehabilitation of Masjumi-PSI, and, since General Suharto then needed to consolidate his position in the ABRI with a view toward ousting President Sukarno, he preferred to adopt a stiff attitude toward Masjumi. On January 6, 1967, General Suharto replied to a letter from Prawoto, former chairman of Masjumi: "Juridical, state, and psychological reasons have led the ABRI to reject the rehabilitation of the Masjumi party." This decision ran counter to a resolution of the third national conference of the Indonesian Lawyers' Association of December 3, 1966, that called for the rehabilitation of Masjumi and PSI, because "their dissolution was not valid from the juridical-formal viewpoint and was unfounded from the juridical-material point of view, and because they were victims of the Old Order."

On March 30, 1967, about two weeks after General Suharto was sworn in as Acting President, Prawoto again wrote him about rehabilitating the Masjumi. Since the People's Consultative Congress (MPRS) had eliminated Sukarno from the presidency, Prawoto thought that Suharto might be more amenable. In March, a Muslim educational organization, the *Persatuan Ummat Islam*, adopted a resolution at its fifth Congress again asking for the restoration of Masjumi, but the General stuck to his position. On April 8, in his first conference as Acting President, he made it clear that he could not allow the rehabilitation of Masjumi because of "treason committed to the *Pantja Sila.*" The demand of some Muslim writers that this accusation be "proved in court" was disregarded. The situation remained frozen; the Masjumi was still a proscribed party.

In view of the Bandung army seminar's support for the idea of mobilizing *all* the forces of the New Order in the political field, presumably including the Masjumi, it is strange that General Suharto's position should be so rigid. He may be cautious about taking chances that might affect government stability. As a result, his government tends to be oriented toward the *status quo* and to move only under the impact of overwhelming forces. Although a pious Muslim himself, Suharto may also be influenced by the secular nationalism of the Central Javanese PNI environment.

Whatever the truth may be, his approach toward the problem of Masjumi cannot be regarded as statecraft or wisdom. His refusal to rehabilitate Masjumi means that Masjumi supporters, who constitute at least 25 per cent of the electorate, will not be able to vote for the party in the next general election.* It means that the progressive elements within the Islamic community are untapped for the work of modernization and nation-building and that Islam as a political force will remain weak and divided.

Meanwhile, circles close to General Suharto say that his position on this matter is not yet final—it is merely a tactical position. We can only hope and wait.

Turning to the attitude of other Islamic parties on this question, one can see why the NU, fearing competition from the Masjumi, might not be very keen to support Masjumi's rehabilitation. The attitude of PSII is similar. Both, however, vigorously support the slogan of upholding *Uchuwa Islamiyah*, or brotherhood among Muslims.

The unsettled problem of the Masjumi is bound to have repercussions within Muslim circles. The Muhammadiyah, which has done a good deal of work in the field of social welfare and education, had had a special status in the Masjumi. When the Masjumi was banned, Sukarno allowed the Muhammadiyah to continue functioning. It became a haven for Masjumi members who wanted to remain active and maintain the morale of the Masjumi rank and file.

Some of the Muhammadiyah leaders, however, compromised themselves and reached an understanding with Sukarno's regime; others did their

* Although originally scheduled for 1968, according to the decision of the People's Consultative Congress (MPRS) at its March, 1968, session, the general elections will take place in 1971.

utmost to maintain a semblance of neutrality. After the PKI coup, the former officers silently retreated into the background, making room for younger leaders.

Although the prospects for the rehabilitation of the Masjumi seem bleaker every day, two groups have appeared within the Muhammadiyah leadership: first, those people who want to transform Muhammadiyah into a political party so as to provide a legal platform for former Masjumi members; second, those who oppose such a transformation on the ground that Muhammadiyah must remain a strictly nonpolitical, social-educational organization. In the Pemuda Muhammadiyah (Youth Group), a similar division is discernible. One group of ambitious young individuals seems bent on seizing the opportunity to occupy prominent positions, preferably in state organizations; the second includes the older people and members of the *Tanwir* (representing the regions), who counsel caution. At present, the possibility of transforming the Muhammadiyah into a political party seems remote. But the search for a way out of the impasse faced by Masjumi continues.

Early in March, 1967, a working committee of twelve formed to study the question of rehabilitation of Masjumi or, if this should prove impossible, to find an alternative. Such prominent Masjumi leaders sit on the Committee as former chairman and Deputy Premier Prawoto Mangkusasmito, former Minister of Religion Fakih Usman, former Premier Burhanuddin Harahap, Anwar Haryono, Hasan Basri, leaders of the Islamic Students Association (HMI), and leaders of the Federation of Indonesian Islamic Workers (*Gasbiindo*). The younger people on this committee favor the formation of a new political party, since there are obstacles to the rehabilitation of Masjumi.

Generally speaking, the younger generation of Muslims insists on being "modern." In current Indonesian political jargon, this means to participate more actively in politics than did leaders of the older generation. In their view, their elders were preoccupied with problems of religion, and because they were rather naïve or inept in politics, the Muslims failed to assert themselves effectively. This view is found particularly among the militant factions of the HMI, with its 200,000 members, and to some extent in the Indonesian Islamic Students (PII), which has 700,000 members among the secondary schools. The young Muslims are critical of former Masjumi leaders, contending that they tend to be dogmatic and rigid and therefore to alienate other Muslims, such as the NU members. They are determined not to repeat their elders' mistakes. They insist that Islam can succeed as a political power only if Muslims construct as broad a front as possible, seeking cooperation and understanding among the various Islamic parties and organizations. Here is a case of a generation gap within the Islamic *ummat*. But despite good intentions on the part of the younger people, nothing concrete in the form of a new political party has emerged as of the spring of 1967.

More promising—or at least so it seems now—is the attempt of former Vice President Mohammed Hatta to start a new party which he calls the

Democratic Islamic Indonesian Party (PDII). Seeing the futility of rehabilitating Masjumi, Hatta has begun to form a new Islamic party, the purpose of which is "to implement Indonesian Socialism implied in the ideal
of a just and prosperous Indonesia blessed by Allah." The PDII is constructed in the spirit of Islam and is a nationalist party, formulated on the
basis of *Pantja Sila*. As explained by Hatta in a pamphlet, *Plans for the
Basis, Program, and Structure of the PDII*:

> The Indonesian Socialism which is created by the PDII guarantees freedom
> of each man to adhere to his own religion and to exercise it according to that
> religion and belief . . . The relation between Indonesian Socialism and
> the ideals of Islam can be described as follows: Islam provides the seed; tra-
> ditional customs and gotong-rojong [mutual cooperation] which mould the
> nation's personality and the Indonesian culture constitute the fertile soil
> that makes that seed grow into a shady tree.[12]

Hatta intends the PDII to be a party for Muslims of all ages, but one
intended primarily for the "1966 Generation" that brought down the
Sukarno regime. His efforts are concentrated on training cadres and starting a movement, after which he will be ready to launch the party. To that
end, he visited several regions outside Djakarta in late 1966 and early 1967
(southern Celebes, Central Java, and western and northern Sumatra),
"campaigning" for the concept of PDII. He met with some good response,
and in early April, 1967, it is said that army circles encouraged him to go
ahead with his movement. But despite this support, Hatta does not seem
to have made much progress.

Some of the former members of Masjumi view Hatta's efforts with mixed
feelings. Some appreciate what he is doing, but there are some doubts that
he is really capable of forming a strong mass organization. Hatta's inclination is toward a cadre party, a view he has held since the days of his Pendidikan Nasional Indonesia in the early 1930's, a cadre party he led with
Sjahrir. The PDII membership would be carefully selected and trained.
The younger generation looks askance at this undertaking, because they
prefer to see Hatta as a nonpartisan father-figure in all respects.

While Hatta is engaged in promoting the PDII, the former Minister of
Religion, Fakih Usman, a prominent Masjumi and Muhammadiyah leader
himself, is seeking to develop another political party. He has reached an
understanding with Hatta that his organization would attract the masses of
the Islamic *ummat*, while Hatta's PDII would concentrate on training the
cadres. Thus, there are two movements working together toward the creation of a new Islamic party.[13]

On May 11, 1967, Acting President General Suharto, shifting his position somewhat, stated that his government had no objection to the creation of a new party, provided all the Islamic mass organizations, such as
the Muhammadiyah, HMI, PII, and so on, ceased to exist as separate en-

[12] "Rentjana Dasar, Program dan Struktur Partai Demokrasi Islam Indonesia" ("Outlining the Program of the PDII"), *Angkasa* (Bandung, 1967), p. 16.
[13] *Nusantara* (Djakarta), May 12, 1967.

tities and were fused into a single political party, and provided the ideology of such a party was based on *Demokrasi Pantja Sila*. The "independents"— those not affiliated with any political party, such as the HMI or PII—seem favorably inclined toward this idea, but elements within the Muhammadiyah oppose its transformation into a political party.

In the meantime, everyone's attention is focused on the 1971 general elections. With the Masjumi most probably still banned, and no alternative in sight, some Muslims see little chance of staging a political comeback. Moreover, their frustration is increased by the difficulty of establishing and maintaining cordial relations with the army.

But the NU, the officially recognized party, also has its share of frustration. The draft election bill that has been submitted by the Suharto government to Parliament contains provisions that are not wholly appreciated by the NU. One quarter of the parliamentary seats have been set aside for the armed forces; in return, military candidates may not run for election for the remaining seats. In March, 1967, NU's first chairman, K. Mohammed Dahlan, charged that 25 per cent was excessive and undemocratic and suggested that 5 per cent would be more reasonable. NU also fears that the election system proposed by the government (single-member constituencies rather than the proportional representation system used in the 1955 elections) will cause it to lose many votes. By the end of May, the discussions in Parliament on the election bill were continuing, and no solution was clearly evident.

In summary, Indonesian Islam has reached a point of crisis. Muslim strength within the population at large is not reflected in Indonesian politics or government. The existence of the *abangan*, the failure of Islam to meet the challenge of modern culture and to become a modernizing force, its lack of unity and organization, its tendency toward exclusivism, and public suspicion that it is working for an Islamic state have all contributed to this situation. Yet the picture is a complex and fluid one. Muslims are increasingly aware of the dimensions of the crisis; new ideas are fermenting. The Muslim parties are zealous and convinced of ultimate success. It is commonly said in Indonesia today that the nation should strive to build the New Order based on democracy, socialism, and *Pantja Sila* and set out to achieve a just and prosperous society. Any truly democratic government, any government that is committed to development and modernization in Indonesia, will have to take Islam into account as a political force and must do everything possible to enlist the Muslims as its supporters.

9

MODERN MEDICINE AND TRADITIONAL CULTURE: CONFRONTATION ON THE MALAY PENINSULA*

ROBERT J. WOLFF†

It has become commonplace to say that the world today is characterized by change. Naturally, people in previous ages have also had to adapt to changed circumstances, but the changes today seem more violent—there are more changes per unit of time.

That is not all, however. Today's changes are not merely technological improvements, they are very basic reorientations.

Some years ago, an irate Frenchman coined the term "cocacolanization" to describe the attempt to replace native wines with Coca-Cola. The real issue, of course, was not whether the taste of one drink was preferable to the taste of another, but whether one way of life would replace another. As wine is a symbol of a certain way of life, so, too, is Coca-Cola—of a very different kind of life.

* Reprinted by permission of the author and the publisher from *Human Organization*, XXIV (Winter, 1965), 339–45.

† This article is based on material collected during 1962–64 in the Malay Peninsula, and supported by USPHS Research Grant GM 11329 (ICMRT); it is a much modified version of a paper read at the ICMRT Advisory Committee meeting, NIH, Bethesda, Md., November, 1963.

Where in France the difference between the old and the new, between *Kultur* and mass culture, were real enough then (and seem to be a problem even now), the differences elsewhere between the traditional way of life and the new were truly staggering. It is no exaggeration to say that the change-over to a new way of life, to new values, to new ideas, is a revolution on a scale perhaps never equaled in the world's history.

Barbara Ward Jackson, in a recent book, *The Rich Nations and the Poor Nations*,[1] lucidly describes this revolution. She points to the sudden and almost universal spread of a number of important *ideas* that are changing the world. The idea that all men are equal, or at least should have equal opportunities in education, in business, in development, is revolutionary and new in almost all areas of the world. Or, the idea that we can and should improve our material, physical well-being in this world rather than wait for compensatory improvement in the next, is revolutionary and new in the history of the world. And the idea that science and technology can and should be applied to the solution of immediate problems of this world rather than to the mystical truths of the universe, is new and revolutionary to many ancient cultures.

MEDICAL SERVICES AS AGENTS OF CHANGE

Modern medicine has been in the vanguard of this revolution. The application of science to problems of everyday living and health, and the idea that the benefits of modern medicine should be made available to everyone, have been instrumental in causing an unprecedented increase in the number of living human beings in this world, and, often, in improving the health of the people.

It may seem strange to us Westerners, who initiated this revolution (and have made it such an apparent success), that others did not actually *demand* the benefits of modern medicine, or modern economics, or modern political systems. Most people did not ask for change. As colonizers, not so very long ago, we imposed our medical science, as we imposed our kind of economics, and as we imposed our kind of government.

Today, however, the revolution of new ideas, which we originally introduced, has led to the establishment of nations with civil services, medical services, and other manifestations of the modern state. It is these services that now bring the changes in their own nations, with or without assistance from outside. Even though the innovations may be carried out by natives, the ideas behind the technological changes are still foreign importations.

Modern medical practices are being introduced by probably all medical services in all developing nations. But modern medicine is not only scientific medicine, as contrasted to traditional medicine, it is, above all, Western medicine. It is important to consider that there might be a difference between the ease with which the tools and the skills of Western medicine

[1] Barbara Ward (Jackson), *The Rich Nations and the Poor Nations* (New York: W. W. Norton, 1962).

are adopted and accepted, and the difficulty of understanding and accepting the ideas underlying the technology of medicine.

It is relatively easy to accept antibiotics, or modern diagnostic tools, or even modern diets—it is difficult to understand or accept the *ideas* that have resulted in the continuing development of antibiotics, diagnostic tools, or diets. For many peoples, it is difficult to accept the idea of causality in health and disease, which we Westerners take for granted because it is so much part of our culture to think in terms of cause and effect; it is difficult for others to understand the idea, which we Westerners now take so much for granted, that we should apply all our scientific efforts to the alleviation of pain and to the prolongation of life; and it is difficult for some to understand that the benefits of modern medical science should be equally available to all, regardless of social class or social importance.

Malaya and Malay Culture

I should like to present a few of the problems inherent in the introduction of Western medical practice as they are manifest in Malaya.[2] Malaya is perhaps not untypical of the developing countries, although it is considerably wealthier than many such nations. Malaya today is going through a period of change, even revolution, on many fronts. Concerted attempts are being made to lift Malaya from a traditional society to a modern nation. Politically, economically, and medically, new tools and skills are being introduced almost daily.

In some ways, Malaya is also perhaps unique in that within a relatively small territory, a number of populations live side by side, each with its own unique culture, and each with its own standards of material civilization. If one counts the island of Singapore in with the total population of the peninsula, there is no majority: Both Malays and Chinese form about 40 per cent of the total population. There is a minority of Indians, about 11 per cent of the total, and a number of smaller minorities, including the group loosely called Aborigines. The Malays dominate the country politically, the Chinese economically. The former consider themselves the original population and think of the Chinese and Indians as guests in their country. Actually, a very large proportion of the Malay population immigrated from Indonesia only one or two generations ago—no accurate figures are available, but it is estimated that in parts of the west coast, up to 40 per cent of Malays immigrated less than two generations ago. At the same time, there is a sizable group of Chinese in Malaya who can trace their ancestors back several hundred years.

Historically, Malaya has always been a crossroads. There have been waves of migrations passing through Malaya; some of the Aborigines are probably descendants of people who moved through Malaya 1,000 or more years ago. There have also been cultural invasions. Even today, there are

---

[2] Malaya, in this article, refers to the Malayan Peninsula—I am not here speaking of the new political unit of Malaysia.

very evident remnants of Hindu, Buddhist, Arabic (Muslim), and, of course, Western influences.

The observable differences between Chinese and Malay cultures are great, and they are exaggerated possibly by the fact that almost all city dwellers are Chinese, whereas almost all Malays live in the rural areas. This means, among other things, that the Chinese, being more urbanized, also seem more Western in many ways; the Malays being more rural, seem more traditional.

The Malays, although they live on the land and use the fruits of the land, do not farm intensively. Only a small proportion of them grow rice commercially, and the rice grown in Malaya is not sufficient for the country's needs—although probably the majority of Malays grow some rice for home consumption. Rice-growing, however, is more a traditional pursuit, a cultural heritage, than a commercial proposition (much as folk-dancing might be a cultural heritage to another people). Many Malays own rubber trees, which they either tap themselves or rent out to Chinese. Malays do not grow vegetables, either commercially or for their own consumption. They own fruit trees but rarely make an attempt to improve yield or otherwise farm more intensively. Despite the fact that the Malays have a long tradition of rural living, their pattern of agriculture seems more like gathering jungle products than growing.

The Malays appear to live a very leisurely life: They are not poor, although they may not have much ready cash. Their houses are simply built but generally airy, cool, and comfortable. Their diet is monotonous, but not because they do not have access to more variety in foodstuffs: It is the traditional way of living.

In contrast, the Chinese generally live in crowded quarters, with less comfort, less space. Their way of life seems very unleisurely. Their diet is simple but varied, and probably more adequate nutritionally than the Malay diet. The unit of Chinese society is the family, not the village.

It would be tempting to say that the unit of Malay society is the village, but this would be a simplification distorting reality. It would be more accurate to say that there is no real unit of society among Malays, that possibly the small nuclear family, in a very vague sort of way, is their unit of society. What binds Malay society, however, is Malay culture, Malay customs and traditions.

For hundreds of years, Malays in this peninsula have been subjected to foreign influences. Long before the invasion of Europeans, there were Indian outposts. Even today, the influence of Hindu culture is readily visible: The language contains many words of Sanskrit origin; Malay shadow plays continue to show the stories of the Ramayana; many of the titles and traditions connected with royalty are Indian. Later, other Indians brought Islam, and today Malaya is by constitution an Islamic nation: By law, all Malays are Muslim. Islam plays a predominant role in the daily life of all Malays. But, as any Malay will point out, this is *Malayan* Islam, not Egyptian Islam. What this means is that Islam, too, is incorporated into the Malay culture.

Perhaps as a consequence of these varied historical influences, Malay culture is a mixture of elements that to an outsider often seem to blend very poorly.

Malays are strict monotheistic Muslims, but, at the same time, they implicitly believe in a host of spirits, demons, devils, and gods, many of them of pre-Hindu origin. Malay society in the villages is strictly egalitarian, or democratic. No man is more than another—and yet, at the same time, Malay society in a larger sense is feudal, with various classes of royalty considered almost as castes. To an outsider, it seems that this astonishing variety of seemingly contradictory beliefs cannot possibly fit into a meaningful whole. There seems no unity, no strong central idea in this conglomeration. For the Malay, this is no problem.

One of the items of furniture sometimes found in a wealthier Malay home is a small cupboard, usually with a glass door (if it is named at all it is usually called an *Almeira,* a Portuguese word). On its shelves is a fantastic array of odds and ends: often a collection of those small sample bottles of liqueur,[3] some dolls, some ashtrays and cigarette lighters, some objects made locally out of straw or bamboo, maybe some knitted doilies. The items usually are not arranged in any particular way. They are generally gifts, not retained because of any economic or aesthetic value, but only because they were gifts. The total impression is very unartistic!

Perhaps Malay culture is like that: It is the cupboard in which are stored all the gifts from other cultures, not arranged in any particular way. There is no connection between the items on one shelf and those on the next—or even any linkage among the items on a shelf. But they are all the possessions of one person.

How does one live with such a collection of gifts? As with the cupboard —cautiously. One is careful not to upset the delicate lack of arrangement. A new gift can always be fitted in, but slowly, cautiously, for fear of upsetting the little china cat on the left or the shell-bird on the right.

Unifying Principles of Malay Culture

Any culture, of course, is the current collection of inherited, acquired, and stolen bric-a-brac accumulated over a long period of time. But must there not be some method to the madness of collecting? It would seem that for a culture to be viable it must have some underlying principles of collection: Some items are rejected because they are not practical, some because they do not fit in with the rest of the items. Anthropological and historical literature is a record of the many principles of selection applied by different peoples at different times. The Malay cultural heritage collection is held together by two principles, mutually dependent. One is that the whole collection is valuable, not for any intrinsic worth but because it is peculiarly Malay. Some of it is old, and so has value as antiquity; some of it is unique—no one else has it. But it is the totality of the collection that makes it really valuable, because it is Malay. The second principle is

[3] Islam forbids the use of alcohol.

the central concept of what might best be termed harmony. The world it-self is perceived as in many ways incomprehensible, consisting of often con-flicting facts. But somehow there is harmony in a live-and-let-live sense. People, too, are different, and they are expected to be. Yet they must learn to live harmoniously. And by harmonious is meant *gentle:* One's ac-tions must be such that they do not cause hurt or embarrassment.

There are two words in Malay that describe this dimension: *halus* and *kasar. Kasar* is coarse, or rough of texture, but it also means large, crude, overbearing, vulgar, boisterous, loud, rude and inconsiderate. *Halus,* in contrast, means smooth, soft, gentle, cultured and refined, small, delicate —and also polite, noble, tender. It even has the connotation of finely chiseled features and smooth skin. Malays are supposed to be *halus,* others are often *kasar*—especially Chinese and Europeans.

No one can escape, I think, the charm of a Malay village. Even a short visit casts the quiet spell of peaceful surroundings and friendly people. At almost any time of day, one can find people sitting around, playing with small children, talking, or just daydreaming. Conversation is low-keyed: A man will need considerable provocation to raise his voice, and a woman who raises hers will be looked upon with amused tolerance. No one ever yells or screams at the top of his voice.

The content of conversation, too, is mild. One expresses an opinion very tentatively in Malay company. No one will contradict; there is always the softly murmured assent from listeners. Disagreement is expressed through stating an opinion rather independently of previously expressed sentiments. This gives Malay conversation a curious tone: The gentle unemotionality may give an impression of vagueness or uninvolved talk about the weather, whereas, actually, important issues may be in discussion. Differences in idea or opinion are always played down; agreement is stressed. And two completely diametrical notions will be expressed as just two side-by-side statements. In extreme cases, disagreement may be expressed by changing the subject or withdrawing from the conversation altogether. This is, of course, a generalization, and it would be most unfair to attempt to char-acterize the totality of a culture by the kind of conversation evidenced. Nevertheless, this is certainly the model of the culture—it is what social intercourse *should* be.

The same model applies to society. Many contradictory elements are apparent in the structure of Malay society, but the contradiction is ignored. Each village or kampong has a village chief who is both appointed and elected, although the process is never as crude as actually appointing or electing. The elders of the kampong will discuss among themselves who would be most suitable for the position, if there is a vacancy. Occasionally, it may be the son of a previous village chief, because hereditary virtues are one of the considerations discussed. A village chief need not be wealthy, although that, too, may be a consideration: His position entails a certain amount of responsibility, and it helps to have some means. He must be a respected member of the community, but, equally important, the sort of person who can handle himself properly outside his own community. Very possibly the district chief will sit in on at least some of these conferences, and he will learn much about the feelings of the elders. He will rarely, however, go so far as actually to ask for the name of a candidate. In the end, the district chief will appoint someone he knows the elders have "elected." If the elders are reasonably agreed, it is a smooth, refined process. If, for whatever reason, one or more of the elders disagrees (this, of course, would never be referred to openly), the process of appointing will be put off, sometimes for years. There is seldom, if ever, a formal meeting of the district chief with the elders of a village to discuss the appointment of a new village chief. Once all parties are agreed through informal discussions, however, the appointment is made officially.

The village chief has little formal authority. His role is not to rule the villagers—they rule themselves, through adhering to the customs of their culture, especially the rules governing human relationships. The village chief will rarely, if ever, be called upon to mediate a dispute. Such a dispute—over land or land use—will be taken to a court or to the district officer, a government servant. All the elders may be asked to mediate a dispute over property. The imam, the religious leader, may be asked to intervene in marital disputes. The *bomoh* (medicine man, or shaman) may be asked to arbitrate disputes over customs. And, of course, it is almost a disgrace to get into a dispute in the first place—and a disgrace, or at least an embarrassment (which is the same thing), to both parties.

The village chief is the "face" of the village—the façade it carries to confront the outside. That is why one of the most important qualities of a village chief is the skill of talking. He must be able to speak properly. This means not only that he speak good Malay, but above all that he be fluent in the proper uses of all the phrases, figures of speech, and addresses that are part of the language. He must say what others expect him to say; he must be well-versed in the elaborate double-talk of the cultured Malay. Yet he must know how to communicate when it is necessary—no mean task. The village chief has prestige, but not much more than other elders. He has influence, but not much more than the imam, the *bomoh*, or any of a number of other individuals. He is not expected to display qualities of leadership—no one is. Nor is he expected to influence opinion, even less, action—no one is. In a sense, he is a figurehead, but it would be unthinkable to treat him as such. It would be considered very rude to march into a kampong to do a survey, or to administer to the sick, or to talk to any of the villagers, without first stating one's business to the village chief. He will be most gracious, invite one to his village, offer his support. But it should be understood that his support is a formal phrase; he cannot guarantee the cooperation of the villagers.

The role and function of the village chief is but one example of the informal but traditional nature of the structure of Malay society. It is a society that provides remarkably few restraints—or rewards—for its inhabitants. Any individual is free to believe what he wants, to act as he wants. The only restriction, and it is a severe one, is that never is one individual to embarrass another. To act aggressively is embarrassing, but it is equally embarrassing to act in such a way that one forces another to be aggressive! The nature of this restraint, however, is cultural rather than social. It is not society, through any channels of authority or law, that enforces good behavior: It is the culture as a whole—the value of being a Malay. The only punishment is ostracism, the only reward is being accepted.

It is perhaps not surprising that in this culture Western medicine and modern medical practices have been accepted in unlikely ways. Malay culture certainly allows for change, for introduction of new practices. It has incorporated many new practices and customs in the past and continues to do so today. However, these new practices must be introduced gently, softly, gradually. And it is the new practices per se that are incorporated, not a new way of looking at things or organizing facts. In the cupboard of cultural bric-a-brac, new customs can always be fitted in, but the system does not allow for the rearrangement of the shelves.

Malays' concepts of disease, treatment, and life and death are as varied as their culture. Disease is caused by bad spirits—and the spirits are bad either because one has not properly propitiated them or because some evil person has manipulated them. But disease is also caused by wind (perhaps a Chinese concept?), and by bad living: If one is not *halus*, it is possible to become violently ill. Disease is also given by God, either as punishment or as a test.

The treatment of disease is, of course, related to these varying concepts of cause: A disease caused by spirits must be treated by manipulating these spirits. Or a disease may be treated by internal or external application of herbs. Or a disease must be suffered. It is not at all unusual to find Malays who treat a disease with all these methods at once. A *bomoh* may be called to exorcise the spirits, but he will, for good measure, prescribe herbs too. He may even use modern Western drugs if he is a modern *bomoh*. If any or all of these treatments fail, it is obviously the will of God, and the patient and those around him must accept this fact.

Hence, it is not surprising that some modern medical practices are readily acceptable. Almost everybody now knows that aspirin brings down a fever and that quinine helps alleviate an attack of malaria (although most people also know that chloroquine is better because it actually cures the disease). Most, too, know or have heard that injections cure yaws and know and accept that certain pills give a mother back her strength after delivery. Today in Malaya, the Malays will readily accept modern drugs, and they know the efficacy of injections. They will consult a doctor (either after having consulted a *bomoh* or at the same time) when they expect the doctor to prescribe pills or injections. They have not accepted surgery, however, saying that it is an injunction from the Koran not to cut or in any way mutilate the body. Their real fear, notwithstanding, seems to be not of the cutting itself but rather of part of the body being removed.

Very generally, the Malays have accepted government-trained midwives, yet rarely to the exclusion of kampong-trained ones. It is recognized that the former may be more skilled than the latter, but, nevertheless, there is seldom an attempt to substitute one for the other.

During a recent outbreak of paracholera, the chief of a village assured me that all the people had had immunizations. A brief investigation showed that perhaps two-thirds of the villagers had indeed been immunized, some of them because they believed in the efficacy of this procedure, most of them because the immunizations were given free. The ones who were not immunized all gave reasons: They were busy at the time, they were asleep when the truck came to the village, they forgot about it, although they planned to get the injection, and so on. Also in this same village, a large ceremony was staged, beginning with prayers in the mosque and ending with a torchlight parade to scare away the evil spirits. Most houses at this time sported a charm outside the main entrance to remind the cholera spirits that the necessary precautionary steps had already been performed. Almost *all* villagers, too, expressed the conviction that cholera was certainly a scourge from God Himself, and that there was little one could do to guard against it.

This, I believe, is an essential element of the Malay attitude toward Western medicine: If a procedure can be fitted into the conglomeration of existing facts, customs, practices, and beliefs, it is accepted—but on a footing of equality with previously held beliefs. The pills and potions handed out by a Western clinic do not *replace* native herbs or traditional medical practices. On the contrary, they are included in the repertoire of the *bomoh*.

POINTS OF FRICTION

Westerners often seem dogmatic to the Malays for this reason: To us a thing is, at least theoretically, either true or false. If it is false, we reject it completely; if it is true, we accept it completely. This, to the Malays, is a very strange, almost unnatural way of thinking. One old man told me when we were discussing this: "Truth cannot be held in the hand—it is something you may see, or rather, guess at—but do not touch it, or put it into words, because it will evaporate." There are two words in Malay that mean truth: *kebenaran*, which contains the root *benar*, meaning real or authentic but also correct; and *hakekat*, an Arabic word having the connotation of essence but also nature. Both words also are used for justice. There is no word for *truth*, however, that has an opposite *falsehood*.

In view of this orientation to reality as something to be circumscribed at best, never pinned down—a point of view that also makes it difficult to accept any kind of manipulation of the external world—it is interesting to examine again the incidents occurring in the village during the cholera epidemic. The inoculation campaign was, of course, preventive, as were the prayers and charms. But it was clear from the number of preventive measures taken that no one believed very much in the efficacy of any of these measures. I am convinced that the people who had availed themselves of three kinds of prevention did not feel any safer than those who had only taken out one kind of insurance—nor did they necessarily feel any safer than those who had not done anything at all.

The radio and newspapers at that time stressed not only the importance of getting "jab-injects," but also cautioned against eating raw vegetables or drinking unboiled water. During this period, the cooking and eating habits of Malays in the village did not change: They still used unboiled water at times (although they might use boiled water if it was convenient to do so).

The Chinese, on the other hand, seemed to take precautionary measures more seriously—because they "believed." It was the Chinese who clamored for mass inoculations and who apparently religiously boiled all their water. It was the Chinese, too, who said frequently: "I do not have to worry any more, I have had my injection." The Chinese took the advice of the government because they believed in the efficacy of these Western medical measures—the Malays availed themselves of the inoculations (when they were brought to their doorsteps) because authority said they should. Since a sufficient number of individuals went along with what the government said, everybody acted properly—no feelings were hurt, no one was embarrassed.

The government medical service was satisfied because millions of cholera inoculations were dispensed. They were especially satisfied because the Chinese appeared to accept not only the inoculations but the idea behind the preventive measures provided by modern medical science. The Malays, on the other hand, although they accepted the inoculations readily enough (free, and delivered to the villages), did not seem to want to substitute Western preventive measures for their own, nor did they seem particularly impressed with the efficacy of this new method.

There are other indications that the Malays may accept new methods but do not seem inclined to make a choice between the old and the new. The government is providing excellent training for midwives, yet it is doubtful that these government-trained midwives are at present replacing traditional midwives, perhaps euphemistically referred to as kampong-trained. Government-trained midwives are accepted, their training is appreciated, but the attitude of many women seems to be that this is no reason to prefer them over other midwives. Partly, perhaps, because to choose might embarrass, partly also because it is a very basic value of Malay culture to accept almost anything without attempting to favor one thing or another, because that would destroy the delicate harmony of the whole.

The government also has started a very ambitious program of providing rural health clinics; these are well staffed and well equipped, yet not always fully utilized. In one village, a number of women told me that they no longer went to the clinic, because the nurses talk roughly.

ANOTHER PERSPECTIVE

It is, of course, not unusual for people to make medical decisions on nonmedical grounds. We might also choose a physician for his bedside manner, and, if he would talk roughly, we might very well consider finding another doctor. Yet there seems to be a difference. We may stop going to a certain doctor because he talks roughly, but more than likely we would immediately try to find another whom we considered at least as well qualified medically. We would not go without a doctor altogether. The alternative to these Malay women, however, was not to go to any clinic at all.

Such behavior seems to us, and to Western-trained Malayans, hopelessly illogical. Nevertheless, it is perfectly logical, of course, in the context of another culture. The idea of gentle harmony binding together often incomprehensible or even contradictory facts, as it underlies Malay culture, is apparently a very workable one. It means that individuals may well have an open mind, may try and use new techniques, but it also means that we should be very careful not to substitute one for another.

At one time, I thought that there might be a pattern to the preference of Malay women in using the services of a kampong-trained midwife, a government-trained midwife, or, in the city, even the maternity hospital. There seemed to be a large number of women who had had their first child in the hospital, if they lived in the city—until it was learned that delivery of a first child was free, the delivery of subsequent children had to be paid for in the hospital. I thought that perhaps there was a predominance of women in the rural areas who had had their first delivery assisted by a kampong-trained midwife, but subsequent deliveries with the help of a government-trained midwife—until I found that the government-trained midwife had only recently arrived in the village and had not been available earlier. A survey of recent deliveries when women could make a choice showed that no choice was actually made. In fact, the determining factor seemed to be whether the kampong-trained or the government-trained midwife discovered the pregnancy first. The mother had no preference, or, at least, was careful not to express any preference.

This seemingly uncritical acceptance of anything new, provided it can be incorporated on an equal footing with the old, is typical of contemporary Malay culture, and probably has been typical of Malay culture in the past. Perhaps this is why the Malays today seem to have accepted Western medical practices—as they have accepted Chinese medicinal herbs, and Indian Ayur-Vedic medical practices—without having accepted Western *medicine*. They have accepted the technology but not the ideas behind it.

Another illustration of this is the Malays' attitude toward hospitals and hospitalization. The importance of hospitals has been very difficult to communicate. The idea of a hospital as a preferred place of treatment is foreign to the Malays, as it is foreign to many peoples. In Malay attitudes toward disease and treatment, there is no precedent for this kind of isolation. All health statistics show that even if one controls for proximity of hospitals, distribution of population, and availability of other medical facilities, the percentage of Malays admitted to hospitals, on either an in-patient or an out-patient basis, is significantly less than comparable percentages for the other population groups.

The assumptions underlying the establishment of hospitals are ideas, and, as such, more difficult, if not impossible, to incorporate in the culture than practices or pills. Unfortunately, these assumptions (ideas) are rarely considered when educating people to the benefits of a better system of medical treatment. The establishment of hospitals is based upon the idea that certain diseases are contagious, and thus patients should be isolated; or that proper care can be given only by properly trained technicians in a properly prepared environment; or that the most efficient treatment proceeds not only from a first diagnosis but from a continuing evaluation of the patient's state of health, best determined by laboratory tests. These assumptions or theories form the very basis of Western medicine.

CONCLUSIONS

For really good medical services to be established anywhere, it is necessary to acquaint the people not only with more modern tools, more efficient techniques, but with a new and acceptable way of thinking about disease, about causation of disease, about treatment of disease.

To the Malay, however, there is no need to assume a single theory to explain the causality of disease—disease, like any other phenomenon of the natural world, is many-faceted and essentially incomprehensible, in the sense that no single theory will cover all known facts perfectly. Where we are satisfied with a theory and accept a number of exceptions to the rules we make in accordance with that theory (until we adopt a new theory), the Malay is satisfied in regarding *all* the facts without the need for any sort of theory to explain all, or even many, of these facts.

Doubtless it is not accidental that there are very few Malay doctors and nurses, since to become a good Western-trained doctor or nurse requires the relinquishing of a basic cultural orientation and the acceptance of *one* explanation of existing facts. Surely it is rather *kasar* to put oneself so squarely in one immutable position, and it is certainly *kasar* to assume a position of opposition or disagreement with any and all of the many other positions others may choose to assume.

It would seem, then, that the introduction of Western medical services to the Malays is difficult not just because there is a conflict of cultures—it is perhaps doubly difficult because the elements of our Western medical subculture are bound together in a meaningful, causal, logical sequence, whereas Malay culture does not recognize any such kind of order, except the order he perceives in the world around him, an order that is the harmony between not necessarily related phenomena.

The conflict between the culture of the Malays and the culture of modern medicine—or, modern medicine as one facet of Western culture—exists under the surface only, where ideas and values underlying the cultures seem incompatible; the fruits of modern medicine, the pills and potions and even injections, are freely accepted. Perhaps this is not an exception, but rather the rule in the world today. Few people in the world will reject nylon, automobiles, antibiotics, and Coca-Cola—but many reject the principles of Western government, production and consumption, medical science, principles that have made possible the development of these "miraculous" fruits of our Western civilization.

It is easy to enjoy the fruits of an alien civilization, but very difficult to change one's own civilization to produce similar fruits. Perhaps the Malays will demonstrate the possibility of the Malayanization of Western cultural elements, rather than the Westernization of Malay culture.

It may well be that Malay society is fortunate in having a culture that can absorb elements of foreign cultures so relatively painlessly. As one village chief told me, "One should never fight progress: the fighting may kill you, as progress may kill you; we accept anything, and then find that it does not change our lives much after all."

10

WESTERN CULTURE AND THE THAI WAY OF LIFE*

MICHAEL MOERMAN

The impact of the West is a subject often painted on a broad canvas. Industrialization, colonialism, nationalism, Marxism have exploded through the world and shaken it, have given to all in common the issues that divide us. In this essay, I do not propose to review the insights of political philosophers and universal historians like Northrop and Toynbee who have observed the great sweep of these forces with which the West has changed Asia and changed itself. Nor do I propose to summarize the work of scholars like James Ingram[1] and Walter Vella,[2] who have recorded the transmission of segments of Western culture to Thailand; my canvas is still smaller than theirs. For the most part, I shall speak not of Thailand, but of one small Thai village. I shall speak not of Westernization, but of specific innovations of Western origin. By looking at my subject through

* Reprinted by permission of the author and the publisher from *Asia*, No. 1 (Spring, 1964), pp. 31–50.
[1] James C. Ingram, *Economic Change in Thailand since 1850* (Stanford, Calif.: Stanford University Press for the Institute of Pacific Relations, 1955).
[2] Walter F. Vella, *The Impact of the West on Government in Thailand* (Berkeley, Calif.: University of California Publications in Political Science, 1955).

the wrong end of the glass, I hope to remind us of some universal qualities of cultural borrowing about which we are all aware, but which we often forget.

Each one of us, especially each of us *farangs*, or Westerners, knows a different Thailand. The elaborate marble beauties of Wat Pho, the social circle of the Gymkhana Club, the hurly-burly of Sankamphaeng, Bangkok's Chinatown, are each, for some of us, the central portal into Thai life. For me, a small village in the isolated northern district of Chiengkham, like the grain of sand which brings forth a pearl, is the core of Thailand. In its houses and humans, its customs and costumes, its fun and its funerals, the village is quite different from anything I have ever known. At home, life is automatic. One sees a face and knows without thought whether to smile or frown, whether to tip one's hat, whether to shake hands. One's public life shapes itself effortlessly. Action follows action, word follows word unconsciously, and so one's energies are left for the few precious things that require learning, creativity, and the deliberate casting of will. In an alien culture, all the familiar cues are gone. Having learned through constant repetition how to open a door, one suddenly discovers it has no knob. Slowly, painfully, albeit with infinite satisfaction, one learns the shape of a new life. Like the Bangkok tourist who runs with relief into the air-conditioned Erawan Hotel, like the expatriate who beams with approval at the Western-dressed cheer-leaders of Chulalongkorn University, I eagerly grasped at anything that appeared familiar. Like every tourist, every merchant, every official, every missionary, every scholar who goes to Thailand, I assumed that anything familiar to me was identical with what it had been when I knew it at home. My experience was limited, my confusion at total novelty great. What could be more natural than to suppose that Thai Coca-Cola or constitutions differed from their American equivalents only in respect to physical location? All of us, both Thai and American, both anthropologist and layman make this error. Past habit, the quest for a comfortable familiarity, the pretense that all men are the same —save that we are a little better than the rest—conspire to make us forget in practice what we assert in theory and know in fact. Human beings live in a world of rich associations. We perceive, we understand, we act only in context. Depending on our training or our faith, we use different words to describe this fact: interaction, configuration, pattern, system, Gestalt, the all, Om. The anthropologist, although he proclaims the integrity and unity of culture, comes upon something borrowed and pretends that it can have been borrowed without change. Constitution equals constitution, as if a dismembered hand were still able to greet and grasp just as it did when on its own arm. Removed from all context, the Thai bottle of Coca-Cola and the American bottle of Coca-Cola are undistinguishable. But removed from all context, they are, by definition, meaningless. Cultures are not like shelves in a supermarket that can be satisfactorily described by taking an inventory of their contents. Bottles of Coca-Cola may look the same, but who in America would think of using one as a religious offering, as it is frequently used in Thailand? The liquid contained therein may be the same, but only in Thailand can a minor official, by drinking it, signal the fact that he is more progressive than the simple villager, who drinks only water, yet less exalted than the district officer, who can afford beer. Elements of culture have meaning only in context. Since no two cultures provide identical contexts, it is unlikely for there to be anywhere a one-to-one correspondence between what is loaned and what is borrowed. The objects, organizations, and ideas that Thailand receives from the West must be modified if they are to enter and sustain the Thai way of life. Numerous foreign advisers are now concerned with Thailand's use of Western culture. They, together with many Thais, often complain that only the form and not the substance of modern customs are borrowed. Some go so far as to suppose that the Thais deliberately corrupt our democracy, transport systems, or bureaucratic procedures. In terms of the analysis I have suggested, such a supposition has little meaning. Things borrowed, whether Europe's Christianity or New York's pizza, are all, of necessity, different in form and substance from the original idea on which they are based. Borrowed traits are universally transformed. This need not preclude us from ever deciding which version of a trait is, in some sense, better. But it should remind us that it is wrong to suppose that the original form is always the best one. When Thailand adapts to its own way of life, our needles and tractors, boy scouts and nationalism, it is childish for us to mutter continually, "No, no, that's not the way to do it." In the evolution of culture, in mankind's common history of creation and borrowing, the inventor holds no patent. We would think it absurd were the Chinese, who invented spaghetti, to insist that Italians eat it with chopsticks. It is scarcely less absurd for us to criticize gratuitously Thai constitutionalism.

The process by which Western customs are altered to fit the Thai way of life should be a source of knowledge, not of complaint. The ways in which Western culture is refined and reinterpreted, adapted and set in novel contexts can tell us about Thailand. Identifiable borrowed elements, by their very transformation, can help us delineate Thai culture and society in much the same way as radioactive isotopes help the physiologist to analyze the organic systems into which he introduces them.

In doing this, we must be careful lest pride make us magnify the West's contribution to the Thai way of life. Thailand has long been a civilization and, as such, a member of world culture; things from the West are no less assimilable to her than was Ceylonese religion or Khmer statecraft. Industrialization is no longer any more purely Western than Christianity is Middle Eastern. One understands the Thai way of life not by the fractional distillation of its components but rather by trying to comprehend the peculiarly Thai way in which they are fitted together.

The remainder of this essay concerns the ways in which items from the West have taken on new meanings in Chiengkham. By describing this cultural confrontation, I hope to suggest some of the main forces which bend borrowed traits, and, by doing so, to demonstrate that the Thai way of life is not a passive receptacle for Western culture.

For about a year and a half, my wife and I lived in a small village in the

District, or *Amphur*, of Chiengkham.[3] The district is an isolated one, with no running water, no electricity, no paved road. During the rainy season, only a single strand of telegraph wire or an unusually strong impulse to travel connects Chiengkham with the rest of Thailand. In the villages, it is rare for anyone to receive mail. Not until 1960 did anyone own a radio in our village. The older villagers are aware only vaguely of the Thai nation; they know still less of any Western country. When we left, one old man, with whom we had often exchanged visits, still thought that I came not from *Amelika*, of which he had never heard, but, rather, from *Lanka*, or Ceylon, of the Buddhist scriptures. These things indicate how well insulated Chiengkham and its villages are from the forces of modernization. This makes it easier to keep track of Western elements. Moreover, it permits me to speak of Westernization as an ongoing process that has not yet been accomplished. Borrowed traits do not strike everyone suddenly and uniformly like a sudden shower. Instead, they flow through a social structure to reach first some persons and places and then others. In Chiengkham, few Western ways have permeated the society so thoroughly that one can no longer trace their route.

I shall first consider some objects of Chiengkham's material culture which are imported or copies from the West. Then I shall turn to a program of community development in order to contrast Western ideology with local practice. Finally, I shall discuss the paradox of European public education, which, in ways peculiarly Thai, has made Thailand more Western. In these three areas—material, social, and intellectual—we shall see a constant dialogue between Western culture and the Thai way of life.

In the village where we lived, there was one shop kept by a Chinese. Nearby it was the house of a young man whose wife, in addition to being a seamstress, kept a few goods for sale. Among the Western-style goods always in these tiny stores were paper packets of cigarettes, made in Thailand but modeled on our own, and cans of sweetened condensed milk imported from Holland or Denmark. It is safe to say that every village household from time to time bought one or the other of these goods. It is equally safe to say that hardly any household ever consumed them. Like disks of wax, sticks of incense, and cheap notebooks, cigarettes and condensed milk are bought by villagers solely for religious purposes. Tied to miniature trees, presented on trays, consumed at the Buddhist temple or by its clergy, these goods are the material expression of village piety. To the American who thinks of canned milk as food for contented babies and of cigarettes as a cause of cancer, the religious nature of these goods must seem somewhat bizarre. This peculiar use of Western culture can help us to delineate major social processes in the Thai way of life. One cannot live long in this village without being impressed by the ceaseless

[3] Amphur Chiengkham is in the Province of Chiengrai. For the opportunity of living there, I am pleased to be able to thank the Foreign Area Training Fellowship of the Ford Foundation.

movement of minor economic goods. Fish, sweetmeats, curries, vegetables, and fruits are forever being given by one household to another. These goods express the intimate reciprocity that ties kinsman to kinsman, neighbor to neighbor. When we came to the village, we began to participate in this exchange of gifts. We soon discovered that some of the things we gave caused surprise, embarrassment, and, as our friends became less shy, frank criticism. For we made the mistake of giving too lightly goods that clearly had been bought for cash. Such gifts should have been restricted to special occasions, to close relatives, and to the temple. Offerings to the clergy are not the currency of quotidian exchange. An especially tasty curry, a carefully contrived paper decoration, an unusually elaborate sample of weaving—these go to the temple and only to the temple. In such a relatively self-sufficient village economy, all purchased goods, like cigarettes and canned milk, are similarly special. They are reserved not for the casual reciprocity of one's fellows but for the far greater reward of religious merit. In addition, cigarettes and condensed milk are inexpensive enough for all to afford. This recommends them as offerings in a community where all are devout supporters of the temple. In an isolated community, such cheap and commonplace items can become part of the currency of sacred life. Elsewhere, where cash and Western goods are more commonplace, other items—shampoo or kerosene lanterns—fall into the category of things that are special yet still within the reach of most. Such goods, I suggest, will be restricted almost completely to sacred usages. Cigarettes and condensed milk are, of course, especially appropriate. They permit the devout to offer their revered priests the maximum comfort that religious restrictions permit. Although prestigious and comforting luxuries, cigarettes and sweet milk do not violate the priestly precepts against durable wealth and intoxicants.

The analysis is tentative and may not prove correct in detail. The point remains, however, that Western material traits have been bent to conform to Thai culture. The foreign observer would be mistaken if he were to allow the presence of paper cigarettes and condensed milk to lead him to assume that their use is the same as in the West. Furthermore, the ways in which these simple goods have been reinterpreted alert the observer to the fundamental reciprocity of Thai social life and to the place of reciprocity in the economies of village Buddhism.

Another of Chiengkham's Western artifacts seems more basic to modernization. Village sanitation is an essential part of public health and welfare. In recent years the Chiengkham district officer[4] has, unsuccessfully, ordered village households to build cement toilets. We all know that this innovation would help to control disease and to provide a more pleasant place to live. But when cultural contexts differ, we cannot blithely assume that an innovation is accepted or rejected for the same reason that motivated its discovery.

[4] In Thailand, each province is administered by a governor, and each district by a district officer (*Nai Amphur*). Both are professional civil servants appointed by the Ministry of the Interior in Bangkok.

At large meetings and small, the district officer rarely fails to urge villagers to build toilets. The reasons he gives them are quite straightforward.
First, he explains that the Ministry has told the provincial governor to tell
the district officers to tell the common villagers that it wants them to build
toilets. Secondly, toilets are desirable to impress any high-ranking officials
who might come to inspect the district. The villagers are therefore directed to build their first toilets near the road where they can be seen and
used by such officials. Thirdly, toilets are part of the vague value of
"progress," or *khwamjarern*, which, while never defined, is a major item
in the vocabulary and the goals of officials. The fourth of the district officer's reasons is related, somewhat pathetically, to this value of "progress."
Taking advantage of my presence, the district officer sometimes pointed
out that I and all other *farangs* would laugh at the villagers and at Thailand if there were no toilets. The district officer has read of the West but
never seen it, has been exposed to Western ideas and persons without ever
really coming to know them. Thus, he has begun to judge himself and his
nation as he supposes that Westerners would judge them.

As might be expected, the arguments that the district officer finds so
compelling have little meaning to the villagers. Although they do not dislike the district officer, they are unwilling to go to so much trouble solely
to earn him the approval of his superiors. Not themselves having had the
mixed advantages of modern education, Western customs are not their
touchstone of excellence. The only villager who seemed willing to build a
toilet was the ambitious headman, to whom official favor is so important.
The rest of the villagers, at the rare times when they discussed the innovation, rejected it for reasons that make more sense to Western ears than
do the district officer's reasons for accepting it. According to an articulate
villager, "A proper cement toilet costs too much for any single household
to afford. If households were to cooperate in building one, they would soon
dispute its ownership and maintenance. The only toilets that we villagers
can afford are simple earthen pits, which are far more dirty and unpleasant
than the forest where we now relieve ourselves. Toilets may be required in
densely populated urban areas, but here there are ample forests and the
rainfall is abundant."

This brief description illustrates some principles by which Western culture is adapted to the Thai way of life. First, innovations are often accepted not for the reasons of pragmatic utility for which we suggest them
but, rather, in order to emulate persons of superior status and so gain
their approval. In more general terms, we see that people adjust their
behavior to conform to the expectations of those who are significant to
them. The higher officials who are a reference group[5] for the district officer are not significant to the villager. Peasants and officials do not have the

---

[5] I use this term as a layman in order to suggest but not participate in the technical
vocabulary of Robert K. Merton and those social scientists who follow his careful
definitions of "reference group."

same understanding of Western material culture, nor do they adopt it for the same reasons. Each interprets Western culture in a manner that accords to his position within the Thai social structure. We must understand that structure if we are to understand the impact of the West.

The last Western material artifact that I shall discuss has changed Chiengkham far more than cigarettes, condensed milk, or cement toilets have. Knowledge of local social structure can help us to understand some of those changes.

Thirty years ago there was not a single wheeled vehicle in Chiengkham. Today, most of its fields are plowed by hired tractors. This dramatic new device was introduced in 1953 by an enterprising businessman from a northern city. Hiring tractors has made it possible to farm a huge tract of land that flooded too rapidly for transplanted rice to escape drowning. With tractor technology, fields can be plowed and dry seed broadcast well before the rainy season. This early rice can keep pace with the rising water. Chiengkham farmers are now able to cultivate 6,000 acres of new land, thereby vastly increasing their production and their cash incomes. These consequences can be understood without much reference to the pre-existing peculiarities of village life. But other results of the introduction of the tractor are intelligible only in terms of local social organization, especially the patterns of residence. In the old days, village-extended families lived together in longhouses that sometimes included five or even seven married couples. All worked together on the longhouse fields, the rice of which fed them. The longhouse and its elders provided for the subsistence needs of its young couples who were thus able, and expected, to buy or clear new lands of their own. These lands produced the "private rice" that would someday provide a couple with the means to found its own household. It took a long time to amass this property. Couples were often unable to leave their parental home until they were middle-aged and their children married. The discovery of the great flood plain was made by young villagers who abortively tried to practice traditional farming on it in order to develop their "private rice" land. The techniques of machine agriculture, which they learned from the tractor owner, permitted them to farm plots much larger than those to which the limitations of human labor had previously confined them. Now, young men, even before they are wed, own significant amounts of tractor-tilled land. As soon as they marry, they are able to build homes of their own. The introduction of the tractor has made for far more and far younger independent households than there ever were before. A second social consequence arises from the first. In all communities, there is probably some conflict of interest between the young and old. In a village that has recently been presented with large numbers of thrilling new stimuli, it would certainly not be surprising to find friction and estrangement between the generations. Only men younger than thirty-five have worked as soldiers or teachers for the national government. Only women younger than thirty have gone to school; only girls younger than twenty have grown up to regard a milling machine as a normal convenience of daily life. In their dress, dialect, deportment, and dreams the young are devoted to things that their elders never knew. There is no evidence, however, that acerbity between the generations is any greater than it ever was. For advice and support, the young still seek their elders. To settle their disputes, they eagerly apply the ancient standards and procedures. For fantasy and romance, they prefer tales of the old days to stories of urban life. At the up-to-date weddings and housewarmings of the modish young, aged guests are vied for. It is hard to believe that the new prosperity of the tractor-tilled fields is irrelevant to this tranquil continuity. When they develop their own fields and, soon after marriage, establish their own households, the young men of the village are aided by their parents. Yet a youth's fashionable luxuries—wrist watch, white shirt, tight-fitting trousers, fountain pen—are provided by money from his own field and not from the grudging generosity of elders, who consider them foolish extravagances. Between young and old there are now greater differences of experience than ever before in the village's history. But because young families can now live alone, because they are helped by parents yet not dependent upon them, guided by parents yet not under their direct control, the young can revere the ways of their elders and need react neither with reluctant obedience nor with destructive rebellion. A dramatic change from the West has modified the rule of residence and thereby helped to preserve the far more basic tradition of affection and respect for elders.

In discussing material culture, I have shown how Western artifacts can help us analyze Thai behavior. I have then indicated that peasants and officials, because dissimilar persons are important to them, do not have the same understanding of objects that seem to us solely utilitarian. Finally, we have seen how social organization conditions the consequences of a technological change. These principles, somewhat refined, also emerge from an example of how Western social culture is modified to suit the Thai way of life.

To those who are concerned with the nonindustrialized world, there are few ideas more exciting than community development. Community development differs somewhat from country to country. Nevertheless, all of its theorists—in America, in the United Nations, in Bangkok—agree that it is essentially a program to meet the total needs of a local community. It is a program of self-help, in which the government provides some guidance, support, and technical assistance to aid villagers in fulfilling their own felt needs. To quote from the Ministry of the Interior, "The national community development program of Thailand . . . aims to encourage the people to exercise initiative to improve their communities and way of life through cooperative efforts on a self-help basis."[6] To allow villagers to express their needs and to encourage their initiative, the Ministry, at the

[6] The quotation is from a typescript copy of the official "Community Development Program for Thailand" kindly furnished me by Dr. Jasper C. Ingersoll, upon whose analysis of community development in Thailand (in a lecture delivered in 1962 to the second group of Peace Corps trainees for Thailand at the University of Michigan) I have leaned heavily.

suggestion of a United Nations adviser, sponsored meetings in each district. I should like to describe the community development meeting in Chiengkham.

Each month, village headmen assemble to be addressed by the district officer. The meeting of November 20, 1960, was extremely elaborate. Headmen had been told to arrive in uniform at 8:30 in the morning, so that they would have time to rehearse their welcome to the provincial governor, who was expected at 10:00. The district's schoolteachers had made a huge banner bearing the legend, "Meeting for the Primary Demonstration of Community Development. First Time: 2503 B.E. Amphur Chiengkham." This was the first indication the headmen were given that the meeting concerned community development. On the stage that the district officer and other high officials would occupy were a microphone, a phonograph, a Buddha-altar, and some placards in Thai, and some in English, illustrating poverty, ignorance, malnutrition, and disease. Although the governor never arrived, these stage properties showed the solemnity and importance of the meeting.

The district officer read for over an hour from a mimeographed address sent him by a superior official in charge of community development. He emphasized and added to the parts of the address that interested him the most. Thus, for example, he quickly read through the qualities of good local leaders of community development and stressed the need for getting rid of bad ones. He spent little time on the need to foster expressions of local opinion, but he elaborated upon the elimination of gambling, repairing roads, keeping villages orderly, and, of course, building toilets. He announced which village had been chosen for development and ordered its headman to make sure that these things were done by the time that a community development official arrived from the provincial capital next year.

Throughout his assigned address, the district officer managed to communicate his faintly puzzled amusement at each reference to the need for community initiative. At one point in his talk, he contrasted the villagers' old attitude of respectful fear toward the officials with the desired new spirit of intimate friendship between them. Here the district officer and his audience burst into laughter, no longer able to contain their amusement at such strange ideas. After lunch, the meeting reconvened for the formation of small discussion groups of teachers and headmen. Each group was to select one of five major problems for community development, discuss it, and report back to the entire meeting. For the most part, only the teachers were active in these groups. The headmen and other villagers sat quietly and spoke only when put a direct question. When a show of hands was called for, they first looked to see how the others were voting, perhaps saying as they raised their hands, "Let's do what the majority wants." The public reports given by the teacher-spokesman after the discussions were recapitulations of the speeches made earlier by the district officer and other officials. At the end of the meeting, the district officer announced that all in attendance had been chosen as local leaders of community development and, as such, would be required to give a voluntary contribution of 30 *baht* to the Red Cross.

Clearly, this meeting for "Primary Demonstration . . . in Amphur Chiengkham" was quite inconsistent with the philosophy of self-help and local initiative. The rehearsal for the governor, who did not appear, the failure to announce the purpose of the meeting, the labor exacted from the teachers, the incomprehensible signs in English, the air of authoritarianism, the emphasis on command, punishment, and conscription all set a tone diametrically opposed to the abstract rules for community development. By dramatizing this contrast, I do not wish to imply either that the rules are misguided or the practice corrupt. Rather, I wish to show how Western ideas become altered as they filter through the layers of which Thai society is made up. When Bangkok officials express the high ideals of self-help and local leadership, they are quite sincere. They understand these Western ideals and have come to value them. They consider village poverty and low productivity to be a major national problem. They regard it as the task of the government to increase village welfare. They wish to accomplish this task through the intimate cooperation of officials and villagers acting as equals. To the people of Chiengkham, on the other hand, whether peasants or civil servants, these ideas are all but unintelligible. Primary principles of Thai society, as they have experienced it, preclude them from understanding and achieving the ideals of community development.

The people of Chiengkham do not share the Bangkok official's view of the role of the state. The government of Thailand has never been oppressive. But it has traditionally considered the maintenance of peace and order to be its sole responsibility. Positive action to increase local welfare and prosperity has always rested with the local community and its individual households. Only slowly, and in obedience to their superiors, have Thai officials taken a more active view of the government's role. It was not until 1874 that the king promulgated "the first assertion in Thailand that the primary responsibility of the government was to the people."[7] After this, the government gradually began programs to build railroads, staff schools, and spread agricultural knowledge. Inspired by the West, the idea that the government serves its people spread slowly down the hierarchy. It has yet to reach most Thais. In Thailand, administration is highly centralized. The nation is divided into about seventy provinces, which, in turn, are each composed of five or ten *amphur*. The district officer is in charge of all government activities in his *amphur*. His responsibilities are vast; his staff quite small. Local administration is thus limited in practice to what it once was in theory: regulation and control. Most older district-level officials still think of these as their sole functions. Their view of the state's role is less Western than that of their Bangkok superiors, who now demand dedication to local welfare and prosperity.

It would be unfair, however, to suggest that district officials, as individuals, are uninterested in the well-being of villagers. Ideally, the official should care for the peasant as a parent cares for his child. Everyone in

[7] Vella, *op. cit.*, p. 339.

Chiengkham agrees that the official is wiser, wealthier, and more powerful than the villager, whom it is thus his duty to guide and protect. To the people of Chiengkham, it is no less absurd for officials to respond to the "felt needs" of villagers than it would be for a parent to request his infant child's advice on how he would like to be raised. Hierarchic relations are at the heart of Thai society. Younger-elder, child-parent, pupil-teacher, layman-priest, peasant-official—bonds between inferior and superior compose the family, the village, and the nation. In return for the service and respect of his subordinate, the superior gives protection and leadership. In none of these relationships is there any provision for the inferior to challenge the wisdom of his superior, to express ideas of which his superior might disapprove, to provide direction to his superior's actions. All initiative comes from above. The exchange of leadership for dependence, of protection for support, of authority for respect is the very stuff of social life. It is also, of course, inconsistent with the Western rules for community development.

The "Meeting for Primary Demonstration in Amphur Chiengkham" showed us how the paternalistic inequality of the Thai way of life bent the Western ideals of community development. Earlier, when discussing village sanitation, I suggested that there is a dichotomy between peasant and official views of the West. We can now see that I oversimplified. The amount and kind of a person's education, the size and sophistication of the community in which he lives, age, sex, social position, and career history all exert major influences on the understanding and sympathy that a Thai has toward Western culture. The impact of the West reverberates through Thai society and is thereby made complex. The very source of this complexity, however, helps us to understand why Thailand seems so receptive to things Western. Thailand has never been a European colony. An alien culture was never imposed upon it. Instead, native leaders have often had a free choice of things Western. The items chosen reach the district and the village only after passing through a *native* hierarchy. In Thailand, Western culture is thus rarely rejected or even recognized as foreign.

The people of Chiengkham will accept radios, neckties, and, ultimately perhaps, even the spirit of community development in order to emulate their leaders. Community development in Chiengkham will represent not grass-roots democracy, but rather the age-old bond of mutual regard between superior and inferior. Like the items of Western material culture, it will become part of the Thai way of life.

Because they have never been colonized, the people of Thailand can learn the Western components of this way of life by watching their own movies, emulating their own elite, buying from their own businessmen. Nothing, however, provides such a major route for Westernization as does the public-school system, which has given new, and Western, meanings to the Thai nation and its culture.

Like cigarettes, tractors, and community development, public education was from its very inception a conscious import from the West.[8] The first

[8] This discussion of the history of public education is based on M. L. Manich Jumsai's excellent UNESCO study, *Compulsory Education in Thailand*, Bangkok, 1958.

secular schools were founded by Christian missionaries in the second half
of the nineteenth century. In 1871, during the Fifth Reign, the king established a palace school for the sons of officials. By 1885, Prince Damrong,
one of the most brilliant men in Thai history and in the history of any
country, had helped the king to establish a number of then still feeble
government schools. In 1898, the ambassador to Great Britain, at the king's
command, submitted a report on the English educational system. This
report, together with a study of Japanese schools made in 1902, became the
model for public education in Thailand. In 1921, public education became
compulsory, although not until 1935 was the law enforced throughout the
nation. Thai government participation in education was stimulated by
Western missionaries, explicitly based on Western models, and consistently
influenced by Western, especially British, advisers.

Moreover, the government's purposes in establishing public education
were Western ones. The Palace School was founded in 1871 in order to
train a generation of officials in the technical skills of administration demanded by Thailand's new relations with Western powers who possessed
those skills. The English language soon became part of the curriculum.
The king sponsored the education of Thais at home and abroad, so that
they might learn Western techniques of government, technology, and
science. Among those so trained were members of the revolutionary group
that overthrew the absolute monarchy in 1932. Their new constitution followed Western political theory by announcing that Western-style representative government would be instituted once half the population was
literate. The source and the goals of Thai public education are Western.
This seems to create a paradox, for in its purpose and consequence, its
organization and content, public education is a major basis for Thai nationalism and for Thai national consciousness. But the paradox comes full
circle. It is precisely these nativistic ideas that are the West's greatest impact on the Thai way of life.

In what follows, I shall indicate how educational administration supports Thai unity and examine national consciousness as taught in the
classroom. This then will permit us to evaluate the West's contribution to
the national culture that is now emerging from both the content and the
organization of Thai public education.

There are few nations whose public school systems are as centralized as
Thailand's. All its teachers are employees of the nation. Each wears the
khaki uniform required of all officials. His status is fixed by a civil-service
rank that has a precise equivalent in every other branch of government. A
district officer can, in practice, call upon teachers to perform almost any
government task. Every teacher in every village, no matter how remote, is
under the authority of the national Ministry of Education. Salaries, pro-
motions, educational policy, standards of instruction, textbooks, school
budgets, and examinations are all determined in Bangkok. This centraliza-
tion makes for occasional inefficiencies. A prominent Thai educator tells
how a school in an area rich in teak was unable to use wood for needed
construction until its request was forwarded up the hierarchy to reach the

ministry in Bangkok. By the time that permission was granted by the Forest Department eight months later, the original construction budget was no longer valid.[9] Throughout Thailand, village teachers frequently complain that the standards and content of the curriculum are inappropriate to the children whom they teach. Thai public education occasions some local objections as the price of the overwhelming national unity of its organization.

The teacher lives much closer to the farmers than does any other official. His dependence on the state and his commitment to it are far greater than any village headman's. The teacher is thus the ultimate contact between the government that begins in Bangkok and the common people of the most backward reaches of Thailand. In what he teaches, just as in his social position, he encourages the unity of national life.

The teacher's foremost force for unity is his language of instruction. Bangkok Thai, the national dialect, is not everyone's mother tongue. Lao, Southern Thai, Shan, not to mention Chinese and Malay, are spoken in many homes. Today, due largely to the public schools, there is probably nowhere a lowland village so remote that no one understands standard Bangkok Thai. In Chiengkham, teachers describe in amusing detail how, during their first few days at school, pupils are unable to understand even so simple a command as "Come here" unless it is said in Northern dialect or accompanied by gestures. Although teachers are ordered always to use the standard dialect, they find that they can only gradually introduce it as the sole language of instruction. Their efforts bear fruit. After the four required years of primary education, all children can understand and speak standard Thai and are literate in it. Even had they learned nothing else, they are able to follow national radio broadcasts, read the publications of government departments, receive advice from official posters, and otherwise share in the written and spoken expression of national culture.

The seminal symbols and substance of this national culture are also taught in school. Throughout the kingdom, the curriculum is everywhere the same. It emphasizes the history of the Thai nation and the glory of its heroes; it teaches the geography and economy of Thailand. It clearly labels its morality and ethics as those of Thai Buddhism. As civics and government, the pupils are told about the Thai state and of their duty and loyalty to its officials and, above all, to its king. The small sons and daughters of peasants whose world barely reached beyond their village are awakened to the past splendors and future hopes of Thai civilization. Once a year, on Children's Day, the primary-school pupils of Chiengkham entertain the townsmen. At one point, little Lao, Lue, Yuan, and Shan—for these dialect groups compose more than 90 per cent of the district's people—come on stage to sing, "Noi, noi, noi, noi, we are Thai children." It is more than an empty skit. Their parents may have few loyalties beyond the kindred, village, and neighborhood. Those who have been to school know of a great nation and know that they are part of it.

[9] Jumsai, *ibid.*, p. 104.

In Thai primary schools, repetition and memorization are the styles of instruction. This is based perhaps on the Buddhist tradition of reverence for knowledge and also on the scarcity of textbooks and teachers. Walking by a primary school, one hears a score or more voices reciting a lesson. The lessons are standardized throughout the nation. On any given day in the school year one can, with only the slightest strain on his imagination, hear the sound of hundreds of thousands of childish voices chorusing in unison.

The idea, form, and goals of Thai public education came from the West. National consciousness, which the schools teach, is also a Western import. The concept of the Thai people—spilling over into what is now Laos, North Vietnam, southern China, and northern Burma—is an old one. The concept of the Thai nation, of Thailand, is far more recent. We *farangs* have by now grown so accustomed to national boundaries neatly drawn in red on political maps that we forget that the idea of the sovereign nation-state was not born in Europe until after the Middle Ages. The idea came to Southeast Asia only in the nineteenth century.

Colonization or, as in Thailand, its threat made "nations" of what had been impermanent aggregates of disparate peoples. When the British ruled the Shan States from Rangoon, and the French claimed Laos as part of Annam, they froze into permanent orderliness the vague, fluid, and sometimes shifting allegiances that had characterized the native polities. Until European powers began to nibble at their borders, and to annex them, the states of Southeast Asia were, in Lauriston Sharp's memorable image, "small umbrellas under the protection of larger and higher umbrellas which in turn were under those still higher and larger."[10]

To protect itself from Britain and France, Thailand became a nation. By the Sixth Reign, early in this century, Western-educated Thais were promoting the new idea of nationalism—the idea that boundaries enclose not only sovereign power but also a sacred integral ethos different from and superior to all others. The backlash of this Western idea has already brought pain to the English, French, and Dutch in Southeast Asia.

The schools, their nationalism, even the nation itself, may be viewed as imports. There is yet another aspect of the way in which public education has brought Western culture into Thai life. The schools are a basis of national unity because they teach the same lessons to all of Thailand's children and require of all of them the same behavior. All children must wear a uniform consisting of Western shorts and shirt for boys, of Western blouse and skirt for girls. Thai clothing—the *phanung* and *phasin*—is forbidden in school. Girls must wear their hair in Western-style bangs. The traditional cropped hair of central Thailand and the topknot of the north are not permitted. Each day begins with patriotic ceremony—a Western-style salute to the Western-style national flag and perhaps the singing of a national anthem inspired by the West. In class, the children learn about Western science. Arithmetic and even standard European accounting procedure may be taught them. They are taught elements of Western hygiene,

---

[10] Thomas M. Fraser, Jr., *Rusembilan: a Malay Fishing Village in Southern Thailand* (Ithaca, N.Y.: Cornell University Press, 1960), p. viii.

so that gradually well-worn brushes replace the more sanitary disposable twigs that their elders used· for cleaning their teeth. Enterprising teachers instruct them in the care of American chickens and in the use of chemical fertilizers. Progressive teachers even proselyte for the virtues of objectivity and task-determined efficiency, and call them superior to the traditional Thai values of amicable face-to-face relationships and reverence for patron. New techniques, new ideas, new values from the West are the core of the curriculum that unites Thailand.

Buddhism and reverence for the king also bind the nation. But in the schools, the king is revered as a constitutional monarch and Buddhism is pervaded by the social gospel that, many scholars feel, came to it from the West.

Thailand is becoming more homogenous. Its citizens share a national culture that distinguishes them from their numerous close relatives among the Thai peoples of China, Burma, and Indochina. A Thai from Bangkok and his compatriot from Chiengkham now share certain understandings not known to the Shan and the Lao. They share what they have learned in school, what they have learned from the West. Western culture provides the distinctive pattern for the loosely woven fabric of pan-Thai custom and belief. The uniquely national components of Thailand's way of life come from the West.

This essay has progressed from small to large, from simple to complex. I first discussed minor material goods in a single village, then social organization in a district and, finally, an idea that affects the entire Thai nation. With each instance, the West seemed more influential. Cigarettes, toilets, even tractors were transformed by the Thai way of life, while in universal education, Western culture seems to dominate. These differences are not fortuitous, but neither are they objective. They result, I think, from the level of analysis employed. If one concentrates on a specific item, like *the tractor*, the weight of the West seems much slighter than it would were one to speak more generally of *mechanization*. Conversely, a particular textbook of Western pattern obviously alters Thai culture much less than does the general idea of universal education.

The influence of something borrowed seems a function of its generality. Indeed, the most influential traits are so vague and thus so subject to interpretation that it is difficult and perhaps misleading to trace them back to their culture of origin. India, Ligor, Ceylon, Angkor—each could correctly be called the "source" of Thai Buddhism. This pursuit of ultimate origins, although interesting and important, tells us little about the religion of Thailand. In similar fashion, the ideal of universal education is not specific to any nation. It is too basic to all modern societies for us to learn very much from the label "Made in the West." Ideas are great when they are sufficiently general for their borrowers to reinterpret them.

This consideration, like that of cultural context, makes one unwilling to picture, as many do, a dynamic West that is always donor to inert underdeveloped nations. The recipient society is also dynamic. The example of community development showed us that even those Thais who are most Westernized have roles to play in their own society—roles that force them to modify what they have learned abroad. As an artifact, an institution, an idea penetrates further into the prism of Thai society, it bends further from its source. It is also given new color by the native values that influence everyone who participates in Thai society, whatever his private beliefs. Thailand, like all viable societies, has its own structure of roles, its own system of values, its own cultural context that alter all things borrowed. As an anthropologist, I have been able to document this principle of transformation. I hope to have helped refine our knowledge by specific demonstrations of how reciprocity, merit-making, hierarchy, reference groups, and nationalism in the Thai way of life transform Western culture. As an anthropologist, I can do no more.

Nevertheless, I feel that few of us are satisfied with so limited an analysis. As citizens, we want to evaluate technical and financial aid. As friends of Thailand, we would like her to use Western culture successfully. To be used, a cultural borrowing must be transformed. Does this make it impossible to decide which version of a Western trait is best? We recognize that mere proprietorship of Western culture gives us no right to judge its Thai modifications. But cannot our long experience with an institution enable us to evaluate its variant forms? I believe that it can, as long as our standards of evaluation are clear and honest. Consider, for example, the way in which community development was modified in Chiengkham. According to an American conference of social workers, community development consists of "organized efforts to improve the conditions of community life, and the capacity for community integration and self-direction."[11] In other words, Western community development has two goals: self-expression and material well-being. We may feel that Chiengkham's program in 1960 was inconsistent with the goal of enhanced individual self-expression. But this in no way prevents it from accomplishing its other purpose of increased material welfare and national productivity. There are a number of rules that we must use when we judge an institutional variant. First, it is incorrect to maintain that a reinterpreted institution can achieve none of its goals because it fails to achieve one of them. Second, it is unreasonable to insist that another nation assign the same priorities to goals that we do. Third, it would be dishonest to permit our dislike of an institution to make us claim that it cannot work. Chiengkham's version of community development, like de Gaulle's version of the "New Europe," may offend us. This does not make it ineffective. Our reverence for human freedom, for example, provides ample reason for rejecting Chinese-style communes. Unless we have economic evidence, however, it would not be honest to say that communes cannot increase production. The fourth rule I suggest is that we compare an institution with its possible real alternatives and not with an abstract standard of perfection. Thus, for example, the historic role of government and the tradi-

[11] Arthur C. Dunham, "Community Development," *The Social Work Yearbook*, 1960, p. 178.

tion of direction from above limit Chiengkham's understanding of community development. Partial community development is still better than none unless, like the Chinese communes, it violates values more sacred than those it achieves.

My message has been too simple and too tied to data for me to summarize with more than an image. I suggest that if we must speak of the "impact" of the West, we should view it in terms of the blows of a diamond cutter, who may either refine or destroy a gem, depending on his knowledge of its structure. Still better, we should think of how soil transforms the seed, and the seed the soil.

11

PROBLEMS OF MANAGEMENT AND AUTHORITY IN A TRANSITIONAL SOCIETY: A CASE STUDY OF A JAVANESE FACTORY*

ANN RUTH WILLNER

The problems of managerial leadership in a transitional society can be examined in many contexts of organizational activity. The one employed in this article is that of an industrial organization in a primarily preindustrial setting in East Java, Indonesia. For the industrial context brings into sharp focus the dilemmas that confront those who attempt to impose unfamiliar organizational forms and norms on a society reluctant or only partially prepared to accept the behavioral innovations demanded by the new organization.

The leaders of most new nations are ideologically committed to industrialization and to the development of concomitant industrial structures modeled on prototypes in advanced industrial societies. Yet, the introduction of new and complex forms of organization, such as a modern factory, in a traditional agrarian environment frequently sets up tensions between the operational requirements of the organization and the cultural norms and expectations of those members of the local community recruited to

* Reprinted by permission of the author and the publisher from *Human Organization*, XXII (Summer, 1963), 133–41.

fill the organizational roles. Where such organizations were introduced under conditions of colonial domination, their operational goals received first priority. These could be attained, in the last resort, through the application of various forms of coercive control by largely foreign management, whose authority could not easily be brought into question.

Political and social changes in nations that have undergone successful revolutions have altered the staffing patterns of organizations and the socio-cultural determinants of organizational behavior. Most intermediate and many top managerial posts are filled by indigenous personnel. However desirous they may be of securing rank-and-file compliance with organizational needs, their problems are more complex than those of their foreign predecessors. For, unlike the latter, they cannot resort to arbitrary measures in maintaining discipline without arousing strong opposition among their subordinates to tactics now labeled "colonial." They must therefore obtain some degree of consensus.

Successful political nationalism, however, tends to produce dissensus in the sphere of authority. On the one hand, it strengthens the claims of those who have learned to advocate and accept rational and utilitarian bases for decision and action. On the other hand, it is generally accompanied by a cultural nationalism that reinvigorates prescriptions traditionally governing social interaction. Thus, there may be little agreement on such questions as to who has the right to be assigned roles of authority or what are the means by which authority can properly be exercised. Every such issue complicates the possibility of reconciling the impersonal requirements of organizational efficiency with the expectations of those who are part of the organization.

These dichotomies are elaborated in the following description[1] of patterns of authority in a Javanese textile factory during two periods of its history. The first period is that immediately preceding World War II, when the factory, which I here call Pabrika, was owned and largely managed by Europeans. In 1954–55, when I observed its operations, it was Indonesian-owned but managed by a Dutchman. With the exception of three other members of the managerial staff of Chinese ethnic origin, the rest of the managerial and supervisory posts were held by Indonesians.

The factory at this time employed a labor force of 1,000, about half of whom were drawn from predominantly agrarian villages outside the small town in which it is located. A seven-hour workday and rotating shifts enabled many to retain some ties with agriculture. One-fifth of the workers were women and one-fifth were migrants from other areas, some of urban provenience.

[1] This is part of an unpublished study, *From Rice-Field to Factory: The Industrialization of a Rural Labor Force in Java,* based on my field investigations. For support of the study I am indebted to Professor Bert F. Hoselitz and the Research Center in Economic Development and Cultural Change of the University of Chicago. What little knowledge I have of the disciplines of Social Anthropology and Sociology I owe to my sister, Professor Dorothy Willner, who cannot be held responsible for its shortcomings.

Traditional Patterns and the Early Factory System

Of the many aspects of the factory routine, those relating to supervision and the enforcement of regulations and discipline appeared to have undergone the most significant changes between the early period of Pabrika's operations and when I observed them. The picture I derived from the reminiscences of older workers and supervisors suggested that this was the area that had formerly provoked the strongest resentment among the workers. For the new recruit, entry into the factory meant not only the necessity to adapt to a new type and schedule of activities. It also meant exposure to an unfamiliar pattern of interaction with rather alien kinds of people. In the first place, he found himself at the lowest level of a hierarchic order, in which all authority emanated from above and unquestioned and prompt obedience was expected from below.

Neither hierarchy as a mode of organization nor obedience as a duty to status superiors seems strange in itself to the Javanese reared in the traditional social environment. For as a young child he becomes aware of a ranking system within the family and within the larger kinship group. He soon learns the different terms[2] by which he must denote and address his immediate and more distant kin and the behavior appropriate to each with respect to degree of relationship, line of descent, and age. He realizes that within the nuclear family, paternal position is paramount and unquestioned and that he also owes a measure of respect and obedience to elder siblings and is owed the same by younger ones. Later, he discovers the ranking system in the village that distinguishes its families on the basis of hereditary rights to land. And he learns to recognize the primacy of the village head and to accede to his instructions. While his encounters with members of the *prijaji*, or gentry, may be rare, he is nonetheless aware of the deference due them from him by virtue of their superior place in the wider society.[3]

Although stratification is a familiar element in almost every group in which a Javanese participates, the particular hierarchy of the factory differs in several respects from the hierarchal structures he knows. In the first place, the factory hierarchy is organized for a specific goal, that of production, and status within it is primarily determined by appointment theoretically based on abilities relative to this purpose. Traditional social groups may serve a multitude of functions. Status within them, as suggested by the above, is allocated by birth, age, and other ascriptive criteria that do not necessarily relate to the achievement of a particular goal. Leadership roles in the factory are specific to factory activity and may not overlap with the exercise of leadership elsewhere. Those with higher ascribed status in

---

[2] These terms indicate not merely degrees of kinship but differentiate between junior and senior kin of the same degree. There are separate terms for elder brother and younger brother, elder sister and younger sister, and similarly for elder and younger brother of parents.

[3] It could well be said that every encounter between two Javanese involves a mutual recognition in gesture, language, and attitude of relative place in a stratified order.

traditional groups appear to exert generalized leadership for a number of activities. Power conferred by leadership positions in the factory tends to be channeled downward and responsibility upward. In traditional structures, those who hold power through status have concomitant responsibility toward those over whom they exercise it.

SUPERVISION—THE NEW ROLE

Moreover, the factory as a work organization introduces a set of intermediary roles generally unknown in groups organized for work in the traditional village. These roles are those of foreman, supervisor, and other positions intervening between employer and the man who performs the visible physical tasks of labor. The wage worker in the village deals directly with the man who wants work done and pays for it. The farmer hires field workers himself, and he or a member of his family exercises whatever supervision may be necessary. Even when farming takes place on a tenant or sharecropping basis, in which several parties profit from the proceeds, neither serves as a "go-between" between the other and the wage workers. Whoever is the cultivator has full discretion over the employment of laborers and the terms of work and payment until the harvest. When the plot is divided at harvest time, each party to the agreement then hires his own harvesters. Similarly, in small industrial establishments in villages and towns, the proprietor is both the direct employer and serves as his own supervisor. And in most organized work activities, the employer works together with his laborers, so that supervision as a discrete function is indistinct.[4]

The direct and face-to-face contact between employer and worker in these situations results in a work relationship in which the personal element is rarely absent. It allows for the continual possibility of negotiation and adjustment between the parties concerned. It makes possible loans and advances to workers in times of need. Thus, there is no analogue[5] in village work structures for the figure who is just a link in a chain of command, directive but not responsive. He who is neither an owner nor visibly engaged in production but merely passes on orders, with no power to negotiate the terms of their execution, is an anomaly.

Nevertheless, however obscure the functions of those directly above him may have appeared to the new worker in Pabrika's early period, he might not have found it difficult to reconcile himself to taking orders from them. For these superiors were mainly Dutch and Chinese. And in the larger colonial society outside the village, a society in which stratification was

---

[4] Even when he does not share the work, his right in the land or his ownership of the enterprise might be seen as the factor authorizing him to direct it.

[5] Perhaps the nearest analogue to the "intermediate" role is that of the village head in his capacity as recipient of orders from higher governmental levels, to which he is expected to obtain village compliance. In the eyes of the villagers, however, he is the only visible authority, besides being the symbol of the community and its intactness. Directives are not given to him in the village but at meetings with sub-district officials at their offices.

partly based on ethnic origin, these people held high status. In the eyes of the villager, they stood in the same relationship to him as his own gentry, government officials, and similar figures of prestige and authority.

However, while the fact of ethnic dissimilarity might have legitimized these unfamiliar roles, this ethnic difference was accompanied by cultural differences affecting their interpretation. The behavior of those who occupied these positions, behavior offensive to the workers, rendered both them and their roles objectionable. The workers were faced with a group of superiors whose demands could not easily be anticipated, whose responses were startling, and whose very language could often not be understood. Even the most submissively anxious worker might not understand instructions barked at him in a mixture of Dutch and Malay or the most crude Javanese. His bewilderment or hesitation, taken for stupidity or obstinacy, was likely to produce impatience, annoyance, and vituperation in these "bosses." Action resulting in errors called down upon him loud-voiced anger and humiliating curses. A worker who stopped to rest or fell asleep from the fatigue induced by a long workday might be cuffed on the head[6] or beaten.

WORK AND TRADITIONAL VALUES

Such conduct offered a great contrast to that displayed by superiors in the customary environment. Perhaps because the Javanese is conditioned from childhood to respect and obey properly constituted authority figures and can anticipate and understand the content of their directives, these figures rarely find it necessary to exert visible effort or force[7] to obtain compliance. Indeed, the very act of doing so might be taken as an implicit admission of their uncertainty of their right to make demands. If those to whom orders are given appear to hesitate in following them or in some other way subtly indicate some degree of resistance, similarly subtle and indirect means of persuasion are applied.

Resistance itself is rarely overt but takes the form of polite evasion. Prolonged non-compliance, which may often be accompanied by outward assent,[8] generally results in the issue being shelved or temporarily deferred until a more favorable occasion arises for obtaining acquiescence. For to bring an issue to the point of open conflict might disturb the harmony of the social order whose maintenance is deemed indispensable in the traditional Javanese view of society.

Such circumspection in avoiding overt discord is not only characteristic

[6] A whack on the head is more than an affront, for the head of an individual is sacred and not to be touched by another.

[7] On the rare occasions when force is resorted to, it is not directly applied by the authority figure himself. Thus, a former district head, recalling that repeated efforts to persuade farmers to plant paddy at the time suggested by the agricultural advisors were of no avail, stated: "I was finally obliged to order two farmers to be beaten as an example to the rest."

[8] It is customary to assent to requests or orders whether or not one has the intention of fulfilling them. Either the tone of voice or the rhetoric of the assent may convey whether it is merely a polite affirmative or substantive, and, in any case, time will tell.

of encounters between social unequals but permeates nearly all face-to-face interchange. Thus, the treatment workers in the factory received from their foreign[9] overseers, in addition to affording sharp contrast with that accorded them by traditional group leaders, also violated their notions of appropriate behavior between human beings, irrespective of status. No matter how incensed a Javanese may feel toward another, he refrains from expressing irritation, anger, or vituperation directly toward that other or in his presence. Incipient or active hostility toward another finds an outlet in making him the butt of humor or in deriding him to others behind his back. But he who expresses an aggressive impulse overtly is regarded as immature, improperly socialized, and deplorably crude. And he who lifts his hand against another,[10] except under the most extreme provocation,[11] is considered no longer a true Javanese, certainly not civilized.

Just as bewildering to the factory recruit, if not as directly humiliating as the supervisory procedures, was his subjection to a strange system of penalties that seemed arbitrarily enforced. For failing to meet a standard of workmanship he might only dimly comprehend, he could lose part of his wages. For infractions of regulations whose purport he could not understand, he could be fined, suspended, or otherwise penalized. Damage to equipment or theft might result in immediate dismissal. What is recalled as having seemed most unjust was the occasional instance, generally involving theft, of the punishment or dismissal of a whole group because none of its members would admit to being the culprit or accuse any of the others. And what seemed least comprehensible was that these penalties were impersonally administered with reference to the offense itself and often without—what to the worker seemed most relevant—concern with intention, cause, or extenuating circumstances.

My observations of work relationships in the traditional settings[12] produced little evidence of an analogous system of sanctions. Neither in the field nor in the handicrafts enterprise does there seem to be a precise standard against which the quality of work is measured. In the first place, since time and speed are not emphasized, there is more opportunity for a

9 Occasionally such treatment was also meted out by Javanese foremen as well, but, if my informants are to be believed, generally upon direct orders and in the presence of those above them. What was more typical of the exploitation of workers under them by Javanese foremen, although perhaps not necessarily regarded as such, was the "commission" taken from the wages of those workers whom they brought into the factory.

10 Even disobedient children are not as a rule spanked or slapped but nipped or pinched.

11 An example I was given of extreme provocation provoking violence was adultery. Even here, according to informants, retaliation is often indirect, such as by poison or soliciting the aid of a "black *dukun*." Outright violence is much more likely to be perpetrated by a group rather than by an individual, and usually after the group has been harangued or has whipped itself up to an emotional frenzy. The most noted type of individual violence—of which I have had no personal experience—is *amok*.

12 Here I am speaking of labor in agriculture and small enterprises in this area and not domestic services. Where I observed the latter in the homes of Javanese aristocrats, especially in the principalities of Central Java, it was not unusual for domestic servants to be sharply reprimanded for unsatisfactory performance and even occasionally physically chastised.

task to be performed meticulously and mistakes avoided. In the second place, approximation is acceptable and exactness of product is not demanded. *Pentjars,* or bundles, of paddy may vary somewhat in size but are paid for at the same rate. Some bricks or tiles or copper kettles are not as well made as others, but only the most obviously unfit are discarded and not paid for at the piecework rate. Sometimes a differential rate is paid to workers according to relative skill (most generally there is only a distinction between apprentices and experienced workers), on the assumption that each sustains over the average the quality of which he is capable, and there are no deductions for pieces that later may be discarded.

In accordance with the prescribed decorum for interpersonal behavior described above, discontent with the performance of an individual is rarely expressed in direct or scolding fashion. A dissatisfied employer is likely to dispense with the services of an unsatisfactory worker with a face-saving pretext, such as telling him that he has not enough work in the near future or that some relative has suddenly turned up whom he is obliged to hire. Or he might, without being in any way sharply critical, convey sufficient lack of appreciation for the worker's efforts to induce the latter to decide to seek a living elsewhere. Similarly, a discontented worker does not complain of conditions of work or payment or announce that he can do better elsewhere, but finds that some urgent situation in the family forces him to sever the connection temporarily.[13]

Direct dismissal as a punitive measure appears to be difficult, in any case, for several reasons. Work associations are rarely a mere exchange of labor for payment. They are often within the context of kin, neighborhood, and village ties involving a number of reciprocal obligations, in which skill or performance may play a minor role. Beyond this, and related to it, is the tradition in agrarian communities that those with land rights, or in other respects in superior economic circumstances, should provide as many as possible opportunities for work for the landless and those in a needy position. This results in the apportionment of available work among as many hands as possible, rather than the recruitment of labor on the basis of efficiency. The converse of this is the implicit recognition of the individual's "right to work" as a concomitant of community membership, apart from considerations of skill or level of performance.[14]

If, despite all precautions, a disagreement should arise in a situation in

---

[13] These pretexts do not, of course, deceive anyone as to the underlying reasons, but they are appreciated and, indeed, expected as a face-saving ritual.

[14] I asked a farmer who was complaining of the high cost of labor why he did not select a few of the faster and more skilled field workers and employ them over a longer period of time, thus cutting his costs. The reply was that he couldn't risk the resultant disapproval of the community and the possible accusations of being penny-pinching and unconcerned with the welfare of his poorer neighbors. A small entrepreneur, who was maintaining two extra hands during the off-season, when he had little work for them in the shop, but tried to keep them occupied with odd jobs around his compound, said: "After all, they cannot easily find other work and they must eat. What else should I do, let them starve?"

which custom has not created a precedent,[15] its resolution would appear[16] to be based on a consideration of more factors than those directly pertinent to the issue itself. Perhaps the most important of these is that tension should be diminished and any sustained bitterness averted. Friends and neighbors often serve as mediators, attempting to press mutual concessions on the contestants rather than trying to assess guilt or support the claims of one to the exclusion of those of the other. Should the issue be taken to the village head or some other prestige figure, the ultimate decision generally favors neither one nor the other completely but is a compromise in which each party obtains some satisfaction.

The problems of supervision and authority can thus be understood in terms of the contrast between the structuring of work relationships in traditional Javanese society and in the factory system. In the early period of Pabrika's operations, this antithesis found little expression within the factory itself. The workers faced the full burden of making the transition, and their problems of adaptation were further complicated by language and cultural barriers. Some managed to overcome the strains of adjustment; many, following the traditional way of withdrawal from stress, quietly retreated to the familiar environment.

THE CURRENT SEARCH FOR ACCOMMODATION

Today, the contradictions between these systems are being acted out within the walls of Pabrika. And they are no longer exclusively personified by the workers on the one hand and the supervisory and managerial personnel on the other. Instead, there exists an uneasy interplay of elements of both systems in the behavior of each of these groups toward the others. In circumstances that can best be characterized as a search for a pattern of accommodation permitting an integrated order, the workers tend to exercise a strong measure of control over the means by which they are controlled. This has come about as a result of the following factors:

1) The replacement of foreign supervisory and managerial staff by those of an ethnic background identical with or similar to that of the workers;

2) the entry of workers who have been exposed to both urban and revolutionary influences and are not reticent in making known their views;

3) the formation of unions through which these views can be channelized;

4) the appointment of a general manager familiar with Javanese values and behavior and capable of employing them himself.

The formal organization of the factory, with its hierarchic structure, has not changed. But the present recruit from the village finds that those in

---

[15] For the disposition of shares of harvest and for the provision of a certain minimum of food to workers, custom is sufficiently strong to preclude the possibility of disagreement.

[16] I have not directly observed the course of a disagreement between wage worker and employer in a village work situation, but I am drawing an analogy from disputes observed over debts and work contracted with artisans.

roles above his interpret them in ways that are not disconcerting. His foreman and supervisor[17] are likely to share with him a common language and a common understanding of how people treat each other. They issue instructions in calm, quiet voices or in gestures that are meaningful to him. They are patient with his initial fumbling, recognizing that he needs time to accustom himself to this new world. Subsequent errors are more likely to arouse not anger but good-natured ridicule that will shame him into avoiding mistakes that are likely to provoke it.

In fact, in the present scene, it is the middle group of foremen and supervisors who are taxed with the burden of reconciling the formal requirements of the factory with the expectations generated by the culture. Discussion with them makes it clear that they do understand the requirements of their roles. They know that their major task is to pass on to those under their jurisdiction the directions they have received from their superiors and to see that these are carried out. They recognize that, with respect to the workers, this involves more or less the following tasks: 1) to make explicit and clear the instructions for the job at hand, 2) to exert continued surveillance over the pace and quality of worker performance, 3) to issue reprimands when called for, and 4) to impose the prescribed sanctions within their competence when necessary.

According to management criteria, only the first of the above functions is consistently and satisfactorily performed by all the supervisory personnel. Although most keep a fairly steady eye on the workers, some appear to observe only sporadically the operations under their control, mainly when their own bosses are present. Fewer reprimand their subordinates with any conviction. And practically none dares to impose penalties without resort to higher authority. In principle, there is delegation of responsibility and allocation of concomitant power down the line. In practice, responsibility is often evaded and the exercise of authority shoved upward. In the words of one department head:

> Only the foremen are supposed to watch and direct the workers; my supervisor is supposed to control the foremen; my assistant should check only on the supervisor and serve as liaison between him and me; and I should spend most of my time in planning and conferences. What really happens is that the supervisor has to keep an eye directly on the workers as well as upon the foremen; my assistant must control the supervisor, foremen, and workers; and I have to be in the shop most of the day to be sure everything goes smoothly.

This department head did not mean that he necessarily substitutes for his subordinates in any specific function, although that takes place also, but that his physical presence is necessary to insure their adequate performance. In his absence, a foreman might turn his back on a group of workers who are not following instructions, pretending not to notice them; the supervisor might somehow neglect to scold the foreman for his inatten-

---

[17] Almost three-fourths of the present supervisory personnel are Javanese, and many have been recruited from the ranks of former workers.

tion; and the assistant might hesitate to inform the head that production is not proceeding smoothly. To affix responsibility for the resulting snarl-up would not be easy. For the foreman would explain that he had been so busy watching another group of workers at a crucial task that he had not had time to notice the first group. The supervisor would have been occupied in explaining the requirements of a new work order to the other foreman. The assistant might admit to an inkling that something was wrong, but since it was not his place to address the workers directly, and there was nothing he could do about it at the time, he had not wanted to disturb his so busy superior.[18]

EXTERNAL STATUS AND FACTORY AUTHORITY

Many of the foremen with whom I talked confessed to a sense of being almost constantly caught between conflicting currents. And although this can be said of the position of foreman in almost any factory, placed as it is at the point where demands from above and pressures from below tend to converge, it is doubly true at Pabrika. For if, on the one hand, managerial staff expect the foremen to obtain compliance from the workers, they also expect this to be done without coercion of the type that would arouse worker hostility and union protest. If the foreman is to gain acquiescence without resort to pressure, it is necessary for the workers to recognize the role of the foreman and to accept the individual assigned to that role. Many of the foremen cannot always depend on such acceptance. When uncertain, they hesitate, in Javanese style, to put their authority to a crucial test.

I have earlier indicated that in the traditional system, he who directs the work of others, with the exception of work performed as a reciprocal obligation, generally has higher status that those who work for him. Obviously, the landholder ranks higher in the village stratification system than the

---

18 An example of this, which was observed in some detail, occurred during the installation of some new looms. On a Thursday morning, under the direction of its foreman, a work crew began on the first loom. A technical advisor stood by, checking the directions on the blueprint. The factory manager came in frequently to survey the progress, and the general manager stopped by several times. By early afternoon, the first loom had been installed. The work on the second loom went faster and was finished by the end of the afternoon. This time, the technical advisor looked in several times, the factory manager twice, and the general manager once, to assure themselves that the complexities of installation had been mastered. On Friday morning, work began on the third loom. The general manager left in the middle of the morning for the city, the factory manager spent most of the morning in conferences and the afternoon at home, and the technical assistant also did not appear after lunch. The foreman seemed to be giving the same instructions, but somehow the work was proceeding more slowly. Two of the members of the crew did not report back after the usual Friday break for mosque attendance. By 4:00 P.M., when the general manager returned from the city, the third loom had not yet been completely installed. Called to account, the foreman explained that he had not been any less explicit or assiduous in giving orders than the previous day, but the workers had responded more slowly and lackadaisically. Slightly stronger pressure on his part had not produced visibly better response. He had not dared to become really rough with the workers. Besides, there had been nobody there to back him up.

workers he employs. The small entrepreneur is often a *hadji* with the prestige acquired from his trip to Mecca. Work on community projects is organized and often directed by the village head, not because of superior organizational skill on his part but in his capacity as village head. Thus, conversely, the right to direct labor may be seen as flowing from status derived from other criteria than the work situation itself.

Some of the foremen in the factory hold such status in the environment beyond the factory. Two of them are leading landholders in nearby villages, and one of these is also well educated by town as well as village standards. It is significant that these two seem to find little difficulty in maintaining discipline among their workers. Another supervisory official who has no feeling that his authority is challenged is a Eurasian who, in the earlier period, was slightly assimilated to the European element in the town and was regarded as such by the Javanese.

It is conceivable that some of the others might have little difficulty in gaining acceptance as authority figures in the eyes of workers recently recruited from the rural area. For even though they themselves may have originally come from low-status groups of the population, by this time they have acquired some of the attributes of higher status. To the villager, their style of living and mode of behavior may seem more comparable to that of the town officials than to his own. And he is likely to regard them, at least initially, with similar respect and a shade of deference.

NON-TRADITIONAL WORKERS' CHALLENGE TO AUTHORITY

Many of the workers, however, are not from the traditional village background. Those with prior residence and work experience in larger centers than Namakota have themselves acquired some of the attributes of urban sophistication, whose possession gives their holders higher status in the eyes of agrarian villagers. Many of them have had equivalent, if not more, education than their foremen, have become accustomed to similar material possessions, and ascribe to themselves the traditionally associated symbolic significance these carry. Those who hold superordinate status in the factory are more likely to be regarded by them outside of the factory as their equals rather than their superiors. This attitude often carries into the factory, where they can be seen retorting freely to admonitions of their foremen and not hesitating to tease and joke with them.

It is not easy to determine what constitutes legitimation of authority for this group. Some of its members appear to consider seniority as the sole criterion for the elevation of others to a position of direction over them. They do not question the right of men who have been in the factory for ten or twelve years to supervise their work.[19] Others seem somewhat amenable to authority exercised by someone whose skill is manifestly superior to theirs, as long as this skill is amply demonstrated. One foreman told me that he constantly hopes for situations to arise in which workers need his

[19] When questioning workers concerning their opposition to a new foreman in circumstances related below, I received numbers of replies to the effect that only a man who has done a certain sort of work for years would know enough to be able to tell others how to do it.

direct assistance. Then his stock rises, and his crew appear to respect him; in between these occasions, they seem to regard his presence as superfluous.

Those workers with a background of revolutionary activity and ideology, most influenced by the new emphasis on democracy and egalitarianism, tend implicitly and often explicitly to challenge the notion of any authority imposed from above. In their minds, such authority carries about it the aura of colonialism and should similarly be abolished. Valid authority over a group, according to their interpretation of democracy, is that derived through selection by and voluntary agreement of the members of the group. This attitude is frequently encountered in other contexts than the political one in which it originated. Within the factory, it finds expression in the intimations that workers should have some voice in the selection of those who supervise them, if not directly, at least through right of rejection.

During the period of my residence, the general manager received a petition, signed by more than forty workers, requesting the removal of a recently appointed supervisor. The major charge leveled against him was that he was "unproductive." When asked to explain what they meant by this term, the leader of the delegation replied that this supervisor seemed to spend most of his time observing and studying[20] and had not been seen working with his hands. Further investigation revealed that there was resentment at what the workers felt to be an aloofness and a sense of superiority on the part of this man toward them. There was also some grumbling at the fact that he was not Javanese but from another Indonesian ethnic group.

This was but one of a number of instances in which workers have communicated objections by means of organized protest rather than individual withdrawal. Previously, there had been overt resistance by workers in one section to taking orders from a foreman brought in from outside. They declared that they would prefer to have someone from their own ranks. This approach had been initially tried and then discarded when those so promoted had proved in management eyes to be even more than normally reluctant to assume effective authority over former colleagues, and the latter even less than normally disposed to accept it from them. This was succeeded by an experiment of transferring workers who seemed to be promising supervisory material to other departments for a few months before returning them with higher status to their original ones.[21] The first retransfer on this basis also encountered worker resistance, from some on the grounds that the individual in question was "too young," from others because he was now "an outsider" from "another department." Ultimately, worker opposition in these cases was overcome by rather skillful rhetoric

[20] Since this was in the dyeing department, which engaged in experiments with different dyes, the new supervisor was also being trained in the technical aspects of dyestuffs.

[21] The underlying rationale was that time and distance might lessen the familiarity that was considered to be the major deterrent on both sides to the assumption of the new relationship, while the added experience might be accepted by the workers as justification for the new status of their former equal.

from top management.[22] But a formula has not yet been found for locating new supervisory personnel who are both effective and acceptable.

The Ambiguities of the Managerial Role

Given such attitudes on the part of even a small number of workers, it is not surprising that few of those in middle-level positions have the confidence to assert authority to the point where it may be challenged. Although none would admit to desiring a return to the "hard old days," it is clear that a situation in which a worker may dare to ignore one of them, turn his back on him, or complain over his head counteracts whatever sense of security is derived from their selection to their posts by management. For many of them share the background of the workers and to some degree are similarly influenced by the attitudes that affect worker recognition of them. Although they have therefore formally mastered the roles assigned to them, they have not yet sufficiently internalized them to implement them adequately.

Traditional Javanese values and modern egalitarian notions also appear to affect the way in which supervisory personnel fulfill the task of transmitting information upward. Yearly wage raises for workers are based upon the three criteria of work efficiency, quality of work, and regularity of attendance. The foremen are expected periodically to give objective evaluation of individual worker performance. It is not at all unusual for a foreman to grade all workers under him as satisfactory on all counts. For, apart from the group solidarity developed through working together, the foreman often lives in the same neighborhood as some of his workers and may have formed a number of other ties resulting from this propinquity.[23] The obligations resulting from such ties make it difficult for him to risk offending them by adverse judgments. They may go so far as to enable workers to induce foremen to record stoppage periods to their advantage. Possibly also bearing on the uniformly favorable grading is the attitude that an advantage should be indiscriminately apportioned, an attitude that may have its origins in the village tradition of sharing benefits and hardships, or perhaps it is derived from the postrevolutionary emphasis on equality.

[22] For example, in the first instance mentioned above, the general manager addressed the delegation, taking as a starting point the comments that the foreman was from another *bangsa*, or ethnic subgroup. He stated that he was shocked to hear that his workers could speak so in this period of national unity. "After all, hasn't Bung Karno (affectionate diminutive for President Sukarno) said that now all Indonesians are one *bangsa?*" Then the delegation was urged by him and other management officials to show by their acceptance of the foreman that they were good supporters of national unity.

[23] I have observed workers and supervisory personnel in joint recreation, such as playing cards and gambling together. One supervisor is engaged in financing credit purchasing of bicycles by workers, that is, he makes the initial payment to the dealers and collects from the workers on an installment basis. On the one hand, this is regarded by the workers as a form of assistance, despite his profit on interest; on the other hand, since collection of debts of this sort reportedly can no longer be legally enforced, he is somewhat subtly intimidated to stay in the good graces of these workers, to insure that they retain their sense of obligation to repay him.

Management's skepticism of the reliability of such blanket approval has resulted in a technique that combines checking of record and attendance books[24] with a sort of bargaining process. The supervisor checks the records with the foremen and generally succeeds in working out with them some downward revisions; the department head engages in the same process with the supervisors and so on up the line. This is done on the assumption that, with each step further removed from the worker, there is less likelihood that personal considerations influence judgment. At the same time, those closest to the workers can avert recriminations from them by attributing unfavorable judgments to pressure from those above.

Many of the criticisms leveled against foremen and supervisors by most of the managerial staff are also applied to the managerial staff by the European general manager. In several respects, he has attempted to follow a different course than that of his predecessor. Whereas the latter made most of the policy decisions unilaterally, he holds daily meetings with his staff for joint discussion and decisions. His predecessor reportedly spent much of his day observing the execution of his instructions and often directly supervising operations. The present general manager attempts to delegate as many functions as possible to his subordinates, appearing only briefly out of his office. He tells them that the department heads are more technically qualified than he, that they have wide latitude in the execution of decisions, and should only resort to him when major problems arise. He defines his task to them as primarily that of planning, coordination, and liaison with the owners.

Thus far, this "loose reins" strategy has been more successful in retaining the good will of his subordinates than in achieving its objective of forcing them to function as executives. Perhaps two have risen to the challenge and perform satisfactorily at the level required of managerial staff by the factory model, without stimulus and pressure from him. The others seem to require at least his presence, if not his occasional prodding, to sustain them, and they tend to relax their efforts in his absence.[25] Like the foremen and supervisors, they are only too eager to pass up to him the responsibility for the enforcement of discipline. The usual reason given in such instances[26] is the desire to avert possible difficulties with the Communist-dominated union.

---

[24] There is a daily book for each section of the factory, in which is recorded the production of each loom or other machine, stoppages, problems, and so on. If a worker complains that errors recorded against him or lower production are the result of the loom rather than of his efforts, this book is used to compare his production rate with that of other workers on the same loom in different shifts.

[25] Although the general manager spends much of this time outside the factory premises, conducting many of its affairs from his home across the street, it is as if his "being on call" serves as a catalyst for the normal conduct of affairs. During a period when he was on home leave, production declined steadily, and he was cabled by the owners to cut short his vacation and return.

[26] One instance I observed when an electrician, careless a second time after a warning, caused a small fire. The regulations provided for immediate dismissal in such a case, and either the foreman of the crew or the supervisor of maintenance, both present,

Implicit in statements of this type is a more basic motive—the disinclination to make embarrassingly obvious the latent ambiguities of their position. For all of the foremen and supervisors, and many of the managerial staff, are also members of the same union as the majority of the workers. Several are even members of the governing body of this union. The development of unions has facilitated the crystallization of worker sentiment, and the participation of managerial personnel in union affairs is an additional factor conditioning their responsiveness to this sentiment. Although such participation could serve as a means of channeling union policy in a direction most advantageous to management aims, and sometimes does, this is limited by the existence of a rival union and competition between the two for membership.

Those in the dual roles of middle-level or higher-managerial officials and active union members or officials profess to feel no real conflict between them. They see themselves in a median or conciliatory position, carrying out the traditional Javanese ideal of maintaining harmony by reconciling divergent interests. It is clear, however, that this inhibits their full identification as members of a distinct "management team." And it may be adduced as another of the factors[27] explaining their inclination to leave any drastic disciplinary action to the very top managerial officials.

In the last analysis, this throws the major burden of decision in the sphere of authority on the general manager.[28] Unable to depend upon unequivocal support from his subordinates and aware of the psychological complexities of their position, he does not try to compel their strict adherence to the formal mechanisms of control as, apparently, did his predecessor. Instead, he assumes the paternalistic but nonauthoritarian role they seem to demand of him and works with them in trying to evolve techniques that outwardly satisfy cultural expectations, while achieving the goal of maintaining the factory in relatively efficient operation. And he is not above employing the circuitous Javanese modes of behavior himself in attaining his objectives.

---

was empowered to discharge him. Instead, they called the factory manager and suggested that he do so; he, in turn, went to the general manager. The latter firmly told the factory manager that it was his affair and he, in turn, prevailed upon the supervisor with the statement that the "big boss" expected him to do it.

[27] It is not easy to attribute relative weights to the various factors that have here been advanced to explain the behavior of this group. For example, in the neighboring British-managed textile factory, there is a separate union for Indonesians above the rank of worker. Nevertheless, the British department heads and supervisors complain that the Javanese supervisors and foremen under them never translate literally their reprimands to the workers but always "soften" them and are generally "too easy" with the workers. The union membership of managerial personnel at Pabrika may be a less important factor than the others.

[28] The three other management officials who are not affiliated with a union are of Chinese ethnic origin. And, although they are not subject to the same inhibitions as their Indonesian colleagues, they also tend to be circumspect and a bit wary because of the peculiar position in the present nationalistic period of even those Chinese who are Indonesian citizens.

FLEXIBILITY AND THE SYSTEM OF SANCTIONS

This is seen most clearly in the ways in which the system of sanctions is enforced. The formal outline of this system has not been greatly altered since the period when it constituted a major source of worker grievance. Workers are still subject to wage deductions for errors, suspension and dismissal for infringement of regulations. However, the regulations themselves are now the outcome of union-management negotiation. Most of the workers I encountered are fairly familiar with them, having been generally informed of them at the time of entry or shortly afterwards. Should one feel himself unfairly disciplined, he has the right of appeal. The very reluctance of his immediate superiors to administer punitive measures means that a worker has a good chance of carrying his case to the highest authorities with the opportunity to defend himself personally.

I received the impression that workers now venture evasion or transgression of regulations in the spirit of a game of chance, in which the player is willing to risk the consequences of losing. In fact, the risk is not so great, for, in practice, the major penalties are rarely administered without investigation of the particular circumstances by higher management officials and often in consultation with the union heads. For example, a worker who has been recorded as dismissed for prolonged absence should not, according to the rules, be reinstated upon reappearance. In actuality, a good weaver stands an excellent chance of being taken back, if he can justify his absence with a plausible explanation or even with an original and entertaining—if somewhat implausible—excuse. Occasionally, a worker trades shifts by private agreement with a worker on an alternate shift in the same department. As long as the machine is not left unattended, such arrangements are not objected to by management.

A worker who proves to be repeatedly inept, careless, or lazy is no longer dismissed on these grounds. Instead, he is exposed to a technique that embodies the utmost Javanese finesse. He is progressively transferred to less demanding tasks that carry with them lower prestige. An ex-weaver assigned to a job that requires him to carry loads through the mill under the eyes of his former colleagues is likely to feel himself so degraded that he leaves voluntarily after several days. As a result, workers who fall below the standard of skill of which they are known to be capable are sometimes brought to rapid recovery by the mere suggestion that they might be happier with a transfer to another part of the factory.

The most drastic penalty of dismissal is generally applied only in cases of theft and action leading to damage or danger to safety. Even here, a concession may be made in extraordinary circumstances. For example, one of the men in the storeroom had worked out an elaborate system of checking and recording supplies, which had enabled him to withdraw and somehow take out of the factory a sizable stock of cloth for three months before he was caught. The offender pleaded at his hearing that his original intention had been to make only a single haul to fill one pressing family need for money[29] but that the system he had evolved forced him to continue his depredations to avoid detection. The staff listened to this explanation and examined the system. They were so impressed with its ingenuity and the intelligence it implied on the part of the worker that instead of dismissing him, they assigned him to a job that would utilize his initiative.

There is no doubt that such pliancy on the part of present management has contributed to the improved morale of the workers and to the growth of a more stable work force. On the other hand, continued divergence of practice from principle may well obstruct the development of integrated and self-sustaining procedures of supervision and authority needed by a factory system. The present ways of reconciling various worker pressures with the requirements of efficient production rely rather heavily on the father-figure of the general manager and on a sort of stop-gap improvisation. But perhaps improvisation is the only mode of dealing with an unstable situation that offers many variables and few constants. The situation in Pabrika is not unique. It merely mirrors in microcosm the confusion prevalent throughout organizational life in Indonesia, as old norms of authority have been wholly or partially repudiated and generally accepted new ones have not yet emerged.

[29] Many of the workers, especially those from the rural environment, cannot understand why they cannot borrow money from the factory in case of personal need and repay in gradual stages through wage deductions. This arrangement, as has been earlier mentioned, is not uncommon in village work arrangements, especially in small-scale enterprises.

12

MYSTICISM IN INDONESIAN POLITICS*

MOCHTAR LUBIS

The Sukarno regime was the ideal model of a situation in which it would be very difficult, if not impossible, to ascertain where the political leader ends and the *dukun* (the medicine man, the fortune-teller, the mystic guru) begins. And if I take up mytho-mysticism in Indonesian politics as the focus of this article, it is not to poke fun at the defunct Sukarno regime nor to draw a caricature of Indonesian political life; it is with the serious objective of trying to understand the role of mytho-mysticism in Indonesian politics, a role that, up to today, has not completely been banished from Indonesian political life and perhaps cannot be banished from our political life for some time to come.

To try to understand political development during the past decade in Indonesia, which might contain lessons for the present and the future, it would be very useful to delve into this mystical world of Indonesia, with the main focus on the Javanese mystical world. To the great majority of the Indonesian people, it is a living world, peopled with a complete set of symbols, powers, meanings, and commands.

* Reprinted by permission of the author and the publisher from *Solidarity*, II (November–December, 1967), 22–27.

During the course of history, Javanese mytho-mysticism has grown in many directions and varieties, but its basic ground pattern suggests some conclusions.

What I mean by mytho-mysticism is the combination of religious or philosophical or mystical experience with mythological and animistic beliefs. Today, in this nuclear age, most Indonesians are still strongly rooted to their animistic past and its successive layers of Hinduism, Buddhism, Islam, Christianity, and Western thought.

Deep in the subconscious of the Indonesian—even in that of someone who is Western-educated and has attended a university in Europe or America—is a belief in mystical, supernatural powers, in spirits that possess the power to aid or hurt man. I can name more than eighty kinds of ghosts, more than fifty devils, and numerous other spirits.

Our people believe in holy *krises* that could bring good or bad luck or even power to their possessors. It was said that Sukarno long possessed such a *kris*, and, some time before the abortive coup, the story went around that the holy *kris* had suddenly left the Merdeka Palace and flown to its home someplace in East Java. This story was told to me by a Javanese intellectual, a very sophisticated fellow, who always talks about rationality, modernization, and common sense. He told it with ringing sincerity and was rather offended when I dismissed his story as an old wives' tale. Of course, he could now tell me how right he had been.

The story also went around that Sukarno had escaped so many assassination attempts because he possessed a very powerful magical charm in his command stick, which he always carried with him. This charm deflected all the bullets aimed at him. (Other reports state that Sukarno also wore a bulletproof vest and rode in a bulletproof car, all made in the United States of America.)

People believe that love charms, the power to make oneself invulnerable to bullets and knives, even the power to reconcile three or five wives at the same time under one single roof, could be bought or, under the proper guru, could be cultivated by fasting, praying, meditations.

Offerings are given to holy graves, and even as recently as two decades ago, many people brought offerings and prayers to a very holy cannon, an old Dutch artillery piece, lying in state, covered by mounds of fresh flowers and incense smoke in Pasar Ikan, named si-Djagur by the people of Djakarta. This relic is now lying in dust in one of the backrooms of the museum in this city, but it was reputed to possess the strongest powers in helping a boy to win the girl he loved, to acquire riches, or to produce offspring. It was only after independence that the old cannon was dragged to its present domicile, because free Indonesians could, of course, no longer worship an ancient Dutch siege gun. But our people, as history has shown, soon enough found new holy things, and more dangerous things, too, to worship.

The syncretic power of our people is not limited to any single group or religion. The Christians of Batakland in Sumatra or northern Celebes, the Hindus of Bali, the Muslims in other parts of Indonesia, the Javanese,

Sumatrans, and so on, all share this strain of animism, which still lurks deep in their subconscious minds.

In 1945, during the first months of our revolution for national freedom, Muslims and Christians were baptized by holy *dukuns*, or gurus, to make them bulletproof. I well remember how, one day, one of the directors of the Antara news agency in Djakarta invited all the editors and staff reporters to such a baptism in the Tangerang River. A holy guru would bathe them to make them bulletproof (the Indonesian version of the American bulletproof vest). Another guru offered to provide us with the power to make ourselves invisible in times of emergencies. These were really great assets at that time, as Djakarta was being occupied by Dutch troops. The Antara office was rather close to the barracks of the Dutch 10th Battalion, and at that time relations between us and the Dutch could hardly be called friendly. Outside Djakarta, I saw the bodies of young Indonesians who died while charging tanks, crying Allahu Akbar, believing themselves to be invincible. During those first months of revolution, our belief in mystical powers caused, I think, more casualties among the Indonesian Republican ranks than did Dutch or British sharpshooters.

And among our people in Java, the Mahābhārata and Ramayana epics grew very deep roots, which neither Buddhism nor Islam nor Christianity nor modern education could budge. Here syncretism works most strongly, blending the ancient remnants of animism with the new influences of Hinduism and Islam, and creating the various schools of Javanese mytho-mysticism, which was going to exercise its strongest influence on Indonesian politics during the Sukarno regime.

For example, Gatotkatja's flight through the skies in the Mahābhārata justified Sukarno's ambition to create an Indonesian space program, in utter disregard of Indonesian realities. During the confrontation period, Indonesian officials began to threaten Singapore and Malaysia with instant destruction by powerful Indonesian-made rockets and missiles. Because Ontoseno, grandson of the god Baruna, lived under the seas, Indonesia must also have the strongest submarine fleet in Southeast Asia. Should some future inventor build a vehicle that could travel beneath the earth, we would be ready for that, too, because we have Ontoredjo, who lived in the bowels of the earth.

The Javanese kings were believed to be descended from Abimayu, son of Arjuna, who received the "wahyutjakaraningrat"—a godlike power. During the height of Sukarno's power, it was said that he had received this "wahyutjakaraningrat" and had fostered this belief by confessing that he had been in communication with God before postulating the *Pantja Sila*. God told him what to do. The giving of the great titles to Sukarno was the mytho-mystical process, which needs outward symbols to strengthen the faith of the believers.

Sukarno and others willingly fostered an aura of semigodliness around his person. Sukarno even dared to claim descent from the Kings of Kediri. As one who had received the "wahyutjakaraningrat," his word was law, his wishes were commands that could not be disobeyed. He could never do wrong; what he spoke could never be other than the truth; whatever he did was always right and true. He was all wisdom and justice, all magnanimity. He was the father; he was god. Anybody who dared to disagree with him, let alone oppose him, was evil. He was Krishna, he was Vishnu.

In addition to this, the teachings of Djayabaya (some say he was a Javanese prince blessed with the power to look far into the future) reinforced the influence of these mytho-mystical beliefs upon the Javanese people. According to experts, Djayabaya had accurately predicted the Dutch colonial period, the short Japanese military occupation, Indonesian independence, the revolts in Indonesia, and even the past dualism in the top leadership of the government before Sukarno was stripped of his presidential powers. Djayabaya spoke about the time of Ratu Kembar, which means Twin Kings, or dualism, and he even anticipated the time when corruption would be rampant in the country, when he wrote:

> we are facing a mad era
> but however profitable it is for
> those who indulge
> themselves in this madness
> those who stay honest are more
> fortunate. . . .

This was a warning to all honest people not to participate in corrupt deals, smuggling, hot-money speculations, hoarding of goods, and so on.

The belief in the coming of a *ratu adil*, a just king, is also still very strong, and in times of stress and great suffering, many people try to find their *ratu adil* wherever they can find him. While Sukarno was looked upon by many people as the *ratu adil*, some also succeeded in having themselves accepted as *ratu adils* in small villages in Central Java.

Religio-mystical movements have developed in several different ways. Some of the Javanese ones want to purify Islam. One of these even forbade its adherents to let their children go to schools or to join a political party, and they were all awaiting the coming of the *imam mahdi*, another symbol of the just king, to deliver them from all evil suffering, and to lead them to achieve the glory of Islam. Another movement, the Ummat Adam Ma'rifat Indonesia, wanted to syncretize the old animism, Islam, Buddhism, Confucianism, and Christianity. Still another (a more interesting one) taught that "godliness" is achieved in sexual union and the satisfaction of all desire. Others advocate puritanism, the clean and simple life, the pursuit of spiritual well-being, salvation.

Mysticism, by its very nature, tends to keep itself aloof from existing religions, regarding itself as superior and as possessing the secret keys to salvation and other desired values. Combining a very strong belief in mythology and the still deeply rooted ancient animism, the present mytho-mystical schools in Java become a potent centrifugal force, a barrier to cohesion, unity, and modernization.

The Sukarno regime itself was a fine model of the mytho-mystical force as exercised not only on a national scale but even in the international arena. All the symbols and the outward trappings were there. At a special conference in Bogor, the title *Waliyul Amri Da-ruri*—whose leadership must be followed by all good Muslims—was bestowed on Sukarno, and the just king emerged as President for life, the Great Leader of the Revolution. He was the Vishnu who could take many forms, the Source of All Law, the Great Fisherman, the Great Peasant, the Great Journalist, the Great Navigator. The unscrupulous Communists cited the Pandawa-Kurawa battle as an example of the struggle of classes, and it was transformed into a war between the true revolutionists (Sukarno's of course) and the subversives and counter-revolutionaries, the NEFOS and the OLDEFOS, the confrontation with Malaysia. And all the litanies were also there: Guided Democracy, NASAKOM, Takari, *Vivere pericoloso*, and so on. Even the high priests were present: Subandrio, Ruslan Abdulgani, Jusuf Mudadalam, Aidit, and many middle-level and lower-level priests and priestesses. Mythomysticism feeds upon irrationality and emotion and easily could become a vehicle for wishful thinking, or, at its worst, be used to mislead the people and oneself. It had twisted the minds of Sukarno and his friends and destroyed, or at least damaged, their objective perception of real facts, and, in the end, they themselves became prisoners of their own mytho-mystical slogans.

Even the Communists, who at the beginning played along (for their own purposes, of course), could not prevail over mytho-mysticism, as Marx and Lenin proved to be much weaker than Gatotkatja or Sunan Kalijogo, Prince Djayabaya or the *ratu adil* or *imam mahdi*, and Marxist-Leninist dialectics pale beside the Mahābhārata and the mytho-mystical teachings of *dukuns* and gurus. When the Communists were at last confronted by the army's power after the abortive Communist coup, millions of their members denounced and left the Party. In many places, public ceremonies were held on the dissolution of PKI's branches and chapters.

Sukarno's complete disregard of economic laws, his utter indifference to a good and clean administration, his twisted view of the actual world situation, his complete lack of understanding of historical trends, and his belief in his own personal superiority and invulnerability, combined to form one supreme example of the heights of folly and distortion to which this mytho-mystical force could raise one person and even, to some extent in the past, a whole nation.

Modern education produces a thin layer of intellectuals, who, while intellectually and materially living apart from the masses, nevertheless remain linked to these tradition-directed masses by their common mytho-mystical experience. They are eager to accept modern technology and modern science to advance their people and country, but, at the same time, they are plagued by suspicion of foreign elements, by bursts of xenophobia. Their modern education tells them to use reason, but their subconscious mytho-mystical experience bends them in the opposite direction. They suffer from inferiority complexes, which they try to hide behind an attitude of superiority, aloofness, or even arrogance.

Although our people had gone through the national revolution for freedom, we failed to spark another revolution, a revolution within ourselves, to cut off roots in our mytho-mystical past. During the past twenty-two years, this nation has been plagued with dissension and strife, power struggles, corruption, and destruction of values, and in such a continuing situation of stress, dangers, emergencies, and desperate situations, our mytho-mystical past gained an even stronger grip on many of our people, so that even decision-making at the highest level of the state's leadership came under the influence of *dukuns* or gurus.

Even today such mytho-mystical schools, with their *dukuns* or gurus, are influencing some members of decision-making centers in this country. A time of great uncertainty could unhinge personality and make people easily subject to irrational and emotional influences and behavior.

That is why it is so vital for us today to achieve economic recovery as soon as possible, to return to a normal situation, where tension and stress, and the sense of crisis and continued emergency, would weigh less heavily on the mind and spirit of the people.

Only continued education in the real sense of the word (education that will enable man to think for himself and shoulder responsibility for his own decisions and actions) will eventually free our people from the bondage of our mytho-mystical past. I realize it will take a very long time before we can achieve this.

But we must return to rationality. We must learn to know our real selves better and not continue in self-deception. I will try to show you how most of us look at ourselves. We always proudly proclaim that Indonesians are basically democratic (the tradition of *musjawarah*); and yet we put up almost no resistance at all against Sukarno's autocratic rule, and millions succumbed to Communist propagandizing. We are a religious people and would never accept Communism; and yet, many *kijajis* in the past used some articles in the Holy Koran to justify their party's collaboration with the Communists under Sukarno. We say that we are absolutely against racial discrimination, but past events have shown how easily we can be tempted to give in to racial disturbances. We regard ourselves as *ksatrias* (noble knights), who always will fight fair and for noble causes (freedom, justice, truth, God), but our recent history is not expressive of freedom, justice, or truth.

All of these are extensions of our mytho-mystical burden; we are easily satisfied with symbols and slogans. By making decisions, by expressing a desire to do something, we think we have done it and have achieved what we have decided. The whole Indonesian administration, if one cares to spend some years looking into it, is completely buried under central committees, special committees, *ad hoc* committees, working committees, national or regional conferences (and their multiple subcommittees, *ad hoc* committees, and so forth), RAKER, MUKER, symposia, seminars, and whatnot.* When some program bogs down or decisions have not been carried out, the first impulse has always been to set up a committee to

* RAKER and MUKER are acronyms for *rapat kerdja* (working meeting) and *musjawarah kerdja* (working conference).

look into the matter, which inevitably will breed numerous other committees. That is why our newspapers print so much news about the setting up of committees but little news on the dissolution of committees that have achieved their purposes.

Indonesians hate to hurry. "I am not the slave of time" is how one of my friends who is habitually late for appointments defends himself. "Our fate is in the hands of God; what is the hurry; tomorrow will be another day" is another favorite remark. Our people's sense of time is still not attuned to the needs of a modern world.

In the case of the Americans and Russians, for example, the sense of space and time must have changed. These countries are already involved in flights into space, to the moon, and to the distant stars. To many Indonesians, distance is still real distance. There are today places where mail from Djakarta may only arrive after two or three months. The concept that we are living in a steadily shrinking world, necessitating better and closer understanding, friendship, and cooperation among nations, is still strange to many of our people. They still think that they have enough space and time to go on wrangling and fighting among themselves, and to carry on with corruption and the preservation of their vested interests. They are not haunted by the possibility that, while they are bogged down in the mess of their own making, the rest of the world might bypass them.

We have no sense of efficiency and of healthy competition. When the price of rubber or coffee goes down, for example, Indonesian growers simply stop tapping rubber and wait till good prices come back. No thought is given to cost accounting and control, better marketing, improvement in quality, better management, and so on. Some years back, Indonesian shopkeepers in Jogjakarta, for example, unblushingly protested to the government about "unfair practices" by a Chinese shopkeeper, who tried to boost his sales by giving away prizes (including motorbikes) to people who came to buy at his store. When the government-owned enterprises lost money, the first reaction was always to increase the price of their services. No serious attempt was made to look into their own inefficiency and mismanagement.

However imperceptibly, some changes in these attitudes are taking place, especially among our younger generation. Modern education, technology, increasing opportunities for a better life, and the creation of a more peaceful and healthier social and political atmosphere will draw more people into the world of rationality.

The modernization of agriculture (the use of machines, fertilizers, and pesticides), medical care, and modern communication will ultimately exert a strong influence, as they will free the peasants from the ancient gods and devils. Fishing boats equipped with engines and helped by modern navigational aids will free our fishermen from the gods of the seas and winds, and in the long run will affect their traditional attitudes.

Another generation or perhaps two will, I hope, bring us to the stage where our society will be able to generate the necessary rational forces to break this mytho-mystical bondage, enabling our people to gaze into the far distance of space and time dotted with the bright stars of a sane and prosperous future.

This is imperative because, if we really want to establish true international cooperation and understanding among nations on this earth, the gap between the rich and the poor nations must be bridged. The rich may be able to understand the poor, but the poor always find it very difficult to understand the rich.

After defeating Communism, we must not let Gatotkatja defeat modernization.

13

THE UNIVERSITY STUDENT IN SOUTH AND SOUTHEAST ASIA*

JOSEPH FISCHER

The widespread and furious involvement of university students in politics is one of the striking features of Asian history in the present century. In India, Burma, and Japan, university students have been initiators and agents in nationalist and independence movements, in the overthrow of governments, and in the rapid growth of radical political factions and parties. In the course of this political activity, student indiscipline has developed in its own well-established traditions in these countries. In Burma, India, and Indonesia, the activity of university and college students in the period prior to independence did not become less intense once independence was attained.

The patterns of student conduct formed in those circumstances have persisted, even though the ostensible objects of student agitation were attained with the advent of independence. In India, "student indiscipline" has been a continuing preoccupation of administrators, and it has claimed the attention of the central and state governments. In June, 1963, the

* Reprinted by permission of the author and the publisher from *Minerva*, II (Autumn, 1963), 39–53.

present military government of Burma, commanded by General Ne Win, was so provoked by rebellious youth that it destroyed the student-union building at the University of Rangoon. Whereas before independence political activities of students were focused on issues of independence from the foreign ruler, and all grievances were given a political tone, today's student agitation in the universities of South and Southeast Asia is much more diffuse and apolitical. It often appears to be disproportionate to the trivialities that occasion it. Bloody student riots in India and Burma have been caused by rises in tramcar fares, grievances against individual teachers and other staff members, the quality and quantity of food in refectories, and shortened holidays. The redress of grievances frequently leaves recalcitrance against academic authority just where it was before.

The fact of the matter is that the alleged grievances often do not at all express the sources of distress in the lives of so many of the young people of these countries. There is a general malaise of educated youth in countries like Burma, India, Ceylon, Indonesia, and Pakistan. Much of the agitation is a response to the strains of modernization in tradition-bound and impoverished countries and its apolitical character represents, in some measure, an advance over the preindependence readiness to think that political changes would resolve all existing difficulties. Nowadays, in South and Southeast Asia, the violent outbursts of the students have generally been directed toward persons and arrangements within the university itself. Teachers, vice-chancellors, deans, principals, examination questions, syllabi, hostels, and university buildings have been the targets.

In Burma, India, and Ceylon, recent agitation has not resulted in country-wide movements that espouse a particular ideology or that seek a major political change. The manifestations of student activity in certain Asian countries outside South and Southeast Asia, such as those that played a large part in South Korea in the past few years, are not reproduced in the countries in which university students once contributed so much to independence. The traditions of Aung San, U Nu, Sukarno, and Subhas Chandra Bose live on in student eruptions against authority, but they have lost their political and ideological "cause."

In the recent revolutions and political disturbances in South Korea, Turkey, Iran, and Japan, the political power of student groups has assumed national proportions and, in marked contrast to that of their South and Southeast Asian contemporaries, has been aimed directly at the government and the political parties in power. In Japan, the numerically small Zengakuren overnight has brought out 10,000 students to barricade the Diet or help to prevent the official visit of the President of the United States. In Korea, students in the face of military force martyred themselves and in large measure precipitated the abrupt downfall of Syngman Rhee. In Turkey, in apparent agreement with the army, university students became insurrectionary heroes in the downfall of the Menderes government. In Iran, despite the existence of a potentially repressive military machine, students of the University of Teheran have constantly flaunted the authority of the government.

In Latin America, too, in the Argentine, Peru, Brazil, and Ecuador, for example, the adherence of youth to movements of political extremism, and the use of violence to suppress them, have been constant features of university life in the present century. Latin America probably harbors the politically most active and powerful body of university students in the world. Why, during a time of such extreme disaffection from the world of their elders, do the university students in the region in question become so apolitical? Why should they be so disaffected, so restless and excitable? This is the fundamental question. Only when we have considered this can we begin to treat seriously the causes of both the political and nonpolitical directions of this state of agitation.

The university in South and Southeast Asia, as it is everywhere outside Western Europe, is an implantation of foreign inspiration, sometimes even of foreign foundation and support. They are largely the product of the urge to modernize.

The period between the beginning of World War I and 1930 was marked by the opening of a great many universities and colleges. In India, the following were established: Mysore and Banaras Hindu University in 1916, Osmania in 1918, Aligarh Muslim University in 1920, Dacca and Lucknow in 1921, Delhi in 1922, Nagpur in 1923, and Andhra in 1926. The universities of Calcutta, Bombay, Madras, and Allahabad date from the nineteenth century (1857, 1882, and 1887). In Burma, the University College was established in 1920 during a time of political crises (Rangoon University as such did not emerge until 1942, but its establishing act was suspended until the end of World War II). The parent college of the present University of Ceylon (incorporated in 1942) dates from 1921. In Thailand, Chulalongkorn University opened its doors in 1917, and Thammasat University in 1934. No universities as such existed in Indonesia during its colonial period. A number of faculties, however, had been established prior to independence; they included the Technical Institute in Bandung (1920), the Faculties of Law (1924), Medicine (1927), and Literature (1940) at Djakarta, and the Faculty of Agriculture (1940) at Bogor. Many of these colleges and universities were established partly to meet increasing political demands on the part of the educated and commercial classes for wider educational and employment opportunities.

When independence was attained, many Asian universities found themselves adrift institutionally with depleted staffs, inadequate resources and facilities, rapidly rising enrollments, and without any significant achievements in science and scholarship to justify self-esteem and public appreciation. Independence was the occasion for the establishment of more universities. The Asian universities—the older ones as well as the newly established ones—found themselves highly vulnerable to the pressures generated by independence. The main, and perhaps only, response of the universities of Asia to governmental and public demands has been expansion. Serious questions of university reform have had to be neglected in order to meet this primary obligation to expand in response to the greatly whetted appetite for educational qualifications that is so characteristic of formerly colonial territories.

Now, as before, Asian governments remain the chief employers of educated persons in their own societies. The recruitment of administrative, technological, and most members of the political elites from university ranks creates a further bond between Asian universities and their governments. With the exception of most of the universities in the Philippines, practically all of the universities of the Asian states are state-financed.

In Ceylon, the University at Peradeniya, though nominally a private corporation, is, despite its income from tuition fees, now primarily dependent upon an annual parliamentary grant. Two Buddhist universities established in 1961 are under the jurisdiction of the Ministry of Education. In India, the universities are almost totally dependent on what they receive from the central and state governments. In Burma, the Universities of Rangoon and Mandalay are private corporations that have in the past received nonaudited block grants from the central treasury; the Ne Win government has now brought these universities under military control. In Thailand, the two state universities (Chulalongkorn and Thammasat) are for the first time experiencing direct government intervention through the recently established National Education Council, which is a part of General Sarit's Prime Minister's Department. In Indonesia, universities are not only entirely dependent upon the resources of the central government but formal control over them, since 1961, has been exercised by a Ministry of Higher Education. However, in such essential matters as the appointment of staff, the content of the instructional programs, and the number of students in various faculties, universities have *de facto* autonomy.

Only in the Philippines are private universities significant. There are no private universities in Ceylon, Burma, Thailand, and Malaysia. Indonesia has two unimportant private universities: the University of Islam in Jogjakarta and Nommensen Lutheran University in Medan. Vietnam has only one at Hué. In contrast, in the Philippines nineteen of the twenty universities are private and enroll about 280,000 of the 300,000 university students in the country. However, despite this, one of the major private sectarian universities (Santo Tomas) receives a government subsidy that meets 60 per cent of its annual expenses. The two major private secular universities (University of the East and the University of the Far East) support themselves almost entirely from student fees.[1]

In view of this dependence of the state on the university for personnel and the nearly absolute dependence of the universities on the state for the employment of their graduates, as well as the absolute dependence of national universities upon the state for financial support, the lack of effective governmental control is remarkable. The great expansion of higher education has taken place practically outside the direction of even those governments that are highly committed to a socialistic pattern of national devel-

[1] The relationship of higher education to government is admirably treated by U Hla Myint, "The Universities of Southeast Asia and Economic Development," *Pacific Affairs,* XXXV (Summer, 1962), 116–27.

opment. Political parties have been abolished or are placed under control, labor unions have been restrained, severe censorship of the press and publication has been instituted, private enterprise has been constructively regulated, yet the higher educational system has, in the main, been left to shift for itself as regards admissions policy and courses of study. It is only in the medium of instruction that the government has intervened. In Ceylon, the government's demand for the use of Sinhalese in the public-education sector has generated intense conflicts. Indonesia has made the greatest break with the language of its former ruler as a medium of instruction, although, remarkably enough, Dutch sources still dominate the offerings of the various law faculties.

On the whole, except for speeches and occasional police actions, the governments do little about the universities' relations with their students. Where government has begun to express serious concern, the unrest of students has already begun to assume proportions that preclude ready governmental mastery of the situation. No effective procedures have been devised to deal with the student indiscipline that has closed universities and caused deaths and injuries at Lucknow, Allahabad, Banaras, Calcutta, Patna, Rangoon, Peradeniya, and Mandalay.

Rangoon University students steal a set of final examination papers, and all students are passed without examinations for the current academic year. Students at Allahabad University barricade the residence of the rector and prevent the delivery of food supplies. Students in Banaras damage the laboratories of the modern medical school to proclaim the need for greater support for traditional Hindu medicine. Students at Dacca University in East Pakistan are provided with a student-union building for "cultural pursuits," and then turn it into a center for political agitation and violence. Politicians in Ceylon, Burma, and Indonesia, for example, often pay submissive deference to even the most violent activities of students. In these countries, to rough up a student is a *cause célèbre*, and a student who dies in protest, be it through self-denial of food, an accident, a police bullet, or a love-suicide, becomes, overnight, a kind of minor hero.

Governmental reactions to the problems of university student indiscipline in South and Southeast Asian countries range from passive and patient deference (India) to angry criticism and, finally, to military countermeasures (Burma). It is not that the political elites of the new states of South and Southeast Asia are entirely indifferent to this student eruptiveness. They are distressed by it. They find it inexplicable, and they are bewildered by it. Many of the political leaders cannot understand the rebellious behavior of youth in countries where colonialism has been terminated, where, they believe, there is a great need for talented and energetic young adults, and where the government does so much for them as compared with what it does for other sectors of the population.

The young adults who attend universities in 1963 form an important and growing body; there are over 300,000 in the Philippines, 50,000 in Indonesia, about 160,000 in Pakistan, about 3,500 in South Vietnam, some

2,500 in Malaysia, about 42,000 in Thailand, about 15,000 in Burma, close to 4,000 in Ceylon, and in excess of 1,000,000 in India. The total for India represents more than a doubling of the university population since 1951. The University of Ceylon student population has grown from 904 in 1942, and 2,392 in 1953, to about 4,000 in 1963. The entire university population in Indonesia in 1940 consisted of 585 students; Gadjah Mada University alone has grown from 387 students in 1947, and 6,529 in 1953, to its present enrollment of almost 17,000. During the period from 1947 to 1963, student enrollment at Rangoon University has increased from 2,636 to about 13,000. In the years to come, these figures will increase, and the human beings that the figures represent will form the bulk of the carriers of public opinion of the country. Technologists, administrators, politicians, journalists, and teachers will come almost entirely from this pool. Their outlook and qualifications are obviously of the greatest importance for the future of their countries. Yet they are being allowed to stagnate and fester.

The causes or conditions of student unrest fall into four general categories. These may be classified as follows: the cleavage between generations, the absence of authoritative models of conduct, the restricted range of opportunities for achievement and conviviality, and the scarcity of socially and economically rewarding opportunities for employment. My observations about these factors were derived primarily from data gained by questionnaires and interviews and from my observations as a teacher and a research worker at universities in Burma, Ceylon, Thailand, Indonesia, and India between 1954 and 1958 and from 1960 to 1962.

In underdeveloped countries, in which traditional systems predominate but where drastic changes in social structures are occurring, the gulf between the older, less-well-educated generation and the younger generation in attendance at universities is much wider than it is in countries where, whatever the differences in education, there is more of a common moral culture shared by less-educated parents and their highly educated offspring. University students between the ages of seventeen and twenty-five represent the group in underdeveloped societies that is most exposed to the institutions and beliefs of modernity and that is, in many respects, most responsive to it. It is the students who study foreign languages, read foreign periodicals, and meet foreigners. The ideas they encounter in their studies come from a very much wider world than that in which their parents live. Their lives as students are hard. Many of them are poor. They live scantily; they have poor places to study in, poor recreational opportunities. Poverty and boredom accentuate the normal intergenerational strain.

During the colonial period of higher education, when entry into universities tended to be more confined to the offspring of already more modernized and educated classes, fathers and their eldest sons held relatively similar views about the world. Since many Asian countries have become independent, it has been possible for the younger sons and even some of the daughters of such families to go to the university. But more important, it has become possible for the offspring of clerks, small traders, and, occasionally, even peasant cultivators to go to the university. More-over, young men who under normal conditions would have been under the domination of quite authoritarian family systems now find themselves at the university, relatively free from that authority simply by being some distance away and immune from its controlling scrutiny; they are now at large in a type of institution and ecological environment that is new to many of them and at which their behavior is relatively uncontrolled. The universities have no way of supervising their pupils—the staff are over-worked as it is.

This emancipation from the familial authorities under whom they grew up goes hand-in-hand with a tendency to look critically at all authority and to regard its demands as oppressive. The emancipation from familial au-thority extends to the refusal to accept institutional and political authority as well. The elites of the new states, even though they were once revolu-tionary students, are now middle-aged and even old men. They certainly appear old—like parents and teachers—and, to the young students, they come to share in the opprobrium that, in their view, the aged and repres-sive parent is accorded. They belong to the "established authorities"; they are thought to be on the side of oppression, of officialdom; they are remote. The order of things that they represent does not recommend itself to young persons in the process of education and emancipation.

There is a further reason, also due to the separation of the youth from the traditional pattern of authority, that contributes to explosive restive-ness.

In the traditional sector of the Asian and South Asian societies in the past, adolescents and youths tended to be heavily impregnated by ex-emplary moral authority. By identification, as well as by precept, a young person learned what constitutes the good life, what makes the wise man, and what knowledge is necessary for an appropriate place in the society. The teacher or guru or *blukkhu* or ulama was such an exemplary moral authority. He was a man of religion and of wisdom; both the spiritual and the earthly were his domains. The evidence of his spirituality and his knowledge lay in their application to his own life. His conduct was his legitimation. The master-disciple relationship between teacher and stu-dent in traditional Asia enabled the young to model their own existence upon that of their teacher. This model was a mentor and a guide; these exemplary teachers exercised great influence upon the young in Hindu, Buddhist, or Islamic societies. The coming of European culture and the establishment of a secular university education destroyed this rule. Re-ligious knowledge and experience were absent from the educational cur-riculum in universities, except as objects of scholarship in the Western style. The teacher became simply a teacher; his subject was the extent of his responsibility; his diffuse moral influence was not integrated with his specific responsibility as a teacher. The other responsibilities that were sometimes officially imposed on the teacher were separate things: the su-pervision of games or wardenship of hostels was specific. They had no diffuse moral overtone. There were, of course, university teachers who were different from the prevailing pattern. There were charismatic personalities, men who cared for their pupils, but they were rare.

This has all taken a turn for the worse with the great expansion of the university student body and the sharp upward movement of the student-teacher ratio. For example, at Gadjah Mada University, in 1960, there were 145 professors and lecturers for 13,139 students, and, of these 145, no more than 60 per cent were in residence on the campus, and more than 20 per cent held more than one teaching position. At Rangoon University, the student-teacher ratio in 1962 was estimated at about 200 to one. In the Philippines, in some private secular universities in Manila, the ratio may run as high as 300 to one, with only 20 per cent of the faculty in residence. Under such circumstances, personal contact between the university teacher and his students has become rarer than it was. Teachers do not have much time, even if they have the inclination. Many of them must pursue other employment in order to supplement the small income that they get from teaching. They do not have rooms where they can receive students. But even if they had more leisure and more inclination, there would still be too many students.

The poor conditions of life and study into which the students are thrown, the need to read in foreign languages in which they are not fully at ease, the all-governing importance of performance in examinations—all of these make the university a distressing place to be in; yet it is one that has an irresistible attraction. Being there is, at the same time, irresistible and intolerable. The university authorities and teachers become the focus of the resentment that these conditions generate in the students.

The situation of the students is rendered more difficult by the deficient opportunities afforded for harmless pleasures in the universities, in the towns in which they are situated, and by the societies of which they are part.

In most Asian societies, young people today have, as never before, become conscious of themselves as individuals. The growth of individuality has been one of the unintended consequences of nationalism, urbanization, industrialization, and the impact of mass media. The individualization of aspirations for achievement, for pleasure, for conviviality has become marked. The university is now the condition and the barrier to the realization of these aspirations, which are now held by far more young persons than ever before.

The student of a South or Southeast Asian university is now in a position in which he must "succeed." This is something new in the culture from which he has come. The student who fails at university is a failure in life, since the certification of the degree is necessary for employment by a public body. (He is also a failure in the eyes of his kinsmen and the people of his village or district, since they set very great store by his satisfactory progress toward the degree.)

Of 2,000 students in Indian, Burmese, and Indonesian universities who were interviewed or who replied to a questionnaire, 60 per cent were primarily concerned with their chances for successfully completing their university studies. Yet the realities of the system in most Asian universities frustrate even the most zealous students, and those whose will to study is weaker are discouraged all the more easily. Much of the frustration grows out of shortages—books, library seats, teachers, laboratories, classrooms, residential accommodation. Many of these deficiencies are functions of economic backwardness, and their solution will depend on economic growth. Some of the irritants and obstacles that trouble the students, however, are the result of institutional traditions that could be modified by determined action more easily than the less remediable shortages of resources.

The university system in most Asian universities is outmoded and unrealistic in the face of exploding populations and pervasive commitments to mass education, to say nothing of the tasks that the elites of these countries claim they wish to face. The examination system is one instance of a practice that has been unthinkingly adhered to and that has pernicious effects. The oral examination that is practiced in so many Indonesian and Indian universities is impossible to administer objectively where student-teacher ratios are 200 to one or more, and where one-third of the staff is inaccessible to the students. An academic system that grants great latitude to the students to request reexamination helps to produce chaos in universities where the enrollment is 5,000 or more, and where constant changes are being made in requirements. Five hundred students in an Indonesian university were asked to estimate how many more years it would take them to obtain degrees. More than half of them said they did not know. These students had no way of determining where they stood; the requirements that governed their study were vague and indefinite. Oral and written examinations, term papers, and lists of books to be read (often in three or more languages), standards varying from teacher to teacher and from department to department, the intrusion of extraneous criteria in determining academic success—these and more are part of the disorder that confronts and frustrates the students' progress through the university. The traditional European view that students are mature enough to be given the responsibility for the allocation of their time, that requirements should be set down only for large blocks of time, and that performance in a few examinations set once a year, or every two years, or even at the end of the entire university course, should be the only measures of success, has in the present-day Asian university resulted in much disorganization among the students.

Alienation from the university system is, of course, the natural result of such conditions. The alienation is reflected in the relative unimportance that students accord to genuine intellectual achievement and in the rarity with which intellectual curiosity, or intrinsic interest in a profession, is aroused among them.

The absence of conditions that might awaken intellectual passion only aggravates the effects of a parallel restriction in opportunities for the pleasures of conviviality. University students have been introduced to ideas about a freer contact between male and female and have sometimes verged on relationships with the opposite sex that are antithetical to the traditions of their own societies. The mere presence of young women, unrelated by kinship, in situations unprovided for by the indigenous culture arouses erotic interest. The experience of films, books, journals, newspapers, radios, and foreigners fosters fantasies and desires that cannot be fulfilled in most Asian educational environments. Since most Asian universities are not physically isolated from all traces of local indigenous society, indigenous traditions still weigh upon the student; they are not strong enough to suppress what they forbid. Moreover, opportunities are in no way proportionate to the new desires. In a series of samples of more than 1,500 students in four Southeast Asian universities, who were asked: "What has been the most serious personal problem that has adversely affected your university studies?" more than 80 per cent answered, "troubles with the opposite sex." This did not mean troubles with females with whom relationships had been established, but rather the inability to initiate any relationships at all with them. The stories are legion of Rangoon University male students who for months follow, from a distance, female students they admire, in the hope that somehow they might be introduced to them. The initiation of the faintest and least erotic heterosexual relationships in Asian universities is hampered by inhibition and uncertainty. Many an Indonesian female student has been confronted by a university youth who has never uttered a word to her until his proposal of marriage. It is hard to imagine relationships between members of the opposite sex in which there is a greater discrepancy between the desired and the actual than those taking place in Asian universities. The liberating theories of sociology and psychology and the impact of foreign media of communication have served to deepen this gap. The sexual propensities of university students in South and Southeast Asia are stimulated on the one side and either repressed or distorted on the other. At a meeting of the World Health Organization in 1962,[2] a marked increase in venereal disease among Asian university students was reported. Inasmuch as any fruitful relationships between the sexes, regardless of their intensity, duration, and quality, that go beyond sitting in the same classroom or bus, and the like, must be conducted clandestinely (and privacy is hardly possible in Asia), the consequences and ramifications are bound to be unsatisfactory to the participants and disturbing to their elders.

It must be remembered that the separation of the sexes is characteristic of most secondary and some public schooling in Asia. This circumstance and prevailing family social codes mean that the university presents youths with their first opportunities for being in the prolonged presence of young women who are not members of their kinship group. The existence of student unions and various other social clubs and groups serves to increase contact and heighten desires, while offering few opportunities

[2] World University Service, *Student Health in Asia.* Report of a meeting held in Ceylon in April, 1962.

for even very mildly erotic satisfaction, such as talking privately to a young woman. The distractions and torments of this combination of excitation and frustration undoubtedly interfere greatly with the students' academic performance, increase their touchiness, and confront university authorities with situations with which, given their present attitudes, they are hardly ready to deal.

One of the few areas where students can find some socially acceptable opportunities for emotional expression is in games and sports. However, even here, existing facilities in Asian universities are far short of what is required. University officials and ministries of education are loath to invest in swimming pools, gymnasiums, and sports fields, when there are shortages of books, classroom, library, and laboratory space, and inadequate salaries for teachers.

The opportunities for the students to engage in extracurricular artistic, dramatic, and literary activities are also very meager. Asian universities have been very backward in providing for student interest and activity in art, drama, dance, music, and literature. The interest of Asian students in traditional and modern arts is really quite extraordinary. The number of Indonesian students skilled in the manipulation of shadow puppets and Indian students skilled in the drum is large. In addition, a sizable number of students are interested in modern painting, drama, and literature. Despite this, there is a general lack of interest among university administrators and teachers in encouraging such cultural pursuits. The university tends to regard cultural activities as only fitting for academic study, and even here the feeling is that the provision for such subjects as music, dance, painting, and drama is a luxury that underdeveloped societies can ill afford. Students, however, seek cultural activities as a means of self-expression; they wish to participate as performers and spectators and have little academic interest in such matters. Funds for cultural activities have to be solicited by the students themselves. Eventually, the effect of this is to dampen enthusiasm and to eliminate yet another possibility of satisfaction for students.

Opportunities for free-ranging political discussion are likewise constricted. In Burma, Thailand, and Pakistan, the boundaries of any type of political discussion are set by military governments. Student activities that touch on politics are permitted only when they are consonant with views of the military elite; they are encouraged only when student groups can be exploited by political parties, such as has been the case in Indonesia, Ceylon, and India. The occasional involvement of the students in politics is considered inherently oppositional by the incumbent political elite and therefore dangerous to its security of tenure. In Burma, the once powerful student associations, because they still took an interest in politics, were deprived of their power by the most drastic procedures. Indonesian university youth groups are permitted to express themselves about political matters only to the extent that they are in agreement with President Sukarno's party and the military group that cooperates with it. In Thailand, political action among university students is practically prohibited. In Ceylon, communal dissension between Sinhalese Buddhists and Tamil Hindus has aggravated student conflict but has narrowed the scope for moderate political attachments.

There is little ease or richness of life for the university students under prevalent circumstances. Students ill-qualified for intensive intellectual exertion and hampered in the pursuit of beneficial routines seek their cultural and intellectual gratification in films and reading the thinnest of novels and stories. A sample of Burmese and Indonesian university students revealed, for example, that more than half spent more of their time at the movies than in the laboratory and library.

Under such conditions, some of the university students who either have no pleasure in their studies or are even bored and bewildered by them, and who are still not completely demoralized, will turn more and more to bitterly alienated groups. The student political groups that are permitted in Ceylon, Burma, and Pakistan—in India there are no prohibitions—largely devote themselves to unrealistic and irresponsible agitation, others less formally organized lead or lend themselves to the disturbance of the peace of the university.

The poor prospects of employment following the degree are fundamental to the insecurity of the university youth. Since the intellectual and humane values of education do not interest most of the students, and the pursuit of learning is rare, the dim practical prospects further the demoralization and alienation of the students. Considerations of status, prestige, occupational security, personal political power, and some vague sense of entry into a charmed circle centering around governmental power motivate a majority of those who participate in the higher educational system. Few aspire to enter an occupation of their own choice. Occupational preferences are traditional, and they are not ordinarily determined by individual aptitude or deliberate choice or a realistic view of employment opportunities or the needs of their society. Law, the liberal arts, and medicine dominate the higher levels of education. Even the chances of entering an uninteresting but dignified post seem to be diminishing as the number of students increases, while the economy moves forward at a much slower pace.

In many Asian countries, particularly in India, Japan, and the Philippines, the absolute demand for highly qualified technicians and technologists is quite high. There are, in addition, considerable opportunities in the private sector of the economy. However, Asian university students generally still seek government employment; indeed in many of these countries there are, in fact, few opportunities outside of the government. However, it is not just the fact that the preference for government service predominates but rather that the vast majority seek *administrative* positions. Administration is, in their minds, synonymous with power, with security of tenure and certainty of advancement, and with the most gratifying position in the world—namely, proximity to the center of society.

It is, of course, true that efficient administration is vital to Asian development, but the hunger for administrative employment has not resulted, as it did in colonial times, in producing an overpopulated class of cadre. It has instead resulted in producing an overpopulated class of indifferent administrators and a system that generates standards leading to much waste of valuable talent. For example, engineers, chemists, and economists prefer to be administrators, while leaving complex technical tasks to individuals who have had little specialized training. Surveys made of the activities of elites in Thailand, Burma, Indonesia, and India indicate that in some fields as many as 60 per cent of those trained are not using their skills or the specialized knowledge that university training has given them. In Thailand, a survey made of 125 chemists, of whom 85 had foreign degrees, indicated that slightly more than half were serving as administrators in positions totally removed from chemistry. In Indonesia, a study made by the writer of the first 900 alumni from all faculties during 1952–60 from Gadjah Mada University showed that of the 85 per cent who entered government service, some 70 per cent were working as administrators in fields in which 45 per cent of these graduates had not received training. To the extent that this is a matter of choice and not of necessity, it reflects, for a considerable number of graduates, a lack of genuinely professional orientation. It is an attitude that appears to have been nurtured by the universities, as well as by the semimodern traditions of colonial societies that accorded primacy to government employment regardless of its vocational content.   .

The incidence of unemployment among Indian university graduates was already severe before independence. In the other countries that had very small university student bodies or none at all, it was not a pressing problem. Then, after independence, those countries, Indonesia for example, which had no indigenous higher civil service before independence and in which, in 1940, there were no more than 1,000 people with higher education out of a population of 60 million, were at first able to absorb all their small output of university graduates. In the latter countries, too, the situation is beginning to move toward the Indian pattern.

In underdeveloped countries where skills are scarce, authority unstable, and economic pressures enormous, the products of the universities have a crucial role to play. They are the generation with the least commitment to maintaining the status quo; they are the least vulnerable to political control and military force; they are the most impressionable, the most energetic, the most secular, the least traditional, and the most uncommitted group in Asia. They are relatively indulged by their societies. They could become the catalytic force in generating change and in demonstrating the extraordinarily beneficial consequences that can accrue to a society from reasonable self-sacrifice. But their energies are being dissipated, and their talents are being left uncultivated. When they do organize politically, they tend to remain outside the process of civil politics, and their role tends to be destructive. Those who might perform useful services to their societies are either thwarted by a resistant academic system, by unsympathetic political and military elites, or by the binding and often frustrating traditions of their families.

Student problems are amenable to solution. Asian governments and their universities have a number of opportunities to bring higher education into line with the demands of the nation and the needs of the individual. To accomplish this, however, education cannot remain what it is at present— the least planned and least evaluated sector of national policy. Entry into the higher levels of the educational system can and must be regulated on the prospective demand and the likelihood of outstanding performances. Control over the flow of students to different faculties lies within the present capabilities of most underdeveloped Asian states, yet very little is being done. Indonesia has established a Ministry of Higher Education but has no plan for control and development of its universities. The new policies of the military in Burma have been directed at preventing any activity by politicized students rather than at reforming the university system. In the Philippines, an attitude of complete laissez-faire exists towards the universities. Only in Thailand and Malaysia have some constructive efforts been directed toward limiting enrollments and toward making higher education somewhat more consonant with national needs. The state has the means, via scholarships, subsidies, and differential salaries, to influence occupational preferences. Governments can encourage and sponsor the development of needed skills and can alter the traditional pursuit of administrative positions. Relatively reliable measures and standards of achievement can be developed. Technological performance can be emphasized and differentially rewarded. The academic system can be revitalized. The talents and energies of educated youth can be rendered beneficial to society and yet satisfying to the individuals involved. The universities and their graduates could then turn out to be the most efficacious of all the available agencies for affecting the magnitude and rapidity of economic and social growth to which most underdeveloped nations have committed themselves.

14

MODERNIZATION IN A MUSLIM SOCIETY:
THE INDONESIAN CASE*

CLIFFORD GEERTZ

As a phrase, "modernization in a Muslim society" begs more conceptual issues in fewer words than almost any I can think of: only the preposition seems straightforward. First, there are the much discussed difficulties implicit in the notion of "modernization." The relationships between "modernization" and "Westernization," the usefulness of sorting cultural patterns and social practices into pigeonholes labeled "traditional" and "modern," the "progressive" role certain "reactionary" institutions such as the extended family, ascribed status or personal clientship seem to play in some modernizing situations—all these have become recurrent concerns in the scholarly literature on the new states. Second, with respect to "a society," considered as a total, bounded unit, the question has been raised as to whether it can be a proper object of scientific study at all, or whether we must not instead resign ourselves to investigating particular ranges of social institutions—family, class, religion—and the specific relations obtaining

* Reprinted with permission of The Macmillan Company from *Religion and Progress in Free Asia*, edited by Robert N. Bellah. Copyright © 1965 by The Free Press, a division of The Macmillan Company.

among them without attempting to talk about society "as a whole." Some have gone so far as to suggest that such entities as "Indian society" or "French society" do not even exist in any recognizable sense, that these terms are merely misleading names of political units—that is, states. But of the three main concepts in my assigned title it is the third—Muslim—that, somewhat surprisingly, conceals the most radical difficulties, for here the sheer possibility of scientific analysis threatens to disappear. Some Orientalists, at least, are coming, as a result of a deepening awareness of the disparate character of "Islam" as a practiced faith from place to place and of the varying nature of the impact of the modern world on different "Muslim" countries, to doubt "whether in *the religious realm* there is either in empirical fact or in theory anything to which the name Islam can meaningfully be given:"[1]

> There is the Islamic tradition which the historian can reconstruct and which is, both in practice and in principle, an accumulating, evolving, observable actuality. For some centuries, this was sufficiently stable for an abstraction called "Islam" to be reasonably significant and academically serviceable. But this was not true in the earliest centuries of Islamic history, and is again not true today. . . . The scholar, if he is historically erudite, can report the accumulating tradition, and if he is sensitive and imaginatively perceptive as well as disciplined, he can report the actual faith of living persons. But can he tell what Islam as a religion "is"? Should he not rather [say] . . . that he has no access to such a thing, in either Heaven or earth?[2]

Thus, like some ancient parchment kept as an heirloom, our very problem threatens to crumble in our hands as soon as, ceasing simply to affirm its importance, we attempt actually to grasp it.

In countering this kind of stultifying historicism, which every significant increase in scholarly realism about social matters seems to bring with it, the anthropologist's response is always to turn again to the smaller canvas, for what in large seems vague and orderless may in small take on more precise and regular outlines. One can overcome many of the apparent failings of "modernization," "society," and "Islam" as abstractions by applying them within the context of a concrete example. The value of such an example does not lie in its typicality or in the possibility of assimilating other cases directly to it. Rather, it lies in the fact that, by viewing social and cultural processes in limited and specific terms, one can isolate some features of them that are truly general, features that, suitably adjusted to special circumstances, are relevant to the analysis of a whole family of cases. Whether or not they are in Heaven, Islam, modernization, and society are on earth. The problem is to know where to look for them.

I shall look for them in Indonesia, and, most particularly, in the religious school system there. This may seem an exceedingly odd place to threaten

[1] W. Smith, "The Comparative Study of Religion in General and the Study of Islam as a Religion in Particular," Colloque sur la Sociologie Musulmane, *Correspondance d'Orient, no. 5*, Publications du Centre pour l'Etude des Problèmes du Monde Musulman Contemporain, Brussels, pp. 1–15.

[2] *Ibid.*

a reduction of serious intellectual problems to matters of mere pedagogy, and scholastic pedagogy at that. But, in fact, the Muslim educational system is the master institution in the perpetuation of the Islamic tradition and the creation of an Islamic society, as well as the locus of the most serious efforts presently being pursued to modernize that tradition and society.

As it was in India, in Persia, or, to a lesser extent, in Morocco, Islam was intrusive in Indonesia, in the sense that it came late into an already well-established, non-Arabic civilization, which it slowly, and with great difficulty, only partly replaced. There are a number of results of this fact, of which perhaps the most important is that even the essentials of the Muslim faith—the Pillars, the acceptance of Koranic authority, the perception of Divine Majesty, and the acknowledgment of the Prophet—had always, and still have, to be maintained in the midst of a number of competing, even hostile, religious orientations of no mean strength, most of them also going, after the conversion of the thirteenth to sixteenth centuries, under the general name of "Muslim." Neither supported by the society and culture within which it grew up as Christianity in the West, Hinduism in India, or Islam in Arabia, nor unchallenged by other "great traditions," as were Buddhism in Burma and Thailand or Islam in Nigeria and the Sudan, Indonesian Islam had to secure its integrity entirely, so to speak, by its own efforts. It had to draw from within itself, from its own organizational and intellectual resources, the power to maintain continuity with its origins, to sustain contact with the distant heartlands of Islamic civilization, and to establish a clear and positive identity on the spiritually cluttered Indonesian scene. In this struggle, never wholly won and never wholly lost, the Muslim school played, and still plays, an absolutely critical role. Without the *pesantren* and, later, the *madrasah* and *sekolah Islam*, Indonesia would not have become even a nominally Islamic society from the simple circumstances of contact.

But beyond this "accultural" aspect, there are at least two other interrelated reasons why Southeast Asian Islam has been so dependent upon the school, which, as they derive from the nature of the Islamic tradition as such, make the Indonesian case relevant to more than itself. There are, first, the highly doctrinal, legalistic, scriptural—that is, basically literary —quality of at least the mainstream of the tradition, and second, the general absence of other social institutions within the religion capable of transmitting this sort of tradition effectively. The school has been important because, even on its mystical side, Islam had leaned heavily toward the scholastic since the other great institutions of scriptural religions—the priesthood, the sermon, even, despite the Friday prayer, collective ritual, have been, comparatively speaking, so weak, undeveloped, or, in the case of liturgy, thoroughly simplified.

Thus, the typical mode of Islamization, of an individual or of a group, has been, like all educational processes, painfully gradualistic. First, the Confession of Faith, then the other Pillars, then a certain degree of observance of the law, and finally, perhaps, especially as a scholarly tradition develops or takes hold, a certain amount of learning in the law, and in the Koran and hadith upon which it rests. The intricate body of norms, doctrines, explications and annotations that make up Islam, or at least Sunni Islam, can be apprehended only step by step, as one comes, to a greater or lesser degree, to control the scriptural sources upon which they rest. For most people, such control never goes beyond accepting, second hand, the interpretations of those who control, or seem to control, those sources directly. But that learning, however crude, access to scholarship, however shabby, is central to becoming a Muslim in anything more than a formal sense is apparent virtually everywhere in the Islamic world, for which al-Azahr is, from some points of view, a better epitome than Mecca. Islamic conversion is not, as a rule, a sudden, total, overwhelming illumination, but a slow turning toward a new light.

Certainly this has been the case in Indonesia. Spread first by foreign traders (Gujeratis, Malabarese, Kalins, Bengalis, Persians, Arabs, and even, here and there, a few Turks) and then by indigenous ones (Malays, Bugis, Makassarese, North Javanese), Islam found its initial foothold in the various spice-trade bazaar ports that grew up around the Straits of Malacca and the Java Sea after the thirteenth century. Very little is known about this formative period, at least on the cultural side, save that the creed as implanted had a distinctly Indian, thus mystical, cast centered around certain semihistorical itinerant teachers regarded as saints. After the Dutch conquest, which began at the turn of the sixteenth century and was reasonably well established, at least in Java and selected points in the Outer Islands, by the turn of the seventeenth, Indonesian Islam became more autonomous, both spreading out from its coastal beachheads and developing a solider, more deeply rooted institutional structure, not only in interior towns but, even more importantly, in the countryside. With the establishment, in the middle of the nineteenth century, of more direct relations with Mecca through the Hadj (by about 1850, transport facilities had progressed to the point that more than 2,000 people could make the pilgrimage each year), more orthodox practices and ideas began to penetrate the Indonesian *ummat* and to transform it into something less completely Indic. By the beginning of this century, nearly 7,500 pilgrimages were being made annually, and in the great boom year of 1926–27, 52,000 Indonesians journeyed to the Holy City, to constitute more than 40 per cent of its foreign population.[3] By this time, reformist ideas, of Al-Azahr and based on the teachings of Muhammad Abduh (1849–1905), were prevalent in the Hejaz—particularly after the triumph in Mecca of Ibn Saud—and a few Indonesians even found their way to Cairo to study at the great university itself. As a result, an Indonesian version of reform Islam—a reading of the ideals of nineteenth-century liberalism and humanism into primitive

---

[3] J. Vredenbregt, "The Hadj: Some of Its Features and Functions in Indonesia," *Bijdragen tot de Taal—, Land—en Volkenkunde* (1962) **118**:91–154.

Islam, as Caskel has characterized it[4]—grew up in the archipelago in opposition both to the orthodox stream and to the popular syncretism of the
mass of peasants. Finally, since independence there has been an almost
desperate search for a way to relate Islam—orthodox and reform alike—to
the modern world in general and to the secular Indonesian state in particular. And at each of these stages of Islamization, it has been one or another
form of the Muslim school that has been the social, structural foundation
upon which the entire, now 700-year-old development has rested.

The generic name for the traditional Muslim school in Indonesia is
pesantren—"a place of religious students" (*santri*)—and, historically speaking, it grew not out of the classical Islamic academy, the *madrasah*, but
out of the Hindu-Buddhist monasteries of medieval Java, secluded com-
pounds in which monks or other adepts studied and composed holy writings, where religious pilgrims rested, sometimes years on end, on their
sacred journeys, and where local youths were instructed in their faith. Except that the scriptures involved became Koranic rather than tantric and
the permanent residents ulama rather than monks, the traditional *pesantren*
was—and, in some places, still is—essentially the same institution. A walled
compound of student dormitories centered on a mosque, set usually in a
wooded glade at the edge of a village, it consisted of a religious teacher,
usually called a *kijaji*, and a number of young, in most cases unmarried,
male students—the *santris*—who chanted the Koran, engaged in mystical
exercises, and seem generally to have carried on the pre-existing Indic tradition with but a slight, and not very accurate, Arabian accent. The student
notebooks—the so-called *primbon*—that have come down to us from this
period are permeated with a heterodox mystical monism directed toward
the same sort of personal release as the explicitly Hindu-Buddhist writings
that precede them. And in such documents as we have—for example, the
late eighteenth- or early nineteenth-century didactic poem, *Serat Tjentini*—
that describe life in these schools before the growth of orthodoxy, the atmosphere seems far more reminiscent of India or Persia than of Arabia or
North Africa.

But even by the time of the *Serat Tjentini*, more orthodox tradition,
demanding a closer observance of the law as written, was appearing, stimulated by the improvement of communications—direct in the case of the
Hadj, indirect in the case of religious publications and Arab immigration—
with the Near Eastern heartland of Islamic civilization. The *pesantren* (or
at least many *pesantrens*) became much more of a proper Koranic school,
headed usually by a returned pilgrim and supported by a religious foundation by the local well-to-do. Though mysticism hardly disappeared, especially in Java, it came to be more rigorously contained within the bounds
laid down by al-Ghazzali and by the orthodox Sufi orders. The *pesantren's*

4 W. Caskel, "Western Impact and Islamic Civilization," in G. Von Grunebaum,
ed., *Unity and Variety in Muslim Civilization* (Chicago: University of Chicago Press,
1955), pp. 335–60.

form changed little, but its content changed significantly as knowledge, or half-knowledge, of the classical Islamic subjects—*figh, tafair, tarich, tawhid,* and so on—increased.

Thus the orthodox revival, which in Arabia took place in the eleventh and twelfth centuries and which, as Gibb has said, "marks the turning point in the history of Islamic culture,"[5] the creation of its still unbroken medieval synthesis, began to take firm hold in Indonesia only six or seven centuries later in the guise of a gradual educational reform that turned the *pesantren* into a mediator of that durable amalgam of *sharia* legalism and *tariqa* mysticism that Ghazzali legitimized.

Though as time passed and shipping schedules improved, the scholastic side of the *pesantren* grew rather stronger and the antinomian rather weaker, it was not until the launching of the reformist attack upon it, and upon the intellectual tradition for which it stood, that this descendant of the Hindu hermitage and the Buddhist monastery became at least a reasonable facsimile of an orthodox *madrasah*. The content of the reform movement is familiar from frequent description—a "back to the Koran" fundamentalism mixed with an "Islam is entirely up-to-date" modernism. But what is less familiar, because less described, is the profound social effect reformism, as abortive as it turned out to be, has had on the mainstream of Islamic orthodoxy. In Indonesia, at least, the ultimate importance of reformism is to be measured not so much in terms of its own success as a social movement, which was local and momentary at best, but in its transformative impact upon that to which it placed itself in opposition and seems ultimately to have been unable to dislodge: the *pesantren* tradition. If the counterreformation has triumphed, at least for the present, the social changes in religious pedagogy necessitated by that triumph mark perhaps another turning point in the history of Islamic culture. And as developments in the archipelago no longer trail those in the rest of the Muslim world, perhaps not in Indonesia alone.

In these terms, the main achievement of the reform movement in Indonesia was the introduction of the modern, graded, partly secularized, formally organized—in a word, rationalized—school into the established Islamic educational tradition. The modern school was not, of course, introduced into Indonesia by the Islamic reform movement, for Dutch government and Christian missionary schools, on a rather small scale, preceded them, and, in fact, acted as an added local stimulus to and model for the reformers' innovations. But the direct impact of these schools was largely confined, so far as the Indonesian population was concerned, either to the uppermost levels of the aristocracy or to the very small confessional minorities, and even when they were not, the orthodox distrusted and shunned them as infidel. For them, the ulama and the *santris* who (both at the *pesantren* and after leaving it for a more ordinary peasant or tradesman existence) were their followers, it was the reform movement that, however bitterly

[5] H. A. R. Gibb, *Studies on the Civilization of Islam,* eds. S. J. Shaw and W. R. Polk (Boston: Beacon Press, 1962), p. 22.

they at first resisted it, made secular learning, modern modes of teaching, and, in fact, the whole drift toward a less medieval world-outlook legitimate. Like the Sufi brotherhood before it, the modern school has become absorbed into the body of the Sunni tradition, and its effects, though as yet limited, may ultimately prove to have been as fateful.

The reformers called their schools *madrasah*, intending thereby to stress the fact (as they saw it) that the *pesantren* had been seriously compromised by a too intimate contact with heterodox local and Indic traditions, and that a thoroughgoing purification of these "backward" or "old-fashioned" institutions was essential before they could qualify for the title of a "genuine" Muslim school. The major innovations the *madrasah* introduced included the teaching of secular subjects (arithmetic, reading of Latin characters, national history and literature, geography, and so on), a curriculum organized along a strict subject, grade, and text-book pattern, complete with class hours, examinations, marks, diplomas, and so on, the employment of teachers who, though believing Muslims, made no claims to be ulama or even especially learned in the scriptures and the law, a day-school rather than a boarding-school pattern, and, perhaps most radical of all, the education (sometimes even the coeducation) of girls. Religious instruction continued, of course, occupying anywhere from three-quarters to a third of the curriculum; but even it was conducted in a novel manner. Rather than the chant-and-echo pattern of the *pesantren*, where the *santri*, ignorant of the meaning of the Arabic words he was repeating, gained what little understanding of the text he achieved from cryptic annotations offered ex cathedra by the *alim* (whose own Arabic was often enough hardly more than rudimentary), in the *madrasahs*, an attempt was made either to understand the Arabic text directly or to work with vernacular translations. Religious knowledge, such as it was, was therefore democratized to some extent, and the *haji-alim*'s role as privileged adept seriously undercut. Since by 1954 there were somewhere around 12,000 *madrasahs* with about 1.5 million pupils, as against about 53,000 *pesantren* with nearly 2 million pupils[6] (before the first decade of this century there were virtually no *madrasahs* in the modern sense at all), the impact upon Indonesian Islam of this most recent transformation in the country's most venerable educational system can hardly have been trivial. The precise nature of that impact is much more difficult to assess, but that it has been in the direction of a loosening of the grip of mindless ritualism and empty legalism seems certain. Secular political leaders and intellectuals, as well as Western scholars, who despair of the narrow confines within which the thought and feeling of the more pious sector of the Indonesian population seems to them to move, might do well to consider what that thought and feeling would have been like if the *madrasah* revolution had not occurred.

[6] *Indonesia*, Subcontractor's Monograph, Human Relations Area Files, New Haven, 1956, Vol. II, p. 422. As these are figures reported to the Ministry of Religion, the *pesantren* figures reported (where no subsidies are involved and a lingering suspicion of the intentions of the government is lodged) are almost certainly much too low.

Whether or not the *madrasah* has made Indonesian Islam modern, it has surely made it, for what must be the first time in its history, critically, even painfully, self-reflective.

The initial reaction of the orthodox to the appearance of the *madrasah* was, as one would expect, sharply hostile. The new pattern of education struck at the very foundations of ulama power. It was now not so important to have made the pilgrimage or to be able to chant the Koran from memory as it was to be able to communicate something of the intellectual content of the Islamic tradition and, beyond it, modern learning in general, and to relate, in some plausible way, the one to the other. But the orthodox reaction, though severe, was surprisingly short-lived. From the very beginning, some ulamas saw the direction in which they must move if they were to maintain their position as spiritual leaders of the more pious element of the Indonesian population. And by 1926, the number of such more perceptive and flexible Koranic scholars had grown to the point that a counterreform organization, called Nahdatul Ulama (the Renaissance of the Ulama), could be formed and, being formed, adapt the reformer's pedagogical innovations to the purpose of the *pesantren* tradition. *Madrasahs* began to appear, led by ulama but assisted and actually directed by some of their more modern followers, first independently of the *pesantren* and then finally within its very walls. For their part, the reformers, exhilarated by success and supported by the times, pushed the evolution of their own schools forward, developing the so-called *sekolah Islam*, Islamic schools, which, rather like Catholic parochial schools in the United States and much of Europe, are essentially secular schools with a place reserved for religious instruction, not *madrasahs*, where secular learning has no autonomous justification but is a mere handmaiden to sacred teachings. Thus the battle shifted from a simple opposition between the *pesantren* "monastery" or "hermitage" pattern and the graded-school pattern, to one between graded schools of varying religious temper, and arguments came to be centered around the proper relations between religious and nonreligious learning, rather than the legitimacy, or even the reality, of the latter altogether. The *pesantren* persists, as the figures I have just quoted indicate. But few now are without some secular education, offered either on their grounds or in a village *madrasah* nearby, which the *santris* are allowed, sometimes even required, to attend. The few institutions that have maintained the older tradition intact and have continued to exclude modern learning entirely have great difficulty attracting *santris* and are slowly fading—relics of an earlier stage of the evolution of Islam in Indonesia—from the scene.

In fact, in the distribution of types of Islamic educational institutions in Indonesia, one can see reflected the whole development of the religion in this, its most distant outlier. The orthodox synthesis of medieval Islam persists in the *pesantrens*, usually slightly modified by some fairly weak modern influences, sometimes not. There are even a few examples of the older mystical pattern still to be found in remoter regions. The reaction of this synthesis to the reformist attack, an absorption of a limited amount of basic secular instruction—reading, writing, and arithmetic—into orthodox study organized along somewhat more systematic lines, is found in the *madrasahs* which nearly every pious village now contains. And the reformers' concept of an Islam at once purified of medieval accretions and adjusted to the modern world finds its expression in the *sekolah Islam* —"parochial" elementary, middle, and normal schools—found mostly in the towns. In the larger cities, there have even appeared a few Islamic "universities." Thus the school—far more even than the mosque or prayer house, whose importance is almost purely ritualistic—is the social structural core of Indonesian Islam, now as in the past. And in the changes in its form is written more clearly than in the development of religious thought, legal, moral, or theological, which in Indonesia has always been more derivative than creative and not especially profound, the nature of the modernization process that Islam has undergone and, beneath the clamor of radical nationalist politics, is still undergoing.[7]

The fact that the renovation of "Islam" as a religious system tends to find its center of gravity in educational reform rather than in a reorganization of an ecclesiastical hierarchy or an alteration in liturgical practice or even, at least initially, in a reorientation of theological speculation, has some important implications for the whole process of "modernization in an Islamic society," not only in Indonesia but fairly generally.

One of the difficulties Islamic reform faces and, perhaps everywhere in the Sunni world save perhaps in Turkey, has always faced is the absence of readily identifiable targets against which to direct its attack. There is no Pope the supremacy of whom can be rejected, no priestly hierarchy whose mediating powers, special privileges, isolating celibacy, or symbolic fatherhood can be dispensed with, no sacraments that can be denied or reinterpreted, not even any official intellectual synthesis that, like Thomism, can be philosophically undermined. There are only the ulama—a loose collection of rather individualistic legal scholars and teachers without any formal status or special perquisites nor, at least until recently, any particular in-

---

[7] A full review of recent experiments in Islamic education in Indonesia would be out of place here, but attempts to set up new forms of religious schools continue. One pattern—started in Gonter, a village in south central Java, before the revolution and attempted after it in Jogjakarta and elsewhere—is to divide the curriculum into thirds: one-third instruction in secular subjects, one-third in religious subjects taught in a more modern fashion, and one-third practical work in fields, crafts, shops, and the like—a revision of the old work-your-way pattern of the *pesantrens*. The proponents of these schools argue that not only will they help to bring Islam "up to date," but that, with their practical, work-oriented bent, they will provide a more suitable education for Indonesian children than the clerk-oriented government schools. What the future of these experiments, most of which have been encouraged and supported by the Ministry of Religion, will be is uncertain, but that they are being planned and attempted shows that the vitality of the Koranic school tradition remains strong. In addition, of course, a great number of ordinary primary and secondary schools have been set up by Muhammadiyah (a modernist social welfare society), Nahdatul Ulama, and other Islamic organizations modeled on the state-run school system but with additional teaching in religious subjects. For a detailed description of the range of religious schools now (1952–54) existing in one region of Java, see C. Geertz, *The Religion of Java* (Glencoe, Ill.: The Free Press, 1960), pp. 177–98.

ternal organization—or the even more elusive and individualistic Sufi
Shaikhs. In such a socio-cultural framework, there is no point at which a
radical break-through, a sudden overturning of the whole system can be
accomplished, or, at least, if there is such a point, no one has yet been
able to find it. All that seems to be possible is a step-by-step attack on the
multiple strongholds of traditionalism, mystical and scholastic alike. The
great intellectual and sociological dramas of the Christian Reformation are
exceedingly difficult to stage in such a setting of dispersed and rather uncertain religious authority, and attempts to do so lead almost inevitably to
fruitless sectarian schism.

It is perhaps for this reason that many Western scholars of Islam seem
to be so disappointed, even personally put out, by the reform movement
and have, at times anyway, rather underestimated its transformative effects
upon the Islamic tradition. Expecting Luthers and Calvins, they have got
instead a collection of, for the most part, rather cautious pedagogues; instead of a few great thinkers of surpassing boldness, there has appeared a
cloud of not terribly distinguished and usually rather unoriginal academi-
cians. This makes history—and history-writing—less colorful; but, in the
same way that Islamization has been in the past a gradual process, a slow
accretion of minor changes rather than a series of spectacular quantum
jumps, so, too, and for the same reasons, may its modernization be. Sixty
years ago the great Dutch Islamic scholar, Snouck Hurgronje, warned his
colleagues in the Netherlands East Indies civil service that Indonesian
Islam, which seemed so static, so sunk in a torpid medievalism, was actually changing in fundamental ways, but these changes were so gradual, so
subtle, so concentrated in remote and, to non-Islamic minds, unlikely
places, that "although they take place before our very eyes, they are hidden
from those who do not make a careful study of the subject."[8]

Today, after four decades of thoroughgoing and quite obvious upheaval
in the Indonesian *ummat* have rendered these words prophetic, the warning
they contain is no less apposite. The tendency to underestimate the dynamic of Islam is as apparent both among the governing elite and among
learned scholars as it was a century ago, a characterization that holds, by
and large, for the leaders of Islamic countries and students of Islam generally.

So far as reorientation and mobilization of traditional values in the modernization process of a Muslim society is concerned, the picture I have
given of the Indonesian case has, if it is accurate, some important policy
implications for the elites of the new states of South and Southeast Asia,
who have found that traditional value systems growing out of long-standing
religious commitments have proved to represent "a much more important
problem in the modernisation process than had been anticipated by most
of these modernisers."[9]

[8] C. Snouck Hurgronje, *The Achehnese* (Leiden; 1906), p. 280.
[9] Soedjatmoko, "Cultural Motivations to Progress: The 'Exterior' and the 'Interior'
Views," in Robert N. Bellah, ed., *Religion and Progress in Modern Asia* (New York:
The Free Press, 1965), pp. 1–14.

By far the most important of these implications is that the continuation of a vital school tradition, and especially of its renovation, is essential to what Soedjatmoko calls "a comparatively smooth modernisation." And this, in turn, leads to what may seem to be a curious paradox: namely, that a strong and active parochial school system (if I may adapt this Catholic Christian term to Muslim uses) is not, in an Islamic country, and certainly not in Indonesia, an enemy but rather an ally of a secularist modernizing elite. It is an ally, not because it promotes the ideals of a militant and totalistic secularism (ideals that only a small minority of these elites themselves hold), but because it allows, and, in fact, encourages, an established religious tradition with a powerful hold on the minds of the population to come to terms with the modern world, neither simply rejecting nor simply capitulating to it, but becoming part of it. More paradoxically yet, it is not a rigid separation of education from religious influence that will make a rendering unto Caesar the things that are Caesar's possible for an Islamic society, but rather the further integration of secular and religious learning in modern-type schools. It is only through such schools that Islam, on the sociological level, and in consequence on the intellectual level as well (for ideas cannot develop in a social vacuum), will be able to come into the modern world. To cut the *ummat* off from this one regenerating institution in its midst by a strict adherence to a state supported and directed secular school system and a vague hostility to "Koranic" schools as "backward," "feudal," or "fanatic" is to insure the rigidification of Islamic institutions generally and, in consequence, Islamic thought.

Today, as in the past, the school is the lifeline of the Islamic tradition, and the reformed school is that tradition's path to the present. It is essential that this path should not be blocked by shallow and short-sighted "modernization" policies that attempt to catch up with the West by a mindless imitation of its external forms.

15

THE "CLERK MENTALITY" IN BURMESE EDUCATION*

JAMES F. GUYOT

Postwar Burma presents the paradox of a nation formally committed to modernization in which the most modern segment, the civil bureaucracy, shows little ability to act as an agent of modernization. Instead, this task has been taken up by the military, a less formally modern body. Of the several available explanations for this situation, the one explored here focuses on the character of the education of Burmese bureaucrats. Two dimensions will be established for classifying styles of education and bureaucratic behavior in colonial and postcolonial settings. One is administrative and distinguishes between generalist and specialist structures. The

* From *Education and the Social Sciences*, edited by Joseph Fischer. © 1970 by the International Textbook Company. Reprinted by permission of the publishers.

This essay was originally prepared for the Comparative Education Conference, School of Education and Institute of International Studies, University of California, Berkeley, March 25–27, 1966. The data utilized here were gathered in the fall of 1962 in Burma, one of the last years that American scholars were able to visit Burma for extended periods. The author is greatly indebted to the brothers and their students at the high school where this work was done, to the Psychology Department of Rangoon University, and to Messrs. Charles M. Dennis, Steven Gifis, and Lee Boon Hiok in the United States.

other is psychological and distinguishes between an achievement orientation and its shadow image, the clerk mentality. Particular attention will be
paid to the achievement motive and the clerk mentality as they appear in
a sample of potential bureaucrats, students in an elite Rangoon high
school. In this way I hope to provide both a theoretical setting and an operational definition for the "slave education" indictment that frequently
appears in postcolonial polemics.

WHY MODERNS DO NOT MODERNIZE

By most standards, the officer grade of the Burmese civil service may be
judged more modern than either the political elite or the army officer
corps. If "modern" is simply defined as Westernized and measured by the
duration and intensity of contact with Western education, Western institutions, and Western individuals, then there is no question about their
modernity. Civil servants as a group have a higher average level of formal
education than their counterparts in the political and military elites.
Where only 30.5 per cent of the active politicians listed in *Who's Who in
Burma* in 1961 held a bachelor's degree and 41.5 per cent had at most a
high school education, 93.6 per cent of the civil servants listed had a B.A.,
and for most of them it was an honors degree. There is little systematic
information available about the formal education of members of the armed
forces, but, among the senior officer ranks, it appears to be slightly higher
than that of the politicians. Typically, a civil servant with training in the
West will have taken an advanced degree at a university, an army officer
may have graduated from Sandhurst or the U.S. Command and General
Staff College, but more likely his stay in the West has been a short training course in a military technical school while a politician will have taken
a three-month leadership tour.[1] In addition, Western technical assistance
teams established long-term working relationships with their Burmese
counterparts in the civil service, while the less numerous military equipment delivery teams were held at a distance by their customers. More
fundamentally, the civil servants are descendants of successive generations
of relatively Westernized families of the colonial period. The politicians
and military men represent a new, and, in some ways, anti-Western, class
catapulted into power during the Japanese occupation.[2]

Even under a more rigorous and theoretically oriented definition of the
concept of modernity—for instance in terms of social differentiation—the

[1] In a carefully stratified random sample of Selection Grade and Senior Branch civil
servants, U Khin Maung Kyi found that 51 per cent had visited Western countries (including Eastern Europe), 30 per cent had attended training courses or study tours of
more than three months, and, of those with professional degrees, 53 per cent had
obtained them in the West. Khin Maung Kyi, "Patterns of Accommodation to Bureaucratic Authority in a Transitional Culture: A Sociological Analysis of Burmese
Bureaucrats with Respect to their Orientations Towards Authority" (Ph.D. dissertation,
Cornell University, 1966), pp. 122–23.

[2] James F. Guyot, "Bureaucratic Transformation in Burma," in Ralph Braibanti and
Associates, *Asian Bureaucratic Systems Emergent from the British Imperial Tradition*
(Durham, N.C.: Duke University Press, 1966).

civil service is still clearly the more modern.[3] The role played by the civil service since independence has been much more functionally specific than that of the army, which was born in politics and violence and branched out into a series of economic and educational activities even before assuming a renewed political role, partially and temporarily as a "caretaker" government in 1958–60, then totally as a revolutionary government in 1962. The politicians, too, have played a wider role both as specialists in violence, with their private armies and occasional underground activities, and as eternal dabblers in administration and in government-sheltered economic activities. Both the army and the civil service have elaborated specialized structures to accommodate the complex tasks of the new nation, but politics remained largely court politics. Distinctions between parties were based little on differentiated interests, except in the case of ethnic parties, more on ideology, and most of all on primarily personal relations. Even the politically associated interest organizations—labor unions, peasant organizations, and youth groups—functioned in rather diffuse fashion where they were not merely "signboard" organizations. Another characteristic of modernity is the separation of occupation from domestic life. For the civil servant, there was some fusion of the two in terms of the community status conferred by his office, particularly in the districts, and a range of housing and medical privileges, but this did not approach the army officer's immersion in garrison life. Not only was the politician's occupational role vaguely defined, but so was his household, which often included a number of resident and itinerant supporters.

If we move from a static description of traits that mark institutions as more or less modern to a dynamic analysis of the process of modernization as the ability to absorb change or to create effective organizations, then our focus shifts from the Burma Civil Service to the Burma Army.[4] Burma's failure to modernize during seventeen years of independent and democratic government has been well documented by foreign scholars.[5] Neither has the point been missed by the local population. As the high hopes and welfare schemes of the *Pyidawtha* plans collapsed in factional strife and administrative malaise, the general public, following the traditional magic formula for transposing vowels, switched the slogan *Pyidawtha* (A Royal

[3] Theories and definitions of modern and modernization abound. An authoritative synthesis and classification is found in James S. Coleman, "Modernization: Political Aspects," an unpublished paper of the African Studies Center, University of California at Los Angeles, 1965, p. 32, mimeographed. On differentiation, see pp. 10–11.

[4] Thus, Pye considers the Burmese civil servants the most modernized people in the entire society but judges the army the more effective modernizing force. See Lucian Pye, *Politics, Personality, and Nation-Building* (New Haven, Conn.: Yale University Press, 1962), p. 215; and Pye, "Armies in the Process of Political Modernization," in J. J. Johnson, ed., *The Role of the Military in Underdeveloped Countries* (Princeton, N.J.: Princeton University Press, 1962), pp. 69–89.

[5] See Everett E. Hagen, *On the Theory of Social Change: How Economic Growth Begins* (Homewood, Ill.: Dorsey Press, 1962); Douglas Paauw, chapter 40, this volume; I. R. Sinai, *The Challenge of Modernization: The West's Impact on the Non-Western World* (New York: Norton, 1964); and Louis J. Walinsky, *Economic Development in Burma, 1951–1960* (New York: Twentieth Century Fund, 1962).

Happy Land) to the stigma *Pyadawthi* (A Pile of Royal Ashes). In contrast to the stumbling progress of the regular machinery of government, the army's eighteen-month caretaker government seemed to many domestic and foreign observers a fresh surge of energy and rational direction. In short order, it cleaned the streets of Rangoon of squatter huts and pariah dogs, made a profit on the state steel mill, ran the trains at night, and organized the citizens for rural and urban uplift. When the army returned to power for good in 1962, more fundamental changes were in order. Foreign and domestic trade were almost totally nationalized, and Indian and Chinese businessmen were driven from the country. Land rents were abolished. Doctors were classified and consigned to needy districts. Lawyers were told to write rather than speak their briefs, and the concept of justice was adapted to the peculiar requirements of the army's revolution. Students on vacation were mobilized to take the census, and workers were mobilized to donate voluntary labor on evenings and weekends. Education was reformed.

After four years of the Revolutionary Government, it was evident that much of the modern sector and some of the rural sector of the society had been changed. A number of quite new organizations were created, among them a totalitarian cadre party. In the economic sphere, the short-run results were over-all economic stagnation, a decline in industrial and agricultural production per capita, rising unemployment, and a collapse of commodity distribution. The new political, economic, and social organizations which the army created did not prove notably more effective than those operating under the democratic government, though admittedly the goals set for them are of a different magnitude. There is a serious question whether the army's reforms increased the society's long-run capacity to absorb change or whether the overcommitment of such scarce resources as organizational talents, ideological fervor, and public energies had an over-all negative effect. Yet, even if the result were not modernization, the point remains that the army accepted and continues to accept the challenge to modernize, whereas the preceding civil-service regime had in fact retreated from the challenge.

The major explanation for the failure of the Burma Civil Service to accept and respond effectively to the challenge of modernization is a political one. Since independence, the civil service has not been in charge of the country as it had been during British rule, nor has it been permitted to behave in rational bureaucratic fashion. Grand goals were set politically, often with little regard to available resources of talent, equipment, or raw materials. The political problem of extensive insurrections restricted progress in the early years, and a decline of political leadership set in toward the end. U Nu's lofty devotion to modernization could no longer come to grips with real issues following his political disenchantment with U Kyaw Nyein, one of the few competent modernizers among the politicians. Any modernizing civil servant in the secretariat or in the districts was harassed by interference from politicians or individuals purporting to be under the protection of politicians. Much of the army's good showing in its first performance as general modernizer may be attributed to its ability to suspend, temporarily, political meddling in administration. This political explanation has obvious relevance for other newly independent nations in which a new political class confronts a bureaucracy tainted with a colonial past.

Another line of explanation for the failure of the civil bureaucracy to serve as a modernizing agent focuses on the bureaucratic structure that Burma inherited from the Indian Civil Service during British rule. The salient characteristic of this structure was that generalist organs and administrative roles thoroughly dominated specialist or technical structures and roles. This "steel frame" of administration, based on the district officer as an omnicompetent agent of government, collapsed under the weight of the wide array of specialized and technical activities required by the welfare and economic development programs of independent Burma. This explanation for the failure to modernize has been vigorously applied to other nations emergent from the British Imperial tradition and even to Great Britain itself.[6]

Several intriguing psychological explanations have been offered for the seeming incapacity of Burmese to meet the requirements for rational performance in an organizational meeting. Lucian Pye[7] uses Burma as an example of the problems of interpersonal trust and identity crisis that face elites making the transition from colonial dependence to autonomous development. Everett Hagen[8] delineates the character and dynamics of the uncreative personality common to traditional societies and demonstrates its role in the Burmese case. Both maladies deflect the Burmese bureaucrat from that orientation toward achievement which appears to be causally connected to developmental action in many cultures.[9]

Education as an explanation finds its most obvious application in the question of quantity. Those countries with higher rates of "investment in human resources" show higher levels of economic development.[10] Faith in this principle is evident in the development plans of many new nations.[11] If Burma's development plans are charted against available domestic supplies of high-level manpower, they reveal an ominous gap, which has never been appropriately filled. Beyond mere quantity are questions of quality,

[6] The best statement of this line of explanation is Ralph Braibanti, "The Civil Service of Pakistan: A Theoretical Analysis," *South Atlantic Quarterly*, 58 (1959), 258–304. A broad theory of the superiority of specialists to generalists is developed in Victor Thompson, *Modern Organization: A General Theory* (New York: Alfred A. Knopf, 1961). He applies this line of attack to problems of development in "Administrative Objectives for Development Administration," *Administrative Science Quarterly*, 9 (June, 1964), 91–108. Applications to Great Britain are surveyed in Robert V. Presthus, "Decline of the Generalist Myth," *Public Administration Review*, 24 (December, 1964), 211–16.

[7] Pye, *op. cit.*

[8] Hagen, *op. cit.*

[9] David C. McClelland, *The Achieving Society* (Princeton, N.J.: Van Nostrand, 1961).

[10] Frederick H. Harbison and C. A. Myers, *Education, Manpower, and Economic Growth: Strategies of Human Resource Development* (New York: McGraw-Hill, 1964).

[11] Joseph Fischer, "Education and Political Modernization in Burma and Indonesia," *Comparative Education Review* (October, 1965), pp. 282–87.

which raise more interesting issues[12] and encompass both the psychological and the structural explanations noted above. In what kinds of administrative, technical, and professional skills are future civil servants trained? What kinds of values and motives are produced by the totality of the educational process? Education is also of particular interest because it lies at the focus of the paradox we began with. The Burmese civil servant who does not modernize is most obviously modern in terms of his education.

Dysfunctions in Two Dimensions

At an earlier period in Burmese history, John S. Furnivall, probably that member of the Indian Civil Service who knew Burma the best, was confronted with a similar paradox: Districts with the highest levels of modern education produced the highest rates of crime. This was no fallacy of ecological correlation. Furnivall[13] was able to demonstrate a causal link between increases in education, in litigation, and in crime. This unfortunate influence operated on two dimensions: morals and skills. The increase in modern education brought about a decline in the traditional monastic schools that had inculcated integrative social values along with Jataka tales and the circular Burmese alphabet. Instead, individuals sought schooling in English for its income-multiplier effect. The study of Western law granted status to the pleader, but the use of Western law shattered community norms for the settlement of disputes. Neither the English language nor the English law contributed much toward meeting pressing public needs for better medicine, improved agriculture, more reliable roads—in short, for a more appropriate development of capabilities in science and technology.[14] Since there was more financial support for the arts, there was little prospect for technical or vocational education, however much a series of commissions recommended schemes for its promotion.[15]

These two dimensions, one defining values, the other skill structure, provide a useful framework for analyzing the relation between styles of education and bureaucratic behavior. As noted above, a strong case has been made that the Indian Civil Service (parent to all subsequent Burmese civil services), with its generalist steel frame and emphasis on guardianship training, established norms of bureaucratic behavior violently at variance

[12] James S. Coleman, ed., *Education and Political Development* (Princeton, N.J.: Princeton University Press, 1965), Part III.

[13] John S. Furnivall, *Educational Progress in Southeast Asia* (New York: Institute of Pacific Relations, 1943); Furnivall, *Colonial Policy and Practice: A Comparative Study of Burma and Netherlands India* (New York: New York University Press, 1956).

[14] The 1931 census for Burma indicates a ratio of 1.57 practicing lawyers for every registered medical practitioner and dentist in the country. This ratio of contentious to constructive allocation of educational resources is reversed in the United States, where in 1960 there were 1.46 doctors and dentists for every lawyer and judge, a ratio that has held for the last fifty years.

[15] For a description of the same problem today in Africa, see Philip J. Foster, "The Vocational School Fallacy in Development Planning," in C. Arnold Anderson and Mary Jean Bowman, eds., *Education and Economic Development* (Chicago, Ill.: Aldine, 1965), pp. 142–66.

with the needs of development in newly independent countries. Even in the post-independence period, the ICS-style guardian is still trained in humanistic and theoretical rather than professional or empirical studies. He strives to become the able amateur rather than the narrow expert. Organizational authority is exercised on the basis of status rather than professional competence. Decisions are made by routine rather than by rational calculation. Consistency is valued above imagination.[16] Nehru claimed that even the British members of the old ICS had about them a certain woodenness; they were "hollow men." He found Indians who served British masters in those days to be a sorry lot indeed. His description is worth examining at length.

> An authoritarian system of government, and especially one that is foreign, must encourage a psychology of subservience and try to limit the mental outlook and horizon of the people. It must crush much that is finest in youth—enterprise, spirit of adventure, originality, "pep"—and encourage sneakishness, rigid conformity, and a desire to cringe and please the bosses. Such a system does not bring out the real service mentality, the devotion to public service or to ideals; it picks out the least public-spirited persons whose sole objective is to get on in life. We see what a class the British attract to themselves in India! Some of them are intellectually keen and capable of good work. They drift to government service or semi-government service because of lack of opportunity elsewhere, and gradually they tone down and become just parts of the big machine, their minds imprisoned by the dull routine of work. They develop the qualities of a bureaucracy—"a competent knowledge of clerkship and the diplomatic art of keeping office." At the highest they have a passive devotion to the public service. There is, or can be, no flaming enthusiasm.[17]

The new India, Nehru asserted, would need a civil service with a new spirit. It would be technically trained and public spirited; no longer authoritarian and no longer privileged.[18]

A central theme in this critique of the British bureaucratic legacy in Asia is the one-to-one correspondence between desirable and undesirable forms of organization, desirable and undesirable classes of values, desirable and undesirable styles of education and bureaucratic behavior. Let us picture organizational and skill structures classified on a horizontal dimension as generalist or specialist, and values classified on a vertical dimension as achievement oriented or its opposite (to be defined shortly). The weight of evidence so far introduced locates bureaucratic practices and the output of

16 Ralph Braibanti, "The Civil Service of Pakistan: A Theoretical Analysis."

17 Jawaharlal Nehru, *An Autobiography* (London: Lane, 1938), p. 439.

18 I am indebted to my colleague H. Arthur Steiner for pointing out the parallel strictures of Nehru's Muslim counterpart, Mohammed Ali Jinnah, who, in a speech at the Dacca University Convocation, March 24, 1948, stated, "the main object of the old system of education and the system of government . . . was really to have well-trained, well-equiped clerks. . . . to create a mentality, a psychology, a state of mind, that an average man, when he passed his B.A. or M.A. was to look for some job in government." *Speeches and Writings of Mr. Jinnah*, collected and edited by Jamil-ud-din Ahmad, Vol. II, rev. ed. (Lahore: Sh. Muhammad Ashraf, 1964), 499–500.

the educational system in underdeveloped societies either in the upper right quadrant—achievement-oriented specialists who are confident, innovative, and pragmatic—or in the lower left quadrant—routine, formalistic, authoritarian, and submissive generalists (see Figure 1).

Nehru's view of the ICS would clearly place it in the lower left quadrant, where it should probably be joined by its postpartition offspring, the civil service of Pakistan, whose probationers are given a year at Oxford or Cambridge after learning law and equestrianism at their own Civil Service

Figure 1

STRUCTURES

	Generalist	Specialist
Achievement Orientation	ICS (ideal) Burma Army	Burma Army Ministry of Finance (Pakistan) Burma Civil Service (professional)
Clerk Mentality	ICS (Nehru) CSP Burma Army (second generation) Burma Civil Service (administrative)	Burma Army (second generation) Burma Civil Service (economic)

VALUES

Academy. Probationers headed for Pakistan's Ministry of Finance, however, do not go to England but instead study economics and learn how to
drive a jeep at their service academy, hence they might belong in the upper
right quadrant.[19] Much, but not all, of the literature on armies in the
process of modernization[20] would place the officer corps in the upper right
quadrant. This is particularly true of analyses of the Burma Army.[21] The
image is one of confident technocrats pushing through pragmatic solutions
to problems that have long confounded their civilian counterparts and
their political masters.

What about the other quadrants? Were there no confident generalists or
timid technocrats? A closer look at the Burma Army suggests that many
members are generalists after all, or at least have been playing generalist
roles. The Revolutionary Council that has governed Burma since March,
1962, consists primarily of former or current field commanders. The assignment of cabinet portfolios in the Revolutionary Government has followed
no particular pattern of specialization. In the fall of 1964, only four of the
fifteen ministers were holding posts in any way related to their previous
training or experience. A more persuasive point is the structure of administration established by the army. It is essentially a reconstitution of the old
steel frame of administration. Power over local officials and the local population, which had slipped from the hands of the district officer, has been
reconcentrated in a Security and Administrative Council (SAC) composed
of the district officer, the district superintendent of police, and the local
military commander. A chain of such locally omnicompetent SAC's
stretches up from the township through the subdivision, district, and division, to the central SAC in Rangoon. Many elements of the old ICS
ideal[22] are here again: confidence, action, initiative, improvisation, responsibility. The army generalist is certainly not the man of letters envisioned
in the generalist ideal as it developed in the Indian setting. Yet he may
come close to the functional equivalent of that ideal in the contemporary
Burmese setting. Macaulay's argument for the selection of scholarly gentlemen was that "whatever be the languages, whatever be the sciences, which
it is in any age or country the fashion to teach, the persons who become
the greatest proficients in those languages and those sciences will generally

[19] Braibanti, "The Civil Service of Pakistan: A Theoretical Analysis."

[20] Johnson, *op. cit.*; Morris Janowitz, *The Military in the Political Development of
New Nations: An Essay in Comparative Analysis* (Chicago: University of Chicago
Press, 1964); William F. Gutteridge, "Education of Military Leadership in Emergent
States," in Coleman, ed., *op. cit.*; and S. E. Finer, *The Man on Horseback: The Role of
the Military in Politics* (London: Pall Mall Press, 1962).

[21] John H. Badgley, "Burma's Zealot Wungyis: Maoists or St. Simonists," *Asian
Survey*, 5 (January, 1965), 55–62; Pye, "Armies in the Process of Political Modernization"; Trevor N. Dupuy, "Burma and Its Army: A Contrast in Motivations and Characteristics," *Antioch Review*, 20 (Winter, 1960–61), 428–40; Moshe Lissak, "Social
Change, Mobilization, and Exchange of Services Between the Military Establishment
and the Civil Society: The Burmese Case," *Economic Development and Cultural
Change*, 13, No. 1, Part 1 (October, 1964), 1–19; and Sinai, *op. cit.*

[22] Philip Mason (Woodruff), *The Men Who Ruled India*, Vol. II, *The Guardians*
(London: Johnathan Cope, 1954).

be the flower of the youth; the most acute, the most industrious, the most ambitious of honourable distinctions."[23] In the age of the army's inception (World War II), the "languages and sciences" it was the fashion to teach were nationalist agitation and the techniques of violence. This training and group legitimation has stood the senior army leadership in good stead, promoting a spirit that facilitates trust and self-confidence. So let us put them in the upper left quadrant. By contrast, some of the younger generation of army officers who did not participate in the brotherhood of the Burma Independence Army have been forced by the weight of responsibilities under the Revolutionary Government to retreat from initiative and buck problems up to their seniors. These may belong in one of the bottom two quadrants.

There remains the lower right quadrant, reserved for professional and technical specialists of a formalistic and subservient bent. Likely candidates are available. U Khin Maung Kyi has classified his sample of higher level Burmese civil servants as administrative, professional, or economic by type of organization. Those in the administrative group scored highest on a measure of "generalized deference to authority," a compound of attitudes associated with traditional Burmese conceptions of authority and opposite to those attitudes deemed appropriate for modernization. The professionals, many of whom are technical specialists, appear to have been trained out of such traditional attitudes. The economic bureaucrats, however, who exhibited most of the other expected characteristics of technical specialists, did not distinguish themselves significantly from the general administrators on the generalized deference to authority.[24] Thus, we may tentatively place them in the lower right quadrant.

Since examples can be found to fill all four quadrants, the "values" dimension carries some significance of its own. There may then be merit in analyzing those particular clusters of values and motives that distinguish an achievement orientation from what I have labeled the clerk mentality.

The concept of achievement orientation has enjoyed such widespread and indiscriminate use as a relevant variable in comparative social analysis that it will be helpful to narrow its meaning for use here. Let us take McClelland's need for achievement, or achievement motivation, as a reasonable equivalent.[25] In the abstract, achievement motivation is defined as competition with a standard of excellence and is expected to share many of the qualities and correlates of Weber's "Protestant ethic." Its relation to economic and other forms of development in any particular society must often be interpreted through a screen of other psychological variables[26] and institutional arrangements.[27] Still, the over-all relation of achievement mo-

[23] Quoted in Braibanti, "The Civil Service of Pakistan: A Theoretical Analysis," p. 266.

[24] Khin Maung Kyi, *op. cit.*

[25] McClelland, *op. cit.*

[26] George A. DeVos, "Achievement Orientation, Social Self-Identity, and Japanese Economic Growth," *Asian Survey*, 5 (December, 1965), 575–89.

[27] Robert N. Bellah, "Reflections on the Protestant Ethic Analogy in Asia," *Journal of Social Issues*, 19 (January, 1963), 52–60.

tivation to development, defined in economic terms, is quite persuasive.

Burmese culture has often struck casual visitors, British civil servants, and trained anthropologists as an unlikely setting for the nurturance of achievement motivation. More often, the outside observer's attention has been fixed on one of the fascinating "negative" aspects of Burmese character. The Burman's peculiar relations to power, to responsibility, and to anxiety have been connected to child-training practices, Buddhism, and the vagaries of colonial history. What concerns us here is the possibility of identifying under one label a cluster of behavioral patterns that are dysfunctional for the operation of modern organizations and occur frequently in the Burmese context. Such a concept is current in Burma as the epithet, "clerk mentality." It is a fairly undefined term associated with most of the evils of bureaucracy—formalism, petty arrogance, routine, insecurity—and it is usually blamed on the British, who provided the Burmese with a "slave education." I will define the term as consisting of two elements: (1) submissiveness toward formal authority, and (2) a ritual devotion to routine tasks under an imminent fear of failure. The first element is related to the Burmese concept, *ana*, or, briefly stated, power and authority of a form that is resented.[28] The second element defines the difference between the clerk mentality and achievement motivation. Both achievement motivation and the clerk mentality may drive individuals to work hard. In the former case, however, a person is impelled by the hope of success, in the latter, by the fear of failure. One individual sets his own goals and employs his resources imaginatively; the other follows out the prescribed path toward an externally defined goal.

INCULCATING THE CLERK MENTALITY

The traditional system of education as it exists today in village Burma seems an ideal prescription for producing the clerk mentality. Manning Nash has observed that

> . . . knowledge, at the village level, is conceived of by both teacher and pupil as a fixed, finite body of information. The teacher is the repository of this knowledge, and the student is the empty vessel waiting to be filled by association with the teacher. . . . The method of teaching is fitted to its tasks: to stuff the mind, to train the memory, and to inculcate a respect for received wisdom. Students are rewarded for feats of memory, for long letter perfect recitations, for knowing the past answers to standard questions.[29]

At the other extreme from the Upper Burma village primary school stands an elite Rangoon high school operated by a foreign missionary order. Yet here, too, much the same approach to education appears. The school prides itself on its discipline, and middle-class Burmese send their boys there to get the discipline they will not get at home or in a govern-

28 Khin Maung Kyi, *op. cit.*, chapter 5.

29 Manning Nash, "Education in Burma: An Anthropological Perspective," a paper presented before the Comparative Education Conference, University of California, Berkeley, March, 1966.

ment high school. The school prides itself on its product, too. Its students maintain an exceptionally high passing rate in the university matriculation examination, and its "old boys" are much overrepresented in the higher ranks of the civil service. I have taken the total population of the high school final and the matriculation classes (ninth and tenth standards), 382 boys in all, as a sample for testing the behavioral correlates of achievement motivation and the clerk mentality in the Burmese educational system.

Achievement motivation[30] and the clerk mentality should have a differ-

[30] Achievement motivation was assessed by means of a six-picture Thematic Ap-perception Test (John W. Atkinson, *Motives in Fantasy, Action, and Society* [Prince-ton, N.J.: Van Nostrand, 1958]), which had been "Burmanized"—picture cards' had been redrawn by a Burmese artist to represent Burmese people in Burmese settings. Clerk mentality scores were derived from stories written in response to two of the six pictures. To develop a measure of achievement motivation that would have meaning in the Burmese cultural context (William Henry, "Projective Tests in Cross-Cultural Re-search," in Bert Kaplan, ed., *Studying Personality Cross-Culturally* [Evanston, Ill.: Harper and Row, 1961], the standard scoring manual for need Achievement had been revised in collaboration with U Khin Maung Kyi, a Burmese with extensive social science training in the United States. There were several questions of concept to be ironed out, such as whether the desire to earn merit in order to attain Nirvana was not "competition with a standard of excellence" in the highest degree. We decided that it was not, in terms of what we wanted achievement motivation to mean. There were also many questions of specific social judgment, such as whether expressed concern with accuracy in a particular kind of work should be scored as craftmanship or routine dili-gence. In the end, a satisfactory level of interscorer reliability (above 85 per cent) was achieved on samples of TAT protocols written by Burmese civil servants. This revised manual was used for the author's scoring of the high school TAT's.

The first element of the clerk mentality, submission to formal authority, was scored for stories written to a picture of an older man and a younger man talking seriously, perhaps angrily, in an office. Stories were rated according to the appearance of various themes along a scale of:

o—no authority theme present;
1—simple authority theme, that is, "the older-looking man is explaining about the business to the younger man";
2—authority or conflict plus fault, that is, "the headmaster is scolding the class master because he has given the test questions to his pupils";
3—authority or conflict plus fault, ending in submission, that is, "the father looks a little severe and he wants his son to be good. The son feels sorry for his mistake."
Where a "rejection of authority" theme is also present, the final score is reduced by one point.

The second element, the "fear of failure" theme, appeared in a picture of a lone man working at a desk after hours. Here the rating scale was:

o—imagery unrelated to any task;
1—statement of a task but no concern with accomplishment;
2—concern only for completion of the task, but the work is perceived as important or rewarding;
3—concern for completion alone;
4—concern for completion of work, which a) results from a personal fault, or b) the noncompletion of which will result in failure.
Here again, a countertheme is possible. If there is some statement indicating a hope for success or an attempt to get ahead of the game, the final score is reduced by one point. An individual's total clerk-mentality score was the sum of the scores received on these two pictures.

Independent research in India by Harry Lasker (1966) developed two "inhibitor variables": (1) conflict avoidance (scored similarly to our submission theme), and ential impact on performance. An individual loaded with achievement motivation should outstrip his less competitive classmate in the arithmetic and vocabulary tests presented in an unusual and achievement aroused situation. Whether or not he performs in equally superior fashion in the normal school situation depends in large part on whether the system rewards initiative and innovation. Our argument is that it does not. Someone endowed with clerk mentality, on the other hand, should be expected to win high marks from his teachers on the basis of conforming and consistent daily behavior. If the clerk mentality is as constricting as has been suggested, those who progress under its pressure should not perform so distinctively in a less structured situation.

By and large, these expectations are borne out in a test of correlations among the two measures of motivation and the two measures of performance, as shown in Figure 2. Achievement motivation and the clerk mentality are clearly antithetical value orientations as shown by the negative correlation between scores individuals obtain on each. Yet both incline students toward high levels of performance. The two kinds of performance are closely related, as indicated by their high intercorrelation, yet they are not the same.

Achievement motivation apparently drives students toward a high level of performance on abstract measures of skill in highly achievement-oriented circumstances. This correlation between achievement-motivation scores and skill-performance scores is respectable, but not impressive. However, it is statistically significant and consistent with expectations. Furthermore, it remains consistent and significant when controls are introduced for four different levels of academic performance and for different ethnic groups (ethnic Burmese, Chinese and Sino-Burmese, Indians, and others). What is impressive is the failure of achievement motivation to connect with aca-

---

(2) defensive set (similar to our fear of failure). Lasker found these inhibitor variables distinguishing clearly between the Indian businessmen who did not perform in more entrepreneurial fashion following a training course in achievement motivation and those who actually did get themselves new jobs or open up more enterprising lines of business. Subsequent research by the author, using a Malaysianized version of the TAT pictures and the same scoring scheme on Malaysian university students and civil servants, reveals differences between Chinese and Malays in terms of this working definition of the clerk mentality. This is reported in "The Two Cultures and the Development Revolution in Malaysia," a paper presented at the 1968 meeting of the Association for Asian Studies.

No apparent language barrier was encountered by having the students write their stories in English, since the median number of words per story produced by the Burmese high school students (64) is not too far below the rate for American high school students (94). (J. S. Veroff, et al., "The Use of Thematic Apperception to Assess Motivation in a Nationwide Interview Study," Psychological Monographs, No. 74 [1960].) The 92 per cent response rate for all measures combined is testimony to the discipline instilled by the brothers.

Measures of two kinds of performance were also obtained. One, skill performance, was the score on tests of English vocabulary and arithmetic given under novel and achievement-arousing conditions immediately after the students had taken the TAT. The other, scholastic performance, was the quartile grade, A, B, C, or D, into which the brothers classified students for purposes of instruction.

Figure 2

Motivation and Performance

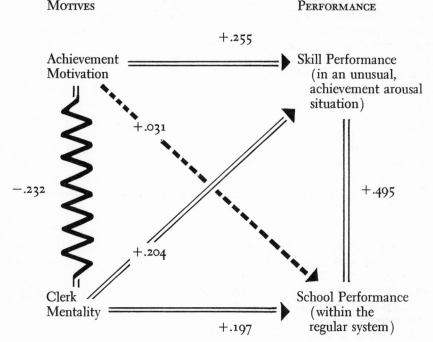

MOTIVES   PERFORMANCE

+.255

Achievement ═══════════════▶ Skill Performance
Motivation   (in an unusual,
                                          achievement arousal
                                          situation)

+.031

−.232   +.495

+.204

Clerk   School Performance
Mentality ═══════════════▶ (within the
                        +.197   regular system)

The coefficients are Spearman's rank order coefficients of correlation. The number of cases in each comparison varies but is always greater than 350. With samples of this size, all the above correlations, except for the one between achievement motivation and school performance, are statistically significant well beyond the 1 per cent level for a two-tailed test. An objection might be raised that the causal connection between the qualities measured by the score an individual received on the test of achievement motivation and the score he achieved on the verbal and numerical tests (skill performance) might actually flow in the opposite direction from that indicated by the arrows above. Someone high in verbal skills would probably write longer stories in the TAT, thus increasing his chances of obtaining a high achievement-motivation score. To some extent, this may have been the case. When the correlation of length of story with achievement score is partialed out, however, the correlation between verbal skill score and achievement score, though reduced somewhat, still remains significant. But it is not necessary to consider all of the correlation between achievement score and story length to be the impact of story length on achievement score. The reverse is equally likely. We could reasonably expect individuals high in achievement motivation to be motivated to produce longer stories than others do. See Veroff, *op. cit.*, and Hubert M. Blalock, Jr., *Causal Inferences in Nonexperimental Research* (Chapel Hill, N.C.: University of North Carolina Press, 1964), chapter 3.

demic performance. Perhaps the brothers' school is no place for entre-preneurs.

St. Paul's students who score high on the clerk mentality, score high in the brothers' books as well, as we had suspected. But they also score high in the less structured, relatively unusual testing situation, which we had not expected. Does this mean that the clerk mentality is a good general purpose motive? Or have we failed to find sufficiently distinct measures of performance? Perhaps there is a transfer of training from regular school work to performance on tests, so that St. Paul's boys with strong clerical inclinations may have done well on the skill-performance tests largely because the tests were so similar to their regular school work. To assess the real relationship of clerk mentality with test performance, uncontaminated by those elements which test performance and school work have in common, we should calculate the correlation while controlling for different levels of school performance. The result is to cut the correlation about in half. Our conclusion is that the clerk mentality, as we have defined it, is congenial with academic performance in the Burmese setting. Whether it is also congenial with performance in a more creative or less structured situation is not as certain. This remains to be discovered once we have devised a more distinct representation of such a situation.

CONCLUSIONS

Clearly the Burmese educational system, even as represented in Rangoon's elite high school, rewards the clerk mentality more than achievement motivation. Education at the university level and examinations for admissions to the civil service also appear to reward the clerk mentality. What is the likelihood of a change in the direction of greater achievement orientation?

In the 1920's, Burmese nationalists began their condemnation of "slave education." After independence, the *Pyidawtha* resolutions called for educational reform to increase the emphasis on training of indigenous scientists and much needed specialists. Some years later, the Revolutionary Government vowed to demolish the "system of education formulated by the imperialists" and to turn education toward science and technology. In addition, the army intended to reverse the direction of the postindependence trend toward lower standards of discipline, university admission, and instruction.

The most obvious results of these reforms have been at the ideological level, primarily in the progressive elimination of English as a language of instruction. Attempts to turn toward science and technology have not suffered from a lack of interest on the part of students, as was the case during British times. In fact, the most popular first choice of our sample of high school students was medicine (30 per cent), followed closely by engineering (18 per cent). These same proportions hold for the first choices of matriculates applying to universities and technical institutes in the fall term of 1965.[31] The difficulty has been to provide sufficient facilities and trained staff in these fields.

While laudable in its own right, this new thrust toward specialist rather

31 *Working Peoples Daily*, October 3, 1965.

than generalist education does not meet the problem of developing an achievement orientation. Neither will the raising of standards (which the army has not yet been able to do—almost all applicants were admitted to some form of higher education) suffice to promote an achievement orientation. The existing standards do, in fact, encourage its opposite, the clerk mentality. The mode of education and the model of the educated man will have to be revised to promote and reward inquiry, creativity, and challenges to doctrine. This the army finds hard to do, since its concern with students centers so much on the problem of control. This concern encompasses not only discipline (university students rioted sporadically throughout the first two years of the Revolutionary Government) but also the content of instruction. History and the social sciences are being revised by party cadres to conform to the ideology of the Burma Socialist Programme Party. Fortunately for the physical sciences, the army's philosophical document, *The System of Correlation of Man and His Environment: The Philosophy of the Burma Socialist Programme Party* is a sufficiently loose mixture of Marxist dialectics and Buddhist cosmology as to have little impact on any hard science save zoology.

16

EDUCATION AND POLITICAL DEVELOPMENT IN MALAYSIA*

ROBERT O. TILMAN

Although now well established in the literature of American social science, there is considerable disagreement on the content of the concept of "political development." The term may be used to describe the sometimes equally vague processes of "modernization" (or "Westernization") in a historical or chronological sense,[1] growing structural-functional differentiation of total social systems,[2] increasing social mobilization,[3] the develop-

---

* Reprinted by permission of the publisher from Université Libre de Bruxelles, Institut de Sociologie, *Education et développement dans le sud-est de l'Asie* (Brussels: Free University of Brussels, 1967), pp. 209–28.

[1] For an example of such as approach, see A. F. K. Organski, *The Stages of Political Development* (New York: Alfred A. Knopf, 1965).

[2] My reference here is generally to the *gemeinschaft-gesellschaft* model of political change in the tradition of Sir Henry Maine, Ferdinand Tönnies, Max Weber, and Robert Redfield. A more specific statement of this model, which is concerned directly with the problem of political development, has been made in the numerous writings of Fred Riggs. See especially his "Agraria and Industria," in William Siffin, ed., *Toward The Comparative Study of Public Administration* (Bloomington, Ind.: Indiana University Press, 1959), and Riggs's *Administration in Developing Countries: The Theory of Prismatic Society* (Boston: Houghton Mifflin, 1964). A contemporary summary state-

228

ment of more universal political loyalties[4] or numerous other phenomena, sometimes even including an increasing commitment to Western-style democracy.[5] The literature on political development is proliferating rapidly in the United States,[6] but, unhappily, so is the confusion.

The present essay will not attempt to achieve methodological purity by rigorously defining and applying one particular conceptual model of political development. My goal here is more to present an interpretive essay on the influence of education on the course of political change in Malaysia. "Political development" is therefore used as a working concept involving two related historical processes that occurred in Malaya (and Malaysia[7]) during the 150 years after 1816. Specifically, I am concerned here with the influence of education on (1) the emergence of political elites, both cooperating and contending as viewed from the perspective of the colonial power, and (2) the emergence of a Malayan political loyalty that transcends traditional communal and geographical boundaries.

Formal education was launched in Malaya with the founding of the Penang Free School by the Colonial Chaplain of Penang in 1816, and this was followed closely by the creation of Raffles Institution in Singapore in 1823. Missionary education was limited, and officials of the English East

---

ment of the political implications of the tradition-modernity continuum is contained in Max F. Millikan and Donald L. M. Blackmer, eds., *The Emerging Nations* (Boston: Little, Brown, 1961), pp. 1–90.

[3] This concept is most frequently employed in the work of Karl Deutsch. See especially his *Nationalism and Social Communication* (Cambridge, Mass.: Harvard University Press, 1953); *Political Community in the North Atlantic Area* (Princeton, N.J.: Princeton University Press, 1957); and "Social Mobilization and Political Development," *American Political Science Review*, LV (September, 1961), 493–514.

[4] See, for example, Clifford Geertz, "The Integrative Revolution," in Geertz, ed., *Old Societies and New States* (New York: Free Press of Glencoe, 1963), pp. 105–57. The work of Karl Deutsch (cited in notes 3 and 27) is also concerned with "political integration," which might in fact well be described as the reverse of the social-mobilization coin. There have been a number of writings, both scholarly and popular, dealing with the general subject of "nation building," in which some aspect of political integration is stressed.

[5] For a general survey of the various meanings of "political development" that differs somewhat from the listing here, see Lucian W. Pye, *Aspects of Political Development* (Boston: Little, Brown, 1966), chapter 2.

[6] In addition to the works cited above, there are two series of volumes related to the subject of political development currently being published in the United States. Sponsored by the Committee on Comparative Politics of the Social Science Research Council and published by Princeton University Press, seven volumes are projected for the series, of which five are already in print. Little, Brown (Boston) is also publishing a Comparative Politics Series in paperback, which includes general theoretical works as well as specific country studies. Thus far, the only country study of a Southeast Asian state is Jean Grossholtz, *Politics in The Philippines* (Boston: Little, Brown, 1964).

[7] Although the terms Malaya and Malaysia will be used interchangeably here, depending upon the time period being considered, it should be apparent that most of the generalizations and observations in this essay are based on the experience of the peninsula. This seems justifiable, since Malaya is the heartland of present-day Malaysia and since Singapore, more influenced by the British colonials and overwhelmingly Chinese, presents many unique problems.

India Company[8] were also reluctant to provide more than token financial support for educational activities. Even in the Federated Malay States (FMS), while the growth of education was steady, there was not a dramatic increase until very late in the colonial period, as the following table demonstrates.

TABLE 1[9]

Government and Government-aided Schools, FMS, 1896–1936

Year	Number of Schools	Enrollment (1,000)	Expenditure (M$ million)
1896	150	6.6	n.a.
1906	285	16.9	0.3
1916	480	28.1	0.5
1921	583	39.7	1.5
1936	1,452	103.4	n.a.

Viewed from the perspective of its impact on the course of political development, the creation of Malay College at Kuala Kangsar, Perak, in January, 1905, was one of the most significant educational events of the colonial era. Malay College drew its inspiration from the kind of thinking revealed in the Macaulay Education Minute of 1835,[10] which was candidly

[8] Until its demise in 1858, the English East India Company governed the settlements in Malaya. Except for a brief period early in the nineteenth century (1805–30), when it enjoyed the status of a Presidency, the Straits Settlements (at first Penang and then later also Malacca and Singapore) was administered as an appendage of Bengal. Between 1858 and 1867, the three component settlements were administered by the India Office and then were transferred to the Colonial Office, where they remained until the Malayan Union of 1946 (which was succeeded by the Federation of 1948) attached Penang and Malacca to the peninsula, and Malaysian *merdeka* (1963) incorporated Singapore into the larger political unit. On the eve of the Japanese occupation in World War II, Malaya consisted of the Straits Settlements, the Federated Malay States (established in 1896 by a multilateral treaty among Negri Sembilan, Pahang, Perak, and Selangor), and the Unfederated Malay States (Johore, Kedah, Kelantan, Perlis, and Trengganu). The intensity and extensiveness of British hegemony varied among the three kinds of structures, but the common thread of British rule ran throughout.

[9] Extracted from the various *Annual Reports* of the FMS for the years listed.

[10] "We now come to the gist of the matter. We have a fund to be employed as government shall direct for the intellectual improvement of the people of [India]. . . . The simple question is, what is the most useful way of employing it? . . . The intellectual improvement of those . . . who have the means of pursuing higher studies can at present be effected only by means of . . . English . . . [or] Arabic and Sanscrit . . . I have never found one among [the Orientalists of the Committee] . . . who could deny that a single shelf of a good European library was worth the whole native literature of India and Arabia. . . . We have to educate a people who cannot at present be educated by means of their mother-tongue. We must teach them . . . our own language. . . . We must at present do our best to form a class who may be interpreters between us and the millions whom we govern; a class of persons, Indian in blood and color, but English in taste, in opinions, in morals, and in intellect." (Thomas Babington Macaulay's Minute supporting the Anglicists on the Committee of Public Instruction, 1834.)

intended to provide a pool of subordinate administrative talent drawn from the "Raja and higher classes" of Malaya.[11] At Malay College, there was a conscious attempt to transplant into a tropical Asian environment the English public school, complete with playing fields, a headmaster, prefects, the high table, and all of the other trappings of an aristocratic English boarding school. The long-range goal of such a school, according to the recognized authority on Malay language and literature, R. J. Wilkinson, who was Inspector of Schools at the time of the creation of Malay College, should be to produce

> a vigorous and intelligent race of young men who will be in touch with modern progress but not out of touch with old traditions; who will be liberally educated but not educated out of sympathy with their own families and people; who will be manly and not effeminate, strong minded but not strong willed, acknowledging a duty to others instead of being a law unto themselves and who will be fit to do something in the world instead of settling down into fops, spendthrifts, or drones.[12]

Not only did Malay College teach exclusively in the medium of English but, by the time of graduation, its students had been thoroughly socialized into an upper-class English cultural environment, which was, of course, the very goal of the original Macaulay educational policies. Some personal reflections by Old Boys of Malay College, though lengthy, provide an excellent insight into the nature of the socialization process at the school.

> Class III . . . was handled by Mr. Hargreaves [the first headmaster] himself. He was indeed a master of method, who had an uncanny insight into the psychology and temperament of each individual student. As if by magic, he would keep us all abreast in our work. We had to move as a team. If any lagged behind he made it our duty to help him along. Without our appreciating it then the headmaster was sowing the early seeds of co-operative effort so valuable to us in later years. Somehow he instilled into us self-discipline in work and in conduct so necessary to character building. . . . He rounded off corners, and gave us the necessary polish for life.[13]

Another Old Boy, the captain of a junior college team (the "Moderates"), recalling one of the greatest football matches ever played at Malay College, recounts the following experience:

> The fame of the "Moderates" soon spread. Our Headmaster was so confident of us that eventually he pitted us against the formidable Perak State Eleven captained by the great international footballer, Mr. Hartley. The team included only one Asian—Mr. P. C. Lesslar, who was then considered the fleetest forward in the country. It was a titanic struggle. We threw all our skill and effort into this game and played like little devils. We succeeded in

11 When the Malay Administrative Service (MAS) was created in 1910, all candidates were recruited from the students of Malay College, a practice that continued until 1921. Although the Malay College monopoly of the MAS was formally broken in 1921, when it began to share its role with other schools, it continued to be tied into MAS recruitment and training schemes until 1941.

12 Quoted in Malay College, *Malay College 1905–1965* (Kuala Lumpur: Straits Times Press, 1965), p. 1.

13 *Ibid.*, p. 9.

forcing a draw with the redoubtable State XI by one all. Wasn't our Head-master a very proud man after that? The names of the team will ever remain fresh in my memory. The team never broke up until the time came for us to leave College. . . . Those were glorious and unforgettable days in College when we learned hard and played hard, inspired by great teachers who gave us, among other things, all that was best of the traditions of English educa-tion.[14]

Finally, an Old Boy, in the quotation below, recalls his feelings before graduation in the spring of 1915.

At the beginning of June, 1915, when I came to realize that the end of my school career was drawing very near, I became conscious of a feeling of sad-ness. The thought that very soon I would part for the last time with the College and its happy corporate life, in the activities of which I had been closely associated for several years, goaded my heart. Memories of many happy days at the College surged up in my breast. Over the years, I had made many friends, some of whom had already left the College to seek their livelihood in the world. Now I was about to follow in their footsteps. So, one bright morn-ing in the month of June, 1915, with a feeling of an unpleasant lump in my throat, I went around to bid farewell to the masters and my friends in the College, before boarding the train, on the first leg of my journey back home. Thus closed a chapter in my life, a chapter crowded with many happy memories which have remained fresh in my mind, undimmed and un-diminished by the lapse of a full half a century.[15]

Until postwar years, there was a direct and formal connection between Malay College, the Malay Administrative Service (MAS), and the elite administrative cadre of the Federation, the Malayan Civil Service (MCS). Until 1953, almost the only avenue of recruitment for local persons into the MCS was by promotion from the junior administrative service, and Malay College was the chief source of talent for the MAS. Thus, it is not surprising that even a cursory examination of any Civil Service List from the time of accelerated Malayanization (1956) onward reveals a large number of Malay College Old Boys in the senior ranks.

Moreover, while their presence is most apparent in the Civil Service, many graduates of the College can be found among the political elite (the best known today is Tun Abdul Razak, the Deputy Prime Minister), and about one-half of the sultans ruling today are also Malay College Old Boys. While the College has by no means monopolized the field of secondary education in Malaya, and, in fact, in purely numerical terms, it has pro-duced only a small minority of the peninsula's graduates, Malay College has generally set the tone for the moderate politics and gentlemanly na-tionalism of Malaysia that are almost unique in Southeast Asia.

Postsecondary education came late to Malaya, and thus exerted relatively less influence on the course of political development than did secondary education. Medical training was available at King Edward College of Medi-cine after 1915, and courses leading to a diploma were offered at Raffles

College after 1928, but it was not until 1949—with the merging of these two institutions—that Malaya had its own university. The University of Malaya (the original campus of which was located on the island of Singapore) opened a branch at Kuala Lumpur in 1958, and this branch, adopting and retaining the original name of the parent, became a fully autonomous university in 1962. At the same time, the Singapore institution was renamed the University of Singapore. That the importance of the university as a channel of elite recruitment is rapidly growing can be seen in the following tabulation of the 257 indigenous MCS officers on the 1962 Staff List. Column one represents the older officers, largely drawn from the Malay College–MAS tradition, who are now retiring and are being replaced by the younger officers of column two, some of whom attended Malay College but many of whom also underwent an educational experience at a Malayan or other Commonwealth university.

TABLE 2[16]

Channels of Recruitment, MCS Officers, 1962 (by percentages)

	Present Elite n = 53	Potential Elite n = 204
Promotion from MAS	79	44
Direct from universities	2	43
Promotion from state services	11	14
Promotion from other services	8	9

Whether considering secondary or postsecondary education, it is apparent that the language of political socialization of the governing elite in Malaya has been English, and that these English-language secondary schools have played a dominant role in shaping the general configurations of Malaysian politics from colonial days to the present time. In addition to the bureaucratic elite, which is drawn entirely from the English stream of education, it is apparent from the following table that the political elite on the eve of the creation of the Federation of Malaysia in 1963 was also heavily indebted to the English stream of education as a source of recruits.

If the English stream of education has produced the governing elites, the vernacular streams have been most responsible for generating the mass support for any contending elite, and, in several cases, for the elite themselves. This is particularly true in the case of the Chinese. The Chinese were willing to educate themselves, and—as the following table dramatically demonstrates—British colonial officials, always mindful of London's demands for administrative economies, were content to let them assume their own educational burdens. As a result, until very recent times, Chinese schools were markedly China-oriented. In addition, the general qual-

[16] Robert O. Tilman, "Policy Formulation, Policy Execution, and the Political Elite Structure of Contemporary Malaya," in Wang Gungwu, ed., *Malaysia* (New York: Frederick Praeger, 1964), p. 352.

TABLE 3[17]

Cabinet Members and Alliance Party Officers:
Major Language of Education, 1962

	Persons Holding Both Cabinet and Party Posts	*Cabinet Members*	*Party Officers*	*Total*
English stream	13	18	22	27
Vernacular stream	0	0	2	2
Vernacular and English	0	0	7	7
Unknown	0	0	2	2
TOTAL	13	18	33	38

ity of Chinese education was unusually low. Despite a larger number of schools and a greater enrollment, Chinese education was much inferior to English education, and, at the primary level, Chinese schools were probably even inferior to Malay and Indian schools.

TABLE 4[18]

Government Schools, Government-aided Schools, and Enrollments,
FMS, 1921

	Government Schools	*Government-aided Schools*	*Enrollment* (1,000)
English	11	30	8.1
Malay	402	0	21.9
Tamil	10	99	n.a.
Chinese	1	0	n.a.

In the late nineteenth and early twentieth centuries, any literate Chinese was regarded as qualified to teach; pedagogic techniques were those used in the village schools of old China, where rote memory was accepted as education; physical conditions, while varying greatly, depending upon the clientele, were generally very unsatisfactory and sometimes deplorable; teachers' pay was pitifully low; each school was managed by a school committee that often took an active hand in the substantive as well as the administrative side of school operations; the subjects of study were almost always Chinese and never Malayan; and, finally, even within the same areas of Malaya, each dialect group maintained its own particular school conducted in the medium of the mother tongue.

In part as a reflection of Chinese nationalism and in part as an effort to consolidate schools and improve the quality of education, leaders of the

[17] *Ibid.*, p. 349.
[18] Federated Malay States, *Report for 1921 on the Federated Malay States* (London: HMSO, 1922), p. 17.

community began to press for the use of kuo-yü* as the medium of instruction in all Chinese schools in 1920, a movement that paralleled similar nationalist drives in China in the decade following the overthrow of the Manchus in 1911. Better qualified kuo-yü-speaking teachers were imported from China, and the standard of education rose considerably in many of the *hua-ch'iao*† schools of Malaya. Along with this, however, also came an increase in the Chinese character of the schools. Teachers who were proficient in Mandarin and who were willing to migrate to Southeast Asia were usually also those strongly committed to the nationalist cause, and they brought with them new teaching material that glorified the revolution and its leaders. So far as the political development of Malaysia is concerned this revitalization of the Chinese school system had at least two important consequences. First, the use of a common Chinese dialect began to bridge the linguistic chasms that had separated even the educated Chinese youth and contributed to a feeling of being "Chinese," rather than being Hakka, Hokkien, Teochew, and so on. Secondly, feeding on this new ability to communicate, as well as contributing to the breaking down of intracommunal linguistic barriers, was a new nationalist spirit that was being infused into the overseas Chinese community by the apparent success of the Chinese revolution and the evidence that a modern China might be emerging on the international scene. But, to further complicate the picture, this was not a monolithic Chinese nationalism, for Marxism-Leninism had also begun to take root in Malaya.

The Malayan Communist Party was established in the peninsula in 1930, and by this time, Marx, Lenin, and Mao were already beginning to receive some attention in the Malayan *hua-ch'iao* schools. In time it was apparent that some schools had been "captured" by the Communists and others by the Kuomintang. In some cases, individual schools had actually split into two competing institutions, each supporting one of the rival ideologies.

In an effort to exercise some control over the content of Chinese education, the FMS began to create machinery for supervision in the mid-1920's, and, from 1924 onward, the government made modest per capita grants to private Chinese schools. However, throughout the period to 1942, this machinery was rudimentary and overworked, and the means of control in the hands of the FMS was minimal.

The dramatic break in the history of Chinese education in Malaya came with the aftermath of World War II. In view of the major involvement of the Chinese community in the Communist-inspired emergency of 1948–60, the Chinese school problem could no longer be ignored. The British colonial administration still failed to suggest any sweeping changes that might integrate Malaya's chaotic educational structure into an orderly system, but the government did at least begin to come to grips with the problem. Increasing control was exercised over school instruction and those schools most blatantly advocating a Chinese ideology were closed, the usual objects

* Mandarin Chinese (Peking dialect)
† Overseas Chinese

of this ultimate sanction not surprisingly being those exhibiting strong Communist leanings. It remained for Malayan leaders themselves, however, to bring about the major educational reforms that were so long overdue.

The theme that Malayan political leaders adopted in formulating educational policy was well stated initially by the Central Advisory Committee on Education in 1951:

> The last racially segregated vernacular primary school in Malaya will cease to exist when the parents of the children attending it believe that a local National School [will] provide a more acceptable education. The Fenn-Wu Report [on Chinese education in Malaya] . . . suggests that day may never come. We believe it will come. We also believe its advent may be hastened by persuasion and inducement but delayed by dictation and compulsion.[19]

Adopting this tactic of gentle but firm persuasion, the government began to offer greatly increased grants-in-aid to Chinese schools willing to undergo increased supervision and improvement of teaching standards. The emphasis here was on content of the curriculum, not on changing the medium of instruction. The Razak Committee of 1955 had as its terms of reference to make recommendations for the creation of

> a national system of education acceptable to the people of the Federation as a whole which will satisfy their needs and promote their cultural, social, economic, and political development as a nation, having regard to the intention to make Malay the national language of the country whilst preserving and sustaining the growth of the language and culture of other communities living in the country.[20]

From the Education Act of 1957, which implemented the Razak Committee Report, to the Talib Committee Report of 1960 and its implementation in the educational reforms of 1962, the emphasis was on the first part of the Razak statement above. The goal was to create a national system, but one that observed, if not fostered, cultural pluralism. From 1962 to the present time, the emphasis has shifted to the second part of the statement—that is, the molding of a national system that fosters national unity while taking cognizance of communal cultures. It is presently provided that full support will be given to Chinese schools that agree to teach at least two-thirds of the curriculum in the Malay or English languages, offer the other one of these as a second language, and relegate Chinese to the status of a third language that can be offered only as an academic subject. The system of partially aided schools was abolished, these either conforming to the new education law and thereby becoming fully aided, or not conforming and losing all public assistance. Universal free primary

[19] Federation of Malaya, Central Advisory Committee on Education, *Report on the Barnes Report on Malay Education and the Fenn-Wu Report on Chinese Education* (Kuala Lumpur: Government Press, 1951), paragraph 21.

[20] Quoted in Federation of Malaya, Educational Review Committee, 1960 [Talib Committee], *Report* (Kuala Lumpur: Government Press, 1960), paragraph 12.

education for all streams of public education was introduced at the same time, thus making it doubly difficult to resist the government's offer of full support. Though there was considerable public discontent expressed in the press, these pressures were highly effective, and by the time of the creation of Malaysia in September, 1963, more than 85 per cent of the almost 1,200 full-time Chinese schools had opted for governmental assistance. In fact, at that time, Chinese remained as the principal medium of instruction in only 120 schools in the Peninsula,[21] and it is likely that this number has been further reduced today.

Although the British colonial government was strongly committed to the support of Malay-language education in the peninsula, by the very nature of the process, the Malay stream produced few political elite, and those that it did produce were more a contending than a cooperating elite.[22] R. J. Wilkinson, as Inspector of Schools at the beginning of the twentieth century, apparently attempted to generate official support for a creative Malay education that eventually might develop an informed Malay population topped by an intellectual class that identified with the political system, as well as contributed much to the cultural life of the country. Some of Wilkinson's ideas came to fruition in the establishment, in 1922, of the Sultan Idris Training College at Tanjong Malim, but, in the end, the college nurtured an intellectual elite that was cut off from the Malay masses and even out of touch with English-speaking colonial Malaya. Despite Wilkinson's brave departures in the field of Malay education, and despite the development of Sultan Idris College (which was novel in that it was along the public-school lines but taught exclusively in Malay), British educational policy, almost without interruption, stressed the importance of keeping most Malays on the land, teaching them to be better farmers, and generally convincing them of the dignity of manual labor.

It is always tempting to ascribe a divide-and-rule motive to British education policy (as to the colonial economic policy), but this would seem to invest the colonial administration with far more rationality than it deserves. The fact is that the Malay education policy was only one part of the more general colonial attitude toward the Malay population. The British saw the Malays as the rightful owners of the peninsula, and they saw their own role as one of paternal protectors of the Malay way of life. British administration, which was heavily Malay-oriented consistently went out of its way to disturb the Malay peasantry as little as possible. It is almost as if the individual colonial administrators saw themselves as good fairies sent to remodel the *attap* hut while the Malay family slept through the night, unaware of the changes that were going on. They were to be seen tiptoeing around the house, refurbishing the interior, directing the

[21] Douglas P. Murray, "Chinese Education in Southeast Asia," *China Quarterly*, No. 20 (October-December, 1964), p. 89.

[22] The discussion here of Malay education draws most heavily from William Roff, *The Origins of Malay Nationalism* (New Haven, Conn.: Yale University Press, 1967). Roff's monograph on the origin and growth of Malay nationalism is the best treatment of the subject available and will stand as the standard reference source for many years to come.

remodeling of the exterior, and all the while doing their best not to disturb the slumbering occupants. In such a role as this, it is not surprising that R. O. Winstedt could, on the one hand, be a serious and devoted student of Malay culture, and, on the other hand, be so determined in his official policies to keep the Malay peasant on the land, with only a minimum of disruptive education.[23]

Vernacular education as a whole (including Indian, which, though not covered in this essay, was largely estate-sponsored and designed to serve the needs of the tapper families) tended to produce a second-class citizenry that was destined to become frustrated when it came into close contact with the world of first-class citizens. Although there were some business and, occasionally, even professional opportunities for the Chinese-educated Chinese, educated members of the community were often frustrated because there was little opportunity for recognition and success within the framework of the colonial political system. Moreover, Malaya was not China, which had been the object of most of their study throughout their school careers. The Chinese had been taught that their culture was superior, yet upon completion of their studies, they found that they had to make their way in the local social environment, however inferior it might have seemed to them. To the vernacular-educated Malay, who longed for a life outside the kampong, the situation seemed almost as frustrating. Regardless of the paternalism of the colonial system, and regardless of the attention and favors that were therefore given to the Malays, a Malay-educated Malay soon found that he was ill-equipped to contest with his English-educated friends for power and prestige. The horizons of an English-educated Malay were almost unlimited. A Malay-educated Malay could be a peasant or a disaffected intellectual. While it is one of the anomalies of Malaysian politics that the second-class citizens from each of the vernacular streams of education were unable to unite in a common cause against the first-class citizens, it is nevertheless true that most of the support for each of the minor parties opposing the ruling Alliance today draws its popular support from one or more of the vernacular-educated communities.

Communal loyalty is not dependent on language alone, but it is apparent that language serves as one of the boundaries of interpersonal contact. And, while the educational system of Malaya broke down some of the intracommunal barriers, it tended at the same time to reinforce or even, in some cases, to redefine these linguistic boundaries. With the adoption of *kuo-yü* as the medium of instruction in the Chinese schools of Malaya, it became possible for Chinese students from different home environments, whose parents had migrated from different areas of China, to communicate

[23] On the attitude of Winstedt, see Roff, chapter 5. Roff does an excellent job of analyzing Winstedt's contribution to Malay education, but he, mistakenly it seems to me, ascribes this apparent contradiction in Winstedt's attitude more to a narrowness of outlook than to the influence of the general colonial belief in protecting the Malay way of life.

and interact almost for the first time, and the resulting homogenization of the Chinese community is a process that continues today. Of course, other influences were being introduced into the Chinese community, and one might hazard a general summary of the evolution of communal solidarity and the intercommunal relations of the Chinese in the following manner. Prior to 1920, the Chinese community was heterogeneous within itself and unassimilated into the indigenous culture. From 1920 onward, for about a decade, the community moved toward increased homogeneity, but in the process its lack of assimilation was becoming even more striking. With the introduction of Communist teachings into some of the schools in the 1930's and the resulting competition between the two ideologies, the community was becoming polarized, but the intensity of this competition made assimilation into Malayan society even more difficult.

Similar, but less marked, developments were taking place in the other communities of Malaya at about the same time. Missionary and some government schools subjected all communities to a common English language, and Malay boarding schools, particularly Malay and Sultan Idris colleges, brought together into a close corporate life rural Malays from all of the Malay states of the peninsula. At both schools, and most notably at Sultan Idris College, a deliberate attempt was made in both housing and extracurricular activities to prevent the segregation of students by region or social class. In this sense, both the English and the Malay vernacular streams of education were contributing to the destruction of provincial loyalties and fostering a more universalistic view of Malaya.

However, having pointed out the integrative influence of the English language, it must also be observed that, as in the case of the Chinese, certain linguistic boundaries to social intercourse still existed. And in some cases, where none already existed, they were created. It is true that English was pancommunal, and—as it will be argued later—the only real social and political assimilation that took place in Malaya occurred among the English educated. It is also true, however, that the English stream of education tended to produce almost a new community, a community whose major bond was more linguistic and cultural than racial, but whose elites increasingly interacted almost exclusively among themselves.

The linguistic boundaries reinforced by the Malay stream of education are even more apparent. Teachers from the various teacher-training colleges in Malaya returned from a training period of varying length and quality to teach, exclusively at the primary level, in the areas of their own homes. No attempt was made to teach these teachers a second language, and they were therefore neither motivated nor qualified to provide instruction for their pupils in another language. It is, of course, true that the proficiency of many colonial officers in Malay, combined with the bilingualism of the English-educated Malay administrative elite, considerably reduced the isolation of the Malay masses from colonial government. But, for the better educated in the Malay stream, life could be very frustrating, for opportunities were severely limited. The elite of this better-educated group, largely the products of Sultan Idris College, became the Malay intellectual leaders of the peninsula, authored most of the modern Malay novels and short stories of the interwar period, and generally formed the core of the Malay nationalist movement. It should come as no surprise that this group was strongly influenced by the Bahasa Indonesia movement in Indonesia, and, as an extension of this, it was impressed by the greater vitality apparent in Indonesian nationalism.[24]

The function of language in the shaping of political loyalties is a much debated subject. Swiss, Belgian, South African, Russian, and Canadian evidence is often cited to demonstrate that linguistic homogeneity is not a *sine qua non* for the emergence of a common political loyalty, but critics sometimes point out that at least several of these examples can be employed to support their side of the argument as easily as they can be used to demonstrate anything to the contrary. Rupert Emerson accepts that "the merits of linguistic uniformity are so obvious as barely to need statement."[25] Karl Deutsch adds the very useful qualification to this generalization that meaningful social communications are essential to the development of a national consciousness, and that linguistic homogeneity contributes to the growth of larger political loyalties insofar as language facilitates more widespread and more meaningful social communications.[26] To this it would seem that a further qualification should be added: It is conceivable (even if unlikely) that an increased ability to communicate, combined with more intensive and extensive communication, could lead to growing dislike and distrust as well as to the opposite. Despite the authority of the heroine of *The King and I*, "getting to know you like me" does not necessarily follow from "getting to know you." "Getting to know you dislike me" (and, conversely, "getting to know that I dislike you") could as easily follow, or, at least it would seem that there is no logical reason for this not being one possible consequence.

In Malaysia today, one necessarily ventures into the realm of speculation when considering the political effects of language. Each side has debated the language issue largely on the basis of faith. Nevertheless, the decision has now been made that Malay will be the national language of the country, the language of government, the common language in all educational streams, and it remains our task in the final section to speculate about some of the implications of these revolutionary changes.

Malayan education contributed directly to the growth of various groups of elites of widely differing political outlooks. From the point of view of the ruling colonials, and this was an important perspective as independence drew near, some were highly "competent and responsible," while there

[24] Roff, chapter 5.
[25] *From Empire to Nation* (Cambridge, Mass.: Harvard University Press, 1960), p. 133.
[26] Deutsch's writings are numerous. The most relevant works on this point are "The Growth of Nations: Some Recurrent Patterns of Political and Social Integration," *World Politics*, V (January, 1953), 183–89; *Nationalism and Social Communication* (Cambridge, Mass.: M.I.T. Press, 1953), and *Political Community and the North Atlantic Area* (Princeton, N.J.: Princeton University Press, 1957).

were others who were seen as "incompetent and irresponsible." On the whole, the former emerged from the English stream of education and were chiefly Malays. Although bilingual, these elites were more at home in an English urban culture than in their kampongs. Not only were they fluent in English (and even to the present time, the quality of English spoken in Malaysia among the English-educated is quite high), but they could be perfectly at ease at an English garden party, a concert, or, in recent years, even at a cocktail party. These elites were indeed capable of aspiring for independence, but, with only few lapses, theirs was a very gentlemanly nationalism. Moreover, the British colonial experience was sufficiently brief, Malaya was sufficiently prosperous, and English-language educational opportunities were sufficiently limited so that this elite never experienced the frustration occasioned by the inability to find places for themselves in the system. Unlike the situation in India, the supply of English-language graduates in Malaya never exceeded the demand.

The vernacular-educated did not find themselves in the same happy circumstances, though among those in the vernacular streams there was probably less frustration and unrest among the Malays than among the Chinese. This was true chiefly because there were some rewards of recognition and prestige available within the colonial system for the well-educated Malay-speaking Malays, however limited these might have been. As for the Malay peasant, his primary-level education had taught him little more than how to be a better peasant, which is self-satisfying so long as higher expectations are not also inculcated.

The most active opponents of colonialism were recruited from among the students of the Chinese stream of education. Confused, frustrated, disrupted by World War II, and alienated from the existing system, they saw little reason to play the game according to rules established by the colonial power. It is no accident that the Malayan Races Liberation Army, which came close to driving out the British after World War II, was almost entirely Chinese in composition. Malaya's Chinese felt that they had little stake in the future of a colonial Malaya, and it was not until it was apparent that the British intended to leave the country anyway that the back of the revolution was broken. It is also no accident that the Chinese middle schools of Singapore and the Chinese university in Singapore (Nanyang University) continue to be politically restive. Even in an overwhelmingly Chinese city such as Singapore there is little future for the Chinese-educated graduate. Salaries of the vernacular-educated are vastly inferior to those of the English-educated, and only the left-wing factions have succeeded in providing a continuing focus of identity for this large, frustrated group.

One function that English education performed was to bridge the communal chasms, at least at the level of the elites. Note the general level of English-language literacy and its comparison to Malay-language literacy at the time of the census of 1957.

It seems apparent that English provided a more useful bridge in 1957 than did Malay, but it should be pointed out that these figures may no longer be an accurate reflection of the situation. Once the decision was

TABLE 5[27]
Literacy Rates, Ten Years of Age and Older, Among Males, 1957

	Malaysian	Chinese	Indian
English	7	14	21
Malay	64	4	6

made in 1967 to convert to Malay as the national language, the government directed a large amount of human and financial resources into preparation for the conversion. As mentioned earlier, the educational system has been reorganized so as virtually to require that Malay be taught in all schools, and a high premium has been placed on Malay-language literacy in both government and business. Government agencies are turning out Malay-language texts, supplementary readings, and dictionaries. It will be interesting to see the effect of this frenzy of activity as revealed in the next census, though it is possible that the next census will not be conducted until 1970.

Language alone and education alone cannot build a nation where other forces are standing in powerful opposition. No one is certain how powerful and how viable the forces of disunity are in Malaysia, but apparently the feeling in government was that without a common language and a common national syllabus the political integration of the plural Malaysian society would be impossible. This unification has now become official policy. For political reasons, the common language chosen was Malay, not English, and now it remains the task of the educational system not only to spread literacy in the national language, but also to convince skeptics in all communities that this is a desirable—or at least a necessary—undertaking. This is a formidable assignment for any educational system. It is no exaggeration, however, to point out that the future of Malaysia, at least as it now exists, is dependent upon the success of this experiment.

[27] Federation of Malaya, Department of Statistics, 1957 *Population Census: Report No. 14* (Kuala Lumpur: Department of Statistics, 1960), tables 9A (1), 9B (1), and 9C (1).

THREE

Politics: Ideology, Identity, and Political Organization

As Harold Lasswell said more than thirty years ago, politics concerns "who gets what, when, how," and we are concerned in this section with questions related to these basic issues. In brief, the states of Southeast Asia, with the exception only of Thailand, were post-World War II creations. All (again with the exception of Thailand) had colonial experiences, all (including Thailand) were affected by the interaction between alien ideas and accepted indigenous beliefs, and all were occupied by Japan. These historical facts have had a significant impact on politics, for history has shaped the make-up of the group that "got" power, it affected the nature of "what" they got, it dictated the timing of "when" they got it, and it influenced tactically "how" they got it.

The essential ingredient in the drive to sever the unequal relationships with the colonial mother countries was the determination on the part of Southeast Asian leaders to achieve independence. Ho Chi Minh, Norodom Sihanouk, Sukarno, Baw Maw, Manuel Quezon, Tunku Abdul Rahman— all of these leaders and many others—valued independence, and to the spirit of this quest for independence, the present generation of political observers assigned the older European term "nationalism." The term is Western, just as is the concept of a "nation" itself, but the raw material is Asian, and this is one of the paradoxes that troubles Rupert Emerson in the first chapter of this section. Emerson's perceptive treatment of the subject was one of the first scholarly analyses of post-World War II Asian nationalism and remains today one of the best. On the other hand, with the advantage of greater perspective, Harry Benda shows us in his scholarly treatment of the impact of Marx on Southeast Asia (and vice versa) that the paradoxes may possibly be more in our own eyes than in those of Southeast Asians. We see contradictions, and because we see them, they exist. Southeast Asians may not see these contradictions, and thus for them they do not exist. Certainly the eclectic and highly emotional nationalism expressed by the recently deposed Sukarno of Indonesia lends support to this view. As Sukarno so eloquently asserts in the selection excerpted here, nationalism, internationalism, socialism, democracy, and religion—all in the Indonesian style—are complementary, not contradictory.

While Sukarno was exhorting his followers to be good nationalists, to become "a people whose soul is aflame with the determination of . . . independence," it is interesting and instructive to view the process of a national awakening from the perspective of a single individual. Probably the memoir of a Lao official reprinted here is atypical of Laos, but it does provide an excellent account of the growth of nationalism in one particular individual. The ingredients described by Emerson, Benda, and others are all present: parents who had already attained minor status in the colonial system; the sudden opening of a new and fascinating world beyond the limits of the village; the deprivation of the Japanese occupation, followed by the even greater disruption caused by the attempted reassertion of colonialism; the fond memories of sympathetic colonial officers in the field; the insults and slights suffered at the hands of other colonials, and the general unfairness of the system itself. From all of these experiences, the young official emerged a committed Laotian, whose nationalism is tinged with a touch of Lao racism.

In the next section we move from the emotional and philosophical bases of the state to its political organization, and here we find less agreement on fundamentals and even more diversity. Almost every basic form of political organization is to be found in Southeast Asia, and the essays in this section deal only with several of the more interesting and troublesome problems faced. There are now three military regimes in Southeast Asia—Indonesia,

Thailand, and Burma. In Indonesia, the army was always a powerful but apparently restrained force, as Daniel Lev shows in Chapter 21; nevertheless, provoked by the left, and threatened by the possible disappearance of Sukarno, it was finally goaded into taking over, and Justus M. van der Kroef describes and analyzes this succession crisis in Chapter 22. Thailand now has a constitution, but the military still rules, and David Wilson, in Chapter 23, shows that this is nothing new, for the Thai military has always had a strong voice in deciding "who gets what, when, how." The third military regime in Southeast Asia is that of Burma, which, as Louis Walinsky points out in Chapter 24, has proved more effective than Burmese civilian regimes in stimulating economic development, but has apparently put a brake on corresponding social and political change.

It is not an easy task to generalize about the impact of the military in Southeast Asia, but, from these three examples, one is justified in asking some hard questions about the nature of military rule. Can the military really govern more effectively than civilian regimes? The answer seems to be in the affirmative in all cases here, though we must qualify this by pointing out that the experience with military government in Indonesia and the experience with unfettered civilian regimes in Thailand have both been brief, thus permitting few valid comparisons within a single culture. What are the political and social "costs" of military rule? Walinsky, the only author who addresses himself to this specific question, obviously thinks they are quite high. As *obiter dicta*, Wilson sees considerable risk in the continuation of military rule in Thailand, despite the fact that the system has worked relatively smoothly in the past. In Indonesia, almost any other political solution seemed promising in 1965, but by 1968 some observers were beginning to ask this very same question.

Two alternatives to military rule are also discussed in this section. Malaysia and the Philippines both have working democracies. In the case of Malaysia, government is based on a precarious communal compromise, which is always in danger of breaking down. Moreover, as K. J. Ratnam observes in Chapter 25, even within the dominant Malay community, a very shaky consensus is threatened by the possibility of a growing Malay nationalism based on religion and racism.

Carl Landé shows us that in the Philippines, while the country inherited the trappings of the American system, democracy functions in a peculiarly Philippine fashion. Parties are formed, candidates are nominated, citizens go to the polls, and governments are elected, but the motivations and behavior of all concerned are more traditional than is the machinery itself. Yet, in both Malaysia and the Philippines, things are changing. "Who gets what, when, how" has been agreed upon for the time, but how long this agreement will last is a question that troubles many. Finally, we come to the only practicing Communist state in Southeast Asia today, and the late Bernard Fall shows us in Chapter 27 that it is not only unique in Southeast Asia—it is also unique within the Communist orbit. But even in a system such as this, it is apparent that "who gets what, when, how" has not been settled for all time.

In the final collection of essays of this section, we examine briefly the personalities, styles, and fortunes of three important Southeast Asian leaders. Norodom Sihanouk, Sukarno, and Ho Chi Minh have several points in common: Each man is (or, in the case of Sukarno, was) the major leader of his country; each led his country to independence; each was strongly influenced by the West; and each has spent much of his time trying to mobilize and unify the people of his state into a single nation. Beyond this, we are dealing with three different personalities, who adopted vastly different techniques and styles in trying to solve domestic and foreign problems and in making the basic political decisions about "who gets what, when, how."

17

PARADOXES OF ASIAN NATIONALISM*

RUPERT EMERSON

Sweeping and remolding Europe in the nineteenth century, nationalism has swept on in equally revolutionary guise to remold Asia in the twentieth century, and is now penetrating Africa. In the study of its impact and development, almost every aspect of human society is involved, positively or negatively, and at least every social science discipline has its part to contribute to the analysis of an exceedingly complex whole. In the Asia of today and of the recent past, we have a whole series of new nations coming forward to assert their claims in the world. A laboratory has been made available, in which we can observe and analyze the growth of nationalism, catch it in its earliest stages, and trace it through to its maturity, as well as at least noting in passing the countervailing forces of the past and present. The raw material, vibrant with a new and dynamic life, is there for our taking, and it would be tragic if we were to let it slip through our fingers without gathering it and subjecting it to the closest possible investigation.

* Reprinted by permission of the author and the publisher from *Far Eastern Quarterly* (now *The Journal of Asian Studies*), XIII (February, 1954), 131–42.

Although the raw material is there, and in abundance, I would be the last to suggest that the task of analysis is easy, or that we now have all the intellectual tools we need to carry it through. Much of what is glibly and habitually said about nationalism rests on a very slim foundation of positive knowledge and, more important, of precise and meaningful concepts. Much of what passes for solid scientific analysis is actually done with mirrors or with a sleight of hand that may deceive the unwary but should not be allowed to deceive the manipulator himself. One of the most seductive and elusive variants of this is the process of ex post facto reasoning: reasoning back from the fact of the nation to the things that must have caused it. Let me suggest two examples. Though it often, and notably, in some parts of Asia, is not the case, a nation is normally assumed to be a community knit together by a common language; but what is regarded for these purposes as a separate language, and what as a mere dialect, is actually likely to be decided after the fact on the basis of the national communities that come into effective existence, rather than on any necessary and objective linguistic principles. With greater assurance, we can assume a nation to be a community knit together by a common experience over a reasonably long past, shaping a common tradition and culture. But any extensive people has a host of traditions, historical experiences, and even cultures, crisscrossing each other in almost every conceivable direction. Those which the observer is likely to put forward as constituting the inevitable national tradition, as integral to the national pattern of life, are those which fit the national mold as it actually develops, to the exclusion or minimization of those—equally real in historical experience—which cut across the nation, as on class or regional lines, or link it with other, external groups.

Behind this ex post facto process, there often lurks the unspoken, but also unquestioned, assumption that the nations that actually appear on the world stage are, so to speak, divinely ordained and predetermined entities that could not be otherwise than as they are.[1] But if one stands back from the stream of history and examines it with a somewhat quizzical eye, it becomes one of the most fascinating of pursuits to attempt to work out why the particular nations that have in fact emerged did emerge, as contrasted with the variety of alternatives that, under different circumstances, might have come to pass. This is far too large a topic for any real exploration here. I suggest it is one worthy of far more attention than it has usually received. Particularly in Asia, new nations have been created, and in some sense are still being created before our eyes, but we have only scanty knowledge of the historical alchemy by which scattered fragments of peoples have been transmuted into communities responsive to the appeal of

[1] This assumption receives explicit, if not quite unchallengeable, statement in a comment by President Sukarno to the effect that God Almighty created the map of the world in such fashion that even a child can tell that the British Isles are one entity—which might surprise the Irish—and that a child can see that the Indonesian Archipelago is a single entity stretching between the Pacific and Indian oceans and the Asian and Australian continents, from the north tip of Sumatra to Papua. *The Indonesian Review* (January, 1951), p. 13.

nationalism. What are the forces that shape the peoples who, at some later stage, come to feel themselves separate and distinctive nations? It is obvious that this is not, and, by its nature, cannot be, any sudden or even speedy process. Over long periods of time, there must be a storing up in the minds of men of a folk sense of shared memories, of common patterns of life, that gives this particular people a deep and profoundly significant sense of sharing a common destiny, from which all the rest of mankind is excluded. At what malleable stage in their history, and under what circumstances, do peoples become so deeply enmeshed in this particular community of the nation that

> In spite of all temptations
> To belong to other nations,
> He remains an Englishman.

It is an attractive theory, and one with a large measure of applicability, that the primary element in the shaping of nations is the existence, at some malleable period in a people's history, of a single political rule, of a common state structure or a reasonable approximation thereof, sufficiently long-lasting and deep-penetrating to make a permanent imprint on that people's social mind. The formation of the separate Philippine and Indonesian nations, despite a large original cultural and ethnic homogeneity, must be attributed primarily to the distinct colonial regimes to which they were so long subjected. Indeed, Quezon is on record as acknowledging that Filipino unity was largely a product of Spanish and American rule.[2] The unity of India is certainly not to be explained without some reference to the unifying force of the British regime—but the splitting off of Pakistan as a separate nation belies the notion that this theory is universally applicable. To understand the emergence of three nations in Indochina—if that is in fact to be the outcome—it is clearly necessary to go back to their ancient pre-French roots, but it is also in order to point out that French rule never really sought to unify them. As the dust gradually settles, will the present colonially determined frontiers survive as the frontiers of nations for the considerable mélange of peoples stretching from Burma across Thailand, into Laos and Cambodia, and up into South China? What national allegiance or allegiances will emerge from the racial hodgepodge of Malaya, where one can only assume that differences were already so deeply imprinted that political unification in the colonial era could not have produced a single communal consciousness. Or, to raise historical "if's," what are the circumstances under which the diversities of China might have been exploited in such fashion as to produce not one but several Chinese nations?

Part of what I have just been saying has already suggested the general range of issues that I should like to consider in this paper. Central to these issues is the fact that it is so clearly and strikingly the impact of the West that has brought to fighting consciousness societies that, in their own roots, derive wholly from non-Western sources. As I have suggested, in at least

2 See Joseph Ralston Hayden, *The Philippines* (New York: Macmillan Co., 1942), p. 21.

some of the colonial areas, even the basic question as to which peoples are to be within and which outside the national community appears to have been determined by the lines drawn on the map by the imperial powers. It seems to me inescapable that, in the future, a great part of the inner dynamics of nationalism in Asia must result from this profound contradiction within nations that derive from an ancient Asian past and yet have been brought to national awareness not only by the Western impact but, even more immediately and insistently, by the revolutionary appeal of their own native Westernizers.

The claim of any people to separate nationhood must rest primarily on the fact that over the centuries—in the Asian setting, I should perhaps say over the millennia—it has developed an identity and way of life of its own. If it is no longer fashionable, as it once was, to speak in Mazzinian terms of the peculiar mission of each nation in the divine harmony of the world, much the same is implied by the currently more palatable, newfangled terms, such as "national character," "pattern of culture," or "value structure." Without being high-flown about it, what presumably drives a nation forward, in its will to live and assert itself, is that its members feel that they share among themselves goals, values, purposes, habits, and outlooks, shaped from an immemorial past, of which only they are properly aware, and which only they can properly bring to bear on the conduct of their collective life.

Every nation that comes to awareness of itself inevitably searches back into its past to single out those things that are distinctive; that have brought it into separate existence, and that serve to demonstrate its unique and illustrious antecedents, be they real or largely in the realm of myth. In the first stage, this search is likely to express itself most vigorously, in the religious sphere, in the form of a revival and perhaps purification of the religion of the country, as a reassertion of the integrity of the national culture, and as a central symbol of difference from the Western intruder. At a later stage, there is a turning away, in the sphere of language, from the alien-imposed European tongues, and an insistence on the adoption and use of a national language that will at once express the national soul and serve as an instrument of national unification. Everywhere there is an effort to re-establish contact with the national past. Sun Yat-sen and Chiang Kai-shek, in their different fashions, look back to the majestic sweep of an earlier China, to the distinctive loyalties to family and clan, to the Chinese discoveries and inventions of past ages. Nehru rediscovers India, Gandhi seeks to build on the ancient Indian heritage, and many Indian nationalists, perhaps particularly in Bengal, turn back to re-explore the religious and philosophic grandeurs of Hinduism; as, later, their neighboring Pakistanis boast the Mogul Empire and the Islamic tradition. Indonesia comes to a new awareness of the empires of Srivijaya and Majapahit, of Borobudur, and of its heritage of music, dance, and art.

But it is a significant part of the paradox that a very large share of the credit for this reopening of the treasures of the past must go not to the Asian peoples themselves but to the Westerners who have delved into the antiquities of India, uncovered the ruins of Angkor Wat, pieced together the ancient chronicles and monuments, and, in this fashion, presented the Asians with an ancestral past, with a rich store of national memories, which had almost slipped from the Asian mind. Indirectly, there was the challenge to Asians of the presence of alien rule, bringing an assertedly superior alien culture; more directly, there was the active work of Western scholars in re-creating a partially forgotten past.

Nationalism, I have been suggesting, is, in part, necessarily a return to the past, to those things that distinguish this nation from the rest of the world. Yet, who are the nationalists? In what parts and segments of the Asian societies do we find them? To put it negatively: The one place where we do not find them is in those parts of the society which are most obviously representative of the cultural heritage and way of life of the past. On the contrary, it is the persons and groups who are most characteristically the product of the Western impact who are the leaders, the storm troopers, and the usual rank and file of the nationalist movements. These are Asian nations that are being roused to life, but it is the disruptive force of the alien European encroachment and dominance that has brought new communities to birth out of the old societies, and the prime movers have been the people most divorced from their traditional worlds. The people who can probably be taken in some sense as the most authentic heirs and perpetuators of the ancient culture and traditions are the rural peasantry, who everywhere constitute the great mass of the population, and such of the old aristocracy as has been able to hold on; but it is very clear on the record that these groups have formed neither the leadership nor the mass-following of Asian nationalism. As far as the peasantry is concerned, this is, of course, by no means to say either that there have not been fringe segments of it that have been drawn actively into the nationalist movements or that, as nationalism has progressed and established itself, the peasants have not come to an increasing acceptance of it. But, in general, the evidence indicates that the rural masses, bound to their villages and continuing the traditional cultivation of their fields, have either been indifferent to the new currents or, at the best and belatedly, passive adherents to the nationalist creed. It is barely necessary to add that, of course, from time to time and place to place, the nationalists, like the Communists, have been able to make effective use of peasant grievances or upheavals, but with no necessary implication that the peasant actors themselves were either nationalist or Communist. The case is similar with the older aristocracy. Obviously, certain members of it—I might cite the Sultan of Jogja and the considerably more equivocal figure of Bao Dai—have played nationalist roles, but, in general, it is a group that either has been pushed aside or destroyed by the colonial regimes, or has become so tainted with colonial "collaborationism" as to have no nationalist standing.

On a geographical, as opposed to a class, basis of analysis, it was in the native states of India and, in lesser degree, of Indonesia that the old ways of life were carried on, in contrast to the greater ferment of modernism in the more directly ruled areas; but these states tended to be backwaters, least touched by the nationalist stream. If one seeks the nationalists of Indochina, it is not to relatively untouched Laos that one turns but to the deltas of the Red River and the Mekong.

Who are the nationalists? Certainly, as far as the leadership is concerned, they are almost exclusively neither of the aristocracy nor of the peasantry, but rather of what must be loosely and somewhat unsatisfactorily defined as the middle class. With only rare exceptions, leaving the special case of Japan aside, they are intellectuals or professional men who have a very high degree of contact with and training in the Western world. Sun Yat-sen was a doctor who secured his lower education in Hawaii and his higher and medical training in Hong Kong. Gandhi, Nehru, and Jinnah were all British-educated lawyers. In the Philippines, Quezon and Osmena were both lawyers with extensive experience of the West. Luang Pradit in Thailand was a Paris-trained lawyer. In Burma, Aung San was a product of Rangoon University and a law student; Baw Maw studied at Cambridge and obtained a French law degree; Premier Nu studied at the University of Rangoon, turned writer, and—a somewhat odd occupation for a Buddhist statesman—translated Dale Carnegie's *How to Win Friends and Influence People* into Burmese.[3] In Indonesia, Sukarno was an engineer by training; Mohammed Hatta, a university student in Holland; and Soetan Sjahrir, an intellectual and writer with an intimate acquaintance with the Western world and its thought. And so it goes, up and down the list. The *Indonesian Review*, in its issue for April-June, 1951, lists the educational background of the members of the Sukiman cabinet of 1951: For one, no academic information was given, and the Minister of Religion received his education at a special Muslim institute; all the rest of the eighteen members of the cabinet had had either a substantial amount of or a full Western-style education; five had studied in Holland or elsewhere in Europe; six were law students; three were engineers; and two were medical doctors, including the prime minister. Surely these are men who, however much of the more ancient tradition they may carry with them, may properly be regarded as products of the Western world and its techniques and outlooks.

To trace down the nationalist following in similar detail is obviously a far more difficult matter because of the necessity of reaching into amorphous and anonymous masses of people. The general conclusion is, however, I believe unavoidable, that the groups and classes who have been most susceptible to infection by the nationalist germ are those who have been most sharply divorced from their old worlds by the impact of the new. Any listing of them must include the students who have enlisted in the nationalist cause with almost unbroken fervor. It would include many of the civil servants, and other elements of the rising middle class, of whom increasing numbers have economic interests that nationalism promotes and protects. An increasing mass following is contributed by the growing urban proletariat and, at least in many instances, by the uprooted workers on

[3] See Virginia Thompson and Richard Adloff, *The Left Wing in Southeast Asia* (New York: William Sloane Associates, 1950), p. 252.

large-scale Western estates and plantations and in other Western enterprises, in mines and oil fields—in brief, the workers in those employments
that are least characteristic of the native society and most characteristic of
the new superimposed Western society. It is no accident that Sun, and the
Kuomintang after him, found so large a measure of financial and political
support among the overseas Chinese in Southeast Asia and elsewhere—a
peculiarly uprooted element. We have many of the bits and pieces from
which a profile and sociology of the nationalisms of Asia might be constructed, but I suggest that there are many studies remaining to be undertaken that would give us a vastly more detailed picture than we currently
have of the inner structure of the nationalist movements, and of the layers
of the population in different countries that have successively taken part
in them.

If we attempt to seek out the sources of inspiration of Asian nationalism,
we again move onto somewhat treacherous and uncertain ground, since
positive proof of intellectual influences and of the ancestry and spread of
ideas is notoriously difficult, but the predominant influence of the West
seems unquestionable. The very idea of nationalism is certainly of Western origin, and there is every reason to assume that the mere element of
imitation in Asia is a powerful one. The strength of the West, which enabled it to dominate so much of Asia, was a thing to be studied and
copied, and a major component of that strength, according to the testimony of the West itself, was the existence of coherent and integrated
nations. The achievement and maintenance of national unity and independence was one of the central themes of the literature and political tradition
of the West to which the Asians were exposed. The writings of Rousseau,
Burke, Mazzini, and the great figures of American independence became
familiar to them, and exercised among them the influence that they had
first exercised in the West itself. More recently, a variant strand of Western thought and political action—the Communist endorsement of national
self-determination—has made its impact through the doctrines of Lenin,
Stalin, and their followers. The evidence of the direct descent of the nationalists of Asia from those who propagated the nationalism of the West
and hymned its praises is too overwhelming to allow of any serious doubt.

This is not, of course, to seek at all to deny that the interactions of the
Asian nationalists on each other, and the stimulus given to one country by
a neighbor, are not of great importance; but it certainly appears to be the
case that, even here, the original spark is derived from Europe and is
passed on through an Asian intermediary, suffering, perhaps, some slight
sea change on the way. As the French Revolution is taken as the conventional date for the starting point of European nationalism, so the rise of
Japan, and particularly the Russo-Japanese War, is taken as the conventional benchmark for Asian nationalism. Sun Yat-sen points to the fact
that the new Japan, transformed into a first-class power, has caught up
with Europe and given the rest of Asia unlimited hope. "We once thought
we could not do what the Europeans could do; and we see now that Japan
has learned from Europe and that, if we follow Japan, we, too, will be

learning from the West as Japan did."[4] But it is obvious from Sun's words that Europe was the true and original model, and he was not averse to drinking directly from the springs of Communist Russia, which gave him both economic inspiration and the political technique of the centralized one-party state.

Particularly for the Vietnamese, so much more influenced by China than the rest of Southeast Asia, Sun himself, the Kuomintang, and, later, the Chinese Communists became sources of nationalist and organizational inspiration; and Sukarno pays tribute to the teaching of Sun. Elsewhere, and most notably in Indonesia in the interwar decades, Gandhi and the Indian National Congress were models to be studied and followed with respect; but nowhere can the nationalism of Asia be traced to Europe with greater assurance than in India.

The wellsprings of Asian nationalism lie in the ideas and political example of Europe, and, despite the praise that, as I have indicated, was frequently heaped on the great past of the several nations, there have been very few among the nationalists who have had their eyes on a restoration of an Asian past rather than on the creation of a Western future.[5] Of the great leaders, only Gandhi's name comes to mind in this connection, with his peculiar mixture of the modern world and India's antiquity. In India, this aspect of Gandhi's life and teaching has been carried on and exaggerated or distorted by the right-wing Hindu groups, such as the Hindu Mahasaba, but it is the modernism of Nehru that has carried the day. In China, Chiang has in some measure preached a return to Confucianism and the time-honored tradition and structure of the older Chinese society. In Indonesia, perhaps Darul Islam and some of the more traditionalist Muslim groups stand for an older world; and in Iran, Kashani has stood up to challenge modernist trends; but the general drift is clearly modernist and Western.

Far from seeking a return to the past, the bulk of the nationalists concentrate rather on bringing to their countries the dynamism, the Faustian drive, of the modern West. That there must be a certain ambivalence in their attitude lies at the heart of the paradox. They are attacking the West; they are seeking to get out from under Western supremacy; but it is the instruments and outlooks of the West that they would have their people master in order to substantiate their claim to an equal and independent status in the world. The nationalism of Asia is no mere xenophobic rejec-

[4] Sun Yat-sen, *San Min Chu I* (Shanghai, 1929), p. 16.

[5] An opposing point of view is stated by F. S. C. Northrop, *The Taming of the Nations* (New York: Macmillan Co., 1952), pp. 68–69, who contends that a study of developments in the Middle and Far East shows that the Muslims and Asians are not pursuing nationalist aspirations as the West understands them: "They are working toward the resurgence of their respective submerged civilizations. What Western reporters have described as the coming of Western nationalism to the Middle East and Asia is really the return of Islamic or Far Eastern ways and values. . . . It is culturalism rather than nationalism that is the rising fact of the world today." But Northrop immediately qualifies this statement by adding that the contemporary mind of Islam and Asia is also seeking to ingraft from the West the factors needed to raise the standard of living of the masses.

tion of the alien disturber, no effort to restore a static and tradition-bound society, but to break with, or at least to build upon, the old traditions in such fashion as to infuse the nations of Asia with the dynamic power that has revolutionized the West.

There is, I believe, at least side evidence of this in the parallel that can be drawn between the development of nationalism in Asia and in the Western world. Although there are some who would deny that any such parallelism exists to a significant degree, I would be inclined to assert that, recognizing the many differences of time and place and circumstance, Asian nationalism has followed a course that coincides strikingly in many essential respects with the classic European models. It would take us too far afield to try to explore this argument in any detail, but I suggest that in Asia, as in Europe and elsewhere, nationalism has been the result of the forces that have characteristically shaped the contemporary world: the stress on individualism, the rationalist and scientific outlook, the commercial and industrial revolutions. It is a product of what one of the recent investigators of nationalism has termed a process of social mobilization[6]— the drawing of more and more people away from the traditional folk culture of village and market town into active participation in the larger society of the modern world. This has come about through the operation of such things as the spread of a money economy, the growth of wage labor, increasing urbanization, the development of communications, and the workings of a rationalized and more intensive governmental structure.

Metternich in the early nineteenth century identified as the revolutionary and nationalist enemies of the old order he wished to preserve, the students, the professors, the intellectuals, and the lawyers: Can we do better in identifying the leaders of the twentieth-century nationalism in Asia? Add to them more generally the rising middle class, the urban workers, and the uprooted peasantry, and you have the groups who have everywhere been the progenitors and the first adherents of the nationalist cause.

I shall leave aside one very baffling question that is, to my mind, all too infrequently asked and to which I have been able to find no satisfactory answer. Why is it that the groups involved in this process of social mobilization should so uniformly turn in the nationalist direction, pour themselves into the national mold? Considering all the other possible bases of community in the world, why should the nation have come to assume the centrality that it has? For example, it is apparent to the good Marxist that, while nationalism may be made use of for his purposes, the real allegiance of the working masses cuts sharply across national lines and is focused on the solidarity of class—or, at least, it should be. It would be interesting in this connection to dig deeper into the group and class make-up of the Communist, as opposed to the more purely nationalist movements, and to see whether or not there is a significant difference in the elements to which they make their appeal, although it is evident on the face of it that such

[6] Karl W. Deutsch, "The Growth of Nations: Some Recurrent Patterns of Political and Social Integration," *World Politics* (January, 1953), pp. 168–96.

an investigation would be complicated by the large elements of nationalism that Communism in Asia has been prepared to absorb.

There is one further line of inquiry that I should like to pursue. What is the relation between the Westernized leaders and the mass of the population which, in varying degrees in different countries and localities, has remained relatively untouched by the impact of the West? The new elite in the contemporary Asian scene is obviously only a minority and often a very small minority, and yet it claims to speak on behalf of the whole of each of the nations. To the colonial administrator, the gulf between the Westernized few and the folk society was frequently one of the justifications of his existence. Seeing himself as a better interpreter and guardian of the interests of the unsophisticated native mass than the clamorous Westernized nationalists, he was inclined to echo the dictum of Lord Lugard in Nigeria that "it is a cardinal principle of British colonial policy that the interests of a large native population shall not be subject to the will . . . of a small minority of educated and Europeanized natives who have nothing in common with them, and whose interests are often opposed to theirs."[7] It was in large part the prevalence of this attitude that led to the bitterest grief of the period of "liberation" after World War II. Assuming that the simple masses would welcome back their true friends and repudiate the Japanese- and Communist-inspired betrayers of the real native soul and destiny, the colonial powers sought to return to 1939. But, despite the great and undeniable gulf between them, the masses in fact gave their loyalty to their new national leaders.

From the standpoint of the leaders, the appeal to the masses of their people was both a political necessity and, I believe, an inherent part of the nationalist creed. To make headway against the colonial regimes or, more broadly, against the imperial powers, it was obviously necessary to build upon a popular base, to enlist as large segments as possible of the people in the political battles. Coming at it somewhat more abstractly, the moral and political justification of their position, of their claim to take over the guidance of their societies, was that they represented the entire nation. What is the nation after all but the whole body of a people knit together by special ties that distinguish them from the rest of mankind? Hence, I suggest, nationalism has in it always a basic democratic element—a democratic element that is not wholly lost even when it is debased into the plebiscitary totalitarianism of a Hitler or a Mussolini.

Under whatever conditions it may arise, nationalism, by its nature, involves an appeal to or, at the least, a reference to the people. Whether the national claim is put forward against a ruler by divine right, against a feudal hierarchy, against a conglomerate empire of the Hapsburgs, or against a colonial regime, nationalism finds its *raison d'être* in the national people for whom it speaks. Furthermore, I would be inclined to advance a tentative hypothesis to the effect that the democratic implications of nationalism are likely to be most effective, for a variety of reasons, in the countries that have had the most intensive experience of colonialism. Even

[7] Report on the *Amalgamation of Northern and Southern Nigeria* (Lagos, 1919).

apart from the fact that there has been a deep and direct indoctrination of the Westernized elements in the theory and creed of democracy, there are other important aspects. In the realm of actual politics there is the inescapable need to mobilize, to nationalize, the general populace. The colonial system has worked to destroy or to devitalize the older traditional, aristocratic leadership, and the new elite must establish its claim to power by winning the allegiance of the people whom it is helping to fashion into a nation. I would suggest that there is a more significant reality in the democratic claims and aspirations of the nationalist leaders of the ex-colonial countries of South Asia than there is in those of, say, Japan, Thailand, and Iran, where the special circumstances and pressures of colonialism were absent. In the colonial countries, the new leadership starts, so to speak, from scratch and has to make its way in the world with the aid of its constituents; in the others, the mighty and the rich and landed groups have established positions, prerogatives, and privileges that the real practice of democracy might well threaten and overturn. Everywhere, nationalism is used as an instrument to win and hold mass support. It would be my contention that in the countries emerging from the colonial era there is a greater and more effective intention to draw the masses into an actual share of political power.

In this sense, nationalism is a unifying force, but I fear that it has also, and perhaps particularly in its democratic manifestations, a strongly divisive element. One authority has suggested that the nationalism of Asia, like its earlier counterpart in Europe, has had the effect of moving toward a territorial base, embracing all the people on the national territory within the nation: "Asia, like Europe, has discovered that modern governments can only function when all are citizens, and all citizens are of equal value."[8] In breaking down the loyalty to religion, caste, and clan, this is likely to be true, but it is also true that, as in Europe, the emergence of nationalism brings with it the emergence of national minorities as well. When the focal point of loyalty is the nation, the state having been created to implement the national will, and when issues are democratically posed for national decision, there is an inevitable tendency to sort out the national sheep from the alien goats. Under a prenational authoritarian rule, the question of membership in the national community may be largely irrelevant; in an age of nationalism, it is likely to become the central question. When it is posed in India, a civil war flares up in which a Muslim Pakistan separates itself from the rest, and in Southeast Asia, the Chinese, the Europeans, the Eurasians, and others find themselves beyond the national pale. Malaya and, in lesser degree, Burma present the most striking instances of this trend. Where there is original unity, nationalism serves further to unite; where there is felt ethnic diversity, nationalism is no cure.

I find myself uncertain as to whether paradoxes are supposed to have answers or not. At all events, I do not claim to have them. The questions sprout up in easy abundance, but the answers are few and far between. We have the basic fact of Westernized elites that have taken command of

[8] Maurice Zinkin, *Asia and the West* (London: Chatto & Windus, 1951), p. 285.

Asian nations, but where they go from here is another matter. Even the elites themselves are inevitably torn by ambivalences. They cannot help but seek to re-integrate themselves in the national traditions, at the same time that they seek to revolutionize their societies into Western modernity. Casting off the control of the West and acutely sensitive to any imputation of inferiority, they are more than ever conscious of the need to draw on the West to build the strength and true equality of their nations. It is of more than symbolic significance that, at a time when they seek to bring Western learning and skills to their people, they move toward the adoption of native, national languages that must tend to diminish the ties to the West.

Prediction in the social sciences is always a hazardous matter, and it is even more hazardous today than yesterday. World wars and world revolutions have changed the old elements in familiar equations and have brought in new ones whose values are still largely unknown. On the face of the record of what has happened in other comparable situations, it is difficult to view the future of the newly risen Asian nations with any great measure of optimism, but in a world undergoing radical transformation, there can be no assurance as to what constitute the relevant points of comparability and analogy. The experience of many other countries over the last century suggests that the most probable outcome is backsliding into a lethargy that pays little more than lip service to the ideals of progressive democracy, but this experience for the most part refers back to an era prior to the more recently fashionable mode of totalitarian dictatorships of the right and of the left. The case of China serves notice that Communist despotism may sweep away both lethargy and the proud hopes of liberal nationalism.

Nationalism is a response to the atomization of society, a turn toward a new form of community to replace old communities that are in process of being destroyed. In our day, it is the nation that legitimizes the state; but what manner of nations are these that are being created in Asia? By any scheme of accounting, they are communities that are all too evidently headed in several directions at once, built on a national unity that has in it more of diversity than of oneness. Will the leaders, holding firm to their democratic and progressive aspirations, be able to carry the masses with them and create a new and stable synthesis, or will they draw apart and form a separate governing caste wielding power for its own sake and enjoying the fruits thereof? Or will they be reabsorbed into a mass that refuses to surrender the ways of its fathers?

18

REFLECTIONS ON ASIAN COMMUNISM*

HARRY J. BENDA

By one of the strangest of history's paradoxes, a revolutionary doctrine hatched in the reading room of the British Museum and primarily addressed to the working classes of the most advanced industrial countries in the West has in part triumphed in, and continues to appeal to, some of the world's least "developed" regions. The specter of Communism, as Karl Marx and Frederick Engels so confidently predicted well over a century ago, has finally come to haunt the world, and with a vengeance. How has yesteryear's remote specter turned into a global threat that in our days is involving hundreds of thousands of Americans fighting in Asia?

Our almost obsessive preoccupation with Communism, the roots of which go back to the Bolshevik Revolution and to our more than justified aversion to Stalinism, and which has been further nourished by the bitter experiences of the cold war, has led us to an oversimplified picture of its nature. This picture, strangely enough, at one and the same time tends to magnify and underestimate Communism. We have magnified it, largely

* Reprinted by permission of the author and the publisher from *The Yale Review*, LVI (October, 1966), 1–16, copyright Yale University.

as a result of the global aspirations so loudly proclaimed—and the conspira-
torial machinations so adroitly practiced—by the Russian Bolsheviks ever
since the consolidation of their power in the early 1920's. But in so doing,
we have stubbornly refused to recognize that the Soviets' attempted monolithism has, as often as not, led to dismal failures. It was, after all, Stalin's
alleged omniscience and the enforced subservience of Communist parties
all over the world that delivered the crown jewel of European Communism, the Communist Party of Germany, into the hands of its Nazi gravediggers. Even before that, Stalin's directives had dictated a course of action
that ultimately facilitated the annihilation of most of the young Chinese
Party's leadership by Chiang Kai-shek in the mid-1920's. And in the immediate postwar era, it was Russian control that, once again, brought many
of the Communist movements in South and Southeast Asia to the brink of
disaster.

If the balance sheet of Russian Communism after World War II looked
more impressive than these momentous errors might indicate, the reason
was not so much that Communism had triumphed in spite of itself (or of
Stalin), but rather that a victorious and imperialist Soviet Union had succeeded in surrounding itself with, initially at least, obedient Communist
satellite regimes in Central and Eastern Europe, as it had already done in
Outer Mongolia before the war, and as it was to do in North Korea after
the war. But both satellitism and imperialism are old historical phenomena
and are not necessarily restricted to contemporary Communist powers. It
is certainly worth noting that latter-day Chinese imperialism vis-à-vis Tibet
and even India has the intrinsic support of Chiang's Nationalist regime in
Taiwan, however much at odds (to put it mildly) the "two Chinas" may
otherwise be.

Our underestimation of Communism is, in a very peculiar way, the
obverse image of our exaggeration. For as we have magnified, if not the
reality then at least the potency, of Communist monolithism, we have also
led ourselves to believe that it was this Russian-directed monolithism that,
in effect, constituted the sum total of Communism everywhere in the
world. This means that wherever there is (or was) Communism, it is (or
was) a creature begotten by the evil demiurges of the Kremlin, and that
if only these brokers of global mischief and their stooges could be checked
in their world-embracing designs, Communism would wither on the vine.
To be sure, there are, so the argument seems to continue, stooges of Communist internationalism in many countries and societies, traitors to their
native lands, ready and willing to sell out for a pot of tainted gold.

Much of this kind of thinking derives its justification from bitter and
undeniable facts of the East and Central European Communist satellites,
where Moscow-trained little Stalins arrived in the wake of the "liberating"
Red Armies and proceeded to impose the harsh, unnational dictatorships of
the 1940's and 1950's. But quite apart from the fact that even these satellites have, in our day, undergone remarkable and "liberalizing" changes,
bringing them somewhat closer at least to "homegrown" Communist governments—still, however, basically dependent upon and hence circumscribed

by Soviet military power—the truth of satellitism does not constitute the whole, or even the most important, truth of Communism: Though there are stooges and satellites within the orbit of "World Communism," it is the nonstooges and the nonsatellites that are the real makers of Communist history. Indeed, a sober examination of the facts would indicate that Communism's most impressive victories were not the easily explained satellites created by Russian bayonets and tanks but those Communist movements nurtured by leaders acting in virtual independence of the Soviet Union: Tito in Yugoslavia and Mao Tse-tung in China. The same is actually true of Vietnam, where Ho Chi Minh came to power four years before the Chinese Communists completed their conquest of the mainland.

Yet it is precisely these historical facts that run counter to the stubbornly held twin notion of satellitism and its concomitant, Communism's intrinsic foreignness to all things human. The roots of that notion reach back to the Russian Revolution itself. To many of the Bolsheviks' most ardent foes, both in Russia and abroad, Communism was not something Russian at all but a dastardly plot foisted upon Mother Russia by the Tartar Lenin and his (mostly Jewish) cohorts. Similarly, Chinese Nationalist propaganda has never tired of proclaiming the innate un-Chineseness of Communism, of its being a Russian export *in toto*. And we are nowadays asserting equally loudly that Communism cannot possibly be genuinely Vietnamese, or rather, and more subtly still, South Vietnamese.

It goes without saying that the unspeakable horrors of Stalin's dictatorship, the harsh rigors of the Chinese and Vietnamese Communists, and of course the shameless brutality of the early European satellites have done much not only to nourish our justified revulsion and apprehension but also to lend credence to what is, after all, an underestimation of reality. Rather than condemning Communism in an act of wishful thinking to the realm of a deviation from human history, if not to that of "antihistory," we must come to recognize that it is, satellitism to one side, a kind of civilization, or rather a variety of civilizations, with a proper claim to historical reality in its own right. And, unlike the Gottwalds, the Rakoczis, the Ulbrichts, and their ilk, the men who made these civilizations, whatever their shortcomings and defects, were and are not hapless stooges. That this is so can be seen from the course of Communism, as it spread from its intellectual origins across the world. Surely no one could seriously accuse Marx and Engels of having somehow forced their teachings down reluctant Russian throats. Though strong on inflammatory propaganda, these revolutionary exiles were after all quite powerless to force others to do their bidding. More than that, they were not even particularly interested in Russia, focusing practically all their attention and efforts on Western Europe. Actually, it was exactly the other way around: It was Russian intellectuals who, having discovered Marxism in print, made the long pilgrimage to London and begged a rather reluctant master for guidance and blessing. It was Russians fired by an idea, not stooges bribed by Germans, who took the initiative and who continued to do the rest all by themselves. By and large, this has been the pattern ever since. Even though in China the Russians did take the lead for some time, with disastrous results, it was, again, Chinese intellectuals who discovered Marxism and made it their own. Indeed, those Russian-oriented and, in part, Russian-trained Chinese Communists who survived Chiang's slaughter in 1926-27 quickly receded into the background, and "home-grown" Chinese Communists—Mao and his followers —then did the rest. The "best" Communists are obviously nobody's puppets, but powerful, intelligent, energetic, ambitious, and usually power-hungry individuals who have creatively adapted Marxism to their needs and environments. What they share is a basic loyalty to a set of ideas—a loyalty often born of pragmatism as much as idealism. What separates them are Communisms uniquely their (or their societies') own.

For such men to become Communists, one thing above all must be true: Marxism must be *relevant* to them as human beings in certain historical conditions. The paradox of it all is that this relevance is actually greatest where the founding fathers of Marxism would have least expected it. Marxism, we might almost say, has triumphed in Asia in spite of itself. Had it not, Communism—like so much of Western political thought, with the exception of nationalism—might in the long run have been of no more than peripheral importance to most of Asia. For, universal though most ideologies claim to be by their very nature, they cannot be successfully transplanted unless they are felt to make sense in their new cultural and social environments. It is easily overlooked that in the early twentieth century, Russia itself was rather close to Asian societies in several important respects. Unlike the countries of the Atlantic community, Russia shared with Asia not only a predominantly rural social pattern but also incipient Westernization, especially in the field of education, and, here and there, also the beginnings of industrialization. Thus, once the adaptation of European Marxism to Russian conditions had been accomplished, once Communism had become Russified—some would even say "Orientalized"—it could begin to make sense beyond Europe. How was it done?

The Communist appeal to the peasantry has obviously little to do with the proletarian theories of classical Marxist doctrine. Good European bourgeois and urban intellectuals that they were, Marx and most of his European disciples had, in fact, nothing but scorn for the peasantry as a social class. Not only did Marxists for many decades ignore or fail to utilize the revolutionary potential of that class in Central and Eastern Europe, but official doctrine remained saddled with the founders' original disdain for the peasants until Mao Tse-tung started to correct (and, even then, gingerly) their sins of omission. But if the main body of Marxist doctrine bypassed the peasants, it yet contained a small seed that yielded a rich, if largely unexpected and unintended, harvest once Marxism got transplanted to non-Western soil. The seed was the Marxist concept of the classless society, the faraway utopia beckoning at the end of a long revolutionary path. In the optimistic nineteenth century, liberals and socialists had often toyed with such utopias, sometimes depicting their promised lands in loving detail. Neither Marx nor Engels was prone to such exaggerated utopianism. On the contrary, theirs was by definition a strictly "scientific" socialism, and they (no less than Lenin) only very rarely allowed themselves to speculate about the contours of the classless society. That historical evolution would, in the end, inevitably lead to such a classless idyll they took for certain, but, knowing it to be beyond the horizon of immediate expectations, they, as well as their European followers, devoted all their energies to the immediate, revolutionary tasks at hand.

It was different when Marxism appeared in the predominantly peasant societies of Russia and Asia. Utopian thinking is, after all, inextricably woven into peasant life in premodern societies all over the globe, including most of Western Europe before the advent of modernization; indeed, it still abounds wherever Europe has remained "underdeveloped" to this very day. Utopianism is a kind of natural safety valve: Wherever the burdens of earthly existence are unbearably heavy, only deliverance from all social ills, the immediate establishment on earth of the Kingdom of God, holds promise of release. Illiterate, unorganized, confronted by a harsh and what must seem perennial social reality, peasants have for centuries sought refuge in dreams of millennial social justice. What is really striking is that these utopian dreams cut across racial, cultural, and religious boundaries. They can be found in the folk religion that illiterates have distilled from the sophisticated creeds of all world faiths—Christian, Buddhist, Hindu, Taoist, Muslim, and others: All of them have their utopian, if not apocalyptic, fringes and traditions. Utopianism may be latent for decades, only to explode in violent movements whenever the old order of things starts to break down and disintegrate. This is what happened, for example, on the eve of the European Reformation in the fifteenth and sixteenth centuries. On a more global scale and more recently, it has been happening where, largely as a result of the meeting of West and non-West, the established social and political order started to crumble. Almost everywhere, with notable virulence in the dying decades of Imperial China and Imperial Russia, its disintegration has been accompanied by outbursts of malignantly utopian peasant revolts. But where urban revolutions capture the headlines in newspapers and history books, primitive peasant uprisings often go unnoticed, the more so since they are invariably doomed to failure.

Doomed and forgotten they are, that is to say, until they can somehow be "modernized" and organized, their vague, anarchical millennial dreams transmuted and energized into more viable protest movements. It is from this universal reservoir that Communism received help, though at first it was unexpected and unprogramed. For whatever the urban-oriented "modern" leadership may have decreed, Communists at the local level quite soon learned to speak—or slipped into speaking—the language of peasant expectations of apocalyptic change leading to immediate justice on earth. Unwittingly reaped by the Bolsheviks, this peasant potential was at long last incorporated into the body of Marxian doctrine by Mao Tse-tung. Communist-led uprisings in colonial Southeast Asia testify to the same pattern of peasant receptivity to Communist utopianism: It certainly was not the dreary pedantry of dialectical materialism or the call to proletarian revolution that won converts among perturbed illiterates, but rather the almost primordial longing for a just, "classless" society, translated into a fascinating half-Marxist, half-native idiom. Only natives could have coined that idiom; it did not exist in scriptural Marxism, nor could even the cleverest foreign plotters possibly have concocted it. What is more, it can hardly be carefully prefabricated, even by indigenous nonpeasants. Doubtless, local Communist cadres, many of them quite likely reared in peasant societies, tried to translate their message into images and notions suitable to their rural audiences, but these audiences may themselves have taken an active, dynamic part in distilling from the new gospel laid before them what they needed and could assimilate, weaving old and new together into a kind of "folk Marxism"—just as they had done for millennia with the gospels of other sophisticated creeds.

The wedding of Communist and indigenous concepts is, however, by no means limited to the primitive level of utopian expectations. While it is easy enough to show the deep cleavages that separate the Communist value-system from that of many, if not most, of the world's cultures, historical experience fairly clearly shows that some aspects of Communism can be made to fit into, overlap, or even merge with certain elements of a wide variety of cultures. If the traditions of Russian Orthodox Christianity constituted a formidable barrier to militant atheism, the widely accepted Orthodox notion of Russia's sacred mission as the Third Rome—indeed, the prevalence of historicist thought among many nineteenth-century Russian thinkers—could be accommodated the more easily to the ardent belief in the Soviet Union as the shining vanguard of all toiling and suffering mankind. And though Communism clashed head-on with Chinese—and Vietnamese—familism and the Confucian virtues of filial piety, it shared with that same Confucianism the postulates for a hierarchically ordered society led by an educated elite jealously guarding an official and monopolistic state ideology. Moreover, most great religions—including, until at least the seventeenth century, Christianity—have denigrated those addicted to the unbridled pursuit of economic wealth. This has been one of the most potent taproots for the Communists' doctrinaire anticapitalism in Asia, where the most conspicuous modern capitalists have been Westerners. It is, therefore, not too surprising that for every Buddhist and Muslim leader who determinedly opposed atheistic Communism in colonial Southern Asia, there were at least several who demonstrably saw no inherent evil in making common cause with it. "Red" monks and hadjis were and are a commonplace in many parts of rural Southeast Asia, and the influence of religious leaders is still of vital significance. Ironically, it was the Comintern's longstanding suspicion of all religions—the "opiate" of the people—that made it difficult for Southeast Asian Communists to exploit this potential source of strength for a very long time. In the end, local Communists, wilfully ignoring Moscow's interdict, exploited it on their own initiative.

The Soviets' professed internationalism—as often as not a convenient cloak for Russian foreign policy—for a long time put similar obstacles in the way of identifying Communism with nationalism. This was especially felt in parts of colonial Asia where fledgling Communist movements were, to their detriment, overly dependent on Russian directives well into the 1940's. In Russia itself, the "nationalization" of Communism had of course been accomplished soon after, if not before and during, the Revolution. Chinese Communism followed suit, once the umbilical cord with the Soviets was severed in the 1920's. The identification of Communism with nationalism was, and is, actually far less problematical than its identification with religion, since, by definition, convinced Communists cannot at the same time also be sincere religious believers. Nationalism, too, has as such by no means been acceptable to Communists on strictly doctrinal grounds (it suffers in their eyes from its alleged historical attachments to "bourgeois" movements and states); yet the dividing line between nationalism and Communism has nonetheless been very thin in much of Asia, where nationalism is quite often also violently and rabidly anti-Western, anticolonial, and anti-imperialist.

Of course, a good many Asian nationalists have held aloof from Communism and some have even set out to fight it with all their might. But it is equally true that Asian nationalism—itself the single most important and successful ideological importation from the West—has frequently been hospitable to socialism, including Marxist socialism, simply because its main enemy was an intolerable status quo created by, and benefiting, the "capitalist" Western world. On the continuum of an intrinsically anti-Western nationalism, Communism thus constitutes one, albeit extreme, variant, not necessarily a deviation. Embracing Communism in such a milieu is not a priori a betrayal of one's patriotism, nor have non-Communist nationalists, especially in a colonial and postcolonial setting, invariably regarded Communists as scoundrels and traitors to the cause of nationalism. Distasteful as Communism doubtless is to many Asians—and there are genuine as well as fake anti-Communists—to some it obviously offers a perfectly legitimate and highly desirable precept for the fulfillment of national aspirations. Nationalism can, after all, coexist with many ideologies, and some pretty noxious ones at that, as experience in Europe and elsewhere should have taught us. Surely there is no reason to assume that national sentiments cast in a liberal, democratic, or even simply anti-Communist mold are somehow more genuine and more "natural" than those in Communist garb. It is only stubborn and blind dogmatism, justifiable at best in terms of Western experience, that can deny Mao's and Ho Chi Minh's nationalism. There are no real grounds to separate them, and others like them, either from the mainstream of Asian history or from the other actors in the historical drama unfolding before our eyes.

As a matter of fact, Communist and non-Communist leaders in much of Asia (with the important exception of Japan) are frequently indistinguishable with respect to social origin, education, and life experience. It must be remembered that Asia, quite unlike many countries in the Atlantic community, remained not only technologically and industrially but also socially "underdeveloped" well into modern times. Where, in the complex modern societies of Western Europe and North America, political leadership has come to be recruited from a wide spectrum of groups and classes

representing diverse interests in society, in Asia, the collapse of the traditional systems was followed by a painful vacuum of political leadership. In
twentieth-century Asia (as well as in Imperial Russia), the most important
claimants to political power were young students more or less profoundly
influenced by Western-type schooling and a whole host of new thought
patterns. Sun Yat-sen in China, Gandhi and Nehru in India, Sukarno and
Hatta in Indonesia are among the best-known representatives of this group
—the intelligentsia, as the Russians called them. It is the prominence of
this particular group on the unfolding political scene that differentiates
the agrarian societies of Asia more pronouncedly still from the industrialized West, where intellectuals at best play a tangential role in the actual
conduct of politics. Even in Asia, there are important exceptions to the predominance of intelligentsia politicians: In countries where the old order has
not broken down to a marked extent (as in Thailand, Cambodia, the
Philippines, and partly in Malaya), but also in Japan, where a new industrial order has largely replaced the old feudalism, intellectuals have so far
remained on the political periphery. But, whether at the center or on the
fringes, very many Asian intellectuals (including semi- and quasi-intellec-
tuals) have all too often been highly susceptible to Communism.

The appeal of Marxism to intellectuals has for long been evident
throughout the world (indeed, in many of the most highly industrialized
countries, far from being the accepted gospel of the proletariat, it tends to
appeal primarily, if not almost exclusively, to handfuls of intellectuals).
The reasons for this attraction are not far to seek. Marxism is, after all, the
product of one of the outstanding thinkers of the nineteenth century;
much of it—apart from the famous *Manifesto*—is only fit for consumption
by patient intellectuals. Even more important in the Asian context, Marxism and especially Leninism (likewise a product of no commonplace intellect) form the most coherent and most sophisticated critique of the
capitalist system—in fact, the only such critique that, whatever its patent
shortcomings and pitfalls, has sought to explain to those on the wrong side
of the fence what is wrong with the world and why. It is thus no accident
that, sooner or later, attacks on colonialism and imperialism tend to borrow from Marxist doctrine. One has only to read such stanchly anti-
Communist writings as Chiang Kai-shek's *China's Destiny* to realize its
profound indebtedness to a Leninist frame of mind. Nor is this all. For
Communism, quite apart from explaining the present, is also, and above
all, a clarion call to revolutionary action, action led by an educated elite.
Though never explicitly placed at the center of Marxist doctrine, the revolutionary intellectual is yet the indispensable pivot of Marxism-Leninism.
Little wonder that the Asian intellectual, who sees himself as the true vanguard of social and political modernity amidst "colonial" or "feudal" backwardness and poverty, finds in Marxism the sanctions for revolutionary social engineering, for the revolutionary philosopher king par excellence.
What is surprising, then, is not that so many politically active Asian intellectuals have flirted with Marxist patterns of thought but rather that so

few of them—Ho Chi Minh being the sole outstanding Southeast Asian example—went all the way and became "card-carrying" Communists.

"Folk Communism" and intellectual Marxism, though they address themselves to two of the most important social strata of changing Asian societies, do not exhaust the audience available to revolutionary doctrines. Slight though modernization and social growth have been in most of the continent, they have yet proceeded apace. Nascent and at best precariously unionized urban proletariats in nineteenth- and twentieth-century China and Southern Asia, and a far more numerous and better organized industrial working class in post-Meiji Japan, have not unexpectedly proved fertile soil for the propagation of "straight" proletarian Marxism, albeit in a simple form, overlaid with utopian overtones for the benefit of workers only one step removed from their peasant homes. Here and there (notably, in central Vietnam in the early 1930's), proletarian and peasant revolts have actually occurred side by side, almost simultaneously. What is true of urbanized Asians—including the increasing stream of migrants who leave crowded hamlets to seek their fortunes in city and town, only to end up in overcrowded urban slums—in almost equal measure applies to the impoverished tenant farmers and the latter-day, often mobile, plantation laborers, living far away from their familiar village environments. To them, too, utopian Marxism, if not the brutally direct appeals of radical Marxism, may sound only too convincing.

Ideology apart, it is not inconceivable that in Asia (as elsewhere), Communist movements as such provide a substitute for decayed or vanishing social institutions. For it is exactly these institutions—the family, the clan, the tribe, or the village community—that have suffered most heavily under the eroding onslaught of the new economic and political systems carried to Asia by the West in the course of the past century or so. Only a few countries of Asia—Japan, Thailand, the Philippines, and Malaya—were fortunate enough to escape the worst consequences of large-scale social disintegration. What direct or indirect Western influence set in motion was all too often completed by decades of rebellions, war lordism, foreign military occupation, and civil wars. Hundreds of thousands, perhaps millions, of socially and psychologically displaced Asians have been left to fend for themselves as bewildered and helpless atoms. In such conditions of protracted near-anarchy, traditional disciplines—secular or religious—tend to break down, and long-cherished notions like filial piety rapidly turn into irrelevant, mocking anachronisms. If iron discipline, rigid hierarchies, and unquestioning obedience are among Communism's most detestable features in the eyes of truly free men everywhere, they may yet spell security, order, and a meaningful place in the world for the social splinters of contemporary Asia. Communist Parties, with their manifold organizational structures, with their intricate fabric of cells, and with their needs of all kinds of skills, are—intentionally or by historical accident—able to provide a new scaffolding on which societies, more particularly their younger members, can be reintegrated. They are thus social organisms of a kind that very few other Asian parties, particularly those patterned on Western models, can and do provide—social organisms that recreate a meaningful closed system, in which each member is once again assigned his firm place and duties. Unfree he will be, almost certainly more rigidly regimented than ever before, but at least he will be freed from the freedom to perish in neglected and harassed social isolation. Were it not so, Communists could not have recruited thousands of devoted cadres, willing to live, fight, and die for their cause, however potent its variegated ideological appeals. This, rather than the brutal and methodical use of terror, is what is really new and important in modern Asian history.

Any assessment of Communism's future in Asia must commence with the sober realization that the progress of decolonization has been visibly gaining momentum during the past decade. The relatively few islands of peaceful modernization apart—and even they are not necessarily forever immune from tensions and disturbances—ferment in much of Asia may well continue for decades beyond the attainment of national independence. As a result, the restraining mechanisms against the growth of Communist movements of the colonial past are rapidly ceasing to operate. The fast-growing number of literates and semiliterates who are attaining political consciousness in an era of unprecedented change, here and there also of visible and tangible social and economic deterioration, can only enhance the appeals of revolutionary radicalism. What aggravates the situation is the growing impatience caused by the failures, presumed or real, of the Western-style political systems that were instituted on the eve of independence in most parts of Southern Asia; in some countries—Pakistan, Burma, and Indonesia, for example—these systems have already been swept away.

Complementing these internal constellations is the demise of Communist international monolithism itself, as a result of which the identification of Communism with national patriotism is likely to encounter fewer and fewer obstacles. Not only are Communists now able to manipulate non-Communist nationalists without fear of outside interference, but even the undecided individual in quest of new political loyalties may find himself more easily attracted to an increasingly independent, more truly "national" Communism. Moreover, regardless of which side in the Sino-Soviet dispute Asian Communists will choose, theirs is no longer a choice of masters but rather one of ideological and tactical models. In any case, this choice can now no longer be determined, let alone enforced, by either of the two contestants for global Communist supremacy, certainly beyond the confines of their immediate military, political, or economic control. The era of polycentrism has, then, brought a greater degree of freedom of action to Communists, especially in Southern Asia, than many of them have enjoyed in the past. Given intelligent leadership, they may conceivably enhance their position, capitalizing on their many-faceted appeals no less than on the legacy bequeathed to so much of Asia by a century of turbulence and upheaval.

A Communist Asia? Certainly not that. And, even though the Asian landscape may one day come to be dotted with some additional and distinct Asian Communist civilizations, there is nothing inevitable about it. Its relevance and attractions notwithstanding, Communism's victories have until now always involved the element of propitious chance. In both Russia and China, it was, in fact, outsiders—Imperial Germany in the one, Imperial Japan in the other—that played important, if not even decisive, roles in helping Communists come to power. Equally important, no Communist movement has yet been able to triumph "legally" as it were; the possession of arsenals of arms, made possible by ongoing war or revolution, has hitherto always been a *sine qua non* for final success. In those parts of Asia, in particular, where social cohesion—whether traditional or modern—is strong enough, Communists may, in any case, encounter great obstacles. But even in those where decolonization is for the moment producing seeming chaos, new and vital forces may well be at work, fashioning new orders whose contours are as yet hard to discern. The very strengthening of Communist movements is, moreover, here and there arousing genuine political jealousies among both civilian and military leaders. As long as these jealousies can lead to forceful institution-building rather than to the more usual sterile anti-Communism, viable growth may yet undercut some of the Communists' appeals and organizational advantages.

19

THE BIRTH OF PANTJA SILA*

SUKARNO

Mr. Chairman:

During three consecutive days the members . . . have made known their opinions, and now I have the honor . . . of stating my opinion also. . . . The Chairman asked this sitting . . . to bring forward the basis for Indonesia Merdeka [Independent Indonesia]. . . .

What the Chairman asked for, in my opinion, is what is called in the Dutch language *Philosofische grondslag* [the philosophical basis] for Indonesia Merdeka. This philosophical basis is the foundation, the philosophy, the innermost idea, the soul, the deepest desire, upon which to build the structure of an Indonesia Merdeka enduring and agelong. . . .

* This is a greatly abbreviated version of one of Sukarno's most important speeches, in which he sets forth the *Pantja Sila*, or the Five Principles, which became part of the basic vocabulary of the Indonesian nationalists. This speech was given on June 1, 1945, before a special assembly called together to discuss preparations for independence in the waning days of World War II. The text used here is the official version contained in Sukarno, *Toward Freedom and the Dignity of Man* (Djakarta: Republic of Indonesia, Department of Foreign Affairs, 1961), pp. 1–21.

MEANING OF INDONESIA MERDEKA

Merdeka for me is political independence. What is it that is called political independence?

In the year 1933 I wrote a booklet . . . called *Mentjapai Indonesia Merdeka*. In that booklet of 1933 I stated that independence, political independence, was nothing but a bridge, a golden bridge. I said in that booklet that on the far side of the bridge we would perfect our society. . . .

I beg you all not to quake at heart, not to think this and that should be completed first down to the last detail, that only when all those things have been done will we be able to be independent. If you are like that, how different is your spirit [from] the spirit of the youth, 2 million strong. These 2 million youth have exhorted me, these 2 million youth are all determined to have an Independent Indonesia now!

Why do we, as leaders of the people, who well know history, grow ponderous, become wavering, while it is not only today that we have broadcast the slogan of Indonesia Merdeka? Decades ago we were already disseminating the slogan of Indonesia Merdeka. Ever since 1932, openly and clearly we have had the slogan Indonesia Merdeka, Now!—even three times "Now": Indonesia Merdeka, Now, Now, Now!

And today we are face to face with the opportunity to establish an Independent Indonesia—and yet, we become ponderous and quaking at heart. I remind you once again, Independent Indonesia, political independence, is nothing but a bridge. Do not waver. . . .

The youth, 2 million strong, all have the slogan of Indonesia Merdeka, Now. If, for instance, the Japanese army today were to surrender affairs of state to you, would you decline it, saying: just a moment, wait a while; asking that this and that be finished first, and only then daring to accept the affairs of state of Independent Indonesia?

Brothers and Sisters: If . . . at this very moment the Japanese army were to transfer state affairs to us, then we would not hold back for one moment, we would at once accept them, we would at once begin with an Indonesian state which is independent. . . .

Brothers and Sisters . . . do we dare be independent, or do we not? This then, my Friends, Mr. Chairman, is the criterion I first bring forward before speaking of matters concerning the basis of an independent state. . . . It is *within* . . . Indonesia Merdeka that we shall make our people independent. . . . On the far side of the bridge, this golden bridge, only then shall we be free to build a society . . . which is self-reliant, strong, and healthy. . . .

UNITY OF PHILOSOPHICAL BASIS FOR INDEPENDENT INDONESIA

Having spoken about merdeka—independence—I will now speak about the basis of the state.

Mr. Chairman: I understand what it is you want. You asked, Mr. Chairman, for a basis, you asked for a philosophical basis, or, if we may use a high-sounding term, you asked for a *Weltanschauung* upon which we shall set up the Indonesian state. . . . What is our *Weltanschauung* upon which to build the state of Indonesia Merdeka? Is it national-socialism? Is it historical-materialism? Is it San Min Chu I, as enunciated by Dr. Sun Yat Sen?

Brothers and Sisters, we have already been in session for three days; many opinions have been expressed—of different kinds—but we must look for agreement, look for agreement of mind. Together we must look for unity of philosophical basis, look for one *Weltanschauung*, which all of us agree to. . . . In short, we must all look for one modus. . . . This is not a compromise, but we are together looking for one thing with which we, in common, are agreed.

What is that?

First of all, friends, I ask: Do we want to set up Indonesia Merdeka for one particular individual, for one particular group? To set up Indonesia Merdeka which in name only is independent Indonesia, but in fact is only to put some individual on a pedestal, to give power to a wealthy group, to give power to a group of the aristocracy? Is that what we intend? Certainly not!

Both our friends called the nationalist group who are present here, as well as our friends named the Islamic group, all of them have *mufakat*, agreed in unanimity, that it is not such a state as this which is our aim. We want to establish a state "all for all," neither for a single individual, nor for one group—whether it be a group of the aristocracy or a group of the wealthy—but "all for all."

NATIONALISM: FIRST BASIS OF FOUNDATION

Thus what has always throbbed in my soul . . . for more than twenty-five years, is this: The first basis, suitable to become a foundation for the state of Indonesia, is the basis of nationalism.

We will establish an Indonesian national state.

I ask . . . the Islamic group to excuse my using the word "nationalism." I, too, am a man of Islam. But I ask that you do not misunderstand when I say that the first basis for Indonesia is the basis of nationalism. . . . What is it that is called a nation? What are the requirements for a nation?

According to Renan, the requirement for a nation is the desire to be united. The people feel themselves united and want to be united. Ernest Renan said that the requirement for a nation is *le désir d'être ensemble*, namely, the desire to be united. According to the definition of Ernest Renan, it follows that what becomes a nation is a group of people who want to be united, who feel themselves united.

Let us look at a definition by another person, namely the definition by Otto Bauer in his book *Die Nationalitätenfrage*, where the question is raised "*Was ist eine Nation?*" and the answer is "*Eine Nation ist eine aus Schicksalgemeinschaft erwachsene Charaktergemeinschaft*" [A nation is a unity of conduct which comes into being because of unity of destiny]. This, according to Otto Bauer, is a nation.

But . . . gentlemen, Ernest Renan's definition is out-of-date. Otto Bauer's definition, too, is already out-of-date. . . . Ernest Renan and Otto Bauer only looked at men alone. They thought only about the *Gemeinschaft* and the feeling of men, *l'âme et le désir*. They were only thinking of character, not thinking of the earth, the earth inhabited by those people, the place. What is the "place"? That place is a country. That country is one unity.

God Almighty . . . created the map of the world. If we look at the map of the world, we can point to where the "unities" are.

Even a child, if he looks at a map of the world, can point out that the Indonesian archipelago forms one unity. On the map there can be shown a unity of the group of islands between two great oceans, the Pacific Ocean and the Indian Ocean, and between two continents, the continent of Asia and the continent of Australia. Even a child can tell that the islands of Java, Sumatra, Borneo, Celebes, Halmahera, the Lesser Sunda Islands, the Moluccas and the other islands in between are one unity.

Similarly, any child can see on the map of the world that the islands of Japan, stretching on the eastern brink of the continent of Asia as a breakwater for the Pacific Ocean, are one unity. Even a little child can see that the land of India is a single unity in South Asia, bordered by the extensive Indian Ocean and the Himalaya Mountains. Even a child can tell that the British Isles are one unity. Greece can be shown to be a unity also; it was placed that way by God Almighty: not Sparta alone, not Athens alone, not Macedonia alone, but Sparta plus Athens plus Macedonia plus the other regions of Greece—the whole of the Greek islands are a single unity.

And so what is it that is called our native land, our country? . . . Indonesia is our country. Indonesia as a whole, neither Java alone, nor Sumatra alone, nor Borneo alone, nor Celebes alone, nor Ambon alone, nor the Moluccas alone, but the whole archipelago ordained by God Almighty to be a single unity between two continents and two oceans—that is our country. . . .

The national state is only Indonesia in its entirety, which existed in the time of Śrīvijaya and Majapahit, and which now, too, we must set up together. Therefore, if you gentlemen, accept this, let us take as the first basis of our state: Indonesian Nationalism. Indonesian Nationalism in the fullest sense. Neither Javanese nationalism, nor Sumatran nationalism, nor the nationalism of Borneo, or of Sulawesi, Bali or any other, but Indonesian Nationalism, all of them together, which becomes the basis of one national state. . . .

INTERNATIONALISM: SECOND PRINCIPLE

But, but—undoubtedly there is a danger involved in this principle of nationalism. The danger is that man will possibly sharpen nationalism until it becomes chauvinism, and think of "*Indonesia über Alles*." . . . We love one country, we feel ourselves one nation, we have one language. But our country, Indonesia, is only just a small part of the world. Please remember this!

The nationalism we advocate is not the nationalism of isolation, not chauvinism as blazoned by people in Europe who say *"Deutschland über Alles."* . . . We must proceed toward the unity of the world, the brotherhood of the world. We have not only to establish the state of Indonesia Merdeka, but we also have to proceed toward the familyhood of nations.

It is precisely this which is my second principle. This is the second philosophical principle which I propose to you, gentlemen, which I may call internationalism. But when I say internationalism, I do not mean cosmopolitanism, which does not want the existence of nationalism, which says there is no Indonesia, there is no Japan, there is no Burma, there is no England, there is no America, and so on. Internationalism cannot flourish if it is not rooted in the soil of nationalism. Nationalism cannot flourish if it does not grow in the flower garden of internationalism. Thus, these two, principle 1 and principle 2, which I propose first of all to you, are closely linked one with the other.

DEMOCRACY: THIRD PRINCIPLE

And now, what is the third principle? That principle is the principle of *mufakat*, unanimity, the principle of *perwakilan*, representation, the principle of *permusjawaratan*, deliberation among representatives. The Indonesian state shall not be a state for one individual, shall not be a state for one group, although it be a group of the wealthy. But we shall set up a state "all for all," "one for all, all for one." I am convinced that an absolute condition for the strength of the Indonesian state is *permusjawaratan, perwakilan*.

For the Islamic group, this is the best place to care for religion. We are Muslims, myself included—do excuse me, my Islam is far from perfect— but if you open up my breast and look at my heart you will find it none but a Muslim heart; and this Muslim heart of Bung Karno's wishes to defend Islam in *mufakat*, in *permusjawaratan*. By means of *mufakat* we shall improve everything, including the safety of religion that is by means of discussions or deliberations in the People's Representative Body. Whatever is not yet satisfactory, we shall talk over in a *permusjawaratan*. The Representative Body—this is our place for bringing forward the demands of Islam! It is here that we shall propose to the leaders of the people whatever we feel is needed for improvement. . . .

SOCIAL JUSTICE: FOURTH PRINCIPLE

I will now propose principle number 4. During these three days I have not heard of this principle yet, the principle of well-being. The principle: there shall be no poverty in Indonesia Merdeka. . . . Do we want an independent Indonesia whose capitalists do their unscrupulous will, or where the entire people prosper, where every man has enough to eat, enough to wear, lives in comfort, feels cherished by his Motherland which gives him sufficient *sandang-pangan*, the basic necessities? Which do we choose, Brothers and Sisters? . . .

Friends, I suggest: if we are looking for democracy, it must not be Western democracy, but *permusjawaratan* which brings life, that is, politico-economic democracy which is capable of bringing in social prosperity.

If we truly understand, remember, and love the people of Indonesia, let us accept this principle of social justice, that is, not only political equality, but we must create equality in the economic field too, which means the best possible well-being. Friends, the body for *permusjawaratan* which we shall make must not be a deliberate body for political democracy alone, but a body which, together with the community, will be able to give effect to two principles: political justice and social justice. We shall discuss these matters together, Brothers and Sisters, in the body for *permusjawaratan*. . . .

BELIEF IN GOD: FIFTH PRINCIPLE

The principle of Belief in God! Not only should the Indonesian people believe in God, but every Indonesian should believe in his own God. The Christian should worship God according to the teachings of Jesus Christ, Muslims according to the teachings of the Prophet Muhammad, Buddhists should perform their religious ceremonies in accordance with the books they have. But let us all believe in God. The Indonesian State shall be a state where every person can worship his God as he likes. The whole of the people should worship God in a cultured way, that is, without religious egoism. And the State of Indonesia should be a state which has belief in God!

Let us observe, let us practice religion, both Islam and Christianity, in a civilized way. What is that civilized way? It is with mutual respect for one another.

The Prophet Muhammad gave sufficient proofs of tolerance, of respect for other religions; Jesus Christ also showed that tolerance. Let us, within the Indonesia Merdeka which we are going to build, declare, in keeping with that: the fifth principle of our state is belief in God in a cultured way, belief in God of noble behavior, belief in God with mutual respect for one another.

My heart will rejoice if you agree that the state of Indonesia Merdeka shall be based upon Belief in the One, Supreme God.

Here, then, in the lap of this fifth principle, all the religions to be found in Indonesia today will obtain the best possible place. And our State shall have belief in God, also. Remember the third principle of *mufakat*, of representation—there is the place for each of us to make propaganda for our ideals in a manner that is not intolerant, that is, in a cultured way!

Pantja Sila: FIVE PRINCIPLES OF THE STATE OF INDONESIA

Brothers and Sisters: I have already proposed the "Principles of the State." There are five. Is this *Pantja Dharma*, the Five Dharma? No! The name *Pantja Dharma* is not suitable here: *Dharma* means duty, whereas we are speaking of principles. I like symbolism, the symbolism of numbers also. The fundamental obligations of Islam are five in number; our fingers are five on each hand; we have five senses, *Pantja Indera*; what else is five in number? . . . And now the number of principles: nationalism, internationalism, *mufakat*, well-being, and belief in God—also five in number. The name is not *Pantja Dharma*, but I named it, with the advice of a linguist friend of ours, *Pantja Sila*. *Sila* means basis or principle. And it is upon those five principles that we shall build Indonesia Merdeka, enduring and agelong. . . .

Principles such as I have proposed to you are the principles for an Indonesia Merdeka which will endure. For decades my heart has burned fiercely with these principles.

But do not forget that we live in a time of war, friends. It is during this time of war that we are going to establish the state of Indonesia—in the midst of war's thunder. I even utter thanks to God that we are going to establish an Indonesian state not under a clear sky, but with the sound of the drums of war and in the fire of warfare. Indonesia Merdeka shall emerge a tempered Indonesia, an Indonesia Merdeka tempered in the fire of war. Such an Indonesia Merdeka is an Indonesian state which is strong, not an Indonesian state which would gradually collapse. It is because of that, that I thank God Almighty. . . .

Conditions for Realization of *Pantja Sila*: Struggle!

If the people of Indonesia desire that the *Pantja Sila* I propose become a reality, that is, if we wish to live as one nation, one independent nationality, if we wish to live as a member of a free world imbued with *perikemanusiaan*, humanity, desire to live upon the basis of *permusjawaratan*, unanimity arising out of deliberation, desire to live a life perfected by social justice, desire to live in comfort and peace, in the widest and most perfect belief in God—do not forget the condition for the realization of this, and that is struggle, struggle, and once again struggle!

Do not imagine that with the setting up of the state of Indonesia Merdeka our struggle is at an end. No! I even say: Within that Indonesia Merdeka our struggle must continue, only its character will be different . . . [from] that of the present struggle, its characteristics will be different. Together, as a united people, we shall continue our struggle to realize our ideals contained in *Pantja Sila*.

And, primarily in this time of war, be sure, realize, implant it in your hearts, that Indonesia Merdeka cannot come if the people of Indonesia do not dare take a risk, do not dare dive for pearls into the depths of the ocean. If the people of Indonesia are not united, and are not determined to death to win independence, the independence of Indonesia will never be the possession of the Indonesian people, never, until the end of time! Independence can only be achieved and owned by a people whose soul is aflame with the determination of Merdeka, Independence—or death!

20

A NATIONALIST AWAKENING *

A YOUNG LAO OFFICIAL

The story of "Smiles and Tears" is a real tale of what has happened to me in the last ten or twenty years. My friends and classmates might forget the troubles that we have had together—eating burned rice, sleeping with bed-bugs, bathing in the Kon Keo River, or hitting the teacher. Some of you may now be *chao muongs*, ambassadors, members of parliament, or govern-ment ministers, but I hope that you officials will not forget the Lao people. I wrote this book three years ago but, having had to go from one place to another, I did not have time to publish it. . . .

From temple school to the city, by merits I accumulated or by sins which I committed during my last life, I parted from my childhood teach-ers and came to the Lycée Pavie in Vientiane. I had a feeling of prestige in coming to Vientiane, the beautiful city of Laos, at that time still a

* This autobiographical account has been reprinted in abridged form from Joel M. Halpern, *Government, Politics, and Social Structure in Laos* (New Haven: Yale Uni-versity Southeast Asia Studies, 1964), by permission of the author of the volume and the publisher. This account was circulated privately in 1960 in mimeograph in Lao, under the title "Smiles and Tears." This translation was made by Sawat Chaichana with the assistance of Kiat Bounthong.

colony of France. Being in the city was a great pleasure to me, because I did not have to get up early with the cocks and sleepily find a lantern to light before starting the fire to cook rice. Sometimes I had to study by fire-light. I was glad not to have to go into the jungle for firewood or to find mushrooms, bamboo shoots, and other vegetables. No more stepping on thorns and kicking stumps. I didn't have to fight off mosquitoes and escape from leeches. No fishing for food. No setting fish traps or bird traps. . . .

Life in boarding school, when I entered the Lycée in 1943, opened the eyes of a village boy far past the temple walls and rice fields, to parts of the world I never dreamed of fourteen years before.

Life at school was very rugged. Just thinking of those old days, I cannot imagine how we survived. The main struggle in life at school was to try not to get behind—not to get behind the teacher's children, who were well brought up and who always had their parents to guide them, not to fall behind the European boys and the Vietnamese, who were well trained in French. Since Laos was under the French until 1947, there were no universities, and the Lycée Pavie was the only school in Vientiane. Despite this, the students were mostly Vietnamese. Lao students had to study hard. In classes which had about forty students, about ten were Lao. From the first through the fourth, or highest, class, the Lao students became less in number, so there were only four or five Lao students who could transfer to higher schools outside Laos. [At that time the Lycée Pavie did not offer the baccalaureate, and was approximately equivalent to junior high school in the American system.] The teachers were European and their wives were Vietnamese, so how could they love the Lao and overlook the Vietnamese? . . . Among the students, there were two groups—the Lao students were separated from the Vietnamese not only in studying but also in playing. Sometimes there were disputes between the two groups, caused by unfair circumstances.

We Lao are easygoing people. It was the system of the Europeans to let the Lao forget the Lao nation, let them become lazy, and let the Vietnamese, who are hard-working people, rule over the Lao nation. This is the policy of the conquerors.

Roads in Laos in those days were in good condition for only five kilometers. Buildings were only one story high. Lao teachers and technicians numbered less than one's own fingers, just enough to help the Europeans rule over the Lao. . . . There is one European who had sympathy toward the Lao. No Lao teachers, students, or farmers will ever forget the name Charles Rochet. We cannot ever forget this man, who was very different from other French. We will never forget that in 1945, during our studies at the teachers' training school, beneath the shady trees along the Mekong River and near the airfield, every student had to get up early in the morning, salute the flag, and do drilling exercises. And every Sunday we went to the Lao Association lawn to drill. We also sang songs. We sang youth songs, Boy Scout songs, and other songs—songs that would not let us Lao forget that Laos still exists in this world. Our European teacher was very kind. He had a very soft voice and ever-smiling face, though he was a very big man. He loved Laos as his own country and never felt that Laos was a colony of France but a country to be helped in guidance and education. While he was trying to help the Lao express loyalty to their own country, other French thought he was disloyal to his own country. The real truth is that every person who knows about Lao culture and philosophies would feel sympathy and love toward Laos. M. Rochet gave a start to the young Lao who are now helping their country. He also gave birth to Lao dramatic plays, the Lao Club, and the Lao Yai bulletin, which has made the Lao feel gratitude and appreciation toward him more than any other European except M. Pavie [French explorer who was largely responsible for establishing a French protectorate over Laos in 1893]. We will never forget that we used to wear our blue shirts and white shorts with a Lao emblem on our pockets, which is a symbol of young Laos. We were well disciplined, which gave us the feeling that the Lao can rule themselves rather than [be ruled by] the French or the Vietnamese, and also we speak the same language. The Lao at that time had just been awakened from a dream. The Lao knew that the Vietnamese and the Cambodians tried to absorb the Lao nation into their own nations as the whites used to do. This policy is quite opposite to human nature, and Great Britain did not succeed in India, Burma, Pakistan, or Malaya. The good deeds M. Rochet showed to the Lao, though only for a short period, we Lao appreciate and feel gratitude for. His name has been written in the history of Laos, and there are many schools and streets which were named after him. It is for the young Lao to remember him always. I pray that his soul, which has shown love and kindness to the Lao, may rest in peace in the great Buddhist heaven.

We used to go on trips to a little pond with sloping banks about five kilometers from Vientiane, where there were shade trees, such as tamarind and jujube. The ground near the pond was salty. People used to take this earth and mix it with water to extract the salt from it. All around this pond are rice fields and fish ponds. During the cold season, the teachers used to take us boys out to play in this place. We used to take our food along— bamboo shoots, ground meat, dried fish and other foods, and also fruits such as bananas. Some of us took our fishing poles along, some took books along to read, some went to meet their girls. We started out early in the morning with excitement, arriving at about eight o'clock. The boys would go out and pick tamarinds and jujubes and eat them with salt. At the same time, we could see the older boys and girls trying to separate from the group. As for us, only thirteen and fourteen years old, we would go and gather brush to put behind the bushes, and then we would try to peep from behind the bushes to see the romantic show. We would then call friends, who would try to break in on the scene. In the afternoon, we would go out fishing with our nets. Thao Khamsing and Thao Bounthong were the most experienced in net fishing. They caught most of the fish, and they were not afraid of leeches. When we had enough fish, we would build a fire and cook them. While we were cooking our fish, we used to talk of the baldness of our teacher and also about his height, because he was about five centimeters shorter than his wife. We left the place quite late in the evening, having had a good time. We were allowed to go to bed early, but in bed we would talk about the fun we had had until we all went to sleep.

The Japanese arrived. The siren sounded for people to get into their bomb-shelter holes. American and Japanese planes were fighting for quite a while. The teacher and his wife ran to their holes. There were a lot of noises caused by the chickens and ducks. Some of the students brought their blankets, and some carried their belongings to the hole, but some of them just put their blankets over their heads and went to sleep as if nothing were happening. There was the sound of bombs, and it was later reported that the bombs were dropped about four kilometers from Vientiane and Tong On, and two people were killed. We did not have much sleep for many days. Some took their bedrolls and slept in the hole all night, while others just slept in their beds as usual. On the morning of March 9, 1945, the Japanese arrived in Vientiane. They went through Chienaimo and Togkhampan, killing two Indian watchmen there. The news reached us, and after breakfast we all prepared our belongings. The head teacher called us and told us not to be afraid and run away. The school was still going to carry on. Some of the students who had packed their things were to stay with relatives, since it was Saturday. But the students who had no relatives in school had to stay on. The sound of guns and explosions, machine guns, and the sound of people was getting louder and louder. The next thing we knew, our head teacher had run away into the woods, leaving his wife alone. The students then left the school to stay with their friends' relatives. The students who lived south of Vientiane were lucky to get a ride on a steamer down the river. Those who lived in the north had to go by oxcart and by the boats which carried salt up river. All students left. . . . I had to go and live in an outlying village again. The school was closed all during the war until the French came back, so during that time we had to put away our books. The Vietnamese who were under the Japanese could do anything they wanted to do in Laos, which caused fighting and killing between the Vietnamese and the Lao. I was then only fifteen. I did not have any relatives in Vientiane, only a friend named Thao Khamsing. We had been friends from the first grade. My friend's father was a Vietnamese, but his mother was a Lao. But both were very kind and industrious and also very honest, which I always admired.

Communication between Vientiane and Vang Vieng was very difficult in the rainy season. I used to go by horse to visit my family when they were stationed at Vang Vieng during my studies at school in Vientiane. Three years earlier, my father had been a *chao muong* there. Later he was appointed governor, but during the Japanese occupation, I did not know whether he was at Vang Vieng or if they had left for Luang Prabang. During my school years, Thao Khamsing and I used to take food to his father at the jail where he was a warden. . . . During my stay with him, I did everything I could to help the family, such as shopping, cooking, and doing housework. But I realized that it was a burden to the family, since the father's income was only 100 kip, which had to be used for a family of ten. I thought of this for many nights. Finally the family decided to go to relatives at a village called Napeng. . . . Everything was settled that night. I took my few belongings and my two books and went with Thao Khamsing and his mother and some of the family by a direct trail. About noon we arrived at Ban Napeng. People came to meet us. Some people brought us vegetables, and some asked for news of Vientiane. I slipped away and went to the pond and then went to Ban No Pa, which was not far from the village, just for a visit. A month at Ban Napeng passed. We were quite well off, because we could go out and find food as we wished. We could go hunting and fishing as usual. The children in the village thought that I was Vietnamese because I was a little bit white and my speaking was a bit different from the others. But soon I made a lot of friends. I now slept in many houses, moving from one to another each night. . . .

There was a boy only fifteen years of age, the same age as I. He came to like me and was interested in the old legends and history of Laos. When I was small, about five or eight years old, my mother used to tell stories to me. My grandfather was a *phya** during the reign of King Sakarine and my mother was a lady-in-waiting in the royal court of Tiao Sisavang Vong for many years, until she was dismissed to marry my father. My grandfather used to tell stories to mother. My mother then told the stories to me. So now I was telling the stories to others. I told many tales about the country and also about my life. I had many friends. The children liked to gather and hear my stories. I was afraid of the Japanese during the night, so I did not go out at night very often, and from the experience of telling stories I became an author. Three years later, when I was eighteen, I wrote a poem about my life which was well accepted by the people.

Another month passed during my stay at Ban Napeng. I wanted to be near my family. The two books which I brought to read while fishing and looking after the ducks were read over and over again. I was more homesick than ever. I wanted to know about my father and mother and my two younger brothers and also my nurse. Was she still living? I then decided to go back to Vientiane and from there to try to get to Luang Prabang.

When I went back everything had changed a lot. All the barracks were now guarded by Japanese. I was very lucky to find out that there were two Lao officials who were going to Luang Prabang and Phong Saly. One of them later became an assistant to my father at Luang Prabang. I asked help of these two officials. They asked me who I was and what I was doing and about my parents. They decided to let me go along. We started out about ten o'clock by oxcart. The journey took us thirty-three days.

We had to stop at Kha and Meo villages which were crowded with itchy insects. We had to go around the river for two days, because a bridge was destroyed. Our group consisted of twenty-four persons. Sometimes we had to sleep in the jungle in the rain; sometimes we were lucky to sleep in a *sala* [temple]. Sometimes we had to build huge bonfires and lead the buffalo near the fire to protect them from tigers. Sometimes we would meet hunters who told about a fierce tiger that had killed two people and

* An honorary title

had not yet been killed. I was then very frightened and hoped that day might soon break.

As for food, it was not at all difficult to find, because we could get food in the forest, but the most difficult thing was when the wood was wet, for it then took a long time to cook. We passed through many villages until we finally reached Xieng Ngeun. I went to the headman there, who told me that my father had been there and had returned to Luang Prabang three days earlier. So I stayed at Xieng Ngeun overnight, and the next day I met my family for the first time in many years.

I was very glad to see my father and mother. They said I had changed a lot and had grown much taller. I asked for my brothers but was told that they were at school. Then I remembered my nurse, but my mother could not tell me. Her eyes were very sad. I went out of the house and looked around for my nurse, but I could not find her. At last my mother told me that my nurse had died many months ago. I was very sad. I cried. I had just met joy and sorrow at the same time. I then went into the priesthood for thirty-three days for my parents and my nurse. During this period in the priest-hood, I published a book with the help of two *mahas*,* under the super-vision of the head priest, who was my father's uncle.

During the Free Lao period, many weeks and months passed. I had no school to attend. I could not work because I was too young. Then came the news of the atomic bomb explosion in Japan. This caused many Japanese soldiers in Laos to commit *hari-kari*.

When the Japanese left Vientiane, there was news that Chinese troops were occupying north Indochina and British were occupying the south, up to the 16th parallel. The Chinese troops ate all of our chickens and ducks. Their money was of no value. They caused a lot of trouble in Laos. They told the people to rebel against the Japanese and then the French. The older people would say, "We seem to have too many bosses." The Free Lao Movement started in Vientiane, then spread to Thakhet, Savan-nakhet, and other provinces. I was still only fifteen, and my father would not allow me to be a soldier, but some of my friends who were older, about seventeen or eighteen years old, were being trained as officers in Vientiane. A new government was established with the purpose of fighting against the French. Tiao Phetsarath was the leader and Phya Khama, the Governor of Vientiane, was the Prime Minister. There were many who were forced to be soldiers. The government placed the Crown Prince in the palace under guard. I witnessed the surrounding of the palace. It started about four P.M., when the soldiers began shooting. My mother pulled me and my brothers into the house, but I was so interested that I slipped out to see the action with my father. The palace was surrounded and guarded by soldiers.

I then was able to join the military with no pay, and worked in the hos-pital. For seven or eight months, I had to work and study in the hospital. In the afternoons, I would go out for drilling and singing, and sometimes go out into the villages to speak to the people about our freedom. The Vietnamese also had their own force, called the Vietminh.

* Monk-teachers

News from Vientiane said that the French had captured Vientiane and many places in the southern area. Many Lao crossed the river to Thailand, and many who were afraid of their crimes also went over into Thailand. The Katay currency [named for Katay Don Sasorith, then Minister of Finance] was used in place of Chinese money, which no longer had value.

Many weeks passed. The soldiers who come to Vientiane were from many nations. There were Thai, Kha, Meo, Vietnamese, and Lao. The ranks were shifted rapidly during two months, and although everything was in chaos, I always thought of school. I could not read French books because others might think that I was with the French. I had to read and study secretly. When the French took over and a *collège* was opened at Luang Prabang, they also taught English. I had learned a little English during the Japanese occupation, so I knew some of the words, but the pronunciation was too difficult for me. The King let his son, Prince Vong Savang, come and study with us. We played soccer together. Sometimes his sisters, Princess Savivan and Princess Dara, would come watch their brother play soccer. Later there was news that the Lycée Pavie was reopening. There were five or six foreign teachers, who were all soldiers, and three or four Lao teachers. The head teacher of the Luang Prabang school called us and told us that peace was restored and that "the government has ordered you to continue your studies at the Lycée. The government needs you! We will all rejoice!"

We had to travel back to Vientiane by boat. Every boat was armed with machine guns. The flags bore the three-headed elephant symbol, which was different from the Free Lao flag, which had a moon in the center. Everyone had his belongings loaded into the boat. I had an ivory image of Buddha around my neck, which was given to me by the high priest. . . . The boat shoved off. Finally, I saw my house and town with the bright golden spire of the Phousi pagoda. We did not hear any shooting from the Free Lao. At that time, the Free Lao had crowned Tiao Maha Siuit as the head of the Free Lao who ruled above the 16th parallel.

It took three days to reach Vientiane. The school had changed a lot. The buildings were remodeled, and the students were many times fewer than before. There were only four classrooms, and each room had only nine or ten students. The beds were all broken. Some had to sleep on their bedrolls on the floor. Our belongings, such as our clothes, books, and stationery, were piled on the floor at the head of each bedroll. The pipes in the bathrooms were broken and torn out, because they had been used as ammunition by the Free Lao in fighting the French. We had to go out in groups to bathe in other places around town. The veranda of the building was used as a dining room. The electric lights were often shut off, and we had to use candles. Though it was the biggest school in Laos, everything was in sad shape due to the war. Books were difficult to get, and we had to study hard all through the twelve months. Many nights we had to go to bed early because the lights were out. When the teacher had gone, we would get up and set up our sleeping mats as a wigwam, putting a cloth over it, and light a candle to study by. It was a very difficult way to study.

. . . We had to pass all our courses in one year. If we failed only one course, we had to study all over again. This is the European system. This system made many Lao fall far behind in education. . . .

Every morning the students would rush in disorder to the dining room; before the war, we used to march in single file. The rice for breakfast was glutinous rice. Our food was little better than the food in a jail. Sometimes the rice was not cooked properly, because the cook got up late. At noon, we had plain rice and curry. The curry was cooked with old buffalo meat. It was very tough. The noodles also were tough. We had to use a special scissor to cut them before eating. Still, those who were late had to go with a light stomach. Sometimes, if we were lucky, we would have chicken and bananas for dessert.

During the crises before Laos became independent, we were interested in politics, but we were spied on all the time. They did not let us leave school to pick fruit. My name and those of some teachers were written in the police black book, but we did not do any harm, and as Laos was our own country, why should we not do anything we wished? I was not afraid that the French might send me to Phong Saly or Sam Neua, because I had no trouble. The French used to send people to an island in the south, but I still sent articles to the newspaper all the time, telling the Lao to prepare for our independence. Later, in Saigon, I set up a Lao Student Association and also broadcast on the radio.

. . . New teachers were coming from France. They did not get along with the students very well. They seemed to be lacking in understanding. We Lao were tired of colonialism, but they seemed to put pressure on us. A new teacher named Levy, who was transferred from the secondary school in Pakse, taught us physical education. He always used bad words and also kicked and hit the students on their ears. He treated us like animals. We did not mind, because we thought that he was only a country man and had no brains. One day, on the school field, this teacher hit a student in the third class, and said, "You Lao are barbarians and the Lao are stupid." So we all gathered around and said, "Why do you talk that way to the Lao? Why don't you scold only one person?" The student got very angry. He took a brick and was going to hit him on the head; it missed, but it struck the teacher's left hand and made it bleed. The teacher was very mad, but he didn't dare do anything. If he had done anything, we would have killed him without thinking. He got on his bicycle and went to report to the head teacher. We gathered around and said that if the head teacher dismissed Thao Bounthong from school, we would all resign. We then all went back to school, and it was talked about all through the day and night. The head teacher told the student to leave school, so he packed his belongings and left. We all went to see the Minister of Education, but did not succeed. We just wanted to tell him our story. We then got together about forty-two students from the first through fourth classes. We decided to write a letter to the head teacher, Lucas. The letter is as follows: "We forty-two students whose signatures are below wish you to give more consideration to your dismissal of Thao Bounthong from school. We would like to have him back and the teacher replaced. If you do not answer our letter, we are all going to leave school with Thao Bounthong at three P.M." We gave the letter to the watchman to give to the head teacher.

From two P.M. on, our hearts began to beat. We waited until three P.M., and started to go see the head teacher. He came out and said, "I have read your letter. It is a letter for me to surrender. I have not seen things like this happen before. I have already dismissed Thao Bounthong from school. If you do not like it, the school gates are open to you all." These words were like a pang in our hearts. We all left with forty-two *samlaws** in a line and had our picture taken as a remembrance. We all prepared to meet the Minister of Education the next day at seven A.M. When we met the Minister, we told him about our problems. He told us to go back to school again. We tried to see him twice after this and did not succeed, so we left school for a whole week. After one week, the head teacher asked us to return to school with Thao Bounthong, and the foreign teacher Levy was moved to Khoueng Noi. I hope he didn't cause any trouble there.

This was the first year that we had our written baccalaureate exams in Vientiane, but we had to go to Saigon to take the oral second exam. Of a total of ten, only four passed the written exams at Vientiane and were able to go on to Saigon for the oral exam. I was one of the four. Two of them were in the lowest grade, while I was in the second grade [approximately equivalent to the twelfth grade of an American high school, the first grade being the highest Lycée grade]. They had moved to Thailand during the Free Lao years, and when they came back, they had to remain in the lowest Lycée class. But they were very bright. That year I got first prize in Lao history, French history, French literature, and French composition. I got second in French geography and English, but in arithmetic and physics I was next to last and just barely made it. I was very glad and very excited to see Saigon. On the oral examinations, it turned out that I failed in French history but passed everything else, so I was very sad and did not enjoy the trip to Saigon at all. I was beginning to think that I had done too much writing of articles. I had to take that exam again during the next three months. I went back to see my family at Luang Prabang. My father had had to flee from the shooting and nearly all his belongings were lost. When I got home, my brothers came around me and asked for presents from Saigon. They did not know how sad I was. My mother said, "Don't be dismayed. We have disappointments sometimes, but we must try again." My father took me out to a coffee shop and told me not to be upset. I did not leave the house, because I was very ashamed of my failure, but after three months, I left the family again to go to Saigon. I did not want to ask for any money from my father and mother. We only had 5,000 kip. My mother gave me 3,000 kip. The remaining 2,000 kip was for the family of four. My father was going to retire soon because he had worked for the government for thirty-five years. During the journey, I was afraid I would fail again, but this time I passed. I wanted to study more, so I put out a publication called *World Statesmen of the 20th Century*. I got the

* Pedicabs

necessary capital of 4,000 kip from two government ministers. The profits of this publication I used for continuing my education in Saigon. There I stayed in the home of a Lao official and got a job in the publishing business. I met a friend who was also working on a newspaper. We both wanted to study abroad together in countries other than France, and eventually he went to America and, as for me, I went to England. My eleven years of experience in Laos and foreign countries and my smiles and tears will continue on. I am trying to use my knowledge and my experience to help the Lao people and the country which I have always loved. I have made a vow to the Luang temple that I will not love any country more than Laos and any people more than the Lao.

21

THE POLITICAL ROLE OF THE ARMY
IN INDONESIA*

DANIEL S. LEV

The major problem that Indonesia's military leadership has had to face during the past decade has been to develop a role for the army in the national political structure that would satisfy its political, economic, and social aspirations. It was never a passive professional army, and its revolutionary origins and continual operations since 1948 against domestic political rebellions[1] have made its officer corps fully aware of national politics. Moreover, as a nontraditional institution,[2] the army has provided an alter-

* Reprinted by permission of the author and the publisher from *Pacific Affairs*, XXXVI (Winter, 1963–64), 349–64.

[1] The Communist rebellion at Madiun in 1948; the fanatical Darul Islam insurrection, beginning in West Java in 1948, later in South Celebes Atjeh, until 1962; the Republic of the South Moluccas after the transfer of sovereignty in 1950; the Sumatra-Celebes PRRI rebellion, 1958–61. On domestic violence and the political role of armies, see Stanislaw Andrzejewski, *Military Organization and Society* (New York: Humanities Press, 1954), pp. 125–26; also S. P. Huntington, *Changing Patterns of Military Politics* (Glencoe, Ill.: The Free Press, 1962), p. 22.

[2] See E. Shils's comments on nontraditional armies in J. J. Johnson, ed., *The Role of the Military in Underdeveloped Countries* (Princeton, N.J.: Princeton University Press, 1962), pp. 31, 54.

native ladder to success—until 1957-58 a short one—for men whose origins did not give them a place among the new republic's political-social elite. From 1957 on, the opportunity existed for these officers to become openly involved in politics. For a variety of reasons, some of which will be discussed here, they avoided seizing power and were forced instead to compete for it. Indeed, only gradually did an awareness that they were competing for power dawn upon most politically inclined officers. So far the result has been an evolution of the army's political role that is unlike that in any other country of Southeast Asia, an evolution in which the intelligent guidance of General Nasution (Army Chief-of-Staff from 1955 to 1962) has played an important part. This article examines some of the problems that it has produced.

Until 1956, the army was on the political defensive.[3] It did retaliate against parliamentary interference, as in October, 1952, when Nasution and several officers tried to force President Sukarno to assume strong presidential powers to the detriment of Parliament.[4] But even this defensive act indicated that the officer corps was seriously divided, a weakness that caused the failure of the attempt and cost Nasution his position for three years. On the whole, with the exception of a few officers like Nasution, Simatupang, and Zulkifli Lubis,[5] the army possessed no ideology, program, or defined political goals.[6] It was constituted as a military, not a political, organization.

Nevertheless, its officers were politically dissatisfied. In 1955-56, there was general discontent throughout the country, resulting partly from the failure of the national elections of 1955 to clear up the political situation, reduce the multiplicity of political parties, end political and ideological strife, eliminate corruption, and put a brake on high-living politicians. Sukarno expressed this discontent late in 1956, when he called for the abolition of political parties and proposed a new Guided Democracy to replace divisive and dilatory "liberal democracy." Army officers, many of whom had been angered by political interference, inadequate supplies, and bad material conditions within the army, shared also in this national discontent. Some officers felt that they themselves must assume the responsibility

[3] For a fuller discussion of the army's early development and its relations with the government, see G. Pauker, "The Role of the Military in Indonesia," in Johnson, *op. cit.* Also George McT. Kahin, *Nationalism and Revolution in Indonesia* (Ithaca, N.Y.: Cornell University Press, 1952), and *Major Governments of Asia* (2d ed., Ithaca, N.Y.: Cornell University Press, 1963); Herbert Feith, *The Decline of Constitutional Democracy in Indonesia* (Ithaca, N.Y.: Cornell University Press, 1962).

[4] The October 17 affair was far more complicated, but this was an element in it. See Herbert Feith, *The Wilopo Cabinet in Indonesia* (New York: The Institute of Pacific Relations, 1958); and Pauker, in Johnson, *op. cit.*

[5] Col. (later Maj. Gen.) T. B. Simatupang was Chief-of-Staff of the Armed Forces until late 1953, when his position was abolished. It was revived in 1962 and given to Lieutenant General Nasution, who was replaced as Army Chief-of-Staff by Major General Jani. Zulkifli Lubis was a dynamic young colonel who later joined the Sumatran PRRI rebellion in 1958, after a period of considerable intrigue, including at least one attempted coup.

[6] See Shils, in Johnson, *op. cit.*, p. 58.

for saving the nation, as they had done in the revolution against Dutch colonialism (1945–50). At the head of the nation's best developed and most powerful organization, they sought to bring the army's presumed dedication, honesty, and skills to bear where civilians had failed utterly.

This powerful feeling was reinforced by the army's own deep involvement in the national crisis of 1956–57. Commanders of military districts in Sumatra and Celebes were at the head of regional protest movements against the central government's economic policies and what they labeled Javanese domination of the archipelago. Huntington's comment that a military involved in politics reflects political divisions seems very relevant here,[7] all the more so because the Indonesian Army's territorial organization, consisting of largely autonomous divisions, most of whose troops came from the areas in which they served, encouraged a political identification under stress between soldiers and civilians of the same ethnic groups. Central control over regional units had never been complete, in part because the various divisions of the army had developed differently in the several islands during the Japanese occupation and the Revolution.[8] Territorial structure reflected and reinforced the regional differences. Civil discontent in the regions thus easily spread to local army personnel, and then, as the most likely men for the job, regional officers took over its leadership. The central army command in Djakarta and most of the officer corps believed that only the army could handle the problems posed by these outer-island commanders. Ultimately, the problems could not be handled by anyone, and rebellion broke out in February, 1958.

In March, 1957, Prime Minister Ali Sastroamidjojo resigned after he and Sukarno had agreed to a proclamation of nationwide martial law (state of seige). Nasution had pressed for this after Colonels Simbolon (in North Sumatra) and Sumual (in Celebes) on their own initiative had declared martial law in their regions. The state of seige gave the army commanders of every district immense authority, subordinating civilian administration to military orders and making it possible everywhere except in Djakarta for officers to exercise paramount influence in government. In Djakarta, too, the army was all-important, but here Nasution and his staff (and the city command) were officially subordinate and politically respectful to Sukarno, the Supreme Commander of the Armed Forces. It is not clear how most army commanders in nondissident areas regarded their new powers initially. During the first several months, they applied themselves to such efforts as starting development projects, trying to make civilian administration more efficient, outlawing gambling, and arresting scores of corrupt civilians.

But martial law was to become the army's political charter, forming the basis for its full participation in the political life of Indonesia—as the political parties were to realize before long. By the end of 1957, martial law also turned out to be the army's economic charter. In December, 1957,

[7] Huntington, *op. cit.*, p. 36. In another sense, the army was also influenced at various levels by political parties, but—though this has been argued—this did not go deeply or extensively. The air force was also politically affected, the navy much less so. Neither is discussed here, for their importance has been far less than the army's.

[8] Pauker, in Johnson, *op. cit.*, pp. 196–97.

Dutch business firms in Djakarta and other major cities were taken over by their employees in connection with Indonesia's campaign to force the Dutch from West Irian. A few days after the action began, the army stepped in to prevent the situation from getting out of hand and assumed control of all the firms, with the approval of Prime Minister Djuanda. Army officers were soon appointed to sit alongside the civilian managers of these companies, which the general staff regarded as a legitimate place for surplus officers. From then on, as one Indonesian writer on the "new [army] elite" has put it, "This group of officers who entered the economy became a new social group with a special place in Indonesia's economic life."[9] It was not long before these officers, and many others who exercised administrative power, became as intoxicated with the social and (often illegal) economic perquisites of their new positions as their civilian predecessors had been.

Army officers brought to politics a political outlook shaped by their army experience. It was by no means a well formulated outlook, nor did all officers think carefully about it. But such as it was, it put great emphasis on national consensus, unity, obedience, and discipline. These predilections were very much in tune with Sukarno's presentation of Guided Democracy, to which many officers gave their full support—short of accepting Sukarno's demand for a cabinet that would include the Communist Party (PKI). Nasution and the general staff were aware of the possibilities that existed under martial law for putting their political ideas into practice. The first major indication of this, beginning in June, 1957, was their attempt to introduce army influence into specialized organizations affiliated with political parties. National military-civilian "cooperation bodies"—Badan Kerdja-Sama (BKS)—were organized by the army among youth groups attached to the several parties, and eventually among peasant and labor organizations, religious leaders, and women's groups. In part this was an attempt to open up communications between the army and significant civilian organizations. It also represented the beginning of an army drive to weaken political parties, unify major interest groups, and put a stop to the proliferation of political organizations. Because of their special relationship with the army, veterans were the one group with which the general staff felt free to deal firmly. In 1958, all veterans organizations save one, most of them tacitly affiliated with political parties, were abolished and reorganized into a single national body controlled by the army.

Neither the cooperation bodies (BKS) nor the National Front for the Liberation of West Irian (FNPIB)—into which the BKS were later organized—were successful, partly because some officers connected with them were corrupt and inept and partly because Sukarno and the political parties

<hr />

[9] See E. Utrecht, *Pengantar dalam Hukum Indonesia* (Introduction to Indonesian Law) (5th ed., Djakarta: 1959), pp. 450 ff., for a discussion of the army's role in the economy after 1957 and its connection with Guided Democracy and Guided Economy, Sukarno's alternatives to "liberal democracy" and "liberal economy." The Dutch firms were nationalized in 1958 and later became state enterprises. Criticism of the malfeasance of some officers eventually forced Nasution to deactivate the new class of officers, making them liable under civil law for their actions in the firms.

opposed them. In 1960, the FNPIB gave way to a new National Front, which might have been intended as the basis for a future single state party, but which until very recently was stalemated by competition for its control between Sukarno and army leaders.

The political parties were justifiably horrified as the army's new role took shape in 1957 and 1958. Military restrictions on party activities and the daily press, not to mention arrests for corruption, made the army threat perfectly clear. The martial law statute became a subject of intense interest.[10] Late in 1957, after two weeks of hard debate, Parliament created a new statute, somewhat different from the old colonial law on the state of war and seige, but this still left the army in control for another year. In December, 1958, martial law was renewed for six months; at the end of that time, another law was passed, but martial law remained, and it was extended several times more. The army held tenaciously to martial law, explicitly threatening a coup late in 1958 if it were not extended. Understandably, the parties wanted it lifted and the army withdrawn from political and economic affairs. Only a very few young leaders understood the inevitability of a politically involved army.[11]

President Sukarno's discomfort with the army was only slightly less than that of the parties. His special relationship with the army requires some explanation. As several writers have pointed out, the dominant political configuration since 1957 has been tripartite, with Sukarno deftly balancing the army against the PKI. Two alliances have been in operation. The first, that between Sukarno and the army, has been the more important. Directed against political parties ("liberal democracy"), it accomplished a major reform of the political system, replacing the parliamentary government in operation from 1950–57 by the far more authoritarian presidential system of Guided Democracy.[12] To this alliance, the army brought physical power, whereas Sukarno brought legitimacy and an ability to articulate ideas and mobilize popular support. Neither Sukarno nor the army has completely dominated this alliance; the rule has been negotiation. It was to avoid being engulfed by the army's power that Sukarno developed the second alliance with the PKI, the best organized and strongest of the political parties. The PKI was and remains the natural enemy of the army, not only because officers regard it as being internationalist, atheist, and under foreign control, but also because the PKI—as a well-disciplined organization with deep roots in Indonesian labor and peasantry and dedicated to radical change—poses a threat to all the political, social, and economic in-

[10] For military leaders as well as civilians. Since 1957, a small flood of books and pamphlets on martial law has appeared. See, for example, Koesnodiprodjo, *SOB* (State of War and Seige) (2 vols. and supplement, Djakarta: 1957).

[11] Imron Rosjadi, a young MP from the Islamic party, Nahdatul Ulama, said in Parliament in 1957 that "There is sufficient evidence that to leave [the army] outside the fence of government is not possible. To separate them from politicians is a holy dream which may be realized by the next generation, who have not participated in the revolution to free Indonesia from Dutch colonialism." *Ichtisar Parlemen* (Parliamentary Debate Summaries), No. 31 (1957), p. 293, session of May 22, 1957.

[12] On the development of Guided Democracy, see the chapter by Herbert Feith in Ruth T. McVey, ed., *Indonesia* (New Haven: Human Relations Area Files, 1968).

terests of the army elite.[13] In exchange for Sukarno's protection against the army, the PKI has supported his policies both at home and abroad, including a few that were too radical for the taste of some army officers. Moreover, the well-known honesty of PKI leaders has made their occasional finger-pointing at the army a useful, though limited, means of control. Also, by threatening to insist on a larger PKI role in the government, Sukarno has been able to add to his bargaining power with the army. The Sukarno-PKI alliance has not been an equal one, the PKI having got itself caught in a debilitating web that permits it only to go along almost completely with Sukarno and be drained gradually of its power, or to rebel and be pounced on by a well-trained and well-equipped army.[14]

The Sumatra-Celebes regional rebellion, which began in February, 1958, and lasted three years,[15] had at least two major consequences for the army. The first was that it eliminated the most radical of the army's officers, among them Colonels Lubis, Simbolon, Husein, and Sumual. General Jani, at present army Chief-of-Staff, once described the prerebellion division within the officer corps in radical-moderate terms on the following issues:[16] (1) radicals had no compunctions about a coup, whereas moderates believed a coup would start a tradition of coups that could not be repressed; (2) a variation of (1), moderates believed that army unity was essential to national political stability, and that a coup would destroy army unity by setting off a fierce struggle for power within the officer corps; (3) radicals felt that if Sukarno stood in the way of their demands, he should be removed, while moderates believed that under no circumstances should Sukarno, Indonesia's foremost leader and symbol of unity, be removed from office or power. If we accept this analysis, it is clear that after the 1958 rebellion, moderates were in undisputed control of the army and committed to a Sukarno government. The position of General Nasution, in particular, was greatly strengthened by the rebellion, several of whose leaders had also favored replacing him with another Chief-of-Staff.

A second major consequence of the rebellion (and its fairly rapid reduction to guerrilla proportions) was that it emphasized the importance of the army and gave it a stronger position in the national government, in

[13] Failure to recognize this implicit antagonism of interests led Dr. Pauker to the analysis that after becoming accustomed to Communists in government, army officers might begin to feel that only the Communists could "give the country strong and powerful government and obtain from outside the kind and amount of aid" Indonesia needed; see Pauker, "Current Communist Tactics in Indonesia," *Asian Survey*, No. 3 (1961), pp. 33–34. Long before army officers conclude that the PKI alone can lead the country, they will conclude, as some have already done, that only the army can do so. The considerable Soviet military and economic aid since 1959 has made no difference to their judgment.

[14] For a discussion of the PKI's plight under Guided Democracy, see D. Hindley, "President Soekarno and the Communists: The Politics of Domestication," *American Political Science Review* (December, 1962).

[15] Although it lasted that long, it was as guerrilla action after the first six months. The loyal army was able to drive the PRRI (Revolutionary Government of the Republic of Indonesia) rebels from major cities of Central Sumatra and North Celebes by June, 1958. See Herbert Feith and Daniel S. Lev, "The End of the Indonesian Rebellion," chapter 33 above.

[16] Interview of October 18, 1961.

addition to justifying the continuation of martial law. Led by a more secure and confident Nasution, politically conscious officers were more than
ever determined to alter the structure of the government, which they
claimed had divided the country and led it downhill for a decade. Especially were they resolved to destroy or weaken permanently the political
parties, which they felt to be the chief source of domestic conflict and
national frailty. The political and administrative integrity of the country
would have to be restored, the central government strengthened, party
influence weeded out at all levels, and discipline and unity inculcated
throughout. These goals the army leaders intended to accomplish under
Guided Democracy. Sukarno agreed with this program, but there was a
great though muted difference between him and the army leaders on the
question of how large a political role the army should ultimately be
allowed to play.

General Nasution was the driving force behind the events that culminated in the restoration in July, 1959, of the presidential constitution of
1945. He had always favored this constitution, which actually was in effect
for only a few months in 1945 before it gave way to a parliamentary cabinet form of government. Nasution thought that it had been a mistake to
remove Sukarno's constitutional powers, for it divided the leadership of the
revolution. Sukarno, as the revolutionary leader of greatest personal authority and popular appeal, should also exercise the greatest constitutional
authority. The parliamentary Cabinet (which was retained in the 1950
constitution) made Sukarno a symbol, but the 1945 constitution had made
him the center of the government, promising strong and unified leadership.[17] In mid-1958, the National Council, a body appointed by Sukarno
in 1957 to advise him and the Cabinet, began to discuss implementation
of Guided Democracy. Nasution, a member of the Council, proposed restoration of the 1945 constitution. It is interesting to note that at that time
Sukarno was reluctant to go along with this proposal—much as he had
been in October, 1952—preferring instead to press for reform of the government, simplification (numerically and ideologically) of the party system, and a restructuring of Parliament to make it more amenable to Cabinet leadership. It may have been that Sukarno did not feel capable of
shouldering the full burden of the presidency under the 1945 constitution,
but it is also likely that he was worried about his ability to control the
army if the political parties were precipitately weakened. The National
Council was compelled to take up Nasution's proposal when the political
parties proved recalcitrant about accepting drastic parliamentary reform.
Sukarno then sped to the vanguard of the movement to return to the 1945
constitution, using the initiative to strengthen his position vis-à-vis the
army. In July, 1959, after the Constituent Assembly had refused to approve
the 1945 constitution and Nasution had temporarily banned all political

[17] Nasution's views on the 1945 Constitution and national leadership are in his
book, *Tjatatan2 sekitar Politik Militer Indonesia* (Notes on Indonesian Military Policy)
(Djakarta: 1955), especially pp. 20, 99, 104. This very important book is filled with
Nasution's frank and perceptive analyses of the army's development, its relations with
the government, army politics, and Indonesia's problems since the Revolution. It is an
excellent introduction to post-1945 Indonesian history and to Nasution.

activities, Sukarno returned from abroad and decreed the constitution into effect.

Thereafter, much of Nasution's program was fulfilled. In the new Cabinet (with Djuanda as First Minister), which Sukarno appointed in July, 1959, there were twelve officers of the armed forces (including police), eight of them from the army.[18] The political-party system was overhauled later, all but ten parties being abolished and the rest partly indebted to Sukarno for their continued existence. Central authority over regional government was reasserted.[19] Army efforts to consolidate labor organizations were not successful, but Nasution's general policy of unifying organizations representing similar interests took hold. One of the first groups to be consolidated was the Boy Scout movement, which before had been divided among several parties.

Finally, an intense ideological program was begun in 1959–60. Sukarno's Independence Day speech of August, 1959, was elaborated by the National *Pantja Sila* and USDEK;[20] it became a basis of an intensive ideological indoctrination effort throughout the nation. This has been nothing less than an attempt to force the consensus that both Sukarno and Nasution see as Indonesia's greatest need. The army has been the chief impetus behind the ideological campaign, taking an implacable stand on *Pantja Sila-Manipol*-USDEK as an ideology for itself—something that the army had lacked in the past. The attempt to force an ideological consensus has also served as a weapon against the parties, compelling them to conform publicly to official doctrine and making it somewhat more difficult (though not insuperably so) to justify their multiple existence.

Since 1959, the dominating theme of political conflict in Indonesia has been that of the army and the PKI. For vehement anti-Communist parties and groups (including the U.S. Government), the army became the center of attention. Among these parties were the modernist Islamic party (Masjumi), the small, intellectual-led Socialist Party (PSI), the Catholic and Protestant parties, and the League of Upholders of Indonesian Independence (IPKI).[21] These parties, while themselves apprehensive about the

[18] The state police force is recognized as part of the national armed forces. In this Cabinet, the chief of the state police became minister of police. The army, navy, and air force chiefs-of-staff were appointed to the Cabinet ex officio. Nasution was also appointed Minister of Security and Defense.

[19] However, at the same time, the powerful position of regional military commanders pushed in the opposite direction, giving the regions more independence than they had enjoyed before martial law.

[20] The *Pantja Sila* is Sukarno's five-point state philosophy: belief in God, nationalism, humanitarianism, people's sovereignty, social justice. USDEK represents (1) the 1945 constitution, (2) Indonesian socialism, (3) Guided Democracy, (4) Guided Economy, (5) national identity. Nasution has always been impressed by the need for a powerful ideology, to which the entire nation would be devoted. See his *Perang Gerilja* (Guerrilla Warfare) (2d ed., Djakarta: 1954), p. 22, and *Tjatatanz, op. cit., passim*.

[21] IPKI, an army-based group, was founded by Nasution in 1954 after he was relieved of his post following the October 17 affair. After his reappointment in 1955, he gradually pulled away from IPKI, maintaining some influence over it but not being influenced very much by it. Masjumi and the PSI were abolished by Sukarno in August, 1960, on the ground that members of the two parties had supported the PRRI rebellion.

army's antiparty commitment, turned to it to achieve their old aim of crushing the PKI. The Nationalist Party (PNI) and the conservative Islamic Nahdatul Ulama (NU) were also anti-PKI, but the closer attachment of their older-generation leaders to Sukarno, in addition to their continued participation in the government, distinguished them clearly from the first group of parties. For the hostility of the Masjumi and others in this first group was directed not only against the PKI, but also against Sukarno, whose protection of the PKI and whose radical nationalism were equally unacceptable to leaders of these parties. In time, they hoped, a democratic government would be restored, after martial law was lifted, with the PKI threat gone and Sukarno weakened (or perhaps also gone).

Army leaders looked at the PKI from a different perspective: (1) as the one remaining powerful political party, whose threat to Indonesia's future was made more serious by its foreign ties; and (2) as a threat to the army's own position. Sukarno's protection of the PKI was resolute, for he saw its destruction as a dangerous threat to national unity and to his own independence.

A second radical-moderate split developed in the army over the PKI issue. The radical position was represented primarily by regional commanders in Java and the outer islands who wanted either outright abolition of the PKI or the imposition of extreme restrictions on it. A few officers on the general staff, including the head of army intelligence, also took this position. They were actively supported by the Masjumi, PSI, and other parties, whose leaders were increasingly preoccupied after 1959 with the attempt to exercise influence over officers in Djakarta and the regions.

The year 1960 saw the greatest tension in this conflict. Soon after the suspension of Parliament in March, 1960,[22] the Masjumi, PSI, Christian parties, IPKI, and a few members of the NU and other parties formed a Democratic League, with the help and encouragement of army intelligence. The League campaigned for restoration of the old Parliament, abolition of the PKI, and, implicitly, for restrictions on Sukarno—an impolitic mixing of goals, as it turned out. Nasution permitted the League to exist but kept it at arm's length, perhaps using it as a political threat for a while in his relations with Sukarno. In the middle months of 1960, while Sukarno was away on a world trip, certain members of the League pressed the army assiduously to take over the government, hoping perhaps that there would be a place for League parties in a new government. But there was no coup, for Nasution was unwilling. Sukarno returned from his trip to deal firmly (though cautiously, at first) with the League, forcing Nasution to withdraw his support from officers involved in it. Thereafter, Sukarno let the League atrophy for a year before abolishing it with ridiculous ease.

During this period, while the League was doing its utmost to convince the army of the necessity of a coup, officers in the regions were moving steadily against the PKI. The radical-moderate split in the army concerning the PKI came to a head in September, 1960. The regional commanders of

[22] It was later replaced by a *Gotong-Rojong* (mutual help) Parliament appointed by Sukarno from political parties (excluding Masjumi, PSI, and unacceptable members of other parties) and functional groups, including the army.

South Sumatra, South Kalimantan, and South Celebes, for whom the absence of tough opposition in their areas made politics seem a rather simple matter, undertook the uncomplicated policy of banning the PKI and its subsidiary organizations in those areas. (The PKI in East Java was also harassed, but its strength in that province made banning it a dangerous policy.) So explosive did the situation become that Sukarno called a national conference of all martial-law authorities, including high civilian officials and military commanders, to ease the tensions. Regional commanders had prepared for a showdown with Sukarno on the PKI issue, several of them having met in East Java beforehand to discuss strategy at the conference. They argued during the conference that, while Sukarno might be able to control the foreign-dominated and atheistic PKI during his lifetime, no one could guarantee what would happen after his death. Sukarno replied forcefully that the PKI was a national party, that it accepted the state ideology, and that therefore it should not be abolished. The regional commanders could not cope with Sukarno or his arguments, and they received no help from Nasution, who, caught between the opposing pressures of Sukarno and the regional officers, remained silent. As a compromise, the conference decided to ban temporarily all political activities throughout the nation. Following the conference, at which they had failed to achieve anything permanent, the regional commanders began to withdraw partially from national politics into the local affairs of their regions. The army's national political leadership was thus left to the moderates of the general staff.

During 1959–60, the army could not abolish the PKI unless it was willing also to consider at least the possibility of a coup against Sukarno.[23] This Nasution and most other officers would not do. There were several reasons for this, in addition to those apparent in Jani's remarks mentioned above. One was that Sukarno was popular and the army was not. Since 1957, as Nasution was well aware, the army had become increasingly unpopular because of its heavy-handedness in dealing with civilians and because of the corruption of some of its officers. Most people wanted the army to withdraw from sight, not to become more involved in the government. Second, Sukarno as paramount leader relieved the general staff of the onerous burden of responsibility that it would have to bear if it tried to run the government alone. It was not only that the army had no program for running the country; also, with Sukarno there, it was easy to put the responsibility on his shoulders for many trying issues that might cause political disruption within the army. Third, the officer corps was divided in its attitudes toward Sukarno, many Javanese officers in particular being personally quite loyal to him. Fourth, these conditions may have led Nasution himself to fear that he would lose in a struggle with Sukarno, as he had lost in 1952.

These are obvious reasons, much commented on by others, but there is

[23] This does not exclude the possibility that the general staff feared that a Communist rebellion would follow upon an attempt to ban the PKI. PKI Chairman Aidit had warned the army of this several times after 1957. Such a rebellion could not hope for success, but on top of the PRRI, it might have caused considerable disorder.

another that merits great emphasis in a discussion of the army's political evolution. This has to do with the way Nasution himself has tried to formulate the army's role—undoubtedly after taking the above factors into consideration—and how he has attempted to direct its participation in the political process on terms other than a coup.

Nasution clarified his conception of the army's role at the end of 1958, when, despite the opposition of the political parties, he was urging profound changes in the political system. He perceived two fundamental facts in the army's political existence. One was that a coup would create more problems than it would solve. The second was that army officers would not brook being forced out of the political and social life of Indonesia. They had fought for independence, and they wanted some of its fruits. In an anniversary speech at the National Military Academy in Magelang in November, 1958, Nasution declared that the Indonesian army would emulate neither the politically active military forces of South America nor the "passive instrument" armies of Western Europe. Between those two poles, it would follow a course that Nasution termed the "army's middle-way." The army as such would not be politically active, but its individual members must participate in determining state policy, even at the highest levels. They must be given an opportunity to make use of their skills in the Cabinet, the National Council, the National Planning Board, diplomatic posts, and elsewhere in government. Otherwise, Nasution threatened, the army might react violently to discrimination against its officers.[24]

The difficulty was that martial law was temporary and under attack. To make permanent the army's right to participate in the direction of national affairs, Nasution claimed for it a new and explicitly political status. At the end of 1958, he insisted that whatever the form of government—whether a revised parliamentary system or one based on the 1945 constitution—the army must have a place in it as a functional group. The functional-group concept originated in 1945, when it was introduced in the constitution as one category of representation. Sukarno had reintroduced the idea of functional groups in 1957, partly as an alternative source of political support, and had appointed to the National Council representatives of such groups as labor, peasantry, youth, intellectuals, and veterans. Neither in 1945 nor in 1957, however, was the military considered a functional group. It was assumed that the army would have authority only so long as martial law was in force. In 1958, Nasution's demand for functional-group status for the military was conceded in the National Council. Later, the National Council tried to persuade the political parties to allocate to functional groups half of Parliament's seats, including 35 seats (out of approximately 260) for the armed forces (army, navy, air force, police). The subsequent refusal of the parties to grant the functional groups control of more than one-third of Parliament was part of the reason for the National Council's decision to restore the 1945 constitution.

Since mid-1959, under the resuscitated 1945 constitution, the military

[24] Nasution's speech was prominently reported in the daily press; see *Pos Indonesia* (a Djakarta daily), November 13, 1958.

(and especially the army) has taken its place in Parliament, the People's Consultative Assembly, the Supreme Advisory Council (successor to the National Council), and, increasingly, in regional government, several officers having been appointed governors and second-level district heads. Functional-group status gave the army rudimentary form as a political organization, guaranteeing it a basis for political participation independent of martial law.

In one sense, this was a crucial reason why there was never a coup. The army's elite was integrated into the political structure of the nation and was satisfied. Little was denied it in the way of political power, economic perquisites, and the social prestige that followed upon political and economic influence. Moreover, the exercise of power—especially among officers appointed to national government bodies—has had a moderating influence. Many officers have, in effect, been absorbed into the national elite, whose attributes, good and bad, they have assumed. This, as well as the restraining influence of Sukarno, has for the time being inclined the army to compete peacefully with its enemies rather than to try violently to obliterate them.

In this competition, the army's most important goals have been to consolidate its political position, to keep political parties generally from ever resuming the control of the government they once had, and, in particular, to weaken and finally destroy the PKI. This latter goal the army leadership undertook to pursue alone, after hoping briefly that the PNI and the NU might help. Those two parties, however, appeared to be too weak, disorganized, and demoralized, and too eager to get rid of the army incubus to be effective allies. Since 1959, the army has been able to restrict the PKI's activities almost (but not quite) at will, obstructing Communist organizational work, forbidding strikes, controlling the PKI press, and in other ways seriously hampering the party. Furthermore, PKI Chairman Aidit's commitment under Guided Democracy to President Sukarno (who is not equally committed the other way) has made a considerable weakening of the PKI almost inevitable. The pace of its decline has been slower than that of the other parties because of its greater initial strength and integrity.

From the army's point of view, however, the mere fact that the PKI could be controlled or gradually weakened was not enough to assure its final demise. More important, the army was not assured of an increase in its own political appeal in the cities and villages where the PKI had been strong. And for army officers this is the other crucial side of the question. In addition to defeating the PKI, they must also buttress their legitimate right to take part in the political life of the nation, and for this they require popular support.

Army leadership has approached this twofold problem at two levels of strategy. At a high level of politics, army-sponsored organizations have attempted to compete with the PKI for control of significant groups in the population. The army was at first not conspicuously successful in this effort; it failed to win full control of the National Front, headed by Sukarno, and it also failed to organize the other functional groups under its wing, partly because political parties also maintained an influence in them. Recently, however, a more significant role has emerged for the functional groups, more or less in alliance with the army but subject to Sukarno's influence. Working through the National Front,[25] younger men who see for themselves a better political future attached to a functional-group block than to political parties, are becoming active in organizational work. Also, other recent organizational efforts of the army have had more success than in previous years. The SOKSI, an army-encouraged organization of labor and management (both "functional workers") in state enterprises, has been able to attract members away from the Communist labor federation (SOBSI), apparently largely because of its ability to distribute government-subsidized commodities in short supply.[26] There is no guarantee that SOKSI will maintain its growth, particularly if economic conditions improve, and it fails to offer its new members other satisfactions, but it is nevertheless more promising than other such efforts have been.

Army leaders, moreover, have played an important role in drafting new legislation for the next national elections, which may be held any time after 1964. Although not yet approved, and although the elections may be deferred for some time, the new law provides that functional groups and the regions, as well as political parties, will send representatives to national legislative bodies.[27] One can assume that the parties' role will be held to the minimum possible, and that the army will support functional groups in the elections, hoping to maintain its influence among them. The army's own representatives in the government will be appointed by the government, presumably with the advice of the general staff or a special army committee.

The other level of army political strategy results from the view that army officers have of the necessity for establishing contact with that great majority of the Indonesian people who live in villages. Nasution and the general staff have been anxious to compete with the PKI where it is strongest. They feel, as do many officers, that by demonstrating its interest in the people's welfare, by helping villagers to develop their roads, dams, bridges, and agriculture, the army can win the respect and devotion of the people. These officers believe that army units were very well received in occupied rebel territory when they set about lending a hand to the local population. If the army could win the same good will everywhere, it could easily undercut the political parties, even the PKI. And, according to this reasoning, there would then be little resistance to the army's continued participation in the government.

The first doctrine to justify a military descent to the villages was terri-

[25] The National Front consists of organizations of every sort, including political parties, as its constituent members. The parties, however, have little to gain from its success and have acted independently of it.

[26] On the initial organization of SOKSI and its stated purposes, see *Suluh Indonesia* (a Djakarta daily), December 27, 1962.

[27] *Suluh Indonesia*, February 2, 1963. The chairman of the government committee to draft a new election law is Brigadier General Wilujo Puspojudo.

torial warfare (*perang territorial*). As Nasution explained it in 1955, terri-torial warfare is a defensive strategy, in which every area of the country is organized and equipped independently to defend itself against foreign at-tack with a minimum of central tactical direction and logistical support. It is well-planned guerrilla warfare, requiring that the army give the country not only military but also proper political, social, and economic organiza-tion.[28] After 1959, the army did, in fact, begin to concern itself with vil-lage affairs in some regions, replacing village heads, training administrative officials, and later putting whole village administrations through indoctrina-tion sessions. As a political program, however, territorial warfare never quite became popular, perhaps because its perspectives were limited by military definitions. But it remained important as a doctrine and is the basis for a new approach to the same problem—"civic action"—now much in vogue in some army circles.

Civic action received its first big boost as a result of Indonesia's success-ful campaign to wrest control of West Irian from the Dutch. As long as the campaign continued, there was every reason to have a large military force, and the army undertook a recruitment program that brought its al-ready bloated size up to approximately 350,000, exclusive of thousands of hastily trained volunteers and short-term "draftees." After the Dutch agreed in mid-1962 to leave Irian peacefully, the argument for a large army suddenly evaporated. Army and government leaders decided that demobilization of scores of thousands of soldiers was out of the question. Unemployed and discontented in the bad economic conditions that have beset the country, they would undoubtedly be the source of disorder and unrest.[29] Therefore, it was decided that the army's manpower would be put to use in a gigantic civic-action program, a policy that Nasution and other officers insisted upon. The army engineer corps, which had already proved its effectiveness in several projects, would undertake to build roads, dams, and bridges around the countryside. Troops would join in and help on simpler projects, wielding hoes and picks instead of guns. The army's civic mission would be dovetailed into national development plans, easing the burden—one might suppose—of the state budget.[30] Civic-action pilot proj-ects were carried out in West Java by Brigadier General Adjie, commander of the regional division, in areas where the recently crushed Darul Islam rebellion had raged.[31]

[28] On territorial warfare, see Nasution, *Tjatatan2, op. cit.*, pp. 199–200; also articles in a new army journal, *Territorial*, first appearing in June, 1961.

[29] The army has been aware of the danger of unemployment in Indonesia. See Major Sajidiman, "Faktor Pengangguran dan Masalah Keamanan" (The Factor of Unem-ployment and the Security Problem), in *Madjalah Sedjarah Militer Angkatan Darat* (Journal of Army Military History), No. 7 (1960), pp. 18–28.

[30] For a detailed discussion of the civic-action program, see Brigadier General Soko-wati, *TNI dan Civic Mission: Suatu Aspek Pembianaan Wilajah* (The Army and Its Civic Mission: An Aspect of Regional Development) (Djakarta: Ministry of Informa-tion, 1963). Sokowati, also a member of the National Front executive council, has long been a popularizer of the territorial warfare doctrine.

[31] *Ibid.* Actually, Adjie began these projects before the civic-action program was con-ceived. See *Territorial*, pp. 38 ff. See also *The New York Times* report by Seth S. King, August 22, 1963, on civic action in Sumatra and its political significance.

Civic action may prove useful in economic development, but that is not its only purpose. Army leaders themselves believe it has profound political significance. The army, they insist, must be "to the people as fish in water,"[32] a quotation from Mao Tse-tung that Nasution has long favored. That the U.S. Government has decided to assist the army in its civic mission, having already provided numerous military technicians, equipment, and technical-training opportunities in America for Indonesian military personnel, also attests to its political significance. In effect, it will be an attempt by the army to compete with the PKI at the grass-roots level.

In May, 1963, martial law was finally lifted, and it has been announced that the military budget for the coming year will be much lower than it has been since 1959. Though no great changes have occurred yet, there are signs that the political parties are stirring and that army leaders feel somewhat insecure. It is probably going too far to say that the determined effort of General Nasution against Malaysia is motivated by a desire to restore martial law, but there may be a slight element of truth in that contention. Nasution has put increasing emphasis on the army's status as a functional group and on its civic mission, reminding everyone that the disappearance of martial law does not mean that the army will withdraw into the barracks.

The development of the army's present political position has not been without internal dissent and tension. There have always been field officers who believed that the army should not be concerned with politics and who resented other officers with political and economic interests. In the civic-action program, there is also considerable dissent, in part from officers who do not want to put their troops to work hoeing in the villages and who feel that their men will resent such unmartial activity. Nasution has called attention bluntly to a division between officers who want a "conventional" army and those, like himself, who want an "unconventional" army, one whose functions are not limited to the military. The Indonesian army, he has said, will not again become a "passive instrument" as it was during the colonial and liberal (pre-1957) periods.[33]

That the army must participate politically is clear; its officers will not relinquish the authority they now exercise. They feel they have as much to contribute as civilian leaders to the nation's development, perhaps more, and ultimately they have the power to maintain an influential position for themselves. But the problem is whether the army can overcome its immersion in the political system to make its role a productive one. No one has yet found a remedy for corruption and high-living among the officer corps —natural concomitants of the army's gradual absorption into the political and social structure of Indonesia. Eventually, however, these problems will have to be dealt with if the army is to fulfill the ideal Nasution has set for it. Otherwise, it may become a half-army, half-party organization, increasingly divisive and ineffective as both. Many officers are aware of this, and they are trying to fashion a place for the army within the broader framework of national political development. How successful they are will

[32] Sokowati, *op. cit.*, p. 52.
[33] Foreword in Sokowati, *op. cit.*, pp. 9–10.

depend to a considerable extent on the wisdom (and political caution) civilian politicians display; this is a responsibility that must devolve increasingly upon younger leaders as the older ones continue to fall away.

One cannot predict the final outcome of a political experiment—and this one has much stacked against it—but the evolution of the Indonesian army as a political organization has so far been unique. It *may* prove to be an excellent solution to the problems posed by a modern army in a rapidly changing society.

22

GESTAPU IN INDONESIA*

JUSTUS M. VAN DER KROEF

On September 13, 1965, President Sukarno of Indonesia, in a ceremony in the Presidential Palace in Djakarta that marked something of an apogee of the prestige and power of the Indonesian Communist Party (PKI), fastened the "Mahaputra" medal on the chest of PKI Chairman D. N. Aidit in recognition of his "extraordinary service and loyalty" to the nation.[1] "Mahaputra" means "Great Son," and Sukarno duly hailed Aidit as an "exemplary patriotic hero." Scarcely two months later Aidit was ignominiously shot and killed, reportedly near a prison wall in Central Java, in an "escape" attempt that proved no more successful than the Communist coup d'état of September 30, 1965, which he tried in vain to direct after it had been virtually crushed within forty-eight hours.[2]

* Reprinted by permission of the author and the publisher from *Orbis* X (Summer, 1966), 458–87. *Orbis* is a quarterly journal of world affairs published by the Foreign Policy Research Institute of the University of Pennsylvania.

[1] *Sinar Harapan* (Djakarta), September 14, 1965.

[2] There have been contradictory stories about Aidit's death. Toward the close of November, 1965, initial reports in a few small Indonesian papers and weeklies were picked up by UPI and Agence France Presse and by a number of Japanese papers, and were given worldwide circulation. Indonesian military spokesmen at first refused to

The surprise abroad over the abortive September coup and the abrupt change in Aidit's and his party's fortunes tends to obscure the long record of Communist pressure tactics in Indonesia and the mounting resistance to them, especially in the past two years. Considering this perspective, it is not so surprising that the GESTAPU affair[3]—as acronym-minded Indonesians have quickly labeled the events of September 30—occurred, but that it, or something like it, took such a long time in coming. An understanding, both of GESTAPU and of the new political alignments in Indonesia today, requires some consideration of the recent maneuverings and interactions of the country's principal triad of power: Sukarno, the army, and the PKI.

The origins of GESTAPU can be traced to the final acceleration of the PKI's drive to power, which began almost exactly two years to the day before the September 30, 1965, coup. On September 29, 1963, just after he returned from Peking (the last leg of a two-month tour of Communist countries that had taken him to Cuba, the Soviet Union, and East Germany, as well as to Communist China), Aidit announced that Asia in general and Southeast Asia in particular had become the scene of the world's most acute "anti-imperialist struggle," opening new opportunities and responsibilities to the PKI.[4] Within weeks, the PKI intensified its ac-

---

confirm or deny Aidit's death. Later, when speculation arose that Aidit might have escaped (according to one rumor, even in a submarine said to have been sent by People's China), army announcements asserted that Aidit had been "sighted" in Central Java (whether dead or alive, however, was not stated). (See *Djakarta Daily Mail*, November 4, 1965.) Peking also denounced the tale that Aidit had escaped to Communist China and generally seemed to intimate that Aidit, whom it described as the "Outstanding Helmsman of the Indonesian Communist Party," was still alive. (*Peking Review*, December 10, 1965, p. 8.)

On December 19, 1965, Japan's semiofficial Radio NHK reported that Aidit had been executed by the army on November 24, 1965, in Central Java. By the following February, supposedly "last" photographs of Aidit being interrogated by army personnel had been published in the Hong Kong and Tokyo press. Little credence has been placed in the assertion of the then Minister for Higher Education, the left-leaning Brigadier Sjarif Thajeb, in an interview in Hong Kong early in January, 1966, that Aidit was still alive and a prisoner, and there has been no contradiction of the Japanese reports and photographs.

It has generally been conceded that if Aidit were alive, he, rather than PKI Politburo member Njono, would have been the star of the special trial staged by the Indonesian military in mid-February, 1966, designed to show PKI direction of the GESTAPU affair. On March 16, 1966, Deputy Speaker of the Indonesian Parliament and Cabinet Minister Ahmed Sainu gave the first official confirmation of Aidit's death. See also *The Straits Times* (Singapore), December 20, 1965, and January 21 and February 8, 1966.

[3] GESTAPU is constructed from the Indonesian *Gerakan September Tiga Puluh*, or "Thirty September movement." Since the GESTAPU affair started late at night on September 30 and in the early morning hours of the following day, it is sometimes also designated as *Gestok-Gerakan Satu Oktober* or "First October movement."

[4] See the essay "Gerakan Komunis Internasional dan Revolusi Asia Tenggara," in the collection of essays by D. N. Aidit, *Langit Takkan Runtuh* (Djakarta, 1963), pp. 24–40.

tivity throughout Southeast Asia.[5] PKI publications, notably its daily *Harian Rakjat*, showed new vehemence in denouncing "revisionism," lending confirmation to reports that Aidit's appeal in his talks in Moscow for greater tactical militancy had met with little Soviet enthusiasm, in contrast to his apparently growing harmony with Peking. On November 12, 1964, Aidit, in a speech to the PKI youth front that was prominently quoted in the Chinese Communist press, noted that the recent downfall of Khrushchev had been due to "the bankruptcy of his home and foreign policies," but that "we must not think that Khrushchev's removal from office means the end of the struggle to smash modern revisionism."[6]

Though Party leaders appear to have been aware of the mounting hostility in Indonesia to their new campaign of pressure, the PKI became increasingly aggressive. One of the Party's "theses" at its forty-fifth anniversary celebration in May, 1965, declared: "The offensive spells success and victory, the defensive means failure and defeat."[7] Boldly proclaimed "revolutionary" and "unilateral action" methods for implementing the government's lagging land-reform program were launched against "recalcitrant landlords" and "reactionary officials." A wave of PKI-directed mass demonstrations culminated in outright seizures of "landlords' land" and in outbursts of violence, in which scores were injured or killed.[8] Despite government regulations, Communist unions also seized control of foreign, especially British-owned, estates. British support for Malaysia, which Indonesia had vowed to crush since early 1963, was the ostensible reason. Initial murmurings of disapproval by the government over these seizures changed by the end of 1964 to official declarations that the estates would remain under government management and Communist-dominated "workers councils." Meanwhile, the PKI-led anti-American campaign greatly intensified, including agitation against American films, attacks on U.S. Information Service libraries, and the burning of "imperialist" books and magazines. In their efforts rapidly to radicalize the public temper, PKI leaders now even appeared ready to usurp Sukarno's role as the nation's chief ideologist. Revealing was Aidit's remark in mid-February, 1965, that Sukarno's concept of NASAKOM (meaning the unity of nationalism, religion, and Communism as the basis of the Indonesian state) had in fact been invented by Lenin "long before it was spoken of in Indonesia."[9] At about the same time, Foreign Minister Subandrio, a particular Party favorite as architect of the developing Djakarta-Peking axis, declared that

[5] For details, see J. M. Van der Kroef, "Indonesian Communism's Expansionist Role in Southeast Asia," *International Journal*, XX (1965), 189–205.

[6] See, for example, *Jen-min Jih-pao*, November 21, 1964, and *Peking Review*, November 27, 1964, p. 18.

[7] *Tesis 45 Tahun PKI (23 Mei 1920–23 Mei 1965)*, (Djakarta, 1965), p. 16.

[8] On the PKI's agrarian action campaign, see especially Kasim, "Surat Hutang Landreform," *PKI dan Perwakilan* (1964), 7–8; the report of Asmu, chairman of the PKI's peasant front, in *Suara Tani*, February, 1965, pp. 6–24; and *Indonesian Observer* (Djakarta), October 27, 31, November 2, 3, 5, 1964.

[9] *Indonesian Observer*, February 15, 1965.

"the Indonesian identity includes Communism, which now belongs to the whole Indonesian people."[10]

Already, in 1963, a handful of intellectuals, some affiliated with the proscribed Masjumi (Muslim) and Socialist parties, had rallied around a so-called MANIKEBU (from *Manifes Kebudajaan*, meaning Cultural Manifesto), an anti-Communist declaration affirming the Indonesian "identity." "MANIKEBU-ism" was banned by the government, but resistance against the PKI continued to gather momentum, and, late in August, 1964, found expression in a new informal opposition group, the "Body to Support Sukarnoism" (*Badan Pendukung Sukarnoisme*, or BPS). Space precludes a detailed analysis of the BPS,[11] except to note its rapidly growing support among newspapers, students, some political parties like the small but influential Titoist Murba (proletarian) Party; elements of the National Indonesian Party (PNI) and the Moslem Scholars Party (Nahdatul Ulama, or NU); the army-influenced Socialist Labor Federation; some cabinet members; top army commanders (including Defense Minister, Gen. A. H. Nasution and Army Chief of Staff, Gen. Ahmad Yani), and others—all of whom spontaneously appeared to be emulating PKI tactics by using Sukarno and his vaguely defined "ism" as a cover for their own "stop the PKI" objective. Especially important was the support of the army, because, until now, army leaders—mindful of a disastrous army attempt to intimidate the Indonesian Parliament in 1952—had sought to develop a professional, disciplined image of identity with Indonesian national ideals above political cabals. To be sure, with the encouragement of Sukarno, always anxious to preserve the domestic power balance, the army had entered into numerous levels of government and public administration. But, thus far, the army had not openly sided with a known anti-PKI organization or lent its name to a popular campaign, such as the BPS, which, through its seemingly innocuous defense of Sukarno's sacrosanct ideology, suggested that his ideology was being attacked by the PKI.

From the start, the PKI bitterly excoriated the BPS, and nothing illustrates the Party's growing power better than the BPS's denouement that soon followed.[12] On November 27, 1964, Communist China's Foreign Minister Ch'en Yi visited Djakarta to implement the Sino-Indonesian political-military partnership, and he reportedly demanded dissolution of the BPS and the Murba Party. Sukarno complied shortly thereafter. On December 17, 1964, the BPS was banned, followed by a temporary and then permanent proscription of the Murba Party. At once, the PKI began agitating for dismissal of the pro-BPS ministers and for the banning of pro-BPS papers. Again Sukarno largely complied. Two Murba Party ministers were demoted, and toward the close of February, 1965, a score of pro-BPS dailies and weeklies, most of them in Djakarta, were banned. Meanwhile Sukarno

---

[10] *Antara Daily Newsbulletin*, March 4, 1965.

[11] For details on the BPS, see J. M. van der Kroef, "Indonesian Communism's Revolutionary Gymnastics," *Asian Survey* (May, 1965), pp. 217–32.

[12] For the PKI reaction to the BPS, see especially the party publication *"BPS" Aksi Reaksi* (Djakarta: 1965).

and other Indonesian officials declared the U.S. Central Intelligence Agency (CIA) to have been behind the BPS.[13] Bitter anti-PKI reaction continued to erupt in the following months, however, as Muslim youth groups and peasants battled Communists in towns and villages in East Java. When Sukarno showed signs of complying with the PKI's heated demands that he outlaw the Muslim Student Association (*Himpunan Mahasiswa Islam*, or HMI), a prime force behind this East Java anti-PKI movement, all principal Muslim parties formed a "defense committee," whose spokesman warned that "even the worm will fight back if it is trampled."[14] Sukarno eventually thought better of the proposed HMI ban.

Sukarno's caution may have been prompted by his realization that the conflict between the PKI and the army was moving swiftly to a climax. Seeking to maintain its momentum of militancy, and encouraged by its successful demand for a ban on the BPS, the PKI by the middle of January, 1965, began a campaign to arm organized workers and peasants. Sukarno at first rejected the notion but then, despite adamant army opposition, seemed to be softening, declaring on February 11, 1965, that "if necessary," workers and peasants would be provided with weapons. Aidit meanwhile sharpened the controversy by suggesting that special "supervisors," properly indoctrinated in the state's ideology, be given positions in the army, but an army conference promptly rejected the idea of a "political commissariat."[15] Subsequently, Sukarno expressed approval for the idea of arming peasants and workers, saying that Chou En-lai had given him the idea some time ago. During his early August, 1965, visit to Djakarta, Li Hsueh-feng, Deputy Chairman of Communist China's National People's Congress, pointedly noted that "in facing the imperialists," it was necessary to arm the whole people of a nation.[16] Given the PKI's pressure, it seemed to many to be but a matter of time before Sukarno would accommodate the Communist demand for a new "people's army," Peking style.

The direction of prevailing political winds became unmistakable when the government announced on August 3, 1965, that the high court of North Sumatra Province shortly would meet, not in its usual location in Medan, but in Djakarta, in order to reach a "more suitable" verdict than

13 *Berita Minggu* (Djakarta), February 21, 1965; *Warta Bhakti* (Djakarta), February 25, 1965; *Antara Daily Newsbulletin*, March 2, 1965.

14 *The Straits Times*, March 26, 1965.

15 For details on this proposed army reorganization crisis, see J. M. Van der Kroef, "Die indonesische Armee zwischen Soekarno und den Kommunisten," *Europa-Archiv* (November 25, 1965), pp. 831–42. The PKI long had desired to have its own paramilitary organization independent of army control. It gave the alleged British military buildup in Malaysia, however, as the reason for its demand for a "Fifth Force" (that is, a military volunteer organization over and above the other four services, army, navy, air force and national police). In January, 1965, Aidit declared that "Recently when I met Gilchrist the British Ambassador to Indonesia at a reception, I said 'thank you' to him, because the dispatch of British troops to 'Malaysia' has provided me with a good reason to propose that workers and peasants be armed." See Aidit's address on the occasion of the anniversary of the Party's daily *Harian Rakjat*, in the PKI monthly *Review of Indonesia* (February, 1965), p. 3.

16 *Djakarta Daily Mail*, June 2 and August 10, 1965.

the fifteen- to twenty-year prison sentences it had just meted out to twenty-three cadres of the PKI peasant front, who had been convicted a few weeks previously of beating to death an army officer.[17] The officer in question, sent to clear squatters from government land, had, according to the Communist press, "provoked" the "people's leaders" (that is, the PKI peasant front cadres); the PKI raised such an outcry over the verdict that the government deemed it wise to order the court to reconsider the case— but this time in Djakarta, a precedent in Indonesia's judicial history and a portent hardly to be minimized. Equally noteworthy was Sukarno's fulsome praise for the PKI at the party's forty-fifth anniversary celebration in May, 1965, and the President's exhortation to "Go Ahead . . . Go Ahead, PKI!"[18] With such assurances, it seemed hardly surprising that Aidit, toward the middle of 1965, kept calling for an "increased revolutionary offensive" and for the holding of new national and local elections, and that Party organs continued to insist that "relations between the people and the Army be strengthened."

It is difficult to say to what degree Indonesia's chronically chaotic economy contributed to the PKI's new momentum, but there is little doubt that Party fronts, particularly Communist trade unions and women's groups, unceasingly exploited it in their demonstrations for lower prices. By early March, 1965, the Djakarta press reported that during the previous year 12,000 people had died of famine in Central Java Province alone, and the index of food prices, which had stood at 2,314 in December, 1963 (1958 is 100), had risen to 7,707 by April, 1965.[19] Sukarno, by the end of September, 1965, complained that the people were "breeding like rabbits," and rice imports, which had risen from 707,000 metric tons in 1958 to 1.2 million tons in 1964, were expected to rise still further, despite the newly-announced policy of *berdirkari*, or economic self-reliance. In April, 1965, the free market rate of the rupiah was about 5,000 to the U.S. dollar (as compared to the official rate of 45 to 1); by September, it had risen to 20,000 to the dollar, as prices continued to soar. PKI exhortations to the Indonesian people to take "quick and proper actions" to bring prices down, and demonstrations by SOBSI (the Communist labor federation) and GERWANI (the PKI women's front) toward the end of September only met with Sukarno's plaintive response that "I can't give any command to lower prices because the problems involved are very complex." On an earlier occasion, Indonesia's President had recounted how he had once challenged his advisers: "Anyone among you who is capable of lowering prices in a short period, I will make a cabinet minister in charge of prices . . . but as a condition, failure—as a cabinet minister—would mean jail. . . . Nobody dared respond to my challenge," Sukarno concluded.[20]

[17] *The Straits Times*, August 4, 1965.

[18] See *Bintang Timur* (Djakarta), May 24, 1965, and *Harian Rakjat* (Djakarta), May 22, 1965.

[19] *Suluh, Indonesia* (Djakarta), March 3, 1965, and *Far Eastern Economic Review* (August 19, 1965).

[20] *Quarterly Economic Review: Indonesia* (London: The Economist Intelligence Unit, October, 1965), p. 8.

Despite the potential advantages provided by the deteriorating economy and the momentum of its own new pressure tactics, major problems confronted the PKI. Though cowed,[21] the anti-Communist opposition remained strong and widespread, as the sudden popularity of the short-lived BPS had demonstrated. The banning of the BPS had not shattered the opposition but merely intensified its bitterness and its search for new organizational outlets. The heightening of political controversy, moreover, amplified another problem for the Party, namely, the relative weakness of its internal organization. The lack of good communications in the country, the profusion of fronts, and the enduring difficulty in maintaining adequate cadre and middle-echelon discipline had been the subjects of frank self-criticism in Party organs for several years.[22] In an atmosphere of struggle and tension, the difficulty of exercising proper "democratic centralist control" over the coterie of regular party units and over peasant, labor, women, student, youth, and other front groups—together comprising more than 14 million members throughout the country by the middle of 1965—rose in proportion. The GESTAPU affair was to demonstrate that poor coordination and a lack of tight, do-or-die discipline greatly contributed, as so often in the Party's past history, to its undoing.

Finally, there was the question of Sukarno and the balance of power. Since the late 1950's, the PKI had successfully hidden behind, leaned on, or fronted for Sukarno in the latter's relations with the army.[23] But, by the beginning of 1965, the prospect that the hard-living Sukarno, at sixty-three old for an Indonesian of his generation and in noticeably failing health, would not be around much longer began to loom ever larger in the Party's tactical calculations. (After the GESTAPU affair, captured PKI Politburo member Njono confessed that the physical deterioration of the President had indeed been a major factor in the preparation of the coup, and undoubtedly Sukarno's Chinese doctors kept PKI leaders well informed about the President's condition.) Party leaders were compelled to plan ahead for the day when the President would be removed from the scene, triggering an open conflict with the army and the rest of the opposition. This, undoubtedly, was the larger meaning of Aidit's demand early in 1965 that

21 Recent army-inspired revelations about the GESTAPU affair should be treated with caution. But not altogether to be dismissed as an illustration of the post-BPS atmosphere in Indonesia, in which opposition to the PKI was quite difficult, is the story of the commander of the army's paracommandos in the Bojolali (Central Java) area: He reported that, well before September 30, 1965, "authorities obtained proof of preparations" by the PKI for "a violent overthrow of the government," but "neglected" to press the matter "for fear of being accused of suffering from 'Communist phobia.'" *Djakarta Daily Mail*, November 30, 1965. Defense Minister Nasution has claimed that, as early as July, 1960, when the PKI published a bitter denunciation of the government, he had attempted to call the government's attention to the "suspicious activities of the PKI." However, declared Nasution, "the prevailing campaign" against anti-Communism at that time "made these warnings politically uncalled for until the so-called 'September 30' movement happened." *Antara Daily Newsbulletin*, December 16, 1965.

22 On the problem of internal party discipline and organization, see J. M. Van der Kroef, *The Communist Party of Indonesia: Its History, Program and Tactics* (Vancouver: University of British Columbia Press, 1965), pp. 175–81.

23 *Ibid.*, especially pp. 82–125, 227–66.

peasants and workers be armed and that "political supervisors" be introduced into the army.

Some students of PKI strategy and tactics have tended toward the belief that the PKI would have had little to gain from a coup, and planned instead to come to power through "popular acclamation" and a tactic of gradually and peaceably mustering overpowering mass organizational influence.[24] Even the eventual death of Sukarno would not force a change in tactics, it has been supposed, because Deputy Premier Subandrio, long considered Sukarno's heir apparent, had shown strong pro-PKI sympathies, and probably would also have been acceptable to the armed forces' leadership.[25] What they overlooked, however, was the cumulative impact on the PKI of the accelerating political crisis, particularly since early 1965; the highly charged day-to-day political situation in Djakarta; the PKI's open rupture with the army; the political suppression of anti-Communist elements; the violent clashes between Communists and their opponents in East Java; the steady but subtle pressures emanating from Peking, which had been largely responsible for Indonesia's withdrawal from the United Nations on January 7, 1965;[26] the rampant inflation and increasingly precarious living conditions; and, last but not least, the continuing radicalization of the public temper through demonstrations and mass agitational campaigns. For the PKI, two lines of tactical analysis began to converge in the course of 1965. First, the accelerating revolutionary militancy, initiated as a matter of policy since 1963, by virtue of its own momentum would demand sooner or later a suitable climax, lest the party suffer a dangerous retrogression. Second, after Sukarno's death, the PKI would probably be provoked into a bloody fight with its enemies anyway, especially in view of the existing bitterness and tensions that the Party's own pressure tactics had unavoidably helped to generate. Far better, then, to prepare for the conflict and, indeed, to strike the first blow.

It cannot be said that no one had wind of the PKI's plans. Already, toward the close of December, 1964, reports appeared in the Malaysian (though not in the censor-ridden Indonesian) press, and in U.S. wire-

[24] See, for example, Guy J. Pauker, "Indonesia: The PKI's Road to Power," in Robert A. Scalapino, ed., *The Communist Revolution in Asia: Tactics, Goals and Achievements* (Englewood Cliffs, N.J.: Prentice-Hall, 1965), pp. 256–89; Donald Hindley, *The Communist Party of Indonesia 1951–1963* (Berkeley: University of California Press, 1964), pp. 301–2; J. M. Van der Kroef, *The Communist Party of Indonesia*, p. 303.

[25] In March, 1965, the Malaysian press reported that Subandrio had been a member of the PKI for the past twelve years. (*The Straits Times*, March 23, 1965.) The report has not been contradicted by any Indonesian source. While Subandrio was less than popular among the anti-Communist army high command, he had a not insignificant following in the officer corps of the Indonesian air force, where pro-Communist influence had long been considerable, in part because of the long-term assistance, both in training and matériel, provided by the Soviet Union in the modernization of the air force.

[26] On Indonesia's policy convergence with Communist China, see my "The Sino-Indonesian Partnership," *Orbis* VIII (Summer, 1964), pp. 332–56.

service dispatches from Djakarta, about a recently exposed PKI Central Committee document describing stepped-up agitation planned for 1965 in preparation for an eventual coup d'état.[27] With each acrimonious exchange in the controversy over the arming of peasants and workers, public conviction grew that the Party was preparing for a final showdown with the army. As late as two weeks before the GESTAPU affair, Bangkok and Hong Kong sources reported on the extensive supplies of arms and explosives being sent to the Indonesian Communists by Communist China via small East and West Java ports and fishing villages.[28] This military hardware was packed in crates supposedly containing building materials being sent by Peking to assist in constructing facilities in Djakarta for the "Conference of the New Emerging Forces," the Sino-Indonesian rival to the United Nations to be held in August, 1966. After the September 30 coup, the military administrative command of the Riau Archipelago, near Singapore, disclosed that recently seized PKI documents revealed a plan for cadres to receive arms from People's China that were to be dropped in the area.[29]

The weapons found their way to all sorts of places: to the teeming, dilapidated native quarters of sprawling Djakarta, where Communist youth and women's front members, "sport" organizations, and volunteer "ward guard" units began to train with them; to a hilly, triangular region in Central Java formed by the towns of Bojolali, Klatèn, and Kartasura at the foot of Mounts Merapi and Merbabu, a stamping ground of PKI guerrillas in earlier years; to cadres in Bandjermasin, South Kalimantan (Borneo), who were busily making plans to kidnap the regional military commander and leaders of Muslim groups.[30] Lubang Buaja (literally, "crocodile hole"), a relatively remote native section on the outskirts of Djakarta and within the terrain of Halim Perdana Kusuma air force base, became a principal Com-

---

[27] *The Straits Times*, December 24, 1964; UPI dispatch, Djakarta, December 23, 1964. According to a purported "confession" made by Aidit just before he was shot by the Indonesian Army—subsequently published in the Tokyo paper *Asahi Evening News*—the PKI had originally set 1970 as its "target year" to seize power, but since word of this planned coup d'état leaked out, Aidit decided to reduce sharply the preparation time and move ahead toward a coup by the middle of 1965. See Arthur J. Dommen, "The Attempted Coup in Indonesia," *The China Quarterly* (January–March, 1966), p. 168.

[28] For details, see *Sabah Times* (Jesselton), September 14, 1965; also *Far Eastern Economic Review* (November 4, 1965), p. 189. Dommen, *op. cit.*, pp. 154–55, quoting "reliable information from private sources," states that the import into Indonesia of these supplies occurred without customs inspection as a result of an agreement reached between Foreign Minister Subandrio and Chinese Foreign Minister Ch'en Yi.

Indonesian Army sources have reported that the PKI was able to finance some of its activities through the illegal export of rubber to China via Singapore. Deputy Premier Subandrio and Minister without Portfolio Oei Tjoe Tat (widely regarded as "Peking's man" in the cabinet and said to have been a *sub rosa* member of the PKI) were the masterminds of this rubber scheme. See *The Straits Times*, March 16, 1966.

[29] *Armed Forces Daily Mail* (Djakarta), December 30, 1965.

[30] For details on PKI preparation for the GESTAPU affair, see *Djakarta Daily Mail*, October 8, November 8–10, 17, and 22, and December 9, 1965. I have also relied on a number of private Indonesian sources, whose identities I cannot reveal.

munist training and staging ground. There is little doubt that the pro-PKI air force high command, particularly Air Force Chief Vice-Marshal Omar Dhani and former Air Chief Suryadarma (both cabinet ministers), knew about and condoned this activity. Indeed, the army has claimed that air force units lent additional weapons to the Communist trainees. And it was from Halim air base, on October 1, when the Djakarta coup had failed, that Aidit flew with Dhani in an air force plane to Central Java. Confessions obtained from GESTAPU participants agree that training at Halim began about mid-August. The profusion of uniformed paramilitary volunteer and civil-defense groups in Indonesia, over which the army had long and vainly attempted to exercise some control, afforded additional cover for the exercises at the base. Even target practice and bayonet training were included. Sexual orgies, designed to promote abandonment of "religious rules" and moral restraints, were also encouraged at Lubang Buaja, according to confessions extracted by the army.

In various parts of the country, meanwhile, PKI leaders launched "Operation Naming Names," during which Party and front members compiled "black lists" of the names of "obstructionists" marked for future elimination. According to the army, if GESTAPU had been successful, mass trials conducted by the PKI were to have been held between October 2 and 5, 1965, culminating in the public execution of 600 KABIRs (*kapitalisbirokrat,* or bureaucratic capitalists, a favorite Party epithet for its opponents, especially in the army).

It is still impossible to say whether the PKI leadership actually wanted the coup to occur when it did. In his confession, published on December 2, 1965, by the army, Politburo member Njono declared that not until a mid-July, 1965, Politburo meeting were he and other Party leaders informed by Aidit that, as a result of Sukarno's deteriorating health, a critical point had been reached and that a "Council of Generals" was planning a coup.[31] Aidit himself assumed command of the campaign to alert Party regional committees throughout the country, and he appears to have emphasized that the army was divided and that the air force would help the PKI. According to Njono, the final decision to seize power was not taken until the end of August, when Aidit advised the Politburo that (1) a "Revolutionary Council" would be established to replace the present cabinet; (2) in order

---

[31] Broadcast, Radio Djakarta (Domestic Service), February 14–16, 1966; *Antara Daily Newsbulletin,* December 7, 1965; *Far Eastern Economic Review* (December 23, 1965), p. 538. Njono subsequently retracted his confession, but under what circumstances is not yet clear. It is difficult to say how many top PKI leaders were aware of the plot or the exact date of the coup. Politburo member Jusuf Adjitorop had been in Peking for medical treatment for some time; Lukman, Sakirman, and Rewang were in various places in Central Java; Njono was traveling with Subandrio in Sumatra. The selection of the night of September 30 and the day of October 1, 1965 (the latter the anniversary of Communist China's "national day"), is also unclear: on October 1, 1965, PKI Central Committee member Sidik Kertapati was in Peking as a member of the official Indonesian delegation (headed by a number of Indonesian cabinet ministers) to the Chinese "national day" celebrations. Chinese sources do not mention any other prominent PKI figures in China at this time. See *Peking Review* (October 1, 1965), p. 6.

to forestall the supposed coup of the "Council of Generals," paramilitary units among the fronts were now to be mobilized; and (3) a political campaign would be launched to demand better living conditions and to reveal the danger of a military coup. But all tactical plans, according to Njono, were coordinated by Aidit alone; he, Njono, did not even know when the coup would actually be launched, until a youth-front courier from Lubang Buaja informed him in the early evening of September 29. Njono's surprising ignorance may well be feigned, but there is little doubt that poor coordination and lack of communication—whether due to extreme secrecy, Aidit's allegedly one-man control, the *ad hoc* character of the PKI's tactics, or a combination of these—almost doomed the coup from the start. On October 2, 1965, for example, the PKI spokesman issued a statement on behalf of the Party Central Committee, dissociating the Party from the coup, and describing it as "an internal affair of the army." Yet, even then, Aidit was rallying GESTAPU guerrilla resistance in Central Java, and, on October 6, *Djalan Rakjat*, a PKI daily published in Surabaya, East Java, printed a letter, purportedly written by Aidit, simultaneously urging all PKI members "to carry out their vital tasks" and declaring that the Party would not intervene in "the September 30 event."

Aidit's assertion to the Politburo that the army was divided was almost certainly correct, but the role of various army leaders in the GESTAPU affair is by no means clear. Unquestionably, the huge PKI had influence among some younger staff and field-grade officers, among them Lieutenant Colonel Untung, an Aidit protegé and battalion commander in the Tjakrabirawa regiment of Presidential security guards, and Colonels A. Latif and Agus Sigit, respectively brigade commander and first battalion commander in the Fifth Military Region Command of Djakarta. To what extent had these officers, some of them veterans of intraservice cabals and motivated by personal grievances (like Colonel Suherman of the Central Java Diponegoro military command) allowed themselves to be "coordinated" by Aidit? To what did they believe they were lending themselves and their units when they voiced support for Untung's "Revolutionary Council" on September 30? Specifically, were they inveigled by Untung, as has been rumored, to aid him, on the assurance that Sukarno knew and approved of the plot? We still do not have the answers. In any case, eventually the GESTAPU rebels were able to muster a force of about five army battalions —two in Djakarta, one in West Java, and two in Central Java. As for the air force, its pro-PKI leadership was apparently not prepared to go beyond the moral support and facilities extended to the Lubang Buaja terrorists at Halim, and no air force units openly sided with the GESTAPU.

In the highly-charged political atmosphere of the first half of 1965, it is not at all unlikely, as Aidit stated, that some army leaders had a "contingency" plan of their own and, like the PKI, were preparing for a preemptive coup and the establishment of a "Council of Generals." In its initial communiqué on September 20, 1965, Untung's "Revolutionary Council" declared that it had acted because the "Council of Generals" had organized a "show of force" and meant to seize power on or before Armed

Forces Day (October 5) by bringing troops from various parts of Java to the capital.[32] However, spreading the tale of an impending coup is the oldest ruse to justify a pre-emptive strike of one's own, and there is no reason why the PKI could not have used such a tactic.

Although we are still in the dark as to the circumstances determining the particular timing of the coup and the nature of the tactical consultations, if any, between Aidit, Untung, and others in the plot, the purpose of GESTAPU itself is a good deal clearer. In the first place, the coup was not designed to establish a full-fledged Communist "People's Democracy" but rather to turn the wheel of policy another hefty thirty or forty degrees toward it. Undoubtedly, some of the army officers who supported the GESTAPU would never have agreed to participate had they been aware of the extent of PKI manipulations behind the scene. This was also true of Untung's forty-five member "Revolutionary Council," proclaimed in Djakarta on September 30 as the new government. At least twelve members of this council were believed to be friendly to the PKI, although no known Party figures were included.[33] A few, like the veteran cabinet official Johannes Leimena, probably had no notion that they had been named, but the great majority of the council were politically colorless military bureaucrats or second-echelon political hacks. This was clearly a transitional body, designed to allay suspicions among the unwary and politically untutored and to be replaced when things settled down.

[32] *Djakarta Daily Mail*, October 2, 1965. For an alternative view, that is, that the coup was instigated mainly by a group of "Young Turk" officers (among them Untung, Latif, and Air Force Major Sujono) "disenchanted with the top army command," which was felt to be corrupt and incompetent, see Lucien Rey, "Dossier of the Indonesian Drama," *New Left Review* (March–April, 1966), pp. 26–40. Untung, according to this view, got his chance when he was put in charge of the parade in Djakarta on Armed Forces Day, permitting him to bring a number of army units sympathetic to his cause into the capital. However, on February 25, 1966, Untung, then on trial, reiterated that the coup had been intended to save Sukarno from a "Council of Generals." Radio Djakarta branded his testimony as false.

[33] Among the pro-PKI figures in Untung's "Revolutionary Council" were two who deserve special mention: Siauw Giok Tjhan, and Mrs. Utami Suryadarma. The former was general chairman of the "Consultative Body for Indonesian Citizenship" (*Badan Permusjawaratan Kewarganegaraan Indonesia*, or BAPERKI), the latter "rector" (or "president") of BAPERKI's University "Res Publica" in Djakarta. Founded in 1954, BAPERKI originally was designed to advance the interests of Indonesian citizens of Chinese origin. But over the years and under the leadership of Siauw, a former editor of the PKI daily *Harian Rakjat*, it became one of the most effective conduits of pro-Peking political influence in the Chinese-Indonesian community and in Indonesian life as a whole, maintaining close ties with the PKI. The dovetailing of PKI and BAPERKI policies is, for example, particularly evident in such BAPERKI documents as *Vivere Pericoloso. Materi-materi Konperensi Pleno Pusat ke-II Baperki, 27–30 Augustus 1964 di Surabaja* (Djakarta, 1965), and Siauw Giok Tjhan, *Gotong Rojong, Nasakom untuk Melaksanakan Ampera* (Djakarta, 1963).

Mrs. Suryadarma, wife of the pro-PKI former Air Force Chief-of-Staff, had done yeoman service for the PKI in the course of 1964–65, in the Party's campaign to ban American films and mobilize anti-American sentiment generally. There is no doubt that, by the middle of 1965, BAPERKI was one of Peking's principal, if unofficial, agencies on the Indonesian scene. BAPERKI headquarters and the premises of "Res Publica" University were among the first buildings to be sacked by anti-Communist mobs in the aftermath of the GESTAPU affair.

A second and probably more immediate and important purpose was to destroy the command structure of the army and to begin elimination of major Party opponents in the provinces. The decimation of top army leaders in the capital was assigned to the Party's youth and women's fronts, and was evidently intended to bring the militancy of these groups, which had been given a major role as "shock troops" in the coup, to the highest pitch. A fifteen-year-old young woman, three months pregnant, who was proclaimed a "Lubang Buaja heroine" by the PKI, described in her confession how she and her associates were trained, were given "small knives and razor blades," and early in the morning of October 1 went to work on one of the six leading generals whose bodies were later found in a well in Lubang Buaja, "stabbing at the victim's private parts and cutting these parts and the body until he died."[34] The GESTAPU assassins came within two generals of wiping out the Indonesian Army high command. The terrorists' failure to make a complete sweep was fatal, for army units outside Djakarta quickly rallied to the personal call of General Nasution who, though wounded, just managed to escape.

Finally, the coup was designed to establish a Maoist "base area" for potential PKI guerrilla activity in the Merapi-Merbabu mountain complex of Central Java, the staging grounds for what the Indonesian press has called "a second Vietnam."[35] Even if—indeed, especially when—the coup had succeeded, this Communist base area was to have provided Party leaders with political leverage as they proceeded with their intended transformation of the armed forces. It was to this planned Communist base area, which two local pro-PKI army battalion commanders in Central Java and police officials in Jogjakarta had helped to establish, that Aidit ultimately fled to make a last and futile stand. And it was from this area that well-armed bands of young guerrillas swarmed out into East and West Java to pillage and terrorize as late as the first weeks of November, 1965, until they were finally destroyed, often by local "volunteer" village guards led by young Muslim fanatics belonging to the "Ansor" youth group (*Gerakan Pemuda Ansor*, or GPA), an affiliate of the Muslim Scholars Party (NU). During this furious guerrilla and counterguerrilla campaign, whole villages and parts of districts in Java were laid waste, and literally tens of thousands were killed—PKI and front members, Party sympathizers and suspected sympathizers, and the usual victims of mere jealousy and personal grudges.[36]

[34] *Sinar Harapan*, November 5, 1965.

[35] See, for example, *Pewarta-Surabaia* (Surabaya), November 16, 1965. See also Boerhan and Soebekti, *Fakta dan Latar-Belakang Gerakan 30 September* (Djakarta, 1966), pp. 126–39.

[36] Estimates of the number killed in the anti-PKI pogrom vary. Sukarno, on January 15, 1966, said 87,000 had been killed, "all but a few hundred" of them Communists and their followers. Sukarno declared that this figure had been given him by a special "fact finding mission." Somewhat earlier British sources put the number killed at between 100,000 and 150,000 (*The New York Times*, January 13 and 16, 1966). The latter figure has also been advanced by the Malaysian government. Later estimates have gone as high as 300,000. Several thousand are believed to have been directly executed by the army, among them such top PKI leaders as D. N. Aidit and

It seems highly probable that Sukarno and heir apparent Subandrio, who headed the civil intelligence agency, knew of the coup and tacitly assented to it. Sukarno's subsequent explanation of his activities on the morning of the coup (he voluntarily went, at the request of his own mutinous palace guards, to Halim air force base, of all places, so that he would be able to fly away "should an unwanted eventuality arise") has only managed to arouse further suspicions, and Indonesia's President has deemed it wiser not to attempt to lay them to rest.[37] Sukarno's endorsement of the PKI's plan to arm peasants and workers and his (and Subandrio's) general attitude toward the PKI and Peking in the preceding year suggest that the coup not only had their approval but, indeed, may have been welcomed as

---

economic expert Sakirman (although toward the close of May, 1966, an army spokesman urged an intensified drive to round up Sakirman and other former PKI Central Committee members, whom he described as still at large). See also *Angkatan Bersendjata* (Djakarta), February 10 and 11, 1966.

Many aspects of the anti-PKI pogrom are likely to remain shrouded in mystery for some time. The extent to which the army passively or actively assisted fanatic Muslim youths in their extermination campaign is one, and the degree to which village *kijajis* (Muslim spiritual leaders) contributed by proclaiming a *jihad* (holy war) against the GESTAPU is another. On the other hand, there have been persistent reports of guerrilla activity being carried out by PKI followers in Central Java and of depradations by a "PKI-malam" (a "night," or underground, PKI) in West Java. See *Armed Forces Daily Mail*, January 26, 1966, and *LKBN Antara Bulletin* (Cologne), May 6, 1966.

Under cover of the pogrom, long-standing personal and ethnic animosities were given free rein. For example, Arab textile manufacturers and distributors, long at odds with their Javanese and Chinese competitors in the batik (native printed cloth) industry, descended upon Surakarta, Central Java, and in the confusion set fire to competing plants and stores there. In many places, mass public beheadings continued well into March, 1966.

[37] *Antara Daily Newsbulletin*, October 6, 1965. U.S. officials, according to *The Washington Post* of October 13, 1965, possess "incontrovertible proof" that Sukarno was, in fact, in league with the PKI in the GESTAPU affair. During the trial of PKI Politburo member Njono, in mid-February, 1966, Air Force Major Sujono testified that Sukarno knew in advance of the September 30 coup. (Reuters dispatch, Djakarta, February 17, 1966.)

There seems little question of the connivance of high-ranking air force officers with the GESTAPU, and air force command statements in the early hours of the coup have generally been regarded as gravely compromising. At 9:30 A.M. on October 1, when the coup still seemed to have some chance of success, Air Force Commander Omar Dhani issued an "Order of the Day," declaring that the "September 30" movement had launched an action to "safeguard the Revolution" and to protect Sukarno against "CIA subversion." The order also stated that the air force would always support the "progressive revolutionary movement." When, by 9 P.M. on October 1, the position of the GESTAPU rebels was becoming untenable in Djakarta, Dhani flew with Aidit to Jogjakarta from Halim base. During the next day, Dhani contacted air force officers in Central Java, urging them to dissociate themselves from the coup, and returned late in the afternoon of the same day to the Bogor presidential palace, where Sukarno had gone. Late on October 2, he issued a statement formally dissociating the air force from the GESTAPU affair. (For various air force pronouncements, see especially "Selected Documents Relating to the September 30th Movement and Its Epilogue," *Indonesia* (April, 1966), pp. 143–49.) By April, 1966, 306 air force personnel had been dismissed from their posts for complicity in the GESTAPU affair. On April 20, 1966, Dhani was arrested.

providing the basis for a settlement of Sukarno's succession. In any case, it is almost certainly impossible that no word of the training at Halim or of the Communist Chinese weapons shipments ever reached Sukarno's own extensive network of informants or Subandrio's agents.

But there is no clarity as to the involvement of Sukarno and Subandrio in the actual timing of the GESTAPU coup. It has been rumored that on September 28, 1965, while making a public address, Sukarno showed signs of illness, and that this may have led Untung and his associates to launch the revolt. On the other hand, without minimizing the factor of Sukarno's health, the rebels may have decided to strike in any case, because of their alleged expectation of a pre-emptive coup by the "Council of Generals" on or before October 5, when large military units would be concentrated in the capital. The Communists might also have feared that the likelihood of such a pre-emptive coup by the army would increase with each passing day, for army intelligence would probably pick up information on PKI plans and alert army leaders.

Why did GESTAPU fail? A complete answer probably cannot be given for some time, but several major reasons can be suggested. For one, the Lubang Buaja terrorists' plan to wipe out the entire command structure of the army failed. As it was, six leading generals (among them the army chief of staff and the chiefs of intelligence and supply), and, outside Djakarta, nearly a score of staff, field, and subaltern officers in vital positions were killed. The fact that the assassins knew exactly where all these officers might be found late in the night of September 30 suggests a degree of planning and involvement by local intelligence services, both the military's and Subandrio's civil agency, that can hardly be overlooked. But Nasution, though wounded by the killers sent to his home, jumped over his garden wall and got away. How well aware the terrorists were of the danger posed by Nasution's escape and how desperate they were to kill him and make a clean sweep is revealed by their efforts to find him: Early in the morning of October 1, when countercoup operations had already begun, one of the principal terrorists, the pro-Communist army colonel Latif, was sent in disguise to the Central Military Hospital in Djakarta, on the assumption that Nasution might be there or else might soon come to visit his five-year-old daughter, who had been severely wounded the previous night by a terrorist bullet intended for her father. But Nasution never came.[38]

Two others marked for death, including an important communications officer, escaped the dragnet simply because by chance they were not where they were expected to be. They soon joined Nasution "in an undisclosed safe place," as the Defense Minister subsequently put it in his account of the escape. Evidently, GESTAPU leaders were convinced that with the army chiefs out of the way and "Commander in Chief" Sukarno inaccessible because he was in protective custody at the Halim base, uncertainty and indecision on the part of provincial military commanders would allow

[38] See the account of Nasution's escape in *Kompas* (Djakarta), October 22, 1965.

time for the rebel hold on the capital to be consolidated; shortly thereafter, elimination of PKI opponents throughout the country would begin. The rebels evidently counted, too, on the psychological effect of a sudden sei- zure of the city of Jogjakarta in Central Java by PKI units moving out of the Merapi-Merbabu area, so that the impression would not be created that the coup was confined merely to the capital. Resistance to the rebels in Jogjakarta was unexpectedly fierce, however, with the city virtually changing hands on several occasions. Meanwhile, Nasution's flight and speedy rallying of his supporters, and the swift communication established and maintained with the loyal Siliwangi division and additional units rushed from nearby Bandung by General Suharto, overwhelmed the rebels in Djakarta after they had barely established themselves in the radio sta- tion and other government centers. With order restored in the capital, the rebel cause in Jogjakarta was soon lost, despite Aidit's apparently personal leadership. The bands of GESTAPU marauders swarmed out into the countryside, eventually to be decimated.

Then, too, GESTAPU leaders had counted on a "popular" uprising and outpouring of mass support in the streets of Djakarta led by Party and front cadres. The cadres did appear on the streets, but their followers soon vanished—despite the PKI Djakarta district committee's last-ditch attempt to rally them with profuse praise in a public statement issued late on Octo- ber 1. Even early demonstrators were greeted by truckloads of Siliwangi division soldiers rushing to rebel strongholds in the city, and with over- whelming armor surrounding Untung's and Sigit's troops. Such discipline and coordination as the fronts possessed wilted almost at once in the face of this display of power. In the past, the Communist ability to mobilize effectively and in time the volatile Djakarta street mobs—when it was known that the military would not interfere—had often seemed to lend impressive strength to Communist demands. This time, the PKI's failure was perhaps most eloquently revealed in the earlier-mentioned exhortation, published in the party paper *Harian Rakjat* on October 2, announcing popular support for GESTAPU, at a time when the coup was to all intents and purposes already crushed. An outburst of massive and sustained revo- lutionary fervor in the Djakarta streets might have turned the tide, for it appeared that in several districts in Java, for example, in Tjilatjap, Ban- juwangi, Malang and Surabaya, cadres and front groups were ready and waiting for action and, indeed, even had begun attacking police and mili- tary posts.[39]

But when Radio Djakarta announced, within hours of the first proclama- tion of Untung's "Revolutionary Council," that Nasution was safe and had re-established control, the rebel offensive beyond the capital, with the

[39] Based on information by private Indonesian informants, whom the author is not at liberty to identify. See also *Djakarta Daily Mail*, December 16 and 20, 1965, and *Armed Forces Daily Mail*, December 21 and 30, 1965, on PKI/GESTAPU activity in the Tjilatjap and Magelang areas. As late as the evening of October 1, junior officers associated with GESTAPU were prepared to hold all or parts of such Central Java towns as Semarang and Surakarta. The turn of the tide in Djakarta and Jogjakarta, however, quickly dampened resistance in Semarang and Surakarta.

exception of the area in and around Jogjakarta, never really mustered any strength. The subsequent crushing of GESTAPU, the pursuit, arrest, and execution of the armed rebels, and the rounding up of thousands of Party and front-group cadres (sometimes in a matter of hours and from all walks of life, even in relatively inaccessible regions), showed a remarkable degree of military and police staffwork, coordination, and control over communication and transport—the elimination of which the plotters had realized was the *sine qua non* to their success. It also strongly suggests that army intelligence, even in the outlying districts, was not altogether unaware of the possibility of a PKI coup and was well prepared to crush it once the signal was given in Djakarta.

The profound repercussions of GESTAPU on Indonesia's political structure are still being felt, but it is possible to trace the outlines of the country's presently emerging power pattern. Perhaps the most significant development in the aftermath has been a new polarization of political forces, stemming from Sukarno's determined effort to rescue the radical left, which in turn involved him in an increasingly sharper conflict with the army.

In the weeks following the September 30 coup, the PKI organization was shattered. Party branches and fronts were banned by military commanders in nearly a dozen principal regions, although Sukarno at first was able to resist a formal, nationwide banning of the Party. Virtually all of the Party's principal leaders from the Politburo to the district level, PKI parliamentary deputies, mayors, or other office-holders, as well as thousands of suspected sympathizers, were either killed or arrested. Party offices were sacked again and again, and Party publications were proscribed. But in the midst of the almost hysterical fury of the anti-Communist pogrom, President Sukarno gave an astonishing performance in trying to save, in effect, a place for Communism in his nation's future development. Again and again, Sukarno warned that the nation should not swerve to "the right," that Indonesia's revolution was and remained a "left revolution," and that even the concept of NASAKOM, which makes Communism an integral part of the official state ideology, should be preserved.[40]

"There must be no more emotional agitation," Sukarno warned on October 16. "What has happened is part of our revolution, only a minor thing in the great ocean we describe as the revolution." The next day, he lashed out at "subversion," not by the PKI or GESTAPU, as his listeners might have anticipated, but rather "of the imperialists, for example, the American CIA." Soon thereafter, Sukarno proclaimed himself "prosecutor and judge" of the GESTAPU, and his counterploys became even more belligerent, as, for example, when he ordered the army to "shoot to kill" during any further anti-PKI demonstrations. By November, Sukarno was asserting that the United States had offered him a bribe of 150 million rupiahs "to spread Western ideas," and he became increasingly critical of

[40] See *Antara Daily Newsbulletin*, November 2, 3, and 10, and December 9 and 15, 1965.

the army-controlled Indonesian press, which, he charged, had been repeatedly guilty of incorrect reporting in connection with the GESTAPU affair. He accused Muslims of violating Islamic law by not burying the bodies of killed and mutilated Communists and, at a time when anti-Chinese feeling was running high and mobs were attacking Communist Chinese consulates and looting Chinese shops, Sukarno called for an end to these demonstrations and a renewal of friendly relations between Peking and Djakarta. As late as February 21, 1966, and again a week later, when his conflict with the army was rapidly coming to a showdown, Sukarno in various speeches insisted that "our revolution is marked with a leftist character," that deviations to the right were "counterrevolutionary," and that any attempt to deter Indonesia from "her leftist course" would fail. On February 14, 1966, at a rally in Djakarta convened to condemn resumption of U.S. bombing of North Vietnam, Sukarno praised the PKI, describing it (amidst jeers) as a Party "which rendered considerable contribution and sacrifice to the independence of the country."[41]

In these exhortations, Sukarno was evidently seeking to preserve the balance of power, which for so long had allowed him to play the PKI off against the army. With the PKI destroyed for the moment, Indonesia's President clearly had no wish to become the army's puppet. This was the meaning of the Sukarno-inspired speculation heard in the capital in mid-November, 1965, that a new "loyal" Communist party might soon be formed. When this proposal met with a storm of opposition, especially among Muslim groups, Sukarno formally proposed, on January 15, 1966, establishment of a new national "left revolutionary" organization, to be called the *Barisan Sukarno* (Sukarno Front), an idea promptly seconded the next day by Deputy Premier Subandrio.

These suggestions were not wholly unrealistic, for there remained significant sources of strength upon which a resurgent radical left might draw. For example, in the left wing of the large but seriously divided *Partai Nasional Indonesia* (Indonesian Nationalist Party, or PNI), in the smaller Partindo Party, a Communist front, which at first survived the aftermath of the coup, and in the radical student groups, Sukarno's appeals fell on sympathetic ears. Moreover, while the PKI's formal party and front structure was destroyed, its popular influence was by no means so easily eradicated. In many parts of Java and Sumatra, the Party had been almost unequaled in its ability to provide organizational focus for and meet some of the needs of the urban poor, the landless proletariat, estate workers, underpaid civil servants, and other groups. Indeed, through its local patronage powers, the Party had given numerous Indonesians a direct stake in its existence as defender of the *rakjat djelata* (the common man), while in the meantime, it had been no secret that the army's involvement over the years in the bureaucracy of government and the economy had frequently been accompanied by spectacular incompetence and corruption, on which

[41] Broadcast, Radio Djakarta (Domestic Service), February 21, 1965; *The New York Times*, October 24, 25, and November 7, 1965, and March 1, 1966; Reuters dispatch, Djakarta, February 14, 1966.

the PKI had always been able to capitalize. Even the most ardent anti-Communist in Indonesia realized that the PKI's destruction would not remove the administrative chaos in which the country was floundering.

But, for the time being, cowed by the violence of the Muslim-led and army-approved anti-PKI campaign, most of the radical left thought prudence the greater part of political valor. Furthermore, it became increasingly clear that army leaders were greatly aroused by Sukarno's continuing attempts to protect the left. As early as October 14, under strong army pressure, Sukarno had replaced Major General Pranoto Reksosamudro with Lieutenant General Suharto as Army Chief of Staff. It was a significant change. Pranoto, an avowed Sukarno supporter with known leftist leanings, had been appointed by Sukarno immediately after the bodies of Army Chief Yani and five other generals, slain by the GESTAPU terrorists, had been found. Suharto, a close friend of Nasution, had mobilized his scattered forces on the morning of the coup and had smashed the GESTAPU in the capital. Nasution himself, with growing vehemence in various public addresses in the following weeks, excoriated "the masterminds and apologists of the counterrevolution," demanded that the perpetrators of GESTAPU not be given a chance "to legalize their activities" or another "opportunity to repeat their crimes," and complained that those responsible for the coup still "have not been totally destroyed."[42] It was only after further army pressure, and not until November 17, 1965, that Sukarno issued a Presidential decree ordering all branches and services of government to purge themselves of GESTAPU sympathizers through special "screening teams." It seemed to be a clear victory for the army. The city council of Bandung proposed that Nasution be appointed to the position of Vice President of the Indonesian Republic, vacant since Mohammed Hatta resigned in 1956. The proposal was quickly taken up in the press, until Sukarno reportedly ordered the army to quash the idea as "inappropriate at this time."

Despite the clamor of student groups and Muslim party leaders, the President refused to issue a formal nationwide ban on the PKI. Known Communists were out of the government, but there was no sign that Sukarno intended a significant revision of policies; figures like Subandrio and others, who had been in the good graces of the PKI, retained their cabinet and other posts. Even the announced "screening" of GESTAPU sympathizers seemed to be only a formality. By the middle of December, 1965, hundreds previously arrested for alleged involvement in Communist activities in several government ministries and departments had been reinstated.

It was against this background that a kind of pamphlet war erupted against the government in Djakarta, Bandung, Surabaya, and other major towns. Anonymous, crudely mimeographed or printed sheets containing

[42] *Sinar Harapan,* November 13 and 24, 1965; *Djakarta Daily Mail,* November 12, 1965. It may be speculated that the vehemence of Nasution and other army leaders at this time was caused, at least in part, by persistent rumors that the army itself had been riddled with pro-PKI supporters to a far greater degree than had been supposed. See *The Straits Times,* November 4, 1965.

inflammatory revelations or accusations, especially against Subandrio—who was fast becoming the symbol of Sukarno's policy of protecting the left— began to circulate widely and found eager readers.[43] Student "action groups," coordinated by a new "command" organization (*Komando Aksi Mahasiswa Indonesia*, or KAMI), staged increasingly massive antigovernment demonstrations, in which the President himself clearly was becoming a target: "*Setop import isteri dari Djepang*" ("Stop importing wives from Japan"), one common picket sign read, an allusion to Sukarno's recent marriage to a Japanese beauty. Many of these demonstrations appeared to have tacit army support, and the army unquestionably in this period was working closely with, if not controlling, such "anti-GESTAPU" civilian "action" groups, including the *Pantja Sila* Front created early in October, 1965. Sukarno himself appeared to be manipulating left-wing student groups,[44] which now frequently began to clash with the followers of KAMI; and in mid-January, 1966, Sukarno and Subandrio urged formation of the earlier mentioned "Sukarno Front," a new mass organization clearly intended to stabilize their own power base. Although the left wing of the PNI and Partindo voiced approval for the "Sukarno Front," local military commanders (with the subsequent approval of Army Chief Suharto) banned the Front's formation "in order to preserve unity."

Throughout the early months of 1966, the power struggle continued. KAMI now took to demonstrating alternately for lower prices, a complete purge of government services, and the formal dissolution of the PKI, and student leaders warned against the emergence of a "neo-PKI." Sukarno first sought to pacify the students, expressing to them his "understanding" of their demands, and even declaring on February 17, 1966, that the PKI had already been dissolved "within the framework of implementing a political solution in an integral manner" to safeguard the national revolution.[45] In the absence of a formal decree banning the party, few took Sukarno's announcement seriously. When KAMI and pro-Sukarno, anti-KAMI students began to battle in the streets, Sukarno declared that he had proof of an underground plot to overthrow him, but he vouchsafed no further details.

In what was evidently a final effort to assert his authority, Sukarno

[43] See, for example, such one- or two-page stenciled pamphlets circulating in Djakarta and Bandung as *Berita Revolusi*, No. 4, November 30, 1965, and No. 6, December 6, 1965, and the leaflet entitled "Subandrio! ! !," signed by one "Anak Rakjat," circulating in Bandung in mid-November, 1965. Subandrio himself in this period did his cause little good by accusing a number of Indonesian newspapers of being financed by the CIA, and then by issuing a "correction" of his statement, which, in effect, was an affirmation of his original charge. See *Angkatan Bersendjata*, October 26, 1965, and *Djakarta Daily Mail*, October 28, 1965.

[44] Among the radical student organizations Sukarno mobilized were such groups as GERMINDO (*Gerakan Mahasiswa Indonesia*—Indonesian Student Movement), PPMI (*Pusat Perhimpunan Mahasiswa Indonesia*—Central Indonesian Student Organization), MMI (*Madjelis Mahasiswa Indonesia*—Indonesian Students Council), and GMNI (*Gerakan Mahasiswa Nasional Indonesia*—National Indonesian Students Movement). These groups were almost entirely Djakarta-based and had been expelled from KAMI. They numbered about 4,000 students altogether. On paper, the groups affiliated with KAMI have three times that number.

[45] Antara dispatch, Radio Djakarta, February 17, 1966.

abruptly announced, on February 21, 1966, that he had reshuffled the cabinet. Nasution was dropped as Minister of Defense. To be sure, the names of Aidit and two other PKI leaders who had held minor cabinet posts were omitted. But fifteen new appointments were made, some of them well-known PKI sympathizers, like the new Minister for Basic Education and Culture, Sumardjo, who had been among the leaders of a teachers association closely involved in the GESTAPU affair, and who for this reason had been suspended from his post only a few weeks earlier. Such figures as Lenin Peace Prize winner Prijono and Oei Tjoe Tat, the latter widely regarded as "Peking's man" in the government, were retained. Former Air Force Minister Omar Dhani, who had resigned as Air Force Chief shortly after the GESTAPU affair and had been immediately appointed by Sukarno to the newly created post of Minister of Aviation Industry, was also kept on. This fact, perhaps as much as the elimination of Nasution, enraged anti-Communist elements, because Dhani was widely regarded as having supported the PKI's ambitions in the September 30 coup. In installing the new cabinet, Sukarno had recourse to Communist terminology, speaking of the "national democratic" phase of the Indonesian Revolution, which now had to be implemented by a "socialist" phase, and calling for a renewed struggle against "imperialism" and "feudalism."[46] It seemed to some as if GESTAPU had never occurred.

But Sukarno lost his gamble. Students intensified their demonstrations and now repeatedly attempted to rush the President's palace. Neither a curfew, nor a formal banning of KAMI by Sukarno, nor the closing of the University of Indonesia to "stop students and nonstudents from using the university for undesirable purposes," halted the agitation. On March 5, several thousand school children, some barely in their teens, stormed Subandrio's office while troops fired over their heads. In defiance of the President's ban but with the obvious approval of the army and police, KAMI continued to march, organize, and press its protest against Nasution's dismissal, demanding a new cabinet purged of left-wing ministers, a formal ban of the PKI, and lower prices.

When it became apparent that leaders of the political parties were reluctant to back him openly against the students, and when it was reported that army units were beginning to concentrate in the area of the palace,[47]

[46] Broadcast, Radio Djakarta (Domestic Service), February 24, 1966. On the concept of the two-stage revolution, with the "national democratic" stage being succeeded by the "socialist" stage, see J. M. Van der Kroef, "The Communist Concept of National Democracy," *Studies on the Soviet Union*, IV (1964), 39–63. Both Sukarno and Aidit used this concept extensively, and it gave the latter the protection of the former in implementing PKI tactics.

[47] What ultimately impelled the army to move against Sukarno is not clear. It may have been that early in March, 1966, the army got wind of an alleged secret agreement between Subandrio and Peking, concluded well after the GESTAPU affair, in which Communist China promised support for Sukarno's proposed "Conference of New Emerging Forces," if the remaining anti-Communist generals in Indonesia were eliminated. The killing of the anti-Communist generals was to have been carried out by civilian assassins or sympathetic military personnel. *The New York Times*, March 16, 1966.

Sukarno, on the afternoon of March 11, summoned army commanders and agreed to a formal ban on the PKI, a purge of pro-Communists, and formation of a new cabinet, in return for continued recognition as head of state and retention of all his titles. On the same day, Army Chief Suharto was ordered "to take all steps" to restore order and the smooth functioning of government, and the next day, Sukarno formally dissolved and banned the PKI. Within hours, more than a score of cabinet members and political leaders, among them Subandrio and Basic Education Minister Sumardjo, were arrested; KAMI agitators also "arrested" three other ministers as students continued to swarm around the presidential palace. A smaller, "purged" cabinet was announced on March 27, in which Nasution returned as Minister/Deputy Commander of the "Crush Malaysia Command" (_Komando Ganjang Malaysia_, or KOGAM), Subandrio was replaced as Foreign Minister by the anti-PKI Adam Malik, and General Suharto emerged as the strong man in the post of Minister of Defense and Security. KAMI and the _Pantja Sila_ Front expressed themselves as only partially satisfied.[48] Even when Suharto ordered a further purge of pro-PKI elements from the government, the agitation did not subside, and periodic clashes between leftist and anti-PKI students continued in a number of towns, particularly in Jogjakarta and Djakarta.

Throughout April and May, 1966, student groups continued their efforts to curtail Sukarno's position and indeed to remove him from office. Initially, the anti-Sukarno elements pinned their hopes on the convening of the Provisional People's Consultative Congress, a kind of superparliament charged with setting forth the state's principal policies (unlike the actual Parliament, which is presumably concerned with the day-to-day implementation of these policies). It was thought that the Congress, which was originally scheduled to meet on May 12, would elect a new vice president—former Vice President Hatta having resigned that office in 1956 after a dispute with Sukarno over the latter's Guided Democracy policies. The new vice president, it was believed, would then begin the process of taking over power from Sukarno with the aid of the army.

But by early May, this strategy had failed, as party leaders fell to wrangling among themselves over the future vice-presidential choice. From various quarters there came increasing demands that only a new general election, in which such banned political groups as the Masjumi (Moslem Federation) and Socialist parties could participate, would restore democratic and constitutional government, and that, therefore, both the Parliament and the Consultative Congress should return their mandates to the electorate. Sukarno's vociferous opposition, moreover, to the convening of the Congress could not be ignored: in Central and East Java, where the President's popularity has remained great, a strong current of political dissatisfaction with the army's attempts to undermine the chief executive was becoming evident. After initial postponement, the Consultative Congress finally met and, on July 5, issued a number of decisions, including revoca-

[48] _Duta Masjarakat_ (Djakarta), March 28, 1966; Antara dispatch, Radio Djakarta, March 29, 1966.

tion of Sukarno's title of "President for Life" (it allowed him to retain the constitutionally meaningless title of "Great Leader of the Revolution"), ordering of new elections by July, 1968, a ban on the PKI and on the propagation of Marxism and Leninism (although "academic study" of these ideologies is permitted), and a "review" of Sukarno's decisions and decrees. On July 25, a new "simplified" cabinet, with Suharto as chairman of the ministerial presidium, was announced, as armed clashes between pro- and anti-Sukarno elements and religious groups continued to erupt in Central and East Java. Even in the armed forces, notably in the marine corps, a quiet mobilization of anti-Suharto officers was begun, presaging future instability. . . . Clearly, the world's largest island republic remains in a period of uncrystallized adjustment to the most far-reaching alteration of its political system in more than a decade.

23

THE MILITARY IN THAI POLITICS*

DAVID A. WILSON

Military leaders have played a dominant role in the politics of Thailand for a long time. This role has not gone unchallenged, and the military has experienced its ups and downs, but for twenty-four of the years since the kingdom became a constitutional regime in 1932, the military, particularly the army, has ruled. Army officers have led the ruling group, dominated the institutions of government, and set the style of Thai politics. An appreciation of the history, organization, and interrelationship of political and governmental institutions is fundamental to an understanding of the reasons for this characteristic of the country's politics. Regardless of which leader is nominally in control, government goes on, and on much the same path. The fact that the ruling class is small and largely overlaps the bureaucracy is at the root of this situation. The ruling class, consequently, is responsive to a political public whose interests it shares to a great extent. Its

* Reprinted by permission of the author, Princeton University Press, and The RAND Corporation from J. J. Johnson, ed., *The Role of the Military in Underdeveloped Countries* (Princeton, N.J.: Princeton University Press, 1962), 253–75, copyright © 1962 by The RAND Corporation (by permission).

political concerns have been narrow, where not actually personal, and conflicts have revolved largely around the basic question of political status—how shall the rewards of goods, prestige, and power be distributed within the ruling class? This state of affairs results from the fact that other institutions that might reflect divergent streams of public opinion, for example, the elected National Assembly (when there has been one) and the private press, are vociferous but weak. The social structure has obstructed the development of effective political parties or social organizations. Commercial interests are often considered to be alien and are politically intimidated. As a result, they seek their ends through personal influence. The great and fundamental class of cultivators, absorbed in a peasant's world of work and religion and largely removed from socially revolutionary pressures, is politically inarticulate.

Some Considerations of Traditions and History

Military officers in modern Thailand have their roots in the traditional bureaucracy. Their historical origins are therefore the same as those of civil officials.[1] There is no indication in the kingdom's history of the existence of any other group comparable to the professional military services and officer corps of the present. Fighting was not an esoteric art to be maintained by a cult or school. All political leaders were soldiers in some sense of the word; all were necessarily prepared and able to organize and lead armies. But there was no warrior class. In effect, the ruling group was bureaucratic and official, and all its members—civil and military—were equally subordinate to the throne.

Although there was little distinction in role between military and civil officials, there were certain characteristics of the traditional organization of the state that account for the historical position of the military in the present Thai political system. One of these characteristics was the formal distinction of title and paraphernalia between civil and military officials, which provided an accepted set of symbols for use in building a modern army. Another was the ancient practice of military officers' holding high political position. The present military officer group is heir to these traditions.

The distinction between military and civil officials became not only formal but also functional during the period of the national reorganization, that is, from the fourth to the seventh reigns of the Bangkok dynasty (1851–1932). In this period, a class of professional military officers was created, and the military became a separate institution. Its outstanding characteristics were centralized organization, professionalization, institu-

[1] Similarly, it is difficult to distinguish in terms of political power the roles of royal and nonroyal officials in traditional Thailand. Office, status, and power were apparently fully merged, and officeholders might be either royal or nonroyal nobles. The differentiation of statuses and roles of various kinds has been a major trend in the history of modern Thailand. For further discussion see George McT. Kahin, ed., *Governments and Politics of Southeast Asia* (Ithaca, N.Y.: Cornell University Press, 1959), pp. 6–7, 12–13.

tional pride, and a dedication to nationalism. But it should be emphasized that while the military was highly bureaucratized, it was not unpolitical. High princes were leaders in the reorganization of the military from the beginning. In 1905, the Crown Prince became by law commander in chief of the army. In 1912, the King became head of a newly created Council of National Defense, which equated military and civil affairs.

The military was a source of considerable pride to the government in this period of national reorganization. Because it had a modern military force, Thailand was able to join the Allied Powers in World War I. This effort, which included sending a small expeditionary force to France, was one of the primary talking points in the negotiations that led to a complete revision of treaties between Thailand and the major world powers in the early 1920's. Moreover, national pride in the military was not diminished by any question of having to share credit with foreign advisers, because the army had been reorganized and rebuilt solely by Thai officials. This process certainly had its influence on the outlook of the national elite.

Military dominance in politics since 1932 is, in part, an outgrowth of the relationship among the parts of the government before 1932. The sovereign power was an absolute monarch. The question of the relationship between ministries and the throne was of such importance that it obscured any potential difficulties between the civilians and soldiers. The ministries drew their authority and budgets from the throne, and whatever conflict and competition there was among units of government took the form of seeking greater influence at the throne. Such conflict was no doubt present in Bangkok prior to 1932. Walter A. Graham, who was a careful and well-informed observer, makes the following remarks in regard to allocation of funds, which indicate that there was debate about the configurations of the budget: "The question of funds is, however, a difficulty. There are many demands upon [Siam's] purse, and irrigation, improvements of communications and other works tending to the development of her natural resources are of the utmost immediate importance if her future welfare is to be assured. At present she is trying to finance her economic reform and to build up a strong war machine at one and the same time, and there are signs of an inclination to starve the former for the benefit of the latter."[2]

Moreover, for much of the period from the late nineteenth century until the coup d'état in 1932, the distinction between political and administrative functions of the government was obscured by a broad common interest in modernization, maintaining independence, revising treaties, and expanding government activities. The question of political power became pressing only with the declining urgency of the struggle for independence and legal autonomy (especially after the renegotiations of treaties in the early 1920's), the impact of world economic depression on the national budget, and the divisive effects of Western antimonarchist thought. It initially centered on the issue of a real or supposed monopoly of power by members of the royal family. On this issue, nonroyal officials—civil and military—held a common position. They were opposed to royal officials,

[2] Walter A. Graham, *Siam* (London: 1924), pp. 318–19.

and any potential conflict between soldiers and civilians was submerged in this more immediately important conflict.

THE MILITARY IN POLITICS: CONSTITUTIONAL PERIOD

Prior to the coup d'état of 1932, the military, along with other Thai bureaucrats, had been subject to a variety of forces that were influential in the formulation of the decision to strike against the government. Military officers regularly, from the late nineteenth century on, had been sent abroad for study in Europe and were infused there with a taste for "progress" and the "up-to-date," if not for democracy. But when they returned home, any expertise or sense of self-importance they had acquired abroad was frustrated by the high princes and their intimates, who held a monopoly of the top posts and the making of important decisions. *Phraya* Phahon Phonphayuhasena,[3] leader of the 1932 coup, once said, "At the very base [of my reasons for joining in the coup] was the birth of the feeling that in the government at that time, high officials and princes acted according to their whim and were not willing to pay heed to smaller people, even though there were reasons for believing them. The big boys mostly felt that the soundness of the opinion of lesser people was not important. What was important was whether or not it pleased them."[4] In addition to the lower officers being generally frustrated, the Ministry of Defense was disturbed in the early 1930's by substantial budget cuts. The extent of this disturbance was indicated by the fact that Prince Bowordet, Minister of Defense from 1928 to 1931, resigned over the cut in the military budget. Such a political resignation was in itself an important event. It could not fail to add to the dissatisfaction among the military. Its impact upon those officers who participated in the coup was sufficient to persuade them to support the noble prince for the position of premier after June, 1932.[5]

The nature of the coup d'état within the narrow political system that Thailand had at that time lends a certain retrospective inevitability to the eventual dominance of the military. The literature on the preparation of the coup, which appears to have begun many years before in Paris, gives no indication that any other method of political action was contemplated. It is difficult to imagine any action that would have had any hope of suc-

[3] Thai usage in personal address is always a source of confusion to the foreigner. This is because of the nearly obligatory use of titles, and because the given (first) name is most commonly used. The terms *Chao Phraya, Phraya, Phra,* and *Luang,* are titles that find their Western counterpart in military ranks, also used in Thailand. Thus, a man can properly be called *Phraya* Phahon Phonphayuhasena but he may also properly be called Colonel *Phraya* Phahon Phonphayuhasena, or Colonel *Phraya* Phahon, or merely *Phraya* Phahon. In recent years, titles have not been granted and are not often used. Thus, Field Marshal *Luang* Phibun Songkhram becomes Field Marshal Phibun Songkhram or Field Marshal Phibun or (for convenience) simply Phibun.

[4] Kulab Saipradit, *Büanglang kan pathiwat 2475* (Behind the Revolution of 1932) (Bangkok: 1947), p. 110.

[5] W. J. Prasangsit, *pathiwat rathaprahan laekabot jalajon nai samai prachathipathai haeng prathet thai* (Revolution, Coup d'État and Revolts in Thailand during the Democratic Period) (Bangkok: 1949), p. 30.

cess without military participation. Furthermore, the civil participants evidently had no misgivings about military participation, since the paramount objective was to isolate and intimidate members of the royal ruling clique.

The events of June, 1932, provided the springboard from which the military plunged into the political life of modern Thailand. Its ability since then to maneuver in the shifting currents has kept it there. The first sixteen months of the constitutional regime were decisive. Although the four senior leaders of the coup were colonels, the role of the military was not overwhelming, and in the initial stages of the new regime, civilians held a dominant position. Military officers comprised only sixteen of the seventy persons named to the House of Representatives. The first Premier was a civilian, chosen, it has been reported, in preference to a candidate put forth by the military. The first constitution was written by a civilian, and the committee appointed to draft the permanent constitution was mainly civilian. Under these circumstances, the civilians might have emerged as the leading force in the government had they remained unified. But they did not. Before the end of the first constitutional government, a serious division developed between the younger men, who had promoted the coup and were fired with the idea of revolution, and the older, more conservative bureaucrats, who had been invited into the government after the coup to lend solidity and respectability to the new regime.

Fractures began to appear in the government in the first part of 1933. After several months of tension, the differences among the discordant elements led to a crisis when a dispute arose between Dr. Pridi Phanomyong, the youthful intellectual leader of the coup, and *Phraya* Mano, the older, more conservative bureaucrat who, although not a participant in the coup, had been chosen to serve as Premier. The dispute, which initially involved an economic plan, developed into a virtual countercoup, in which *Phraya* Mano closed the National Assembly. This was a blow at the coup group as a whole. Several military leaders of the group, with the approval of many high civilian officials, reacted by seizing power and reopening the Assembly. Their position, which might be considered a prototype for subsequent reactions on occasions of military intervention, was characteristically lofty and impartial. They were opposed to the ideas of Pridi and the methods of Mano. Thus, for the second time in a year, the proponents of constitutional government revealed their dependence upon military support.

The indispensability of the army having been demonstrated. the important question for the future was who was to turn the army into his personal constituency? The answer to the question was complicated. Within the ruling group, the military and civilian elements were in uneasy balance and the period of *Phraya* Phahon's government (1933–38) was one of inner conflict in the military. *Luang* Phibun Songkhram, because of his role in the seizure of power from *Phraya* Mano and in the suppression of a rebellion in October, 1933, emerged as the most prominent of the young army officers. In 1934, he became *Phraya* Phahon's Minister of Defense. The dynamic manner in which he built up the military, as well as the ruthless way in which he suppressed opposition to himself and the regime, cemented his grip on the army organization. During his tenure, the budget of the defense establishment doubled. He also undertook a campaign of public relations which emphasized the indispensability of the military to the nation. He made speeches comparing his administration favorably with the royal administration and saying that a strong military was necessary to prevent other countries from bullying and oppressing the kingdom.[6] By his activities, he constructed a solid constituency in the army. Thus based, his influence surpassed that of his rival, Dr. Pridi, and, in 1938, he succeeded *Phraya* Phahon as Premier.

Between 1938 and 1944, Phibun Songkhram and the army were firmly in control of the country. Phibun instituted a nationalist policy directed initially against the Chinese minority in the country and then against France on the borders of Indochina. The latter conflict brought Thailand under the umbrella of Japan's developing strength in Southeast Asia. In December, 1941, Phibun took Thailand into Japan's camp and linked his fate and the political position of the army to Japan. Phibun's coming to power and the increasingly warlike situation in which the country found itself meant greater influence for army officers in the government. Civilians continued to cooperate, although with less and less enthusiasm. One by one, the more important civilians withdrew or were ousted from the government. Thus the military established their role of political dominance.

The Army in the Postwar Period

The overthrow of the Phibun cabinet in 1944 was the first direct challenge to the position of the army in politics after the take-over in 1932. It occurred when, confronted by the decline in power of Japan, with whom the armed forces had associated their fortune, and by increasing hardships in Bangkok, civilians took heart and moved against Phibun and the group of officers around him. With Phibun on the side lines, the influence of the military went into a decline. From his ouster in 1944 until the coup d'état of 1947, only five army officers held posts in eight cabinets.

In the process of revising the constitution in 1946, the civilians—Pridi and his followers—who had come to rely heavily on parliamentary strength, attempted to use the rationale of a professional government service as a barrier to military politicians. Section 66 of that constitution prohibited permanent officials (including military officers, of course) from holding political posts. This provision was maintained in the three constitutions that were in effect between 1946 and 1951, but it did not appreciably deter ambitious officers of the services. Despite this constitutional support, the military dramatically returned to power in the coup of 1947, in an action that was fundamentally against Dr. Pridi's civilian parliamentary group. Initially, the coup group had the cooperation of the Democrat Party, a civilian parliamentary group opposed to the incumbent regime, but this cooperation dissolved within a few months. Of the thirty-six leading figures

[6] Kenneth P. Landon, *Siam in Transition* (Chicago: University of Chicago Press, 1939), pp. 54–55.

of the coup, thirty-three were army officers, two were air force officers, and one was a police officer.

In the words of its leader, the coup of 1947 was carried out to "exonerate the honor of the army which had been trampled under foot."[7] At the same time, the military leadership assumed the authoritarian role of savior of the nation from "the dishonesty and evil of various kinds of the government circle,"[8] and thereby took as its trust the guarantee of orderly and good government. Such a posture served admirably to rationalize the authority of military leaders in politics.

The three services did not support the coup with equal enthusiasm. The leaders of the coup were predominantly from the army, and there were competing groups with support from the navy and marines, as well as in the National Assembly.[9] The coup leaders beat back two serious challenges to their power from other military groups—one in 1949, and the other in June, 1951. As early as 1948, an attempt to undermine their control of the army itself was stopped short.

Encroachment by parliamentary politicians was tolerated, while opposition within the armed forces was a potential threat. But in late 1951, after a thoroughly unsuccessful attempt by navy leaders to seize power, the National Assembly was dissolved. On the authority of the coup group, the constitution of 1932 was reinstated, including the tutelage provision by which half the assembly was appointed by the government. By means of this consolidation, the leadership of the coup d'état group achieved overwhelming political power. By putting loyal officers and followers in all controlling posts, the army has been able to maintain its control and authority over the bulk of the government's organization.

CONTROL OF THE ARMY

It is difficult to distinguish by observation between an army leader with a political role and a politician whose constituency is in the army. But analytically there is a distinction. It is clear that in Thailand, only an army officer can call upon the loyalty of the army to support him. But it is not clear at what rung on the political ladder an officer ceases to be an army man and loses his personal contact and influence with the action units. Wherever that may be, he comes to rely on his manipulation or placation of intermediate officers, who themselves have other alternatives.

The events of 1952–57 are instructive in this regard. After institution of the half-appointed Parliament in November, 1951, the coup d'état group

[7] W. J. Prasangsit, *op. cit.*, p. 170.

[8] *Ibid.*

[9] There are three military services in Thailand—army, navy (including marines), and air force—as well as a paramilitary police force. The three services are administered by the Ministry of Defense, and the police is a department of the Ministry of Interior. All of these services have distinct political roles, and each has at least some troops available for deployment. The political distinction among them appears to be less ideological than organizational. This is not the place to elaborate the cliquish nature of Thai political life, but it is relevant that the various services have been from time to time associated with one or another conflicting clique, which may or may not be mainly military.

was firmly in control of all the military services, the police, the administration in general, as well as the National Assembly. But within the group were three cliques or potential cliques: the first centered on Phibun Songkhram, the second on Phin Chunhawan-Phao Siyanon, and the third on Sarit Thanarat. In retrospect, it appears that in 1952 the leaders of these three cliques each had a different level of relationship to and influence over the army. Field Marshal Phibun Songkhram lost his direct contact with the army commanders of regimental level probably no later than 1944, when he was retired from the Supreme Commander's post by Pridi. When the group came to power in 1947, he was important because of his great fame, and because he symbolized the honor of the army. But it was General Phin Chunhawan who was active in recruiting army commanders to the coup. In 1952, Phin was making his last stand as army commander. His political activities had already extended far beyond the army into business and a variety of other matters. His clique was being transformed by his son-in-law Phao into a complex organization that combined control of the police, the government parliamentary group, and other activities.

By 1952, General Sarit, who had joined the 1947 coup as a regimental commander, was in command of the army in Bangkok, and thereby probably in effective control of the army's political activities. He replaced Phin as Commander in Chief of the Army and was promoted to Field Marshal in 1954. By this time, the coup d'état group was in a process of dissolution. What evidently happened was that as General Phin became more involved in political activities outside the army, he lost control of it. His position came to depend on the power of his son-in-law General Phao, whose influence in the army was meager. At the same time, Field Marshal Phibun's position in power depended upon the mutual support of Field Marshal Sarit and General Phao, who were about the same age and inevitably in competition to succeed Phibun as leader. These two cliques were mutually exclusive, and the rise to the top by one of them would be incompatible with the expectations of the other. Between 1955 and 1957, the cliques intensified their differences, the Phibun and Phin-Phao groups finally being ousted by Sarit, who, backed by the army, moved in to "clean up the mess."

New elections, administered by a caretaker government appointed by Field Marshal Sarit, were conducted in December, 1957. They were carried out in a quiet atmosphere, and public interest was low. After the election, Sarit tried to form a new parliamentary group, which was intended to amalgamate the various elements of parliamentary support, appointed or elected. Sarit, suffering ill health, named his immediate deputy in the army to the Premier's office and went abroad for medical treatment.

The new government was faced with a number of financial and political troubles that weakened its authority. Falling revenues obstructed the drafting of a satisfactory budget. Disparate elements in the government's military and parliamentary support presented conflicting claims and demands, and the difficulties were exacerbated by opposition politicians and newspapers. The government was not capable of decisive action. The situation moved from one minor crisis to another until October, 1958, when Field Marshal Sarit suddenly returned to the country and, in another bloodless coup, overthrew the constitution and set himself up as a military dictator.

In January, 1959, a new temporary constitution was decreed. It provided for an appointed assembly with the dual function of a legislative body and a constitutional assembly. The government was given broad discretionary powers. The Field Marshal took the Premier's office himself. A tough line was proclaimed against dissident elements and corruption. A number of the loudest parliamentary and journalistic opponents of the government were jailed, and a few men were executed for political crimes. The Sarit group had again established tight army control on the machinery of the government in the pattern of the coups of 1947 and 1951.

THE ARMY AS A POLITICAL ORGANIZATION

What is the reason behind the fact that the relative power of the army among the various bureaucratic agencies has been overwhelming since 1932? Is it not that an army is a bureaucratic agency par excellence? There are certain characteristics, inherent in an army, whose combined effect is an ability to act decisively at the opportune moment. In this regard, the army is superior to rival organizations. Not the least of these characteristics is control over weapons. But arms alone are not sufficient to explain the phenomenon.

After armed strength, the most outstanding of the army's characteristics is the nature of its organization. The organizing principle of a modern army is its unequivocal hierarchy. This principle, whatever troubles it may have caused the armies of modern Western democracies, is admirably fitted to the traditional modes of social organization in Thailand. Even though the Thai army is historically an innovation, its hierarchical structure is completely harmonious with Thai attitudes.

Research in connection with the psychological content of social organization, carried out in the village of Bang Chan in central Thailand by associates of Cornell University, is very suggestive in this context. The research of the Cornell group is based on limited sources, namely, a few villagers, and extrapolation, of course, has its usual risks. Yet the homogeneity of Thai society makes plausible the extension of some of the Cornell conclusions. Given Thai social organization, urban as well as rural, political as well as domestic, military as well as civilian, these judgments are reasonable.

The essence of the analysis is that the Thai understand social organization only when patterned in subordinate-superordinate terms. In the words of L. M. Hanks, Jr., and Herbert P. Phillips, "Group coherence depends on status inequality. It is difficult for an equal to give anything of value to an equal or to command his 'respect.' Indeed he stands as a potential competitor for favors. Group solidarity requires . . . framing unambiguously the relative rank of each."[10]

The military is, of course, very successful at "framing unambiguously the

[10] "A Young Thai from the Countryside: A Psychosocial Analysis," in Bert Kaplan, ed., *Studying Personality Crossculturally* (New York: Harper, 1961). . . .

relative rank of each." In a society with a social-psychological taste for hierarchy, a military organization (*qua* organization) will likely be a strong one, particularly in comparison with that which seeks to follow more egalitarian principles. To strengthen its organization, the Thai Army can call upon the disciplines of loyalty and swift punishment. Respect, deference, and loyalty to one's superiors are also important elements of traditional Thai social thought, and its army is able to tap these feelings without being embarrassed by any novel ideas of equality and freedom. Such feelings, which lead naturally toward good discipline, are also reinforced by a system of courts martial.

The army has further means to develop solidarity and *esprit de corps*. With its own distinctive uniforms and insignia, ranks and titles, and other symbolic apparatus of the organization as a whole, or of particular units, members of the army can be expected to have an allegiance to the organization, as well as to individuals in it. Members of the army, particularly the officers, become concerned about the place and role of the organization on the national scene. The army's honor becomes an issue of personal honor. The fate of the army is the fate of each officer. This *esprit*, built upon an in-group psychology, can be further intensified by a general attitude of patriotism. The army's role as the defender of the nation makes it appear uniquely important that its dignity and honor be upheld.

Soldiering, moreover, is now a profession. The esoteric arts of government are combined in the army with the esoteric arts of warfare. The management of large units of men is matched by the management and operation of large machines and weapons. The sciences of tactics and strategy are in the possession of the army. The fate of the nation, it is maintained, depends upon the degree to which army officers are permitted to practice these arts and sciences unencumbered by petty and niggling demands. *Esprit de corps* and in-group attitudes, while to some extent characteristic of all governmental units in Thailand, are practically nonexistent outside the bureaucratic organizations. Hence the ability of the military, particularly the army, to mobilize large numbers of men for coordinate action has given it a distinct advantage in controlling political action.

Since the beginning of the constitutional regime, the Ministry of Defense has enjoyed a high degree of autonomy, and within the ministry the army has been the dominant service. The ministry's appropriation is succinctly stated in a few lines in the annual budget, and there is no indication that nonmilitary agencies make inquiries into the military's expenditures. The ministry itself is staffed almost entirely by officers under discipline. The position of the army is indicated by the fact that all ministers have been army officers, as have been the permanent undersecretaries. The army's share of the defense budget invariably has been greater than that of the other services.

The Ministry of Defense engages in a number of extra-military activities. It directs several industrial enterprises, including a fuel-distribution organization and factories producing batteries, leather goods, glass, woven cloth, and canned food. Military units operate a majority of commercial radio broadcasting stations in the country. The ministry is a major shareholder in the Military Bank (Thanakan Thahan), a private commercial venture. This type of administrative autonomy is widespread in the government, but in the military it is highly developed, for two reasons. One is the very simple consideration that the army wants it that way and can insist on it. The second is that the military has control of far greater financial resources than other agencies and therefore has an unusual degree of flexibility. Such administrative free-wheeling has a tendency to run away with itself and has become increasingly difficult to bring under outside control.

The military not only enjoys great administrative autonomy but is judicially independent. Soldiers live under strict military law and are tried in military courts. The sway of military law has at times been extraordinarily broad. For example, in 1939, when a group of conspirators was brought to trial for revolt, it was decided by the government, then under Phibun Songkhram's firm control, that because some of the accused were army officers, all of them should appear before a special court under military law.[11]

Finally, the recruitment and training of its own personnel make up perhaps the most important aspect of the autonomy of the armed services. These activities are particularly important in regard to the officer corps. The army, as well as the other services, maintains cadet academies that receive large numbers of applicants because of the prestige of the military officer's role. The staff, consequently, can be quite selective in choosing personnel, a process that in itself helps to create the image of the officer corps as an elite group. The graduates of the military academies are generally freed from routine administration, which is left to graduates of civil universities, who are obliged to spend a period of time in the service. Control over education permits the army to mold the mind of the officer candidate, including his attitude toward politics. Under such circumstances, it is not surprising that military officers in Thailand share certain attitudes and ideas that distinguish them from civilians.

It may help to explain the soldier's role in politics if we consider some of his allegiances. The first has to do with his attitude toward the nation. One of the most important justifications of the military is its purpose as bearer of the national honor, defender of national independence, and symbol of national status in the world community. In a selection of messages to the army on Army Day in 1955, we find the following statements that support the above view. "It is a matter of certainty that the Thai Army is an up-to-date army equal to the armies of other countries. . . . It is a certainty that the army is capable of maintaining the independence of the Thai nation very firmly and in a way that is fitting to the honor of the Thai nation as well. . . ."[12] "Thailand is a country which is independent and fully sovereign; so it must have an army to shield, defend, and maintain its independence and sovereignty undivided. . . . During the time that I was Commander in Chief of the Army, I tried to the best of my

---

[11] *Bangkok Times Weekly Mail*, February 6, 1939, p. 23.
[12] Field Marshal Phibun Songkhram in *wan kong thap bok* (Army Day) (Bangkok: 1955), unpaged.

ability to bring about rapid progress in the army so that it would be the equal of the armies of independent nations of the same rank, and I tried fully to develop our army speedily beyond those of our neighbors which have just recently joined the ranks of independent nations. . . ."[13] "The highest duty of a soldier is to shield and defend the nation from the threats of its enemies so that the people can live happily and at peace. Soldiers receive the highest honor and trust from the nation. . . ."[14]

A second allegiance of the Thai officer is to the simple virtues: love of duty, love of honor, and love of nation, to mention only the foremost. [And] the academy seeks to inculcate these virtues in the young officers. . . .

Finally, the soldier is oriented toward action and leadership. The military academies put a great deal of emphasis upon qualities of leadership in the training program. One may assume that decisiveness and even aggressiveness are rewarded to a greater extent in the army than elsewhere in the Thai bureaucracy.

Imbued with a sense that the nation's fate and honor depend on him, along with a somewhat limited view of moral and political virtue, and a tendency to act rather than to reflect, the Thai officer does not long hesitate to press his case and that of the army itself. What is good for the army is good for the country. His ethics make few demands on restraint or patience, and his conception of virtue sustains a self-confidence that is reinforced by his experience as an army officer who is seldom questioned or challenged by subordinates. In short, he tends to be decisive, active, and assured.

In contrast with the indoctrinated and politically minded officer, the common soldier of Thailand is generally indifferent to politics. His social horizon is not likely to extend far beyond his village, and his education is at best four years of elementary school. In the services, he is schooled in loyalty and obedience to superiors. As a two-year conscript his devotion to the army is limited. In short, he is a politically indifferent and docile pawn in the leader's political game.

In addition to strength of organization and tendencies of character that fit the army well for the game of bureaucratic politics, qualities that are not exclusively associated with the army, there are others peculiarly its own. They fall under three heads: mobile force, leisure time, and effective rationale.

Because control of the capital means effective control of the government, the army units based in Bangkok are crucial for maintaining the political role of the army. They are under the single command of the First Army. Precisely how many troops there may be in the Bangkok area is not public knowledge, but the figure is certainly much higher than any other group could muster. The men are all compactly located to the north and east of the city and can be rapidly activated by telephone. Among the troops stationed in Bangkok is at least one battalion of tanks, which inevitably ap-

13 Field Marshal Phin Chunhawan, *ibid.*
14 King Phumiphon, *ibid.*

pears at each periodic declaration of emergency. Since the declaration of an emergency is not an unusual occurrence, one may assume that the army has a standing plan for such occasions. The orderly establishment of patrol by army units at key locations in the city at times of declared emergency is one of the more impressive displays of organized activity to be observed in the city of Bangkok. Its significance is surely not lost on politicians.

In the many coups and revolts since 1932 that have involved a show of force or sustained fighting, the army has never failed. On the six occasions when the army took the offensive to change the political situation, namely, June, 1932, June, 1933, November, 1947, November, 1951, September, 1957, and October, 1958, the seizure of key points in Bangkok and the arrest of certain leaders proved sufficient for success. On the three occasions when fighting took place, October, 1933, February, 1949, and June, 1951, the army successfully beat back moves to oust it from power. In the first of these—the Boworadet Rebellion—the fighting was in fact between certain upcountry garrisons and the combined force of Bangkok army garrisons and navy ground forces. In those of 1949 and 1951, the army fought with the cooperation of the air force and the police against naval and marine troops. This history of the use of force in politics clearly indicates that the army has been sufficiently determined and strong to impose its will on its opponents, and probably will continue to be.

The leisure time that an armed force enjoys in a state that is the size and in the position of Thailand has to a large extent been devoted to political activities and intrigue. As has been indicated, the military has served occasionally as an instrument of diplomacy, as in World War I and in Korea, in both of which Thailand was represented by token forces. Presumably the military would ordinarily devote its attention to planning for defense from external attack, and considerable staff effort does go into such work. But there must be serious doubts about the Thai military as an instrument of national defense.

Such doubts arise not from an inability or unwillingness to fight. It is rather a question of whether the defense of Thailand is or will be a matter of its own independent military action. Early in the twentieth century, when Thailand was squeezed by France and Britain its only defenses were diplomatic. From 1909 to 1941, Thailand lived at peace under the umbrella of European imperialism. Japan substituted a parasol in 1941, with little resistance from Thailand. The switch back in 1945 came without fighting. At present, Thailand is on the marches of the free world, its fate largely in the hands of the United States and China. Whatever its capabilities, the Thai military has been largely untried.

The army leadership, freed, perhaps unconsciously, from a sense of responsibility for defense, has therefore been at leisure to plan action in the political arena. In this respect, the military has an advantage over all other government organizations, since the latter have continuing administrative obligations to keep them occupied. The police, for example, who share the use of force with the military, are charged with such a variety of duties that they cannot undertake strong political action against the military.

The third function of the army—the maintenance of internal security—furnishes a rationale sufficient to justify the army's political activities. The question of what actually constitutes a threat to internal security is a subtle one, as any student of the history of civil liberties knows. In the recent history of Thailand, the military on various occasions has taken it upon itself to judge this question and has overthrown governments, suppressed dissident elements, and beaten back countercoups in the name of civil order.

THE ARMY IN THE SYSTEM

By its success, the army is confronted with the tensions that pervade the Thai political system: an authoritarian tendency, at once welcomed but illegitimate and irregular; and an egalitarianism, which is legitimate but does not work. At present, the authoritarian pattern, demonstrated by the army's dominant position, is ascendant and is bolstered by social tradition. The removal of the throne from politics in 1932 by no means ended traditional attitudes toward authority characterized by uncritical acceptance of orders from above. As has been indicated, such attitudes survive in the psychological content of social relations, and the army has become their most powerful repository. In turn, they form the basis of much of the army's own solidarity and, given their pervasiveness throughout the government, provide the psychological means (supplemented by organizational strength and arms) to control the government. In its relationship with other groups and institutions, the army seeks to subordinate rather than to eliminate. There is no indication that the army's leadership has any desire to revolutionize the nation's social or economic system. In general, it has been conservative and in some respects reactionary, and this in spite of the fact that its dominance is a result of the reduction of royal power. The army has always accepted the view that it should rule the country through the bureaucracy, a bureaucracy that by Asian standards is very successful. The army has also developed such congenial working relationships with business interests that they are not likely to be precipitously destroyed.

But, at the same time, its own authority to rule is extralegal. Its legitimacy is open to challenge from any group that dares. Such challenges, under the circumstances, tend toward open power conflicts occasionally involving shooting. To give the appearance of some legitimacy, the army has made a show of adherence to constitutionalism, and in doing this has repeatedly created problems for itself. The National Assembly, as a symbol of constitutionalism, has been particularly troublesome in this regard. Those members who are appointed can, of course, be controlled, but elected members have resisted the more subtle techniques of authority. Their stentorian voices have often been stilled, but only by offices, privileges, and other bribes. An increase in tension has been evident in recent years, and perhaps only by such means as Sarit's current practice of postponing constitutional decision can peace in Thailand be maintained.

24

THE ROLE OF THE MILITARY IN DEVELOPMENT PLANNING: BURMA*

LOUIS J. WALINSKY

Two words in my topic title require definition. Development can be narrowly construed to refer to economic development only, or it can be construed more broadly to embrace social and political development as well. Planning similarly can be interpreted literally and narrowly to embrace only the planning function. It can, alternatively, be interpreted broadly to include also the programming, policy making and implementation functions. Because my subject matter so requires, and because the concept of development planning in Burma—at least during my direct acquaintance with it—was broadly construed in both these respects, I, too, shall follow these broader constructions.

The role of the military in relation to development planning in Burma falls historically into four phases. The first of these, and the longest, was the Anti-Fascist People's Freedom League (AFPFL) period from early 1948 to the fall of 1958, which began with formal independence and terminated with the political split of the ruling coalition party and the advent of the first military government. The second phase covered the life of the military "caretaker" government—which lasted some eighteen months into the spring of 1960, at which time General Ne Win voluntarily surrendered power to a newly elected civilian government under U Nu, in accordance with a pledge made at the time of take-over that he (Ne Win) would assume power only long enough to insure free and fair elections. The third phase lasted roughly two years, until March, 1962, when the military

* Reprinted by permission of the author and the publisher from *The Philippine Economic Journal*, No. 8, Second Semester, IV (1965), 310–26.

peremptorily seized power, this time without reservation or pledges to observe the Constitution. The fourth phase has been in process ever since, and bids fair to continue for an indeterminate time into the future. I shall develop my topic in relation to these historical phases.

PHASE I—THE AFPFL PERIOD OF CIVILIAN RULE

The AFPFL government, which took on responsibility for governing independent Burma in 1948, was, as is well known, dominantly Socialist in composition, views, and aspirations, and dedicated to the creation of a welfare state under a system of parliamentary democracy. With the exception of two Communist splinter groups (the Red Flags and the White Flags), one paramilitary group (the PVO's) and one large indigenous minority group (the Karens), all of whom soon went into underground opposition to the government and continued to wage guerrilla warfare against it through the years, the AFPFL government was virtually unopposed. Legal opposition parties were few, weak, and irresponsible. Burma had, in effect, a one-party system during these years.

The military, it should be noted, shared the government's socialist, welfarist, and neutralist ideologies. The new military elite, significantly, were not professional soldiers. The officer corps, during the period of British rule, had been comprised largely of Indians and members of the indigenous minority groups—the Karens, the Chins, the Kachins—rather than the Burmese majority. After independence, the new officer corps, and especially its elite, was, however, drawn from the same group of Burmese nationalists who led and won the freedom fight. They were, in Brigadier Aung Gyi's words, "not soldiers who became Socialists." They were rather "Socialists who became soldiers." This fact has considerable significance for all that follows and may make the Burma case a highly special rather than a general one.

This change in the composition of the officer corps was accompanied, though in a lesser degree, by a similar change in the ranks. Whereas the enlisted men during the British time had also been drawn predominantly from the minority peoples, their ranks were now swelled by Burmese who, coming in the main from the impoverished peasantry, were ardent followers of the AFPFL. There were, thus, no distinctions or latent conflicts of caste, race, class, or political views between the officer elite and the men in the ranks, just as there were none between the military and the political elite. We begin, therefore, with a military leadership that shared fully the ideology and aspirations of the civilian government and that supported fully its program of economic and social development under a constitution dedicated to socialist gradualism, welfare, and reform. While the army saw as its own immediate task the suppression of armed insurrection, it recognized that its longer-run task was to modernize and, thus, develop a capability to meet its responsibilities for safeguarding the national security. This, in turn, rested on the country's successful development.

Throughout the AFPFL period, the military's relation to development planning was tangential rather than integrated. The military did not participate in the long-term planning or annual budgeting processes, either as participating staff or at the interdepartmental review level or at the policy-making level. Their plans were separately and autonomously developed and were expressed in annual budgetary demands, both current and capital. These demands were not screened or even examined by the planning and budgetary staff and authorities, and certainly not by the foreign advisers, who recognized at the very outset of their service that such an activity on their part would be inappropriate. Military budget demands and plans were separately reviewed at a political level within the Prime Minister's office, and the current and capital budgetary provisions there determined were taken as given by the planners. Military claims had, in a real sense, a first claim—and a heavy one—on resources. In a setting of general disorder, when no other investment could possibly deliver a greater income response than could progress toward law and order in the countryside, such a priority was not only warranted but indeed mandatory.

There were several other ways—still in this Phase I—in which the military through either their activities or their views impinged on the development planning process.

The military early developed an interest in and a rapport with their opposite numbers in Israel. This coincided with a broader rapport developed on a political level between the two governments, which began with their association in the Asian Socialist Congress. So far as the military were concerned, they were especially interested in the colonization activities of the Israeli army and in its universal registration and mobilization plans. The Burmese military were interested in the colonization of sparsely settled areas near their borders, not only for national security reasons but also to create employment opportunities and to minimize potential unrest among discharged soldiers, who might otherwise swell the insurgents' ranks. Their interest in Israel's universal registration plan was with an eye to its role in promoting internal security controls and the eventual introduction of a military draft. These areas of collaboration were supplemented by others—training in military aircraft operation and maintenance, in military hospital personnel staffing and training, in physical rehabilitation, and so on. And their cooperation on the military level opened the way to a much broader program of technical cooperation and assistance between the two countries which soon extended to agriculture (irrigation, experimental farms, and general planning) and public enterprise, marketing and management.

Another military activity of interest during this period, although it became consequential to development in major degree only later on, was the creation of the Defense Services Institute—a kind of military post-exchange, where many common consumer items were sold to military personnel at discount prices. The volume of business transacted became quite large. But more important than this was the development of an organization and staff with a procurement and marketing capability and a capability for considerable future expansion as well.

So far as other projects are concerned, I suspect that the views of the military played at least a contributory role in the planning decisions to build a steel mill and to build or rebuild certain roads. Perhaps the decision to build a large pharmaceutical plant was influenced by them as well.

I come now to a more tenuous and delicate relationship between the military forces and development. Partly because of a growing mistrust of one another among the civilian political leaders and groups, and perhaps also because some political leaders lacked full confidence in the army, several other paramilitary groups were brought into being or were strengthened—the national constabulary, local volunteer militia forces, and so on. Some of these groups took on the coloration of private armies. Their discipline was poor, and many suspected that they contributed to, rather than pacified, disorder in the countryside. As the years passed and political tensions within the AFPFL became exacerbated, the existence, indiscipline, and suspected personal and partisan loyalties of these groups—and their potential role in a civil war between the split political groups—were an important factor in the first political take-over by the military leadership.

The fear of civil war was not the only factor in the decision of the military to assume power temporarily in 1958. The military elite had watched with dismay, with scorn, with a wounded sense of national pride, and with a growing sense of shame the fumbling and inept administration of the development effort by the civilian government. They had seen too many evidences of captious, irresponsible, and impetuous planning decisions and of essential decisions too long deferred and evaded. They had seen the administrative and policy-making functions of the government constipated by red tape and indecision, the public enterprises mismanaged by policy makers who would not delegate authority to professional managers, who were not interested in accounts, records, or performance, and who would not call those responsible to account. The military knew that orderly decision making and efficiency needed to be brought into public affairs. They were confident of their ability to provide them. This, as much as the political chaos that had been created by the split within the ruling AFPFL, motivated the military in their initial assumption of political responsibility.

PHASE II—THE MILITARY CARETAKER GOVERNMENT

The circumstances I have just described, together with General Ne Win's pledge to set up a "caretaker" government that would hold office only long enough to establish law and order and to insure that free and fair elections could be held, explain the relationship of the military to development planning and the development process during the next year and a half. The primary aims of the first military government were to restore law and order, to instill discipline, and to "tidy up the (administrative) mess" created by the politicians. I have described the details of this effort elsewhere, and it will not be necessary to repeat them here. Crispness in decision making, delegation of authority and responsibility in a clear-cut chain of command, efficiency and discipline were the order of the day, and, indeed, much was accomplished by these emphases, albeit with a certain degree of ruthlessness and disregard of human sensibilities.

These priorities were concerned naturally with the implementation of development rather than more narrowly with its planning. Administration, policy, and management were all involved across the entire spectrum of widespread public-sector activities. Improved law and order, increased efficiency in governmental offices, services, and enterprises, and the introduction of a new climate of dynamism and social responsibility all had significance for social and political, as well as economic development.

Specifically, among its more important contributions, the military caretaker government emphasized more intensive farming methods and improved yields, and improved the efficiency of the land nationalization and distribution program. It terminated the ban on cattle slaughter and thus relieved pressure on fish and fowl supplies and prices. It enlarged the capital of the State Agricultural Bank and enforced repayment of outstanding agricultural loans. It paid price premiums for improved paddy and for better grades of milled rice and improved teak milling and marketing. Completion of a major hydroelectrical project was expedited. Greater utilization of capacity in state-owned manufacturing plants was achieved, and improved accounting pointed the way to remedy their operating deficiencies. Industrial investment legislation was enacted, and an industrial development bank was established. Tax collection was tightened. Private firms were allowed to participate more fully in rice exportation, and incentives were provided to stimulate other exports.

These and other measures I have not paused to mention were notable and constructive, even though they represented almost entirely proposals that had long awaited action by the AFPFL government without success. Over and above their actual effects, they created an atmosphere of action and achievement which was itself important to further development efforts.

While General Ne Win himself was reluctant to undertake new development projects, the Defense Services Institute previously mentioned did expand its activities enormously, under the aggressive management of Ne Win's then right-hand man, the talented and driving Brigadier Aung Gyi. Mostly by taking over existing private enterprises, but also by initiating new ones, the DSI within a short period was operating a huge economic complex that comprised banking, department-store merchandising, road construction, ocean shipping, fishing. shoe manufacture, radio assembling, restaurant operation, coal and coke imports, and still other commercial activities. The formula for DSI's apparent success was simple: expeditious, beneficent governmental assistance in providing supplies, markets. licenses, and whatever else was necessary, plus professional managers, to whom was delegated a relatively free hand to run the enterprises in a businesslike way. While the latter alone could not have sufficed in the absence of the former, this delegation of managerial authority struck a fresh and badly needed note in the field of public-enterprise management in Burma.

The policies and activities of the first military government were not all of a positive nature. Chauvinistic antipathies against minority and alien groups—chiefly Indians—were indulged. These found expression particularly in discriminatory and repressive measures against trading and some manufacturing firms and inhibited both private investment and the contribution of the talents of the minority communities. Even more important was the general atmosphere of fear imposed by the domineering attitude of the military generally. Talent, initiative, and independent thinking were repressed. The government not only prohibited dissent, it was intolerant of criticism as well. In such a climate, physical progress might be made. But real development—the economic, political, social, and cultural flowering of a people—could not take place.

The real test of this was not to come until later. In the spring of 1960, the military permitted free elections to be held. Significantly, the electorate voted overwhelmingly for the return of U Nu and his new Pyidaungsu Party. While many factors contributed to the electorate's decision, an important element in their choice was the popular belief that the military government favored the election of U Nu's Socialist opponents, the "stable" AFPFL group led by U Ba Swe and U Kyaw Nyein.

Phase III—The Brief Return of Civilian Rule

Short though the life of the military caretaker government was, it lasted long enough for several fissures to appear in what had originally been the monolithic façade presented by the military. The first of these separated the politically minded from the nonpolitical soldiers, who believed that the military did not belong in politics, that political intervention would damage the military image and ultimately weaken the armed forces as an instrument of national defense. This officer group was, however, unorganized, operated for the most part in field assignments, and played a relatively passive role in the military's decisions. The second fissure separated those officers who were genuinely development-minded from those who were not. Brigadier Aung Gyi was the outstanding example of the former group; Ne Win, at least during the caretaker-government phase, was seemingly inclined toward the latter position. A third fissure separated those aggressive and ambitious officers who believed that, having seized political power, it would be a mistake to surrender it. Brigadier Aung Shwe and Colonel Maung Maung were leaders of this group. And finally, another and less visible fissure separated those officers who were weak and venal enough to seek personal profit from those who were honest and idealistic enough to do their duty without seeking material rewards.

Upon the return of the civilian government to the center of the political stage and to power—a power limited this time by the fact that the military stood watching in the wings, ready to exert a veto over individual measures, or to assume full control again whenever they chose to do so—two of these divisions within the military elite became increasingly important. Prime Minister U Nu, perhaps because he desired to direct the military's energies into constructive channels, perhaps because he sought allies within their ranks, encouraged Brigadier Aung Gyi to continue expansion of the DSI's economic activities and program and even negotiated a huge development credit with Mainland China, in the utilization of which Aung Gyi and the DSI would obviously participate in major degree. Steps were taken to convert the DSI into a civilian organization—the Burma Economic Development Corporation—with the proviso that military officers who wished to remain in charge of its operations and manifold activities would have to don civilian attire.

Second, the political extremists within the military agitated for a second take-over of governmental responsibilities. Since Ne Win was not, as early as 1961, prepared to do so, they apparently plotted to seize control without him. This plot was nipped in the bud, and Brigadier Aung Shwe, Brigadier Maung Maung, Colonel Tun Sein, and others were neutralized in typical Burmese fashion by being dispersed and dispatched on far-flung overseas diplomatic assignments.

The role of the military during this third phase resolved itself into one of watchful waiting. This may be charitably interpreted as waiting hopefully to see whether the politicians had indeed learned enough from the 1958 debacle to settle down to serious, responsible, and effective government. It can, perhaps more realistically, be interpreted as waiting patiently for the civilian government to provide sufficient occasion and excuse to justify a second, and this time permanent, military take-over without obligation to pretense at observing constitutional mandates. Whichever of these was actually the case, the occasion was not long in coming. Prime Minister U Nu's new party soon developed still another internal and serious split. U Nu himself, interpreting democracy to mean universal consent, condemned himself to inaction on vital issues. New long-term development plans were mooted but not really seriously. The old indecision and inefficiency returned. And the minority hill peoples—Shans, Chins, Kachins, Karens—who had been pushed around by the military caretaker regime and wished to safeguard themselves against more of the same in the future—pressed for greater autonomy within the Union and even for separate status. U Nu's posture in response to these pressures was too soft to please the military. By March, 1962, General Ne Win and his colleagues felt the time was ripe. They believed they could now as patriots seize power in violation of the constitution—this time for keeps. And so they did.

PHASE IV—THE "REVOLUTIONARY MILITARY GOVERNMENT"

Since that time, the military have concentrated first on consolidating their political power and suppressing dissent; second, on wholesale nationalization of the economy, pursuant to their decision to find "a Burmese Way to Socialism"; third, on attempts to negotiate peace with the insurgent forces; fourth, on ridding Burma of alien minority groups—chiefly Indians; and finally, on stepping up the pace of capital formation and economic development.

The consolidation of power involved, variously, abrogation of the constitution; dissolution of the Parliament; arrest and confinement without charges or trial of practically every political figure of consequence, from the President, the Prime Minister, and the Chief Justice of the Supreme Court to leaders of the minority peoples and lesser politicos, and of potential critics as well; the ouster and political neutralization of Brigadier Aung Gyi, who was apparently out of sympathy with the pace of nationalization and other extremist measures; the take-over of mass organizations; the intimidation of university students; and so on. Related to this consolidation of power were the sharp reduction of contacts with the diplomatic community, the ouster of nondiplomatic Western personnel and activities, such as the Ford and Asia Foundations and the British Council, the denial of entrance or stay visas to journalists or visitors, and the virtual closing of the exit door to Burmans who desired to leave. Whether this regressive withdrawal from outside contacts was motivated by a desire to shun "corrupting" influences, or by a fear of exposing themselves to objective and possibly critical eyes, may be debated. What cannot be debated is that the military have created in Burma virtually a closed society. Finally, the program of consolidation of power included an attempt to create a new and reliable political party of "national solidarity"—with what success I do not know.

As regards the nationalization of enterprises, it is necessary to recall that, even under the AFPFL civilian government, the public sector already embraced major transport and communications, electric power generation and distribution, virtually all large manufacturing plants, rice and teak exports, major sawmilling, and the import and distribution of many essential consumer goods. If one considers joint enterprises in which the government was involved as a full partner as also constituting public-sector activities, then major mining and oil extraction and refining were also included. To these the military have added virtually all other enterprises, with the exception of farming and indigenous petty trade and manufactures. Banking, insurance, wholesaling, department stores, larger general stores, some medium-sized manufacturing, all exports, imports and their internal distribution, and so on have been nationalized, as have been all foreign-owned operations. Thus, agriculture remains virtually the only economic activity of major consequence in private hands.

Concomitant with the consolidation of power, withdrawal from the international community, and nationalization, resident aliens have been leaving the country en masse. The largest group to be affected comprises Indian nationals, long residents in Burma, who are being involuntarily evacuated by the shipload, leaving all their property and possessions behind. This extends, I understand, even to the wedding rings on women's fingers, although evacuees are being permitted to take with them the equivalent of some $15 in currency. Among these evacuees are not only the merchants and traders but also doctors, lawyers, engineers, mechanics, artisans, and persons of other sorely needed talents and skills whom Burma can ill afford to lose.

During its first year or so in power, the Revolutionary Government made every effort to conclude peace with the various insurgent groups. Negotiations were conducted at some length, but with little success. Communists of two varieties, and representatives of almost every important indigenous group—Shans, Kachins, Chins, Karens—continue to conduct guerrilla warfare against the government.

Lastly, as of the adoption of the budget for the 1963–64 fiscal year, the military decided to embark on a much enlarged capital-investment program, with special emphasis on agriculture and industry—the results of which will not be apparent for some time.

The motivations underlying the nationalization decision must be related to some judgment on the part of the military as to why the AFPFL government and program failed. The judgment here could have been that the AFPFL government extended the area of public-sector responsibility far beyond its capacities for efficient administration. The military by their decision appear to have concluded (a) that the AFPFL weakness was a weakness of planning rather than of execution, administration, management, and policy; or (b) that the AFPFL failure resulted from timidity, in not going far enough with nationalization rather than from going too far; or (c) that their own administrative capabilities were so considerable that they could carry successfully an even greater burden than that which broke the back of their civilian predecessors. Perhaps all three judgments were involved. I suspect, however, that other elements also entered significantly into the decision. In a puzzled search for answers to why the golden expectations that attended the country's independence had not been realized, the failure to build quickly a fully socialized economy remained one of the few as yet untested hypotheses. Since the key military leaders were, for the most part, as simple-minded and unsophisticated in their knowledge of socialism as they were about most other areas of knowledge, and since they were by profession activists, the decision to nationalize fully must have been a tempting one to make. Reinforcing these was the desire—perhaps even the inner need—to justify their violation of the constitution, which only a radical departure in basic policy and program could provide. Finally, and not to be underestimated, was the need to undercut the programmatic appeal to the underground insurgent Communist groups—an appeal that might otherwise spread rapidly among a population resentful of military control.

It will have some relevance for our topic if I observe that the military appear to believe that all these programs I have mentioned are essential to Burma's future development; that they appear to view long-term development planning with some suspicion and prefer to plan from year to year, using the budget-making process as the vehicle for this annual planning; that they appear to be mobilizing resources rather effectively and allocating them in a rational, pragmatic manner; and that their international trade and balance of payments policy is mercantilist in character, being designed apparently to build up as large a volume of foreign exchange reserves as possible, even though this was accomplished till recently at the expense of tremendous increases in the privately held money supply. (The privately held money supply was substantially reduced during fiscal year 1963–64 by the demonetization of currency notes of larger denominations, which were called in for exchange, but which will be redeemed only if the authorities are satisfied as to how they were acquired. For the most part, the demonetization constitutes an expropriation obviously aimed at the Indian community but which has undoubtedly hit hard many Burmese as well.)

It is too early to evaluate the impact of the military on that most general of development measures—the gross domestic product (GDP). In fiscal year 1962–63, the first full fiscal year of this government, the GDP rose some 5.2 per cent in constant prices. Increases were recorded in almost every sector, particularly in agriculture and manufacturing. In fiscal year 1963–64, however, despite a budgeted rise in public investment of more than 50 per cent as compared with estimated capital outlays in 1962–63, the GDP is reported to have declined by 1.8 per cent in constant prices and by more than 6 per cent in current prices. Declines in agricultural and manufacturing production appear again to have been chiefly responsible, as they were for the increase the previous year. While the official Economic Survey of Burma attributes the fall in agricultural production in 1963–64 to bad weather, one suspects that this is not the entire story. And the reasons for the declines in private sector investment, manufacturing, and other activities are all too clear.

Such, in brief outline, is the record thus far. What does it mean and what does it portend? It seems to me quite conceivable—quite likely, even —that the military will accelerate the pace of Burma's economic development, at least in physical, material terms. Agriculture, industry, electric power, transport and communications, forestry, fishing, mining—these all bid fair to progress, provided the military are not so foolish as to attempt to extend the nationalization process to the nation's farms, and provided they are flexible enough to permit at least a partial return of domestic and foreign trade to the private sector if they find—as perhaps is already evident —that the government cannot adequately perform these functions. We must recognize that whatever their naïveté, their lack of moderation, and their ruthlessness, the military really have been the revolutionary government they set out to be. They have effected basic changes in the country's economic structure and relations and may well continue to build on these rearranged foundations. In this respect, they resemble General Nasser's Egypt far more closely than they do other military regimes.

The Burmese military have displayed some imagination and much daring. They have obviously brought sorely needed organization, decision-making ability, drive, determination, and administrative competence to the development process. They obviously have the will to modernize—in the ways, that is, that they understand. And, importantly, they have undoubtedly inflicted a sense of culture shock upon the entire nation, which was perhaps necessary to jar and bring into question the entrenched traditional culture that stood as an almost immovable obstacle in the way of effective national development.

But development is more than economic. It is part of a nation-building process based on individual human beings. It embraces men and institutions in their social, political, and cultural, as well as in their economic, relations. In terms of these broader criteria, we are confronted with quite a different picture. For the military have been in these fields a regressive, not a constructive, force. They do not communicate; they give commands. They do not encourage men to initiate, to innovate, to grow taller than they are; they require them uncritically to comply and even to bow.

Repression—rule by force rather than by consent—necessarily involves a basic instability. The military have progressively alienated almost every important group in the national community—civil servants, intellectuals and students, businessmen, the numerous indigenous minority peoples, and, very importantly, the Buddhist clergy. Although the government has extended agricultural credit at moderate cost to the nation's farmers on a massive scale—a strategic and constructive move—it is doubtful whether even so positive a factor will suffice to offset the numerous other factors influencing the peasantry against the military government. Important among these are the peasant's affectionate loyalty to the still-imprisoned U Nu, their devotion to the clergy, and the enforced purchase of their produce by the government at controlled prices. Finally, there probably exist severe strains within the officer corps itself.

Economic prospects are thus threatened by social and political tensions and instability. These are perhaps as likely to bring on civil war, or to deteriorate over time into apathy under a series of corrupt military regimes on the historic Latin American model, or even to open the door to a foreign master, as they are to bring the benefits of modernity to Burma.

Development under the Burmese military is therefore necessarily limited in scope. It is not the fuller development that can be achieved only by a free society. And although the military regime may serve ultimately as a transition to a freer society—even as Soviet society seems at long last slowly and painfully to be evolving—we cannot, as democrats, believe that development of this kind and at such human cost is worth the price.

25

RELIGION AND POLITICS IN MALAYA*

K. J. RATNAM

Until the end of World War II (and, with some modifications right up to 1957, when Malaya achieved its independence), British administration in the Malay States was based on a system of indirect rule.[1] A characteristic

* This paper was presented in slightly different form at the Twenty-seventh International Congress of Orientalists (Ann Arbor, Michigan, August, 1967) and is published here by permission of the author. "Malaya" is a shorthand term employed here to mean the eleven peninsular states of western Malaysia.

[1] The Straits Settlements of Singapore, Malacca, and Penang were administered as a colony. The Malay states were divided into two categories: the Federated Malay States (comprising Perak, Pahang, Selangor, and Negri Sembilan) and the Unfederated Malay States (made up of Kedah, Kelantan, Trengganu, Perlis, and Johore). As implied by the names given to the two categories, British rule was more direct in the former group of states.

There was a brief period after the war when indirect rule was abandoned: between 1945 and 1946, when there was a military administration, and between 1946 and 1948, when the ill-fated Malayan Union proposals were in operation. (The Malayan Union was abandoned mainly as a result of Malay opposition. Although this opposition was aimed primarily at the drastic liberalization of citizenship rules that allowed vast numbers of non-Malays to become citizens, an important factor was the severe reduction in the prerogatives of the sultans, including their control over religious affairs.)

feature of the agreements between the British Crown and the Malay rulers, on which the system was based, was that the latter had full authority on matters concerning the religion and customs of the Malays. This naturally helped to soften the impact of British rule, and the fabric of Malay society was generally left undisturbed. The non-Malays, not being seriously affected by this arrangement, found little cause for complaint. Further, at least before the war, they were essentially a transient population and did not involve themselves to any great extent in local political affairs. Another important feature of this period was the absence of representative institutions. This helped to keep political competition between the communities to a minimum; consequently, the Malays had fewer anxieties about their political status vis-à-vis the other communities, particularly since the non-Malays had not by this time begun to enjoy the rights of local citizenship.[2]

It is only since the immediate preindependence period that religion has come to assume any serious political significance in Malaya. The factors that gave it this significance are not difficult to understand.

As soon as independence was imminent and the process of drawing up a new constitution was set in motion, a vigorous controversy developed over those features of the constitution that would determine not only the broad framework of government but also the manner in which political and economic power should be shared between the different communities.[3] A viable equilibrium had to be found between the need to provide certain safeguards for the Malay community (which, as the indigenous community, had been accorded a "special position") and the necessity, at the same time, of guaranteeing full citizenship rights to the non-Malays, who, by this time, had become a part of the settled population.

The Malays had two important preoccupations, both arising from their desire to safeguard their political pre-eminence in the country: first, they wanted the constitution to serve as an instrument that would give Malaya certain external features of a Malay state; second, they wanted to secure political and economic advantages that would help them improve their position in relation to the other communities. Islam, being regarded as a chief component of Malay identity, naturally became involved in the efforts to promote the first goal. In the event, there was not much difficulty in having it established as the state religion [4] although it was necessary to assure the sultans that the creation of a state religion would not undermine their own status as heads of the faith in their respective states. It was, how-

[2] In the Straits Settlement, however, no political distinction was made between Malays and non-Malays, since all were equally regarded as British subjects.

[3] The Malays constitute just under 50 per cent of the total population of Malaya, which stands at about 8 million. The Chinese constitute about 38 per cent and the Indians about 12 per cent. Although no single community forms a clear majority, it is important that the indigenous population is slightly outnumbered by the non-indigenous. The Muslim population (which includes all Malays), however, slightly outnumbers the non-Muslim.

[4] The Malay character of the state was also promoted by certain other provisions, such as the preservation of the sultanates, the creation of the post of Yang di-Pertuan Agong (the Supreme Head of the Federation), and the acceptance of Malay as the national language.

ever, not the intention of those responsible[5] for establishing Islam as the official religion of the Federation that Malaya should thereby become a fully theocratic state. Care had to be taken not to provoke any new fears among the non-Malays, and one way of doing this was to emphasize the purely symbolic content of the constitutional provision in question, while guaranteeing that other faiths would not in any way be made to suffer disabilities.[6] Thus, it is stated in clause (3) of article 11 of the constitution that every religious group has the right, "(a) to manage its own religious affairs; (b) to establish and maintain institutions for religious or charitable purposes; and (c) to acquire and own property and hold and administer it in accordance with law." As regards educational rights, clause (2) of article 12 states: "Every religious group has the right to establish and maintain institutions for the education of children and provide therein instruction in its own religion, and there shall be no discrimination on the ground only of religion in any law relating to such institutions or in the administration of any such law; but federal law may provide for special financial aid for the establishment or maintenance of Muslim institutions or the instruction in the Muslim religion of persons professing that religion."[7]

Although it was not intended that Malaya should become a theocratic state, it was unavoidable that the mere fact of establishing Islam as the state religion, in combination with the strong undercurrent of communal politics in the country since independence, would generate conflict over the practical consequences that should or should not be implicit in such a provision. Put simply, there has been a continuing agitation from some sections of the Malay community that the purely symbolic value attached to the constitutional provision that elevates Islam to its national status is not satisfactory. Leaders of the Pan-Malayan Islamic Party (PMIP), for example, have been steadfast in maintaining that article 3 of the constitution (which establishes Islam as the state religion) has turned out to be nothing but a dishonest political maneuver by the Alliance, and that if their own party came to power they would see to it that genuine "Islamic principles of administration" were adhered to.[8] On more specific matters, controversy has ranged from matters like the adequacy or otherwise of government financial support for Islamic religious schools and the recognition of qualifications obtained in them, to whether alcohol should be served at state functions and whether it is proper for Muslim girls to participate in beauty contests.[9]

[5] In effect, the Alliance, headed by the United Malays National Organization (UMNO), on whose recommendations the entire constitution was based.

[6] The major festivals of all main religious groups, for example, are declared public holidays.

[7] There is one exclusive safeguard that Muslims enjoy. This is contained in clause (4) of article 11, which states: "State law may control or restrict the propagation of any religious doctrine or belief among persons professing the Muslim religion."

[8] Although this assertion is frequently made, the PMIP has never been explicit about the actual content of "Islamic principles of administration."

[9] In late 1966, there were protests from certain Malay organizations about the impropriety of Malay girls taking part in beauty contests. The Penang Malay Youth Patriotic Organization, for example, set up a special "Banning of Beauty Contests"

Although a decade has now passed since Malaya achieved its independence, the feeling has persisted among the Malays that "Malay nationalism" still has an important role to play in the country. Not surprisingly, this nationalism derives its inspiration from the belief that the Malays are the true "sons of the soil" and that Malaya therefore is, or should rightly be, a Malay country. The goals of Malay nationalism are, therefore, at least partly based on communal antipathy toward the non-Malays, and are, to this extent, a result of the frustrations felt by the Malays in having to accommodate themselves to a multiracial society where they are slightly outnumbered. Despite the attainment of independence, they feel unable to claim full ownership of the country and resent being inhibited in their efforts to promote their own language and culture. An important residue of nationalist aspirations thus continues to be of relevance in determining the political outlook of the Malays.

Given this continuing importance of "nationalist" appeals, one can see why many Malay political leaders (notably those in the PMIP) have attempted to bring about a more effective political unification of their community. It is also not difficult to understand why these attempts should have included references to the religious identity of the Malays, since this clearly constitutes an important source of communal solidarity. But before we go on to evaluate the substance of religious appeals, it may be useful to have a brief account of the UMNO and the PMIP, the two main contenders for Malay support. Such an account will enhance our understanding of the main postures that have been adopted in appealing to the Malay communal vote, and will also give some indication of the role played by religion in Malayan politics.

The United Malays National Organization (UMNO) is both the oldest and the most prominent political party in Malaya. It was founded in 1946 to lead Malay opposition to the Malayan Union scheme. It harnessed the emerging nationalist sentiments of the Malay community[10] and succeeded in unifying that community on a scale that was surprising in the light of prewar experience. As a result of the party's activities (which involved the mobilization of mass protest on a large scale), the Malayan Union scheme

---

Committee and urged the Islamic religious authorities in the country to take action on this matter, stating: "We are protesting against participation in such contests by Muslim girls purely on religious grounds. . . . It seems to us that Muslim girls in this country are beginning to get enthusiastic over beauty contests. Some of them have even gone beyond the religious limits and trespassed Islamic and cultural decorum." (*The Straits Times*, November 3, 1966.) But these protests failed to find receptive ears in the highest circles. The Prime Minister failed to see anything in Islam that forbade the participation of Muslim girls in these contests (*The Straits Times*, December 20, 1966), while the Minister for Education (who is also the Secretary-General of the UMNO), commenting on criticisms that had been leveled against a Malay school teacher who had participated in a beauty contest, observed: "Anyone who is pretty and has the potentialities is entitled to take part in a beauty contest. . . . As for her posing in a bikini, all I can say is that she was exercising her constitutional rights." (*The Straits Times*, October 17, 1966).

[10] These sentiments, although directed at the colonial government, were provoked to a large extent by fears of non-Malay domination.

was withdrawn and replaced by the more pro-Malay Federation of Malaya Agreement.[11] Thus, during its early years, the UMNO was without question a party that dedicated itself solely to the cause of protecting Malay interests by firmly opposing the claims of the non-Malays to increased political rights. Indeed, so strong were its suspicions of the non-Malay communities that it chose to allow its president, Dato' Onn (who could have claimed considerable personal credit for the popularity of the UMNO and the withdrawal of the Malayan Union Scheme), to resign from the party rather than accept his proposal, made some two years after the Malayan Union Scheme had been withdrawn, to allow non-Malays to become associate members of the UMNO.[12]

However, by 1952, when municipal elections were first held in the country, the UMNO had lost some of its earlier intransigence. It was willing to form a partnership with the Malayan Chinese Association (MCA) in Kuala Lumpur, where the first elections were held, in order to defeat Dato' Onn's newly launched Independence of Malaya Party (IMP). But this was purely a local election alliance, in which the primary concern did not involve the formulation of a common platform; the chief aim of the two parties was to maximize their chances of success by presenting a united front against the IMP and by apportioning seats in such a manner between themselves that UMNO candidates would be put up in Malay wards and MCA candidates in Chinese wards. Success at this and subsequent municipal elections, however, encouraged the two parties to consider their partnership more seriously, and this led in 1953 to the formation of the Alliance Party. Just before the first federal elections in 1955, the Malayan Indian Congress (MIC) was brought into the fold.[13]

With the formation of the Alliance, the UMNO unavoidably had to moderate its earlier outlook to accommodate its non-Malay partners. From being a party whose horizons did not go beyond serving Malay interests, it became a party which, while retaining this characteristic, nevertheless had to satisfy certain non-Malay demands. While it originally saw Malay and non-Malay interests as necessarily in conflict with each other, the UMNO now had to view these admittedly divergent interests as being capable of

[11] Among other things, the Federation of Malaya Agreement restored the sultans to their prewar status, imposed more stringent regulations regarding the eligibility of non-Malays to become citizens, and gave official recognition to the "special position" of the Malays, which entitled them to certain privileges in recruitment to the Civil Service, the awarding of scholarships, and the issuing of business licenses.

[12] After his resignation from the UMNO, Dato' Onn founded the noncommunal Independence of Malaya Party (IMP). When this party failed, he reverted (but without much success) to his original role as champion of Malay rights through Party Negara, another party which he helped to found.

[13] The Alliance Party is thus made up of three component units, and individual membership is confined to these units. It exists only at different coordinating levels (constituency, state, and national) and comprises delegates from the member bodies. Although the party represents intercommunal ideals and contests elections as a single unit, its strength lies basically in the support given directly to its constituent organizations.

accommodation within a common framework of intercommunal partnership.

The PMIP is undoubtedly the most extreme communal party in Malaya. Although its name might indicate a preoccupation with religion (and Islam undeniably constitutes an important cornerstone of its appeal), it is a communal party in a more general sense, in that its activities cover all aspects of Malay welfare.[14] It is unwilling to concede that the non-Malays have a legitimate place in the country and sees its goal of protecting Malay rights primarily as an effort to stave off the "non-Malay threat." The party's support is concentrated in the predominantly Malay states in the north and northeast, the most tradition-bound and economically backward areas in the country, where it has been able to put its religious and anti-Chinese themes to profitable use. It also has the advantage of being the UMNO's only serious rival, as a result of which it automatically becomes the chief beneficiary of Malay dissatisfaction. It is, however, worth pointing out that although the PMIP's uncompromising stand on communal issues gives it a basic core of support and enables it to profit from Malay protest, the same stand is also an important weakness in that it virtually rules out all chances of the party's coming to power at the national level. Not only will non-Malay support never be forthcoming,[15] but even Malays in the more advanced states of western and southern Malaya will find many of the party's present attitudes repugnant.

A convenient and effective way of assessing the significance of religion in Malayan politics would be to focus attention on the importance of religious appeals during elections. This could be done by looking at the relevance of religious issues in election campaigns and by evaluating the role played by religious elites in mobilizing party support.[16]

The main debate on religious issues has tended to be between the PMIP and the UMNO. At first glance, this may appear a little curious: If the religious theme is essentially a part of Malay nationalism, how is it that the conflict on religious issues has not been between the PMIP and the strongest non-Malay party, but rather between the two main Malay parties in the country? The explanation lies almost entirely in the fact that the chief contenders for support in the rural areas, where the population is predominantly Malay, have been these two parties. It would certainly be unrealistic to conclude that the non-Malay parties in the country are any less opposed to the PMIP's platform, or that they do not fear any increase in that party's support; at least during elections, they have had to concentrate on winning seats in the areas where their candidates were contesting (that is, in the predominantly non-Malay urban areas), and attacks on Malay religious extremism would not have been too relevant to the issues that

[14] The fact that the Muslim population is almost entirely made up of Malays has no doubt made it easier for the PMIP to play this dual role.

[15] In 1964, the non-Malays constituted about 45 per cent of the total electorate.

[16] For a detailed account of these aspects of the campaign in 1964, see K. J. Ratnam and R. S. Milne, *The Malayan Parliamentary Election of 1964* (Kuala Lumpur: University of Malaya Press, 1967).

separate them from their opponents.[17] Further, non-Malay politicians have also felt reassured that the UMNO, not only because of its electoral rivalry with the PMIP, but also because of its partnership with the MCA and the MIC and its belief that the PMIP's obscurantist policies are not in the best interests of the Malays, will do their work for them. These leaders have perhaps also realized that the UMNO's attacks on the PMIP will be far more effective than attacks by non-Malay parties.[18]

As pointed out earlier, one of the PMIP's chief complaints has been that the adoption of Islam as the state religion has not in itself been sufficient either to elevate the status of that religion adequately or to produce the desired practical consequences. In this connection, the party has bitterly attacked the UMNO, allegedly the custodian of Malay interests, for having overlooked an important element of Malay welfare and identity, namely religion. In a similar vein, the UMNO has also been accused of sacrificing spiritual advancement for material progress of dubious promise, and, in any case, of being unqualified to represent Malay interests because of its collaboration with "infidels." The party's alleged disregard for the tenets of Islam was further conveyed by the PMIP during the 1964 elections in the form of certain specific accusations—for example, that the Alliance government had allowed Chinese to rear pigs near Malay homes, and that the Tungku had danced the twist with girls who had been competitors in a Koran-reading competition during Ramadan, the Muslim fasting month. It was reported that the PMIP had also, in the course of its door-to-door campaign, warned Malay voters that they would be going against the dictates of Islam if they voted for non-Islamic parties or even parties (like the UMNO) which worked in close collaboration with non-Muslims.

The UMNO's response to these tactics and allegations has rested on two main arguments. First, it has maintained that the PMIP's interpretation of the Koran is perverse and likely to damage not only the prospects of peace and harmony in the country but also the future progress of the Malay community. The PMIP's attempts to create a religious basis for communal unification and Malay political protest have frequently been condemned as both unnecessary and irrelevant when the true interests of the Malay community are considered. Several examples have been given of the party's irrational and obscurantist approach. During both the 1959 and 1964 elections, it was alleged that the PMIP had made rural Malay voters swear on the Koran that they would vote for its candidates. Apparently votes were solicited on the grounds that the contest between the PMIP and the UMNO was not merely one between the candidates of the two political

---

[17] It should be made clear that the effective contest in most urban constituencies tends to be between candidates from different non-Malay parties.

[18] Since there is no risk of non-Malays being attracted by Malay communal propaganda, it is only the Malay voters who have to be persuaded not to endorse the PMIP's extremist platform. Given the importance of communal politics in Malaya, non-Malay attacks on Malay communalism, particularly in Malay-dominated areas, may backfire by producing greater communal solidarity among the Malays. Malay leaders are therefore more likely than others to receive a sympathetic hearing when they campaign against the PMIP's extremism.

parties but between "messengers of the prophet" and "infidels." The party was alleged to have insisted that it was *haram* (forbidden) for Muslims to cooperate politically with non-Muslims, and a great deal of attention was given to its alleged "whisper campaign" in the less sophisticated areas of Kelantan that those who supported political parties that had non-Muslims in them (for example, the Alliance) would be regarded as infidels who, in addition to suffering various other calamities, would have their marriages annulled in heaven. In Kelantan and Trengganu, the PMIP was accused of having made use of talismans, chain letters, and even love charms.[19] It was linked with the circulation of certain allegedly "seditious" pamphlets, which contained quotations from the Koran and Hadith and which purported to serve as "guides for Muslims during elections."

This kind of politics, the UMNO has argued, is not merely obscurantist —it is also likely to endanger the future of democracy and communal harmony in the country by giving the Malay community the false impression that it is at odds with its political environment. This view was expressed with unmistakable firmness by the Prime Minister, who, in the course of an election rally in 1964, observed:

> I have warned the PMIP before to cease inciting the people [to fight] each other. This time I will take stronger action. If they dare defy me, go ahead. I'll fight back. I will arrest those who want to destroy the unity of our people. Democracy should be pursued through persuasion. That is the essence of democracy. We cannot force people into accepting our point of view, leave alone incite them to wage a holy war against those who are not members of the PMIP.[20]

At another rally he had this to say:

> [The PMIP's] policy is particularly dangerous because there are almost the same number of Malays and Chinese living in Malaysia. No party should ever play the game of religious and communal politics. If ever the people accept the policy and propaganda put out by the PMIP and other Opposition parties, then there will be trouble and chaos in the country. Malaysia might even end up worse than Cyprus.[21]

The second argument used by the UMNO in countering the PMIP's allegations has been that it is at least as concerned as its rival in promoting the interests of Islam, and that, unlike its rival, it has solid achievements to back its claims. In this connection, great political capital has been made of the vast sums of money that have been spent by the federal and (Alliance-controlled) state governments in building mosques and small prayer houses. The PMIP, in contrast, has been said to be unable to boast of any

---

[19] The talismans apparently urged Muslims in the country to wage a holy war against non-Muslims. The love charms were allegedly sold to unsuspecting kampong women with the warning that they would not produce the desired consequences in the case of those who voted for the Alliance!

[20] Quoted in Ratnam and Milne, *op. cit.*, p. 122. A few PMIP men were, in fact, arrested in 1964, under a law that prohibits incitement to communal hatred.

[21] *The Straits Times*, March 31, 1964, quoted in Ratnam and Milne, *op. cit.*, p. 124.

similar achievements in Kelantan, where it has been in power since 1959;
it had come to power there by posing as the champion of Malay rights and
Islamic principles of administration but had promoted neither during its
period in office. In its campaign pamphlets issued during the 1964 elections, the Alliance also claimed credit for promoting such things as Koran-
reading competitions (which are held, not infrequently, at state, national,
and international levels), religious education, and pilgrimages to Mecca.

Turning now to the role played by religious elites in political campaigns,
the first thing to note is that the local (that is, sub-state) rather than the
national elites constitute the most relevant groups. High-ranking religious
officials seldom pronounce on political issues and do not generally become
involved in partisan activity. At the village level, however, local religious
elites are often active in promoting the interests of the party of their
choice. Secondly, the activities and influence of these elites should, ideally,
be studied in relation to those of other local elites (particularly the local
administrative elites, like the *penggawas*, *penghulus*, and *ketuas kampong*),
because they operate in a common milieu and either compete with or com-
plement each other's activities. It is, however, well beyond the scope of this
paper to attempt a general discussion of all categories of local opinion
leaders.

The political influence of religious elites is by no means widespread
throughout Malaya, but, by and large, is confined to those areas where the
competition between the UMNO and the PMIP is keenest. In areas where
the PMIP is weak, or where the population is unresponsive to religious
appeals, these elites are naturally reluctant to embark on serious political
activity; such activity would be unrewarding. Also, in the absence of any
PMIP threat, there would not be the same incentives for the UMNO to
conduct its campaign through persons whose main value would lie in their
ability to counteract the PMIP's appeal. It is, therefore, not surprising that
the rivalry for the support of religious leaders has been keenest in Kelantan
and Trengganu (and, to a lesser extent, also in Kedah and Perlis); these
states provide fertile ground for religious propaganda, and they have witnessed a close rivalry between the UMNO and the PMIP.

Among local religious elites, four groups may be mentioned: religious
schoolteachers, imams, *mubhalirs*, and gurus. In some ways, those in the
first group have only an indirect political influence; they do not campaign
openly during elections,[22] but, because of their contact with parents, are
able to exert a certain degree of influence. There are, however, other ways
in which they have made their political importance felt. Together with
Malay schoolteachers, they have constituted an important pressure group
that has endeavored to goad the government into adopting more "positive"
measures in promoting Malay as the national language. The influence of
this pressure group has, needless to say, been enhanced by the fact that,
between them, its two component units represent the areas of Malay cul-

[22] The reference here is only to government religious schoolteachers. Private religious schoolteachers have been known to campaign vigorously, usually on behalf of the
PMIP.

ture (namely, language and religion) that are politically the most sensitive and therefore receive considerable attention from those who want to promote a more explicitly Malay identity for the state, and who wish to confirm Malay pre-eminence in the country's political life.

The next two groups, the imams and the *mubhalirs*, are part-time officials of the State Religious Councils and are, to that extent, semigovernment servants. As such, they are precluded from active political participation, particularly when their state government is not controlled by the party they wish to support. But the religious significance of their duties, and the fact that they come into frequent contact with the people, gives them a fair amount of political influence, particularly in the more traditional rural areas. In Kelantan, where they were active during the 1964 elections, both the UMNO and the PMIP were agreed that the support of these groups was an important factor in deciding the outcome of the elections.

The final group, the gurus,[23] are in many ways the most influential. They are private religious teachers who enjoy informal recognition as the main spiritual guides of the communities in which they operate. While the other groups mentioned are civil servants of one kind or another (and, to that extent, perform duties that are at least partly of a routine kind), the relationship between the gurus and the communities they serve is highly personalized. They have closer and more intimate contact with the people than the other groups have, and, being the main stalwarts of the traditional society, naturally have an easy rapport with the rural population in the less developed states, notably in Kelantan. They are regarded with some reverence as men with a genuine spiritual calling who have dedicated their whole lives to unfolding the true meaning of Islam. Not being government servants, they also have the advantage of being more free than the other groups to participate actively in political campaigns.[24]

In Kelantan, the PMIP clearly enjoys the active support of the majority of the religious elites discussed above, and it owes its success to this fact. In the other states, the situation is less one-sided; in fact, the UMNO often has a slight edge, but this is not of equal significance, because in these states the religious elites are both less active and politically less influential. The difference, as indicated earlier, can be best explained in terms of the more traditional nature of Kelantan society, which has helped to sustain the influence of traditional opinion leaders. Because of the continuing importance of traditional values and relationships, there are also more religious leaders in Kelantan than in the other states. Although the PMIP, in its efforts not to be outdone by the Alliance, created an elaborate election organization in 1964 based on a functional decentralization of responsibility right down to the village level, it was apparent that this was aimed at bolstering the morale of rank-and-file members, by giving them individual

[23] Referred to as *tok* gurus in Kelantan and *tuan* gurus in the other states.

[24] In fact, it was the gurus who were alleged to have been responsible for distributing the talismans referred to earlier. They were also believed to be the ones who most actively encouraged, and played on, religious superstitions.

duties to perform, and partly at preventing the Alliance from having an advantage by being the only well-organized party in the rural areas. It was evident during the campaign that the PMIP relied less on its formal organization than on individuals outside it (namely the religious leaders) for the success of its campaign.

In conclusion, it is worth emphasizing that religion does not derive its political significance in Malaya from the conflict between different faiths. The issue must be viewed primarily as a component of the more general rivalry between the Malays and the non-Malays. Religious appeals for political ends are confined to the Malay community and are, in the main, directed at unifying that community by emphasizing its separate identity and interests. Religious and anti-non-Malay slogans almost always go hand in hand and are aimed at persuading the Malays to be more vigilant in safeguarding their pre-eminence in the country's political life and, as a corollary, to be less compromising in their relations with the other communities.

But one cannot completely dismiss economic underdevelopment and the continuing pulls of traditionalism as being irrelevant. As shown in the preceding pages, these factors at least influence the forms and the content of political persuasion, in that religious appeals and the use of religious elites in political campaigns are more rewarding in the less-developed and tradition-bound areas of the country. However, the most crucial factors that explain the political importance of religion are to be found not in the traditional versus modern but rather in the Malay versus non-Malay continuum. The conflict between traditional and modernizing interests might have become the dominant factor only if the Malays had constituted the entire population (or at least a very substantial part of it), or if the communal differences between the Malays and the non-Malays had failed to assume much political significance. In actual fact, however, intra-communal differences have tended to be very much overshadowed by the more serious conflicts *between* the Malays and non-Malays.

26

POLITICS IN THE PHILIPPINES*

CARL H. LANDÉ

THE PREMODERN CHARACTER OF PHILIPPINE PARTIES

Perhaps comparisons of the Philippine party system with those of other countries will better illustrate some of its distinctive features. Present-day Western Europe offers nothing comparable, but the American party system has several parallels. In fact, one may say that the Philippine party system accentuates the peculiarities of the American system. Thus, in the United States, parties are not very far apart in their positions on most questions of public policy; Philippine party positions do not differ at all. In the United States, interest groups and political parties operate independently of one another, though certain groups tend to throw their support in an election to the party whose traditional policies are more acceptable to members of the group concerned; in the Philippines, interest groups are not only organizationally independent of the political parties but over the long run treat both parties with fine impartiality. In the United States,

* Reprinted by permission of the author and publisher from Carl H. Landé, *Leaders, Factions, and Parties: The Structure of Philippine Politics* (New Haven, Conn.: Yale University, Southeast Asia Studies, 1965), pp. 101-23.

parties continue to be to some degree what Maurice Duverger calls "cadre parties" of the nineteenth-century type, that is, a "grouping of notabilities for the preparation of elections, conducting campaigns and maintaining contact with candidates." Though a partial evolution into "mass parties" of the twentieth-century type is evident in the American system of primary elections, Philippine political parties are in almost every respect "groupings of notabilities."

It is particularly interesting to note the many ways in which the intra-party and cross-party factional rivalry of provincial and municipal politics in the Philippines resembles the factional rivalry found in the United States within the dominant Democratic Party in the South, a region whose social and economic systems have a good deal in common with those of the Philippines.[1] What large portions of the American South and the Philippines have in common, of course, is that both, to a high degree, are agrarian societies characterized by sharp differences in wealth between a landowning gentry and a class of poor farmers, some of whom own their land, but many of whom work as sharecropping tenants or as agricultural laborers upon other people's land. The closest parallel to the Philippines in the American South is to be found in the "black belt" regions, where Negro tenants and laborers work on land owned by white landowners. But the parallel must not be pushed too far. The racial division between white landowners and Negro tenants and laborers has permitted the former largely to disenfranchise the latter, a state of affairs not found in the Philippines. Equally important, the presence of a lively two-party system in all parts of the Philippines means that most local as well as national election contests in that country are dominated by two leading candidates, who, in turn, are supported by groups whose more or less permanent rivalry leads them to align themselves fairly steadily with the two competing national parties. In the American South, stable bifactionalism is found only in some states, such as Tennessee, Virginia, and Georgia, and in these states the rivalry of state factions is unrelated to the national rivalry of the two major parties.

Yet the fact that the Philippines and the American South do resemble each other in many respects, both in their social and economic systems and in their factional politics, is of considerable interest to a student of both countries, for it focuses attention upon that which distinguishes both of them from the northern United States and from modern Western Europe: The fact that the economic, social, and political systems of both the Philippines and the American South are largely preindustrial, agrarian ones characterized by marked differences in wealth between the rich and the ordinary tillers of the soil.

An even closer parallel to the Philippine pattern of political organization can be found in early eighteenth-century England. The structure of politics in the two political systems, separated in time by two and a half centuries, is remarkably similar. So are the aims of politics. So are the tac-

[1] V. O. Key, Jr., *Southern Politics in State and Nation* (New York: Alfred A. Knopf, 1949), *passim*.

tics and the style. Walcott has written an excellent account of English politics during this period, and I take the liberty here of quoting pertinent passages from his book. In English shire constituencies, though the franchise was extended to all forty-shilling freeholders, "knights of the shire did not come from the yeoman class nor from the small landowners, but were drawn almost exclusively from the upper ranks of the landed gentry" who were the "natural leaders" of the society.[2] Many constituencies were dominated by particular families so that a change in their representatives in the House often meant simply that the new member replaced a relative in the same family borough or a noble's nominee gave way to another nominee of the same nobleman. Walcott writes that:

> Theoretically the freeholder could make an independent choice, but in practice this freedom was limited to choosing between candidates previously fixed upon at informal meetings of the local landowners. Moreover, the freeholder was often a tenant for some other land and amenable to pressure from the landlord. Add to this, open polling, treating, and free transport to the often distant polls, and it becomes obvious how easily elections could be managed by the leading local families.[3]

Yet "local grandees, of course, often fell out among themselves," with the result that "ruinously expensive election contests were common in more than half the counties."

Several anecdotes told by Walcott reveal conditions very familiar to Filipinos today, for example, the tale of the young lord who charmed his constituency with his personality and the gift of a "large Fire Engine."[4] In another, we are told that despite "the most lavish promises and the most varied and elaborate methods of influence," the competitive nature of elections meant that "few corporations stayed long in anyone's pocket. At Malmesbury Lord Wharton was overthrown on one occasion, 'after he had treated and threatened the town for ten days together,'" whereupon he retired temporarily "after 'a farewell Benediction that, as they had been an ungrateful and perfidious Corporation to him, so he would endeavour to extirpate them as such and would never more be seen within their villainous town.'"[5]

Just as it does in the rural Philippines today, electoral politics in the early eighteenth-century English rural constituency revolved largely around the personal rivalries of leading members of important landed families, supported with varying degrees of steadfastness by the little people who were their clients. The outcome of an election there, as in the Philippines today, often depended on the ability of one candidate to surpass his rivals in his ability to buy the votes of those little people sufficiently independent of any gentry-candidate to be able to play off several candidates against one another.

[2] Robert Walcott, Jr., *English Politics in the Early Eighteenth Century* (Cambridge, Mass.: Harvard University Press, 1956), p. 9. Unless otherwise noted, most of the analysis of English politics of the period is drawn from this source.
[3] *Ibid.*, pp. 9–10, 102.
[4] *Ibid.*, p. 45.
[5] *Ibid.*, pp. 16–17.

The spectacle of the little people choosing great landowners to represent them in Parliament did not seem to strike contemporary observers as incongruous. The outlook and interests of the estate owners, Walcott suggests, were not widely divergent from those of their tenants, with the result that:

> The political organization of parliament . . . would interest an eighteenth-century politician far more than an analysis of occupational and social groups. He would want to know, not whether a Member was well-born or in trade, but whether he was connected with Lord A—or Lord B—; not whether he was a landowner or a barrister, but whether or not he would vote with the Court.[6]

The same may be said for the typical twentieth-century Filipino politician. He, too, finds that, viewed in terms of the universal demand for roads, bridges, irrigation works, fertilizer, and the like, the outlook and interests of the landowners are not widely different from those of their tenants. He, too, finds the occupation or social status of his fellow politicians a matter of little relevance for an understanding of politics. To him, too, the network of personal alliances, the siding of politicians with or against the president, is what matters.

There is a similarly close parallel between Philippine factions and the personal blocs into which English politicians in the early eighteenth century grouped themselves. Bound together in large part by bilateral kinship, marriage, and friendship, these blocs formed "family connexions" much like the "family constellations" of Philippine politics. The main difference is the sphere of action: In England, the rivalry was for control of Parliament; in the Philippines, familial rivalry is essentially confined to the politics of individual provinces. Walcott identifies seven family connections in the House of Commons of 1701–2, the largest having sixty-four members and their combined total amounting to 212 of the 512 members of the House. These family connections, which were usually led by members of the House of Lords to whom the members of Commons were related, together with the "Court interest" (a separate group composed to a large extent of officeholders under the Crown), constituted the "fundamental units of party organization."[7] It is the rivalries and alliances among such family connections, rather than the opposition of Tories and Whigs, Walcott argues, that best explains the structure and process of early eighteenth-century English politics.

The Philippine Congress differs from the House of Commons of 1701 in that it does not contain these large family connections. Within the Congress, the struggle for power goes on, instead, between two clear-cut if not very highly disciplined political parties. It is true that parties with

[6] *Ibid.*, p. 33.

[7] Walcott, pp. 32–33, finds that, of the ninety-seven members of Commons in 1707 who were closely related to members of Lords, "only seven belonged to a political group opposed to that of their titled relative." Walcott also finds that, in addition to these ninety-seven close relatives of peers in the lower house, "as many more members of Commons were attached to [peers] by equally strong ties: of friendship, gratitude for favours received, and the hope of more to come."

names—Whigs and Tories—were to be found in the eighteenth-century Commons as well. But they played a far less important or less structured role than do parties in the Philippine Congress. Even in 1760, six decades after the time discussed by Walcott, "the political life of the period could be fully described without ever using a party denomination."[8]

There is, nonetheless, an important point of similarity between the internal makeup of the early eighteenth-century House of Commons and the mid-twentieth-century Philippine Congress. In neither do groupings for the capture of power and groupings for the promotion of public policies coincide. In both, the two types of groupings are distinct and cut across one another. In the early eighteenth-century House of Commons, as described by Walcott, the Whig and Tory "parties" appear to have been not much more than loose divisions of members who took similar positions on certain questions of public policy, notably those involving the Church and the royal succession. And even with regard to such matters on which there were distinct Whig and Tory positions, there were many members who were neither consistently Whig nor consistently Tory in their voting behavior. As for the second function performed by modern political parties, collective action to win and exercise power through the running of party candidates in nationwide elections and the support of party administrations, the Whig and Tory "parties" were rather deficient. It is true that there were contests between Whig and Tory candidates for the speakership of the House. But Walcott reports[9] "no examples of a single party in office faced by a single opposition party." And there was certainly nothing resembling a nationwide organization to support the campaigns of Tory candidates or Whig candidates for election to Commons. Essentially, then, the Whig and Tory "parties" appear to have been not two organizations but two points of view.

The struggle for power in Commons and the organization of administrations were carried on by other structures, that is, family connections. As none were large enough to form governments by themselves, these family connections formed coalitions for this purpose. An administration, then, ordinarily would be headed by the leader of one connection, with lesser posts going to leaders of other connections temporarily or otherwise allied. Parliamentary support would be obtained primarily from the relatives friends, and clients who made up the connections of these leaders, and from those courtiers who could be counted upon to support any administration.[10] Neither individual connections nor alliances of such connections were uniformly Tory or Whig. Walcott notes that "the various groups tended to be 'Whig' or 'Tory' in general, but on specific issues in parliament and particularly during the intervals between the great debates all

---

[8] L. B. Namier, *The Structure of Politics at the Accession of George III* (London: Macmillan, 1929), I, vii.

[9] Walcott, *op. cit.*, p. 4.

[10] The pattern somewhat resembles the factional politics of the Japanese Diet, with the important difference that Japanese parliamentary factions (*habatsu*) compete for power within their respective parties but work together with a high degree of party discipline in confronting the opposing party.

the groups followed distinctly individual, though sometimes parallel courses."[11] As for the stability of alliances among family connections, Walcott reports that "no combination of leaders could hold together their combined following for long in the face of disagreements among themselves and defections to the Court."[12]

Another Walcott observation pertinent to any study of twentieth-century Philippine politics is that though there was, on questions of policy, a rough division of Commons into Whig and Tory parties, there was also a quite different division between the "Court party" and the "Country party." The "Court party" consisted of those who voted in favor of the Court's position on such issues as, for example, a bill banning placemen from the House; the "Country party" of those who on such issues could be expected to take the opposite view. Some members, in short, who did not vote consistently Whig or Tory did vote very consistently for or against the government of the day. As late as 1702, "it was commonly assumed that 'Court' and 'Country' were the normal divisions of politics."[13] To understand the division of Commons on questions of policy, Walcott concludes, the set of Whig-Tory coordinates is insufficient: Another set of coordinates running at right angles to the first, that of Court-Country, is equally important.[14]

In the Philippine Congress, too, alignments for the promotion of public policies and alignments for the capture of power do not coincide. (Nor do they entirely coincide in the U.S. Congress, though more so than in the Philippines.) But in contrast to the parties of the eighteenth-century House of Commons, "political parties" in the Philippine Congress would have to be designated as almost exclusively alignments for the capture of power.[15] The alignments that promote public policies in the Philippine Congress are not the parties but the legislative blocs, which regularly cut across party lines. Among the most powerful are the "sugar bloc," the "tobacco bloc," and the bloc of legislators who take a special interest in the welfare of the new Filipino industrialists.

Unlike the typical "modern" party of present-day Western Europe, which serves both as the instrument for the advocacy of a common and coherent set of policies and as the instrument for the capture of power, the parties of eighteenth-century England and of the present-day Philippines performed, or perform, but one or the other of these functions. The fact that the other function in each case falls to a different alignment whose membership cuts across the lines of party may help to explain why in neither situation do party unity and discipline become as strong as in countries where ideological commitment and organizational discipline reinforce one another. Attesting to the fluidity of party lines is the ease with which

11 Walcott, *op. cit.*, p. 156.
12 *Ibid.*, p. 5.
13 *Ibid.*, p. 92.
14 *Ibid.*, pp. 92–93, 157.
15 The difference, probably, is due to the fact that twentieth-century Filipino politicians had for their models of "parties" those of nineteenth-and twentieth-century America and Europe, which, whatever else they do, certainly serve as the main instruments for the capture of power.

alliances are reshuffled in the cases of both eighteenth-century England and the Philippines.

Why, in these two political systems, do we find so little correspondence between alignment for the advocacy of policy and alignment for the capture of power? In the Philippines, the answer may lie partly in the fact that the great mass of political actors—from ordinary voters to a large proportion of the political elite—are but dimly aware of the major policy decisions a modern state must make or, aware, do not see the choices facing their government in categorical terms. Politics is seen as the struggle for power, and in this there are natural allies—relatives, friends, townmates, coreligionists, patrons, dependents, or other such people bound by "primary ties." Alignment is made with these natural allies in the struggle for power rather than with people sharing the same views on highly theoretical questions of public policy.

A reading of Walcott's description of politics in early eighteenth-century England suggests that this was probably the case there as well. And it may well be that this is the case in many other "developing countries"—so long, at least, as their peoples have not been subjected to massive doses of indoctrination by modern-minded leaders, whether Marxists or others, who want to reform their habits and teach them to think and act categorically.

Even the principal leaders in the Philippines, who compete for the highest positions in their parties and in the government, seem by and large to be preoccupied with the struggle for power per se. The formulation of policy, either in line with ideological positions assumed a priori or, more commonly, in response to the pressure of "interests," is for them an important but, on the whole, distinctly secondary matter. The conversion of Filipino politicians into power-shy ideologues or docile public servants devoted to the task of "aggregating interests" lies some distance in the future. The taming of politicians—a process far from completed even in much older democracies—must await the day when the electorate has learned to a greater degree than it has up to the present to think programmatically and to force its leaders to do the same as the price for investing them with public offices.

DEMOCRACY IN THE PHILIPPINES

The character of the political process that takes place within the framework of the Philippine party system suggests certain conclusions concerning Philippine democracy. Some insight into those ways in which the Philippine political system may be said to be democratic and into those ways in which it falls short of the democratic ideal may be gained by measuring the Philippine political process against such general criteria of a democratic political system as these: (1) That there be free and, hopefully, lively competition between rival aspirants or groups of aspirants for control of the key positions in government and between rival substantive proposals for the conduct of government. (2) That it be possible for the electorate to hold those who occupy important policy-making positions in government collectively responsible for their conduct of public affairs. In the large, modern, constitutional democracy this usually means that there must be "responsible party government." (3) That political influence be distributed widely among the country's citizens. (4) That, insofar as possible, political influence be distributed equally among these citizens.

Competition in Philippine Politics

Like the party systems of many other present-day democracies, that of the Philippines is characterized by the rivalry of two major parties, but, in contrast to the state of affairs in most contemporary democracies, these two parties are for all practical purposes identical. This fact, perhaps more than any other, sets the Philippine political system apart, making party lines neither a strong incentive to intraparty discipline nor much of an obstacle to interparty switching and demonstrably affecting the nature of political competition, the range of the voters' choices, and the content of political goals.

In some respects, certainly, there is lively competition between parties, among individual candidates for office, and among diverse proposals for governmental action. At least since the end of World War II, there has been close competition between two major parties throughout the country. By and large, in almost every constituency during these years, each party has had a reasonable chance of winning a good number of elections—and neither party, having won control of a constituency anywhere in the country, has been able to take its continued hegemony for granted.

Equally important, both between and within the two political parties there is lively competition among candidates for public office. The margin of victory in most elections has been narrow and has become ever narrower over the years. Though in most congressional elections the winner and the runner-up have represented opposite political parties, no "official" candidate of either party has been able to count on having a clear field insofar as the votes of his party's supporters are concerned. In fact, because of the write-in ballot system and the associated sample-ballot campaign device, an official candidate is never secure on election day against challenge from "rebel" candidates among his own party-mates. Such intraparty rivalry at election time—more likely to plague the stronger of the two parties than the weaker one—further lessens the margin of victory between the two major parties and increases the importance of the voting decisions made by the uncommitted voters.

The political competition continues between elections, as the Filipino citizen seeks practical assistance from elected officials. Whether a big man or a little man, the Filipino citizen can depend on the readiness of the politicians of his locality—if he has supported them—to promise him and on the whole make a serious effort to supply him with whatever he chooses among a wide variety of benefits, appropriate to his social stratum, which the government can supply.

But when we look more closely at the actual choices between parties, candidates, and substantive benefits offered the voter, we are struck by the fact that the choices are largely of a particular rather than a categorical nature. Thus, we find that the voter can choose between different parties but not between different *types* of parties; the major parties, as well as most of the minor parties of recent years, have been all but indistinguishable. Similarly, we find that the Filipino voter can choose among various candidates but not among many *types* of candidates; most of the men who compete for public office at any particular level of government are much alike in background and point of view. Though the active voter has a wide range of choice among specific benefits he may obtain for himself through his connections with politicians, he rarely has an opportunity to express a choice between two distinctive, let alone comprehensive and coherent types of programs for the government of his country. He cannot (except on the rare occasions when an atypical candidate runs on a personal program which differs from that of most of his party-mates) indicate by his vote that he is for or against more heavily progressive taxation, that he is for or against a broad program of land reform, or that he favors the interests of local manufacturers as against the competing interests of those who produce commodities for export. At most elections, both parties and the great majority of politicians offer the voter essentially the same bundle of compromises designed to satisfy as best as they can the diverse needs of all sectors of society.

Responsible Party Government?

The argument for responsible party government, put forward by various American political scientists concerned with their own country's system of government, has been summarized by Austin Ranney and Willmore Kendall[16] roughly as follows: In a large modern state, a high degree of popular participation in the daily affairs of government is not feasible. If such a state is to be democratic, its system of government must permit the electorate to exercise a high degree of control over government. For there to be such control, the voters must be able, at the polls, to choose between several—and ideally two—distinct and comprehensive programs of public policy. A majority of the voters having expressed their preference for one or the other program at election time, the electorate must be able, after the elections, to hold someone accountable for the enactment of that program into law and for its implementation through executive action. This is what is meant by "responsible" government.

Responsible government can only be achieved, it is argued, if responsibility for the formulation, propagation, enactment, and implementation of each of the competing programs is assumed collectively by a group of politicians sufficiently large to ensure joint control of all branches of government whose cooperation is needed for the execution of such a program, a group sufficiently united and disciplined to assure that such cooperation will, in fact, take place, and a group of politicians who are sufficiently stable in their commitment to their program to be able to carry it into

16 Austin Ranney and Willmore Kendall, *Democracy and the American Party System* (New York: Harcourt, Brace and World, 1956).

execution over a number of years and to enable the mass of the electorate to learn which group of politicians stands for which program.

In the modern democratic state, the group that can best perform this function is the political party. But not all parties or party systems are equally well fitted to do so. The American party system, for example, is thought to be less suited for this task than is the British party system, for American parties are less united and disciplined than British parties and the difference between the programs of the two major American parties is less clear-cut than is the difference between the programs of the two major parties of Great Britain. In the U.S. Congress, in fact, members of both parties usually can be found voting on both sides of an issue. As a result, as Ranney and Kendall have pointed out, much American legislation must be regarded as nonpartisan or bipartisan legislation, for which neither party as such can be held fully or solely responsible.

If the American party system falls short of being a responsible one, that of the Philippines does so to a much more striking degree. In the Philippines, party unity and discipline are even less in evidence, and lasting differences between the policies of opposing parties are even smaller—if discernible at all.

The results of this fact are more or less predictable: In the Philippine Congress there is little evidence of any kind of party planning in the sense that, in directing the legislative business of their two chambers, the congressional leaders of the majority party aim toward a set of clearly envisioned, long-range goals, as embodied in programmatic pre-election commitments and rooted in a distinctive, coherent, and lasting body of party principles. Nor is there in Congress the kind of party discipline that would enable a party to enact a broad program of legislation if it had one. Such party discipline as is to be found in Congress is displayed mainly in matters involving the organization of the two houses and in the appropriation, by the majority party in each house, of a disproportionate share of patronage and spoils. I have myself had the opportunity to attend many meetings of the majority caucus of the House. With few exceptions, these meetings were devoted almost entirely to the division of the public-works funds. Even on the rare occasions when an attempt was made, in caucus, to commit the members to adopt a common position on a really controversial piece of legislation, caucus members asserted the right to ignore caucus decisions when the bill in question came to a vote on the floor of the House.

If the two parties in Congress lack the unity and discipline needed to enable them to plan and enact broad and coherent programs of legislation, is there no planning at all? Is the output of a legislative session no more than a random collection of laws introduced by individual senators and congressmen, and pushed through the legislative mill individually and haphazardly, without central guidance? Is the program of Congress no more than the resultant of the personal desires of 128 senators and congressmen?

It is certainly more than that. Planning does take place in each house. Leadership is exercised. A measure of unity is displayed in voting for substantive legislation. But planning and direction do not emanate from a single party center, and unity is based only in part upon party identification. A case in point is the influence wielded by specialized economic and other interest groups. Avoiding an exclusive alliance with either party, these interest groups create legislative blocs by cultivating senators and congressmen of both parties who, for one or another reason, are willing to give fairly consistent support to legislative measures considered advantageous or to oppose all measures considered objectionable by the particular group. In the Philippines, both the "sugar bloc" and the "tobacco bloc" have among their members senators and congressmen of both parties. The leaders of these blocs, in or outside the Congress, can and do plan. And they can and do mobilize bipartisan majorities capable of giving legislative effect to their wishes. Not infrequently, the size and discipline of these blocs enable them to challenge and defeat legislative measures of the Philippine president himself.

But such legislative blocs do not pretend to usurp the role of political parties. In the first place, their objectives are of limited scope. Though an interest group may develop and obtain the enactment of various measures designed to benefit a particular industry, there is no attempt to formulate really comprehensive programs for the government of the country as a whole. In the second place, while a political party presents its program to the country openly, it is a characteristic of special-interest blocs in the Philippine Congress that they deny, or at least do not make a point of publicizing, their existence except to those whose special interests they champion. Thus, while the existence of the sugar bloc is a matter of common knowledge among politicians, sugar men themselves go out of their way to deny its existence or at least to denigrate its importance. Unlike political parties, whose business it is to nominate candidates to run for public office on party platforms, special-interest blocs do not as a rule put candidates into the field. When they do so, such candidates do not advertise their bloc affiliations but run, ostensibly, as party candidates. Several of the leading aspirants for the presidential nomination in the Nacionalista convention of November, 1964, were closely tied to special-interest blocs but none made a point of advertising this fact, except, perhaps, in his home region. Clearly, supraparty blocs, whose programs are partial ones, who shun publicity, and whose candidates do not make explicit their bloc affiliation, provide no substitute for responsible party government.

In the Philippines, a program that is comprehensive, that is presented to the country at election time, and for the enactment and implementation of which someone can be held accountable does not come from the parties as such or from bipartisan legislative blocs but from presidential candidates —and as individuals rather than as spokesmen for their parties. The distinction is an important one. To a decidedly greater extent than in the United States, and to an immeasurably greater extent than in the United Kingdom, the program of a Philippine administration is the personal program of the president rather than the program of his party. This personal program will reflect his own convictions, his accommodation of the demands from different sectors of society which no president can ignore, and his choice of allies among the numerous competing interests that propose policies to him and offer him their support. His party supplies little, if any, guidance in the formulation of his program, and his party-mates may or may not share his enthusiasm for the program, once formulated. Yet, because parties as a whole do not develop programs, a president's party-mates in Congress must, to some extent, go along with his personal program: It is the only program the party has. Though, as we have seen, party loyalty is weak when compared with that found in most other countries, those members of a president's party who do not happen to be feuding with him are more likely than are members of the opposition to support his measures, if these do not conflict with the interests of their constituencies, with their private interests, or with the interests of those who lend them financial support. Unless a president's relations with his party's leaders in the Senate and the House of Representatives have deteriorated badly—by no means an unusual state of affairs—these leaders will make some effort to persuade their party-mates in Congress to support the president's measures. Nonetheless, a Philippine president usually dispenses lavish amounts of patronage, spoils, and sometimes cash to win the votes of members of his own party for important administration measures. And even this is not enough to assure solid support. Hence, presidents ordinarily must court the support of various senators and congressmen of the opposition party in order to assure passage of administration measures.

Deprived of disciplined party support, a president begins his term with a serious handicap. Though the electorate holds him responsible for the enactment of the program on which he campaigned for office, he lacks adequate means to carry out his mandate. There is a helpless rhythm to the appearance of every postwar president, after a short honeymoon, painfully explaining to the country why he has failed to fulfill his election promises. Ironically, in the absence of united and disciplined parties capable of bridging the gap between the two political branches of government, the American system of checks and balances becomes in the Philippines a serious obstacle to effective and responsible government.

A further unfortunate consequence of not having loyal, disciplined parties is the lack of continuity in presidential party policy. As a president's term in office lengthens and his inability to fulfill many of his promises becomes increasingly evident, and as his popularity declines, support for his program becomes increasingly hard to obtain. When he leaves office, his program is likely to die with him, and the program of the next member of his party to occupy the presidency may be quite different. Carlos Garcia's program differed markedly from that of Ramon Magsaysay. Conversely, a rather similar program may be adopted by a president of a different party. This has been the case with the land-reform programs of Presidents Magsaysay and Macapagal, the former a Nacionalista and the latter a Liberal—but both sons of families of modest means and natives of Central

Luzon. And why, indeed, should there be continuity between two administrations of the same party, when one of the presidents was perhaps a newcomer to his party when he ran for presidential office? Or why not rather similar programs in two administrations of different parties headed by men who, at one time, were party-mates? Can one expect the members of the two parties in Congress to differ significantly in their response to presidential policies, when many members of the president's party, including a good many chairmen of standing committees, are recent defectors from the opposition, with minimal concern for the long-term welfare of their new party?

If there is continuity in the programs of the Philippine government from one administration to the next, it is not because of a party's faithfulness to a party program but because of the similarity of the pressures playing upon succeeding administrations. If there is some change, it is not because one party has won the presidency and another lost, but because a different individual occupies the presidency or because the mood of the country has changed. Change, in short, is not cyclical change, associated with the regular alternation in power of the two major parties, but change that is both essentially unpredictable, in that it stems from the assumption of office by a new president with a distinctive personal program, and secular, in that it reflects the changing configuration and relative power of competing interests in the country and the changing mood of the Filipino electorate and their local leaders.

Public Participation in Government:
The Wide Distribution of Influence

While the Philippine political system fails to provide for responsible party government, it can be said that to a high degree it fulfills another criterion of a democratic political system: a wide distribution of political influence. A large proportion of the Filipino public has an opportunity to participate in the making of the decisions that affect the staffing of government and the determination of its substantive "outputs," albeit these decisions are confined largely to choices that are particular rather than categorical in nature.

The substantial influence that the ordinary voter exerts upon decision-making is explained, in large part, by the unrestrictedness, the closeness, and the intensity of competition for elective offices at all levels of government. The fact that party nomination is not a prerequisite for candidacy for offices lower than those of the presidency, vice-presidency, and senatorships—that is, the fact that no party stalwart is secure against challenge by an upstart in his own party—as well as the narrow margin by which most elections are won give the individual voter a good deal of leverage at election time, for a relatively small number of votes can mean the difference between election and defeat. An awareness of this fact is reflected in the behavior of politicians. In talking to leaders at the lower levels, the foreign observer is amazed at their detailed knowledge of the probable voting behavior of each family head and at the great efforts willingly made to win his support.

The intensity of competition among candidates of substantial means, that is, the great importance they attach to winning, leads to phenomenal spending for the purchase of votes. It is normal for votes to be bought for between five and ten pesos each, and in very hard-fought elections with several wealthy candidates much larger sums—reportedly as high as twenty or thirty pesos—have been paid for the good will of a single family head. Under such conditions, the ordinary voter becomes well aware of the fact that as an individual he can have a good deal of influence upon one form of political decision-making: the selection of those who hold public office.

The ordinary voter also learns that what he does can have a direct effect upon certain substantive "outputs" of government. He knows that, rather than sell his vote for cash, he can trade it for the promise of a public-works job, free medical care in a government hospital, protection against harassment by a local policeman, or exemption from the payment of taxes. In short, he is far more aware than his American counterpart that what he does on election day can have a direct and immediately perceptible effect upon the outputs of government insofar as they concern himself. The high sense of participation in the political process that this engenders accounts in large part for the surprising amount of information about politics possessed by the ordinary Filipino and for the intensity of his interest in politics.

Concomitantly, a good deal of leverage accrues to anyone in the Philippines capable of mobilizing and delivering even a relatively small bloc of voters. Village- and municipal-level politicians, petty leaders though they be, have collectively and individually considerable bargaining power in their dealings with the national party leadership. Similarly, even a relatively small interest or policy-oriented group, if it has sufficient discipline to vote as a group, can exert a surprising amount of influence upon the selection of candidates and the allocation of governmental outputs. The most notable group of this sort at the present time is the Iglesia-ni-Kristo, a small religious sect whose members account for only 1 per cent of the population, according to the census of 1960, but who are known among politicians for their disposition to vote as their leader directs. Candidates for various offices, from the presidency downward, take extraordinary pains to cultivate the good will of the Iglesia's leader.

It seems fair to conclude, then, that while the Philippine political system does not provide responsible party government, it is a highly *responsive* system. The ordinary Filipino voter can claim a real measure of participation in the business of government. So, too, by and large, can every group aware of a common interest and also able and willing to enter the political arena in order to promote or defend it. This is true of new groups as well as old, for Filipino politicians are highly sensitive to the appearance of any new group with the means and the willingness to press claims for governmental action. These means may consist of wealth, strength of argument, or numbers. Thus, the last decade bears witness to the growing influence, upon administrations of both political parties, of the new Filipino industrialists, of nationalistic intellectuals and—to an extent that may be debated but that, in the writer's view, is substantial—of a welfare-minded peasantry. Because of the ability of political newcomers to make their weight felt through constitutional processes, one may hope that in the coming years the Philippines will be spared the danger that large and po-tentially powerful sectors of the population, denied access to those who control the government, will escape the notice of the decision-makers until they suddenly make their presence known through extraconstitutional out-bursts of mass violence.

Of course, the obverse of the high sense of effectiveness possessed by the voter who obtains some tangible benefit from the government in return for his vote is an acute sense of deprivation on the part of the voter who sees his neighbor obtain such a benefit but fails to obtain the same for himself. This kind of frustration never seriously disrupts the political system, how-ever, because those deprived at any one time do not fall into a distinctive social or occupational category, hence are not united in their envy of an-other category of favored persons, and because those who find themselves deprived of governmental favors today can hope to be among the favored another year. The frustration of the deprived reveals itself mainly in a widespread but directionless undercurrent of dissatisfaction with "politics" among the electorate at large or, more acutely, in a disposition to throw out the current holders of office at frequent intervals and to "give a chance" to other politicians and their followers. There is, further, some yearning and periodic talk of the need for a third party, that is, for leaders who, somehow, are better men, less corruptible men, men more determined to keep their promises than the average run of the politicians with whom the voters are familiar. But here, again, the remedy for the excesses of politics is seen, largely, in terms of personalities and individual performance rather than of policies. It is remarkable how few of the educated Filipinos who talk of a third party suggest that such a party should institute really significant substantive changes in governmental policy. Better men, it is assumed, will do everything better. Practically no one thinks of remedies in categorical terms.

The Unequal Distribution of Influence

While political influence may be widely distributed in the Philippines, it would be unrealistic to say it is distributed equally. On the contrary, it is distributed in a markedly unequal fashion. This stems from the fact that though in the counting of votes the ballot of each elector has an equal value, each Filipino does not control a single vote. One of the most notable features of Philippine society is that there are to be found in each town numerous individuals—some of them professional political leaders but many of them not—who, because of their wealth, have varying numbers of clients dependent upon them. In the past at least, these clients could be depended upon to vote as their patrons directed. Though the ability of such patrons to direct the votes of their clients is declining to some extent as the little people "get wise," as one politician put it, many of these little people are ready, nonetheless, to sell their votes to the highest bidder among the candidates for office. This means that persons of wealth, either because they can deliver the votes of their clients or because they can supply the funds with which a politician can buy votes, have a bargaining power vis-à-vis these politicians that far exceeds that of the ordinary villager, who has nothing to offer in the political marketplace but his own vote and maybe his family's. This helps to explain why a disproportionate share of the benefits dispensed by government does fall to the middle and upper classes, even though, in contrast with the autocratic or oligarchic governments found in so many other developing countries, the Philippine government is highly responsive to the demands emanating from the innumerable little people. A more equitable distribution of political influence will come presumably only after the little people learn to use their votes with greater skill. In certain respects, the growing disposition of the villager to sell his vote rather than to vote blindly as directed by his patrons is a sign of progress. It means that the ordinary voter has learned to deal directly with those who control the government and, in effect, to eliminate the middlemen. The next step, one may hope, is that he will learn not to trade his vote for a mess of election-time pottage but to use it to bring into office candidates capable not only of distributing particularistic benefits to their followers but also of devising and implementing more lasting programmatic measures to improve the lot of the common man.

National Unity and the Future of the Philippine Party System

National Unity

Thoughtful Filipinos are among the first to see the shortcomings of their system of identical parties, beginning with the lack of a real choice between the parties. Throw out one set of politicians, they say, and in comes another set, no better than the last, and with no more coherent program for the government of the country. One may well sympathize with their complaint.

Yet the similarity of the two parties itself offers certain advantages, and these are often overlooked by Filipino critics of the party system. Perhaps the most important side effect is the contribution to national unity. The fact that competition in Philippine politics is restricted to parties and politicians with programs that differ but little from each other and to candidates who are alike in seeking to represent all regions of the country, all social strata, and all organized and unorganized interests does much to mitigate the potentially divisive consequences of the existence of differences in the needs of diverse regions, social strata, and interests. The rivalry of parties at election times does not, as it does in some countries, become an occasion for the clash of the interests and the exacerbation of hostility between diverse regions and social classes. On the contrary, this is the time when each party, fearing that its rival might deprive it of its supporters in some important region or among some influential group, will go to great lengths to match or outdo the opposite party in catering to every region and every group. It is at election time that politicians travel far from their home bases to seek votes in places where they are not well known, and it is at election time that upper-class candidates throughout the country take the most pains to win the good will of their lower-class constituents by showering them with material benefits and—equally important—with expressions of good will.

Not only does the similarity of the two parties foster unity—or at least minimize conflict—among various sectors of the public but between politicians of the opposing parties as well. The lack of intraparty unity and discipline, which arises largely from the lack of palpable distinction between the parties, forces Philippine presidents and the legislative leaders of the two houses of Congress to seek votes among opposition senators and congressmen in order to enact their legislative measures. This strengthens the bargaining power of the opposition and produces a far less hostile atmosphere between members of the two parties in Congress than is the case in the Japanese Diet, for example, where the discipline of the Liberal-Democratic Party's majority assures the passage of virtually all government measures, deprives the Socialist opposition of effective legislative bargaining power, and justifies, in the minds of many Japanese, acts of both intraparliamentary and extraparliamentary violence designed to protest the "tyranny of the majority." In the Philippines, on the other hand, the opposition member of Congress has reason to hope to influence the course of legislation through the shrewd and independent employment of his vote in committees and on the floor. Aware of his power, wooed by diverse interests and party leaders, invited on occasion to take counsel with the President himself, the opposition member of Congress in the Philippines feels that he plays an important part in the government of the country. As in the United States, bipartisan legislative efforts preclude real enmity between the opposing parties, make the opposition an essentially "loyal opposition," and contribute to the unity of the country at large.

The competition of identical parties, neither of which has a clear and consistent program for the economic development of the country, and both of which seek to maintain themselves in power through the haphazard, particularistic distribution of largesse to all individuals or groups, has serious disadvantages for the country, not the least being the great waste of the nation's resources. Yet, in an age and a part of the world where the rivalry of classes, regions, and communal groups has often played into the hands of those who would abandon attempts to create institutions of constitutional democracy in favor of the institution of dictatorial rule either by a single strong party or by a strong individual leader, these shortcomings hardly seem too high a price to pay for the preservation of individual liberty and economic opportunity under what has become a lively yet remarkably united and stable democracy.

Prospects for the Future

What are the prospects for a major transformation in the Philippine party system? What are the chances that, in the foreseeable future, the Philippine party system will come to resemble that of most other modern democracies? That the identical parties of today will be replaced by parties

which, over the long run, adhere to really distinctive positions on fundamental questions of public policy and which draw their support from quite
different sectors of Philippine society?

It seems reasonable to suppose that, in time, parties with distinguishable
positions will emerge in the Philippines as they have emerged elsewhere.
There is, however, no evidence that such a realignment is beginning to
take place today, nor is there any reason to believe that it must take place
in the near future. What may appear to be evidence of such realignment
is misleading. In recent years, for example, the tobacco-producing Ilocos
region of northern Luzon has leaned more strongly toward the Liberal
Party than has the rest of the country, but this stems from an accident of
postwar history rather than commitment to a particular party on ideological grounds. After the end of World War II, when the old Partido Nacionalista split in two, the vice-presidential candidate of the Liberal Party,
Elpidio Quirino, happened to be a native of the Ilocos region of the north.
On the death of President Manuel Roxas, Quirino became president, and
during his presidency, he made a point of giving special attention to the
needs of his home region. The legacy of Quirino's favoritism for the north
remained after his term in office and has been reflected in recent years in
a heavy northern vote for Liberal candidates. But no better proof of the
personal basis of the Liberal voting preference could be found than the
probability of a switch in the 1965 elections, when the north's new favorite
son, Senate President Ferdinand Marcos, a recent defector from the Liberal Party, will be running as the Nacionalista Party's presidential candidate.* It is being confidently predicted that a good many northern Liberal
leaders will join the Nacionalista Party and that the north's recent bias
toward the Liberal Party will decline and possibly change to a bias toward
the Nacionalista Party.

Similarly, the fact that most sugar-growers in recent years have been
Nacionalistas is essentially an accident of recent history. It will be recalled
that before 1953, the leaders of the "sugar bloc" were Liberals. One of the
principal figures of the sugar industry, Fernando Lopez, was Vice President
under Liberal President Quirino. When Lopez failed to win the Liberal
Party's vice-presidential nomination in 1953, his bloc, aware of the declining strength of the Liberals, switched to the Nacionalista Party. Since
then, most leaders of the bloc have been Nacionalistas. But when, in 1961,
a Liberal once again captured the presidency, it surprised few in the Philippines that the head of the Federation of Sugar Cane Planters, a man
closely allied with the Nacionalistas, resigned from his post to be replaced
by another planter who happened to be a Liberal. The incident is a typical
example of the almost exclusive reliance of special-interest groups on their
members' personal connections with powerful government officials.

What of the peasantry? What of commerce and industry? And what of
urban labor? Is there any evidence that either party will succeed in the near
future in winning special and continued support from one of these sectors
of the population? At the first postwar elections in 1946, central Luzon,

* Marcos was indeed elected President.

the traditional region of agrarian unrest, threw 33 per cent of its votes to the left-wing Democratic Alliance, while giving 56 per cent of its presidential vote to the Nacionalista presidential candidate, Sergio Osmeña, who was thought to have more sympathy for the peasantry than his opponent. But since the collapse of the Democratic Alliance in 1946, the two major parties have split the vote of all social strata in central Luzon as elsewhere. Ramon Magsaysay, who as President was to make a strong appeal for the support of the peasantry, was no stronger in central Luzon than in the nation as a whole (68 per cent in both cases) when he ran for the presidency in 1953. How he would have fared in central Luzon had he lived to run for re-election in 1957 one cannot say: His lieutenant and political heir, Manuel Manahan, running under the banner of the short-lived Progressive Party of the Philippines (PPP), did somewhat better in central Luzon than in the nation as a whole (28 per cent as against 21 per cent). Emmanuel Pelaez, another Magsaysay lieutenant and an erstwhile PPP and Grand Alliance member who ran as Liberal party vice-presidential candidate in 1961, also made a somewhat better showing in central Luzon than in the nation as a whole (43 per cent against 38 per cent). These special friends of the peasantry have run under various party labels, however, and there is still no evidence that either major party has become more sympathetic than the other toward the peasantry as against the landowning class—or vice versa.

As for the urban interests, business and labor, there is again no evidence that either party is prepared to make a special appeal to one of these groups to the extent of alienating the other. Business organizations have made a point of being nonpartisan. Individual businessmen can be found in the ranks of both parties in approximately equal number. The commercial and industrial community does its best to influence the policies of whichever party controls the presidency, and prominent businessmen have held key cabinet offices in all recent administrations. Urban laborers, whose interests as wage earners conflict with the interests of their employers, have been equally bipartisan. In contrast to the large American cities, where labor has been mostly Democratic while business has been mostly Republican, party rivalry in Manila remains the rivalry of two groups of ward-heeling politicians, both of which have appealed equally for the votes of all social strata. Every politician has his own neighborhood following among the common people and deals in much the same way as every other politician with the city's businessmen, native and foreign. In short, the main features of the party system as found in the rural Philippines are reproduced with but minor changes in the metropolis. And there is little evidence that even in Manila a major party realignment will soon take place. The most significant characteristic setting Manila off from the rest of the country is that the city traditionally has rallied to opposition parties to a greater extent, or earlier, than have the provinces. In prewar days, when the Nacionalistas were the permanent majority nationally, Manila showed sympathy for any minor party that dared to challenge the entrenched Nacionalistas. Since the war, Manila has leaned away from whichever party was in power and toward the party destined to replace it, with fine impartiality.

There is, in short, no evidence of the development now or in the foreseeable future of clear and persistent distinctions between the two parties. And as long as the leaders of both parties continue to be able to win support from all classes by providing them with particular benefits of diverse kinds, they have no reason to commit their parties permanently to positions that might alienate any important sector of society or any major region of the country. It is unlikely that this pattern will change, as long as the little people in most parts of the country continue to accept as a matter of course the political leadership of their patrons among the big people of their respective communities. So long, that is to say, as political organization continues to be structured by vertical dyads of patronship and clientship rather than by a categorical sense of common interest based on region, industry, or class. No doubt the time will come when the latter type of structure will replace the former as it has in the West. Certainly, Filipino voters follow their leaders less blindly now than in an earlier day and show a greater readiness to play big people off against one another so as to benefit from their rivalry. But, on the whole, they still accept the leadership of "big people" as a class. How long they will continue to do so will depend in large part upon the willingness of the privileged members of Philippine society to satisfy the needs of the great mass of the "common tao" who live in the countryside. Those of a conservative bent who feel that the past successes and the hope for the survival of constitutional democracy in the Philippines rest in large part upon the existence of an informed, public-spirited, and socially responsible upper and middle class can only hope that this elite will not, to its own disadvantage and that of the country, allow its own quite understandable preoccupation with the country's industrial development to obscure the need for flexible responses to the rising demands of less fortunate countrymen.

27

NORTH VIETNAM: A PROFILE*

BERNARD B. FALL

Larger geographically than the three Soviet Baltic republics combined, and having—as of 1964—a population of about 18.2 million, North Vietnam ranks fourth in both area and population among the countries of the bloc. The Democratic Republic of Vietnam (D.R.V.N.), dating its birth from September 2, 1945, is also the second oldest "people's democracy" after Mongolia, and it stands alone with Yugoslavia in having come into being without the help of Soviet bayonets or the presence of a larger Communist power.

These factors alone warrant a close study of the North Vietnamese regime, for they suggest a far greater degree of solidity and cohesion than is usually found in a small Communist country. As one French observer has correctly remarked, the D.R.V.N.'s "communism is not the result of an alien overlay . . . but the product of a long-maturing and hardening process in the course of the anti-French struggle,"[1] and—one may now add—

* Reprinted in somewhat abridged form by permission of the publisher from *Problems of Communism*, XIV (July/August, 1965), 13–25.

[1] Julien Cheverny, *Éloge du colonialisme—Essai sur les révolutions d'Asie* (Paris: Julliard, 1961), p. 177.

in the equally long fight for the eventual control of South Vietnam. The same factors also have a profound influence upon the attitude that Hanoi has thus far taken toward the Sino-Soviet split, as well as upon the D.R.V.N.'s approach to its confrontation with the United States in the South Vietnamese conflict. A look at the historical, political, and economic background of North Vietnam will serve to bring the whole problem into clearer focus.

From Clandestinity to Resistance

Like many of the Communist movements in former colonial countries, that of Vietnam started abroad—among Vietnamese living in France, Russia, and China. Under the name of Nguyen Ai-Quoc [Nguyen-the-Patriot], the D.R.V.N.'s present President, Ho Chi Minh, was a co-founder of the French Communist Party when the latter split off from the French Socialist Party in 1920. By 1923, Ho had risen high enough in the French Communist hierarchy to be sent to Moscow as a delegate to the *Krestintern* (Peasant International), and later to attend the Fifth Comintern Congress in 1924 as a French colonial delegate.[2] It is worthy of note that he intervened very strongly in the 1924 Congress debates on two specific points: namely, the importance of the anticolonial struggle (he asserted that Stalin was one of the few Communist leaders who attached proper weight to the colonial question); and the importance of the peasantry in the revolutionary movements of colonial and semicolonial areas. In the latter connection, Dr. Ernst Kux, noted Far Eastern specialist of the Swiss newspaper *Neue Zürcher Zeitung*, recently observed that Ho had been well ahead of Mao Tse-tung in advancing "the thesis that Communist revolutions in the colonial areas must be carried out by the peasant masses under the leadership of the party." Kux goes on to remark: "Ho's assertion that practical acts and leadership of the revolution are more important than the formulation of ringing theses became the mainstream of his own future activities. In fact, he almost repeated it verbatim at the meeting of Communist parties in Moscow in 1961."[3]

This pragmatic trait has manifested itself throughout Ho Chi Minh's career to this day, and it has also marked the whole approach of the North Vietnamese Party leadership to the thorny problem of relations with the Party's competing Soviet and Chinese mentors. Ho's personal loyalty to Stalin during the 1930's perhaps explains why he survived the various purges that sent almost all of his early Comintern associates to death or into exile, and there is absolutely no evidence that the North Vietnamese Communists ever swerved from their pro-Moscow sympathies until Stalin's death in 1953.

Ho's stay in the Soviet Union in 1923–24 marked the first shift of Vietnamese Communism away from a West European (mostly French) to a

---

[2] There is no full-length biography of Ho Chi Minh. The author has attempted a biographical essay in *The Two Viet-Nams* (rev. ed., New York: Frederick A. Praeger, 1965), pp. 81–103. Also see this volume, chapter 30.

[3] Ernest Kux, *Die Satelliten Pekings* (Stuttgart: W. Kohlhammer, 1964), pp. 38–39.

more specifically Soviet orientation. His own assignment, in December, 1924, to Mikhail Borodin's Soviet mission to Sun Yat-sen's Chinese revolutionary government in Canton as an "interpreter" (actually to work as a Communist organizer of Vietnamese exiles in South China) strikingly underlined this new orientation toward Moscow—the more so because of the Chinese context. Within a few days after his arrival in Canton, Ho addressed a preliminary report to the Executive Committee of the Comintern, in which he described his principal future task to be "the unification of various Vietnamese nationalist groups under Communist leadership."[4] The task was not to be an easy one, since many of the Vietnamese exile groups either were hostile to the Communist ideology or, if sympathetic, had come into contact with Communist ideas in France and were reluctant at first to accept the authority of the totally unknown Russian-trained Vietnamese organizers in Canton. But the Canton group had several important assets in its favor: (1) It had official Comintern support; (2) it was able to utilize Chinese Nationalist military academies for training cadres;[5] and (3) it had Ho Chi Minh as its leader.

Vietnamese Communist reliance on Soviet and Comintern support only increased after Chiang Kai-shek's break with Moscow in 1927, which led to the expulsion of the Soviet mission from Canton and the near-destruction of the Chinese Communist Party (CCP) apparatus. Ho and his associates switched operations to the nearby British crown colony of Hong Kong, which offered excellent liaison with the outside world because of its direct location on the shipping lanes to both Western Europe and Vladivostok. It was in Hong Kong that the final differences among the three existing Vietnamese factions of the Third International (there was also a strong Trotskyite group) were hammered out. Confronted with a communication from the Comintern, which stated that the existence of these differences "under present circumstances is a grave error and an even greater danger,"[6] the leaders of the various factions finally came to terms. On February 3, 1930, the *Dong Duong Cong San Dang* (Indochinese Communist Party, or ICP) was born. . . .

A CHECKERED COURSE

The ICP soon experienced its first crisis in the course of a peasant uprising in the central Vietnamese province of Nghe-An—Ho Chi Minh's province of birth—in the spring of 1930. There has thus far been no definitive account of the uprising, and existing sources conflict as to its interpretation. Basically, it grew out of a totally non-Communist mutiny of native soldiers in Tonkin (North Vietnam), which then spread to the peasantry as a consequence of drastically falling commodity prices caused by the "Great Depression." A Vietnamese Communist, evaluating the uprising in

[4] Kux, *op. cit.*, p. 40.

[5] According to North Vietnamese Premier Pham Van Dong (*Le président Ho Chi Minh* [Hanoi: Foreign Languages Publishing House, 1961], p. 52), "more than 200 cadres" were trained during 1925–27 at the Chinese Nationalist military academy at Whampoa and in Russia.

[6] Pham Van Dong, *op. cit.*, p. 57.

1960, admits to "serious errors"—notably that the rebellion was entirely based on the small peasantry, rejecting the support, on the side of the French, of all other bourgeois elements. That error was, in fact, duly condemned by the Far Eastern Bureau of the Comintern in May, 1931, as "leftist and sectarian" and "not in accordance with the principles of communism."[7]

The ensuing repression of the Vietnamese Communist movement rendered it almost leaderless (and well-nigh memberless) for nearly five years, until the advent of a Popular Front government in France brought about a softening of anti-Communist police activity in Indochina. Tran-Phu, the first secretary-general of the ICP, was among those arrested by the colonial authorities in Indochina, dying in prison in September, 1931. Ho Chi Minh, who was still in Hong Kong, was arrested there by the British in June, 1931, but was released later that year and went underground in Shanghai before returning to Russia and Western Europe, where he remained until 1938. The ICP's second secretary-general, Le Hong Phong, stayed abroad until the more lenient Popular Front policy took hold in Indochina.

In July, 1936, the ICP Central Committee officially adhered to the "Dimitrov Line" as laid down at the Seventh Comintern Congress and withdrew the slogans "Down with French Imperialism" and "Down with Feudalism." A short period of political collaboration with the French followed, but the honeymoon was interrupted by the Molotov-Ribbentrop Pact of August, 1939, and the outbreak of World War II. Le Hong Phong was arrested and died on the guillotine in 1940. By the end of that year, the whole senior ICP apparatus had again withdrawn to China—but not to the areas held by the Chinese Communists; instead, it chose warlord-held Kwangsi province, bordering on Vietnam, as its base of operations.

A new secretary-general, Truong Chinh, was elected by the reconstituted ICP Central Committee in May, 1941. (His real name is Dang Xuan Khu, and his adoption of the pseudonym "Truong Chinh"—the Vietnamese term for the "Long March" of the Chinese Communists—reflects his long-standing personal admiration of the CCP.) Meanwhile, Ho Chi Minh had rejoined the Party apparatus in Kwangsi but had subsequently antagonized the local Chinese warlords by resisting their pressure for integration of the ICP-in-exile with Vietnamese nationalist elements under their aegis. Arrested by the Chinese, Ho was kept in jail from August, 1942, until September, 1943. This presumably left Truong Chinh a fairly free hand to staff the Party apparatus with his own men. Although he has never, to this day, attained the popularity and charisma of Ho or of General Vo Nguyen Giap, the victor of Dien Bien Phu, Truong unquestionably played a major role in the ICP's well-organized take over of the Vietnamese anti-French revolution in the summer of 1945, which he himself has described in a small book that deserves more attention than it usually gets.[8]

[7] Tran Huy Lieu, *Les Soviets du Nghé Tinh* (Hanoi: Foreign Languages Publishing House, 1960), p. 52.

[8] Truong Chinh, *Primer for Revolt: The Communist Takeover in Viet-Nam* (New York: Frederick A. Praeger, 1963).

It is vital to remember that, unlike any other successful Communist movement, the Vietnamese Party fought its way to ruling power in virtual isolation. In Eastern Europe, Soviet troops were always present in the countries where Communist take-overs took place; in fact, they were an essential ingredient. In China, the turnover to the Communists of vast stores of Japanese arms by the Soviet forces in Manchuria was of vital importance to the CCP's military success, and the Russian military presence in North Korea insured the creation of a "people's democracy" there. In Albania, Tito's partisans played the role of Soviet troops elsewhere. In the Vietnam of 1945, on the contrary, the D.R.V.N. had no such support from either the Soviets or even the Chinese Communists (then bottled up in the hills of northwestern China); and connections with the French CP, then just emerging from four years of clandestinity, were probably non-existent, for the simple reason that the first postwar ships to go from France to Indochina only reached Saigon in late September, 1945—and these were troop transports bringing the vanguard of the French Expeditionary Force. In other words, the Vietnamese Communists literally had to play their revolution alone and "by ear."

With practical political realism, Ho played down the Communist character of his regime and movement. The ICP was formally "dissolved" on November 10, 1945, and replaced by an "Association of Marxist Studies" under Truong Chinh. For a time, Ho also succeeded in getting his followers to adopt what was openly called the "Brest-Litovsk" doctrine, involving readiness to accept a partial and temporary return of French influence to Vietnam in order to get rid of a Chinese Nationalist military presence which, by virtue of its sheer numbers, threatened to become permanent. It was largely because the French were unwilling at this stage to consider relinquishment of their colonial sovereignty that the upper hand in Hanoi eventually passed to those who preferred the risk of all-out revolutionary war to the risk of being nibbled to death by ever-increasing encroachments of French military power. Ho's own failure, during negotiations in France in the summer of 1946, to sway even the French CP to support his viewpoint[9] must have heavily influenced his decision to press for a military contest. On December 19, 1946, the first Indochina War broke out. It ended seven and a half years later with the defeat of the French and the Geneva agreement of July 21, 1954, partitioning Vietnam at the 17th parallel.

VIETNAMESE "WAR COMMUNISM"

The war with the French in a way simplified some of the problems of Vietnam's Communist leaders. The fact that the struggle was a "resistance" movement against the colonial power made it easier to attract into an *union sacrée* many Vietnamese elements who otherwise would have eschewed association with the Communists. It also removed the ambiguity

[9] The French CP was then a member of the government coalition in France and had solid hopes of taking over the government. In that event, all French colonial areas would automatically have passed under Communist control. See Fall, "Tribulations of a Party Line: The French CP and the Indochina War," *Foreign Affairs* (April, 1955).

arising from the negotiations with the French, which had laid the Communist leadership open to charges that it was ready to negotiate away "true" independence for the sake of short-range political gains. And lastly, it permitted the Communists to take some drastic steps in many fields under the guise of strengthening unity and discipline in the war effort.

The first constitution establishing the formal governmental structure of the D.R.V.N. in 1946 was enacted by an assembly from which all but two opponents of the Communists had been removed, but it discreetly made no mention of the Communist character of the state. This document remained in force until 1960, when it was replaced by a wholly new constitution making that character fully explicit.[10] Throughout the period of anti-French hostilities from 1946 until 1954, a Standing Committee of the National Assembly fulfilled all legislative functions, except for the convocation of an Assembly session in 1953 to enact a land-reform law. In actual fact, governmental functions were carried out at the central level by Ho's council of ministers, assisted at various subordinate levels by "Committees of Resistance and Administration" (CRA), combining civilian, military, and Party elements.

Wherever feasible, the village-level CRA's were chosen by election. Needless to say, these elections were strongly influenced by the presence of "Vietnam People's Army" troops, although in many instances, locally popular village chiefs managed to win positions as committee chairmen. Communist control, however, was ensured by a *can-bo* (cadre), who saw to it that the local CRA chairman did not deviate from the official Party line. Furthermore, under a decree of November 11, 1948, the government gave the higher-level CRA's more power, not only to override decisions by the local committees "contrary to higher order" (article XII) but also to designate a provisional local CRA to replace a recalcitrant one (article XIII).

On the political side, the "League for Revolution and Independence" (better known by its abbreviated title of Vietminh), which had been created in Kwangsi in May, 1941, was supplemented in May, 1946, by an even broader "united front," including non-Communist elements that had not been part of the émigré groups in China. This new front, the "League for the National Union of Vietnam" or Lien-Viet, also embraced a large number of subsidiary "national salvation" (*Cu'u Quoc*) groups, such as "Women for National Salvation," "Catholics for National Salvation," and so on, thus making it appear that the regime had the backing of a broad variety of parties.

External developments brought the next major political change. In December, 1949, Red Chinese troops arrived on the North Vietnamese border, providing the D.R.V.N. for the first time with direct access to the Communist bloc and all that this meant—that is, plentiful military supplies, a sanctuary for casualties and training camps, and, above all, easy exchange of political delegations with the Communist countries. This made recognition of the D.R.V.N. by members of the bloc more than an empty gesture, and by the end of February, 1950, all the bloc countries, as

10 For a full English text of the 1960 constitution, see Fall, *The Two Viet-Nams.*

well as Yugoslavia, had extended such recognition. It meant further that the regime was no longer as dependent as hitherto on the internal support of non-Communist and bourgeois elements.

The result was that in March, 1951, the old ICP was resurrected in the form of a specifically Vietnamese (rather than, as before, "Indochinese," that is, including Cambodia and Laos) "Workers' Party," or Dang Lao-Dong. Its secretary-general was the same Truong Chinh who had previously been ICP Secretary-General and later chairman of the succeeding "Marxist Studies Association." The radicalization of its posture was reflected in a new slogan: "The anti-imperialist and anti-feudal struggles are of equal importance."

At the same time, the Vietminh was merged into the broader Lien-Viet front, and traditional Vietnamese Communist predominance in the revolutionary movements of neighboring Cambodia and Laos was reasserted through a meeting (March 3–11, 1951) between Ton Duc Thang, later Vice President of the D.R.V.N.; Prince Souphanouvong of Laos, the leader of the Pathet-Lao movement; and Sieu Heng, the head of the "Khmer [that is, Cambodian] Liberation Committee." A Communist source provides clear evidence of the importance of the conference:

> It was decided to set up a Viet-Nam-Khmer-Lao Alliance which called on the people of the three countries to coordinate their fight to defeat the colonialists. It was on the basis of these decisions . . . that Vietnamese volunteers later entered Cambodia and Laos to fight side by side with the Khmer Issarak forces—by then the Khmer National Liberation Army—and the Pathet-Lao.[11]

The effective satellization of the Cambodian and Laotian Communist movements under Vietnamese aegis was clearly illustrated at the Geneva conference of 1954. There, after some initial skirmishing, the Communist side accepted the fact that the Khmer and Lao "resistance movements" would not be seated at the conference table, and Brigadier General Ta Quang Buu, the Oxford-educated Vietnamese senior military representative, signed the Cambodian and Laotian cease-fire agreements on behalf of the "Khmer Resistance Forces" and the Pathet-Lao.

The Geneva conference signaled the emergence of the D.R.V.N. as a full-fledged power. Its political and administrative institutions were in place, and it boasted a formidable army capable not only of waging a protracted revolutionary war but also of fighting standing battles against relatively well-armed Western forces.

AFTER PARTITION

The 1954 Geneva cease-fire left the northern sector of Vietnam above the 17th parallel in the hands of the D.R.V.N., while the somewhat larger southern part, now inhabited by about 14.8 million people, came under the rule of the anti-Communist government of Ngo Dinh Diem. It is still not entirely clear why the D.R.V.N. accepted the compromise of a "tempo-

---

[11] W. Burchett, *Mekong Upstream* (East Berlin: Seven Seas Books, 1959), pp. 89–90.

rary" division of Vietnam, inasmuch as the prospects of the holding of a reunification election within two years, as provided by the Geneva agreements, seemed fairly slim from the outset. Soviet pressure on North Vietnam for the sake of improving Russian relations with France—more specifically, for the purpose of inducing Paris to block the creation of a European Defense Community including West Germany—may well have been the main factor behind Hanoi's agreement.

Another probable factor was the pragmatism of the North Vietnamese Communist leadership. Ho Chi Minh had characteristically settled for a safe half-loaf rather than fight to the finish merely to prove a point. Moreover, the consolidation of Communist power in North Vietnam after four years of Japanese depredation, one year of Chinese pilfering, and eight years of scorched-earth war with the French was a formidable enough problem to tackle. To be sure, South Vietnam's rice surplus would have been of value to the North, but it must not be forgotten that the 1954 agreements provided for unhindered trade between the two zones. The fact that this never materialized no doubt contributed to the D.R.V.N.'s later decision to attempt a settlement by force.

Following the Geneva accords, the D.R.V.N. settled down to the task of transforming itself into a full-fledged "people's democracy." A "Population Classification Decree" issued in March, 1953, had divided the population into distinct social categories, and the regime now proceeded to eliminate all landlords by methods of force and terror reminiscent of the Chinese Communists—and with similar results. Exact figures remain unavailable, but the number of peasants killed during the North Vietnamese land-reform drives from 1954 to 1956 is variously estimated at between 50,000 and 100,000.

This brutal policy led to the outbreak, in November, 1956, of a veritable peasant rebellion in Nghe-An Province—the same region that had been the seat of the pro-Communist peasant uprising of 1930. Ho stepped in, as he often had before, to save the unity of his movement without making irreconcilable enemies of the losers—in this case, Truong Chinh and the pro-Peking wing of the party, which stood for all-out collectivization of peasant land. Truong himself was dismissed as Party secretary-general, though retaining his Politburo seat, while lower-ranking agricultural officials were purged altogether. (Ho assumed the secretary-generalship himself, occupying the post until 1961, when he relinquished it to Le Duan, a South Vietnamese Communist.) In the ensuing "rectification of errors" campaign, tens of thousands of people were released from prison camps, and the Lao-Dong Party saw its membership drop from 700,000 to 420,000.[12] It is doubtful that such drastic actions would have been taken had de-Stalinization not been the order of the day, but the Khrushchev speech at the Twentieth Party Congress in February, 1956, had apparently not fallen on deaf ears in Hanoi. From the Nghe-An outbreaks of November, 1956, until the spring of 1957, the North Vietnamese press freely published graphic accounts of life in D.R.V.N. prison camps—something that was matched

[12] Kux, *op. cit.*, p. 74.

only years later in the Soviet Union, and never in Communist China, even during the "Hundred Flowers" period.

The relative political calm that followed, coupled with a succession of two good crops in 1958–59, made the situation propitious for a gradual change-over from the makeshift wartime pattern of governmental administration to a more permanent system. At the lower levels, the old CRA's were reorganized in 1958, divorcing the military and Party elements (at least officially) from the administrative structure. The new machinery of government was patterned fairly closely after the Soviet model, with locally-elected people's councils, each of which in turn picks an administrative committee from its midst. At the village level, the administrative committees are composed of at least a chairman, vice-chairman, and secretary, while those for larger administrative divisions are correspondingly more elaborate.[13] Interestingly enough, the functioning of this machinery has been criticized even in the Lao-Dong's own newspaper, Nhan-Dan (Humanity), which charged that members of the people's councils often fail to listen to the complaints of their constituents and are not familiar with local problems, causing a "loosening of the ties between the government and the people."[14]

In the matter of territorial organization, the D.R.V.N., unlike South Vietnam, maintained the established provincial boundaries from the French period, thus leaving the population by and large within a familiar administrative environment. Two "autonomous zones," each embracing several provinces, also were created to accommodate the bulk of the 2.5 million minority tribesmen living in North Vietnam: The Thai-Meo Zone (now renamed Tay-Bac, which simply means "northwest") was created in May, 1955; and the Viet-Bac (northern Vietnam) Zone in August, 1956. Both have their own zonal assemblies and administrative committees, whose chairmen in both cases are former People's Army generals of tribal origin, as well as their own militia forces.

CENTRAL POLITICAL STRUCTURE

The most important institutional changes, however, affected the central government. From November, 1946, until May, 1960, the D.R.V.N. had operated with the same National Assembly, but the membership of this body had shrunk from 444 to 202 owing to purges of its non-Communist members, the desertion or capture of others during the war, and normal attrition. The low standing of the Assembly was evidenced by the passage of a resolution in January, 1957—that is, after the 1956 uprising—requesting that the Assembly's parliamentary immunities be respected and that bills proposed by the executive be presented for legislative approval within the proper deadlines.[15] These complaints led the regime to scrap plans for a perfunctory revision of the original 1946 constitution and to charge the

[13] D.R.V.N., Law on the Organization of People's Councils and Administrative Committees of October 27, 1962.
[14] Nhan-Dan, November 24, 1962.
[15] Fall, The Two Viet-Nams, p. 140.

committee appointed for this purpose with framing an altogether new constitution. After a year of preparatory work by the committee, in which Ho took a personal hand, the draft constitution was presented for public discussion in April, 1959, and, after many amendments, was adopted by the legislature on January 1, 1960.

Consisting of 112 articles divided into ten sections, the 1960 D.R.V.N. constitution is set apart from the run-of-the-mill constitutions of the other "people's democracies" by the virulence of its denunciations of the West and the doctrinaire extravagance of its praise of Communism and the personal role of President Ho Chi Minh. The extremely long preamble is a recital of Vietnamese history over the past twenty years and a paean of homage to the "farsighted leadership . . . of President Ho." The latter is vested, in practice, with almost unlimited power, inasmuch as the vice president, who is empowered by the constitution to "replace the President by proxy [sic] in all of his powers," happens to be Ton Duc Thang, an old and faithful friend of Ho's, who is in his eighties and hardly likely to step into Ho's shoes. The premier and five vice premiers wield very little authority, and the unicameral National Assembly—like its prototype, the Supreme Soviet of the U.S.S.R.—is a mere rubber-stamping body.

North Vietnam's judicial system also merits a few comments. While nominally guaranteeing the independence of the courts, the constitution practically nullifies this guarantee by making the courts "responsible" to the people's councils at each level and placing the Supreme Court under the authority of the National Assembly and its Standing Committee. In addition to the courts, the constitution makes provision for a brand new apparatus of "People's Control Organs," which seem to combine features of the Soviet Communist Party's "Control Commission," the Soviet Procurator's Office, and the Chinese Nationalists' "Control Yuan." The People's Contol Organs have both civil and military sections and seemingly are a law unto themselves, except that the Supreme Control Organ (now headed by a reliable old Communist guerrilla leader from South Vietnam, Pham Van Bach) is, like all other government organs, nominally subject to supervision by the National Assembly. A law promulgated in July, 1960, gives the Control Organs the power to bring to justice all cases under inquiry, as well as to "suspend prosecution, [to] participate in judicial processes, and [to] appeal judgments of lower courts."

It is readily apparent that the structure of the North Vietnamese state as fixed by the 1960 constitution contains little that offers any real prospects of liberalization. Elections held since the adoption of the constitution have amply confirmed this. The elections of May 8, 1960, for the new national legislature followed the standard Communist pattern, with 99.8 per cent of the voters casting ballots for a total of 458 candidates "competing" for 404 seats. Two small minority parties (Democratic and Socialist), whose existence is tolerated as long as they obediently collaborate with the Communists, were permitted to put up candidates in certain districts (notably in Hanoi) and won a few seats, but for the most part the voters were offered no choice. The latest regular legislative elections, held in April,

1964, brought little apparent change, except for a reduction of the number of seats to be filled to 366, for which 448 candidates ran.[16]

Thus, North Vietnam has become a full-fledged Communist state, backed by a strong army and a ubiquitous Party. The intellectuals, who enjoyed a brief taste of freedom of expression during the period of relaxed intellectual controls in late 1956 and early 1957, have since been brought thoroughly into line and find themselves literally "frozen out" of any real participation in public affairs. North Vietnam's "Hundred Flowers" period, which took its cue from Communist China, lasted less than six months. Phan Khoi, one of the most brilliant Vietnamese intellectuals, succeeded in publishing only five issues of a new literary journal entitled *Nhan-Van* ("Humanism"—a word play on the name of the Communist daily *Nhan-Dan*, meaning "Humanity") before it was banned. As elsewhere in the Communist bloc, the ensuing crackdown covered all branches of the arts from painting to music, and the repressive measures taken by the regime ranged from forced self-criticism—as in the case of one intellectual who was obliged to confess to the sin of reading the French liberal newspaper *Le Monde*—to outright trial for subversive activity. Five intellectuals, including one woman, were tried in January, 1960, on charges of having collaborated with *Nhan-Van* and were sentenced to prison terms of up to fifteen years. Phan Khoi himself died before going on trial, and his son, Phan Thao, died from unexplained causes seven months later. Thousands of other intellectuals, along with high school and college students, have been conscripted into "education-and-work" programs similar to those instituted in Communist China. . . .

In sum, the North Vietnamese Communists have succeeded in building a solidly-entrenched, totalitarian regime, based upon a disciplined Party structure and the largest land army in Southeast Asia. On the other hand, North Vietnam—like almost every other Communist state—is plagued by a disastrous agricultural situation and cannot find a solution of its acute food problem within the confines of the bloc. It has also become directly engaged in a military contest in which it urgently requires outside support; yet, the availability of such support from Moscow is jeopardized by the Sino-Soviet conflict, while acceptance of large-scale military assistance from Communist China would not only mean committing North Vietnam to Peking's alternative of "liberation war *à l'outrance*," but would also involve sacrificing a relative freedom of maneuver for which Ho Chi Minh and his associates have struggled for almost forty years.

[16] *Viet-Nam Information Bulletin*, May 30, 1964.

Leaders

28

PRINCE NORODOM SIHANOUK OF CAMBODIA*

ROGER M. SMITH

Prince Norodom Sihanouk of Cambodia shares with several other prominent Southeast Asian nationalist leaders the experience of having been in
the forefront of their countries' political development during all of their
adult lives. But few of his Southeast Asian colleagues share his distinction
of also having been the principal leader in his country during most of this
period, and, for many of the last fourteen years, chief of state and head of
government.

Prince Sihanouk is not only chief of state, but, in a very real sense, he is
the essential strength, the apex of the popular pyramid in Cambodia. As
the former king in a country where the monarchy is one of the principal
unifying symbols, tremendous prestige has accrued to him automatically.
Moreover, as king, he won independence for Cambodia, and for this he is
popularly acclaimed as the "Father of Independence." Today, more than a
decade since he abdicated the throne, Prince Sihanouk continues to dominate the executive, legislative, and judicial branches of government in

* Reprinted by permission of the author and the publisher from *Asian Survey*, VII
(June, 1967), 353–62.

Cambodia. He is his country's chief diplomat, its foremost political thinker, and its formulator of ideology. He is, moreover, a great popular leader.

In all of these roles, the youthful Sihanouk (he was forty-three on October 31, 1966) displays a lively and seemingly inexhaustible vitality. He is an indefatigable public speaker, and it is not an unusual day when, between breakfast and dinner, he delivers six speeches in as many different parts of the kingdom. In these public appearances, he shuttles easily between Cambodian and French, and, when speaking Cambodian, between the language of the court and the vernacular. Spontaneity is one of his chief attributes, and his words ring with the emotions that stir within him. His informality and obvious rapport with the common man are especially evident in the manner in which he conducts his popular audiences, where even the most humble peasant is encouraged to come before him with his grievances, suffered often at the hands of public officials and local authority.

An exceptionally gifted man, Prince Sihanouk's talents are many and varied. He is not only an accomplished composer and jazz musician, but also an equestrian, an actor in plays and films, which he writes, directs, and produces, the publisher and chief editorial writer of three Cambodian publications, the captain of championship volleyball and basketball teams, an enthusiastic sailor and water skier, and a student of Cambodian history. His energy and talents are often skillfully employed to evoke interests and attitudes he would like to have his people adopt. Thus, to demonstrate that locally produced textiles can be as attractively utilized as imported ones, he has personally designed clothing from them that he and his children have modeled for state publications. To persuade Cambodians that to work with one's hands is not disgraceful, he participates energetically in manual-labor projects, such as the building of a new railway, schools, and hospitals.

So much has Sihanouk identified himself with his country and people that any criticism of them is regarded by him as a personal affront, and any attack on him is considered as an insult to Cambodia's dignity and honor. He is a voracious reader, and all literature—journalistic, scholarly, or otherwise—that pertains to Cambodia receives his careful scrutiny. Any slur on Cambodia's integrity is immediately noted, and the Prince himself takes pen in hand to defend his country through letters to foreign governments, the editors and correspondents of the world's leading newspapers and news magazines, and to American housewives who seem compelled from time to time to lecture the Prince on the attributes of Western democracy.[1] Moreover, the Prince's prodigious memory and endless curiosity extend beyond events pertaining to Cambodia, and many of his expositions reveal his familiarity with and understanding of Western classical literature, history, philosophy, and religion.

Prince Sihanouk is guided by his capacity to feel sincerely, observe clearly, and act courageously. He has an alert and clear mind that enables him to strike swiftly to the essence of problems. He also has a remarkable

[1] See, for example, the exchange of letters between the Prince and Mrs. Shirley E. Bush, published in *Le Sangkum* (Phnom Penh), No. 5 (December, 1965), 30–31.

feeling for all the nuances of language. He knows how to simplify the most complicated issues and problems and to arouse in his listeners and readers a sense of urgency.

The obvious and central fact of Cambodian politics for much of the last decade is the power that Prince Sihanouk has exercised in public affairs. He has not, however, always enjoyed this omnipotence.

In April, 1941, as a youth of eighteen engrossed in Greek and Latin studies at the Lycée Chasseloup-Laubat in Saigon, he was called back to Cambodia by the French to succeed his grandfather, King Sisowath Monivong, on the throne, because he was believed to be submissive and malleable. There were more likely candidates for the throne, and, indeed, the remoteness of the possibility that he would be seriously considered was reflected in Sihanouk's upbringing and education, which in no way prepared him for the monarchy.[2] Because of his early accession to the throne, he was unable to pursue a formal college education. Today, he takes a certain amount of pride in being, as he said recently, "a man who for the past twenty-three years has been in politics without ever having learned its sciences."[3]

Sihanouk's political acuity was honed during the turbulent post-World War II days, when he had to face simultaneously the problems of negotiating Cambodia's independence from France and of tempering the anti-French nationalism and antimonarchical sentiments of the chief political body of the time, the Democrat Party. Although he owed his crown to the French and was sufficiently foresightful to anticipate the economic and political chaos that would likely result from the abrupt removal of France's power, Sihanouk was also shrewd enough to appreciate the momentum with which nationalism was spreading and to assume an active leadership role.[4]

He pursued independence in earnest, but with reason rather than fervor guiding his action. Negotiation rather than armed revolt was the method he elected, for he felt that it was only in this way that he could get the French Army off Cambodian soil and yet preserve French amity, upon which he hoped to rely for assistance in the difficult postcolonial years. For this tactic, he became the object of attack by the Democrats. Sihanouk was accused of being a playboy and of being in collusion with the French. They attempted to discredit the monarchy, which the Democrats charged had outlived its usefulness to Cambodia and was now the instrument of French rule.

2 See Norodom Sihanouk, "La Monarchie Khmère: Mon Accession au Trône et le Début de Mon Action pour l'Indépendance de Mon Pays," *Le Sangkum*, No. 9 (April, 1966), 21.

3 Lecture at the Faculty of Law, University of Paris, June 26, 1964, quoted in *Réalités Cambodgiennes* (Phnom Penh), July 4, 1964.

4 For details of this period, see Philippe Preschez, *Essai sur la Démocratie au Cambodge*, Fondation Nationale des Sciences Politiques, Centre d'Études des Relations Internationales. Série C: Recherches, No. 4 (Paris: October, 1961), 14–55, and Roger M. Smith, "Cambodia," in G. McT. Kahin, ed., *Governments and Politics of Southeast Asia* (2d ed., Ithaca, N.Y.: Cornell University Press, 1964), pp. 604–18.

Sihanouk was hurt by his assailants' thrusts and offended by their malevolent vilification of the monarchy. Taking advantage of a constitutional provision that all power resides in the king, he assumed charge of the government, dissolved the Parliament, and took upon himself a mandate to achieve independence and establish political stability within two years. Once independence was attained in 1953, as a result of his personal "royal crusade," Sihanouk was able to forestall the campaigns of those who sought to undermine him. Those who had opposed him now found it in their interest to serve him or, if this was not practicable, to quit the country.

With independence won, Sihanouk strove to make it meaningful. He realized that the loyalty and support of the people that his recent victory had won for him would not necessarily guarantee the high degree of national unity he believed to be essential for a modern nation. It would be necessary, he was convinced, to revolutionize the monarchy and to link the people to a conception of government that combined both conservatism and social and economic reform. New governmental structures would have to be created to cope with domestic problems; a stable and sensitive mechanism would have to be devised that could relate the people's interests and demands to political power; and a political consensus would have to be attained. The people themselves, not merely the actual governing body, Sihanouk felt, must develop a sense of responsibility for and participation in the process of political and social modernization.

It was this conviction that led him, in early 1955, to propose a number of constitutional reforms.[5] Elite opposition to his proposals, however, served to convince the king that only by stepping down from the throne—which by custom is above politics—and becoming an active participant in the political arena, could he work effectively toward his announced objectives. On March 2, 1955, therefore, King Norodom Sihanouk abdicated in favor of his father, Prince Norodom Suramarit.

Almost immediately after his abdication, Sihanouk founded the *Sangkum Reastr Niyum* (People's Socialist Community). The *Sangkum* was conceived by the Prince as his chief instrument for creating and maintaining national unity. It was designed not as a political party but as a common meeting ground for all Cambodians who wished to vote into office men loyal to the monarchy, who would strive to institute the Prince's reforms. The people responded enthusiastically to Sihanouk's new role as an active political leader, and it was with their support that he was enabled to block opposition to his ideas. In time, most of the country's political parties dissolved themselves, and their members joined the *Sangkum*. Since then, with nearly unanimous popular support, Prince Sihanouk has dominated Cambodia's political scene.

With the government and the legislature both under the control of the Prince, political stability should have ensued but has, however, remained elusive. Although the *Sangkum* has won every election since 1955, political rivalries within the *Sangkum* and the pursuit by the elite of narrow per-

---

[5] See Norodom Sihanouk, "Étude corrective de la Constitution accordée par S. M. le Roi du Cambodge en 1947," *France-Asie*, XI, No. 108 (May, 1955), 654–63.

sonal interests have continued to characterize political life in Phnom Penh. In addition, new and unforeseen problems have undermined the constitutional reforms Sihanouk had hoped would provide for stable and unharassed government. These have included deteriorating relations with Cambodia's neighbors and the United States, foreign-supported subversive plots, the death of King Suramarit in 1960, and the clamor of the young elite for positions of political power. These issues have generated a succession of ministerial crises, which have resulted in the increasing concentration of power in Sihanouk's hands. They have also led him to exploit fully the institutions of "direct democracy," which he has created as a part of his design to involve the people directly in politics.

One such institution is the National Congress, a biannual forum at which the people are given the opportunity to discuss current issues of domestic and international importance with Sihanouk and his advisors and to voice their complaints against government officials and legislators. The National Congress has met regularly since 1955 on the palace grounds in Phnom Penh. In practice, the agenda of each Congress is conceived and arranged in advance by the *Sangkum*, and although the peasants trek from all over the country to attend it, they usually constitute by choice a passive audience. Here important legislation is initiated, which the National Assembly is directed to enact. Prince Sihanouk presides at the Congress, and through his opening remarks and commentaries interjected throughout the proceedings, he is usually able to influence the course of the meeting. The term "direct democracy" may not be appropriate as a description of the Congress, but there is no doubt that, during the last eleven years, the Congress has helped to create a popular awareness of Cambodia's problems and has created new channels of communication between the government and the people.

Of course, Prince Sihanouk himself is the most important institution of "direct democracy" in Cambodia, and it is in his relationship with the people that this fact may be illustrated. It is part of his genius that during his public career he has been constantly aware of the need to meet and talk with Cambodians from all walks of life, to speak candidly with them about the country's problems and of his hopes for them, to make himself their personal leader, to enlist their aid, and to try to bring them to an understanding of the new attitudes and values they must adopt if Cambodia is once again to take its place as an equal among nations.

Prince Sihanouk is a superb actor. He knows how to seize dramatic opportunities, and he can evoke and maintain in his audience an attitude of breathless attention and expectation. Wherever he goes, whether to a provincial capital, the remotest village, or his residence in the suburb of Chamcar Mon, where he holds frequent audiences for the people, they greet him with a mixture of joy, affection, and reverence. With a salty joke or two that provoke hearty laughter, Sihanouk quickly dispels any feelings of shyness or tension that the people may feel upon meeting him. Almost always planned, but sometimes impromptu, these meetings with the people are usually conducted by the Prince in the Socratic manner. At times, Sihanouk delivers sustained speeches on the problems confronting Cambodia and on his plans for the future. To these, the people listen intently, and they respond to them from time to time with signs of agreement. He lectures, taunts, scolds, and encourages them in turn. To the people, Sihanouk is still king, and they respond to his admonishments and praise by addressing him as *Samdech Euv*—Papa Prince—and by disclosing to him their grievances and problems. More than any other ruler in Cambodian history, Sihanouk in this way has fostered intimacy with the people, and his genuinely benevolent and paternal concern for them has won him their indestructible loyalty.

In seeking, as he declared in his abdication speech, "the realization of the union of all our compatriots," Prince Sihanouk has tried to impart to them a new, powerful, and meaningful expression of old traditions, attitudes, and values. Among other things, he has sought to inspire nationalism through an appeal to history, in particular by recalling the grandeur and power of the once extensive Khmer empire. In his campaign, which is carried to the people through the press, radio, school texts, and by Prince Sihanouk in person, the monarchy is portrayed as representing the continuity of Cambodian culture and history and the present regime's wise political conservatism. As this symbol has become personalized in Prince Sihanouk himself, it no longer arouses an image of a remote power indifferent to the needs of the people, but one of a benevolent paternalistic authority, upon whose judgment rests their welfare and the nation's destiny. Great stress is placed on the suggestion that, throughout Khmer history, the leaders of the nation have been the kings, whom their subjects trusted and to whom they looked for guidance. Thus, the efforts of the government today in social welfare and education are directly associated with the reign of Jayavarman VII in the thirteenth century, when a system of hospitals and roads was extended throughout the kingdom. Prince Sihanouk frequently speaks of the roles played by the kings and people in ancient times. In 1960, he declared:

> Angkor does not only symbolize our victories in war, but also, and above all, the high point in our civilization, expressing itself not only in an incomparable burgeoning of great monuments affirming the mastery of our architects, but also in immense engineering works, irrigation systems, communication networks, and works of art, hospitals, libraries, etc. Would we have had "rois soleils" if they had not been surrounded by scholars, architects, artists, engineers, doctors, men of letters?[6] . . .

In appealing to the past for guidance he has also noted the lessons to be drawn from the decline of the Khmer empire.

> During the Angkorian period, our people were without doubt very united, very well disciplined, and very dynamic, since they were able to make Cambodia a great Asian power. . . .

[6] Quoted in *Réalités Cambodgiennes*, January 22, 1960. For a detailed discussion of the relation in Cambodia of the past to the present, see Milton E. Osborne, "A Note on History and Kingship in Contemporary Cambodia," *Journal of Southeast Asian History*, VII (March, 1966).

Our egocentrism was born from the post-Angkorian decadence. Four centuries have lessened the force of our character. The intoxication of recovered liberty incited us to place our rights before our obligations, although the first gave rise to the second.

Today, we must find again the source that gave grandeur and prosperity to our country during many centuries. This source is made up of union, discipline freely accepted, self-denial and mutual self-help [of people and government].[7]

Another cultural symbol that Prince Sihanouk has injected with new significance is Buddhism. Buddhism, like monarchy, ties the people with their historic past and, by providing them with a common philosophy, acts as a cohesive agent. Among the Buddhist values that Prince Sihanouk extols are brotherhood of man, self-help, and self-sacrifice for the good of the community. These values have been used as a foundation for a highly unorthodox type of socialism that seeks to foster national unity based on the application of socialist measures appropriate to local conditions. According to the Prince:

Buddhism is socialist in its fight against social injustice. Buddha's fight did not cease in the course of his life. He pursued it against dishonesty, thievery, deceit, and lying as well as against the privileges of the upper classes. One often forgets that Buddha was a revolutionary preaching in a feudal society love of one's neighbor and equality among all living beings according to the beautiful formula: "men are judged by their actions." . . .

This temporal and dynamic aspect of Buddhism expresses itself finally in an effort to go beyond man in his personal search for truth, as in Buddha's sacrifices to aid his fellow men. . . . and it is in this form that it makes the best ideal for animating our socialism.

There exist a thousand forms of socialism applied in the daily life of our people. Our rural communities offer many examples which concern themselves, e.g., with large agricultural works, including planting and harvesting, accomplished in common, in the sense of equality and justice that inspires the workers in the fields and towns . . . in the sense of aid brought to the poorest and the disinherited . . . in the sense of a care for the common interest and of a fundamental incapacity to exploit the misery of others.

The rural society which forms the soundest base of our people is as egalitarian and democratic as it can be. The *theories* of socialism are most certainly—and happily—never attained here, but the rural society lives and applies its socialism. And it is precisely by this applied, natural socialism that we wish to enlarge the spirit of the nation.[8]

These views, in turn, are directly related to Sihanouk's belief that political stability depends on the extent to which the people actively engage in the political process and are imbued with a sense of nation. The concept of nation is a relatively new one to the people in Cambodia. Long accustomed to village life that received little attention from the capital, the average Cambodian is only now beginning to comprehend this notion.

[7] Quoted in *Réalités Cambodgiennes*, April 5, 1958. See also Osborne, *op. cit.*

[8] Quoted in *Neak Cheat Niyum* (Phnom Penh), April 30, 1961. See also, *Le Sangkum*, No. 1 (August, 1965), 18–19.

Furthermore, the view that the political elite, on the one hand, and the people, on the other, are irreconcilable groups having different interests and objectives, has had to be overcome. Prince Sihanouk has tried to do this by equating his own interests with those of the nation and, thus, of the people.[9] He has also tried to make the two groups equally active participants in Cambodia's socio-economic development by recruiting from both the labor force required for the construction of schools, roads, bridges, and other public services. At the same time, he has urged the elite to exercise moderation in their ostentation and has tried to inculcate in the people the idea of their equality under the Buddhist religion and before the law. He has also tried to extend their thinking beyond the villages by keeping them informed of national problems.

Prince Sihanouk's success in winning the loyalty and support of the people and infusing them with the feeling of solidarity has not been lost on the political elite; only a few persons have attempted since 1955 to challenge his authority, and they have failed in their efforts because of their inability to attract popular support. In the few instances when his programs have been confronted by vociferous opposition, he has, characteristically, appealed directly to the people, confident that he would receive reaffirmation of their support. Thus, for example, in 1957, when the Democrats accused the National Congress of being little more than a political instrument of the *Sangkum* and of having usurped the constitutional prerogatives of the National Assembly, Prince Sihanouk proposed to the people that they resolve to write the Congress into the constitution. This was done, and the Assembly was induced to adopt the amendment without dissent. He has also used the referendum as a means of alerting his opponents to the near unanimity of popular support for his policies. Still another tack is seen in the Prince's occasional threat to resign from his position of leadership—a suggestion that has invariably resulted in an outpouring of popular sentiment in his favor.

In other instances of opposition, for example, among the young elite in the National Assembly, the mere hint by the Prince that he would not allow them to ride on his coattails in the next election has usually been enough to bring the recalcitrants back into line.[10] Whenever it has been possible, however, Sihanouk has sought to avoid antagonizing potential opponents. This has particularly true with respect to the young Turks, whose obstructionism has been motivated not so much by the extraordinary political power that Sihanouk himself exercises, as by their frustration at being denied positions of power and responsibility in the government by the old guard. In an effort to dissipate their discontent, Sihanouk has

[9] See, for example, Sihanouk's discussion of this point in his interview with Senator Mike Mansfield, November 29, 1965, published in *Kambuja*, No. 10 (January 15, 1966), 17–22.

[10] In the September, 1966, legislative elections, Sihanouk withheld his endorsement from all candidates. By thus throwing the elections wide open, he hoped that many of the rightist and leftist deputies whose quarrels and criticisms of his policies were disrupting the work of the government would be eliminated. Most of them, however, managed to win re-election.

awarded some of them ministerial portfolios. At the same time, he has warned that, if they do not fulfill their responsibilities, he will replace them. With only a few exceptions, his young appointees have worked diligently to meet his expectations.

This is not to say, however, that Prince Sihanouk is no longer troubled by discontent. There is evident among the youth a growing dissatisfaction. Constant princely appeals to them have tended to inflate their sense of self-importance; but when they finish their schooling, the majority of them find little opportunity for work that meets with their ideas of the positions they should occupy. A growing restlessness is also to be found among the civilian and military elite, who have become increasingly dissatisfied with the Prince's economic policies, and who feel that he is doing Cambodia a disservice by quarreling with the United States and by taking up the cause of the National Liberation Front of South Vietnam. But Prince Sihanouk's great popularity among the people, the absence of another personality who could command their loyalty and respect, the lack of consensus among his critics, and the Prince's maneuvers among them have so far enabled him to avert a major crisis over his policies and to forestall any moves to replace him.

One of Prince Sihanouk's greatest strengths is his ability to detect and employ effectively men of considerable talents. In his search for the most able advisors, he has not allowed himself to be distracted by personal differences and dislikes. Some of his present advisors at first not only disliked Sihanouk, but openly opposed him. But Sihanouk, knowing his own weaknesses, chose men who were able to offset them. Among the men upon whom the Prince relies most for advice and counsel are Penn Nouth, a former prime minister who gained prominence during the crusade for independence; Son Sann, Sihanouk's chief economic advisor and long-time Governor of the National Bank; General Lon Nol, who was appointed Prime Minister following the 1966 elections; General Nhiek Tioulong, Inspector-General of the Royal Army; Tep Phan, the energetic mayor of Phnom Penh; Prince Sisowath Sirik Matak, a cousin of Sihanouk's; and Prince Sisowath Monireth, Sihanouk's uncle, who, in late 1966, was given charge of the Prince's own military staff. If, because of death or illness, Prince Sihanouk should be removed from office, some of these men, probably under Prince Monireth's direction, would most likely emerge as Cambodia's new rulers.[11]

In retrospect, it appears that Prince Sihanouk's great political success has been due to his remarkable foresight, a shrewd understanding of his people, and his ability to multiply his effectiveness through the creation of new institutions and the enlistment of popular effort.

At an early stage in Cambodia's postwar development, Prince Sihanouk saw that the world was a very different place, that in order for Cambodia

[11] A few years ago, Prince Sihanouk designated one of his sons, Prince Norodom Naradipo, to succeed him as head of the *Sangkum*. However, Naradipo, until recently a college student in Peking, is generally considered to be too young and inexperienced to take charge of the government.

to once again take her place as an equal among nations, she had to undergo political evolution—a process wherein the new opportunities made available to the people would in the long run probably make the positions of the elite, including his own, untenable. Some changes in Cambodian life had to be effected. The most important of these—the one that has altered the whole fabric of Cambodian political life and for which Prince Sihanouk must be given full credit—was the direct involvement of the people in the modernizing process. As a result of his efforts, political liberties were extended to the people and political institutions were created that have given the people a regular means of voicing and settling their grievances and of finding satisfaction for their demands. Moreover, Prince Sihanouk's earnest efforts to launch programs intended to improve their lot and permit fulfillment of their aspirations have assured their commitment to the continuation of the new social and political structure and to the Prince, himself, who has become a significant expression of the Cambodian people's will.

29

SUKARNO AND HISTORY*

BERNHARD DAHM

Sukarno has never lacked high-sounding official and semi-official titles, especially after the implementation of his Guided Democracy in 1959. He was Commander in Chief of the Indonesian Armed Forces, President, and, after 1963, President for Life; he was also the Great Leader of the Indonesian Revolution, the Creator of *Pantja Sila*, the Father of Marhaenism and the Great Son of West Irian. In addition, he received honorary academic degrees from twenty-six universities all over the world. He was Doctor of Law, Doctor of Technical Sciences, Doctor of Political and Social Sciences, Doctor of Philosophy, and Doctor of Islamic Sciences—but it was not until almost the end of his political career that he was praised as a great historian: On December 23, 1964, Sukarno received the honorary degree of Doctor in the Science of History from Padjadjaran University in Bandung.

* This paper was presented originally at the 1968 Annual Meeting of the Association for Asian Studies, Philadelphia, March 23, 1968, and is published here by permission of the author.

THE RELEVANCE OF MARXISM

In his presentation speech, Professor Ruslan Abdulgani pointed out that, for Sukarno, history was not the mere knowledge of facts and dates but a source of inspiration and a guide to action, and that history had given him a telescope to look into the future. To use the words of Ruslan Abdulgani, Sukarno's view was "historic-telescopic, historic-visionary, and therefore historic-optimistic." It was historic-visionary because Sukarno had predicted the outbreak of a Pacific war as early as 1928, and historic-optimistic because Sukarno, even in dark times, was unshakably convinced of the final success of the Indonesian independence movement as a historical necessity. To quote Ruslan Abdulgani again, Sukarno had used historical materialism in analyzing history and drawing lessons from it. With the "sharp knife of Marxism" he had "dissected" the historical events from the time of Genghis Khan down to Hitler. That already would be sufficient to promote Sukarno to a Doctor of Historical Science. But—so Ruslan Abdulgani continued—Sukarno had done more: He had analyzed the history of culture and the history of the idea of God and found a promising new synthesis in his concept of NASAKOM, the cooperation and solidarity of nationalism, religion, and communism—a synthesis, said Ruslan Abdulgani, that is more sublime than the synthesis of Jean Jaurès, who combined the historical materialism of Marx with the mysticism of Michelet and the hero-worship of Plutarch. The synthesis of Sukarno, however, contains a message for the world, the spirit of tolerance, and that places him even ahead of Jaspers and Toynbee among the historians of the world.[1]

The arguments of Ruslan Abdulgani—at that time often considered "his master's voice"—suggest how Sukarno saw himself at the zenith of his career. In his vote of thanks, Sukarno fully agreed with his pupil and gave a number of examples of the use of the "sharp knife of historical materialism," a term he obviously liked. The new Doctor of History told his audience that it would be a mistake to think that the French Revolution had been caused by the demand for *liberté, égalité,* and *fraternité.* No, it was the political and economic exploitation of the Third Estate by the Church and the feudalists that had led to the capture of the Bastille and subsequent events. It was similarly a mistake to think that the rise of Hitler was due to his program or his appeal to the German people. Instead, Sukarno insisted, Hitler was a tool in the hands of the capitalists, who needed a cudgel against the growing movement of the workers. And it would be yet another mistake to think that the foundation of Malaysia was a particular act of malice by Tunku Abdul Rahman: Abdul Rahman, probably without knowing it, was an instrument of the imperialists and colonialists who had created Malaysia as a last attempt to rescue their interests in Southeast

---

[1] See *Indonesia, Ajam-djantan-sedjarah dunia baru (Indonesia, the cock heralding the history of the new world),* speeches of Sukarno and Ruslan Abdulgani on the occasion of Sukarno's receipt of the honorary degree of Doctor in the Science of History, Padjadjaran University (1965), pp. 29 ff.

Asia. But we know from history, Sukarno concluded, that Malaysia will vanish from the earth, whether there is a Sukarno or not.[2]

One week later the still omnipotent president withdrew Indonesia from the United Nations. The fact that Malaysia had been admitted to the Security Council was for him an undeniable proof that the world organization was dominated by the imperialist powers.

We are not concerned here with the influence of Sukarno's ideology on Indonesian politics; that subject has been competently studied in a recent work by Donald Weatherbee.[3] The point here is that Sukarno's interpretation of history was not a product of his later years, a mere legitimation of his confrontation with Malaysia. The same arguments can be found in earlier articles, in which Sukarno dealt with the French Revolution or the rise of Adolf Hitler. His interest in historical materialism and the dialectical process reaches as far back as 1926. Sukarno is an outstanding example of the appeal of Marxism in a world where, to use the words of Harry J. Benda, "the founding fathers of Marxism would have least expected it."[4]

What appealed to Sukarno most in the theory of Marxism was its prophetic character, the dialectical assurance of the ultimate victory of the suppressed classes at a time when no other hope was left. After World War I, the colonial powers very quickly recovered from their wartime setbacks, and the nationalist movements in Asia, which had temporarily been able to take advantage of the consternation caused in the European world by the outbreak of the Russian Revolution, were again restrained.

Knowing that no existing power could fight the colonial masters, Sukarno's hope for progress in the independence movement was rooted in the dialectic, in the knowledge that action creates reaction, that a thesis has its antithesis. The preconditions for a class struggle did not exist in Indonesia at that time; Sukarno, moreover, did not like the idea of splitting the Indonesian people into rival groups. So he who had always fought for "strong" unity in the independence movement attached the Marxist prophecies to the antithesis between the friends and foes of Indonesian independence—an interpretation that differed from that of the founding fathers themselves. Sukarno argued that the nationalist movement had been created by foreign domination; its suppression would call forth an even stronger reaction; and this dialectical process would finally lead to the victory of the ever-growing independence movement. It was this ideology —what Sukarno early in 1933 called a wedding of nationalism and Marxism —that turned class-struggle into race-struggle. Sukarno tried to keep his antithesis—often identified with the color-line between white and brown— as sharp as possible.[5]

This dialectical process, however, did not work, for the simple reason that one could not merely substitute an antiforeign sentiment for the material-

[2] *Ibid.*, pp. 11 ff.

[3] Donald E. Weatherbee, *Ideology in Indonesia: Sukarno's Indonesian Revolution* (New Haven, Conn.: Yale University Southeast Asia Studies, 1966).

[4] Harry J. Benda, "Reflections on Asian Communism," this volume, chapter 18.

[5] See Bernhard Dahm, *Sukarnos Kampf um Indonesiens Unabhängigkeit* (Frankfurt and Berlin: 1966), pp. 72 ff. and 116 ff.

istic base of Marxism. Right from the beginning, therefore, Sukarno looked for allies for the Indonesian independence movement in the outer world. The application of historical materialism to conditions in Southeast Asia provided more hope than did its application to the Indonesian scene alone. The activities of the great powers in Southeast Asia opened the prospect of a clash in that part of the world that Indonesia could make use of. Although Sukarno had spoken in 1928 about the possibility of a Pacific war, it was the Communist Tan Malaka who was the first Indonesian to argue, in 1925, that the clash between Japan and Western powers was a historical necessity.[6]

Sukarno, who used Tan Malaka's pamphlet as reading material in his cadre courses, accepted the latter's analysis because of its "scientific foundation," and, in his speeches, he publicized the idea of a war in Southeast Asia and its possible consequences for Indonesia. Even before the judges in his trial on charges of subversion in 1930, Sukarno confirmed that he had spoken of—and still believed in—the possibility of such a war as a logical consequence of the economic competition of the big powers in Southeast Asia.[7]

In later years, after Sukarno had been exiled from Java in 1934 and was isolated from the independence movement, he tried to apply the method of historical materialism to both historical and political events. He saw indications of a decline of capitalism all over the world, and particularly clearly in Italy and Germany, where Fascist parties were needed to protect the interests of the monopoly capitalists. The beginnings of the same development were to be seen in England and the United States. In the United States, however, the challenge to the ruling classes was not yet so acute, he wrote in 1941, that they needed to play with the whip.[8] And, finally, the steadily growing initiative of Japan offered promising aspects to a banished nationalist waiting for his chance to return to the Indonesian independence movement. In earlier times, Sukarno wrote in 1941, he had liked the theory of Marxism; nowadays it was a part of the peace of his soul.[9] Therefore, the long-awaited outbreak of the Pacific war was no surprise to him at all: It was the final confirmation—as he put it at that time—of the "relevance of Marxism in dealing with political, historical and social questions."[10]

The Function of Indonesian History

If historical materialism provided a method for predicting Indonesia's future, it did not determine Sukarno's attitude toward Indonesian history.

[6] See Tan Malaka, *Menudju Republik Indonesia* (Djakarta: 1962), pp. 58 ff. This is an Indonesian version of his *Naar de Repoeblik Indonesia* (Canton: 1925).

[7] See Sukarno, *Indonesië klaagt aan* (*Indonesia Accuses*) (Amsterdam: 1931), pp. 91 ff.

[8] See Sukarno, *Dibawah Bendera Revolusi* (*Under the Banner of the Revolution*) (Djakarta: 1963), p. 601.

[9] *Ibid.*, p. 511.

[10] *Ibid.*, p. 510.

Whereas he strictly denied any influence from the ideologies of the French Revolution, the rise of Hitler, or World War II, he tried to strengthen Indonesian nationalism precisely by stimulating awareness of the greatness of the past. In his defense in December, 1930, he told his judges that he and his Partai Nasional Indonesia had attempted to promote nationalism by telling the people that they had a glorious past, by intensifying the notion that the present time is dark, and by showing the masses the promising future.[11]

Quoting this, Bambang Utomo, writing in D. G. E. Hall's *Southeast Asian Historians* some ten years ago, pointed out that Sukarno was "one of the first Indonesians to formulate ideas on their people's past."[12] I do not subscribe to this statement. In my opinion, Sukarno's interest in Indonesian history was very limited. He could sum up the major kingdoms of the past, it is true; he liked to speak about the greatness of Majapahit, of Srivijaya and Mataram, and to say that the Indonesian flag was flown and honored as far away as Madagascar, Persia, and China, but not without adding that it was a feudal past that nobody would like to see revived.[13]

The glorious past served Sukarno as a contrast to the present; it was a means of arousing self-respect and the will for independence in his audiences. The function of Indonesian history was determined: it was object rather than subject of his interest. There is not a single article among his many known writings of the 1920's and 1930's dealing with a special problem of any of the ancient empires, not even with the life or the ideas of an Indonesian hero. There is no esteem for the Borobudur or the Prambanan, the great temples of the Buddhist and the Hindu past in Middle Java; there is no attempt to interpret the Nāgarakĕrtāgama, the Pararaton, the Sejarah Melaju, or any other chronicle of early times, though all had been published by Dutch scholars in the first decades of the twentieth century.

The honor of first having formulated ideas on Indonesian history should go to E. F. E. Douwes Dekker, a nationalist as fiery as Sukarno, as much attracted by the Marxist way of thinking, and as often persecuted, jailed, and banished as the latter—but a man who nevertheless found the time for intensive study of the past, for the simple reason that he was interested in it. In Dekker's *Guide for the Indonesian Nationalist*, published in 1921, there are more than 200 pages dealing with the historical, social, and cultural conditions of empires, the names of which Sukarno barely knew.

Even the Indonesian Communist Party (PKI) of the 1920's seems to have been more aware of Indonesian history than was Sukarno. When Party members prepared their revolution of 1926 in December, 1925, they met at Prambanan under the eyes of Shiva, Vishnu, and Brahma, thus conjuring up the spirits of the past. When Sukarno founded his Partai Nasional Indonesia in 1927, he chose as the founding date the fourth of July.

[11] See Sukarno, *Indonesië klaagt aan*, p. 64.
[12] See D. G. E. Hall, ed., *Historians of Southeast Asia* (London: Oxford University Press, 1963), p. 75.
[13] Sukarno, *Indonesië klaagt aan*, p. 65, and *Dibawah Bendera Revolusi*, p. 623.

It was a test of the magical strength of American Independence Day, which should also lead the Indonesian movement to its goal.[14]

For Sukarno, digging in the past and searching for hidden treasures in history meant wasting time. He admired the greatness of the past, as he repeatedly stated, only as a milestone on the way of the people, as a proof that in earlier times Indonesian society was dynamic and would have developed, had there not been interference from outside. Once this was perceived, the study of history was no longer necessary. Writing in 1941 about his attitude toward history, Sukarno asked:

> May we love the greatness of the past as such and forget about the demands and requirements of the present? May we become ancient culture-maniacs, whose thinking and imagination is filled with temples, Nāgarakĕrtāgamas, Mpu Tantulars, Panuluhs and other old relics like that? The bygone times are nice but they are dead. I could compare them with a pretty girl who has died. Look at her nice body lying on a golden bench calling forth emotion and ardent desire. O, bring flowers, blossoms of jasmine, wreathe the face of the lovely goddess, put the flowers into her black hair so that they liken glistening stars in the darkness of night. Oh, how beautiful is our holy goddess! Our hearts are affected, our hands join as in a prayer, our knees sink down to the floor and our soul is touched. But the beauty we adore is dead. We may cry until blood flows from our eyes, but she will remain dead. The lips of our goddess are cold, the color of her face is pale; no sign of breath moves her lovely bosom. There is a smell of incense in the room, and everything is oppressed and grieved.
>
> And I ask you: Can we admire a beauty like this in our daily life? To be sure, we have not got the time for that kind of corpse-cult and worship of the dead![15]

How, then, to draw "the lifeline of the dynamism of the olden times into our very days?" This Sukarno regarded as the main task of the intellectuals. For the majority of the people, Indonesian history was an embarrassing multitude of names, and just as meaningless as for Sukarno himself. In his attempt to promote nationalism, he needed something else. In the same article, we find the remark: "Better than to desire the nice corpse is to admire Gatotkatja, who is alive!"[16]

Thus, Sukarno referred to the interest of the Javanese population in mythical stories that had been handed down from generation to generation, the affection of the masses for the Javanized Hindu epics, the Mahābhārata and the Ramayana, which formed the major part of the Indonesian shadow play, the *wajang*. From its performances all classes of the population drew—and draw—their ethical principles and maxims for daily life. They knew the stories of the Pandavas and Kauravas, of Rama and Hanoman, of demons, gods, and heroes almost by heart; but they were again and

---

[14] In Sukarno's journal, *Suluh Indonesia Muda* (*The Torch of Young Indonesia*), attention was given to the "coincidence of the days." For the meeting of the PKI at Prambanan, see Ruth T. McVey, *The Rise of Indonesian Communism* (Ithaca, N.Y.: Cornell University Press, 1965), p. 311 ff.

[15] Sukarno, *Dibawah Bendera Revolusi*, p. 621.

[16] *Ibid.*, p. 624.

again fascinated by the interpretations and allusions of the *dalang*, the performer of the plays, which lasted from early evening throughout the night until dawn.

This was the milieu Sukarno needed. In his speeches, the *wajang* puppets came to life; friends and foes of the Indonesian movement were identified with the heroes and demons of the myth. It is well known that Sukarno himself drew strength from his heroes' fates in times of depression,[17] and that since his early youth the *wajang* had been his favorite entertainment.[18] So he knew how to attract the masses and to give them an idea about his party and its aims. For instance: The goddess Devi Sita had been taken by force by the demon Rahwana, but her husband, the God Rama, and his ally Hanoman were on the way for her liberation. There was no difficulty in indicating that Devi Sita was Indonesia, that the demon Rahwana was the colonial power, and that Rama and Hanoman and his army of apes were the Indonesian movement, and everybody knew the story's end.

The mythical stories thus completed history and supported it in its task of arousing nationalism and strengthening the liberation movement. In dealing with the Indonesian past, Sukarno followed other principles than those of historical materialism. Of course, there are some references to feudalism but again—as could be noted already in his attempt at applying dialectics to the Indonesian nationalist movement—little attention is paid to historical materialism. For the progress of the movement, he relied on race-struggle, based on antiforeign sentiments rather than on class-struggle; when dealing with Indonesian history, he saw dynamism, spirit, and ideas rather than the productive forces as the prime movers. The same observation can be made about Sukarno's interpretation of the history of Islam, whose function for him was similar to that of Indonesian history, namely, the strengthening of the independence movement.

Sukarno's explanation of the orthodoxy and backwardness of Islam in the Middle Ages was that the later Muslim generations grasped the ashes rather than the "fire" of the teachings of the Prophet and of the time of the first caliphs; they did not follow the spirit and the great ideas, but stiffened in formalism.[19] The same metaphor (which Sukarno had taken from Jean Jaurès) was used in his concluding remarks on Indonesian history: If the Indonesian intellectuals only admired the past, they would grasp only the ashes. Taking the fire from the spirit of Śrivijaya, the spirit of Mataram, the spirit of Majapahit, would mean the realization of the "lifeline of history in our own days," which he then described as "the fire of democracy, the fire of liberty, the fire of manliness, and the fire of human thoughts which flame from the olden days down to the present, and from our days into the future."[20]

Little is left of historical materialism. Here history is no longer a dialectical and mechanical process as he had perceived it in the French Revolu-

[17] See, for example, Cindy Adams, *Sukarno* (Indianapolis, Ind.: Bobbs-Merrill, 1965), p. 101.
[18] See Dahm, *op. cit.*, pp. 17 ff.
[19] *Ibid.*, pp. 138 ff.
[20] See Sukarno, *Dibawah Bendera Revolusi*, p. 625.

tion, in the rise of National Socialism, in the decline of England and America, or in the creation of Malaysia; here it is instead an inspiring force and guide to action. A similar approach to history can also be noticed in his comments on developments in India, Turkey, and even the Soviet Union. Sukarno's political division of the world into friends and foes—of the Indonesian independence movement in earlier years, of his so-called New Emerging Forces in more recent times—also ran straight through his interpretation of history: the history of colonial, Fascist, and imperialist powers strictly follows the laws of historical materialism, while the history of Indonesia and its allies depends on the decisions of men, whether they choose the fire or the ashes.

Materialism on one side, idealism on the other. From this, it is obvious that history for Sukarno has always been a weapon to promote nationalism and progress on the one hand, to attack imperialism and colonialism on the other. As long as he was fighting his enemies, he stood behind the shelter of Marxist philosophy; as soon as he tried to strengthen the solidarity of his allies, he emerged as a prophet, calling on spirit, ideas, and the fire of human thoughts.

HISTORY AND SUKARNO

Does Sukarno, then, represent a break with the Indonesian past; can he be regarded as one of the populist leaders of the world and separated from Indonesian history? I doubt this, despite the fact that he had little interest in Indonesian history as such.

So far, no distinction has been made between Indonesian and Javanese history. For Sukarno, they were one. Right from the beginning of his political career, he worked for Indonesian independence rather than a Javanese revival. In his eyes, only the empires of Śrivijaya and Majapahit were "national states." He saw local kingdoms that did not try to establish their rule over wider parts of the archipelago as representatives of regionalism and tribalism, whether they had their merits in fighting the Dutch or not. For Sukarno, the unity of Indonesia was unquestionable. As he put it in his famous *Pantja Sila* speech on June 1, 1945: "Even a child, if he looks at the map of the world, can point out that the Indonesian archipelago forms one entity."[21]

However, Sukarno himself can hardly be understood apart from the Javanese environment, the Javanese past, and the Javanese way of thinking. We have seen that he was strongly aware of the significance of Javanese myth, and we venture to assert that his division of the world into friends and foes, into wickedness and righteousness, has its origins in the world of *wajang* rather than in Marxism, which was later welcomed as a scientific confirmation of a future victory.

Marxism and Islam were considered as allies and were married with Indonesian nationalism. In 1941, Sukarno wrote: "I am a convinced nationalist, a convinced Muslim, a convinced Marxist. The synthesis of these

[21] See Sukarno, *The Birth of Pantja Sila* (Djakarta: 1950), p. 22, and this volume, chapter 19, p. 270.

trends is living within myself; in my own eyes it is a powerful synthesis."[22]

And here we encounter another decisive imprint of Indonesian history on Sukarno, that is, the legacy of Javanese syncretism. Unconsciously, as a schoolboy, Sukarno had already tried to combine elements of the various ideologies, and throughout the years to come, he strove to erase the contradictions of his synthesis. He told the Marxists that opposition to religion was a misunderstanding of Marxism, boldly stating that philosophical materialism was mere speculation and that Marxism meant historical materialism and nothing else.[23] He urged the Indonesian Muslims to accept the Marxists as allies, and he was furious about the so-called anti-Communist phobia. He was utterly convinced that Islam and Communism could work together harmoniously, if they did not fall into dogmatism but took the "fire" of the teachings of their respective prophets.

For Sukarno, nationalism, Islam, and Marxism were more than casual allies: they were essentially one. In his thinking, belief in Allah represented the category of profundity, Marxism represented the category of time, and nationalism the category of space. In a typically Javanese drive for a harmonious order, he had thus combined the heterogeneous trends for which he later found the NASAKOM formula. He thought these doctrines could solve the problems of a divided world and lead to eternal peace, once imperialism had been finally defeated.

The tragic events of 1965 have shown that Sukarno's message failed, even in Indonesia. But even after the mass murders, Sukarno insisted upon the practicability of his ideas. In his last public address, in August, 1966, he declared: "You cannot leave history." As he understood history, it was his historical role to reconcile the different ideologies; so he stood by NASAKOM, although he knew that this meant the end of his political career.

Indonesian students used his phrase, "You cannot leave history," for a wordplay. From its Indonesian version, "Djangan sekali meninggalkan sedjarah," they formed the acronym, DJAS MERAH, that is, "red jacket," to indicate that Sukarno was a Communist in disguise. But we had better take Sukarno's phrase literally, for the gist, the essence, of his ideology was syncretistic; it was Javanese.

[22] See Sukarno, *Dibawah Bendera Revolusi*, p. 513.

[23] Sukarno made this point for the first time in his article, "Nationalisme, Islamisme, Marxisme," in 1926 (see Dahm, p. 57). He has reiterated it since then in his lectures on *Pantja Sila* (*Pantja Sila Sebagai Dasar Negara* [Djakarta: 1961], p. 84), in public speeches, even before congresses of the Communist Party (see H. A. Notosutardjo, ed., *Kepribadian Revolusi Indonesia* [Djakarta: 1964], p. 135), and also on the occasion of his receipt of the Doctor of History degree (see *Indonesia, Ajam-djantan*, note 1, p. 404).

30

HO CHI MINH, LIKE IT OR NOT*

BERNARD B. FALL

"You know, it's damned difficult to tell people to hate a guy who looks like a half-starved Santa Claus" was the way an American member of the Saigon psychological-warfare services explained one of his problems to a journalist recently. Another American, an officer faced with the hundredth affirmation that, no matter what his politics, Ho Chi Minh was the George Washington of Vietnam, said: "All right, so he *is* the George Washington of Vietnam. But do *we* have to get stuck with all the Benedict Arnolds?"

These near-desperate statements sum up a major difficulty in making the whole Vietnamese war credible. Public opinion was easily rallied in the age of Hitler, Mussolini, and Tojo, men who not only looked loathsome but *were* loathsome. Stalin made a plausible hate-figure too, and Mao Tse-tung doesn't do badly, with his Red Guards playing the Yellow Peril out of Central Casting.

But with Ho Chi Minh, we enter the era of the Hate Gap. It isn't easy for the United States to convince us that a frail seventy-seven-year-old

* Reprinted by permission of Esquire Magazine © 1967 by Esquire, Inc., from *Esquire* (November, 1967).

gentleman with a wispy beard and rubber sandals, ruling a country the size of Florida with an army about as big as the Swiss militia and a hundred-plane air force, is a "threat to the freedom of Southeast Asia" and to America's position in the world. True, North Vietnam is a Communist state, and Ho is a Communist, and North Vietnam is indubitably involved in the Vietcong insurgency in the South. And it is equally a fact that, with Ho as president of the country, a land reform was rammed through in 1953–56 that, even according to North Vietnamese sources, caused "many unlawful executions." Unfortunately for the Hate Gap, though, it is also true that Ho himself stopped these land-reform excesses and fired the party hacks who were directly responsible.

Unlike other world leaders on whichever side of whatever tattered curtains remain, Ho constantly underplays himself. He has thus far abstained from expressing his views on art in general or portraits of himself in particular; he does not pretend that assiduous study of his writings will overcome all problems; he has confined his literary efforts to one brief comic sketch, *Le Dragon de bambou* (1923 vintage, and a flop to such a point that it never reached Hanoi), and to brief political pamphlets and speeches. An exception is a slender volume of poems written while he was in a Chinese Nationalist prison in 1942–43. One poem, *The Leg Irons*, reflects his feelings at a time when he was totally at the mercy of others:

> With hungry mouth open like a wicked monster
> Each night the irons devour the legs of people:
> The jaws grip the right leg of every prisoner:
> Only the left is free to bend and stretch.
>
> Yet there is one thing stranger in this world:
> People rush to place their legs in irons.
> Once they are shackled, they can sleep in peace.
> Otherwise they would have no place to lay their heads.

Finally, there are as yet no mountains, towns, or even international airports named after Ho, at least officially. There is, of course, the torturous and inhospitable Ho Chi Minh Trail, but this was named by the French Army, and the name was inherited by the Americans.

To unconditional enthusiasts, all this reflects a real passion for humility, in the same sense that Communist Chinese leaders wear unadorned uniforms. Yet the latter were—at least until the dust settled around the Red Guards—as slavishly adulated as leaders ever were anywhere in the world. Ho also wears a suntan version of the Stalin-Mao uniform jacket. But as a Japanese legislator noted when he visited him in 1966, the jacket was badly frayed at the collar, as if, in a poor country at war, he could not afford a new one. And that precisely is the point of difference. Ho may not be as egregiously humble as certain other uniform-wearing types, but he is a simple man with simple tastes and honestly prefers to dress this way. He knows what he likes. *Time* magazine, which attempts to be well-informed at least about small things, once informed its readers that Ho, who in 1955 smoked Philip Morris cigarettes while offering local brands to visitors, has now switched to Salems.

The apparent precision of these details of Ho's life conveniently hides large unknown areas, gaps of four or five years in which he *may* have been married, *may* have lived in Boston, Massachusetts, *may* have been with Mao in China, *may* have studied at the Lenin School in Moscow. Even the Communist press has never quite been able to make up its mind about Ho. His birth dates are mangled as to day, month, and year, and, in 1932, the London *Daily Worker* published an eloquent obituary of "Comrade Nguyen Ai-Quoc," his pseudonym of the time. (In fact, the ever-vigilant French Sûreté got a good identification photograph of one of Ho's ears in the early 1920's, and I am assured that recent photographs tally with that, thus making rumors of a second Ho Chi Minh rather implausible.) The same kind of confusion seems to hold true for Ho's personal life. Even Mao Tse-tung is acknowledged to be a family man—in fact he married a very pretty actress who may yet turn out to be a political power in her own right—and so was Stalin, up to a point. None of this applies to Ho, who many panegyrists claim has devoted his whole life to the Cause. To this day, no one has been able to pin down the story that he once had a wife and daughter who died in the 1940's, while the Vietminh were fighting for liberation from Japan.

Actually, Ho was born on May 19, 1890, at Kim-Lien, about fourteen miles from the now much-bombed city of Vinh in central Vietnam and north of the 17th parallel that now divides the country.

Vinh is the capital of the province of Nghe-An, an area that has always produced more than its fair share of strong-willed men. Ho's father was one of these. He was an ardent patriot, and he joined eagerly when a new, young Vietnamese emperor, Ham-Nghi, ascended the throne in 1884 and opened war against the French. The bemused French colonialists were at first unable to cope with this result, led by the country's elite and aptly dubbed The Intellectual's Rebellion, but by 1888, they had managed to crush it.

Ho's father, heartbroken, vowed not to serve the colonial power or the native administration it controlled, and returned to Kim-Lien, where he still owned a house and a plot of land (a normal procedure for Vietnamese officials in disgrace, and one of the reasons why they will, to this day, own a farm in their native town, regardless of how much other wealth they may possess). Ho was thus born into a family where the presence of the French was bitterly resented and in which patriotism was an article of faith. At Ho's birth, his father gave him the family name of Nguyen (the Vietnamese equivalent of Smith) That Thanh (Who Will be Victorious). By the time the boy was old enough for school, he was carrying messages for the anti-French underground, and when he transferred to the French lycée at Vinh, he was promptly expelled, probably in 1905. "Poor grades," the teachers said. "Politics," say North Vietnamese historians.

Next, Ho's father enrolled his son in the Lycée Quoc-Hoc in the imperial capital of Hué. Quoc-Hoc was an experiment: it blended the best of

French education with a solid groundwork in Vietnamese culture. The school was later to become a hotbed of passionate intellectual Vietnamese nationalism. At the time, it was, like the rest of Vietnam, under French control, and Ho dropped out around 1910 without a diploma, thus ending his formal education. (Accordingly, he has no claim to the title "Doctor" that many Asians bestow upon him.)

But, even without a degree, Ho now had more education than all but a small elite of his compatriots. His next step was to teach school in the sleepy southeast Vietnamese fishing town of Phan-Thiet, where there was a nationalist curriculum patterned after that of Quoc-Hoc. But, as everywhere else, teachers were paid starvation salaries, and, by 1911, Ho was in Saigon attending a trade school, probably in the field of cooking and baking, since for a Vietnamese such a specialty was a sure way to lucrative employment in a European household. (It has by now probably been forgotten that a minor flap ensued in Washington when it was rumored that Mrs. Kennedy was trying to hire away the Vietnamese cook of the French Ambassador.)

In the summer of 1912, when he was twenty-two, Ho landed a messboy's job on the French liner, *Latouche-Tréville*. His selection of a French ship on an Atlantic run symbolizes a key political decision he had made: Instead of turning for guidance and inspiration to China or Japan, as did more conservative fellow Nationalists, he had opted for the West against the East. North Vietnam's main Party theoretician explained Ho's choice in a small book published in Hanoi in 1966: "What attracts [Ho] to these [Western] countries is their ideology of freedom, of the sovereignty of the people, of democracy, of science and technology. . . . He thought that to fight the French colonialists with the help of Japanese militarists would be to 'hunt the tiger only to be eaten by the wolves.'"

A few months before World War I broke out, Ho settled down in London. During his time at sea, he had perfected the already superb French acquired at school and had learned good English. Now he found a job at the posh Carlton Hotel, where the incomparable Escoffier held sway as the greatest chef of his time, to the point that Frenchmen would go to London in order to dine. Escoffier liked the slim, quiet Asian youth and soon promoted him to the pastry division, a choice spot. Here Ho had ample chance to see the constant side-by-side existence of riches and poverty, even in a world capital. To supplement the meager salary (of which he sent a portion to his family in Kim-Lien), he shoveled snow at London schools before going on to his hotel job. It is said the experience with Escoffier has left him with a gourmet's taste and, like some American presidents, an occasional urge to take his turn in the kitchen.

What exactly Ho did next is lost in mythology and hagiography. But at some point, in London, he made his first politically significant contact, with the Chinese-dominated Overseas Workers' Association. This organization, originally concerned with improving working conditions of foreign laborers who were usually excluded from local unions, had begun to address itself to the political life of its members once they had returned to their homelands. Yet, at the age of twenty-four, Ho was little more than a naïve young Asian trying to make a living, like thousands of West Indians and Pakistanis in London today. There is strong circumstantial evidence that he *did* return to sea on the dangerous transatlantic wartime runs, visiting Boston and New York and Gulf Coast ports: he later wrote vivid accounts of what his present Prime Minister, Pham Van Dong, calls "the barbarities and ugliness of American capitalism, the Ku Klux Klan mobs, the lynchings. . . ." A pamphlet written by Ho in Moscow in 1924, and entitled *La Race Noire*, seems to be in part based on what he saw and heard in the United States during the years 1914–16.

Late in 1917, Ho went to war-torn France, and, this time, he was moving directly into a political storm. At home in Vietnam, a rebellion against French colonial troops led by a new young emperor, Duy-Tan, had just been put down, while in France itself, a mutiny within the French army was put down by General Pétain with the help of loyal Vietnamese military-police units. Tens of thousands of Vietnamese, themselves restless, were seeing cracks in the veneer of the "omnipotent" whites.

But something else happened in 1917. A Communist revolution had broken out in Russia under Lenin. The tenets of the heady new faith included immediate independence for all colonial territories, not only at home but throughout the world. To Ho, the Russian Revolution came as a flash of recognition: here was *his* program, clearly presented and part of a seemingly coherent philosophy identifiable with a political party that would accept him. In France, that party was the French Socialist Party. He joined enthusiastically. By the end of World War I, he was a fully accepted member of the French Socialist hierarchy and met on a basis of equality with almost every politician who was to hold power in France through the 1950's. To this day, whenever he meets Frenchmen, he immediately begins to ask about *mes amis*.

Meanwhile, he had to make a living. Ho's Chinese calligraphy, laboriously learned as a child, suddenly proved useful in the profession of photoretouching. The Socialist Party's newspaper, *La Vie Ouvrière*, of 1918, carried small classified advertisements testifying to Ho's adventure into free enterprise under a new name, Nguyen Ai-Quoc (The Patriot): "You who wish a living remembrance of your relatives, have your photographs retouched at Nguyen Ai-Quoc's. Handsome portraits and handsome frames for 45 francs."

Apparently the business did not exactly flourish, and Ho, with the war at an end, began to travel throughout France as a political agitator among the almost 100 thousand Indochinese in France who awaited the few and long-delayed repatriation convoys. These Asians had seen Europeans at their worst through four war years; they had also seen, as Mao Tse-tung was to express it only a few years later, how much power was really growing out of the barrel of a gun. And Ho, as well as other Vietnamese exile leaders, now put all their hatred of colonialism into words. It is no exaggeration to say that the Indochina war against the French, and now against the United States, began in the repatriation camps of 1918–19.

The next formative shock for Ho was the great 1919 Versailles Peace

Conference. America's President Woodrow Wilson had hoped that this Conference would be the cradle of a just peace for all and would bring the right of self-determination to nations yet unborn. But in a white man's world, *nobody* was about to back independence for any African or East Asian country—a lesson that the Gandhis and the Nehrus, the Haile Selassies and Ho Chi Minhs had every intention of remembering. Ho and some of his friends laboriously drew up a modest eight-point program and had it printed over Ho's signature. The finished product did not look very impressive (the French printer even misspelled Ho's name), but Ho, in a second-hand pin-striped suit, pinch-waisted overcoat, derby, and a tan muffler tossed over his left shoulder, was off to Versailles by suburban railroad.

Ho and his friends had wasted their time and money. Versailles nowhere records that a petition for "Annamite" (as the term then was) independence had been officially taken under consideration, and Ho's petition never even got a hearing. At Versailles died Ho's hopes for a "liberal" solution for his country, and he also heard other complaints among unsuccessful petitioners, the Irish in the lead. Armed revolution was the answer, they muttered: the road to power via the terrorist's bomb and the gun barrel. One large country, absent from Versailles, was at that very moment proving that point—the Soviets in Russia—and their example was wildly debated in every socialist party in the world. There were anarchists throwing bombs in the United States, red flags flying in Milan, huge strikes racking Britain, as the more radical elements pressed for world revolution—*now*.

In France, the clash came on Christmas Day, 1920, at the Eighteenth National Congress of the Socialist Party. Ho participated, according to the record, as "Comrade Indochinese Delegate." A period picture shows us a sallow young man with shining, deep-set black eyes, speaking before a crowd of well-fed, jowly French faces. With incredible single-mindedness, Ho pleaded for the colonials. "In its selfish interest [France] conquered our country with bayonets. Since then we have not only been oppressed and exploited shamelessly, but also tortured. . . . I cannot . . . reveal all the atrocities that the predatory capitalists have inflicted on Indochina." He ended with a passionate plea that the Socialist Party act to "support the oppressed natives." Among the delegates, there was an uncomfortable silence.

For Ho, this apathy was appalling. On December 30th, the last day of the Congress, he decided Communism was the only way out for Vietnam, on pragmatic, nationalistic grounds, and he became a founding member of the French Communist Party.

His life was changed. From an isolated young man in a hostile community, he was now a sought-after Party official in a world-wide, charismatic movement with the financial backing of a powerful state: the Soviet Union. Funds suddenly became available for more lecture trips inside France; Ho started the Intercolonial Union in 1921 as a "front" to attract members. The Union's paper, *Le Paria* (The Outcast), reflected Ho's own direct style, hammering away at concrete problems, never bothering with doctrine.

As one reads Ho's writings forty years later, one can only be amazed at

how difficult it is to pin down the "essential Ho" to a small booklet of his
quotations, as was done with Mao Tse-tung's writings; for Ho, throughout
his life, has never sought to convert the world to anything except the existence of an independent, united Vietnam. In fact, that single-mindedness
about a country nobody had ever heard of often irritated the senior Comintern leaders at the time, since they felt they had done everything that
was necessary once they had passed a few resolutions condemning colonialism. But the published records of the Comintern Congresses between 1922
and 1924 are full of statements by "Comrade Nguyen Ai-Quoc" about the
necessity for colonial revolution. In fact, in 1924, Ho made an impassioned
prophecy at the Fifth Comintern Congress that the way to defeat the industrialized powers was *not* by labor agitation in the West, but by a ceaseless series of debilitating colonial wars of liberation. Ho turned out to be
right.

By now, the Comintern had appointed Ho to its Southeast Asia Bureau.
He began to sign articles with a new pseudonym: Nguyen O-Phàp ("Nguyen
Who Hates the French"). This was a little too much for the French Communist leadership, and he was told to tone down his statements. Instead,
Ho decided to return, at last, to the Far East, to put into practice what he
had been preaching. In South China, the antiwarlord elements of the Chinese Republic had regrouped, and one of their generals, Chiang Kai-shek,
was setting up a modern army under Russian guidance. Ho's job, nominally
to serve as secretary-interpreter, in fact consisted of reorganizing the Vietnamese exile community in South China.

Adopting the name of Song Man Tcho (the actual list of all his pseud-
onyms is almost endless), Ho was in his element: talking with his own
countrymen, organizing them for liberation. Soon he had established an
efficient "Revolutionary Youth Association," whose members, after training in China, began to reinfiltrate Vietnam and to organize strikes in
schools, plantations, and mines. Heavy-handed French repression only won
new recruits for Ho. Among them was the son of a high-ranking mandarin
of the Vietnamese imperial court. Soon he became Ho's most trusted lieutenant, and today Pham Van Dong is Ho's prime minister.

Other recruits brought only problems. Some of the young Vietnamese
had no special feeling of loyalty to Moscow, and their return to Vietnam
after training would only have endangered Ho's underground. Their names,
therefore, were often conveniently "leaked" by Ho to the French Sûreté.
This factionalism remains a constant bane in Vietnam. Between 1925 and
1930 alone, the Vietnamese somehow managed to have *three* bitterly-
quarreling Communist parties that were not above selling out their Trotskyist and nationalist competitors, who in turn revealed what they knew
of the Communists. It was a mutual decapitation leadership that, to this
day, accounts for the instability of institutions in South Vietnam.

Now events began to move quickly in the life of Ho. When Chiang and
his Russian advisers split over the role the rising Chinese Communist Party
was to play, Ho escaped the ensuing massacre of the Communists by fleeing
to Buddhist Thailand. The Vietnamese community there gave him shelter,

and he began to preach in the villages, traveling in the disguise of a saffron-robed, shaven-headed Buddhist monk. In 1928, presumably financed by the Soviets, he appeared mysteriously in Brussels, at a Communist-sponsored Congress against Imperialism; he then traveled to Switzerland, Fascist Italy, worked in a Berlin racked by the rise of Nazism, probably touched base in France; in 1930, he took up residence in Hong Kong (being an unwelcome —or, conversely, a most-wanted—guest in Nationalist China).

With all this going on, Ho received a message from the Executive Committee of the Third International to clear up the factional mess in his own country. Since it would have been sure death to begin such a project inside Vietnam, warily, one by one, the leaders who were to work with Ho filtered outside to Hong Kong. (There is an element of high comedy in the fact that the earliest of these reunification meetings took place in the bleachers of the Hong Kong stadium while a wildly disputed soccer game was in progress. The noise blanketed the equally wild disputes of the Vietnamese Party factionalists.) On February 6, 1930, Ho was able to report that a unified Indochinese Communist Party was now in existence.

But that success bore little fruit. The most important Party members in Vietnam—Pham Van Dong and others—were arrested by the French and sentenced to long jail sentences. Ho himself was arrested in Hong Kong, and he was given a six-month sentence. That seemed mild enough, except that Ho, technically a French subject, had been sentenced to death *in absentia* by a French tribunal in Vinh, his native province, for subversive activities and rebellion, and now the French were demanding his extradition.

Legality, however, prevailed in the genteel world of Hong Kong's Anglo-Saxon law. Defended by Sir Stafford Cripps before Britain's Privy Court, Ho was found not subject to extradition since he was a political refugee. Still, the British did not want him, and he was a marked man. He slipped out of Hong Kong, into the nearby but isolated Chinese province of Fukien.

Somehow, only a year later, Ho was in Shanghai, the only foreign place in Asia at that time where a substantial Vietnamese community could be found. He was desperately seeking contact with the Comintern apparatus, which was now prudently concealing its operations in China. It was understandable that what was left of the Chinese Communist Party outside of Mao's forces was not about to advertise its presence all over Shanghai. But there may have been another reason as well for Ho's difficulties in making contact with the Communists: Ho had been released from British prison for reasons which a suspicious Communist might find difficult to swallow. To a Communist apparatus emerging from the blows it had been subjected to in the early 1930's, it was normal procedure to isolate Ho Chi Minh as a potential *agent provocateur* until more was known about what he had said and done while in British custody.

Finally, Ho made contact, and, early in 1934, the Communist apparatus smuggled him back to Moscow, where he had been preceded by a fairly large group of Vietnamese trainees studying in many fields, from engineering to plain *agitprop* (agitation and propaganda). He naturally turned to the latter.

Ho first attended the Institute for National and Colonial Questions in Moscow, and then the famous "graduate school" for senior Communist leaders, the Lenin School. Moscow, in 1935–38, also provided an education of a far different sort: the Stalin purges. It would be interesting to know what Ho's feelings were as he saw some of his best friends accused, convicted, and executed for crimes that they patently had not committed. What is remarkable is that Ho, as a well-known member of the Comintern group, was not purged right along with them, for hundreds of thousands of people of lesser distinction than he became victims of Stalin's mania. One reason for this may have been his absence from the U.S.S.R. when the major break came between Stalin and the "internationalist" wing of the Party structure; another may be that Ho, as a doer rather than a theoretician, had never participated in the fundamental debates between Stalinists and their opposition; and, lastly, Ho probably was then unconditionally loyal to Stalin, and Stalin knew it. This became particularly clear when Nazism began to loom as a threat, and the Communist parties decided in 1936 to apply the policy of "popular fronts" with the Western democracies.

This policy was a bitter pill for the colonial Communist Parties, such as that of Indochina, for it meant giving up advocacy of outright independence in favor of a policy of cooperation with the French colonial regime. But Ho, returning to Communist bases in northwest China in 1937, gritted his teeth and rammed this line down the throat of his reluctant following in its most minute vagaries, and his report on the results, addressed to the Comintern in 1939, demonstrated his success.

It was probably Ho's lowest point. He had to forswear publicly all he had stood for, had to cooperate with the French, the people he hated most, and had to sell out the Trotskyist allies who had helped the Communists from time to time in beating French-sponsored candidates for elections in Cochin China (a French colony, then part of the Federation of Indochina which, as a protectorate, enjoyed a measure of legislative representation). And the worst was not yet over. Not authorized by the Comintern to expose himself through a premature return to Vietnam, he now worked only as a low-level communications operator to the Chinese Communist Eighth Route Army, then fighting the Japanese. In the meantime, everything had gone wrong: the "popular front" was a total failure, as Stalin and the Western democracies could not agree to agree about the Axis powers; Stalin did a turnabout and made friends with Hitler; and the colonial Communist parties, which had operated very much in the open for three years, were destroyed by the police when France and Britain went to war with Germany. Much of what was left of the Party inside Vietnam found itself in French prison camps, and some of its leaders went to the guillotine. As in the case of the Chinese Communists in 1927, Moscow had blundered miserably again in sacrificing local Parties to its own interests.

The physical divorce from Russia created by the outbreak of World War

II turned out, though, to be a real boon for the Asian Communists, for now their own local needs could for once take precedence over Moscow. For Ho, this meant that he could resume his anti-French *and* anti-Japanese lines, as well as his outright struggle for national independence. In 1941, the only power relevant to that struggle was China—not the China of Mao (then a small-time guerrilla holding in the northeast), but that of Chiang Kai-shek, which then controlled all the border approaches to Vietnam. In late 1940, Ho became the political commissar of a Red Chinese training mission sent to train Nationalist guerrillas, including a nucleus of Vietnamese exiles, at Liuchow, Kwangsi Province. In February, 1941, after an absence of exactly thirty years, Ho set foot on Vietnamese soil.

During the spring of that year he lived in Cao-Bang Province, thinking, writing orders, planning the future. (The Museum of the Revolution in Hanoi today carefully preserves the battered rattan suitcase and the other few belongings he had during that period.) On May 10, 1941, the badly-depleted Central Committee of the Indochinese Communist Party (ICP) met to discuss its new tactics. Ho was ready with his plan: the French would be defeated by the Japanese, the Japanese in turn would be defeated by the Allies, and in the resulting vacuum, the Vietnamese Communists, as the only really well-organized party in the country, could gain power, if there was mass support. But if there was to be such mass support as well as Chinese Nationalist support, the movement could no longer be overtly Communist-run. Thus, Ho proposed a new "front" organization of his own. After nine days of discussions, his suggestion was adopted. Called the League for Independence, contracted in Vietnamese to Vietminh, it was born on May 19, 1941, Ho's fifty-first birthday. It was probably then, when his last pseudonym, Nguyen Ai-Quoc, would have lost him much Chinese support as a known Comintern agent, that he first used the name "Ho Chi Minh."

But Ho's troubles were not yet over. Since he was unwilling to accept Chinese demands to include a majority of pro-Chinese "Quislings" in his Vietminh leadership, he was arrested by a Chinese warlord on August 28, 1942, on the interesting, if somewhat conflicting, accusations of being (1) a Communist and (2) a French spy. Chinese prisons, regardless of political coloring, have never been known for the loving care of their inmates, and Ho not only lived in stocks but was shifted from jail to jail in heavy shackles and on foot. It was a time of bitter trials, and it was then that he found solace in writing poetry.

When he was finally released on September 16, 1943, Ho was a sick man and had learned a hard lesson about dealing with Chinese warlords. He agreed to work with them on their terms (at least on the surface), while casting about for allies.

All Americans who knew him then agree that he was an "awfully sweet old guy," who, far from selling the Communist line, was interested only in one thing: national independence. His hatred of the French seemed unquenchable. How much of this was show and how much of it was real is hard to fathom: in other areas of Vietnam, stay-behind French detachments operated harmoniously with the Vietminh. Perhaps Ho, sensing the anticolonial feelings of his American guests, put on a "show" for them, just as often happens in Saigon today, where public demonstrations of anti-French feeling for the benefit of Americans are immediately followed by private apologies to whatever Frenchman is handy. In any case, American aid to Ho was of a minor nature and probably had not been subject to a high policy decision, and Ho soon discovered that the Americans, for all their personal friendliness, were not going to be much use in backing him against two of their major allies, the Chinese or the French.

There was nothing left for him but to rely on speed, organization, and his own native cunning. As Japan was collapsing in the first days of August, 1945, Ho convened a "National Congress" at Tan Trao, north of Hanoi, with the aim of taking control of Vietnam before the Allies arrived, so as to confront them with the *fait accompli* of "people's power." Similar tactics had worked beautifully in Poland and had almost worked in Greece; now they also worked in Hanoi and Saigon. Three days after V-J Day, Ho's forces in Hanoi joyously dedicated themselves to the Vietminh. On August 25, in the imperial capital of Hue, the abandoned Japanese-backed conservatives, under Emperor Bao Dai, handed over the Grand Seal to Ho's representative, while 700 miles south, Tran Van Giau, one of Ho's most ruthless associates, took over Saigon. On September 2, 1945, in Hanoi, Ho proclaimed the independence of the "Democratic Republic of Vietnam" to a delirious crowd of half a million. Until then, it had probably been the swiftest and most bloodless Communist take-over on record.

But Ho understood that Chinese Nationalist support had gone as far as it could. If further relied upon, it might swallow Vietnam as it had done several times in the past. Yet the alternatives were pitifully few: Russia was far away, preoccupied with the huge devastation at home; the Chinese Communists were in deep trouble themselves; the Americans seemed to have lost all interest in Vietnam as anything more than a tiny southeast appendix to China, which was where their interest really lay. That left the hated colonial power, France, with whom one would have to come to terms. It must have been a bitter decision to make.

On March 6, 1946, Ho and the French signed an agreement permitting French troops to return for five years, with France recognizing the Democratic Republic of Vietnam as a "Free State within the French Union." On May 31, 1946, Ho and his entourage left for a state visit in France to negotiate the final treaty.

What follows next is a story of blunders. Involved in their perennial government crises (it was not until July 6 that the French even had a government to negotiate), France left colonial matters to the "specialists," that is, the ultraconservatives of the Ministry of Colonies. Ho, for his part, naïvely overestimated the strength and willingness of his old Socialist and Communist friends in Paris. Settled down in a minor hotel near the Place de l'Étoile, graced for the occasion by a red carpet as is protocol for a chief of state, Ho had time to ponder, as all the fine promises made by French liberals in the spring were slowly whittled down. Another nationalist awaiting a change in his country's fate, David Ben-Gurion, future Prime Minister of Israel, noted wryly that Ho's descending fortunes could be measured by the progressive shrinking of the protocolary red carpet. On Ho's arrival, it had extended from the sidewalk to his room. As the summer wore on, it was limited to the lobby, then to the staircase, and, finally, simply to the corridor in front of Ho's suite.

On September 14, 1946, in a dramatic night session, Ho and the French Overseas Minister, Marius Moutet, signed a *modus vivendi*, an "agreement to disagree," after Ho had pleaded vainly for a softening of the terms. But the French had proved unyielding on the unification of Vietnam, and Moutet, "boxed in" by his own "hawks," could not yield. Ho understood that this meant eventual war with France. As he walked back to his hotel room, he found that the remaining red carpet in front of his door had disappeared altogether.

On December 19, 1946, at 8:00 P.M., nearly all the French electrical plants in Vietnam, carefully sabotaged in advance, blew up. The lights went out as Ho's Vietminh shock troops began to attack French garrisons from south of Saigon to the Chinese border. The war for the reunification, with minor cast changes in the South, is still going on.

For Ho, at fifty-six, this meant a brutal change of roles. Until now, he had been the underground agent, writing reports and holding together networks of agents. At best, he had been a guerrilla leader. Now he was *in* Vietnam, a country that he actually knew less well than he knew France, Russia, or China, and that was isolated from any major source of Communist power. He had access to nobody, until December, 1949, when Communist Chinese troops finally reached the Vietnamese border. Yet he fought on, and against a French Communist-backed government, for nothing else but purely Vietnamese national objectives, and that fact is terribly important. He was not interested in proving that capitalism was on the way to the scrap heap; that the war of "liberation" (the word, of course, was used but had not yet been discovered by the Pentagon) was the wave of the future; or that the French (and the United States, which began backing them in 1950) were "paper tigers." He fought because he felt that a viable Vietnam must be one single state and because Vietnamese national dignity was being trampled upon.

This became quite clear in May, 1947, during the first of at least four unsuccessful peace attempts with France, when the war was only a few months old. The French, though seemingly on top militarily, sent a highly competent negotiator to meet Ho just inside Vietminh lines. He was Professor Paul Mus, one of France's most renowned Vietnam specialists and a consistent advocate of Vietnamese independence. The French Army had given Mus a set of negotiating points with a certain amount of leeway, but on one point it was adamant: Ho had to surrender to the French all the foreign specialists who were serving with his forces. These included a bevy of Japanese officers, who were afraid of Allied war-crimes courts, and even a sprinkling of Germans from the Nazi missions in China, as well as some Foreign Legionnaires of various nationalities. In the absence of any outside aid, these foreigners were of tremendous importance to Ho, for they were the only men capable of training his forces in the use of the Japanese, French, and American weapons (the latter bought from the Nationalist Chinese or smuggled in by boat or plane from the Philippines) with which they were equipped. This was the one chink in his armor; if he yielded on that point, he was quasi-powerless to resume the struggle. In addition, by surrendering people who had sought asylum with him, he would dishonor himself in front of his own people. Mus, who knew Vietnamese mores well, had argued that this point would surely abort the peace talks, but the French High Command remained adamant: Ho would surrender his specialists, or the war would go on until victory.

As Mus presented Ho with the French proposals in a small thatched hut near the bridge of Hanoi where he and Ho were to meet, Ho rapidly went over the various points: return to the status quo of December, exchange of all prisoners, resumption of political talks—all these he could accept. But then he came to the surrender of the specialists.

Unblinkingly, Ho looked at Mus and said slowly:

"*Monsieur le professeur*, you know us very well. If I were to accept this, I would be a coward. The French Union is an assemblage of free men, and there can be no place in it for cowards."

He said it, shook hands with Mus gravely, and walked back into the jungle for seven more years of war. A war that Ho Chi Minh won.

Since then, Ho and the regime that he heads have changed little. As in the past, now we have "Hanoi-ologists" who claim that he is (1) "senile," (2) a tool in the hands of Party leaders, and (3) Peking's stooge.

The hard fact is that Ho, at seventy-seven, is as old as de Gaulle and younger than either Adenauer or Churchill were when they led their countries in some notably difficult situations. On the basis of his past experience with the French and Chinese, or, for that matter, with Stalinist Russia, he is likely to distrust any arrangement from which he cannot pull back if events turn against him. As Ho sees the world, his trust (in Stalin, in China, in the French, and in the Geneva participants of 1954) has always been betrayed. And when it became clear that the reunification elections that were to take place in 1956 were not going to be held, the callous non-support of both Red China and Russia must have shown him how little trust he could place in his allies when their own interests happened not to coincide with Vietnamese interests.

Ho and his closest associates have a hard-headed faith, thus far not contradicted by events, that the Vietnamese people (and particularly those in the North) will take an immense amount of punishment if the issues seem to them simple and clear, that is, they are the ones who are aggressed against, and their goal is reunification of their country, even if it were to take twenty years and involved the destruction of Hanoi and Haiphong (events that Ho, in a nationwide speech on July 17, 1966, predicted would happen). Ho, for all his cosmopolitanism, is essentially a product of the Vietnamese village. In 1946–47, he almost immediately abandoned to the French every city in the country: Saigon and Hanoi, as well as "vital"

Haiphong, fully realizing that what was really vital in that kind of war was not the cities, nor the bridges, nor industries, but the allegiance of his people.

When I saw him last in Hanoi in 1962, the Vietnam war was still a localized conflict between a huge South Vietnamese regular army with 11,000 American advisers facing a small guerrilla force. But Ho had few illusions.

"It took us eight years of bitter fighting to defeat you French, and you knew the country and had some old friendships here. Now the South Vietnamese regime is well-armed and helped by the Americans. The Americans are much stronger than the French, though they know us less well. So it may perhaps take ten years to do it, but our heroic compatriots in the South will defeat them in the end."

That was before the bombing of the North began, and it was also before almost half a million Americans were sent to Southeast Asia. But Ho continued:

"I think the Americans greatly underestimate the determination of the Vietnamese people. The Vietnamese people have always shown great determination when faced with a foreign invader."

Perhaps Ho will, in the next few months, show himself ready to settle once more for the half-country he has consistently been forced to settle for ever since the day that the French finally and irrevocably rolled up the last segment of the red carpet on him in Paris back in 1946.

Or perhaps he will settle down to ten years of war, just as he settled down to seven years of it when Professor Mus faced him with unacceptable demands.

In that case, according to Ho's own timetable, we have only five more years to go.

FOUR

Internal and International Integration

In modern Southeast Asia there are few, if any, nation-states in the classical European sense. International borders divide ethno-linguistic groups in almost random fashion, and few countries are blessed with natural homogeneity. Given the demands placed on states in the present-day world, it is small wonder that nation-building has received such high priority throughout the area. The six essays reprinted here attempt to tap three dimensions of the problem, but in all of these we can do no more than to scratch the surface. Almost every state has experienced problems stemming from unassimilated minorities within its borders. Clamor for a greater voice in policy-making may spring from militant regionalists, or new international disputes may arise from old intercultural differences.

In brief, we are concerned here with three kinds of social and political relations. First, our essays focus on the interaction of identifiable social groups within the borders of the state, groups that do not, in general, have one or several areas of well-defined territorial concentration. The identity of these groups stems more from the fact that they are Chinese, Indian, Malay, or Thai, for example, than from the fact that they may live in Cholon, Rangoon, Pasir Mas, or Maha Sarakham. Both of the groups examined in this section are minorities in Southeast Asia, and it is as social groups, not as regions, that they must reach some accommodation with the indigenous majorities. Are these minority groups destined to remain forever as identifiable entities? While the myth is that the Chinese, in particular, are unassimilable, Maurice Freedman clearly shows that "once a Chinese, always a Chinese" is an oversimplification. Our view of Chinese assimilation, Freedman argues, is myopic, for more profound changes have taken place in the Chinese communities than most scholarly observers and practicing politicians have been able (or perhaps willing) to recognize. Similarly, in the case of the Indians, Ronald Hatley finds that the various communities are increasingly becoming Indians of the hyphenated variety —Malayan-Indians or Burmese-Indians. One can, of course, legitimately raise some difficult questions on this aspect of nation-building. How long will it take to "nationalize" these minorities? Do the wielders of power in the various states of Southeast Asia actually desire such a nationalization? Even if it is desirable and possible, what will be the nature of the transitional period? Is assimilation permanent? Or will some external event (for example, the emergence of the mother country as a powerful international force) contribute to what Maurice Freedman once called in another context "retro-assimilation"? No one can answer these and many other related questions at this time, but the two authors here, in analyzing what has happened in the past, provide us with many clues and suggestions about the future.

In the next three essays, we shift from social groups to territorial units as the building-blocks of nationhood and deal with the problems of nation-building as it relates to integration of identifiable geographic areas into the larger national unit. In the first of these, Herbert Feith and Daniel S. Lev document the rebellious response of parts of Sumatra and the Celebes to a Java-centered Indonesian national government and demonstrate how this disintegrative threat was met by Djakarta. As the authors show, while it was the force of the Indonesian Army that brought the rebels back into the fold of the central government, in the end, a lack of consensus within the guerrilla movement itself contributed to its failure. Just as the absence of a consensus created the revolt, so too did a lack of consensus bring about its disintegration. In the second essay, A. Thomas Kirsch, working among the Phu Thai of northeast Thailand, thoughtfully questions two myths that have long been accepted by many scholars and practitioners. First, Kirsch's research among the Phu Thai reveals a regionally based society far less static and far less isolated from the influence of the central government than its physical location and our stereotype of the tradition-bound peasantry would seem to suggest. Secondly, Kirsch raises a question that cannot now be answered but which must be asked eventually—is economic assistance to the northeastern peasant likely to make him a better Thai citizen, or might it actually "aggravate the specifically political dimensions of the problem"? While we have little hard evidence to go on at the present time, Kirsch clearly implies that he cannot accept the often unquestioned assumption that economic betterment and political conservatism go hand-in-hand. In the third essay of this section, the editor has tried to analyze one specific case of failure in territorial integration—the breakup of the seemingly logical association between Malaysia and Singapore. In the course of this analysis, it becomes apparent that the process of nation-building is vastly more complex than we have often been willing to recognize, and even the useful distinction between social and territorial integration employed here must be cautiously used lest it obscure more than it reveals. In all five of these essays, we can see how territorial and social-group identities are inextricably interrelated, and how the autonomous social or regional subsystem is only an ideal abstraction of a very complex reality. Finally, all five essays should alert us to the difficulties that lie ahead for the leaders and followers of the "nation-states" of Southeast Asia.

In the final essay of this section, Bernard K. Gordon takes us beyond the domestic problems of the nation-states and into the realm of contemporary international relations. At the very beginning of this volume, we raised some fundamental questions regarding the existence of a "Southeast Asia," and here Gordon shows us that, for many Southeast Asian leaders, the area is indeed assuming an identity of its own. For some, this might be viewed as a logical continuation of the "nation-building" process, but, if nation-states are so far from becoming realities in Southeast Asia, how much further away must be a meaningful regional association? The question is frequently asked by many observers, but as Gordon seems to suggest, perhaps—and just perhaps—it might be irrelevant. Could it be that the viable nation-state is not a necessary precondition for meaningful and viable regionalism? Or, to go one step further, might regional association have an even better chance in an area where the idea of nationhood is still in embryo?

31

THE CHINESE IN SOUTHEAST ASIA:
A LONGER VIEW*

MAURICE FREEDMAN

Longer than what? And why? The subtitle of this lecture is an encouragement to try to avoid certain misunderstandings of the position of the Chinese
in Southeast Asia. On the short view, our eyes myopically focused on the
present day, the Nan-yang Chinese, that is to say, those Chinese living in
the region which stretches from Burma in the west to the Philippines in
the east, seem to be some 12 million misplaced persons, a restless and insecure population acting as the markers of a vague outer frontier for a politically expansive homeland. This is the "present." The trouble with it is
that it confirms the prejudices of both those who dislike or distrust the
Chinese and those who worship them. Everywhere in Southeast Asia there
are visible and viable Chinese communities, great and small, which serve
at once as "proof" of the anti-Chinese contention that the Chinese are
always alien and unassimilable entities, and as "evidence" in aid of a pro-
Chinese thesis that Chinese culture is so superior in fact and in its evalua-

* This essay was given as a lecture to the China Society, London, in 1964 and
originally appeared as *Occasional Paper*, No. 14 of the Society. It is reprinted here by
permission of the author and the publisher.

tion of itself as to be able to withstand the impact of other Asian influences and of Westernization.

Both views are wrong and unjust, as a longer perspective on Southeast Asian history will, I think, demonstrate conclusively enough. Chinese have certainly been assimilated in large numbers in various parts of the region and have effectively disappeared off the map of the Nan-yang. And when they have not been so assimilated, their specifically Chinese culture has often been weathered away. The present is deceptive because, although the chapter of Chinese immigration to Southeast Asia has been virtually closed since Communism conquered China in 1949, the effects of recent immigration are still clearly to be seen a mere decade and a half later; and because, while Portuguese Timor and British-protected Brunei are now the sole remnants of foreign rule in the region, the colonial atmosphere still hangs about our thoughts. We live in a postcolonial era, but it is yet so new that we need to make a great effort of the imagination to come out from beneath the shadow of its predecessor. And it is important to add that, having made this effort and emerged, we run the further risk of being seduced by the new myths of latter-day nationalism, "neo-colonialism," and *le tiers monde*.

Let me try very briefly (and amateurishly, for I speak as an anthropologist, not a historian) to survey the story of Chinese movement into the area we have come, increasingly since World War II, to call Southeast Asia. The present Chinese diaspora known to us as the Nan-yang ("southern ocean") rests historically on early merchant ventures from southeastern China powerfully reinforced during the colonial period. The term Nan-yang itself stresses the sea connection with China; in fact, it originally meant the coastal area of Southeast Asia plus the islands of the Philippines group and the Indonesian archipelago. In earlier times, Vietnam, Burma, and Thailand were reached from southeastern China by land routes. For the Chinese, the Nan-yang was in the first place an area for trade and only in a minor degree an arena for the exercise of political power (although the imperial might was more than once shown in Southeast Asian waters). Trade was encouraged by both official policy and official capital during Sung and Yüan times, and while the early Ming rulers put restrictions on the trade, their successors eased them in order to continue the commercial tradition laid down by the previous dynasties. At the turnover to the Ch'ing dynasty in 1644, the southern Chinese with Nan-yang connections formed an important part of the resistance to the new regime, and it was then for the first time that the Nan-yang came to be a significant factor in the political life of the empire. It is important to note that the Nan-yang traders were concentrated in the two southeastern provinces of Fukien and Kwangtung and that this region of China held out against the new Ch'ing rule until the 1680's. And even when open resistance had ended, anti-Ch'ing sentiment remained. It was institutionalized in the secret societies (the "Triad" and others) which came to form an important element in the social life of the southern Chinese who stayed at home and of those who moved overseas. Ch'ing policy, based on a view of China as a land power and unsympathetic to the attachment of the southeastern provinces to the sea, was set against ties with Nan-yang. But while overseas trade was hindered, it was not stopped. Indeed, one of the unintended consequences of imperial action seems to have been precisely to promote the overseas settlement which it deplored; for Chinese traders, fearing the difficulties and dangers created for them at home by the officials of the new regime, now established themselves *in partibus infidelium* where formerly they had gone temporarily to trade.

In the course of the eighteenth century, the Chinese trade with Southeast Asia became heavily dependent on Western enterprise, as the European presence made itself increasingly felt in the region; and from this bracketing of the Chinese merchants with Western power springs the anti-Chinese view of the present day that Chinese economic dominance has been one of the attendant afflictions of Western imperialism. When the Dutch in the East Indies were the chief among the Western traders, the Indies were the center of Chinese commerce, but with the founding of Penang (toward the end of the century) and of Singapore (early in the nineteenth century) as British settlements, the Malay Peninsula came to the fore as the geographical focus of Chinese trading activity. (Originally a Portuguese acquisition and subsequently Dutch, Malacca was added to the list of British possessions early in the nineteenth century. With Penang and Singapore, it came eventually to form the Straits Settlements, a British nucleus in the peninsula from which has emerged in our own day the western part of Malaysia.) At the same time, as Chinese commercial talent was being deployed in the East Indies and the Malay Peninsula, Chinese were making an economic niche for themselves in Thailand, although here independently of Western enterprise and influence. In this fashion the historical basis for the modern concentration of the Nan-yang Chinese in the three countries of Malaysia, Indonesia, and Thailand was laid.

But it was not until well into the nineteenth century that migration from China took place on the grand scale, to man the modern agricultural and mining enterprises, to populate the growing cities, and to cover the region with a network of small businesses. Especially after about 1850, the Chinese overseas became preponderantly composed of poor working men, the coolie element (recruited from the peasantry of Fukien and Kwangtung, in a drive which swept Chinese into the Americas and Australia as well as Southeast Asia) swamping the merchants who had hitherto characterized the Nan-yang.

When, as a result of the Opium War, Hong Kong was established as a British colony and the first treaty ports of China were opened to the West, Chinese commercial enterprise in the Nan-yang began to operate with securer bases at home, the final blow having been delivered to the Ch'ing policy of restraining ties with the non-Chinese world. Chinese business empires grew up which linked various parts of Southeast Asia with financial centers such as Singapore, the hub of the Nan-yang, Shanghai, and Hong Kong. And with every advance of the frontier of Western control in Southeast Asia (for it is important to realize that the effective colonial government of the region did not reach its maximum extent very long before it was shattered by the Pacific war), the Chinese expanded their economic interests, until by 1941, a framework of Chinese commercial and industrial relationships covered the whole region.

As Ch'ing fortunes began to decline at home, the Nan-yang Chinese repeated their role at the beginning of the dynasty by forming a base for revolutionary activities, and we have merely to remind ourselves of Sun Yat-sen's comings and goings in Southeast Asia to underline the significance of the Nan-yang in the political life of modern China. Since the establishment of the Republic in 1911 until the present day, the various governments of China (whole or divided) have sought in greater or lesser measure to watch over the interests of their overseas subjects (for a long time defined as *all* the descendants through males of men from China) and make use of their resources in capital and skill for China's economic development. During the rise of modern China, and under the encouragement of its government, the Chinese overseas became "overseas Chinese," having come to think of themselves as an entity with rights and duties vis-à-vis their homeland. In brief, China was their political focus and their cultural model.

The new nationalism (pride in their homeland and consciousness of their connection with it) was reflected in the modern education of the Nan-yang Chinese. Even before the 1911 revolution, Mandarin had to some extent been taught as the national language among Chinese overseas. (Mandarin was, of course, a foreign tongue to people whose homes lay in the linguistically peculiar provinces of Fukien and Kwangtung.) It was not long before a Mandarin-speaking school culture was well established in the Nan-yang. Postimperial China, as seen through the eyes of overseas Chinese educated in the new schools, became the yardstick for cultural judgment and the point of reference for political thinking. Political activity in the Nan-yang, to the extent that it was ideologically inspired, was oriented to the homeland. Domestically, in each of the various countries of Southeast Asia, the Chinese were narrowly concerned with protecting their special interests. In the colonial territories of the region, the Chinese were not typically anti-Western (except as they reflected China's radical rejection of its Western harassers), and this fact, coupled with the economic strength which the Chinese built up under the umbrella of colonialism, earned them the suspicion from local nationalists which still bedevils the position and security of the Nan-yang Chinese.

I apologize doubly for the potted history. It is both inelegant and, although in this form necessary to the argument, inaccurate in its brevity. I hope presently to redeem myself by going more deeply into the facts of the most important of the Chinese communities in Southeast Asia. But before I do so, we shall need to set out the basic population figures of the Nan-yang as a whole. We have seen that there are some 12 million Chinese in the region (say, 5 per cent of the total regional population). But what kind of a fact is this? It is the vaguest of statistical notions about a mass of people who are in some sense Chinese. What does "Chinese" mean? In one country, it means anyone who says he is Chinese in answer to the census-taker's question. In another country, it means anybody who bears a Chinese name. The 12 million include Chinese who speak Chinese, are citizens of China, live in domestic surroundings similar to those to be found in southeastern China, wear clothes such as are worn in China, eat Chinese food. No problem about them. But in the global figure there are also people who do not know a word of Chinese, are citizens of the Southeast Asian country of their birth, and live, dress, and eat in fashions which would be intolerably exotic to a Chinese fresh from China. One may imagine the variations possible between these two extremes. "Chinese," therefore, begins to emerge as a label for some kind of political and social status (varying as between countries) and to recede as a name for a way of life or culture.

In Burma, the Philippines, Cambodia, and Laos, Chinese numbers are relatively small. They are particularly small in the last of these countries, while they fall below half a million in each of the other three. There are about a million Chinese in the two Vietnams. The giants, for historical reasons which we have already glanced at, are Malaysia, Indonesia, and Thailand. In the first of these countries, there are 4 million Chinese in the western part (that is, the Malay Peninsula, including Singapore) and over a third of a million in the eastern (Sarawak and Sabah). The Malaysian figures are based squarely on census returns, and we may assume that they account for virtually everybody who thinks of himself as a Chinese. In Thailand, we may say that there are between 2.5 and 3 million Chinese; it is a hit-or-miss figure, for reasons which will become clear when we consider the Thailand case later on. The Chinese population in Indonesia was last counted by a proper census in 1930, and then by roughly the same principles as applied in Malaya and British Borneo; for recent times, we have to rely on less satisfactory statistical sources. We may estimate the present-day Chinese population of Indonesia to be 2.5 million. It will be clear, therefore, that as far as our figures go, the three giants of the Nanyang account for some 80 per cent of the Chinese in Southeast Asia.[1]

We have established that not all the 12 million Southeast Asian Chinese are Chinese by culture. Not all of them are "racially" Chinese in the sense of being descended exclusively from Chinese forebears. Not all the people descended exclusively or partly from Chinese immigrants in Southeast Asia are accounted for in the 12 million Chinese. The Chinese cultural heritage has been whittled away. The Chinese biological heritage has been dispersed. Let us try to see how this has come about. I shall begin with the case of western Malaysia, which up to 1963 could be discussed as the Federation of Malaya and the State of Singapore. I shall refer to it simply as Malaya for the sake of convenience.

As we have seen, Chinese settlement in Malaya began in Penang, Malacca, and Singapore. From these British bases, Chinese moved out to trade and mine tin in the Malay States even before the extension of British

---

[1] See the various population estimates contained in Table 17 of the Appendix to this volume.

rule to them, which began in the 1870's. Despite this earlier movement into independent Malay territory, however, we may say that the Chinese experience in Malaya was essentially a colonial one. As a result of this experience (the wielders of ultimate power being British) and of the fact that the indigenous people with whom they came in touch were Muslims, there was little inducement to the immigrants to stop being Chinese. It was open to them to be converted to Islam; as converted Muslims, they were welcome in Malay society. And it is fairly clear that over the years, men in a Chinese community very short of Chinese women sometimes found their way to a new religion and a wife. They entered Malaydom, as the Malay expression has it, and were lost to the Chinese. But the numbers of Chinese-turned-Malay were small; and, in fact, the main infusion of Chinese "blood" into the Malay population has come about in a different manner: Since the time when Chinese women have become more numerous, and right up to the present day, unwanted babies (nearly always girls) in Chinese families have often been sold to Malays to grow up as full members of Malay society.

In the early phase of Chinese settlement in the country, there was a reverse flow of Malay "blood." The first Chinese merchants in Malacca took women from among the strange people in whose midst they lived. (The women were probably for the most part slaves and non-Muslim.) From these early unions, there sprang a Chinese population to which the name Baba came to be applied. The significance of this population lies not in the fact that it was "racially" mixed but in the cultural amalgam for which it was responsible. Beginning in Malacca, and thence spreading to other parts of the country, the Babas carried forward into our own day a Malay-ized Chinese culture which demonstrated that it was possible in the Malayan context to be unambiguously Chinese without the full Chinese cultural apparatus that would have been demanded in China. The Babas spoke a dialect of Malay; their prayers, folklore, and literature were put into this dialect; their music, food, costume, and manners were all heirs to the Malay tradition. But the Babas were Chinese—and so much so that throughout the nineteenth century, although decreasingly toward its end, they were a dominant element in Malayan Chinese society, a kind of elite which enjoyed riches inherited from previous generations and could communicate with the Malays in Malay and with the British in English (for many of them took advantage of the first opportunities in Malaya to gain a Western education). Forming a superior stratum of Chinese society, they attracted to them and absorbed ambitious Chinese immigrants ("China-men," they condescendingly called them), to whom they gave their daughters in marriage.

The first lesson the Babas teach us, then, is that Chinese culture does not in all circumstances enjoy the vitality and viability which many Sino-philes lovingly attribute to it. But, in fact, there is an even more striking lesson to be learned from the history of the Malayan Babas: Chinese culture may die to be reborn again in a different guise. Having moved away from Chinese culture to Malay, all the while remaining Chinese, the Babas have in more modern times shifted back to the culture of the majority of the community of which they form part—having become Malayan. The Baba sector of the Chinese community was progressively reduced in size as more and more people came into Malaya from China; at the end of the nineteenth century, the Babas formed perhaps 10 per cent of the Chinese population in the Straits Settlements and certainly a smaller percentage in the Malay States. For a time, they kept their lead of the Chinese community and its institutions, but economically they began to lose out to successful immigrants who were no longer willing to be absorbed by them; more women were being brought from China and a self-subsistent immigrant Chinese group became possible. During the early part of the twentieth century, although some Baba families retained their riches, the Babas as a whole declined to a less significant point on the economic scale and ceased to constitute an elite for the Malayan Chinese.

By this time, Chinese culture in its modern nationalist form had entered the Malayan scene. True, one or two Baba intellectuals were already teaching themselves Chinese and trying to bring about a Chinese renaissance before the end of the last century, but, for the great part of them, it was the growth of the modern Chinese school system in the period between the World Wars and its florescence after World War II that turned them into Chinese speakers, or at least gave them the feeling that they were heirs to Chinese culture. (Baba Malay literature passed out of existence in the late 1930's, as far as I have been able to judge. The costumes and ceremonies specifically associated with the Babas were still to be seen after World War II, but were clearly giving way before the competing symbolism of nationalist Chinese culture.) Of course, the Chinese language "reacquired" by the Babas was Mandarin; it was not the Chinese spoken by their (largely southern Fukien) ancestors. The "folklore" they now assumed was that of Chinese nationalism; it was not the tradition of their forebears. But in the very process of becoming, so to say, more Chinese, the Babas were, in fact, fitting themselves for the latest phase of Malaya's history, in which to be a Malayan a man must have an identity as a Malay, Chinese, Indian, or Eurasian. The Malayized culture of the Babas had not made them Malay; to be Malayan they had to grow more Chinese.

The story of some of the leaders of present-day Singapore is, in this connection, illuminating. Baba in origin (although by their day, the name Baba having become pejorative, it had been replaced by "Straits Chinese"), they fought their way to the head of an overwhelmingly Chinese colony by identifying themselves with the hopes of the culturally aggressive Chinese. (To do this, they learned Chinese and to think as nationalist Chinese, while using the skills taught them by their English education in order to operate within a British political framework.) From this position in the van of an army of enthusiastic Chinese, they have sought to guide their followers into a Malayan (and subsequently Malaysian) nation which, ironically enough, must in the long run relegate the Chinese language to a poor third place behind Malay (the country's national language) and English, and put an ever-increasing distance between the culture of the Malayan Chinese and that of their congeners in China (a "homeland" of diminishing significance).

The growth of Chinese cultural nationalism in Malaya in the twentieth century was, in one sense, a response to the colonial situation; in order to react to colonialism, the Chinese, not being part of any local nationality, could respond only as Chinese. And as Malaya has emerged as an independent country, Chinese cultural nationalism has declined. We can most clearly see the relationship between the two processes in the history of Chinese education. While Malaya was under British rule and the Chinese were regarded, and largely regarded themselves, as sojourners on foreign soil, their school system was, as to form and content, modeled on that of China. Chinese school culture then became one of the chief instruments in modern times for the expression of anticolonial sentiment, most dramatically so in Singapore, where, during the 1950's, the Chinese schools formed a major center of ideological ferment and political action. But in independent Malaya, where the state can intervene more decisively in educational policy than its British predecessor and where a Malayan ideology can compete with Chinese, the old purely Chinese school system is already virtually dead. Again, the establishment of the Nanyang University in Singapore in 1956, which to its sponsors and supporters seemed to be the logical extension of the Chinese educational systems of Southeast Asia and the final step along the road to Chinese cultural independence, a mere decade later already looks as though it will prove to have been at best a brave gesture. The splendid irony of change has been that, since the withdrawal of the British from Malaya, it has been English education which has begun to capture the allegiance of the Chinese.

In the old Malaya, the Chinese were not assimilated by the Malays. They are not now being so assimilated, although I should guess that Islam will seem to be a decreasingly difficult barrier to some Chinese ambitious to reach the peak of national power. But even if there should prove to be no absorption of Chinese into the Malay ranks, Chinese culture and Chinese views of themselves must undergo a radical transformation. Every new Malayan institution is an incentive to Chinese to act as Malayans and to abandon a parochial Chineseness. It is true, of course, that the network of Chinese commercial and industrial life, by means of which the Chinese play a dominant role in the Malayan economy, is an inducement to the Chinese to stay within an ambit which minimizes contact with people of other "races." It is also true that the constitution in certain particulars favors the Malays against Chinese, Indians, and the other ethnic groups and restricts the access of non-Malays to some central points in the bureaucracy. But within the framework of a political system which is seen to rest on the collaboration of the various "races" (a collaboration formalized in the dominant Alliance of Malay, Chinese, and Indian parties), the Chinese are constantly wearing down their particularity and moving toward a Malayan meaning of "Chinese."

Yet, to the visitor to present-day Malaya, Chinese culture must seem very vigorous still. He should realize, however, that what he sees is not simply a straightforward heritage of the Malayan Chinese past. It is, on the contrary, a refashioned Chinese culture, which took its standards from the homeland via the modern school system. That system, as we have seen, flourished up to the time of Malayan independence, and was increasingly affected by left-wing Chinese nationalism after World War II. For the young Chinese who had been through the system, what the Malays stood for was looked down upon, and to the extent that the new education promoted local political ambitions, they were concerned with the assertion of Chinese (not general, Malayan) rights against the British rulers. But if we examine Chinese culture in twentieth-century Malaya a little more carefully, we shall see something that at first sight seems highly paradoxical: While it rejected English (except for purely practical purposes in business and administration) and saw little to emulate in the behavior of the British on the local scene, it was in fact Westernized to a high degree. The Malayan Chinese of this century took their standards from China; China took many of hers from the West. For this reason, foreigners like myself, who knew both Chinese-educated and English-educated Chinese in preindependence Malaya, were often more impressed by the former; through their Chinese culture, they had a window on the world. They saw it distorted, no doubt, but at least they saw it. The English education provided in Malaya served to give Chinese a practical linguistic skill without arousing in them any great interest in things outside the range of their immediate experience.

Turning our attention to the most recent years, we see another twist in the fate of Chinese culture in Malaya. Chinese education, as we have noted, is beginning to decline. Elsewhere in Southeast Asia, Chinese school systems have suffered some grievous blows from unsympathetic governments. That is not the case in Malaya. The government there has certainly not repressed the Chinese schools. Rather, as a postcolonial Malayan society has been taking shape, Chinese ambitions have been turning in directions to which "modern" Chinese education (now itself old-fashioned) is less relevant. By a wisely formed and executed policy, the Malayan authorities have stressed the importance of the national language (Malay) and of English, and have provided means by which the Chinese schools may be built into a national system of education, shedding their exclusive preoccupation with the Chinese language and things Chinese.

Malaysia (and with it Malaya) is, in the context of the Nan-yang, a special case. The 4 million Chinese in Malaya are neither numerically nor politically a minority. They are 44 per cent of the total Malayan population and fractionally more numerous than the Malays. They form a powerful economic and political bloc. It seems to follow that cultural pluralism is not merely the basis of Malaya's history but also its destiny, and no wise Malayan politician has ever tried to bring about a future in which the Chinese would cease to exist as in some sense distinct in their cultural heritage and social identity. It cannot be part of the idea of Malayan citizenship that those who bear it have a uniform set of values and a standard style of life. A rigorous attempt to realize in Malaya the nineteenth-century ideal of a coincidence of folk and polity would remove the possibility of a single society surviving within its present frontiers. The riches, the votes, and the organization of the Chinese assure them their survival as Chinese. What "Chinese" will mean in Malaya a generation or two hence we cannot now foresee, but it is at least certain that it will have little interest for Sinologues in search of a "pure" Chinese culture outside China.

We have only to take a hint from current diplomatic practice and confront Malaysia with Indonesia to see how numbers matter, culturally as well as politically. The Chinese in Indonesia are well over half as numerous as those in Malaysia, but they are a mere fraction (between 2 and 3 per cent) of the total population of the republic. Under Dutch rule, the Chinese of the East Indies could hold their own; legally and politically, a place was allotted them in the plural society which Furnivall and others have described for us; economically, they were well entrenched. But in a nation-state which detests the stranger within the gates and believes its survival to depend on the elaboration of an indigenous culture, the Chinese as a minority are under the threat of cultural extinction. It would be foolish to imagine that the extinction will inevitably be consummated, but twenty years after the Pacific war, we can already see that a great part of the Indonesian Chinese are moving toward a "nationalization" that empties the description "Chinese" of nearly all its cultural content.

Malaysia and Indonesia are not merely neighbors (and, for the moment at any rate, rivals); they have much of their history in common. Their Chinese communities grew up in much the same manner and went through similar processes of adaptation. Let us consider again the case of the Malayan Babas, this time in the light of the Chinese who parallel them in Indonesia, the Peranakans. As a result of the great flood of immigrants to Malaya in the latter part of the nineteenth century, the Babas came to form a small minority of the Malayan Chinese. When their economic futures declined relatively to those of many of the immigrants, and when the Chinese nationalism of the twentieth century undermined their confidence in their own Malayized culture, the Babas began to move back into the Chinese cultural fold. The Straits Chinese, as they are now called, are still to some extent identifiable as a special area of the Chinese community, but one cannot drive a hard line through the community to arrange Straits Chinese on one side of it and "immigrant" Chinese on the other.

Yet something of the sort may be done in Indonesia, at least in Java, which is, of course, the heart of the country. Here the Peranakans, the analogues of the Babas (and often related to them across the international frontier by kinship and marriage) have managed to survive into our own day as a large, self-subsistent, and relatively independent Chinese community. The Chinese with whom we contrast the Peranakans are the Totoks, the "immigrants" (but not necessarily literally so for many of them are Indonesian-born). In Java, at any rate, they have emerged as a separate kind of Chinese, counterposed to the Peranakans, only in the twentieth century; for before then, the rate of Chinese movement into Java being relatively low and steady (and, as elsewhere, composed almost exclusively of men), the immigrants were absorbed by the Peranakans, as at one time the Babas ingested the immigrant Chinese in Malaya.

Again like the Babas, the Peranakans sprang from unions between Chinese and local women. A Peranakan culture was formed which was expressed in one or another of the languages of Java and in customs some of which are readily traceable to Javan origins. But it must not be supposed that the contrast between this culture and that of the Totoks in the twentieth century is a simple one between, say, half-Chinese and full-Chinese, for the word "Chinese" has here a slippery meaning. True, the Totoks, being of more recent derivation from China, were fully Chinese in their speech, their general mode of life, and their evaluation of things-Chinese-from-China. But they were "modern" Chinese and reproduced in Java many of the features of republican Chinese society and its ideology; whereas the Peranakans (being from this point of view fossil remnants of imperial China) carried forward to our times many traditional Chinese characteristics within the framework of their Javanized culture. Paradoxically (and the point holds true *mutatis mutandis* for Malaya), the Peranakans are in some sense more Chinese than the Totoks.

I shall try to illustrate this paradox very briefly. Although the Peranakan system of family and kinship has been heavily affected by its need to adapt to local (non-Chinese) values and to new urban and economic conditions, Peranakan family affairs are conducted more conservatively and ceremoniously than those of the Totoks. Indeed, the family seems to carry more weight in Peranakan than in Totok social organization, while domestic ancestor worship (which we naturally think of as being a hallmark of Chinese culture) is apparently carried out by more families and more regularly among the Peranakans. Certainly, nobody who has seen a Baba wedding (and I assume the same to be true of a Peranakan wedding) and has been able to compare it was a wedding among the "immigrants," can fail to be convinced that, in certain respects, Baba-Peranakan culture is Sinologically more interesting than the strident nationalist Chinese culture of modern times. At a Baba wedding, one may feel that one has had privileged access to the Chinese past. At a "modern" wedding, one is more likely to be impressed by the Chinese version of Western symbolism.

Peranakans and Totoks in Java have emerged as socially separate groups and culturally distinct entities of very roughly equal size. Yet—and the point brings us back to the strategic importance of formal education in the shaping of Nan-yang destiny—the boundary between the two groups and their cultures has not been steadily maintained. Under the influence of nationalist enthusiasm in the early part of the century, many Peranakan children walked the road to modern Chinese culture in the Mandarin-speaking schools set up in Java, their parents having been caught up in the movement, essentially Totok in inspiration, to unify the Chinese in the Indies as a coherent group and to press for greater political privileges within the framework of the colonial society. At this stage of Peranakan development, Dutch policy intervened sagaciously. From 1908 onward,

Dutch schools for Peranakan children were created by the government. And the Dutch accorded the Peranakans legal and political privileges which helped to steer them away from identifying themselves with the nationalism of the Totoks.

A second period of Peranakan-Totok rapprochement came during the Japanese occupation and its aftermath. Chinese self-consciousness was heightened, and an interest in Chinese education promoted. In Java, the Peranakans continued their interest in Chinese education for some years after the end of the war; when in the uncertain years of the Dutch return it was not clear that they were soon to go forever, many Peranakans were unwilling to make common cause with the Indonesians; and during the early years of the republic, there was enough in Indonesian behavior toward the Chinese to convince the Peranakans that they had little to gain by abandoning whatever they had of a Chinese heritage. But by the late 1950's, the general situation had changed, and we have since then been witnesses to a sharpened divergence between Peranakan and Totok. It would appear that at the present time only Totok children attend Chinese schools, and that almost all Peranakan children are being educated in schools where the language is Indonesian, that is, the modern language of the Republic, based on Malay. (But these latter schools are for the most part run by the Peranakans themselves; the education is Indonesian but structurally separate.) Peranakans and Totoks have disentangled themselves from each other in fields other than education; above all in associational life, so that the two halves of Java Chinese society operate without a common leadership and with few relationships to tie them together. As G. William Skinner, our chief authority on the Indonesian Chinese, has it: ". . . today the chief links between the two communities are the now anomalous Chinese-educated Peranakans and the diminishing number of Peranakan women married to Totoks."

The wedge now driven between the Peranakans and the Totoks squeezes the former into closer and closer identification with the Indonesians and the latter into a sullen defense of their national and cultural integrity. "Indonesian" has two meanings. On the one hand, everybody who is a citizen of the republic is an Indonesian; and. although the citizenship issue is fantastically complex, we may assume that most, perhaps nearly all, Peranakans are Indonesians in this sense. On the other hand, the word is used for the indigenous peoples of the country to the exclusion of such ethnic outsiders as the Chinese who, in this context, are said to be not real (indigenous, *asli*) Indonesians. (There is less confusion in the parallel terminology across the water in Malaya, where "Malayan" or "Malaysian" describes citizenship and cannot be used to distinguish Malays from their fellow citizens of other "races.") We may say that the Peranakans, having become Indonesian in the first sense, are straining after acceptance in the second.

What makes their effort the more striking is that both official policy and public attitudes do not go very far toward matching their enthusiasm. Indonesian citizens of Chinese descent are discriminated against, above all in economic life, where the old Chinese dominance of local trade and some forms of industry is met by the preferential treatment (in the granting of licenses, credit, and so on) to "real" Indonesians. Of course, as elsewhere in Southeast Asia, the attempt by the government to gouge Chinese out of their economic niches and replace them by "true" citizens has had the effect of promoting alliances between Chinese capital and skill on the one hand and the licenses and contacts with officialdom of "true" citizens on the other. And the bonds so set up in economic activity between Chinese and non-Chinese are one basis for Peranakan hopes that they may be eventually accepted fully within the Indonesian fold. It would appear that at times when alien Chinese have been under attack (as was outstandingly the case at the end of 1959, when foreign Chinese were prohibited from engaging in trade in the rural areas, and in West Java were forcibly evicted from the countryside), the Peranakans have for the most part held themselves aloof, either having little sympathy for Totoks or at any rate not wishing to jeopardize their own *modus vivendi* with the Indonesians by demonstrating solidarity with foreigners.

"Assimilation" is now a plank in the Peranakan political platform. What this is meant to imply in the predominantly Muslim parts of the country (for not all Indonesian "Muslims" are in fact Muslim; some indeed are hostile to Islam) is not clear. But there seems to be no doubt that influential members of the Peranakan community foresee some kind of cultural merger, the first steps to which have already been taken. (It should be particularly shocking to cultural Sinophiles that, in recent years, an increasing number of Peranakans have been giving their children Indonesian names and suppressing their Chinese surnames.) The voices raised in favor of "merger" are by no means all crying for the immediate disappearance of the Peranakans as a separate entity. Indeed, a policy of "integration" seems to command the largest following. The Chinese of Indonesian citizenship have, in the last decade, been organized chiefly within the framework of an organization known as BAPERKI, through which, and by taking part in politics acceptable to the rulers of the country, the Peranakans have achieved what appears to be a fairly stable relationship with the society englobing them. The Peranakans are therefore still a distinct and organized entity within Indonesian society. One day, possibly, they may cease to be. Meanwhile, contrasted with the Totoks, from whom they have been increasingly differentiating themselves in recent times, they show us a Chinese identity stripped of much of its Chinese culture.

In neither Malaya nor Indonesia have the Chinese in any considerable numbers been assimilated to the point of disappearing as Chinese, although in the latter country the thing may yet happen. Thailand, the third country I have chosen to talk about, illustrates the opposite case: mass assimilation has taken place. Just as Singapore or Kuala Lumpur looks like a good argument for assuming that Chinese culture has always flourished in Malaya, so Bangkok today seems to be certain proof of the persistence and viability of that same culture in Thailand. The common-sense inference happens to be wrong, for what we can now see in Thailand is the not yet assimilated portion of a much larger historical population of Chinese. This is a country which in two major respects stands contrasted with the others we have looked at: It was never a colony, and its dominant religion is Buddhism.

Once more we must have grateful recourse to Skinner's work. This careful student of the Chinese (both at home and overseas) asserts—and supports his assertion by a mass of sociological and historical evidence—that there has been a steady stream of Chinese into the Thai population since the eighteenth century. And it is probable that this old process will continue, perhaps to the point where all the Chinese landmarks, except for "archaeological" monuments and literary remains, will have vanished from the kingdom.

I must content myself with the barest outline of the facts. While Chinese newcomers to the country were free to build up for themselves an economic position which both local and international economic circumstances encouraged, and which their social organization and its values prevented the Thai from occupying, the Chinese were at the same time given a license to merge into Thai society, shedding their Chinese identity completely. Their economic roles, and the social organization created about them, made Chinese immigrants a distinct sector of Thailand society. But the descendants of these distinctive immigrants moved into general society with ease, more especially because they were children of the Thai women whom the Chinese immigrants found little difficulty in marrying. But immigration from China was not, of course, once for all; new Chinese kept coming into the country to take the place, so to say, of those who had disappeared from the ranks of a distinct Chinese enclave. Chinese society in Thailand was, as it were, a kind of staging post along the road from the society of southeastern China to the Thai-speaking Hinayana Buddhist society of Thailand.

In examining part of the history of the Chinese in Malaya and Indonesia, we have had to take account, however cursorily, of the impact of the form of Chinese nationalism we associate with the rise of the Chinese republic in the early years of this century. We must do the same in the case of Thailand, noting that in the same period, Thailand itself was undergoing the experience of a modern nationalist awakening. The two nationalisms in interaction produced a sharper confrontation of Thai and Chinese on Thai soil, and the line between the two was further entrenched by the appearance of women in considerable numbers among the immigrants from China. Intermarriage, hitherto the order of the day, decreased in significance as a bridge over which Chinese might pass easily and fairly quickly into Thai society.

Once Chinese in Thailand were defined as foreigners (instead of being welcome strangers), they could be subjected to official pressures to curb their economic strength, their cultural idiosyncrasy, and their competing nationalism. The list of these pressures is a long one, and as tedious to recite as they were painful and offensive to the Chinese who experienced them. Certainly, the attempts made by the Thai government in modern times to hinder immigration, to lever Chinese out of their economic strongholds, and to suppress Chinese culture (notably by placing severe restrictions on Chinese schools) might seem to be unambiguous evidence of a serious anti-Chinese policy—a policy likely to make the Chinese close their ranks and resist the forcible assimilation to which it pointed. But there are two very important points to be borne steadily in mind when we try to interpret the history of the fate of Chinese in Thailand.

The first point is that anti-Chinese policy in many of its aspects was directed against organized Chinese society, not against Chinese as such. The numerous Thai of Chinese descent have not generally been made to suffer for their foreign antecedents. On the contrary, the definition of "Thai" being operatively cultural, Thais of Chinese ancestry have fared outstandingly well. Naturally, economic policy aimed at reducing Chinese strength bore heavily on individuals, but it does not appear to have been intended to starve the Chinese out.

The second point is that it is characteristic of the Chinese in noncolonial Thailand to look up to and not down on the "foreigners" among whom they live, in contrast to the behavior of their congeners in colonial Southeast Asia. The Thailand Chinese have been attracted to their hosts who, being masters in their own house, have not labored under the disadvantages of Malays or Indonesians as subject peoples. Some Chinese in Malaya could aspire to behave like Englishmen and be socially acceptable to them; and there have been some fair Chinese imitations of Englishmen in Malaya. Some Chinese in the East Indies aimed similarly to consort with the Dutch; in modern times, they could acquire certain legal privileges open to the "assimilated." But no Chinese could *become* an Englishman or a Dutchman. In Thailand, a Chinese could become a Thai. And the repressive measures taken in Thailand to curb the Chinese seemed to have worked, in the sense that they gave the Chinese an extra push in the direction of committing themselves finally to adopting a Thai identity. All in all, it looks as though anti-Chinese policy in Thailand may be interpreted to have been more halfpence than kicks.

At the present time, the situation appears to be something after the following picture. There is a small Chinese society alongside the Thai society. (At its maximum extent, this Chinese society cannot contain more than 10 per cent of the total population of the country.) Each of the two societies is a crystallized entity. A Chinese may participate in both of them, assuming a personal name and language to suit his alignment and associations of the moment. Many Thailand Chinese of the second and subsequent generations move back and forth in this fashion, but the movement is, in fact, very sensitive to changes in national policy. In periods when the pressure is taken off, the movement is unhampered, and a man does not need to throw in his lot finally with the Thai. But when repressive measures are applied, he must make his choice. The whole time, whether or not the government of the country is being officially anti-Chinese, the process of assimilation goes on (although at differing speeds), and—which is particularly important and interesting—it serves to cream off the leaders of the organized Chinese community. It seems that once a Chinese gets to the top of the Chinese social hierarchy, he is paradoxically in a fair way to being a Chinese no longer; for Thai society offers him great rewards of prestige to lure him in. And while he himself may never cease to belong to the Chinese community in some sense, his children will be more definitely committed to the dominant society. Perhaps the most illuminating single fact about the Chinese in Thailand is that, despite the unbroken history of Chinese settlement in the country since at least the fifteenth century, "even fourth-generation Chinese," in Skinner's words, "are practically non-existent."

If it is true that assimilation is taking place with regularity, although at different rates at different times, then "the Chinese" cannot survive in Thailand, for here, as is the case generally in the region, the gates have been pretty well closed to immigration since 1949. It follows that the Chinese minority will be eroded away. Then—if we may toy with the fancy of being alive to witness this consummation—we shall be able to say "So much for the superiority and self-satisfaction of Chinese culture."

There is a final point to be made on the case of the Thailand Chinese. When in Malaya and Indonesia we think of the Chinese changing their culture (becoming acculturated, as some anthropologists put it), we can envisage the process as one in which Chinese grow less and less Chinese and more something else (although in Malaya, in contradistinction to contemporary Indonesia, that something else falls well short of a non-Chinese identity). And since the process will not operate at a uniform rate for everybody, and not everybody will have started to move along the path at the same time, some Chinese will be culturally less Chinese than others, the newcomer from China at one end of the scale and the modern versions of the Baba-Peranakan at the other. This kind of model will not take us far in perceiving the realities of the situation in Thailand as it exists today. There the terminal points for a scale of acculturation can certainly be found: the most recent immigrant Chinese from China and the man of Chinese descent in whom Chinese culture is barely perceptible. But the bulk of the Thailand Chinese cannot be strung along a line between the two points to form a scale, for they have that "double identity" which one of the writers on them, Richard J. Coughlin, has chosen for the title of his book. Culturally, most of the people we call Chinese in Thailand are both Chinese and Thai, although with varying emphases.

Thailand is by no means the only Southeast Asian country in which Chinese have been swallowed up in numbers, although it is the most dramatic case of such cultural ingestion, principally, no doubt, because of its exemption from colonial rule. But to attempt now to talk about Burma, Laos, Cambodia, Vietnam, and the Philippines would be very rash, not only because I should be abusing the hospitality offered by a single lecture, but also on account of the fact that the sociological groundwork for the study of these smaller manifestations of the Nan-yang is for the most part yet to be done.

May I take the liberty of reminding you of the two points I have set out to argue? It is wrong to imagine, first, that the Chinese are an unassimilable lump in the digestive tract of every Southeast Asian country, and, second, that Chinese culture is highly resistant to being worn down by other cultures. The clamorous (and, to tourists, colorful) "Chinatowns" are but one aspect of a long history of Chinese settlement in the Nan-yang —and not necessarily its most significant. The 12 million Chinese in present-day Southeast Asia are of different nationalities, speak many languages, follow several religions, and live many styles of life. And, as some of them have painfully discovered by going back to one of the two Chinas, many are so little Chinese in their outlook that they are foreigners in several senses in the land of their forefathers.

Yet it by no means follows that the Nan-yang has completely lost its meaning in the 1960's, or that in the context of Southeast Asia the adjective "Chinese" has come irretrievably adrift from the noun "China." The Chinese in one Southeast Asian country are certainly aware of the fate of those in another; and the awareness may enhance or decrease their satisfaction with their own lot. They have a fellow feeling for their congeners dispersed about the region, and may sometimes indeed be related by family ties to many of them. And China itself, now occupying a position in world affairs which is at least unambiguous in its importance, stands for the inhabitants of the Nan-yang as an ancestral land, however remote it may be in a distance measured by generations, knowlege, or political sympathy. These facts are not a discredit to the Nan-yang Chinese, yet they often stand to their disadvantage. They make the Chinese seem to be rootless cosmopolitans in a world where narrow-minded nationalism requires a more straitened discipline of loyalty. It is true that some Chinese in Southeast Asia, being Communists, are doubly a risk to the countries where they live: They stand not only for Communism but also for a giant China. It is also true that some Chinese businessmen show a greater concern for their own commercial interests than for the economic policies of their rulers (although in this they are sometimes of greater benefit to the economy than are their rulers). But the longer view of the Nan-yang, for which I have tried to plead in this lecture, should suggest that "Chinese" does not automatically mean alien, that the presence of Chinese in Southeast Asia does not entail the subversion of national integrity, and that—although in keeping my lecture close to the subject of changes in culture I have neglected this theme—the economic benefits, in capital-formation and entrepreneurial skill, which the Chinese have brought to Southeast Asia would, in a just world, earn them more gratitude than jealousy.

A Note on Sources

The literature on the Nan-yang is very big, and it is not always easy to identify the most useful items in it. Moreover, many of the most valuable items have been published in out-of-the-way places and journals. Victor Purcell's *The Chinese in Southeast Asia*, London, 1951, is now, of course, out-of-date, but a revised edition of it, announced for 1965, will presumably take account of recent historical and sociological research.

The history of the Chinese in Southeast Asia is best approached through a remarkably concise and sophisticated pamphlet: Wang Gungwu, *A Short History of the Nanyang Chinese*, Singapore, 1959. On the key question of Chinese education in the Nan-yang, see for a very useful survey, Douglas P. Murray, "Chinese Education in South-East Asia," *The China Quarterly*, No. 20, October–December, 1964.

It will have been obvious to anybody who knows the field that I have relied very heavily in this lecture on the shrewd analyses of the Thailand and Indonesian Chinese made by G. William Skinner. But my reliance on his work in no way involves him in any mistakes or misinterpretations I may have slipped into. In connection with the main theme of the lecture, I may suggest the following of Skinner's works to the reader: *Chinese Society in Thailand: An Analytical History*, Ithaca, N.Y., 1957; "Change and Persistence in Chinese Culture Overseas: A Comparison of Thailand and Java," *Journal of the South Seas Society*, Singapore, Vol. XVI, parts 1 and 2, 1960; and "The Chinese Minority," in Ruth T. McVey, ed., *Indonesia*, New Haven, Conn., 1963.

The work by Richard J. Coughlin referred to in the lecture is *Double Identity, The Chinese in Modern Thailand*, Hong Kong, 1960.

Important contributions to the study of the Chinese in Indonesia are to be found in the following works: Lea E. Williams, *Overseas Chinese Nationalism, The Genesis of the Pan-Chinese Movement in Indonesia, 1900–1916*, Glencoe, Ill., 1960; Donald E. Willmott, *The National Status of the Chinese in Indonesia 1900–1958*, Monograph Series, Modern Indonesia Project, Cornell University, Ithaca, N.Y., rev. ed., 1961 (mimeo); Mary F. Somers, *Peranakan Chinese Politics in Indonesia*, Interim Report Series, Modern Indonesia Project, Cornell University, Ithaca, N.Y., 1964 (mimeo).

In speaking about the Chinese in Malaya, I have drawn on my own experience as well as the considerable literature on the country. The following work provides the best framework for understanding the present position of the Chinese: J. M. Gullick, *Malaya*, London, 1963. R. B. Le Page, *The National Language Question, Linguistic Problems of Newly Independent States*, London, 1964, takes Malaya as one example of the problems it discusses. Some of the cultural questions mentioned in the lecture are touched on in the following pieces I have published: *Chinese Family and Marriage in Singapore*, H.M.S.O., London, 1957; "Immigrants and Associations: Chinese in Nineteenth-Century Singapore," *Comparative Studies in Society and History*, Vol. III, No. 1, October, 1960; "Chinese Kinship and Marriage in Early Singapore," *Journal of Southeast Asian History*, Vol. III, No. 2, September, 1962.

POSTSCRIPT, 1968

This lecture was delivered in 1964, since when some important political changes (chiefly, the re-emergence of Singapore as a separate entity and the revolution in Indonesia) have altered the circumstances I discussed. I would not dare, in a mere postscript, to try to assess the significance of the changes for the overseas Chinese. In the last four years, the scene has changed in another respect: The literature on the subject of the Chinese in Southeast Asia has increased. In the recent publications, I would draw attention to W. F. Wertheim, "The Trading Minorities in Southeast Asia," in his book, *East-West Parallels*, The Hague, 1964; Lawrence W. Crissman, "The Segmentary Structure of Urban Overseas Chinese Communities," *Man* (n.s.), Vol. II, No. 2, June, 1967; The Siauw Giap, "Religion and Overseas Chinese Assimilation in Southeast Asian Countries," *Revue du sud-est asiatique*, No. 2, Brussels, 1965. In addition, there have appeared two important works dealing with countries not discussed in the lecture: Edgar Wickberg, *The Chinese in Philippine Life, 1850–1898*, New Haven, 1965; and W. E. Willmott, *The Chinese in Cambodia*, Vancouver, 1967. But whatever the changes in fact and study, I stand by the main lines of the argument in my lecture.

32

THE OVERSEAS INDIAN IN SOUTHEAST ASIA: BURMA, MALAYSIA, AND SINGAPORE*

R. HATLEY

The map of Southeast Asia clearly delineates the boundaries of contemporary nations; yet, within these borders are many autonomous or semi-autonomous communities. These differentiated populations can be divided into indigenous and immigrant minorities,[1] but it is the latter, the "alien" communities, that present the greater challenge to integration and modernization.[2] Whatever "modernization" may mean, the problem of identifying

* This is an abridged version of a study prepared for a seminar on political integration at Yale in Spring, 1967. Material on Ceylon, which was originally included, has been omitted. The essay is published here by permission of the author.

[1] For a recent study dealing largely with immigrant minorities in Southeast Asia, see Guy Hunter, *South-East Asia: Race, Culture, and Nation* (London: Oxford University Press, 1966).

[2] The crisis of "identity" has been called by Verba the most basic issue to be dealt with by the developing states in their drive to be modern nations. See Lucian Pye and Sidney Verba, eds., *Political Culture and Political Development* (Princeton, N.J.: Princeton University Press, 1965), p. 560.

with a political entity larger than the primary group is basic to the growth of the nation-state.[3]

The various communities of the overseas Indians in Southeast Asia are among these immigrant minorities whose primordial attachments[4] differ from those of the assimilated populations in the various states. The Indian communities in the countries[5] considered here exemplify some of the problems faced by "plural societies" in reducing the primordial sentiments of the various groups to the "civil order" of the nation-state. This process of integration, when accompanied, as it usually is, by increasing social mobilization, seems more often to increase rather than reduce communal differentiation.[6] When these nation-building processes are at work in a state in which there is a community whose identity is subject to question between that state and another, as is the case with the immigrant Indian communities, then integration becomes even more of a challenge.[7]

This essay attempts to describe the relations of the overseas Indians with their adopted homes and to evaluate their progress toward, and their prospects for, political assimilation.[8]

The History of Indian Migrations

That India and Southeast Asia have been in communication for a very long time is evident from the many similarities of their cultures. During at least the first millennium of the Christian era, Indian culture was the dominant external influence in Southeast Asia, particularly in the form of Hindu and Buddhist religious-cultural systems. And migrations to and from India were obviously important in the exchange of goods and ideas throughout India and Southeast Asia.

[3] For a general survey of the various meanings of political development, see Lucian W. Pye, *Aspects of Political Development* (Boston: Little, Brown and Co., 1966), chapter 2.

[4] Clifford Geertz calls this reduction of "primordial sentiments" to "civil politics" in the new states "integration"; Clifford Geertz, ed., *Old Societies and New States* (Glencoe, Ill.: The Free Press, 1963), pp. 105-57.

[5] For the purposes of this paper, the overseas Indians of Malaysia and Singapore will be treated together. And, depending on the historically relevant period, the terms Malaysia and Malaya (both including Singapore, unless otherwise noted) will be used.

[6] The most instructive model of the interrelation of social mobilization and assimilation is found in Karl Deutsch, *Nationalism and Social Communication* (2d ed.; Cambridge, Mass.: Massachusetts Institute of Technology, 1966), especially chapter 6. Deutsch has also provided definitions of many concepts that are used in this paper; see especially *ibid.*, chapter 4.

[7] Karl Deutsch, "External Influences on the Internal Behavior of States," in R. Barry Farrell, ed., *Approaches to Comparative and International Politics* (Evanston, Ill.: Northwestern University Press, 1965), pp. 5-26, has elaborated a model (p. 9) describing the relationship of a foreign minority as that of a "linkage group" between its mother culture and the host state.

[8] Here I am suggesting that integration (and assimilation) requires the cooperation of both the minority (differentiated) and the majority (assimilated) populations. It may be required in the process of nation-building that *all* communities reduce their primordial communal attachment in favor of a more comprehensive civil identification. See Geertz, *op. cit.*, pp. 119-20.

These migrations of earlier centuries, however, have little relation to the contemporary Indian communities in Southeast Asia. The current Indian populations in these countries are a result of the nineteenth- and twentieth-century migrations of Indian laborers, businessmen, and financiers to take part in the commercial development of the European colonies. Indians migrated in significant numbers only after the abolition of slavery had disrupted the traditional labor supply, in order to sustain and develop the plantation enterprises and concomitant transportation, communication, and administrative facilities of a number of British colonies, and, to a lesser extent, some French and Dutch colonies.

The first migration of Indian laborers, to Mauritius in 1834, came at a time when employment was difficult in India.[9] Colonial plantations continued to attract laborers until World War II, despite working conditions that were sometimes little better than slavery, apparently because this was still more attractive than employment in India.

Patterns of settlement, methods of recruitment, and the numbers of Indian laborers going to the British colonies nearer India (Ceylon, Burma, and Malaya) differed greatly from those of Indian workers migrating to more distant points. Until World War II, most Indians went to Burma, Ceylon, or Malaya to work for a short period (generally five to seven years) and then returned to India.[10] The transience of Indian communities militated against identity with local populations and claim to permanent residence. However, increasing numbers of Indians did settle in Burma, Ceylon and Malaya. Indeed, today these three countries have the largest overseas Indian populations.

An indenture system of recruitment and the distance and expense of repatriation (although provided for) meant that immigrant Indian laborers tended to remain in the more remote countries. Labor for Burma, Ceylon, and Malaya, however, was recruited under different circumstances. A former laborer returning to India would recruit new workers, often within his local community, on the basis of his family and social connections, and then return with his recruits to the overseas plantation, where he served as their supervisor. Abuses under this system were frequent, often taking the form of indebtedness of the laborer to the *kangani* (or *maistry* in Burma), as the recruiter was called.[11]

[9] For the most useful analysis of Indian migration during this early period, see I. M. Cumpston, *Indians Overseas in British Territories, 1834–1854* (London: Oxford University Press, 1953).

[10] Of the 1931 Indian population in Malaya (including Singapore) of 621,847 (14.3 per cent of the total population), only 21.1 per cent were locally born. Of the 1931 Indian population in Burma of 1,017,825 (6.9 per cent of the total), only 28.1 per cent were locally born; and if Arakan, which is contiguous to India, is excluded, only 17.6 per cent of the Indians of Lower Burma were born locally. Of the 1921 Indian population of Ceylon comprising 602,735 (13.4 per cent of the total), 31 per cent were locally born.

[11] Details of the indenture, *kangani*, and *maistry* systems of labor recruitment are given in C. Kondapi, *Indians Overseas, 1838–1949* (Madras: Oxford University Press, 1951), pp. 8–16, 29–39, 45–49.

But while the abuses suffered by Indians overseas were apparently many and harsh,[12] they were not severe enough to curtail migration. This was partly because the European planter, through his pressure on the Colonial Office in London, had almost total control over Indian emigration, until the Government of India Emigration Act of 1922 vested this responsibility in the Indian legislature.[13] This act ended immigration to all countries other than Burma, Ceylon, and Malaya, and suggested wage guidelines and welfare safeguards for the laborers. In fact, however, its impact was minimal. Almost no economic disruption was caused in other countries by cutting off Indian migration, and in Burma, Malaya, and Ceylon, welfare measures and wage safeguards were gained through enactments of local administrations, rather than as a direct result of this act.[14]

Perhaps the most striking feature of the migration back and forth for more than a hundred years was that very few of these migrants or their descendants lost their Indian identity. Three important factors seem to have contributed to this fact: the often temporary nature of the Indian's residence overseas, the geographic and social isolation of the Indian settlements on the agricultural estates and in the public-works labor quarters, and the highly visible physical, cultural, and religious differences that further distinguished Indians from the assimilated population.

One reason for the maintenance of the resulting "plural society" was the low level of social and economic mobility in colonial society—the Indians' occupational training skill and literacy were sufficient only for their jobs as laborers. Secondly, even in the new environment, Indians were still guided by social values derived from the Indian milieu, in part because of a recruitment system that helped to maintain family and social ties with the Indian villages. Finally, it was in the self-interest of estate operators to maintain a minimally qualified and docile labor force, and the protestations of Indian civil authorities usually went unheeded by a Colonial Office more susceptible to the persuasions of the planters. All things considered, it is little wonder that overseas Indian laborers became neither mobilized nor assimilated.

Smaller numbers of overseas Indians, however, did rise to conspicuous positions as "white-collar" workers in the technical, administrative, and professional fields. Although far less numerous, their political roles were far more important, since it was they who first came into contact, competition, and conflict with the indigenous populations.

---

12 *Ibid.*; see also George Netto, *Indians in Malaya* (Singapore: published by the author, 1961).

13 M. K. Muhammad Kunhi, "Indian Minorities in Ceylon, Burma and Malaysia," *The Indian Year Book of International Affairs*, part 1 (1964), 408. This long article (pp. 405–72) gives a most useful historical account, but it tends toward a legalistic analysis and is based almost exclusively on Indian sources.

14 J. Norman Parmer, *Colonial Labor Policy and Administration* (Locust Valley, N.Y.: J. J. Augustin, 1960) gives an excellent account of the labor situation and policy enactments and effects for the Malayan rubber-plantation industry.

Overseas Indians in Southeast Asia

Burma

Although the British occupied Tenasserim and Arakan in 1824 after the first Burmese War, the immigration of Indians into Burma on a significant scale began in 1852, when the British gained control of the Irrawaddy Delta of Lower Burma.[15] The development of the delta as a major area of rice production and export was directly related to the influx of Indian labor and capital and to the Indian demand for rice. Whereas Burmese subsistence agriculture had not been able to provide the skills and capital necessary to develop a commercial rice economy, nearby India was in a position to supply both.

The Burmese, however, could provide labor for rice cultivation. The total population of Lower Burma grew from 2,747,148 in 1872 to 7,765,614 by 1931, while the Indian population in the same area grew from 136,504 to 849,381.[16] In 1931, at the high point of rice cultivation and Indian immigration, only 5.7 per cent of those engaged in agricultural cultivation in the delta were Indians. Thus, "it is evident that it was not primarily Indian labour that developed the Delta."[17]

Other Indians, in smaller numbers, came to dominate the nonagricultural labor market in the developing Burmese economy. They engaged in occupations related to trade, transport, communications, the civil service, rice-milling, and, eventually, mining and oil. In addition, seasonal labor in the agricultural sector attracted large numbers of Indians.

Finally, despite these significant labor migrations, as Pearn has correctly pointed out, "above all, it was by the provision of capital that the Indian made his contribution to the economic development of Burma."[18] Capital for the purchase of equipment and seeds was supplied to the Burmese cultivator principally by the Chettiar moneylender from South India. Thus in terms of capital and consumption, the development of Burma was accomplished almost entirely by and for the Indian. Indeed, Burma was even governed as a province of India until 1937, and it was in part the ever-increasing presence of the Indian in Burma that led to a reaction against the very real threat of absorption by India.

Perhaps the first consequences of Indian immigration into Burma were felt after the introduction of the Montagu-Chelmsford Reforms in India. The exclusion of Burma from these reforms, though it still constituted a province of India, evoked political agitation that resulted in the eventual extension of the reforms to Burma. Their implementation brought communal legislative representation, which only further emphasized the fact that the Burmese were not Indian and led to demands in the 1920's for the

---

[15] B. R. Pearn, *The Indian in Burma* (Ledbury, England: Le Play House Press, 1946), pp. 5–6. This brief study is the most concise and useful historical account of the Indian in Burma until World War II.

[16] *Ibid.*, p. 14.

[17] *Ibid.*

[18] *Ibid.*, p. 15.

separation of Burma from India. This separation was finally provided for by the Government of Burma Act of 1935, which came into operation on April 1, 1937.

But before political separation from India was finally granted, the economic disruptions after 1929 tightened the Indian hold on Burma's economy. "One of the results of the economic crisis was that the Burmese began to compete with the Indian workers."[19] Unemployment among the Burmese heightened the conspicuousness of the Indian presence, especially in the public sector of the Burmese economy. Many Indians also became unemployed as the price of rice fell, but they could at least return to India, and many of them did. At the same time, Indian immigration into Burma subsided, causing a net reduction of Indian residents. It was not unnoticed among the Burmese that when privation threatened, the Indian asserted his Indian identity.

It was in urban Rangoon that the effects of the depression unemployment were most acutely felt: "The first anti-Indian riots of 1930 were the direct result of the competition between the Burmese and Indian worker: and the apprehensions of the Burmese majority over the dominant economic position of the Indian minority."[20] At least 120 persons died during the rioting, which began in the dockyards where Burmese, driven from their land, had replaced striking Indian stevedores. More important, perhaps, than the death toll was the communal nature of the disturbance, in which the contention was directly between Indians and Burmese.

An additional aggravation brought about by the depression was the increasing alienation of land from the Burmese cultivator, most notably by the Chettiar moneylender.[21] With the falling market, the Burmese cultivator found himself unable to repay his loans, and foreclosures gradually began to take place. While the Chettiar may have had little desire to be a landowner, much less a farmer, he now found himself owner of foreclosed land mortgages that no one had the capital to purchase. Furthermore, when the Indian moneylender came into possession of land, he often pre-

[19] Kunhi, *op. cit.*, p. 414.

[20] *Ibid.*, p. 430.

[21] The seriousness of land alienation may be seen in the following table derived from Usha Mahajani, *The Role of Indian Minorities in Burma and Malaya* (Bombay, Vora and Co., 1960), p. 20, the most important study of the Indian economic and political role in these countries from 1930 to 1955:

Land Alienation in Lower Burma
(in thousands of acres)

	1930	1934	1938
Total rice-growing area of Lower Burma	9,249	2,335	9,732
Area owned by nonagriculturalists	2,443	4,460	4,971
Area owned by Chettiars	570	2,100	2,468
Percentage of Chettiar land to nonagriculturalist land	19	47	50
Percentage of Chettiar land to total rice-growing land	6	22	25

ferred Indian to Burmese tenants, thus depriving the Burmese of his principal occupation.

Essentially, the Burmese felt the Indian presence most severely in economic terms. The fact that the Burmese had been forced off the land was only part of the problem, for in seeking employment outside agriculture, he found that Indians held nearly all the jobs in commerce and industry, not only as manual laborers but also as white-collar workers. With the development of higher education in Burma, large numbers of young Burmese who had been educated to hold government jobs now found Indians entrenched in the colonial bureaucracy. Indeed, the colonial regime in Burma must have been much more Indian than British. Thus, land alienation and competition for jobs in a time of economic challenge to the colonial system provided perhaps the most important stimulus to the awakening Burmese nationalism.[22] And the fact that this nationalism partly stemmed from antipathy toward him could not help but affect the future role of the Indian in the Burmese nation.

In 1938, during this period of rising Burmese national sensitivity, riots broke out upon the publication of a book by a Burmese Muslim that contained passages criticizing Buddhism. Although the conflict began in Rangoon and was initially directed against Burmese Muslims by Buddhist *pongyis* and their supporters, the riots spread, eventually pitting Burmese against Indians (Muslims and non-Muslims alike) throughout the country.[23] "One of the direct results of the 1938 riots was the Immigration Agreement concluded between India and Burma in 1941."[24] With the separation of Burma from India in 1938, Burma had gained the right to control immigration. And, in effect, the Indian in Burma became an alien, no longer under the protection of the government of India. The agreement was intended to regulate immigration and to define the legal status of Indians in Burma, but before it could be implemented, the Japanese invaded Burma.

The depression and its aftermath—coupled with Burma's separation from India—had awakened the Burmese to the extent of Indian influence in Burmese affairs, but the Japanese occupation proved an even stronger impetus for Burmese self-assertion. After the war broke out in Burma in December, 1941, nearly half the Indian population there fled to India; those left behind were mainly the poorer classes and many of those long domiciled in Arakan.[25] This fact underlined the lack of identity the Indians felt with the Burmese nation. The Indians remaining in Burma were subjected to various cross-pressures that affected their attitudes; many asserted their nationalism through the activities of the Indian Independence

[22] *Ibid.*, p. 21.

[23] Approximately 200 Indian and Burmese lives were lost in the rioting, and property damage, especially to Indian shops, amounted to £1.3 million by official valuation, although Indian claims amounted to more than £4 million. Pearn, *op. cit.*, p. 28.

[24] Kunhi, *op. cit.*, p. 433.

[25] Of approximately a million Indians in Burma, nearly 500,000 evacuated successfully; approximately 10,000 are believed to have died on the way. Mahajani, *op. cit.*, p. 173.

League.[26] On the other hand, the isolation of the Indians left in Burma during the war years probably made them more aware of their identity with Burma and their growing remoteness from India, and changes in Burmese attitudes toward their own identity also took place during the Japanese occupation. Burmese skill at managing their own affairs was augmented by the Japanese-sponsored Baw Maw government, which added to the Burmese drive for full self-rule, free from either British or Indian influences.

Thus, when the British recognized Burmese independence on January 1, 1948, many changes had already occurred in the role of the Indian in Burma. Since independence, this role has been even more radically altered. Because of the various disruptions during and after the war, the number of Indians in Burma and their position in the Burmese economy have been difficult to assess.[27] We must assume that their economic stature is much diminished, especially after events of the 1950's and 1960's.[28]

After Burmese independence, it seems to have been fairly easy for an Indian to identify with Burma (at least legally) if he chose to do so. Regulations in the Burmese Constitution provided citizenship for any person

[26] For a discussion of the activities of the Indian Independence League, see Joginder Singh Jessy, "The Indian Army of Independence" (B.A. thesis, University of Malaya, Singapore, 1958); see also Mahajani, *op. cit.*, chapter 5.

[27] The last complete census was taken in 1931. In 1931, the total population of Burma was 14,667,146, of which 1,017,825 (6.7 per cent) were Indians. For Lower Burma, less Arakan, Indians comprised 9.3 per cent of the population. The city of Rangoon had a total population of 400,415 in 1931, of which 211,692 (52.9 per cent) were Indian. In addition, 80 per cent of the Indian population in Burma was born outside Burma. The war itself displaced half the Indian population of Burma (see footnote 25). With the end of the war, about 246,000 Indians returned to Burma. A partial census in 1953 listed the urban population of Burma as 2,940,704, of whom 287,903 (9.7 per cent) were Indians. In Rangoon, of a total population of 737,079, 140,396 (19.2 per cent) were Indian. An estimate of the Indian rural population of approximately 300,000 would bring the total Indian population of Burma in 1953 to nearly 600,000 (4 per cent) of the population of Burma. See Mahajani, *op. cit.*, pp. 172–73.

[28] The last complete census yielded the following totals (adapted from Pearn, *op. cit.*, pp. 8 and 11):

Economic Position of the Indian in Burma, 1931

	Total Population	Indians	Indians in Total Population (*per cent*)	Indians in Total Population of Lower Burma, Less Arakan (*per cent*)
Public force	30,816	13,995	45.4	40.0
Public administration	44,867	13,762	30.8	52.1
Professions	198,890	10,418	5.2	11.1
Domestic services	44,689	24,326	54.4	67.9
Agriculture	1,605,556	95,692	5.3	4.0
Mining	39,503	14,752	37.3	31.4
Industry	664,376	104,767	15.8	36.3
Transport	222,055	101,536	45.7	65.8
Trade	557,248	96,211	17.3	24.0

born in Burma, or born in the Commonwealth and resident in Burma for eight of the ten years immediately preceding independence. Under these provisions, Indians returning after the war, among them many Chettiars and other businessmen, would not qualify for citizenship. But for the majority of the Indians then in Burma, citizenship was theirs for the asking. By 1961, only 6,800 of them had taken advantage of this opportunity.[29]

The Land Nationalization Act of 1953 prohibited landholdings of more than fifty acres, and noncultivators could not own land. This measure most affected the Indian landowner in Burma, but it was directed toward all landlords. After the Ne Win government took power in 1962, all major industries and all banks were nationalized. Licenses for moneylending, importing, exporting, retailing, and wholesaling were open only to Burmese citizens. Foreign remittances were curtailed, cutting off the outflow of funds to India. Consumer industries, warehouses, and retail and wholesale shops were nationalized in 1963.[30] "While the nationalization of lands, banks, and the export and import business hit the Chettyars and the other landlords and big financiers, the taking over of shops has mainly hit the small traders."[31] After the nationalization of banks and industries in 1963, Indian departures from Burma began as a trickle. When the shops were taken over, the trickle became a stream, with the result that, "according to [Burmese] Government statistics, more than 177,000 foreigners [nearly all Indians] have left Burma since April 1963."[32]

Despite protestations of the Indian government, little could be done to help the alien Indian in Burma who had failed in, or was prohibited from, becoming Burmese—at least by citizenship. "General Ne Win maintained that his government was pursuing goals based on a socialism that was not discriminatory against foreigners, but applied equally to all . . . and that foreigners desiring to stay in Burma 'must merge themselves with the common people in building a socialist economy.' "[33] Thus, the Indian in Burma has found his Indian identity untenable in the Burmese nation-state, which is based increasingly on Burman cultural values. His role as a "linkage group"[34] is ending, as he is either being absorbed, integrated, or in some way assimilated into the Burmese polity, society, and community, or his alienation is being emphasized to the point of his physical expulsion. For the estimated 450,000 overseas Indians in Burma, the choices are no doubt becoming more clear.

Malaysia and Singapore

Indians have migrated to the Malay Peninsula for many years. The presence of the Malacca Chettiars, descendants of South Indian traders who

[29] Kunhi, *op. cit.*, p. 457.
[30] Robert A. Holmes, "The Politics of Burmanization," *Asian Survey*, VII, No. 3 (March, 1967), 190–92. See also Kunhi, *op. cit.*, pp. 458–61.
[31] *Ibid.*, p. 461.
[32] Drew Middleton, "Burmese Urged to Produce More," *The New York Times*, May 1, 1967, p. 9. Since May, 1967, Chinese have also fled Burma in large numbers.
[33] Holmes, *op. cit.*, p. 192.
[34] See footnote 7.

settled in Malacca before the coming of the Portuguese in 1511, testifies to this fact. Indian assimilation into Malayan society is exemplified by this group, which, while retaining certain aspects of its Indian identity—particularly the Hindu religion—has come to identify Malaya as its home and Malayan society as its own.[35]

But these at least partially assimilated "overseas Indians" came far earlier than the great bulk of the Indians who now live in Malaysia and Singapore. The influx of Indians to cultivate spices and sugar for export began in the 1830's, when only the Straits Settlements were under British control. European (largely British) plantations created the greatest demand for Indian labor, beginning with sugar in the 1840's, coffee in the 1870's, and, finally, rubber in the 1890's.[36] Additional Indian laborers were imported to build and maintain the transport facilities needed to develop the Malayan export economy.[37]

At various times until 1897, immigration to Malaya and the Straits Settlements was restricted by the Indian government, largely for health and welfare reasons, and immigration sometimes failed to meet the labor demands of the estates and public-works projects. After 1907, the Tamil Immigration Fund was set up, assessing estate employers to pay for transportation, medical aid, and repatriation of laborers.[38] This not only assured a stable supply of labor for the planter but also brought benefits to the Indian laborers. Abuses in recruitment and working conditions were reduced by further regulations instituted by the Colonial Office and the Malayan Planters' Association. For example, wage policy in Malaya for Indian estate workers always provided an income adequate to meet the costs of food and other necessities. "But . . . aspirations, however feeble, to anything more than simple existence were discouraged. Indeed they were not permitted to arise."[39]

The depression of the 1930's in Malaya, as in Ceylon, most severely affected the primary export sectors of the economy. And, as in Ceylon, Indian (largely Chettiar) moneylenders had not been so dominant in the economy as they were in Burma, and thus had acquired little land by mortgage foreclosure.[40] In addition, most land under cultivation was reserved for Malays or leased to European and Chinese estate owners, and thus little was subject to alienation. The Indian estate laborer, however,

---

[35] Mahajani, *op. cit.*, pp. 101–2.

[36] For an excellent account of the role of immigrant labor in Malaysia, see R. N. Jackson, *Immigrant Labour and the Development of Malaya* (Kuala Lumpur: Government Press, 1961); see also N. Jagatheesan, "Immigration of Indian Labour into Malaya, 1867–1910" (unpublished B.A. honors thesis; University of Malaya, Singapore, 1954).

[37] Javanese and Chinese were alternative sources of labor, but Dutch emigration regulations impeded an adequate supply of Javanese, and the Chinese found more remunerative occupations, especially among their own communities, which were being established in Malaya independent of British control. The indigenous Malay seemed satisfied with his own subsistence ecology and could not be induced to labor in the plantation export economy being built up by the Europeans.

[38] Parmer, *op. cit.*, pp. 42–45.

[39] Mahajani, *op. cit.*, p. 100.

[40] *Ibid.*, p. 258.

felt the fall in prices in the form of 40 to 60 per cent wage cuts.[41] Repatriation of approximately 130,000 of them to India did occur as a last resort after work had been spread as thinly as possible.[42] By 1934, the immigration of Indian laborers was renewed, but a surplus of Indian labor had built up, and wages continued to be reduced, although Indians were still said to be better off in Malaya than in India. By 1938, emigration of unskilled labor was halted by the Indian government at the recommendation of the Central Indian Association of Malaya, a commercial and quasi-political organization serving as spokesman for the Malayan Indians.

With the rapid Japanese occupation of the Malay Peninsula, only 5,000 Indians managed to flee to India. There were surely many more who would have preferred that alternative, but the rapidity of the Japanese advance made escape impossible. After the war, there was a rush of about 80,000 Indians back to India. The war experience had profound effects on the Malayan Indian. His prolonged isolation from India, the disruptions in the plantation economy, and, perhaps most important, the increasing politicization of the Indian communities, which was led by the Indian Independence League (IIL) under Japanese auspices, were factors that created a new situation for the overseas Indian in Malaya. While the IIL was promoting Indian independence, the Malayan Indian was learning his "nationalism" in Malaya and at the same time was undergoing a profound mobilization, which brought him into contact with other communities of Malaya.[43] It may well have been isolation from India and the mobilization forced upon him by the disruption of the plantation economy and society that caused the Malayan Indian to identify more closely with his adopted country than did the overseas Indians in Ceylon and Burma.

World War II had a lasting effect in awakening the communal and national consciousness of all three major communities residing in Malaya and Singapore. And, in many ways, the Chinese, Indians, and Malays identified with the aspirations of China, India, and Indonesia (although the Malays probably felt a stronger identity with Malaya itself, since they considered themselves, or were considered, to be the indigenous population).[44] With each community asserting its identity and none having a majority in the Malayan population, compromise among the various communities seemed almost obligatory. The most generally conceded accommodation is Chinese control of the economy and Malay control of politics. The Indians, constituting only 10 per cent (735,038) of the total population of Malaya in 1957, were apparently not considered in this arrangement.[45]

The presence of the Chinese, always in greater numbers but usually not

---

[41] Parmer, *loc. cit.*

[42] *Ibid.*, p. 259.

[43] Ravindra K. Jain, "Migrants, Proletarians or Malayans? South Indians on the Plantation Frontier in Malaya" (Ph.D. thesis, Australian National University, 1965; to be published by Yale University Press), pp. 59–60, 133.

[44] For some of the varieties of Malay perceptions of and loyalties toward Indonesia and Malaysia, see Peter J. Wilson, *A Malay Village and Malaysia* (New Haven: Human Relations Area Files Press, 1967), pp. 34, 52–54.

[45] Hunter, *op. cit.*, p. 31.

so disproportionately represented in the Malayan society and economy as the Indians, has tended to de-emphasize the importance of the Indians as an alien minority.[46] Thus, the principal communal confrontation has been between the Chinese and the Malays. This holds true also for Singapore, where the Indians constitute only 8.4 per cent (140,000) of the 1960 population of this predominantly Chinese city-state.

While a disproportionate share of agricultural workers are Indians, compared with their share of the total population, the Indian population has two other surprising characteristics, which contradict the usual image of the Indian in Malaya as an estate worker. In 1937, 68.2 per cent of the estate-labor population was Indian, but in 1947, Indians made up only 50 per cent of the estate workers. In 1955, this figure was 53.7 per cent.[47] And while the total figure for the Indian estate-labor population in Malaya of 164,896 in 1955 would imply a current estate-oriented population of approximately 300,000, a total Indian population in Malaya of 735,038 indicates that at least half the Indians are not employed on the estates. And, of course, in Singapore, where there are few estates, such workers account for a very small percentage of the Indian population.

Indians constituted 8.7 per cent of the urban population of Malaya in 1957 (13.8 per cent in 1947 and 17.8 per cent in 1931).[48] Of the total Indian population in Malaya, 30.5 per cent was urban in 1931; in 1947, the figure was 39.0 per cent, and by 1957, 42.1 per cent of the overseas Indian population of Malaya lived in gazetted towns.[49] One other factor besides urbanization has made the Malayan Indian more aware of his Malayan identity. Whereas, in 1931, only 21.4 per cent of the Indians in Malaya were locally born, in 1947, the figure was 51.6 per cent; this rose by 1957 to 64.5 per cent.[50]

Equally important have been the rather liberal citizenship laws, which

[46] As some indication of the disproportionate role of the Indian in various occupations in Malaya, see the following table adapted from Hunter, *op. cit.*, p. 71:

Percentage of Each Ethnic Group in
Selected Occupations, 1957 Census

	"Malaysian"	Chinese	Indians
Total economically active	48.4	36.8	14.8
Agricultural occupations	62.5	24.5	13.0
Administrative, executive, managerial	22.0	65.2	12.8
Clerical	29.0	49.6	21.4
Sales	15.6	67.3	17.1
Craftsmen, production workers	23.9	56.7	19.4
Total population (not including "others")	51.0	37.6	11.4

Note: All figures are percentage figures on the sum of the three population groups listed in the table and hence *not* on the total population of Malaya. Thus, occupational (line) percentages above total 100 per cent.

[47] Adapted from Mahajani, *op. cit.*, pp. 109–10.

[48] K. J. Ratnam, *Communalism and the Political Process in Malaya* (Kuala Lumpur: University of Malaya Press, 1965), p. 2.

[49] Mahajani, *op. cit.*, p. 113.

[50] Ratnam, *op. cit.*, p. 10.

provide that all persons born in Malaya after independence (August 31, 1957) are automatically citizens, and that those resident in Malaya for eight of the ten years preceding independence are eligible for citizenship. Singapore citizenship laws are almost the same as those of Malaysia. Politically, the Malayan Indian has been able to play a role in the delicately (communally) balanced politics of Malaya through the Malayan Indian Congress, a member of the tri-communal Alliance Party.[51]

Thus, we see that with communalism as the basis of Malayan politics and society, there has evolved in Malaysia what might be called a "plural national society." Several events since Malaysia's formation on September 16, 1963, are indicative of the instability, or, at least, of the tenuous nature, of this integrative accommodation. Singapore's expulsion, the political disquiet in the Borneo states, and the recent communal riots in Malaya suggest that all may not be well with the Malaysian political society. Although the various communities of Malaysia have learned to work together (out of necessity perhaps), the building of the kind of "national" identity that is needed to weld the various communities into one nation may require even further integration—and perhaps assimilation—into a system of commonly shared values.

Conclusion

The historical events and circumstances of the overseas Indian experience in Burma, Malaysia, and Singapore have laid the foundation for the maintenance of the Indian identity and for the political, social, and economic integration of the overseas Indian into the Southeast Asian nation-states. On the one hand, the development of the plural society in these Southeast Asian countries under an externally imposed colonial rule set up formidable barriers against the development of a common social will among the disparate communities and hence formed a major obstacle to national integration.[52] But the introduction of these countries into the

[51] Indian political power in Malaya is shown in the following table adapted from Ratnam, *op. cit.*, p. 207:

Percentage Communal Distribution of Political Power

	Population	Electorate	Constituencies	Seats	Cabinet Appointments
Malays	50.1	57	63.5	64	67
Chinese	36.9	36	36.5	27	25
Indians	11.3	7	—	9	8

Note: Population column does not total 100 per cent.

[52] Furnivall's concept of the plural society is defined as "a unit of disparate parts"—"groups of differing race and culture living side by side in economic symbiosis and mutual avoidance"—"which owes its existence to external factors, and lacks a common social will"; M. G. Smith in the Preface (p. vii) to his *Plural Society in the British West Indies* (Berkeley: University of California Press, 1965). Smith's discussion of Furnivall's concept is most useful. See also John S. Furnivall, "Some Problems of Tropical Economy" in R. Hinden, ed., *Fabian Colonial Essays* (London: Allen and Unwin, 1945), pp. 167–71; and *Colonial Policy and Practice* (London: Cambridge University Press, 1948), pp. 303–12.

international trading community by the very forces that created the plural societies exposed them to the processes of modernization and social mobilization, which made the plural compartmentalization of the societies untenable.

While the inertia of the colonial experience maintains, and even reinforces, the plural society, the revolutionary factors of economic intercourse, increased communication, and social mobilization have imposed severe demands on all elements of the segmented societies. The isolation of the overseas Indian community primarily on the rural agricultural estates and in the public-works labor lines is breaking down with urbanization and occupational mobility. Where the colonial situation had enforced the social, political, linguistic, religious, and cultural differentiation of the Indian from other communities, and, at the same time, had not fostered either a means of intercommunal communication or a unifying educational system, the phenomenon of urbanization, by providing job mobility, has facilitated contact among the various communities of the Southeast Asian plural societies. But this contact between members of various communities has not necessarily resulted in an increase of shared values, for it is in precisely this situation of intercommunal contact and competition that the recognition of one's differences from the members of other communities and of one's similarities to one's own group—in short, one's identity—becomes most acute. The common values that facilitate everyday communication go unnoticed, while the lack of shared values leads to communication failure and the anxiety of contention and conflict among perceptibly dissimilar competitors.

The extension of educational opportunities has also had unforeseen outcomes. One might suppose that the spread of literacy under a nationally sponsored and unified system of education—moreover in a common language—would further communication and the sharing of values among members of various communities. While all three countries have carried out extensive educational expansion programs with a national curriculum, the maintenance of Tamil-language schools in Malaysia, Chinese-language schools in Malaysia and Singapore, and English-language schools in all three countries may encourage communal distinctions, for it only further increases the perception and articulation of the differences between communities. And the imposition of the "national" language on all communities within each country has apparently increased communal conflict, whereas the "unifying" role of English (among the educated elites of the various communities) has produced perhaps an even deeper cleavage between the leaders and the masses.

The increase in employment opportunities brought about by urbanization and education among overseas Indians has also proved a mixed blessing. While individual mobility and intercommunal contact have increased, so has intercommunal competition for jobs that were formerly reserved for one community or another. Such competition has been particularly evident during times of economic stagnation or depression, or when competition for land among communities has arisen. During times of economic prosperity, for example, throughout the colonial period (save the depression of the 1930's) and during the Korean War boom, intercommunal economic competition has been very low.

The overseas Indian has become more aware of his identity as his political participation increases. In Burma, political participation is confined to citizens, thus excluding most Indians. In Malaysia, where most Indians have become citizens, the communal character of political activity has emphasized the distinct identity of the Indian through his relationship to the Malayan Indian Congress, as opposed to other communal parties.

The factors of mobilization that have affected the accessibility of India to the overseas Indian seem, however, to have lessened his identity with India. Longer, if not permanent, residence in the Southeast Asian country brought about by a secure employment, war, and now national sovereignty controlling migration, has caused changes in the attitude of the overseas Indian toward his adopted country and also has lessened the "Indian-ness" of the Indian community. While the Indian "community" in any Southeast Asian country has never been monolithic but rather comprises different linguistic, religious, caste, and culture groups, the isolation of these Indians from the proscriptions of their native villages has made caste, religious, and cultural strictures less binding. Intercaste marriage has become common and, indeed, the various Indian communities have become more uniform. At the same time, the Indian community has adapted many local features of language and culture to its new identity. Isolated from their India, the overseas Indians are now less Indian than they are Malayan— or Burmese—Indians. But while in fact they may have become less Indian, in their own view and to their neighboring communities, they seem to have become more Indian as contact between them and other communities has increased.

Social mobilization leading to intercommunal contact, the communication of ideas, and dispersal of goods, services, and jobs among the various communities, have put a severe strain on the continued compartmentalization of the plural societies in Southeast Asia. The minority overseas Indian communities, given the legacy of the plural society for which they are partially responsible, would perhaps have suffered more anguish had social mobilization broken down the plural social structure faster.

Three significant events have profoundly influenced the role of the overseas Indian in Southeast Asia. The economic depression of the 1930's first brought him into severe economic competition with other local communities and made the question of relative deprivation most noticeable. This was particularly true in Burma, where the overseas Indians were in economic competition with the mobilized indigenous population, and where the alienation of land to the Indian moneylender reached high levels. In Malaya, these effects of the depression were less significant; the Indian was relatively isolated on the plantations, and the existence of the Chinese as economic middlemen tended to divert attention from the Indian as an alien minority. In somewhat the same way, the Chinese in Burma have distracted some hostile attention from the Indians in that country. The effects of depression, forcing many unemployed laborers to take temporary refuge from the market collapse in India, probably reinforced the Indian identity of the overseas Indians.

World War II had perhaps even more far-reaching consequences for the overseas Indian in Burma and Malaya. The disruptions brought about in the economic sector, compulsory labor for the Japanese, the political organization and awakening brought about by the Indian Independence League, and the enforced isolation from India must have made the Indian more aware of his Indian identity in a multicommunal and colonial setting and also made him conscious of his opportunities as a member of the "nation" in which he resided. Even the "lowly" overseas Indian laborer must have had an enhanced self-esteem as an Asian.

The hierarchical social structure of the colonial plural society placed the minority communities in a position that militated against their assimilation with the majority population. Intermediary between the European colonialists and the indigenous population as functionaries of the colonial apparatus, these minorities viewed absorption into the majority population as a loss in status.[53] Yet their aspirations to equality with the Europeans were thwarted. Born of colonialism and wedded to it, the favored minorities saw their position threatened by colonialism's demise.

Independence from colonial rule thus proved the most profoundly influential event for both the plural society and the overseas Indian within it. The transfer to the independent states of the power by which the colonial governments had maintained the inimical plural societies meant that the new states could define their own national society. The overseas Indian found himself a minority in a nation-state that was becoming defined more and more in terms of the values of the largest and now most powerful community in the nation. In addition, he became subject to the political authority of the newly independent state. Where he did not embrace this authority, and to an ever increasing degree the values of the community behind this authority, he became an alien. Complicating his choice was the fact that the independence of India permitted him to fully assert his own Indian identity. While Indian nationalism had from the beginning of the twentieth century been a factor in the assertion of his Indian-ness, now Malayan and Burmese nationalism could only limit this self-identification, while the achievement of Indian independence sanctioned his desire to remain Indian.

Thus, at the very time when the mobilization of the overseas Indian in Southeast Asia encourages the articulation of an exclusively Indian identity, the Indian finds it politically necessary to assume an identity based on a set of values by which Burma, Malaysia, or Singapore is defined. The fact that the overseas Indian in these Southeast Asian nations remains identifiable—and it may be disputed whether he is *first* a Burman, Malaysian, or Singaporean, *or still*, in some ways, an Indian—shows the extent of his integration into these countries. It becomes obvious that Karl Deutsch's conclusion about assimilation and differentiation accurately describes the

[53] On this point, the author is indebted to Harry J. Benda.

integration of the overseas Indians with the other communities of the countries of Southeast Asia: If mobilization of the various communities is growing faster than their common culture, an "acute recognition of their differences and their common, mutual experience of strangeness, and more conspicuous differentiation and conflict may result."[54] And the rapidity with which mobilization has proceeded, coupled with the reinforcing co-incidences of economic, religious, linguistic, and cultural characteristics, rigidly differentiating the communities of the plural societies in Southeast Asian nations, suggests that the growth of common values required for integration of these communities—including the overseas Indian—into coherent national states in Southeast Asia will not be secured without increased communal conflict.

[54] Deutsch, *Nationalism and Social Communication*, p. 126.

33

THE END OF THE INDONESIAN REBELLION*

HERBERT FEITH AND DANIEL S. LEV

The Indonesian regionalist rebellion ended in 1961. More than three years after it began in February, 1958, with the proclamation of a "Revolutionary Government of the Republic of Indonesia," almost all of those who had fought for it voluntarily surrendered to local army posts in Sumatra and Celebes (Sulawesi), most of them after negotiations with government army commanders. They brought in with them the leaders and followers of two earlier rebellions with which they had become allied—the Atjehnese Islamic rebellion, dating back to 1953, and the Kahar Muzakar rebellion of South Celebes, which broke out first in 1950. Almost 100,000 men left the path of rebellion, bringing about 20,000 weapons with them,[1] and Suma-

* Reprinted by permission of the authors and the publisher from *Pacific Affairs*, XXXVI (Spring, 1963), 32–46.

[1] The figure 100,000 exaggerates rebel fighting strength. As most commanders maintained ratios of from 1:2 to 1:4 between arms and men, it is likely that not more than 60,000 of those who abandoned the rebellion were full-time fighters. The others were members of the rebels' families and villagers who had some link with the rebels and came in with them, possibly in the hope of participating in government rehabilitation schemes. Probably about 10,000 had been members of the Indonesian Army at the outbreak of the rebellion.

tra and Celebes are now virtually free from all rebel activity. This development is highly significant for the course of Indonesian politics henceforth. But it is also important for what can be gleaned from it about the dynamics of rebellion in contemporary Indonesia, and about Indonesian potentialities for national unity. This article discusses the rebellion principally from this point of view.

The PRRI* rebellion had its origins in the turbulent period of mid-1956 to mid-1958, a period of transition from an open and pluralistic political system to a far more authoritarian one. Indeed, the rebellion and its rapid reduction to mere guerrilla proportions played a major part in making that difficult transition possible. Not long after the national elections of September and December, 1955, which had disappointed the high hopes Indonesians placed in them for political regeneration, the existing political order came under challenge. The loose postrevolutionary consensus began to break up, with nationalist, Islamic, Communist, military, Javanese, non-Javanese, and other elite groups looking about for new roles to play.

In the course of 1956, two groups staked out claims to leadership of a new and changed regime. One was the group of "regionalists"—several army commanders of areas outside Java and their civilian supporters, most of whom were members of the modernist Islamic party, Masjumi, or the much smaller Socialist Party. This group served to focus the widespread general dissatisfaction of the time upon Djakarta, charging the national government with overcentralization, "bureaucracy," neglect of the outer regions, corruption, and too much tolerance of the Communists. Some army members of the group blamed the nation's troubles on civilian influence. The second group was headed by President Sukarno himself, initially allied with supporters of the small national-Communist Murba (Proletariat) Party. As an alternative to regionalist and militarist proposals for change, the President blamed the prevailing dissatisfactions on "liberalism" and the political parties. He argued that the ills of the political order were rooted in the existing party system, and particularly in Indonesia's choice of an imported brand of democracy rather than the democracy that existed in its own traditions.

In 1956 and much of 1957, the political initiative lay with the regionalists. The first stage of their challenge unfolded between May and July, 1956, when army commanders in the rich exporting areas of North Celebes and North Sumatra organized large-scale smuggling of copra and rubber, arguing that this was necessary because of Djakarta's neglect of their areas and the welfare of their troops. Although the cabinet under the Nationalist Party's Ali Sastroamidjojo was eventually able to stop this by-passing of its (highly unrealistic) exchange rate, it failed to persuade the commanders to hand over any part of their revenues from imports.

The second stage of the regionalist challenge consisted of a series of bloodless coups, in which army-led councils took power out of the hand of civilian governors in Central, North, and South Sumatra in December, 1956, and in East Indonesia (Celebes, the Moluccas, and the Lesser Sundas) in

---

*Pemerintah Revolusioner Republik Indonesia (Revolutionary Government of the Republic of Indonesia).

March, 1957. Here again, Djakarta was largely powerless. It did succeed in undoing the seizure of power in North Sumatra by organizing a successful counter coup within that area's military command. Later, it reduced its challengers' power in East Indonesia by dividing that single military district into four. But the other areas remained under vociferously anti-Djakarta administrations, which enjoyed sympathy and some active support from military and civilian groups in most areas outside Central and East Java, the area of the ethnic Javanese.

A deadlock persisted for the rest of 1957, Djakarta refusing to recognize the regionalist councils but nevertheless negotiating with their heads, the military commanders. The councils insisted that they did not want to undermine the unity of Indonesia, and declared that they were willing to return the powers they had seized from Djakarta if the Sukarno-Hatta duumvirate were restored. This was in effect a demand for the Sumatran and Masjumi-Socialist oriented Hatta (the one-time prime minister and recently resigned vice president) to return to the post of prime minister.

President Sukarno, however, was strongly opposed to such a solution and looked to the radical nationalists and Communists for support against it. In February, 1957, the President developed his conception of Guided Democracy into a twofold practical proposition, which he then put to the various parties. First, he said, there should be a cabinet consisting of the four major parties, thus including the Communists as well as the three parties of the current coalition (Nationalists, Masjumi, and the conservative Muslim Nahdatul Ulama). Secondly, a national council should be established, based not on parties but on functional groups—workers, peasants, national businessmen, artists, and so on. Such a council, which would be led by the President and take decisions by unanimous agreement, would give advice to the cabinet, solicited or unsolicited, and would serve as a bridge between the government and society.

Support for this double proposition proved to be limited to the Nationalists, Communists, Murba Party, and smaller groups. The Masjumi, Socialists, Nahdatul Ulama, and the two small Christian parties declared their opposition. In these circumstances, the Djakarta leadership of the army came to play an independent political role. Under Chief of Staff Major General Nasution, whose own position was threatened by the regionalist military officers, the army leaders presented themselves as arbiters between the regionalists and Sukarno and his supporters. On the one hand, they shared anti-Communism and "anticivilianism" with the regionalists, and on the other, they agreed with Sukarno on the importance of maintaining central-government authority. As their formula to help resolve the hostility between the regionalists and Sukarno, the army heads proposed nationwide martial law. This was proclaimed in March, 1957. Its effect was to legalize the greater powers already assumed by the regionalist military commanders, and also to increase the civil powers of the commanders who had not become associated with the regionalist cause.

The tug of war between Djakarta and the regionalists continued until late 1957. In November, the government launched a major domestic campaign in support of a pro-Indonesian motion on West Irian then under discussion in the U.N. General Assembly. President Sukarno himself threatened that if Indonesia should fail again, as in 1954 and 1956, to obtain the necessary two-thirds majority in the Assembly, actions would be taken that would "surprise the nations of the world." But the Assembly failed to give the motion two-thirds support. Tension reached a high pitch on the following day, November 30, when a fully organized attempt was made on the President's life. Three days later, labor groups declared that they were seizing several Dutch enterprises. These expropriations had the President's support, and, with the cabinet sharply divided on how to respond, they spread to more and more firms. By December 13, virtually all of the large Dutch business establishments, estates, banks, trading and industrial firms, and the large interisland shipping line (KPM) had been taken over, and on that day Major General Nasution used his martial-law powers to place them under military control. Most of the 46,000 Dutch nationals remaining in the country prepared themselves for immediate departure.

Both the assassination attempt and the take-over actions appear to have worked to the President's political benefit, and, to the extent that he became politically stronger, the likelihood of tough action against the regionalists increased. As a result of the acute crisis in shipping that followed the take-over of KPM, the regionalists became more determined than ever to manage their own foreign trade; Djakarta was quite as determined to stop them. Moreover, government-protected youth groups and similar organizations actively harassed a number of top Masjumi leaders in December, with the result that three of them, all former prime ministers (Natsir, Burhanuddin Harahap, and Sjafruddin Prawiranegara, who was then governor of the central bank) fled from Djakarta to Sumatra. Tension mounted further when the regionalists heard that a central government arms-buying mission was leaving for Eastern Europe.

After numerous meetings in West Sumatra between the regionalist leaders and Djakarta politicians who sympathized with them, an ultimatum was issued on February 10, 1958, by Lieutenant Colonel Husein, spokesman of the group. It demanded that the existing Djuanda cabinet resign within five days, that Parliament allow Hatta or the Sultan of Jogjakarta to form a new business cabinet, and that President Sukarno assume a constitutional position again.[2] The cabinet rejected the ultimatum, and on February 15, the regionalist group proclaimed the Revolutionary Government of the Republic of Indonesia (Pemerintah Revolusioner Republik Indonesia) in Padang, West Sumatra, with Sjafruddin Prawiranegara as prime minister.[3]

---

[2] After the Ali Sastroamidjojo cabinet returned its mandate in March, 1957, President Sukarno took the unprecedented step of appointing himself *formateur* of a new cabinet when two attempts by the Perserikaten Nasional Indonesia (PNI) leader, Suwirjo, to form a cabinet failed. He also established an extraconstitutional national council, and in other ways began to play a much more active role than before.

[3] The PRRI cabinet included, among others, Burhanuddin Harahap, Sumitro, Simbolon, Warouw (a former commander of East Indonesia), and Dahlan Djambek.

Initially, it was unclear how much support this rebel government would attract, in particular how much support from other regional army commanders and how much foreign support. There was also great uncertainty about how Djakarta would respond to the direct challenge. But soon a pattern began to emerge. Most important was the fact that open support for Padang came only from Central Sumatra, Tapanuli in North Sumatra, and North Celebes. In all other areas outside Java, and particularly in the very important regionalist-controlled area of South Sumatra, the attitude was one of "wait and see."

Foreign support came in covert forms. Before and for a short time after the rebellion began, modern American automatic rifles, bazookas, machine guns and radio transmitters were dropped in West Sumatra, reportedly by American government agents. And U.S. officials made a number of statements that indicated a degree of support for the rebel government. But no state recognized the PRRI or accorded it belligerent status. Sjafruddin's appeal to the U.S. Federal Reserve Bank to freeze Djakarta's funds went unheeded. Furthermore, the Caltex oil company, with installations in Central Sumatra, continued to pay foreign exchange to the central government.

In Djakarta, there was marked disagreement on how to act. The Indonesian Air Force made some minor attacks on rebel areas, and the Navy began an active blockade, but, at the same time, Sukarno went to see Hatta, and for a while, the two appeared close to a formula of settlement. Some opponents of military action argued from experience with the costly and long-deadlocked rebellion of the extremist Darul Islam, and also pointed to the possibility that government officers and soldiers might refuse to fight their fellow Indonesians. However, others asserted that some clear-cut solution was imperative if Indonesia was to survive as a nation, and stories of foreign military support for the rebels served to strengthen their case.

On March 7, government paratroopers landed in oil areas of eastern Central Sumatra, partly, it is possible, to show that Djakarta was able to protect American oil personnel, and in this way to forestall a feared American intervention. Rebel soldiers offered no resistance, and on March 12, the town of Pakan Baru was retaken. By this time, the government's choice of military action was clear.

A rapid series of Djakarta successes followed. Padang fell on April 17 and Bukittinggi on May 5. The PRRI troops made little or no effort to defend their area, and by the end of May, the Sumatran half of the rebellion was reduced to guerrilla action. There was much more fighting, some of it very hard, when the central government's troops landed in North Celebes. But there, too, the government had marked success, and by the end of July, no major town remained in rebel hands.[4] Rebel guerrilla ac-

[4] The North Celebes arm of the movement most frequently called itself PERMESTA (literally Over-all Struggle) after the name of the regionalist council which took over control of the East Indonesia military command in March, 1957. But the use of this name does not imply that the North Celebes leaders regarded themselves as distinct

tivity continued for the next two-and-a-half years, and no important rebel leaders were captured. But Djakarta's victories were major and had been achieved much faster than had been expected by most observers.

The rebellion and its early defeats, coming on top of the seizure of Dutch enterprises, was a turning point in Indonesian politics. The power of the Masjumi in national politics was drastically reduced, as was that of the Socialist Party and of other groups with similar attitudes. Those Masjumi leaders who had not joined the rebellion were in the difficult position of having to justify their own continued participation in national politics without too strongly condemning their former, and still much admired, party leaders. The claim of the Masjumi and the Socialist Party to a legitimate place in Djakarta political institutions remained shaky, and it was their attitude to the rebellion that served as grounds for the government's decision of August, 1960, to dissolve them. This decline in the Masjumi's strength contributed notably to a weakening of all the parties in the face of military and presidential opposition to the party system.

By removing the regionalists from the political and military scene, the rebellion cleared the way for the emergence of a new set of power relationships. Of the three main political forces of 1957 (the President, the central army leadership, and the regionalists), only the first two remained by mid-1958, and these continued to be markedly distinct and, in many ways, competitive with one another. But they also had many goals and interests in common. They have shared government power up to the present, together fashioning a more and more fully authoritarian political order.

A great deal remains to be said about why the rebellion was started, why the regionalists went so far as to make threats that, if taken up, might result in a war for which they were not prepared. Perhaps their ultimatum and the proclamation of the PRRI were a last-trick bluff, but one from which developments did not permit them to back down when Djakarta finally replied forcefully. In addition, a full explanation has yet to be given of why the rebels fought as badly as they did between March and July, 1958.[5] But the question to be discussed here is why the PRRI failed as a guerrilla movement, and why almost all of its leaders eventually decided to return to the Republic of Indonesia. Part of the answer lies in the PRRI's internal development.

The most striking point about the rebellion's internal politics is that it suffered from the same affliction that had eaten away at the nation since independence—a lack of consensus and purpose. Many of the divisions that had characterized national politics in earlier years appeared rapidly among

---

from the PRRI, although some of the Celebesians were inclined to take a particularist view of their rebellion against Djakarta. Sumatran and Celebese leaders remained in contact with one another until early in 1961, when radio transmitters in Celebes broke down. However, none of the PRRI cabinet ministers from Celebes attended PRRI cabinet meetings, all of these having been held in Sumatra.

[5] For one discussion of this problem, presenting a highly readable but occasionally inaccurate account of the rebellion's beginning, see James Mossman, *Rebels in Paradise: Indonesia's Civil War* (London: Jonathan Cape, 1961).

the rebels, and the number of small cliques was almost as great in the ranks of rebel leadership as in Djakarta.

Some of the divisions were largely personal. Mutual suspicions and antagonisms were great between different leaders of the rebellion, and were aggravated by frequent accusations, charges that a leader was corrupt and immoral or that he failed to prevent wanton behavior among his soldiers. One particular basis for mistrust was the matter of distribution of arms. This led to conflict on a large scale in Minahasa, North Celebes, and resulted in a major massacre in October, 1960, with the death of Colonel Warouw, a PRRI minister, and 125 others.

But most of the clique conflict reflected more than personal dislikes. One major line of cleavage was that between officers and civilian politicians. The rebel military commanders tended to blame the civilian leaders for the rebellion's failures, just as they had blamed civilians for national troubles before the rebellion; and some of the civilian politicians threw the allegation back at the officers. But the most important division was ideological. Appeals were one of the PRRI's greatest problems from the beginning. The rebels were clear in what they opposed: Communism and President Sukarno.[6] But what were they for? They needed ideals more attractive than "regional autonomy" to make men lay down their lives. Religious appeals were one possible alternative. But to fight for God would be compelling only for Muslims as such, or Christians as such, and the rebellion was a Muslim-Christian alliance. (Of the four main ethnic groups involved, two—the Minangkabaus of West Sumatra and the Mandailing Bataks of South Tapanuli—were predominantly Muslim, and the other two—the Toba Bataks of North Tapanuli and the Minahasans of North Celebes— were chiefly Protestant.) So the question of "What ideals are we fighting for?" was a persistent source of division within the rebellion, and particularly because it was linked with two other questions: "What is the outcome we are hoping for?" and "Who are to be our allies?"

For the Masjumi leaders—Sjafruddin, Natsir, and Burhanuddin Harahap —and certain of the military officers, such as Colonel Dahlan Djambek, Islamic appeals were of great importance. These men argued that Islam should be an important aspect of army organization and general propaganda in areas where the population was predominantly Muslim. They were generally opposed to negotiation with Djakarta. And they wanted maximum cooperation with the Darul Islam, the original West Java rebel movement dating back to 1948, and its loose affiliates in South Celebes and Atjeh.

Most of the military leaders, however, took quite a different approach. The Christians among them, men like Colonel Simbolon, were fundamentally opposed to the use of Islamic ideology, and a number of Muslim offi-

[6] There was an initial reluctance to attack the President, for fear that this would be interpreted as opposition to Indonesia as a unified entity. Most military officers, certainly, believed that the President continued to be a symbol of national unity. After their ultimatum, however, the rebel leaders became increasingly open in their hostility to Sukarno, until his removal from office became, for many of them, a necessary goal of the rebellion.

cers like Lieutenant Colonel Husein were with them in preferring the more inclusive and permissive *Pantja Sila* (the five principles of the one deity, nationalism, humanity, people's sovereignty, and social justice) as a state ideology. Having no sense of fighting for a holy cause, members of this military group found it much easier than the old Masjumi leaders to consider early negotiations with the government. By the same token, most of them were cool toward ideas of combining with the Darul Islam. Although they could see military advantages in such an alliance, they also saw it as likely to strengthen the strongly Islamic groups in the PRRI leadership, and as likely to militate against their own hopes for a favorable negotiated settlement with Djakarta.

This conflict was never resolved. In practice, each group of leaders operated with its own appeals. Sjafruddin and Djambek gave arms to Masjumi high school students and village youths in the Minangkabau and Mandailing areas. Husein, operating in other parts of the Minangkabau area, used the appeal to Islam much more sparingly. And the Christian Toba Batak followers of Simbolon, fighting in the Toba area, had numerous Bible-teachers working in their midst. Husein and Simbolon did, in fact, negotiate with the central government, or rather with its army, at various times during 1958 and 1959. But these negotiations, held in Singapore, Hong Kong, and Geneva, all failed to produce an acceptable formula of settlement, and a rebel envoy sent to Djakarta was arrested in May, 1959.

After early 1959, there were radio discussions within the PRRI leadership, and between its civilian leaders and the Darul Islam, on the possibility of combining the various anti-Djakarta forces into a unified movement. These discussions began to achieve some success at about the same time as efforts to negotiate with central government army leaders were failing. Consequently, PRRI cabinet meetings held in August and October, 1959, were able to agree on a major constitutional recasting, which led to the proclamation in February, 1960, of the Republik Persatuan Indonesia (RPI, or Indonesian Federal Republic).[7] Under this arrangement, there were ten constituent states—including the Islamic state of Atjeh and a state of South Celebes, but not, significantly, an Islamic state of West Java—in different parts of the archipelago.[8] The federation was bound together by a constitution that was an elaborate attempt to be Islamic and non-Islamic at the same time, each member state being free to choose its own ideology. The RPI had little significance as a political entity. But progress toward it was important, along with arms gifts from the PRRI, in persuading the Atjehnese rebel leader, Daud Beureueh, to break a two-year truce with Djakarta. Daud began fighting again in September, 1959. There had been military cooperation earlier between the PRRI of North Celebes and Kahar Muzakar in South Celebes.

[7] Literally translated, "Republik Persatuan Indonesia" means "United Republic of Indonesia," but "Indonesian Federal Republic" was the official translation.

[8] The states were as follows: the Islamic state of Atjeh, Tapanuli, East Sumatra, West Sumatra, Riau, Djambi, South Sumatra, North Celebes, South Celebes, Moluccas, South Moluccas.

The establishment of the RPI was something of a victory for Sjafruddin and the other civilian leaders. But the ideological rifts in the PRRI had only been papered over, and the formal link with the Darul Islam served only to heighten the inclination of Simbolon and the Christian Toba Bataks (and, farther away, of the Christian Minahasans) to negotiate with Djakarta. Moreover, a conflict developed in Sumatra over the status of Central Sumatra, to whose division into three states (West Sumatra, Riau, and Djambi) Husein objected, apparently for reasons for Minangkabau ethnic solidarity. And, finally, the military advantages to the old PRRI of the new fighting in Atjeh turned out to be not very great.

Government operations in 1960 aimed at isolating the rebel fighting units further and obtaining control of their areas of supply.[9] At the same time, much attention was given to propaganda and, especially, to contact work among nonfighting but rebel-sympathizing groups in rebel areas. Chief of Staff Nasution himself met with numerous religious leaders in Sumatra and Celebes in May and July, 1960, making every effort to persuade them that the army was not antireligious and that it was opposed to Communism. Similarly, there were efforts to persuade leaders of rebel-sympathizing communities that the economic recovery of their areas would be possible only with the end of the rebellion. A government-organized meeting of North Tapanuli community leaders, held in February, 1961, brought forth a resolution threatening customary sanctions against rebels who would not stop fighting. Considerable evidence of this sort indicates that the army leadership did not regard the rebellion solely as a military matter.

By late 1960, the PRRI military commanders faced acute difficulties. Ammunition was running out, especially in Sumatra, where resupply had been irregular since the invasion of Padang. Bringing in ammunition from Singapore had always been difficult for the Sumatran PRRI, largely because of the difficulties of crossing the broad belt of east-coast swamp, and the possibility of buying arms from government troops decreased as government operations became more successful. One group of soldiers in northern Central Sumatra had only ten bullets each by early 1961. In October, 1960, the government forces had succeeded in forcing the rebels out of their major headquarters in the village of Koto Tinggi, near Bukittinggi. Some of them, including Natsir, Sjafruddin, and Burhanuddin Harahap, were thus prevented from living in villages and forced into the tiger-infested jungle. With the government forces offering reasonable terms to rebel soldiers who surrendered, it became increasingly difficult for the leaders of the rebellion to keep their followers with them.

Problems of morale were probably almost as serious as low supplies for the rebels in Sumatra. Younger rebel troops, who provided the real fighting strength of the PRRI, could see no future for themselves as perpetual

[9] The rebel forces had been scattered in many small units since shortly after the capture of Padang by government troops in April, 1958, and the smaller units often lost contact with one another. However, fairly large forces remained with Husein, and Simbolon was able to operate with a sizable number of troops after he left Central Sumatra for North Tapanuli in 1959.

rebels. They had lost years of education, and by the end of 1960, they were probably thinking and talking about making new lives for themselves. Many small rebel groups began to accept government offers of amnesty early in 1961, though most troops directly under the commands of Husein and Simbolon seem to have held together until the end. But the increasing number of surrenders probably had some influence on the troops who remained in the rebellion.

The rebel forces in North Celebes appear to have been much better supplied, and their attacking capacity remained considerable, even late in 1960. However, internecine conflict in the leadership was particularly bitter and demoralizing in this area.[10] One result of this was that the able and highly respected Colonel Kawilarang, who was formally the PRRI's commander in chief, became thoroughly disgusted with the whole rebellion. By late 1960, moreover, it was becoming much more difficult to bring in ammunition from the outside. This was partly due to the increasing effectiveness of the Indonesian Navy, and partly a result of the conclusion of an agreement between Djakarta and Manila for joint control of smuggling in the waters between North Celebes and Mindanao. The Philippine government had previously seemed to drag its feet in negotiating this treaty, but later abandoned its reservations.

This raises the question of how important American attitudes were in the rebels' eventual decision to stop fighting. There is no doubt that U.S. support was, to some extent, instrumental in making it possible for the PRRI to receive supplies in the period after mid-1958. It has been suggested that some of the military hardware that the rebels bought in Singapore was secured at prices that had been lowered drastically by dumping. Some was certainly supplied to the Celebes rebels from Taiwan, apparently as a result of the work of Professor Sumitro, the rebels' most active representative abroad. But the U.S. seems to have pressed Taiwan late in 1960 to stop sending aid to the rebels.

Nor was this a matter of ammunition only; it was also an important indication of U.S. thinking on the rebellion. By the end of 1960, the U.S. evidently believed that it had sufficiently strong and reliable allies inside the Indonesian government—particularly the Army under Nasution's leadership—to enable it to dispense with the rebels, and that it was merely hurting those allies by the earlier policy of helping to keep the rebellion alive. To the extent that the rebel leaders were aware of this change, it probably strengthened their inclination to stop fighting.

What then were the rebels fighting for? A military victory had always been out of the question, and it was clear by the end of 1958 that the PRRI could not topple the central government by economic strangulation. Some rebel leaders believed the repeated predictions of Professor Sumitro that the central government would collapse as a result of economic deterioration, but this idea had lost much of its force by 1960. Economic deterioration

[10] For an eyewitness account by a Dutch mission doctor who lived for eighteen months in rebel-held North Celebes, see F. J. van Rootselaar, "Een ontvoering in Noord-Celebes" ("A Kidnapping in North Celebes"), *De Groene Amsterdammer*, January 16, 1960.

continued, but the Djakarta government showed no signs of collapse. What hopes remained then to sustain the rebel forces in their fighting? Some PRRI men hoped for a settlement after the expected death of President Sukarno. But others, especially among the military leaders, believed it would be sensible to negotiate more promptly, and argued that this might enable the PRRI group to strengthen the position of the army vis-à-vis Sukarno.

It was most important for those rebel leaders who did want to end the rebellion that a bridge back to the Republic of Indonesia existed. This was especially true of the rebel military commanders, who felt that their former army colleagues were prepared to give them reasonable terms. Here one sees a crucial aspect of the rebellion, that it was in a sense a war between friends. The leaders on both sides, particularly the military officers, had a great deal in common. Their social and educational backgrounds were similar. Many of them had fought together against the Dutch and were bound together by the symbols of that fight. Some were even related by marriage, and genuine respect and affection existed between many of them.[11] The officers of the rebellion were not radically alienated from the Indonesian state, its history, its symbols, or its army. In this sense, they were not revolutionaries but rather a group of leaders of what they themselves had earlier called a "corrective movement," who had made bigger and bigger threats to achieve their ends and had eventually found themselves outside the limits of legality and political toleration.

This goes a long way toward explaining the remarkable absence of ruthlessness that characterized both sides in this rebellion. There was, of course, some mutual hatred and bitter resentment, particularly in the later stages of the rebellion, but the quip that this was history's most civil war has a large grain of truth. Unlike the Darul Islam in West Java, the PRRI perpetrated few atrocities. They engaged in little scorched-earth warfare; in Sumatra, at least, they were reluctant to blow up bridges, for that could only hurt the economy of their own regions. Casualty rates were low on both sides.[12] Clearly the military commanders of each side were reluctant to fan the passions of warfare too high. Partly, no doubt, the absence of ruthless fighting is a cultural phenomenon. Cruelty and fanatical zeal are rare in Indonesian behavior, and the Darul Islam may thus be seen in terms of social pathology. But it is equally clear that this was something of a phony war.

On February 10, 1961, one of the Celebes commanders, Laurens Saerang, surrendered with 10,000 followers, including 6,000 troops. The government temporarily conscripted some of these men and indicated that if they proved their loyalty they would be restored to their former positions in the army. Two months later, Colonel Kawilarang of North Celebes for-

[11] Colonel Jani, commander of the force that took Padang, asked the British journalist Mossman to give his regards to Colonel Simbolon, adding, "we used to be old comrades . . . he's what you would call a gentleman." *Rebels in Paradise*, pp. 159–160.

[12] According to an Army report of September, 1961, 2,499 government troops had been killed in the rebellion, 4,098 had been wounded, and 198 were missing. The same report claims that 22,174 rebels were killed, a figure that is undoubtedly grossly exaggerated. *Suluh Indonesia* (Djakarta daily), September 9, 1961.

mally delivered 27,000 men to the government command, and again there were indications that the government was giving generous terms.

News of Kawilarang's return came as a great surprise to the rebel leaders in Sumatra, and led Simbolon and Husein to intensify their efforts to reach a settlement with Djakarta. It was not only that the loss of the respected Kawilarang made the rebel cause seem close to defeat; in addition it was clear that with the PRRI virtually at an end in Celebes, the government would be able to bring far greater military pressure to bear in Sumatra. After radio discussions with one another in April, Simbolon and Husein decided to disavow their connections with the RPI and established themselves as an Emergency Military Government (Pemerintah Darurat Militer), headed by Husein. After protracted negotiations, Husein surrendered to the government forces with 13,500 men in June, and Simbolon did the same with 11,000 men in the following month.

The group of Sjafruddin and the other Masjumi leaders had little fighting strength left and so was forced to give up soon after Husein and Simbolon. In a declaration issued on August 17 (Independence Day), 1961, Sjafruddin urged all RPI followers to lay down their arms, and most of them did so in the course of the next seven weeks, which the government declared to be an amnesty period. Those returning included the various former Masjumi leaders and Colonel Zulkifli Lubis, and most of the PRRI representatives abroad, but not Professor Sumitro. Lieutenant Colonel Sumual, the one remaining rebel leader in North Celebes, surrendered in mid-October, his return being officially backdated to the last day of the amnesty period. The long rebellions of Daud Beureueh in Atjeh and Kahar Muzakar in South Celebes were quietly wound up at the same time. Peace was restored everywhere except in West Java and a small area of South Sumatra.[13]

All the major surrenders were negotiated, but the conditions differed widely from area to area, the Celebes rebels generally obtaining better terms than the Sumatrans. Kawilarang won particularly generous terms; most of his troops who bore arms did not have these taken from them, and it was agreed that a large group would be restored to their positions in the army after a period of retraining and indoctrination. Former civil servants who had joined the rebellion would be reinstated, and the Minahasa area would be allowed to trade directly with the outside world for some time.[14] Furthermore, relief supplies began to arrive on a large scale to repair the great damage that warfare had wrought in Minahasa. The liberality of these terms may have been due largely to the army's conjecture that once Kawilarang had left the path of rebellion, the rest of the PRRI would soon have to follow. Certainly it worked out that way, but it is also

[13] In June, 1962, S. M. Kartosuwirjo, head of the Darul Islam of West Java, was captured by the army. He subsequently ordered his followers to lay down their arms, and many of them did so, but it is not clear at the time of writing how far this has gone toward the elimination of rebel and bandit activity in the long disturbed area of West Java. The remaining South Sumatran PRRI rebels surrendered in August, 1962.

[14] It is not clear whether this was to be a temporary arrangement only, merely to enable accumulated stocks of copra to be sold fast, or whether it was to operate much longer.

true that Kawilarang's troops had remained a force to be reckoned with militarily; as late as the end of 1960, they had shown themselves capable of launching an attack on Minahasa's capital, Menado.

The PRRI leaders in Sumatra were given three promises: that there would be no prosecution of the returnees, that the government would take care of former rebels, and that surrenders would not be made to look like surrenders, thus avoiding humiliation. There was no question of rebel soldiers being admitted or readmitted to the army, but a monthly allowance was paid to many of the returnees for a period of three months. Many of the leaders were obliged to take oaths of loyalty to President Sukarno personally and to the President's Political Manifesto, as well as oaths to the state and the constitution.

Much less is known of the terms granted in Atjeh and South Celebes. The Atjeh rebels under Daud Beureueh appear to have obtained somewhat better conditions than those of the Sumatran PRRI, some men gaining admission to the army. In South Celebes, where the Kahar Muzakar group apparently kept much of its fighting capacity to the end, the terms seem to have been better, possibly like those granted to Kawilarang in Minahasa. Here the shroud of secrecy was particularly thick at the time of the returns, partly perhaps because it was feared that Kahar might lead his followers back to the jungle, as he had on a previous occasion, if publicity made it seem that he had "surrendered." But it is probably significant that the oath he took on his return was a triple one—to Sukarno, to Defense Minister Nasution, and to the strongly anti-Communist military commander of South Celebes. Colonel Jusuf Kahar apparently was in a strong bargaining position.[15]

Officially, no terms were granted to any of the rebels. The official assumption was that "returning to the fold of the Republic" could only be an act of unconditional trust. But news of the good terms that some of the rebel groups had received was quick to reach Djakarta, and facts and rumors surrounding the returns became of major importance in the politics of the capital. When former rebel troops from North Celebes were brought to East and Central Java in the second half of 1961, initially for retraining and indoctrination, many people suspected that the general staff intended to use them to fight Communist influence there.

Until about the middle of 1961, negotiating the end of the rebellion had been very much the army's affair. The various sets of terms were arranged largely by Nasution, sometimes without President Sukarno's knowledge. Some efforts were made by immediate associates of the President to negotiate with the rebels independently of the army, but these were unsuccessful. The rebel leaders, civilians and officers alike, looked to the army for a settlement, expecting greater leniency from it than from the civilian political leadership in Djakarta.

However, once the rebels began to return in force, there was no longer any question of permitting the army alone to determine policy. Too much

---

[15] Kahar has, however, since gone back into the jungle, but without a sizable number of followers.

was at stake for the Djakarta political factions. In the Communist press and, to a lesser extent, that of the PNI, voices were raised against too much leniency toward the rebels, and these evoked favorable responses among many outside those two parties. In these circumstances, it was possible for President Sukarno to regain the initiative in the treatment of the rebels, and a number of the concessions that had been granted were subsequently whittled down. A secret Presidential instruction issued late in July provided that the ex-rebels should be politically quarantined for an undetermined period. They would not be restored to full political rights until they had proved their loyalty. Thus, they would not be able to join any governing institutions, or the army, police, or civil service. In addition, a number of rebel leaders were obliged to live virtually under city arrest in scattered towns in Java.

The surrenders were a victory particularly for the army, which, under Nasution's leadership, had fought, negotiated with, and, finally, brought back the rebels. Army leaders were rewarded by increased prestige, and many observers expected that they would be able to take political advantage of this. But whether or not they could have done so, by taking further measures against the Communists or forcing President Sukarno to do their will, they did not. One reason for this is that the growing tension of the West Irian campaign quickly absorbed both their military and political energies. Now that West Irian has finally been signed over to Indonesia by the Netherlands—and this fact also works somewhat to the credit of the army —it is possible that the army leaders may concentrate their undivided attention on their domestic political interests.

The Sukarno-army regime as a whole gained from the collapse of the rebellion, in that there is now no longer an alternative focus for the loyalties of ethnic groups hostile to Djakarta. With the rebels' return, a major blow was dealt to centrifugalist politics. The grievances that gave rise to the rebellion have not been removed; export-producing groups in Sumatra and Celebes continue to resent the economic policies of the central government, and responses to the President's ideological claims are as cool in these areas as they were in 1957. But interregional relations have been stabilized nevertheless, partly because of the suppression of the rebels, partly because of the enforced termination of public ideological debate, and partly because great power has been left to the regional military commanders. These men now have very great freedom to respond to the pressures of their regions, subject only to the demands of military organization as set by the army's general staff, and the demands of ideological conformity as set by President Sukarno and his supporters.

With the army now far stronger and more united than it was in 1958, and with major increases in the size of the navy and air force, it seems that Indonesia's territorial integrity is far more firmly established than in prerebellion days. The authoritarianism of the post-1958 period has been bought at a high cost, in economic performance as well as in law and public liberties. But its gains have been major too, if only because it saved Indonesia from the threat of separatism and made possible a fairly stable settlement of the problem of potentially separatist movements. . . .

34

DEVELOPMENT AND MOBILITY AMONG THE
PHU THAI OF NORTHEAST THAILAND*

A. THOMAS KIRSCH

Both popular discussion of northeast Thailand and its problems and more programmatic statements defining development aims seem to be rooted in certain conceptions about the "kind" of people northeasterners are. Northeasterners are conceived, for example, as people with strong commitments to a particular mode of life, that of rice farmer; to a traditional set of village-based social relations and customs; and to particular localities, whether native villages or the northeastern region in general. That is, northeasterners are seen as "typical peasants." Given this conception of the way that northeasterners are, and the massive fact of the economic under-development of the northeast, solutions to the region's problems have been seen largely in economic terms. Since it is recognized that northeastern farmers have adapted as well as can be expected to the ecological conditions of the area,[1] typical solutions focus on improvements within the tra-

* Field work among the Phu Thai was supported by a National Institute of Mental Health Fellowship and by a National Institute of Health research-grant supplement. Reprinted by permission of the author and the publisher from *Asian Survey*, VI (July, 1966), 370–78.
[1] Hans Platenius, *The North-east of Thailand, Its Problems and Potentialities* (Bangkok: National Economic Development Board, 1963).

ditional mode of technology, for example, improved seed, some diversification of crops (both cash and subsistence), improved irrigation and water control, encouragement of indigenous home and handicraft industry, such as silk, and the provision of an improved infrastructure of transportation, communication, and education. . . . In return for a better standard of living, peasants apparently are expected to give political support, or at least to remain politically apathetic.

I would like to raise two questions: *first,* is the picture of the northeasterner as a typical peasant bound to a traditional peasant mode of life accurate? I would be inclined to argue: only in part. *Second,* will the economic solutions proposed for the northeast's problems be effective? It seems to me that the major problem facing the northeast is one of political commitment, and it is, at best, problematical whether such political problems can be solved by economic means.

With regard to the first question, it will be fruitful to consider the various channels of mobility operative in the northeast, because such mobility channels provide clues to goals and aspirations. Although the channels of mobility that I will consider are found generally throughout the northeast, my remarks are based on observations among the Phu Thai, with whom I worked in 1962–63.

The Phu Thai entered Thailand from Laos about 125–40 years ago, during the reign of Rama III. They now occupy four localities in the northeast: (1) in Sakonnakhon province in the vicinity of Nong Hang; (2) in Kalasin province in Amphur Kutchinarai, and at two localities in Nakhon Phanom province; (3) at Renu Nakhon near That Phanom; and (4) in Amphur Khamcha-ee, some twenty-two miles due west of Mukdahan. There are reportedly clusters of Phu Thai scattered throughout Laos, and there is another group of Phu Thai located in the central region of Thailand near Phetburi, where they are known as the Lao Soong. My work was done primarily with the Phu Thai of Khamcha-ee. Nong Son, the village in which I worked, was a "commune" (*tambon*) center for fifteen villages and was larger (population more than 1,400) and organizationally more complex than other nearby villages.

The Phu Thai of Khamcha-ee have tended to adapt to a fairly specific ecological niche in the valleys near the highlands that border the Mekong River. When they first settled in Thailand, the Phu Thai were an isolated and semi-autonomous ethnic enclave with their own local ruler (*caw myang*). Although the Phu Thai speak a dialect of Thai and share a common Buddhist culture with their neighbors, they appear to have had little contact with the larger society surrounding them. The only available ethnographic accounts of the Phu Thai of northeast Thailand[2] portray them as relatively isolated, backward, and "superstitious" well after the turn of the century. They are far from that today.

Following the reorganization of the northeastern administrative struc-

[2] Erik Seidenfaden, "The So and the Puthai," *Journal of the Siam Society,* XXXIV, part 2 (1943). See also Erik Seidenfaden, *The Thai Peoples,* I (Bangkok, 1958), 112; and Frank LeBar *et al., Ethnic Groups of Mainland Southeast Asia* (New Haven, Conn.: HRAF Press, 1964), p. 228.

ture initiated by King Chulalongkorn in the late nineteenth century, the Phu Thai abruptly lost their semi-autonomous status and have been increasingly assimilated within the national Thai framework. The Phu Thai world was suddenly shifted from a narrowly circumscribed locality to a larger social universe.

Today the Phu Thai have a reputation among their neighbors for being hard-working and industrious, and this reputation is supported by production figures comparing Phu Thai and Thai-Lao communes within the same district. The Phu Thai of the Khamcha-ee area had already diversified their economy somewhat, producing traditional and new subsistence and cash crops—for example, rice, livestock, maize, jute, sesame, and silk. Nong Son had an active group of indigenous traders concerned with marketing not only traditional specialties, such as livestock, but more modern cash products as well. The Phu Thai of this area were also characterized by active, locally initiated attempts to manipulate their physical environment—for example, through water-control projects locally conceived, financed, and implemented. We might say then that the Phu Thai were economically more active and generally more prosperous than the nearby Thai-Lao. Indeed, compared with other groups of the northeast, the Phu Thai approximate the ideal that many development planners call for. Aside from their industriousness, the Phu Thai also appeared to be politically more aware and more active than their neighbors.

I will briefly note four channels of mobility operative among the Phu Thai that served to pull individuals (perhaps only temporarily) away from their particularistic—or peasant—bonds and commitments, orienting them to a larger, more universalistically defined society transcending peasant commitments. These four channels are: (1) the Buddhist monkhood, (2) official status, (3) advanced secular education, and (4) the familiar *pai thiaw*, or "going around" pattern. The operation of these channels of mobility suggests that, for many villagers at least, desire for social-status mobility in a society larger than that of any rural village may outweigh particularistic ties to a peasant mode of life or to particular localities.

THE BUDDHIST MONKHOOD

The Phu Thai share with other Buddhist Thai groups an explicit ideal that every man should serve for a time as a monk, and monks, of course, have considerable prestige. It is worth noting that the prestige of monks is not confined to their own village or locality but is common throughout the country. In all probability, the principle that every man should serve as a monk was never met in actual practice, but in Nong Son, 59 per cent of the eligible households had members who had met this ideal. Although data on monastic service are difficult to interpret, and my data are not strictly comparable, Blanchard reports that about 55 per cent of the eligible men in a "typical" Thai village serve as either monks or novices,[3] which suggests that Phu Thai men approximate the ideal somewhat more closely

[3] Wendell Blanchard *et al.*, *Thailand, Its People, Its Society, Its Culture* (New Haven, Conn.: HRAF Press, 1958), p. 113. Discussions with Charles Keyes suggest that this high degree of monastic service may be a common feature in the northeast.

than these "typical" Thai. I also have the impression that Phu Thai men tend to serve, on the average, somewhat longer in the monkhood than other Thai groups; however, comparative data to verify this are not available.

With respect to the conception of the northeasterner as committed to a peasant mode of life, we might note that not only does the monk not "work" but monks are specifically forbidden to engage in agriculture—the typical peasant's occupation. Entrance into the monkhood formally cuts a young man off from his ties to secular roles and to kinship ties, opening a path for geographic and social mobility that might be hindered by such ties. Indeed, as a part of the ritual of becoming a monk, the young man's parents might be said to "give away" their son to the monkhood, while the young man simultaneously gives up his old ties and identities to be a monk. Although there are formal restrictions on travel for monks during the rainy season, when most young men enter the monkhood, during the remainder of the year, monks are inveterate travelers. Not only do monks get special rates or free rides on public transportation facilities, but every village or town that has a temple is a potential home. Many young men leave their village temples to seek ecclesiastical advancement, or perhaps merely to move about from temple to temple, sometimes never to return to their home village or the peasant mode of life.

This channel of mobility has served in the past to bring young men into rural villages from other similar environments. For example, seven men of varying ages living in the village of Nong Son had been drawn into the village from outside the district through this channel. Young monks come to local temples, stay for awhile, perhaps become attracted to some local girl, leave the monkhood, marry, and settle down. This mechanism for recruiting men into the village is still operating today. The monastic institution serves to pry men out of villages and into other contexts as well.

Ecclesiastical advancement pays off for the individual not only in terms of religious self-satisfactions but also by adding an increment of social prestige when, and if, the individual leaves the monkhood. It should also be noted that the training available within the monastic system, both historically and at present, is not unimportant with respect to secular status achievement. For example, advanced monastic education is open to young men who may be cut off from advanced secular education—preparing these monks for better jobs if they leave the monkhood.

It seems that formerly, in the Phu Thai region, monastic mobility was rather diffuse and random, although important regional centers, such as the temple at That Phanom, were effective in structuring such movement. Today, ecclesiastical achievement is probably more important than ever before, and it has become increasingly formalized and tied to the national monastic organization. The increased articulation of ecclesiastical achievement with the national *sangha* has tended to structure this channel of mobility more firmly into certain directions, most notably toward larger urban centers, on up to the Buddhist universities in Bangkok. In 1963, five young men from Nong Son became involved in this striving for monastic achievement in large urban centers. The operation of this channel of mobility and the very ideal that all men should serve as monks for a period suggest that a Phu Thai villager's commitment is not simply tied to the peasant style of life nor to a locally based relational system.

AN OFFICIAL STATUS

For contemporary Phu Thai, achieving an official position within the national bureaucracy is the way par excellence of secular status advancement. Presumably, when the Phu Thai were semi-autonomous, achievement of such political status was closely tied to considerations of locality and to kinship bonds and alliances. Legendary materials suggest that such political advancement was important even before the Phu Thai entered Thailand. Today, Phu Thai who are seeking secular achievement see this largely, if not exclusively, in terms of an official position within the national bureaucratic framework.

With respect to the northeasterner's commitment to a peasant mode of life, we might note that officials (like monks) follow a way of life that is considerably different from that of the peasant, and desire for such a change in status involves at least a readiness to cast off ties to a peasant mode of life, ties to close kin, and ties to localities.

In the past, there was a radical gap, both socially and geographically, between the Phu Thai villager and the government official. As the national bureaucracy has expanded and penetrated more deeply into remote rural regions, this gap has, to some extent, diminished. In particular, the penetration of the national educational system has promoted the presence of the schoolteacher as a *kind* of official on the local scene. In Nong Son, for example, there were fifteen schoolteachers, although only eight of them actually worked in the local school. The other teachers commuted to their more isolated schools from the more "civilized" commune center.

While aspirations for any kind of bureaucratic position are widespread among young Phu Thai villagers, the desire to be a teacher has been especially common. In 1963, for example, nine of the teachers living in Nong Son were ethnically Phu Thai, though not all from the Khamcha-ee area, and a number of young people were away from the village studying in teachers' colleges. The role of the local teacher is an important one. He serves not only to implant national symbols, ideologies, and values in the rural village, but, perhaps more significantly, he serves as a proximate living model of secular status achievement, as well as indicating the means of achieving such status—that is, education. Aside from this, in the Phu Thai case at least, the presence of a group of schoolteachers on the local scene, with a prestige base transcending the traditional village or locality prestige system, has had important implications for status-striving within rural villages.

It is worth noting that, although many young schoolteachers are recruited from rural contexts and eventually return to work in rural areas, they are by no means wedded to the idea of working within such rural villages. Most young teachers are more likely to aspire to achieve within the framework of the Ministry of Education, hoping in particular for a scholarship to study in Bangkok, or, better, abroad. (One locally-born man had received an M.A. from an American university and had a good job with the Ministry of Education.) One of the most frequent complaints of the young schoolteachers of the northeast with whom I came into contact was that the quality of education in their area is so low that they cannot hope to compete for such scholarships with people educated in the central region. Indeed, the situation of northeastern schoolteachers may be an especially important instance of the ironic situation in which programs of the central government aimed at alleviating the problems of the northeast actually contribute a new dimension to these problems.

Advanced Secular Education

This channel of mobility might well be viewed simply as a subtype of the previous channel, that is, the desire to achieve an official position. For most young people, the desire for an advanced secular education is firmly tied to aspirations for a position within the national bureaucratic system. Advanced secular education is seen today as the key means to such achievement.

Although the teacher's role is extremely popular among the Phu Thai, and this role is likely to bring the individual into closest contact with the peasant mode of life—to which northeasterners are believed to be committed—the teacher's role is certainly not identical with the peasant mode of life. In fact, aspirations for a government position are likely to be far more general than being geared specifically to such roles as the teacher's role. One reason why the teacher's role is so popular is because it is easier to achieve and more accessible than other official roles. This is due in large measure to the structure of the secular educational system itself, as well as to official government policy. That is, it is simply more feasible for Phu Thai villagers to get into a teachers' college than to get into one of the Bangkok universities. Advanced education that does not carry any connotations of advanced status (for example, technical and vocational training) is, in general, neither popular nor aspired for. We will note here only that advanced secular education is not seen as preparing individuals for a peasant style of life. It is seen as a mechanism for social-status achievement and aimed at freeing individuals from the peasant style of life. This is explicitly recognized by the parents of the young people seeking such advanced education, many of whom were themselves the village elite—local schoolteachers, wealthy villagers, and the like.

Traditionally, education was associated with the local temple and the monk-teacher, and was confined largely to religious subjects. To some extent *both* religious and secular status achievement were tied to this predominantly religious style of education. Today, religious and secular education are more differentiated, although by no means totally separate. However, the secular educational system and the modern bureaucracy have opened up channels of mobility for women that were formerly limited or closed to them. Of the twenty-three young people away from Nong Son in 1963 getting advanced education, ranging from university study in Bangkok to secondary schooling in nearby urban centers, sixteen were men and seven were girls.

THE PAI THIAW (OR "GOING AROUND") PATTERN

The Phu Thai share with the central Thai and the Thai-Lao the pattern of "going around," in which young men, individually or in small groups, leave their home villages, often going to urban areas or to the central region to obtain wage labor of some sort, or occasionally to engage in intermittent, wandering trade. Although this pattern is closely tied to economic activities of one sort or another, it would be a mistake to view it in narrowly economic terms. In particular, young men do not leave their villages on such ventures simply because of the pressures of poverty. Poverty is more likely to force them to remain within their home village. This movement of individuals is tied more closely to ideas of "fun-seeking"—indeed, this is the literal Phu Thai equivalent of the central Thai *pai thiaw*, or *pai din*. In commenting on similar phenomena in the central region, Phillips has very aptly referred to the attitudes of such young men as, "almost a Dick Whittington view," as they go out to seek their fortunes.[4] Although there is often some general destination in mind and some plan for work, as well as, perhaps, an intention to return to the native village, there is no assurance that the destination will be reached, the plan followed, or that the young man will return—although, in fact, most are likely to do so. In some cases, the young man will find some girl in a distant village and settle down with little apparent thought of his home and little regret at leaving his kin. However, some of these men will remain in and around urban areas, as a sort of free-floating "proletariat," following the shifting vagaries of wage-labor opportunities. Most of the men who remain in such a context are likely to have moved out of the lowest laboring levels, working, for example, as foremen and "pushers," machine operators, and interpreters on development projects involving foreign companies.

The important thing to note is that, while following out the *pai thiaw* pattern, these young men are engaged in activities that are far removed from the traditional peasant's role. Such young men, while engaging in wage labor, are very rarely working as farmers, and by involving themselves in this pattern have indicated at least a willingness to give up—if only temporarily—their ties to the traditional peasant way of life, their village-based solidarities, and their regional ties.

This pattern has a long history within the Phu Thai region; indeed, the pattern seems to be shared with all Thai-speaking ethnic groups. The pattern has undergone important changes, however. Formerly, it seems to have been a relatively diffuse and unstructured movement of individuals, as likely to shift from one rural context to another, as from rural regions into urban environments. That is, this pattern was effective in recruiting men

[4] Herbert Phillips, *Thai Peasant Personality: The Patterning of Interpersonal Behavior in the Village of Bang Chan* (Berkeley: University of California Press, 1965), p. 28.

into Phu Thai villages from far-off areas, as well as in sending young men out of the village. As patterns of trade and communication have become rigidified following the lines of the modern transportation system, and as large-scale government projects have increased in importance for wage labor, this pattern has become increasingly structured in the direction of urban areas or regions where government projects provide work. For example, although eight individuals had been recruited into Nong Son from as far away as northern Thailand through the operation of this mechanism, the last man recruited *into* the village by this means entered over twenty-five years ago. In 1963, there was a total of fifty-one individuals away from the village, who had left, at least ostensibly, to follow this pattern.

The Phu Thai pattern contrasts in two ways with that of the neighboring Thai-Lao. First, the Phu Thai rarely move seasonally. Typically, they go for two years or more. Secondly, the Phu Thai of Khamcha-ee virtually never go to Laos to work. Surprisingly, the largest number of men away from the village went to Yala province, one of the southernmost provinces of Thailand, located in the Malay Peninsula.

What implications might be drawn from these observations about the operation of the mobility channels in the Phu Thai area? I believe that there are several that may have general relevance to solutions to the problem of northeast Thailand. Let me briefly note four implications:

(1) While the picture of northeastern villagers as typical peasants may be descriptively accurate for a large number of those living in rural villages, such a picture overlooks the aspirations of a significant and strategic segment of the rural population—most notably, young men.

(2) Many of these young men display an openness of commitments, a readiness to give up a traditional peasant style of life, if they can achieve status in some other sphere of activities. Phu Thai villagers, perhaps in contrast to rural peoples in other areas of the world, do not conceive of the peasant way of life as the "best way of life" and a repository for certain pristine values. This is not to say that villagers conceive of the peasant way of life as the worst possible, for the peasant style of life does have some positive value. It may be better to be a little "somebody" in a rural village than to be an insignificant "nobody" in an urban environment.

(3) The spheres of activity that are most attractive to these young men are largely in the direction of ecclesiastical or political achievement. It should be noted that both these spheres of advancement are also "traditional." Purely economic advancement as such tends to be a residual sphere in terms of structuring aspirations for achievement.[5]

(4) Mobility channels have become increasingly rigidified and structured, particularly in the Phu Thai case, in the direction of the central region and the national framework. It seems likely that these mobility channels have also become increasingly important.

[5] I have noted some of the historical evidence on this point and tried to link this patterning of aspirations to various cultural factors, largely religious, in a paper, "Buddhist Values and Thai Sex Roles," read at the meeting of the American Anthropological Association, November 20, 1965.

We might return now to the second question with which we started: Will the purely economic solutions to the northeastern problem prove adequate? I would suggest that, far from solving the problems of the northeast, such measures are likely to aggravate the specifically political dimensions of the problem. If villagers' income levels are raised within the traditional economic framework, and if life is made easier and more comfortable for the rural villager, the levels of aspirations among young men are also likely to rise, and the means of achieving such aspirations—for example, freedom from poverty, better educational facilities—will be available. Thus, more young men are likely to want to achieve social status outside of the rural village and outside of the peasant style of life. But most plans for development of the northeast do not seem to take into account the possibility of such an increase in aspiration, for northeastern villagers are viewed as an undifferentiated mass with common commitments to a peasant style of life. Unless efforts are made to keep channels of mobility open, and to expand them, we are likely to find a crucial segment of the northeastern population thwarted in their aspirations—perhaps an easy prey to those who might offer alternative commitments and alternative opportunities for status achievement.

Frequently, discussions of the development of northeast Thailand present a pessimistic picture, primarily because of the magnitude of the problems involved and the presumed characteristics of the northeastern population. Considering these problems from the standpoint of the aspirations and goals of northeasterners leaves room for some optimism. With imaginative and effective planning, aspirations for status achievement may be used as a lever to help solve at least some of the problems—for example, by providing organizations that both will be attractive as relatively permanent occupations and will simultaneously diversify the economy, thereby lightening pressures on arable land. However, consideration of these aspirations also suggests that solutions to the northeast's problems must be dealt with on both a national and a regional scale, for while the technical and economic problems of the northeast are largely regional in scope, the political problem is national, extending beyond the confines of the northeast.

Many of the discussions of the problems of the northeast appear to reify the economic problems facing the population of the region—which are considerable and important—and fail to take into account such factors as aspirations for status mobility. This tendency to excessive stress on the economic situation seems to stem from stereotypes about the characteristics of the northeastern population. In formulating plans for the development of the northeast and its integration into the Thai nation, active steps must be taken to link the already existing aspirations and interests of northeasterners firmly to the nation.

35

MALAYSIA AND SINGAPORE:
THE FAILURE OF A FEDERATION*

ROBERT O. TILMAN

On the surface, the union formed between Singapore and Malaya[1] in 1963 seemed so logical and realistic that few observers would have predicted its swift dissolution in 1965, despite political problems in Kuala Lumpur and

---

* This essay was originally a section of a much longer report on Malaysian foreign policy for the Research Analysis Corporation. It has been slightly edited here and reprinted with the permission of RAC.

[1] The use of the terms Malay, Malaya, Malayan, Malaysia, and Malaysian demands some explanation. Prior to the Japanese occupation of the area, "British Malaya" consisted of the nine "Malay States" of the Malayan Peninsula, plus the crown colony of the Straits Settlements (Penang, Malacca, and Singapore). Immediately after World War II, Britain created the "Malayan Union," which incorporated all of these units, with the exception of Singapore. Because of "Malay" opposition to this political arrangement, in 1948, Britain substituted for it the "Federation of Malaya" (which still excluded Singapore). This political unit gained independence under the same name in 1957. The Federation of Malaya was expanded in 1963 to include Singapore, Sarawak, and Sabah (formerly known as British North Borneo), and was then renamed the Federation of Malaysia. The Malays constitute the largest ethnic group within the Federation of Malaysia, but are not a majority. "Malaya" no longer exists, but the term is often still used to designate the territories of the former Federation of Malaya and is

490

Singapore. Singapore needed a hinterland—a market for its manufactured goods, surplus capital, and technology, and a convenient source of raw materials for its rapidly growing industrial complex. On the other hand, Malaya, Sarawak, and Sabah, the other members of the new Federation of Malaysia, seemed to need Singapore's industrial, trade, and port facilities. Both Singapore and Malaya seemed to recognize the mutual benefits of political association. In the four years between 1961 (the first mention of the possibility of a Malaysian federation) and 1965 (the withdrawal of Singapore from Malaysia), integration between the island and the mainland seemed to be increasing, just when the political seeds of separation were sinking their roots. The first part of this essay will document increasing interaction between the two areas in terms of some accepted indicators of integration, while the second part will attempt to explain this apparent paradox.

POINTS OF CONTACT

Most students of political integration have become increasingly wary of transaction flows alone as a measure of political integration, yet increasing exchanges between two areas do have political significance.[2] In the case of Singapore and Malaya, some of the increasing contact between the two areas is quantifiable (trade, air travel, mail), and some is not (newspapers, radio-television services). However, the way certain communications media are used may itself be a source of discord.

Trade. From 1961 to 1965, trade between Malaya and Singapore showed a steady, if not dramatic, increase in both relative and absolute terms. The value of this trade grew from M$1.61 million in 1961 to M$1.82 million in

---

so used in this chapter. Similarly, although the term "Malayans" no longer has any legal meaning, it is often used, and is used here, to describe in political terms the inhabitants of the former territory of Malaya. The term "Malaysian" is now accepted to mean one who lives in Malaysia, regardless of ethnic origin. To complicate matters even more, in the past, some social scientists (notably geographers) have used the term "Malaysia" to include Indonesia, and the 1957 *Census Report* of the Federation of Malaya applied the term "Malaysian" to the Malay, aboriginal Javanese, and Sumatran inhabitants of the Malayan Peninsula. In this essay, I shall use "Malay" as an ethnic (or, more correctly, a communal) term, while reserving the terms "Malayan" and "Malaysian" for more general application to the members of all communities (Malay, Chinese, Indian, native, and so on) resident in Malaya or Malaysia.

The labeling of Malaysian political parties has also shared in this terminological confusion. The Alliance, the governing party in Malaysia, is now known as the Malaysian Alliance, and includes the Alliance parties in the states of Sabah and Sarawak. However, its strongest segment is the federation of the three communal parties of the peninsula—the United Malays National Organization (UMNO), the Malayan Chinese Association (MCA), and the Malayan Indian Congress (MIC)—and this federation is still referred to as the "Malayan Alliance." (In Singapore, the ruling Peoples Action Party, or PAP, of Lee Kuan Yew sat on the opposition side in the Federal Parliament.)

[2] For a convenient discussion of some indicators of integration, and numerous warnings about their use, see Phillip E. Jacob and James V. Toscano, eds., *The Integration of Political Communities* (Philadelphia and New York: J. B. Lippincott, 1964), especially the introductory chapter by Phillip E. Jacob and Henry Teune and chapters 2 and 3 by Karl Deutsch.

Figure 3
TOTAL IMPORT-EXPORT TRADE
SINGAPORE – FEDERATION OF MALAYA
1961–65

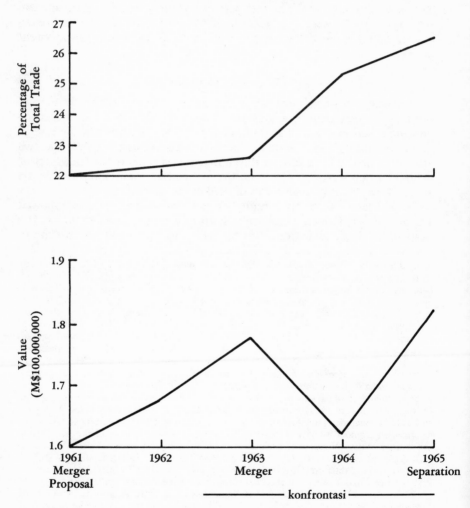

1965. More significantly, Malaya accounted for 22.1 per cent of Singapore's total trade in 1961 and 26.7 per cent in 1965 (see Figure 3).

The Press.[3] It is impossible to quantify the circulation of newspapers across state lines in Malaysia, because some regionally based newspapers have both Malayan and Singapore editions and a national readership. Malays of both territories were reading the same Malay-language press, while many Chinese in both areas depended heavily on the Singapore Chinese-language press. This "national" press did, however, pay some attention to local news stories. Since January, 1966, Kuala Lumpur has banned newspapers actually printed in Singapore, while permitting the circulation of Singapore newspapers with presses in Malaya, although Singapore has no corresponding prohibition against newspapers printed in Malaysia.

There are four newspapers that can qualify as national, despite regional printing. One of these, *Utusan Melayu*, is Malay in the Jawi script; two are Chinese, *Nan-yang Shang-pao* and *Sing-chew Jit-pao*; and one is English, *The Straits Times*. Three of these produce both Malayan and Singapore editions, although the two editions are almost identical, except for advertisements and some local news.

Utusan Melayu was originally published in Singapore, but is now published daily in the more cordial environment of Kuala Lumpur; its papers are delivered by air to Singapore. It claims a circulation of 50,000; 25 per cent of this is in Singapore, which has a population of some 262,000 Malays. There is also one Romanized Malay-language newspaper of limited circulation, *Berita Harian*; it is owned by the Straits Times Press, and is similar in many ways to *The Straits Times* itself.

It is estimated that Chinese readership in Singapore and Malaya for the two major Chinese-language papers has grown from about 85,000 in 1959 to some 120,000 at the present time. Prior to 1959, the national newspapers joined in chartering a daily flight to take their Singapore editions into the Malay Peninsula. The first to break out of this pattern and open its own presses in Kuala Lumpur was *The Straits Times*. In 1961, *Nan-yang Shang-pao* opened its own presses in Kuala Lumpur, and, in May, 1966, *Sing-chew Jit-pao* began facsimile transmission of its Singapore edition to new presses in Kuala Lumpur. The extent to which these Chinese newspapers are national is revealed by their circulation figures. *Nan-yang Shang-pao* has an actual circulation of 65,000, of which 40 per cent is in Singapore and 60 per cent in Malaya. *Sing-chew Jit-pao* has a circulation of 55,000, with 55 per cent in Singapore and 45 per cent in Malaya.

The English-language press is dominated by The Straits Times enterprise, which publishes numerous magazines and newspapers, although only *The Straits Times* is truly national. The decision to open presses in Kuala Lumpur was triggered by the Singapore elections of 1959; the restrictions the victorious Peoples Action Party (PAP) seemed inclined to place on journalists' activities threatened the paper's Singapore operations. At present,

---

[3] Where not otherwise documented, much of the following material on Malaya-Singapore relations derives from a series of interviews and informal discussions in Singapore and Kuala Lumpur during the period July 12–29, 1966.

The Straits Times has a total circulation of about 125,000; some 60 per cent of its papers are printed and sold in Singapore.

Increasing press contacts between Malaysia and Singapore cannot be demonstrated graphically, but, since 1959, a general trend toward increased circulation of the national press throughout Singapore and Malaya has been accompanied by the tendency to install presses in each territory and to print similar, but separate, Malayan and Singapore editions.

Air Traffic. Malaysian Airways (now Malaysia/Singapore Airways), which has a monopoly of air travel within Malaysia, has expanded dramatically in the past five years and now has domestic routes linking nineteen cities throughout Malaysia and Singapore in addition to a small international service to Hong Kong, Bangkok, and Manila. In 1967, there were fifty-four round-trip flights per week between Kuala Lumpur and Singapore, and these provided a total of 2,730 seats in each direction. Although Figure 4 also includes the Hong Kong and Bangkok international flights, it is at least suggestive of the growth of air-travel facilities within Malaysia and between Malaysia and Singapore. While Malaysian Airways did not formerly provide figures on air travel within Malaysia, statistics compiled by Singapore airport authorities clearly reveal increased communications between Singapore and Malaya. Both absolutely (numbers of passengers) and relatively (percentage of total traffic traveling between the two areas), air travel between Singapore and Malaya was increasing rapidly between 1961 and 1965, as Figure 5 reveals.

The Flow of Mail. Statistics of mail flow can only be partially quantified. The postal services had been a pan-Malayan department for almost half a century, and thus postal authorities did not distinguish between letters posted or received in Singapore and Malaya.[4] However, the Singapore government did record the weight of mail transported by air, and this provides a fair sample of all first-class mail. There is no special domestic air-mail postal service throughout Malaysia. The rule of the postal services is that domestic first-class mail will be transported to its destination by the most expeditious means. In practice, this has meant that first-class mail going to Kuala Lumpur and the north goes by air except for late-afternoon postings, which reach the north more quickly by the night train to Kuala Lumpur. Mail destined for areas south of Kuala Lumpur usually goes by rail or road.

The picture presented in Figure 6, below, clearly reveals the trends toward increasing correspondence between the mainland and Singapore between 1961 and 1965. Moreover, the increase could have been even more dramatic than this graph reveals, for it does not include mail flowing between Singapore and southern Malaya, and presumably one communicates at least as much with near neighbors as with more distant ones.

Radio and Television Services. The control of broadcasting services was one of the more obscure parts of the final Malaysia Agreement. In principle, radio broadcasting was a federal matter, at least so far as "general

[4] A similar postal situation obtains between the United States and Canada, except that, according to the Director of Posts, Singapore, in the past, even the Pan-Malayan Post Office did not keep its own statistics on Singapore-Malaya mail.

Figure 4
MALAYSIAN AIRWAYS OPERATIONS
1960–65

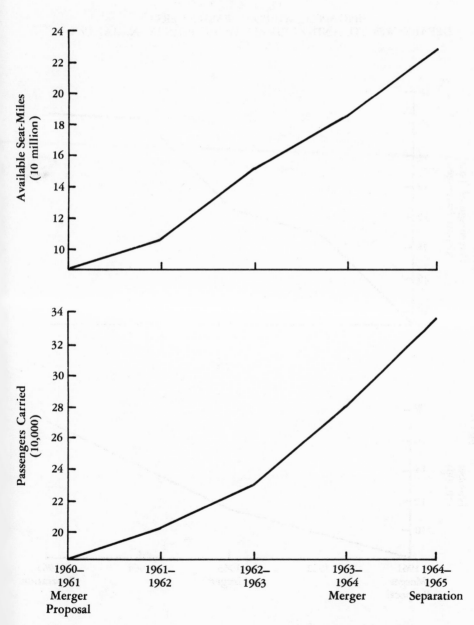

Figure 5
SINGAPORE AIRPORT PASSENGERS:
DEPARTURES TO, AND ARRIVALS FROM, POINTS IN MALAYA
1961–65

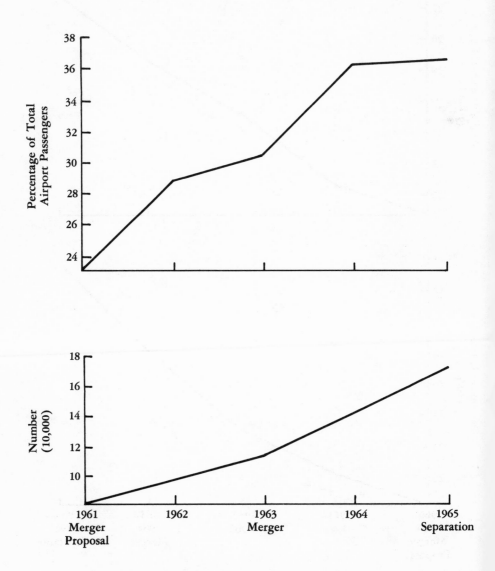

Figure 6
MALAYAN MAIL RECEIVED AND DISPATCHED
SINGAPORE AIRPORT,
1961–65

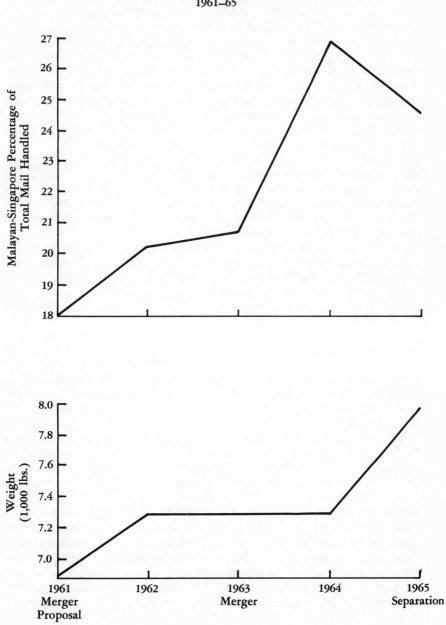

policies" were concerned, but in practice, there were so many loopholes in the final agreement that one could only conclude that the issue had been postponed and that both parties had merely agreed to disagree at some future time. There is some evidence that Malaya never adequately understood the potential impact of the Singapore radio and television services. In terms of quality, Singapore programs tended to be somewhat better than those originating in Malaya, reflecting the greater availability of performing and technical talent in Singapore, and also longer experience in the entertainment field. In radio, Singapore not only operates several medium-wave transmitters covering the island and southernmost Malaya, but it also feeds the regular Chinese, Malay, and English programs into three fifty-kilowatt shortwave transmitters, which together provide excellent signals from Borneo to Bangkok. It is my impression from my own personal and highly unsystematic observations, that Radio Singapore may be considerably more popular among the Chinese of Sarawak than Radio Malaysia, Sarawak. Singapore television, which is also somewhat more experienced than TV Malaysia, can be received clearly throughout much of the important southern Malayan state of Johore. While Indonesia well understood the potential impact of Singapore television, and accordingly banned television receivers in the nearby Riau Archipelago, Kuala Lumpur either failed to perceive its potential importance or else was waiting for a more opportune time to assume control.

Whatever the reason, the birth of Malaysia had little effect on the operations of Singapore broadcasting. Singapore did make minor changes, broadcasting daily news bulletins from the capital city, several film reports from Malaya, and providing direct television coverage of the 1964 general elections in the peninsula via microwave relay from Kuala Lumpur. Although the microwave services were available at all times, it is interesting that they were used for direct television programming only once. Again, the federal government seems to have failed to recognize the potential of television, or perhaps it wanted to postpone any action. Network services requested by Singapore were twice refused: once at the time of the creation of Malaysia (the celebration had to be filmed and flown to Singapore), and once when TV Singapura proposed a regular Malaya-Singapore national television network.

There is some evidence, however, that thinking in Kuala Lumpur was beginning to change by mid-1964. Ministers seemed to be becoming increasingly sensitive to the coverage they were receiving in Singapore, and, in fact, in order to avoid the risk of statements being carried out of context, Kuala Lumpur directed that TV Singapura could not edit the speeches of federal ministers it broadcast. From mid-1964 on, there were also increasing reminders from the Ministry of Information in Kuala Lumpur that broadcasting was a federal matter, but these warnings resulted in little concrete government action. Thus, Singapore's dominant position in radio-TV, and the failure of the government to recognize the potential impact of, and to exercise jurisdiction over, the media, makes it difficult to argue that the radio and television services were increasing the knowledge Malaysians and Singaporeans had about each other, but it is apparent that the structures, at least, existed.

In sum, the objective realities of increasing interaction between Malaysia and Singapore in terms of trade, newspaper circulation, air traffic, and radio-TV coverage suggest that Malaysia and Singapore should have continued their association. On what basis, then, was the Federation of Malaysia formed, and why did a split occur?

SOURCES OF CONFLICT

In Malaya, it was Prime Minister Tunku Abdul Rahman who had led the drive for Malaysia, and for this he eventually earned the title of Bapa Malaysia, or the Father of Malaysia. Once the Alliance leadership had fallen in behind the prime minister—a relatively simple matter in Malaya —the success of the scheme there was almost certain. In Singapore, it was an entirely different problem. Lee Kuan Yew and his immediate followers in the PAP were almost the only reliable supporters of the Malaysia scheme. The situation was precarious in the Singapore Assembly, where they faced a mercurial left-wing *Barisan Sosialis* that opposed the Malaysia plan. How Lee overcame these odds and pushed through not only a bill in the Assembly, but even a popular referendum, has been told elsewhere and need not be repeated here. It was, however, masterful leadership on Lee's part.[5]

A closer look at the motives behind each territory's attitude toward the creation of Malaysia reveals some fundamental differences that help explain subsequent tensions. Malaya had always been cold to any suggestion of union with Singapore, largely because this would upset the delicate racial balance. However, by 1961, Malaya had become even more concerned about the implications of internal developments within Singapore. If the extreme left wing there continued to erode Lee Kuan Yew's majority in the Assembly, Lee's government would suffer the fate of the governments of David Marshall and Lim Yew Hock, both of which fell victim to a young, expanding, and restless electorate. Britain, Malaya, and Singapore each had one of the three votes in Singapore's internal security committee, and Malaya could join with Britain to guarantee the maintenance of peace and order in Singapore, but this provision was most likely to become one of the dominant issues in the review of the Singapore constitution scheduled for 1964. Thus, Malaya could easily foresee a fully independent Communist state just across the causeway. Malaya had brought its own Communist insurrection to a successful conclusion only in 1960, and the thought of a Communist-controlled Singapore at its doorstep was, therefore, doubly alarming.

Singapore's prime minister shared many of these concerns. He also recognized that the state of Singapore needed a secure noncolonial association to assure its long-term viability, and, most of all, that a rapidly developing island economy needed raw materials and markets—a hinterland for its

[5] The best account of the Singapore referendum is contained in Willard A. Hannah, *The Formation of Malaysia* (New York: American Universities Field Staff, 1964), chapter 13.

port. A superb politician, Lee also undoubtedly realized that if he could maneuver Singapore into a new Malaysian federation, it would be good, not only for Malaya and Singapore, but also for the PAP and Lee Kuan Yew.

After the creation of Malaysia, Malaya apparently hoped that life in the peninsula would remain much as it had been. For the most part, Singapore would be left alone to enjoy its autonomy, but since it was now formally a part of the federal state, any trouble that might occur there could be controlled. Part of the new bargain with Singapore involved the allotment of seats in the lower house of the federal parliament, the Dewan Ra'ayat. On the basis of population, Singapore might have expected at least twice as many seats as it actually received. On the other hand, other states on the peninsula had been subjected to a highly centralized political system; Singapore was not; it enjoyed considerable local autonomy, particularly in the fields of education and taxation. Also, as was pointed out earlier, until very late, Singapore operated its own information services, radio, and television with almost no intervention from the federal government. In brief and admittedly oversimplified terms, although both Malaya and Singapore had a vague common goal of stability, each also saw union as the means to its own individual ends. The merger took place on this basis on September 16, 1963.

Once the merger had taken place, satisfying the immediate objectives of Lee Kuan Yew and the PAP cabinet on the one hand, and Tunku Abdul Rahman and the Alliance leadership on the other, differences arose in regard to national goals. To Lee, who conceived of Singapore's association with Malaysia in terms of economic progress as well as of political stability, economic modernization implied, or perhaps even required, social modernization, and thus his message of social revolution gradually took shape. The somewhat conservative leadership of Kuala Lumpur was more concerned with stability—in the sense of law and order—for only in a stable, secure, politically predictable environment would one have the climate for a continuing inflow of foreign capital. While the PAP advocated social revolution, the Alliance was content with social evolution.

Differences of a communal nature also played an important role in tensions between Singapore and Malaya during Singapore's membership in the Federation of Malaysia.[6] Before the union, Malaya was not "socially homogenized," in that members of the various communities did not really interact

---

[6] The population of Malaysia in mid-1964 was officially estimated to number about 10.9 million; 90 per cent lived in Singapore and Malaya. There were more than 4.5 million Chinese throughout Malaysia; they accounted for 75.2 per cent of Singapore's population of 1.8 million and for 36.8 per cent of the 7.8 million population of Malaya itself. Malays were the second largest group in the Federation of Malaysia, but, even in Malaya, comprised only 50.1 per cent of the population. In addition, about a million Indians have settled in Malaysia, mostly in Singapore and Malaya. Dayaks are the largest population group in Borneo, but many Chinese and some Malays have settled in the cities. (Malaya last conducted a census in 1957; Singapore, Sarawak, and Sabah, in 1960. The estimates given here are taken from official Malaysian and Singapore sources and are the most reliable figures available.)

as individuals without reference to their native communities. During the period of British rule prior to 1957, Malays were regarded as likeable, rural people, whose interests were best served by leaving them as they were; the British allowed members of their nobility or near-nobility to retain traditional titles and privileges and encouraged some of them to pass through the English stream of education and eventually emerge as the political, administrative, and symbolic elite of the country. The Chinese and Indians, on the other hand, worked Malaya's tin mines and rubber estates, repaired the roads, and generally provided the goods and services for the country as a whole. When Malaya became independent, this social differentiation was widely accepted, although sizable numbers of all communities had already become dislodged from their traditional occupations. The belated discovery of this fact further disrupted Malayan social integration. One got along with the members of the other communities, not because of common goals, but because this was the best means to further the interests of one's own community. Only at the level of the top elite would it be possible to speak of an agreement on national goals, and even here some reservations must be made. Until most recently, the Alliance has been a federation of three communal parties, not a single political party.

In Singapore, the picture was somewhat different. Three-fourths of the population were Chinese and thus formed a far more homogenous community than Malaya. As long as issues were not defined in communal terms, cleavages were along other social lines. However, almost as soon as Malaysia became a reality, relations between Kuala Lumpur and Singapore took on a communal flavor, and, when this happened, the differences within the Singapore Chinese community receded in importance, while the population's awareness of itself as Malaysian Chinese grew. Kuala Lumpur had succeeded in bringing Singapore into the Malaysian fold, but it had not yet realized that Singapore's inclusion would affect the social and political balance of the Federation as a whole.

One of the immediate issues was that of communal "equality." With the single exception of the Pan-Malayan Islamic Party (PMIP), all of the major Malaysian political parties were committed to an egalitarian ideology, but "equality" meant something different to the different groups. Many Malays did not wish to follow the lead of other Southeast Asian states in harshly oppressing the resident Chinese plurality, but at the same time sought to retain the established privileges of the Malay community, which were designed to permit the Malays to compete on more even terms with the Chinese. In part spontaneously, and in part as a result of conscious government policy, increasing emphasis had been placed on Malay privileges as a means of bringing the Malays up to the point where they could compete with the Chinese (or, as it was so often described by the golfing ministers of Malaysia, the less skilled players were simply being given a reasonable handicap). As a result, Malays were beginning to enter business and the professions—traditionally, the Chinese and European sectors of the economy. Dissension increased with the institution of the practice of Malay preference in business and the professions in Malaya.

This practice made it increasingly difficult for the Chinese to get licenses, permits, and scholarships. The demand for Malay privileges also rose upon the discovery that the Chinese themselves were not observing the unspoken symbiotic bargain; they were, in fact, entering government service in larger numbers than the Malays, although this sector had previously been the preserve of Malayas and Europeans. For many Chinese, to be "equal" meant to give the better qualified Chinese a chance to maximize their advantages and thus to permit them to pull further ahead of the disadvantaged Malays. It was within this context that the PAP chanced upon the phrase "Malaysian Malaysia" to convey the Chinese concept of communal equality. This catchy phrase kept Malayan leaders constantly on the defensive until the union broke apart. The dilemma was the most serious for the Malay politicians of the Alliance, for to deny that one stood for the principle of a Malaysian Malaysia would have been highly offensive to the non-Malay members of the Alliance; on the other hand, to admit that one accepted the goal, with all of its implications, would have been suicidal within the context of UMNO.

Communal differences between Singapore and Malaya inevitably assumed a political dimension both before and after the formation of Malaysia. The union of Malaya and Singapore could not help but raise the issue of a national political base for parties whose previous roots had been in either Malaya or Singapore. General elections were held in Malaya in 1955, 1959, and 1964, and in Singapore in 1959, 1963, and 1968. Although the 1963 and 1964 elections were held within the framework of Malaysia (the 1963 Singapore elections were actually held on the eve of the creation of Malaysia), their purpose was to elect representatives to the Federal Parliament and the State Legislative Assemblies only from the territories concerned. Neither set of elections was, in fact, a Malaysia-wide election, for these were seen as transitional elections leading to a planned all-Malaysia general election about 1968.[7] Both the 1963 and 1964 elections provided opportunities for bitter rivalry between the Malayan and Singapore political parties.

The United Malays National Organization, the dominant voice of the Malayan Alliance, had always presumed that it spoke for the majority of the Malay population throughout Malaysia, and that the influence of the PAP was limited to the Chinese of Singapore. The PAP, however, regarded both Singapore Malays and Singapore Chinese as its own preserve. Thus,

[7] Malaysia has a parliamentary system of government modeled on that of Britain but superimposed on a federal structure that borrows heavily from the American experience. As in Britain, the lower house (the Dewan Ra'ayat, or House of Representatives) is far more powerful than the upper house (the Dewan Negara, or Senate). Because of the composition of the Senate (which synthesizes the U.S. Senate and the British House of Lords) and the general nature of the constitution, Malaysia is, in fact, a highly centralized Federation. Singapore, which has a one-house parliamentary system, enjoyed unique constitutional privileges in its association with Malaysia, and had considerably greater autonomy than the other thirteen states of the Federation. Each of the thirteen states of the Federation has a state legislature (known by various names but usually called in English the State Legislative Assembly) and each of these practices some form of parliamentary government borrowed from the British experience.

UMNO entered the Singapore elections of 1963 fairly confident that it would get a large part of the Malay vote (Malays constitute some 13 per cent of the Singapore electorate) and almost certain of capturing seats in the three overwhelmingly Malay wards of the Southern Islands, Kampong Kebangan, and Geyang Serai. However, the PAP won 37 out of 51 seats, including the predominantly Malay wards. UMNO realized that even if the PAP message of modernism was still admittedly in its formative stage, and even if it did not actually appeal to the Malays, at least it did not deter them from supporting the party that was taking Singapore into Malaysia. UMNO realized that it would need to carry out an active campaign of proselytization among the Singapore Malays, and probably decided to do so at about this time, despite potential conflict with the PAP.

By early 1964, the more Malay-oriented wing of UMNO had begun to carry its message to the Singapore Malays, and on the other side of the coin, Lee Kuan Yew had decided to do some poaching of his own to try to expand the influence of the PAP beyond the Johore causeway. In what some PAP leaders now admit was probably a strategic error, Lee Kuan Yew chose to contest selected seats in the 1964 Malayan elections. Apparently there was a considerable difference within the party on this issue until the very last moment. Some argued that the PAP should not enter the elections at all, while others thought that if it chose to run, it should do so on a massive scale. The compromise, which was probably made by Lee himself, was to put up a token fight; the party would try to capture six or seven of the nine seats they decided to contest and would thus demonstrate to Kuala Lumpur their potential rather than their actual power. The party, however, was handicapped from the very beginning. First, the party structure was poorly organized. Secondly, the PAP tried to direct its attack specifically against the MCA (see note 1), while praising the leadership of Tunku Abdul Rahman and the Alliance. This anti-MCA but pro-Alliance stance (which Lee apparently hoped would split the MCA away from UMNO and MIC and thus provide the PAP with an opportunity to join the Alliance) was too subtle and contradictory for the electorate. In the eyes of the electorate, the MCA was a part of the Alliance, and another party had to either be for the Alliance or against it. In the end, the PAP was resoundingly defeated, capturing only one of the nine seats it had contested in the 104-member Parliament.

If the meaning of the election contest had escaped the voters, it did not, however, escape the leaders of the Alliance. It was clear by that time that Lee and the PAP had no intention of restricting their political activities to the island of Singapore. The PAP slogan for a Malaysian Malaysia had been heard all over the peninsula. Worse still, perhaps, Lee had led a movement to create a Malaysia Solidarity Convention from among the disparate opposition to the Alliance, and the Manifesto of this predominantly non-Malay confederation sounded suspiciously like the language embodied in the working papers of the hated Malayan Union scheme of 1945.[8] The

---

[8] Lee envisioned the Malaysia Solidarity Convention as a confederation of all the opposition parties of Malaysia that were politically to the left of the Alliance (this includes

Malayan Union had been opposed because it threatened the position of the Malays, and if this new message aroused a serious response, it could threaten the entire integrated structure of the Malayan system.

Although the attempt by Lee Kuan Yew and the PAP to gain a political base throughout Malaysia had been at least temporarily stymied, the new UMNO appeals to the Singapore Malays were destined to be considerably more successful. The vehicle that carried the message to the Singapore Malays was the Jawi script newspaper, *Utusan Melayu*. For many months, *Utusan Melayu* had published increasingly inflammatory reports of PAP repression of Malay rights in Singapore and had generally painted the party as the chief threat to the Malays of all Malaysia. Probably for the first time in history, the Malay community of Singapore was able clearly to identify, and be identified, with the Malays of the Peninsula. The message consistently carried by *Utusan Melayu* during this period was plain: the PAP wanted a Chinese Malaysia; Lee was a traitor; the Singapore Government was oppressing the Malays of Singapore, just as it would oppress the Malays of Malaya, if given the opportunity, but the Malayas of Singapore need not worry too much, because, as part of the larger Malay community of Malaysia, they would be looked after by the Malaysian Government.[9]

By mid-July, 1964, leaders of the two major communities were no longer urging their followers to work together, even as a means of achieving their individual ends. *Utusan Melayu* was carrying a message of strong Malay nationalism and calling for even stronger measures, while the PAP slogan of a Malaysian Malaysia signified Chinese domination for many Chinese and Malays. The confrontation led to bloody riots during the course of the celebration of the Prophet's birthday in Singapore on July 21, 1964, and, with the advantage of hindsight, we can see that, from this point on, both territories probably began to give some thought to formulating alternative political arrangements. Communications between citizens of the two territories had, indeed, become more intensive and extensive—as the first section of this essay demonstrated statistically—but the messages were hardly conducive to integration.

By the fall of 1964, the union of Singapore and Malaya was no longer

---

virtually all of the opposition except the Pan-Malayan Islamic Party of the Peninsula, a Malay chauvinist group). Its general goals, as originally stated, were the complete equality of all Malaysian citizens, regardless of communal and social origin. This position was very similar to that taken in the idealistic statements of the British Labor Government at the close of World War II. The working papers of the Labor Government became the guidelines for the creation of the short-lived Malayan Union, which was opposed by the Malay nobility, who successfully mobilized popular Malay support against this threat to traditional Malay privileges. The Convention was never a major political force, since its leadership came from Singapore, and Singapore withdrew from Malaysia shortly after the Convention was created.

[9] The most blatant and obvious example of this line is a long report of a speech given by the then Secretary-General of UMNO, Syed Ja'afar Albar, before a Malay crowd estimated at more than 12,000 at Pasir Panjang in Singapore on July 12, 1964. The speech itself was highly inflammatory, and the *Utusan Melayu* report of it played up every bitter detail (*Utusan Melayu*, July 13, 1964, p. 1).

attractive to either of the principals. Considerable pressure was building up in UMNO to have Lee arrested, and it was not certain how long the moderate Malaysian prime minister could contain these forces. In the period 1961–63, Lee had feared that he might be the victim of the threatening left wing of Singapore politics, but by 1965, he was in much firmer control of the situation. The 1963 elections had given him a sizable, and, most important, a reliable majority in the Assembly, and the PAP had further consolidated its position after this. Finally, the Singapore prime minister had traveled widely throughout the world during the period 1963–65 and had probably gained increased confidence in the ability of Singapore to compete internationally.

Malaysia was disenchanted with the union because Lee's drive for a Malaysian Malaysia was apparently disrupting the social fabric of Malaya. Secondly, one of the major arguments in 1961 for incorporating Singapore, the threat of a Communist base at the tip of the peninsula, seemed considerably less real by 1965. Finally, the moderate leadership of the Alliance recognized that the Singapore–Kuala Lumpur dispute was bringing the radical elements of UMNO into prominence, and, unless this tide could be turned, the future of both the Alliance and Malaysia looked bleak.

After preliminary suggestions in late 1964 and early 1965 that some new confederational arrangement might be attempted, the complete break between Singapore and Malaysia was announced to a stunned Parliament at 10:00 A.M. on August 9, 1965. Simultaneously, in Singapore, Lee Yuan Kew proclaimed the independence of that state before a hastily summoned press conference. The reaction in Kuala Lumpur was at first one of disbelief, and later of some relief, that the dispute had ended at last. In Singapore, the prime minister shed tears on TV, and the people celebrated with firecrackers and dancing.

36

REGIONALISM IN SOUTHEAST ASIA*

BERNARD K. GORDON

INTRODUCTION

Southeast Asian leaders began in the 1960's to give much more attention to achieving meaningful progress toward the old goal of "regional cooperation" in their area. To leaders of small and medium-sized Asian states, faced with a resurgent China and uncomfortable with the prospects of long-term dependence on either the United States or Japan, regionalism today looks much more attractive than it appeared in the 1950's. To some, it even appears as the only feasible approach to their long-term security problem. As a result, among leaders in states such as Thailand and Indonesia, the concept has received a priority that would have been remarkable a few years ago.

The measure of this change is in the pace of developments specific to

* This is an abridged version of "Regional Cooperation in the Asian-Pacific Area, ca. 1980," which was originally prepared for Washington Center of Foreign Policy Research, "The Balance of Power in the Asian-Pacific Area, ca. 1980" (The Johns Hopkins University, School of Advanced International Studies, 1968, mimeo.), chapter 11. It is published here by permission of the author.

Southeast Asia, and the clearest reflection is in ASEAN (Association of Southeast Asian Nations), the five-nation group established in August, 1967. ASEAN is both the logical product of much that has been taking place in the 1960's and the likeliest format for future trends in Southeast Asian regional cooperation. Because it borrows heavily from an earlier regional grouping known as ASA (Association of Southeast Asia, composed of Thailand, Malaysia, and the Philippines), and because its development is likely to proceed along lines first established in that smaller organization, the discussion here will focus initially on ASA before moving on to ASEAN.

THE ASSOCIATION OF SOUTHEAST ASIA (ASA)

ASA operated during 1961–67 and marked a second phase in the development of Asian regionalism. Because of the special and highly favorable circumstances of its termination in 1967, ASA warrants more attention than might ordinarily be given to a three-nation group with a life-span of only six years. ASA, however, was not terminated because it had in any way failed; rather, it was the most successful of efforts thus far in Asian regional cooperation, and its success had much to do with the creation of ASEAN. Indeed, within a few weeks after ASEAN was established in August, 1967, spokesmen for Malaysia, the Philippines, and Thailand announced that most ongoing ASA activities and plans would be incorporated into ASEAN. In essence, the creation of ASEAN (which also includes Indonesia and Singapore) means that ASA, rather than disappearing, has simply been enlarged and given a new name.

The sense in which ASA represented a "second phase" in the development of Asian regionalism was in its indigenous and pragmatic nature, for, unlike ECAFE,[1] the Colombo Plan, or SEATO,[2] ASA was not created on the initiative of extraregional powers, nor did it include any. Moreover, unlike the Asian Relations Conference of 1948 or the Afro-Asian Conference at Bandung in 1955, ASA established permanent administrative machinery providing for multilateral meetings and working sessions at regular intervals. Most important, ASA was not highly ideological. In the words of Tunku Abdul Rahman, the Prime Minister of Malaysia and one of the ASA's first sponsors:

. . . this organization is in no way intended to be an anti-Western bloc or anti-Eastern bloc, or, for that matter, a political bloc of any kind. It is not connected in any way with the various organizations which are in existence today; it is purely a Southeast Asian Economic and Cultural Cooperation Organization and has no backing whatsoever from any foreign source.[3]

[1] United Nations Economic Commission for Asia and the Far East.

[2] Southeast Asia Treaty Organization—Philippines, Thailand, Australia, New Zealand, Britain, France, and the United States.

[3] Federation of Malaya, *ASA, Report of the First Meeting of Foreign Ministers* (Kuala Lumpur, 1961), p. 4. A Thai preliminary working paper circulated in 1959 also emphasized this point: "The cooperation will be practical in the sense that the South-East Asian meeting to be convened shall not deal with conflicts of ideologies and

To the extent that any ideological basis did exist, it lay in a sense of Southeast Asian identity and regional consciousness, a feeling that the countries of the region constituted a geographical and cultural family distinct from other such families in the world. In the view of many Southeast Asian leaders, this family had been separated by colonialism and by surviving postcolonial trade and political patterns, and, through association, the ASA countries hoped to rediscover old linkages, promote a new regional identity, and, most important, promote economic development through cooperation. In practice, the last was stressed, giving ASA a somewhat pragmatic, even conservative, stamp.

ASA's Political History

Abdul Rahman is generally credited with initiating the idea embodied later in ASA. He hoped that such an organization, encompassing both pro-Western states and neutralists, would help destroy the conditions of poverty in the region, which he is convinced facilitate the expansion of Communism. In 1959 and 1960, Rahman sought to interest other non-Communist Southeast Asian governments in the proposed association and won quick support from the Philippines and Thailand. The "neutralists," however, feared that the new organization would be "too political," and Indonesia was disdainful of any initiative not its own. Consequently, even though Thailand hoped for almost two years that Burma might join, none of the nonaligned states did.[4]

On July 31, 1961, the foreign ministers of Malaya, the Philippines, and Thailand met in Bangkok and issued a declaration that formally created ASA. They were careful to assure a maximum degree of flexibility in the organization and to leave the door open for new members. For this reason, a simple declaration, rather than a signed treaty, was issued. The aims and purposes of the association were left vague, so that almost any kind of cooperation could be incorporated within the framework of the declaration.[5]

During the following two years, ASA gained momentum as the three countries first identified, and then carefully screened, the projects on which collaboration seemed useful and most feasible. Some of the earliest planning focused on joint arrangements in shipping, technical cooperation de-

---

the so-called East-West issue, except as passing references. . . . Such meeting shall concentrate its attention and efforts mainly on matters which affect directly the region as a whole or some countries of the region, and on questions whose solutions will directly benefit the region or some of its members."

[4] For elaboration see Bernard K. Gordon, *The Dimensions of Conflict in Southeast Asia,* (Englewood Cliffs, N.J.: Prentice-Hall, 1966), pp. 165–72.

[5] The aims of ASA were to establish effective machinery for "friendly consultations, collaboration and mutual assistance in the economic, social, cultural, scientific, and administrative fields"; to provide for exchanges of use of facilities and information in these fields; to promote regional studies; to provide machinery for cooperation in resource use, trade promotion, industry, and transport; to study problems of commodity trade; and "generally, to consult and cooperate with one another so as to achieve the aims and purposes of the Association as well as to contribute more effectively to the work of existing international organizations and agencies."

signed to improve agricultural productivity, trade agreements (with a view to establishing uniform tariffs), and even commodity-producers agreements, with the hope of establishing better bargaining positions vis-à-vis world purchases of such products as rubber, tin, and rice.

Progress was slowed after mid-1963, however, because Philippines President Macapagal resurrected an almost-forgotten private Filipino claim to British North Borneo (Sabah), which at that time was about to be joined with Malaya and Sarawak in the new Federation of Malaysia.[6] The claim led to numerous irritants between the Philippines and Malaya and eventually to the recall of ambassadors—although ASA committees continued to meet throughout this period. Then, when Malaysia actually was formed in September, 1963, Manila declined to grant immediate recognition, because to do so would imply that it had given up hope of ultimately winning sovereignty over North Borneo. The effect, of course, was to break relations with the newly formed Malaysia, and although that situation was remedied not too many months afterwards, relations remained strained for the next two years.

Despite these tensions, ASA did not go out of existence; Thailand's Foreign Minister Thanat Khoman insured that Malaysian and Philippine leaders were in contact with one another indirectly, and each of the three governments stressed that its national ASA staff would continue work on proposals for collaborative action. No decisions were taken during this period, of course, but the net result of that two-year suspension, it now seems clear, was merely to slow ASA cooperation. When circumstances improved, ASA resumed almost where it had left off, thus supporting the view of those officials who had stressed in 1963–65 that the "idea" of cooperation would weather a temporary disagreement between two of its members.

The inauguration of new Philippine President Ferdinand Marcos in December, 1965, paved the way for a Filipino-Malaysian rapprochement. ASA was reactivated on March 2, 1966, and full diplomatic ties between Malaysia and the Philippines were restored on June 3. Concomitantly, the ascendancy of new political forces in Indonesia encouraged a favorable Indonesian policy toward regional cooperation, leading to the creation of ASEAN a year later.

ASA's Organizational Structure

The Bangkok Declaration of 1961 set out the principal elements of ASA's structure: the annual Foreign Ministers' Meeting (the highest policymaking body); the Joint Working Party, expected to meet a month before the Foreign Ministers' Meeting to review past progress and make recommendations; and the Standing Committee, composed of a host foreign minister and the ambassador of the other ASA countries in that foreign minister's capital. This committee provided permanent machinery and oversaw special projects. ASA scheduling in practice was flexible; a special Foreign Ministers' Meeting was convened in April, 1962, only seven months

[6] For elaboration see Gordon, *op. cit.*, pp. 9–41.

after the Bangkok meeting, but the next meeting was delayed several months because of the growing estrangement between the Philippines and Malaysia. Similarly, the Joint Working Party was convened as much as four months before the Foreign Ministers' Meeting and also held one special session.

Unlike the superstructure, the lower committee structure, where most of the spadework was done, underwent a number of changes, reflecting the increasingly pragmatic orientation of ASA. Three permanent expert committees were established in 1963, and existing functional committees were subsumed under them, or these were replaced by *ad hoc* committees. Because of the hiatus in 1964–65, most of these *ad hoc* committees were unable to meet until the autumn of 1966, and at that time, many of them found it desirable to resume permanent status.

ASA considered, but did not establish, a central secretariat. Part of the reason was the problem of the location of any central headquarters, and to avoid this problem, ASA originally set up three national secretariats. Meetings and conferences rotated among the capitals. This system has both strengths and weaknesses. On the negative side, problems of duplication and coordination were intensified, and there was probably less continuing contact among nationals of the three countries than there would have been in a multinational central secretariat. On the positive side, the use of national secretariats encouraged intensive national participation in the work of ASA along procedural lines already familiar to the participants. The feasibility of establishing a central secretariat remained under discussion when ASA "merged" into ASEAN, and the new group will probably face the same dilemma. The desire for a central institutional base is strong, however, and it is not unlikely that ASEAN will decide to establish one.

The slow evolution of the ASA organizational structure illustrates one of the hallmarks of the organization—the continual pragmatic adjustment of structure and goals in the course of operation.

ASA Projects

ASA was established amid dreams of a common market, interlocking development plans, an ASA international airline, and a joint shipping line. These grand goals have not been forgotten, but the ASA participants discovered that they could not be achieved in a short time by simple agreement on the ultimate ends. To achieve these goals involves many small steps. There are long bargaining periods during which the difficulties become apparent, compromises must be made, and the projects reduced to a manageable size. Small agreements then become the basis for expanding the areas of cooperation later.

During its first year, ASA's main activities centered on finding projects suitable for cooperative efforts. By the time of the second meeting of the Joint Working Party in November, 1962, a great number of these had been considered and the initial difficulties identified. The Working Party was able to divide its recommendations to the foreign ministers into three categories: those to be implemented immediately, those "subject to further clarification," and those "which require further study with a view to implementation in the future."

When the Joint Working Party met in April and July, 1966, there was a new sense of urgency—a feeling that ASA must redouble its efforts to make up for time lost, and thus prove that it was indeed a viable institution. It was felt that ASA would spread itself too thinly by grasping at every straw, and the Working Party therefore gave priority to the most promising cooperative endeavors. Others, useful but less likely to reach fruition, were de-emphasized and eventually disappeared from the agenda of ASA meetings. The final report to the foreign ministers was a concise, 24-page document, listing 34 recommendations, whereas the 1962 Joint Working Party's report had been 60 pages in length and had listed 171 recommendations.

While a detailed examination of some of the specific projects would be instructive, it must suffice to point out that there were some successes recorded. Although no major or tangible economic cooperation projects were completed, certain potential areas for regional cooperation were identified for the first time. Moreover, even where ASA was largely unsuccessful in meeting its stated goals, there were often significant unanticipated fringe benefits.

The Meaning of ASA

ASA, though a small and short-lived organization, deserves to be viewed as more than a one-time attempt at regional cooperation in Southeast Asia. Although it achieved few tangible results of its own, ASA must be viewed as something of a success. It was an unprecedented step, largely in that it was originated by Southeast Asians. Both the fact of its establishment, as well as the favorable circumstances under which it was superseded by ASEAN, demonstrate that the concept of regionalism, especially in Southeast Asia, has a remarkably strong appeal to the political elites of many of the countries.

This appeal must be weighed against the political, cultural, and economic obstacles that impede cooperation. In ASA, the political problems were never major—though the Philippines' off-and-on claim to North Borneo continues to be troublesome. Instead, it is more likely to be the divergencies in cultural and administrative patterns and the presently low levels of economic interaction that will impede cooperation in Southeast Asia. The small volume of intraregional trade militates against initially broad commercial contacts; in the longer perspective, however, the similarity of economies increases the scope for exchanges of technical information and joint research related to economic development. It also enhances the opportunities for what some economists and senior ECAFE specialists call "harmonization of industrial development" among Southeast Asian nations.

As long as ASA was restricted to only three nations, however, it was unlikely that significant progress could be achieved along such grandiose lines. The absence of Indonesia, in particular, reduced the potential of ASA. Indeed, it was partly in the hope of ultimately attracting the neutral Southeast Asian states, especially Indonesia, that the three ASA members regularly played down some of the important political reasons that had led them to attempt regional cooperation in the first place. It should be understood that ASA's ostensibly nonpolitical label was never altogether accurate, and this fact, while never publicly acknowledged, is part of the "meaning" of ASA.

One overriding political goal—to limit the appeal of Communism by improving Southeast Asian living standards—had been involved from the outset. This is apparent not only from the private memoranda circulated (in 1959) before ASA's birth but also from a public statement made by Tunku Abdul Rahman at the April, 1963, Foreign Ministers' Meeting:

> We are determined to make a success of this organization because we believe sincerely that the best possible way of preventing the Communists from trying to destroy the lives and souls of our nations is by improving the lot of our peoples. Believing this thoroughly we must make ASA an inspiration and an example of sustained effort in growth and development. We must not allow anything to come in our way or to distract us from our common purposes.[7]

There are three implicit premises underlying this statement: (1) Containment of Communism in Asia involves primarily combating internal subversion (and in this it differs tactically from containment in Europe, where strategic balance plays the principal role); (2) internal subversion is facilitated by economic discontent and low standards of living; (3) regional cooperation is one of the instruments that can be used to improve standards of living.

Communists in Asia have emphasized internal subversion as their primary vehicle for expanding influence, and the ASA countries—because they cannot by themselves hope to affect the over-all strategic balance—probably judged correctly that their best contribution to security would lie in improving the environment. Moreover, economic performance in the ASA countries has, on the whole, been satisfactory, and while subversion has been a problem to them, too (notably in Thailand), it is fair to say that such non-ASA states as Indonesia and Burma have been more plagued by political instability. Although it is impossible to demonstrate statistically a high degree of correlation between poverty and internal subversion, the relatively stronger economies of the ASA states at least seem suggestive of such a correlation. This observation, of course, is not meant to suggest that ASA has contributed in any important way to the economic performance of Malaysia, Thailand, and the Philippines. ASA had an effective life of only three years, but, when the leaders in five Southeast Asian states formed ASEAN, they retained a firm belief in the direct connection between cooperation and improved development. Only considerable experience with regionalism in developing countries, for which there is as yet no useful precedent anywhere in the world, will allow for a judgment on the correctness of their belief.

In political terms, however, it is easier to see that ASA brought some

[7] Federation of Malaya, ASA, *Report of the Second Meeting of Foreign Ministers* (Kuala Lumpur, 1963), p. 30.

benefits. Among the most significant of these is probably the increased level of communication among its members. Without question, the role that Thailand played in the Filipino-Malaysian dispute was enhanced by the common ASA membership of the three. Both Filipino and Malaysian leaders constantly reiterated that they had a stake in the continuation of ASA, and developments in that difficult period do suggest that an informal peace-keeping role can be one of the most useful by-products of an ostensibly economic grouping. But ASA's most significant political contribution lies simply in its survival, for thus it helped to maintain the remarkably strong appeal of the regional concept to indigenous Southeast Asian elites.

THE ASSOCIATION OF SOUTHEAST ASIAN NATIONS (ASEAN)

Indonesian Participation

Indonesia's participation in ASEAN is one of the best evidences of the growing appeal of regional association, and, by virtue of Indonesia's membership, it is now possible for the first time to say that the regional concept may acquire genuine political significance. Indonesia's participation helps remove two of the major drawbacks of previous attempts at Asian regionalism—too small a membership and too clearly a "Western-oriented" membership. Aside from adding the world's fifth largest state to the group, Indonesia's participation will help make it more feasible for neutrals such as Burma and Cambodia to participate in the ASEAN format.

From Indonesia's standpoint, Southeast Asian regional cooperation has considerable attraction. The concept provides a legitimate means of exercising what is regarded as a proper leadership role, and this is one of the reasons why ASEAN has met with such widespread acceptance in Djakarta. It should be stressed very emphatically that both military and civilian elites in Indonesia share a strong and favorable attitude toward Southeast Asian regionalism. The army in Indonesia is likely to remain the dominant political group for a number of years, and even under circumstances in which it begins to share leadership more effectively with civilians, army positions on foreign policy matters will be critical. Consequently, the fact that the senior army officers are advocates of greater Southeast Asian collaboration reinforces the support of the civilian leadership.

The Indonesia imprint is clearly visible in the development of ASEAN; indeed, it would be most accurate to say that ASEAN was created to provide a place for Indonesia. Part of the reason derives from the tendency of Indonesian leaders to view ASA as a Western creation. It was not, but whatever the facts, it was clear that Indonesian participation in regionalism could only be accomplished by creating an altogether new body. Such a new body, moreover, would have to incorporate at least some of the appearances of the group known as MAPHILINDO—the only other regional effort in which Indonesia has participated.[8]

[8] MAPHILINDO was created in 1963, and although it was only a loose consultive body of the three "Malay" nations (MAlaya, PHILippines, and INDOnesia), it caught the attention of outsiders rather more than ASA ever did. The explanation lies in the two relatively useful by-products of MAPHILINDO. First, Indonesia's participation did

The idea for a new Southeast Asian group can be traced primarily to the new Indonesia government—in particular, Foreign Minister Adam Malik. Malik, as soon as he came to power as part of the triumvirate led by General Suharto, was inclined to achieve a relatively sharp break from Indonesia's policies of the immediate past. As part of this inclination, Malik was in the forefront of those who were urging President Sukarno's removal from power, and he was anxious to bring about a quick end to President Sukarno's "confrontation" against Malaysia. The final element in his desire to reshape the foreign image of Indonesia has seemed to be Malik's strong personal interest in the concept of Asian—especially Southeast Asian—regional cooperation.

The opportunity to express these sentiments arose late in 1965 and continued through the early months of 1966, as Indonesian officials inaugurated a series of informal "peace feelers" with the Malaysians. The confrontation itself came to a formal end with talks convened in Bangkok in June, 1966, and it is likely that Malik's views were communicated even earlier.[9] It is certain, however, that "regional cooperation" was one of the agenda items when formal talks took place under Thanat Khoman's auspices.[10] Malik announced in June, 1966, that he had proposed a new regional group and that the three ASA countries already had decided to join.[11] This estimate was premature, and while officials probably were considering a new "Southeast Asian Association for Regional Cooperation" (privately termed SEAARC), little more seems to have been achieved until the end of 1966.

The reasons for the delay centered on Indonesia and the question of precisely in what way Djakarta would associate itself with states that were already members of ASA.[12] The problem essentially was whether Indone-

---

represent a change in policy, for until 1963, its leaders had carefully avoided anything approaching regional cooperation in Southeast Asia. The utility of this by-product became apparent in 1966–67, the period during which President Sukarno was gradually being toppled. It was possible for his successors during that uncertain time to speak about and work for regional cooperation without fear of breaking entirely new ground. The second useful by-product of the MAPHILINDO experience—and this may help explain why MAPHILINDO gained more attention than ASA—lay simply in the fact of Indonesia's participation. The dramatic Manila summit talks, which gave birth to MAPHILINDO, reminded observers once again of Djakarta's importance in the region. More specifically, MAPHILINDO helped to bring home the point that, without Indonesian participation, any effort at regional cooperation in Southeast Asia—such as that represented by ASA—would be at best a limited achievement.

[9] Malik, it should be pointed out, is a relative of the senior Malaysian civil servant responsible for foreign affairs, Tan Sri Ghazalie bin Schafie. In a conversation with this writer, Ghazalie described Malik as his "cousin," but I am not certain how close the family tie is. The two are, however, on a friendly basis, and Ghazalie feels quite at home in Malik's house.

[10] For reports on these negotiations and discussions, see articles in *The Washington Post*, May 19, 1966, and May 31, 1966, as well as *The New York Times*, June 7, 1966.

[11] *The New York Times*, June 3, 1966.

[12] In an interview in October, Thanat Khoman suggested that while there were difficulties, he expected to find a format for Indonesian participation in a "new Asian group" (conversation with the author, New York, October, 1966).

sian leaders, who believe that their nation is the natural "leader" of the region, would be willing to "ask" for membership in a new regional group. Such a request might have the appearance of humbling Indonesia before Malaysians and Filipinos, and, until Sukarno was removed, it was especially important to avoid any charge that Indonesia was aligning itself with Western-associated nations.[13]

By late in the summer of 1966, a way was found out of this dilemma, perhaps as a result of talks between Malik and Thanat Khoman. When Thanat arrived in Djakarta late in August, he said that part of his visit was in connection with an Asian search for a Vietnam solution, but that regional cooperation, too, was very much on the agenda.[14] When he was asked whether that meant SEATO, he said emphatically, "I did not come here to discuss SEATO." Indeed, only several days before Thanat's visit, the Foreign Minister of the Philippines (Narciso Ramos) had also visited Foreign Minister Malik in Djakarta. Their joint statement reaffirmed "the importance and urgency of meaningful regional cooperation among the countries of Southeast Asia, especially in the economic, social, technical, and cultural fields."[15] Given this background and given Thanat's reputation for extraordinary negotiating ability, as well as his strong personal interest in Southeast Asian regionalism, it seems quite certain that much of his discussion with Adam Malik was concerned with regionalism. Both ministers shared an interest in furthering the concept, but the question was who would act and when.

The approach that the two leaders apparently agreed upon called for Malik to make his views known to Thanat, who would then circulate a Thai invitation to the ASA members. This would avoid the necessity for Indonesia to "ask" for ASA membership. The invitation would also probably benefit from Thanat's prestige in both Malaysia and the Philippines.

The SEAARC Proposal

In late 1966 (probably in December), a "Draft Joint Declaration" was sent from Bangkok to Manila, Djakarta, and Kuala Lumpur.[16] The gist of the document can be summed up by saying that it represented a careful

---

[13] In March, 1966, while still in power, Sukarno attempted to persuade the Filipino government not to re-establish diplomatic relations with Malaysia (*The Washington Post*, March 8, 1966). By May, when his power was in its period of rapid decline, Sukarno expressed his discontent with the talks then taking place with Malaysian leaders in Bangkok. It was apparently at this time that the Indonesian President was requested to make no more speeches on foreign-policy subjects (*The Washington Post*, May 31, 1966).

In addition, as late as August, 1966, other leading Indonesians complained about the end of the confrontation, and they were not always leaders closely aligned with President Sukarno. For example, Mohammed Dahlan, Chairman of the central committee of the Muslim Scholars (a party that claims about 8 million members), demanded a return to the agreement signed in Manila in 1963. This called for elections in Sabah and Sarawak, and it implied that Indonesia should not establish peaceful relations with Malaysia until Sukarno's demands of three years before were satisfied.

[14] *The New York Times*, August 30, 1966.

[15] *The New York Times*, August 24, 1966.

[16] At this stage, Singapore, as a non-ASA member, was probably not contacted formally.

and conscious melding of the purposes of ASA, along with much of the style and flavor of MAPHILINDO.[17] The preamble, for example, is distinctly reminiscent of the phrases incorporated more than three years earlier in the Manila Declaration, and those sentiments—in contrast to the organizational format of MAPHILINDO—owed much of their inspiration to former Indonesian Foreign Minister Subandrio. Thus, when Subandrio met with the Malayan and Philippine Foreign Ministers in June, 1963, they issued a "Report," which declared: "The ministers were of one mind that the three countries share a primary responsibility for the maintenance of the stability and security of the area from subversion in any form or manifestation."[18] A few weeks later (at the end of July, 1963), Sukarno himself went to Manila, and, because he wanted a specific reference to foreign bases, even stronger phrases were incorporated. Filipino and Malaysian leaders, to mollify Sukarno, agreed to words on foreign bases unlike anything their governments had ever said before.

Today, it is very instructive to see how those 1963 Indonesian sentiments have stood the test of time, for they are almost identical with the words Thanat Khoman of Thailand used in his 1966 and 1967 drafts, which led to ASEAN. The 1963 Declaration read in part:

> The three heads of government further agreed that foreign bases—temporary in nature—should not be allowed to be used directly or indirectly to subvert the national independence of any of the three countries. In accordance with the principle enunciated in the Bandung Declaration, the three countries will abstain from the use of arrangements of collective defense to serve the particular interests of any of the big powers.[19]

In comparison, Thanat Khoman began his new "Draft Declaration" with these words:

> The Ministers of Foreign Affairs of Indonesia [and] Malaysia, the Secretary of Foreign Affairs of the Philippines . . . and the Minister of Foreign Affairs [of] Thailand, . . .
> Believing that the countries of Southeast Asia share a primary responsibility for ensuring the stability and maintaining the security of the area, . . .
> Being in agreement that foreign bases are temporary in nature and should not be allowed to be used directly or indirectly to subvert the national independence of Asian countries, and that arrangements of collective defense should not be used to serve the particular interest of any of the big powers.[20]

If a close comparison is made of the texts of MAPHILINDO, SEAARC, and, finally, ASEAN, the origins of at least the preamble of the new Southeast Asian group become very clear. Moreover, it is precisely the evident

[17] The "Draft Declaration" was shown to the author by an official of one of the foreign ministries, during a Southeast Asian visit in January, 1967.

[18] This also appears as Paragraph 4 in the Joint Communique of the Foreign Ministers Conference, Manila, June 7–11, 1963, and is published in *Malaya/Philippine Relations* (Kuala Lumpur, 1963), Appendix VII, p. 26. See also Gordon, *ibid.*, p. 102.

[19] Appendix VIII, *Malaya/Philippine Relations*, in Gordon, *ibid.*, pp. 100–104.

[20] From the draft, "Joint Declaration, Southeast Asian Declaration for Regional Cooperation," probably mid-December, 1966. It is also interesting to note that Indonesia is listed first in the "Introduction" to the Draft Declaration.

similarity with MAPHILINDO phrases that helped delay the establishment of ASEAN until August, 1967. Neither the Filipino nor the Malaysian government was initially enthusiastic over Thanat's effort to mollify
Indonesia again, even though the format for SEAARC did not borrow
much from MAPHILINDO other than the preamble. The rest of it, especially the structure of the group and its purposes, were clearly patterned
after ASA. In part, the misgivings of the Philippines probably derived from
President Marcos' tentative thoughts about proposing his own format for
regional cooperation and also from his uncertainty about the prospects for
Sukarno's return in Indonesia.[21]

In Malaysia, these same anxieties existed and were reinforced by the
prime minister's still negative view of Indonesia growing out of the confrontation. Thus, when Thanat Khoman wrote to Tunku Abdul Rahman
late in December, the premier began his reply with the phrase, "I have
certain grave misgivings." He went on to caution about the dangers of associating too closely with Indonesia: "As long as Sukarno is there . . . it
would be dangerous for us to embark on such an enterprise." But his letter
made it clear that more was involved in his negative response than merely
doubt about Sukarno's role and his potential return to power (still an
anxiety early in 1967). The Tunku took pains to reaffirm in this letter his
enthusiasm and interest in ASA. He wrote to Thanat: "I would not like to
see us sacrifice ASA . . . to create a wider regional association, which I am
convinced in the present circumstances has little chance of success." He
added, finally, that while it was a noble goal to somehow try to help Indonesia (and the stability of the region, too) by incorporating it into a new
regional group, this could be a mixed blessing. The Tunku apparently felt
that Indonesia's own interests and behavior might so diverge from those of
the three ASA nations that the risks involved in a new regional group
might outweigh any potential benefits. Among other things, he reminded
Thanat, "Indonesia's behavior has been to leave any organization when
and as it suits her."[22]

Over the next six months, these misgivings were softened, largely because

[21] Early in 1966—shortly after President Marcos took office in Manila—he asked
for and received from Foreign Secretary Ramos a memorandum outlining a Philippines
posture toward regionalism. Ramos wrote that "if it is intended to divorce from. the
past and from existing rivalries in Southeast Asia power politics, there seems to be a
need for a fresh approach to Asian problems under the new administration." After
noting that Manila was well suited to take a lead in new approaches, partly because
the Asian Development Bank had just been established there, Ramos wrote that "the
fact remains, however, that with the prospective resumption of normal relations between
the Philippines and Malaysia, the reactivation of the ASA will become a pressing issue.
While the Philippines is committed to all that the ASA stands for, it would not be to
its national interest to pronounce a sentence of doom for MAPHILINDO, which Indonesia might construe as a rebuff against her.

"Hence, it seems rather advisable if in favoring its reactivation, ASA *should be spelled
out as a transitory arrangement, a stepping stone, toward the formation of an organization of Asian states*, with a call for wider collective action to achieve Asian progress."
("Memorandum from Secretary of Foreign Affairs, Narciso Ramos, to President Ferdinand Marcos, January 6, 1966. Subject: Proposed Organization of Asian States" [type-
script, emphasis added].)

[22] From a draft letter of January 3, 1967 (typescript).

Thailand and Indonesia were willing to give a remarkable amount of time and energy to the task of creating a new multination association for regional cooperation. Indonesian Foreign Minister Adam Malik and his senior deputy (Anwar Seni) made a series of trips throughout the region in April and May with two purposes in mind. The first was to inform the neutral states of Burma and Cambodia of Indonesia's plans for a new regional group, for Djakarta hoped either to gain their support or at least persuade them not to condemn the effort publicly. The second purpose was to undertake with Thai, Malaysian, and Filipino leaders the specific negotiations necessary to launch the regional group.[23]

Thanat and Malik divided their responsibilities, and both tasks were reasonably well accomplished. Malik, while unable to gain Burmese or Cambodian participation (unlikely anyway at that early state), was pleased to have their assurances of friendly interest in the proposal.[24] Moreover, Thanat, almost up to the eve of ASEAN's creation in August, was required to bend all his efforts to persuade the Malaysian prime minister to accept Indonesia's new foreign-policy course. Because many others in the Malaysian government were already prepared—even anxious—to resume intimate ties with Indonesia, this problem was more superficial than real, for the generation that will succeed the Tunku in Malaysia's political and bureaucratic elite contains many persons who already identify very closely with Indonesia. Looking ahead into the 1980's, one of the most promising aspects of Southeast Asian cooperation is precisely the strong likelihood that Indonesian-Malaysian relations will be remarkably close. In 1967, however, the Tunku's understandable pride in having initiated the steps that led to ASA also led him to resist its inevitable disappearance once ASEAN was formed.

Thanat Khoman, on the other hand, while equally responsible for ASA's creation, understood even in 1959 that it was not to be seen as an end in itself. To Thanat, regional cooperation is only an instrument for far more basic political purposes. Thus, in 1967, and in contrast to the Tunku, Thanat was quite willing to bury ASA in favor of a wider grouping. He recognizes and stresses that tight bipolarity in Asia is not only dangerous, but especially uncomfortable to Thailand, and for that reason he hopes for a return to multipolarity as the structure of East and Southeast Asian international affairs. Multipolarity requires a more cohesive Southeast Asia, and it is with that goal also in mind that Thanat has so enthusiastically worked for regional cooperation.

[23] Reports of Malik's travels appeared in *Antara* (Indonesia's press agency) dispatches of April 12, 16, and 21, 1967. In Bangkok, Malik announced that preparations for the new group "are almost complete," and added that it would cover technical, economic, and cultural fields and "be more perfect than MAPHILINDO."

[24] Accounts of Malik's talks in Rangoon and Phnom Penh, as well as letters between General Suharto and Prince Sihanouk, appear in *Antara* dispatches of May 16, 25, and 31, 1967. Prince Sihanouk, in a reference to the divisions resulting from the Vietnam war, said, "Cambodia will fully cooperate with Indonesia to promote the cooperation in question after all nations in Southeast Asia have again received their free and complete independence."

The Meaning of ASEAN

The creation of ASEAN must be seen as something of a triumph for aspirations that the Thai foreign minister has entertained for several years. But it is potentially much more than that, for ASEAN is the first *general*, *indigenous*, and politically *neutral* effort in Southeast Asian regional cooperation.

ASEAN must be distinguished from regional groups devoted to a specific functional purpose, such as the Mekong Development Committee and the Southeast Asian Ministerial Conferences on Education (SEAMES) and Transport. Such bodies have the support of the particular ministries involved and can probably achieve given cooperative tasks of importance, but there is little evidence that they attract wide and high-level participation and interest in each government. In a word, and in contrast to the sort of political support that led to ASA and ASEAN, such single-purpose ventures are narrowly based, functionally specific organizations.

The *indigenous* nature of ASEAN must also be stressed, for this is the single most important characteristic missing from all other efforts at "regional" cooperation. Even the recent Ministerial Conferences on Transport and Education just referred to, to say nothing of the obvious cases of SEATO and the Colombo Plan, have been based to some extent on the support and frequently the initiative of states outside Southeast Asia. The Ministerial Conferences draw at least half of their fiscal support from the United States alone, and it is altogether unlikely that they could exist without the constant encouragement of their patron. This is not to condemn such efforts—but it must be stressed that much of my judgment that ASA and ASEAN reflect very high-priority interests of the regional states themselves stems from the consideration that the two organizations are altogether the work of Southeast Asian governments.

Finally, much of the potential significance of ASEAN derives from Indonesia's participation, which helps remove the "Western" stigma that afflicted ASA. ASEAN represents a major departure in Indonesia's foreign policy, and, for the first time, it is possible to expect that its considerable foreign-policy energies can be channeled into endeavors within the region. For its own benefit, moreover, participation in ASEAN opens the possibility for Indonesian collaboration with states that have had successful developmental experience. Thailand and Malaysia stand out in this regard, and the statement of ASEAN's "aims and purposes" suggests that—like ASA—the group will emphasize pragmatic goals.

ASEAN is still quite young, and it is too soon to make any definitive judgments about the implementation of the organization's statement of purposes. At the same time, the mere statement of these reflects such a major change in the Asian environment—compared with even a decade before—that no analyst can ignore the political forces behind them. It is clear by now that leaders in Southeast Asia are no longer content to have their region regarded as another Balkans, and it is also apparent that previously vague calls for "Asian regionalism" have found in Southeast Asia a very receptive environment. In many cases, the explanation is the simple recognition that the crucial task of Southeast Asian leadership—development—can probably be greatly aided by collaboration with nearby states. In addition, for some of these leaders who recognize that another major task is provision for security, collaboration with neighbors seems an equally logical step.

It is no accident, for example, that both Malaysian and Indonesian leaders have begun to speculate openly about "regional defense collaboration," and this can be attributed to recent changes in their perceptions of the Asian environment.[25] The most significant change is the disappearance of certain fictions in the postwar world. In the Malaysian case, the fiction was that Britain would continue to look after the security of Malaya and Singapore. Malaysian leaders must now realize that Britain simply does not have the capacity to play that role. In the Indonesian case, the fiction was that exhorting "Afro-Asian solidarity" was identical with having a foreign policy. For different reasons, both states are now forced to recognize that they must act to insure their own security. Since they cannot rely permanently upon the United States for this purpose, they have almost simultaneously begun to search for ways in which regionalism can help resolve their security problems.

The significance of ASEAN is that it reflects these developments, which in turn reflect a fundamental change in the Asian political environment generally. This change was well summed up by President Johnson, when he said in 1966 that "the nations of Asia are casting off the spent slogans of earlier narrow nationalism. . . . One after another, they are grasping the realities of an interdependent Asia."[26]

PROSPECTS FOR REGIONAL COOPERATION: CONCLUSIONS

There is little reason to expect that the concept of regional cooperation will have application to the entire Asia-Pacific area during the next decade and into the 1980's. Instead, present trends show a very strong tendency toward cooperative efforts among the states of Southeast Asia—primarily among Indonesia, Thailand, Malaysia, the Philippines, and Singapore. It is possible, however, that in the wake of a Vietnam settlement, both Cambodia and Burma might also affiliate themselves with already initiated regional efforts. The states of Southeast Asia are the weakest in Asia, and, in strong contrast to both India and Japan, are precisely the states that can benefit most from cooperative efforts with their neighbors.

[25] The most specific endorsement for the concept has come from General Panggabean, Chief of the Indonesia Army staff, and generally regarded as the most influential officer after General Suharto. In his call for defense cooperation in the region, General Panggabean said, for example, that "like it or not, it is an absolute condition of peace and stability in Southeast Asia that the Southeast Asian nations themselves should have the ability to maintain their own defense. . . . Indonesia must play a role . . . consistent with its active and independent foreign policy." *Djakarta Times*, February 28, 1967.

[26] From the President's speech in Hawaii, October 17, 1966, in *The New York Times*, October 18, 1966.

The main uses of regional cooperation for these states will probably be found in two fields, both ultimately related to stability and security in the Asia-Pacific region. The first use is in the field of economic development, because a large number of Asian and Western specialists strongly believe that regional cooperation can bring marked advantages to relatively small developing states. States in Southeast Asia, with strong outside support, are already operating on this assumption. It is prudent to conclude that a more cohesive Southeast Asia, based on economic cooperation related to development programs, is a likelihood in the next several decades. To deny this is to deny the meaning of important steps taken since 1965, most notably the establishment of the Asian Development Bank (with very strong Japanese and American financial support), the creation of ASEAN, and the marked reduction in intraregional political tensions (as compared with the early 1960's). These steps reflect and represent the major political forces in Southeast Asian international affairs, and there are few indications that these forces will significantly decline during the next decade.

Consequently, although it is impossible to predict precisely the outlines of economic cooperation, it is reasonable to expect that by 1969–71 major planning steps will be completed to coordinate specific developmental efforts in Southeast Asia. It is likely that concrete measures for "harmonization" of industrial efforts, especially in certain light industrial fields, will be undertaken first. Similarly, early in the 1970's, measures can be expected to establish joint research centers, especially in fields related to the agricultural and industrial productivity of the region. Only in the late 1970's is it likely that intraregional trade patterns will be perceptibly affected by these and related steps. Nevertheless, it is possible to project that increased intraregional trade, especially in consumer goods and products of light and medium industry, will result from industrial programs even now under way, and industrial harmonization will accelerate this tendency.

By the early and mid-1980's, therefore, it is probable that Southeast Asia will show considerably greater economic interaction than is presently the case. The needed first steps, in terms of the likely direction of economic cooperation, have been taken in the 1960's. These have been the result of remarkable political support for the concept of cooperation even in a period when there has been little or no real achievement to show. If the products of economic cooperation are reflected in accelerated rates of economic growth, the present major justification for such cooperation, then it is reasonable to expect a continuation and probably an enhancement of political support for regionalism. Simultaneously, an improvement in economic conditions, while often itself the source of some dislocations and instabilities, should help reduce the appeals on which insurgents and subversives have relied since the 1950's.

Nevertheless, it has to be assumed that Southeast Asia will remain a relatively fertile field for subversive efforts through the 1970's. Combating subversion is already a high-priority concern of several Southeast Asian nations, and any benefits from patterns of economic interaction and political consultation probably will spur interest in regional defense measures. Interest in defense cooperation is already apparent, although only at the earliest stages of discussion. Compared to cooperative measures in trade and development, which could take concrete shape in the mid-1970's (because they have already been talked about for a decade), regional defense measures ought not be expected in the same time frame. Yet, the lines along which Southeast Asian defense collaboration could proceed are discernible even now, and the decision of Great Britain to withdraw militarily from Southeast Asia after 1971 is likely to accelerate the pace of cooperative defense planning. But that is the subject of another discussion that cannot be undertaken here. What can be said is that the increasing pace of efforts toward regional cooperation in Southeast Asia holds the potential for fulfilling the hope of the United States that multipolarity, rather than dangerous bipolarity, will once again characterize the international politics of East and Southeast Asia.

FIVE

The Quest for Economic Progress

In the final part of this collection of essays, we come face to face with one of the most pressing problems of contemporary Southeast Asia—the problem of economic progress. In the euphoria of the early days of Southeast Asian decolonization, much of the domestic policy of the underdeveloped states was based on the assumption that economic development was an almost automatic concomitant of political independence, and much of the policy of the developed world grew out of the equally fallacious assumption that the new states needed only a quick stimulant to enable their economic machines to take off into self-sustained growth. It was satisfying to think in terms of another Marshall Plan without stopping to consider the profound differences between industrial Europe and pre-industrial Southeast Asia. In Europe, the industrial machine only needed repairs; in Southeast Asia it had to be built. The implications of this simple observation are enormous. How does one create an industrial machine in an agricultural setting? Where is the skilled and semiskilled manpower to come from? What happens if the potential labor force resists the attempts to industrialize led by the Westernized elite? How can one account for individual successes and failures in Asia? To what extent is economic change taking place even among the most apparently static societies? What are the implications of this for the future?

In this concluding part, many important subjects must remain untouched. In order to avoid technical essays on economics, I have excluded a number of valuable studies dealing with the goals, strategies, and performances of economic systems, and I have, perhaps inexcusably, not ventured into the entire field of demography and population growth; however, the reader with more specialized interests can find several of the most important works concerning these subjects in the bibliography at the end of this volume. Here we shall focus on economic development as it affects the individual, who is unhappily too often lost in the welter of aggregate data detailing economic performances.

The first two essays deal with the long-debated problem of the apparent conflict between social values associated with preindustrial society and those of an industrialized one, and, so far as Southeast Asia is concerned, both reach rather pessimistic conclusions. Mya Maung concerns himself with the question largely from the perspective of the peasant and concludes that Burma is no exception to the general rule that pretechnological values impede economic modernization. Eliezar Ayal, in the second essay, qualifies this generalization somewhat in demonstrating that an indigenous value system may be developmental or antidevelopmental, and, to support his thesis, he draws on the experiences of Japan after the Meiji Restoration and Thailand after the coup of 1932. This essay is instructive not only for its qualifications of the more general thesis about pretechnological value systems, but also because it raises some doubts about the utility of the "Japanese model" of economic development, which is frequently mentioned as useful for providing some guidelines for the developing economies of Southeast Asia. In the third essay, Michael Moerman provides us with the anthropologist's worm's eye view of economic change, and here we discover that, regardless of how it might look on the surface, significant changes are taking place in the realm of values. Meaningful modernization has been introduced in rural Thailand and is being accepted, not through a revolutionary overthrow of the old order, but through a subtle reinterpretation of the still-accepted indigenous values. (In an essay above on Muslim education in Indonesia [Chapter 14], Clifford Geertz reached similar conclusions.) In summary, these three essays show us that some kinds of indigenous values may indeed obstruct rapid economic change, but the societies of Southeast Asia are far from static; change is occurring, though it may be difficult to measure or even to discern.

In the final essay of this volume, we shift from the level of the individual to the level of the total economic system and look at the statistical results of the quest for economic progress in Southeast Asia. In an essay that has stood the test of time, Douglas S. Paauw confirms the findings of Mya Maung, Ayal, and Moerman: Economic advancement in Southeast Asia is a slow and painful experience. Some states have performed more impressively than others, but Paauw points out that much of this stems from rehabilitation of the economies, not from new growth. Paauw's final caution—that there is little reason for optimism about continuing self-sustained growth in most Southeast Asian economies—has unfortunately been borne out by more recent data, some of which are presented briefly in the appended statistical summary.

37

CULTURAL VALUE AND ECONOMIC
CHANGE IN BURMA*

MYA MAUNG

The process of economic change can only be understood as an inextricable part of a more complex process of cumulative social change. In Burma, as in any society, economic change occurs in conjunction with changes in other sectors of the society. Throughout the period of independence, however, successive governments of the Union of Burma seem to have maintained a position contrary to the preceding assumption, either because of political necessity or nationalism. The objective of a *Pyidawtha* (welfare state) and the recent proclamation of the "Burmese Way to Socialism" are based on the assumption that it is possible to have radical economic changes while keeping the traditional cultural values largely intact. This apparent contradiction in approach to economic development is similar to the resistance to social change that can be observed in many less-developed traditional societies, where one can see conflicting ideologies simultaneously being pursued.

One of the problems of economic change in Burma is the price, in terms

* Reprinted by permission of the author and the publisher from *Asian Survey*, IV (March, 1964), 757–64.

of cultural change, that must be paid in order to achieve economic progress. In Burmese society, the impact of Buddhism[1] upon the economic life
of the people has been uniformly great. Indeed, a glance at the recent history of Burma indicates that the role of religion and the cultural values
that it fosters has been immense in every phase of social and political
emancipation. Resistance to British rule took the form of politico-religious
organizations, such as the Young Men's Buddhist Association (since 1906)
and the General Council of Buddhist Associations (since 1912). Looking
at the history of independent Burma, the popularity of the ex-Prime Minister U Nu, the policy of adopting Buddhism as the state religion, and the
failure thus far of the Communists bear witness to the fact that Buddhism
is the basic cultural substratum in Burma. As J. L. Christian rightly remarks: "To a Burman, Buddhist and Burmese are almost interchangeable.
Buddhism has come into the life of these people as religion has rarely
affected the life of any other nation."[2]

In order to relate the impact of Buddhist cultural values upon questions
of economic change, three fundamental factors will be considered, borrowing from the concept of the "will to economize" advanced by W. A.
Lewis.[3] Namely, we seek to evaluate the impact of Buddhist cultural values
upon the attitude toward material goods, the availability of opportunities,
and the stimulation of effort.

For the time being, we are not concerned with differentiating among
classes or groups with respect to the desire for material well-being. First,
the general image of the people regarding betterment of material life must
be examined in relation to the ascetic codes of Buddhism. It is undeniable
that the principles of Buddhism, through such concepts as the "Four Noble
Truths," *samsara* (*thanthayah*), and *karma* (*kan*), prescribe a lesser valuation of material goods than of the ascetic life.[4] In essence, the Four Noble
Truths stress an outlook of indifference to one's role and status in society.
By the First Noble Truth (*dokka*), life and existence are explained as the
sum total of sufferings, the prolongation of which lies in the desire for
material wealth (*tanha*).[5] The philosophy of "becoming," as put forth in
terms of *samsara*, and the Doctrine of the Three Signata[6] suggest the futility of a desire for goods, wealth, position, and power, all of which are
impermanent (*anatesa*). The concept of *karma* likewise emphasizes the
uselessness of effort to improve one's economic position in the absence of a
good *kan*, which one inherits from the previous life. To what extent these
cultural values have a dampening effect on economic motivation in Burma

[1] I shall confine myself to the *Theravada* Buddhism as actually practiced in Burma.
[2] J. L. Christian, *Burma* (London: Collins, 1945), p. 48.
[3] See W. A. Lewis, *The Theory of Economic Growth* (Homewood, Ill.: Richard D.
Irwin, 1955), p. 23.
[4] The words in parentheses are Burmese variations of Pali.
[5] See, for a detailed account, Ledi Sayadaw, "Manual of the Four Noble Truths,"
translated in *The Light of the Dhamma*, VI:1 (Rangoon: Union of Burma Buddha
Sasana Council, 1959).
[6] See Bhikkhu Ananda Metteyya, *The Religion of Burma* (Madras: Theosophical
Publishing House, 1929), pp. 112–78.

is difficult to determine in measurable quantities, yet their qualitative effect on Burmese economic life can be assumed to be considerable. One may, of course, concur with Lewis that their effect is insignificant when opportunities to improve the standard of living are available. Yet, this cannot be assumed for tradition-directed social groups, whose input of effort is a function of the degree of difficulty in the procurement of material goods.

Direct contact with the rural population of Burma would seem to confirm the observation made by J. G. Scott more than fifty years ago: "If anyone escaped the curse of Adam, it is the Burman. He does not need to earn his bread with the sweat of his brow, and riches having no attraction for him, when his patch of paddy has been reaped."[7]

This, indeed, poses the question of the role of acquisitiveness in Burmese cultural life, even when opportunities to enhance material well-being are open to the rural villager. Lack of economic anxiety, which has so often been attributed to Burmese society, may either be caused by the affluence of basic necessities or by the limited horizon of desire for better living imposed by the cultural values. Both factors seem to operate strongly on the economic motivation of the average Burmese, and in some cases the latter exercises a greater influence. For example, when the author interviewed a number of villagers who belonged to agricultural producers' cooperatives concerning their attitude toward equality of effort, ability, and status, most of the answers were directly oriented to Buddhist cultural values, in which inevitable differences of role and status among individuals are determined not by the effort of the present life but by the immutable law of *karma* in its impersonal and determinate form.[8] This attitude, of course, in no way deters a Burmese cultivator from enjoying credit privileges or other forms of governmental support that involve little or no effort. The crucial point is not whether the Burmese want to improve their living conditions,[9] but rather the extent to which their valuation of such opportunities affects their incentive to work. My findings on agricultural cooperation in Burma suggest that the leisure-preference function of an average Burmese cultivator is determined by at least three important factors: the festive environment molded and preserved by the Buddhist culture, the lack of challenge that can be traced to certain cultural values, and the recent liberal economic policy of the government with respect to easy procurement of credit and other forms of support.

Indeed, the social environment of Burma is imbued with cultural activities that encourage heavy spending on religious festivities. The Buddhism of Burma is often described as a religion of gaiety and festivities[10] that seems to encourage spending rather than saving. This is closely linked to the norms of conduct and the philosophy of being that are an integral part

[7] Shwe Yoe J. G. Scott, *The Burman, His Life and Notions* (London: Macmillan, 1910), p. 67.

[8] These interviews were part of a study of agricultural cooperation in Burma financed by The Asia Foundation during 1961–62.

[9] See Lewis, *op. cit.*, p. 25.

[10] R. L. Slater, *Paradox and Nirvana*, Ph.D. Dissertation (New York: Columbia University, 1950), p. 23.

of Buddhism. Under the concept of *samsara,* life and existence are conceived as a whirlpool of birth-death-rebirth, or a cycle of incarnation in the thirty-one planes of existence.[11] The escape from such a wheel of endless existence, the route to *nirvana* (*nibban*), lies not in attachment to property or wealth or in the accumulation of material wealth but in the performance of deeds of merit (*a-lhu* or *dahna*), one of the Eightfold Noble Paths in Buddhism. For instance, a Burmese Buddhist often saves a large sum of money earned from years of toil, which is then spent on the initiation of his son into Buddhist novicehood or on his daughter's ear-boring ceremony. The cost of such ceremonies ranges from hundreds to thousands of *kyats,* depending on the social and economic position of the family concerned.[12] Since the annual per capita income of Burma is around 200 *kyats* (roughly U.S. $40 at the official exchange rate), such expenses constitute a tremendous cultural obstacle to economic change in the direction of frugality or private capital formation. From the daily offering of rice to monks to ostentatious spending on cultural festivities, thrift for a better economic future in the present life is almost meaningless, since the objective in spending on cultural occasions is the attainment of a good *karma* in the future, which stretches to life after death or to the achievement of *nirvana.*

The lack of challenge in Burma is both cultural and economic. The cultural inhibition against acquisitiveness manifests itself in the attitude toward entrepreneurship, which traditionally is given a low status in the Burmese social structure. Although this attitude toward entrepreneurship may not apply as strongly to the urban population, the educated class, and the articulate section of the population of Burma as a whole as it does to the tradition-abiding rural population, the attitude toward business in general, called in Burmese *konthe,* bears the mark of traditionalism. Traditionally, the class of traders (*a-the*) has been looked upon as socially inferior to the classes of those who serve the king (*min-mhu-done*), ordinary civil employees (*a-mhu-done*), and even cultivators.[13] The pervasive carry-over effect of such a social preference-function has been strengthened further by colonial rule and by socialist criticisms of capitalists; and, in modern Burma such professionals as lawyers, magistrates, civil servants, military officers, and teachers are much more highly esteemed than businessmen. These professions symbolize authority, power, and prestige, which once were the monopoly of the Europeans,[14] and which, moreover, are not so conspicuously acquisitive and deviant from the traditional norms. Even these professions lack challenge in terms of competition and performance of ability, since traditional outlooks and methods still persist strongly. In teaching, administration, and official enterprises, for instance, disagreement, skepticism, and criticism are rare. Traditionally, the status of teacher, parent, or elder is considered as equal to that of the Buddha, whose authority is final

[11] Refer to Narada Thera, "Outline of Buddhism," *The Light of the Dhamma,* XI:2, *op. cit.* (1954).

[12] The minimum cost averages around 500 *kyats.*

[13] See Shwe Yoe, *op. cit.,* chapter 45.

[14] See Theodore Morgan, "The Economic Development of Ceylon," *The Annals,* CCV (1956), 96.

and unchallenged. Moreover, the impact of colonial rule with absolute authority of the superior continues to prevail in many aspects of administration.

Hirschman's thesis of group-focused image in a transitional traditional society applies forcibly in its particular aspect of intolerance to individual deviation in performance based upon ability from the norms of conduct approved by the society at large.[15] Thus, in contemporary Burma, students, the newly educated, and those who are educated and trained abroad, constitute the most frustrated group. The recurrent student strikes are in part a manifestation of rebellion against authority in a deviant mood, although, in another sense, they also represent resistance to change. Since independence, the socialist mass-education movements in Burma have produced a glut of educated unemployed after the vacancies demanded or created by economic and social programming have been filled.[16] This phenomenon of a reserve army of the educated unemployed is a serious social and economic problem, requiring an adjustment in the rate of expansion in human resources to the rate of development of the country.[17] The rate of expansion in human resources not only requires the over-all expansion of education but also necessitates certain cultural changes in the acceptance of new values attached to professions that may be against accepted traditional norms. The lack of challenge or demand in a society with rigid patterns of social approval of professions is even more a problem of cultural change than of economic development.

The lack of challenge in Burma is also a normal economic condition, which is best exemplified in the proud Burmese saying that there are no deaths due to starvation in Burma. This is not an overstatement; even in its worst economic crisis, Burma has never faced famine conditions like those of its giant neighbors, China and India, which have been plagued by famine throughout their history. This sufficiency of basic necessities is one factor responsible for the lack of economic anxiety in Burmese society. Yet its significance must not be exaggerated, for many countries with a similar or even better state of natural affluence have made longer strides in economic development. The real economic challenge to the Burmese has been posed by the economically more aggressive Indian and Chinese communities, whose dominance of trade, industry, and even agriculture has been one of the hardest problems to solve in independent Burma. This situation has led to a series of agrarian reforms, cooperative movements, nationalization of land, and socialization of trade and industry. Despite these measures, Burmese entrepreneurship has still lagged far behind that of the Indians and Chinese in Burma. Even with the stupendous assistance of the government in recent years, the grip of the money-lenders on the Burmese economic life is far from being removed. The problem of indebtedness,

15 See A. O. Hirschman, *The Strategy of Economic Development* (New Haven: Yale University Press, 1959), pp. 11–14.
16 See Hla Myint, "The Universities of Southeast Asia and Economic Development," *Pacific Affairs*, XXXV (Summer, 1962), 116–27.
17 *Ibid.*, pp. 398–400.

agricultural indebtedness in particular, has remained unsolved in Burma. The Burmese nationalist leaders trace the roots of this problem to the colonial heritage and the capitalist economic organization that accompanied colonialism, leading to the exploitation of the majority by a few.[18] But this ignores the role that cultural factors have played in encouraging indebtedness. The Report of the Burma Provincial Banking Enquiry Committee in the 1930's laid stress on the Burmese cultural pattern of extravagant spending as one of the causes of agricultural indebtedness.[19] Even today, in the so-called socialist economy of Burma, where the primary and secondary economic sectors are directly controlled by the state, more than 50 per cent of the cultivators are found to be consistently in debt, private or governmental.[20] Due to the enormous accumulation of interest rates on governmental loans which were in default of repayment, the direct governmental loans had to be written off with effect from September 30, 1961.[21]

In order to solve the age-old problem of agricultural indebtedness and landlessness, the successive governments of Burma have nationalized the land and relied upon the cooperative approach on a grand scale. From 1940 to 1961, the number of cooperative societies rose from 2,047 to the phenomenal figure of 11,865 societies.[22] It must be noticed, however, that only about 40 per cent of the societies on the roll in 1960–61 were actually working societies. The Department of Cooperative Societies and the State Agricultural Bank are the two most important governmental organizations designed to aid the agriculturalists through a liberal credit policy. It has been found that the liberal credit policy and the large-scale farm-support programs, through such agencies as the Agricultural and Rural Development Corporation and the Department of Agriculture and Forests, have not been particularly effective in stimulating efforts to improve agricultural yields. Indeed, they seem to encourage a reduction of effort because of the availability of easy credit and other privileges.[23] The continuous support of the government in agriculture and industry alike has augmented the spirit of dependency that is deeply rooted in the Burmese family's structure. For example, a large majority of the members of agricultural producers' cooperatives believe that cooperation is the task and responsibility solely of the state.[24]

The problem of indebtedness is not only confined to the rural areas but

[18] See *The Land Nationalization Act of Burma, 1948* (Rangoon: Government Printing and Stationery, 1950), p. 2. Also, *Pyidawtha Conference, Resolutions and Speeches* (*August 4–17*) (Rangoon: Ministry of Information, 1952).

[19] *Report of the Burma Provincial Banking Enquiry Committee* (*1920–1930*) (Rangoon: Government Printing and Stationery, 1931), I, 55–64.

[20] Estimated on the basis of my findings.

[21] Government of the Union of Burma, *Announcement No. 2 of the Ministry of Agriculture and Forests* (Rangoon: January 31, 1962).

[22] *The Union of Burma Co-operative Manual* and *Reports on the Working of Cooperative Societies* (Rangoon: Government Printing and Stationery, 1948, 1951, and 1961).

[23] Based upon my survey on agricultural cooperation.

[24] More than 95 per cent of the members of producers' cooperatives expressed this view.

also extends to the urban population. The outright spending of a year's earnings at the end of each harvest in rural areas has its urban counterpart in expenditures for movies, Burmese entertainments, such as *pwes,* and other cultural festivities. For the government to permit such cultural patterns of spending while attempting to effect radical economic changes without concomitant cultural transformation, is more utopian than realistic.

The cultural resistance to economic change in Burma is provided by the three most outstanding institutional factors: religion and the clerical order, nationalism and the political leadership, and traditionalism and the uneducated masses. This is not to deny that Buddhism in Burma contains certain dynamic elements that can be made to be compatible with modern economic life, but rather to assert that the bright image of achieving economic development without impairing the traditional culture[25] is not as simple and easy as it is assumed to be by the Burmese government. To embrace and practice a socialist economic system may not be so difficult on the leadership level, but incorporating modern socialist values into the traditional society of Burma on the cultural level must be based upon the criterion of "social acceptability."[26] Unless this is taken into serious consideration in the formulation of economic policy, the economic programming will not achieve the results expected. The government of the *Pyidawtha* Burma and the current Revolutionary Council Government seem to follow an identical policy in their utilization of nationalistic and traditionalist slogans in appealing to the masses to endorse their socialist ideology. The official philosophy of the *Pyidawtha* government was stated thus: "The new Burma sees no conflict between religious values and economic progress. Spiritual health and material well-being are not enemies: they are natural allies."[27]

Similarly, the present government has declared in "The Burmese Way to Socialism" that: "In whatever situations and difficulties the Revolutionary Council may find itself it will strive for advancement in accordance with times, conditions, environment and ever-changing circumstances, *keeping at heart the basic interests of the nation.*"[28]

Upon reading the socialist proclamations of the governments, one perceives an uneasy sense of contradiction between two extremes: radicalism in economic change and conservativism in cultural change. This is reflected in the term "the Burmese Way to Socialism," by which capitalism is rigor-

25 See B. F. Hoselitz, "Non-Economic Barriers to Economic Development," *Economic Development and Cultural Change,* No. 1 (Chicago: University of Chicago, March, 1952), p. 11.

26 See E. E. Hagen, "The Allocation of Investment in Underdeveloped Countries, Observations Based on the Experience of Burma," *Investment Criteria and Economic Growth* (Cambridge, Mass.: Massachusetts Institute of Technology Press, 1954), p. 60.

27 *Pyidawtha, The New Burma* (London: Hazel Watson and Viney, Ltd., 1954), p. 10.

28 *The Policy Announcement of the Revolutionary Council: The Burmese Way to Socialism* (Rangoon: The Revolutionary Council, April 30, 1962) (in Burmese), point 4, or *The Philosophy of the Burma Socialist Programme Party: The System of Correlation of Man and His Environment* (Rangoon: Ministry of Information, 1963), p. 44.

ously abused and rejected, although in cultural transformation, traditionalism is discordantly tuned to the radical philosophy of socialism. The abuses of cutthroat capitalism, private property, and profit-motivation are exposed and explained through the traditional Buddhist concepts of suffering (*dokka*), greed (*loba*), and immorality of conduct (deviation from *thila*).[29] The Marxist theses of historical change, exploitation, and dialectic method are introduced and explained under the cloak of impermanency (*a-nate-sa*) and the Buddhist metaphysical concept of the world of being (*loka*). The best examples are to be found in the recent book published by the Ministry of Information entitled *The System of Correlation of Man and His Environment*, which states: "In any case, whatever the beginning of man might be, the history of society is but the history of the bodily, verbal, and mental activities, in all the three periods of time, the past, the present, and the future, of man in whom *Rupa* and *Nama* (matter and mind) exist as correlates."[30]

Before the book reaches such a conclusion, however, it has already concluded a priori that "the flux of mind depends on his [man's] aggregate of matter; his mind cannot exist without this aggregate of matter on which it must continually depend."[31] This classic Marxian psychology is carried out further to enunciate the Law of Correlation by which the generic causality of man is reconciled with "the spiritual life of the preceding and the present periods."[32]

Whatever the political philosophy may be, the primary issue of economic development in Burma is a problem of change that must be no less cultural than economic. If the alleged environmentalist theories of Marx were correct, perhaps the problem of cultural change as a time-consuming process could be discarded. It is the opinion of this study that such a philosophy may be justified on nationalist political grounds, but that in reality cultural change and economic development must exist as correlates in the cumulative process of social change. Whether or not the political leadership can relate the traditional cultural values to the modern socialist environment in actual policy implementation is for the future to see. The basic dilemma of Burma in modernizing its society is the political and cultural necessity of preserving the traditional heritage and the need to introduce and diffuse modern ideas, socialist or others, technology, and values to achieve economic progress. In this respect, Burma is no exception to the problem of cultural change or cultural resistance to economic change that has been experienced by all pretechnological societies.

[29] *Ibid.*, pp. 43–47.
[30] *Ibid.*, p. 38.
[31] *Ibid.*, p. 3.
[32] *Ibid.*, p. 15.

38

VALUE SYSTEMS AND ECONOMIC DEVELOPMENT IN JAPAN AND THAILAND*

ELIEZER B. AYAL†

Traditional economic doctrine does not provide a satisfactory explanation for differences in economic behavior. The question is not whether economic factors are important determinants in the process of economic development. They are. There is no evidence that any appreciable economic development can take place without changes such as capital accumulation and developing money and commodity markets. The question is, rather, why some societies do, and others do not, behave in ways that bring about sustained economic progress. For this, we need to reach beyond the boundaries of economics. A full understanding of the causes for, and the process of, economic development requires interdisciplinary cooperation that would, hopefully, result in a comprehensive theory of social change.

* Reprinted by permission of the author and the publisher from *Journal of Social Issues*, XIX (January, 1963), 35–51.

† The research for this paper was financed by the Ford Foundation Faculty Research Fund, Department of Economics, The University of Michigan. The author is indebted to Professors Clifford Geertz, Samuel P. Hayes, Michael Moerman, Chandler Morse, James N. Mosel, and Herbert Phillips for valuable comments. Special thanks are due to Dr. Alvan J. Obelsky for permission to utilize some material included in his Ph.D. thesis: "Pre-Conditions of Economic Development: An Analysis of the Japanese Case" (Ann Arbor: University of Michigan, 1961).

The aim of this paper is more modest. It seeks to demonstrate the important place that must be assigned the value system[1] in such a theory. It further supports the proposition that changes in political and social institutions, or investments by foreigners, will not, by themselves, bring about sustained economic development, unless the fundamental human values in the society are conducive to development.

This is done through a comparative study of two Asian countries that, while showing clear divergence in their economic performance, had many common features and faced similar external stimuli. The relevant external stimulus is the familiar one facing the underdeveloped countries—that of exposure to Occidental culture and challenge. That mere exposure to the West and the availability of Occidental technical knowledge and favorable natural resources do not insure development is a matter of historical record.[2] To avoid possible complications arising out of colonialism, the two Asian countries selected were those that remained politically independent —Japan and Thailand. Japan was the first non-Western country to achieve self-sustaining growth, while Thailand's economy still resembles that of its ex-colonial neighbors.

A Japan-Thailand comparison has numerous advantages. There was a striking chronological similarity in the histories of the exposure of the two countries to the West and in the nature of their contacts with the West. Both countries possess traditions of selective cultural borrowing over a long historical past, and both are within what might be loosely called the same general Oriental culture area (as opposed to the Western-Christian area). The similarities extend to factors often mentioned as important for the economic development of Japan: Both countries maintained their political independence; both were characterized by a homogeneous culture, awareness of national identity, a high degree of authority enjoyed by the central government, and an early realization by the rulers that it was imperative for national survival to learn Western methods. Even in more direct economic factors there were similarities, especially in that both had ample markets abroad for the principal foreign-exchange earner (silk for Japan and rice for Thailand).

In spite of these similarities, there was a wide disparity in the economic development of the two countries. The Japanese case represents an example of highly successful economic development involving a large part of

[1] For the purpose of this paper, the value system might be viewed as the syndrome of general rules, sanctions, and goals underlying the activities of a society. The term "institutions" in this paper refers primarily to concrete organizations. For example, the church is an institution, but its widely accepted precepts are part of the value system. The schools and the educational system are institutions, but what is being taught in the schools and the mutual expectations of the teachers and students reflect the value system. The structure of bureaucracy is an institution, but the prevailing concepts that guide actual superior-subordinate relationships are parts of the value system.

[2] See, for example, E. E. Hagen, "Changing Parameters into Variables," *American Economic Review*, Papers and Proceedings, May, 1960, pp. 623–28. He lists four countries by degree of exposure to the West: Indonesia, India, China, and Japan. The order of development seems to be in the opposite sequence.

the nation. In terms of the limited total resources, the rates of saving and investment in the first three decades after the Restoration were quite impressive. Significant progress was achieved through improvements in methods and techniques, best exemplified by agriculture. Between 1878–82 and 1913–17, net agricultural production increased by about 120 per cent. While there was an expansion of some 35 per cent in cultivated land, the bulk of the increase was a result of increased productivity. Ohkawa and Rosovsky[3] estimate the rise in land productivity during the period at 80 per cent, and of labor productivity at 136 per cent. This increase in productivity was primarily due to technological improvements, double-cropping, and better fertilizers, and involved relatively small investments.

Industries expanded rapidly, with the textile industry being the first to experience acceleration. Until World War I, however, industrial development was mostly in light and small-scale industry, much of it developing in the so-called traditional sector that involved numerous small-scale entrepreneurs. Heavy industry, although strongly encouraged by the government from the beginning of the Meiji period, developed more slowly but picked up vigorously with the advent of World War I. Economic historians (for example, Allen)[4] explain this time lag essentially by the higher cost of capital equipment required for such industries and the greater requirements for scientific knowledge and skilled technicians. Once these obstacles were overcome, however, the paucity of natural resources did not deter Japan from developing practically all modern branches of industry by engaging heavily in foreign trade.

Throughout the period under discussion, there was in Japan a very high rate of saving, both voluntary and forced, a high degree of plowback throughout the economy, with little spending on conspicuous consumption or luxuries, and a very vigorous absorption of Western techniques and methods. There was also an ample supply of entrepreneurs and innovators at all levels.

Thailand, too, did not stand still during this period. The data for Thailand are much more sketchy than those for Japan, but available evidence indicates that after the Bowring Treaty of 1855, which removed trade barriers, there was a fairly substantial increase in rice production. The labor for this was provided from these sources: the freeing of the slaves, increased population, substitutions of rice production for other crops, and some movement of farmers into the delta of the Chao Phraya River, where land more suitable for exportable rice was located. It would then be erroneous to say that the Thai farmers (the vast majority of the population) did not react positively to the market incentives provided by the growing external demand. The important thing, however, is that this reaction was confined to rice production. Moreover, there was no change in the methods and techniques of rice production, which were centuries old. From available

[3] Kazushi Ohkawa and Henry Rosovsky, "The Role of Agriculture in Modern Japanese Economic Development," *Economic Development and Cultural Change*, IX, No. 1, part II (October 1960), 43–68.

[4] G. C. Allen, *A Short Economic History of Modern Japan, 1867–1937* (Rev. ed., New York: Frederick A. Praeger, 1962).

data, we can say with some assurance that the productivity per acre either remained the same or even declined. The only other significant exports that showed some increase were tin and teak. But these industries were operated by aliens, mostly Chinese, and practically no Thais were involved in any stage of their production or sale. Whatever Thai manufacture existed, such as home-spinning, it declined rather than expanded. The only exception was some development of resident Chinese handicraft, in which no ethnic Thais were involved. The contrast between the two countries is clear.

The range of possible explanations for this wide divergence in economic development narrows down substantially by the similarities listed earlier. Assigning major responsibility to differences in climate and resource endowment is also ruled out, for reasons that have been dealt with by others.[5] We must, therefore, concentrate on factors that more directly condition, motivate, and channel human and social activities. Such include the value system, the personality traits, the social structure, and, to some extent, the institutional framework. In spite of the mutual interdependencies, especially in the long run, between these factors, I will concentrate on the value system as the one providing the most comprehensive explanation. Some oversimplification is unavoidable in a paper of this length, and the case for the value system is slightly overstated to drive home the point.

As for methodology, I am not following a current approach that takes a developed society as the model and judges the "nearness" of other countries to this ideal type as indicative of their development prospects. This approach is rejected mainly because it is by no means clear (1) what aspects of present-day modern, developed societies are the results and what are the causes of development; (2) what features of these societies, although present, were not contributory to, and could even have been a drag on, development. A good example is individualism, which is often mentioned as a factor favorable to or even essential for development. The present paper will in fact show that the great importance of individualism in the Thai value system was detrimental to the development of Thailand's economy.

An alternative method, and the one employed here, is to try and find some causal relationship between the value system and modes of behavior associated with economic development. The transmission of the general orientation of the value system into action is conceived here as being materialized through the intermediary of "propensities." This shorthand term stands for internalized, behavioristic, and instrumental values, or predispositions to action, which have their origin in the value system.

In order to facilitate the identification of the relevant elements in the value system, the following propensities were singled out as required for sustained economic development: to accumulate capital, to work systematically and diligently, to cooperate in organizing effort in pursuance of

[5] See, for example, Douglas H. K. Lee, *Climate and Economic Development in the Tropics* (New York: Harper, 1957), and Hagen, *op. cit.*

goals, and to innovate. While the specific nature of action indicated by the first three propensities is self-evident, a word about innovation is called for. It has been pointed out, in the literature discussing the nature of innovational and entrepreneurial activities, that there is a probable connection between the "original" technological innovations in Europe and European scientific and logical tradition. Here, however, we are concerned with "induced" development in underdeveloped countries. The distinction that is more relevant for these countries would be that between the adaptation, by an enterprising group or individual, of foreign technology to local conditions, and the adoption of these already adapted techniques by large segments of the rest of the population. The function of adapting the new technique might be called "secondary innovation" and the adoption by others, "acceptance of innovation."

My thesis here is that, in order for economic development to come about, it is essential that the value system fulfill two functions. First, it has to provide goals, either public or private, that can be promoted by increased production. The ultimate goals may be, but do not have to be, economic, but economic activity must be a path toward the achievement of the ultimate goals. They could be, for example, greater power and prestige, greater social welfare, and so on. Second, the value system must generate, include, or at least sanction the means—namely, the propensities, and the activities associated with them. The degree of fruition of the propensities in actual performance depends upon the environment, such as physical conditions, institutions, availability of knowledge, and the like. But without the appropriate value system, a favorable environment would not bring about development. The appropriate value system is then a necessary though not a sufficient condition for development.

The components of the value system may be identified primarily from religious (defined broadly) and ethical teachings. The justification for this procedure is based, in part, on practical considerations. Elements of the value system are generally seen in clearest and most easily identifiable form in the dominant religious and ethical movements. This need not commit us, however, to the role of religion as the major determining factor in the make-up of social values. It is reasonable to assume that religious beliefs affect the value system, but it is equally likely that values originating elsewhere are accommodated by the religious system. In either or both events, the social values of established traditional society can be identified, for the most part, within the body of prevailing religious teaching. It is necessary, at the same time, to be prepared for instances where a social value may, in fact, be present and motivate behavior without receiving ethical or religious sanction. In such instances, the particular value may, however, appear in marginal ethical movements that depart, to this extent at least, from the dominant system.

The remarkable economic performance of Japan in the Meiji period was preceded by a substantial array of economic activities during the pre-Meiji period, namely, before the big push provided by the Restoration. As a number of studies show,[6] commercial activities allied with a sophisticated credit system were already conducted on a large scale (these were only partly a result of the *sankin kotai* system); progressive agricultural techniques were widely disseminated, and manufacturing based on Western techniques was becoming a significant feature of clan activities early in the nineteenth century and onward. Thus, without slighting the substantial institutional changes effected during the Meiji period, we may observe that the factors operating to provide economic development were evident much earlier. This is consistent with my proposition regarding the crucial role of the pre-Meiji value system, whose relevant elements remained substantially the same for the Meiji period.

On the surface, the Japanese value system did not have a unifying focal point in a single religion, such as is provided by Theravada Buddhism in Thailand. There was a proliferation of religious and ethical sects throughout much of Japan's history, incorporating and reinterpreting the teachings of three major religions or ethical systems: Confucianism, Buddhism and Shintoism. There was, however, substantial agreement concerning ethical values, although different movements did not always give the same emphasis to the same ethical values.

The significant elements of the Japanese value system that can be readily identified were: *active* fulfillment of obligations of class status and loyalty, asceticism and frugality, development of expertise in carrying out one's tasks, and diligence in performing these tasks. The practical character of these values reflects the small regard the Japanese had, from earliest times, for the metaphysical and doctrinal aspects of religion, and testifies to the eminence of political values in the central value system.

The political orientation of the value system is evident in the schools of Confucianism and Buddhism that were most widely adopted, the nature of their evolution in the Japanese climate, and the form that Shinto assumed at its most highly organized stage. Often, the function of religion was merely to provide sanctions for forms of activity that the politically oriented value system encouraged; indeed, some secular obligations took on aspects of religious duty.

In the prevalent Japanese version of Confucianism, these values (especially political loyalty) were seen as necessary elements of a smoothly functioning organic society. Confucianism was metamorphized into an official ethic forming the basis for the system of administration and law throughout the Tokugawa and allied domains.[7] In Japanese Buddhism, behavior

---

[6] See especially: Thomas C. Smith, *The Agrarian Origins of Modern Japan* (Stanford, Calif.: Stanford University Press, 1958) and "The Introduction of Western Industry to Japan During the Last Years of the Tokugawa Period," *Harvard Journal of Asiatic Studies* (June, 1948), pp. 130–52; Eijiro Honjo, *Economic Theory and History of Japan in the Tokugawa Period* (Tokyo: Maruzen, 1943); Charles D. Sheldon, *The Rise of the Merchant Class in Tokugawa Japan: 1600–1868* (New York: J. J. Augustin, 1953).

[7] Even the *tozama* ("outside") feudal lords tended to follow rather closely the administrative pattern of the Tokugawa. See, for example, Kanichi Asakawa, *The Documents of Iriki* (New Haven, Conn.: Yale University Press, 1929), pp. 11–12. The result was that the system of administration and law, as well as the underlying ethical principles, were widespread and uniform.

consistent with the prevailing values became a means for acquiring religious merit.[8] Shinto was, in effect, a religious form of nationalism, clearly serving the function of intensifying the loyalty to the state. In all, the first claim to the loyalty of the individual or subcollectivity was held by the superordinate collectivity represented by its head, ultimately the emperor. This loyalty called for cooperation with other individuals in active performance of duty. In view of this, the apparent ease with which many Japanese transferred their loyalty from their own lords to the emperor or the national state is not surprising. They attempted to fulfill their duty now with the same intensity as before. Active loyalty became, as it were, second nature to them.

The clearest expression of the dominant values was to be found, however, not in the religious teachings but rather in the *Bushido,* the code of ethics for the *samurai* class. The *samurai* ethics provided the model for other ethical movements and the ideal ethical image for all social classes. It might be pointed out that the peculiarly activist nature of service based on loyalty, which received great emphasis in *Bushido* in particular, and the value system in general, had its derivation outside the system of religious belief.

For specific references to economic activities, we have to rely more on individual ethical movements, which were organized characteristically on a class basis. While for most purposes these movements were but branches of the dominant official ethic, emphasizing such virtues as diligence, abstinence, and loyalty to political authorities, they gave varying degrees of emphasis to the various virtues and included elements that were even sometimes deviant from the mainstream of official ethics. Judging from actual behavior, some of these deviant ideas were more representative of prevailing values than might be inferred from the size of these movements.

A good example is provided by attitudes toward commercial activities and the making of business profits, both of which were fairly widely engaged in during the Tokugawa period. The Buddhist *Shin* sect legitimized commercial activity, although it ran counter to the traditional Confucian and, for that matter, the stricter Buddhist views. Indeed, the successful accumulation of wealth through commercial endeavor became, in *Shin,* an index of religious merit in somewhat the same sense as in the "Protestant Ethic."[9]

Shingaku (not to be confused with *Shin*), which was primarily the ethical movement for the commercial urban class, provides another good example.[10] This was a highly eclectic and educational movement that sought

[8] Even some dissident Buddhist sects, especially the "pietiest" such as Jodo, Shin, and Nichiren, who refused at first to accede to the principle of the primacy of political loyalty to the Bakufu, devoted increasing (though secondary) attention to obligations of a political nature.

[9] The following is attributed to the early *Shin* leader, Rennyo: "If we engage in Business we must realize that it is in the service of Buddhism." Quoted in A. K. Reischauer, ed., "A Catechism of the Shin Sect," *Transactions of the Asiatic Society of Japan,* XXXVIII (1912), 384.

[10] For an excellent study of the movement, see Robert N. Bellah, *Tokugawa Religion* (Glencoe, Ill.: The Free Press, 1957), especially pp. 133–76. The present analysis of the Japanese value system has benefited throughout from this pioneering work.

to legitimize the role of the urban commercial class in a society where commercial activities, while in fact widespread and important, were beyond the pale of respected status. There is little in the movement that departs from the ethical principles already enunciated in the official doctrine, except for the defense of the legitimacy of business profit and of the useful role of the merchant class in society. It is characteristic that the arguments employed rely on a comparison of the role of the business class with that of the prestigious *samurai*. Business profit, for example, was equated with the *samurai* stipend, both representing necessary rewards for useful social functions performed.

Of special interest is the *Hotoku* movement, which addressed itself to the farmers. It interpreted the central values in terms that sound very much like our economic propensities. It had fundamental economic principles that revolved around increases in production and productivity. This was to be achieved through hard work, cooperation, and rigorous voluntary restriction of consumption.[11] While part of the surplus was destined for tax purposes, underlining the obligation to the state, the remainder was to be invested for increased productivity in subsequent periods. The peasant role was conceived as one of acceptance of the existing social order and values and the proper discharge of his specialized obligations within the total social scheme. Although *Hotoku* had only a small formal membership, its teachings emphasized, if overstated, fairly widespread interest in increased productivity and innovation in the Tokugawa farm communities.

The activist quality of the components of the value system can be seen in the concept of *on* (favors). The idea was that the individual, in coming into being or in accepting protection or status within a group, automatically becomes a recipient of favors and is thereby placed under obligation to the source of favors.[12] These obligations are met not by retiring from mundane activities but rather by service, by active physical participation. Although of secular origin, this quality also found expression in religious movements, most notably in the "Tosa School" and the *O-Yomei* variants of the official *Shushi*.

From this summary of the Japanese value system, we can see that the highest value was active loyalty to the superordinate collectivity that, during the Meiji Restoration, was explicitly identified with the emperor and nation. The strengthening of the nation and the maintenance of its power and prestige was the ultimate goal. The challenge presented by the Western powers threatened both and called for countervailing action. Because

11 Consider the following quotation attributed to Ninomya Sontoku, the founder of the movement: "Work hard, earn much, and spend little. Gather plenty of fuel, and burn as little as possible. This is the secret of making a country wealthy. . . . We must save and provide for the future by industrious effort, the earnings of this year providing for the necessities of next year. Saving is the virtue of self-denial." In R. C. Armstrong, *Just Before the Dawn, The Life and Works of Ninomya Sontoku* (New York: Macmillan Co., 1912), p. 232.

12 A schematic table listing the various kinds of obligations and their reciprocals is found in Ruth Benedict, *The Chrysanthemum and the Sword* (Boston: Houghton Mifflin, 1946), p. 116.

of the demonstrated interdependence between the economic and military power of the Western countries, modernization along Western lines seemed the obvious solution. The major contribution of the Meiji leaders, in this context, lay in the identification of the national goal with economic development. Thus, our first condition for development—that the value system's ultimate goals can be pursued through economic means—was fulfilled.

There is also strong evidence for our second requirement—that the value system promote and legitimize the means—namely, the economic propensities. The injunction that one has to work diligently at whatever task one is engaged in was universal both in the central value system and in the somewhat dissident movements. Almost as universal, especially because of its intimate link with the effective performance of loyalty, was the propensity to cooperate. The propensity to accumulate was explicit primarily in the non-*samurai* ethical movements. But its counterpart—the propensity to save—was implied in the teachings of asceticism that were an integral part of the central value system as well. The willingness of the Japanese to adopt Western methods, techniques, and customs ("propensity to innovate") was phenomenal. This was no new experience for the Japanese. The religious and some of the other elements of the value system were themselves an adaptation of imported ideas. While no explicit "value" of adopting new ideas can be pointed to, this theme was present throughout Japanese history.

All of the above was accentuated by what is probably the most important characteristic of the Japanese value system—the fundamental emphasis on activism. By dynamizing the activities indicated by the propensities, the emphasis on activism was responsible for the quick pace of Japanese development. The very occurrence of development in Japan could be ascribed to this factor. One specific example would suffice: Much has been made of the increasing loss of function and prestige suffered by the *samurai* as a major cause of Japanese development.[13] This, however, is only part of the story. The question is, why did the *samurai* not resign themselves to their new position, as happened to declining classes in a number of other countries, rather than look for unfamiliar ways to bring about change? I suggest that the explanation lies in the activist character of the value system, which was particularly strong among the *samurai* with their intense sense of duty.[14]

We have seen that in spite of the numerous historical similarities, including the time and nature of the Western challenge, no economic devel-

[13] See, for example, E. E. Hagen, "How Economic Growth Begins: A General Theory Applied to Japan," *Public Opinion Quarterly*, XX (1958), 389.

[14] It is very interesting to note that McClelland made a similar observation on Hagen's argument, and assigned the responsibility for the "frustration" of the *samurai* to their high need-achievement. (David McClelland, *The Achieving Society*, Princeton, N.J.: D. Van Nostrand, 1961, p. 370.) It would not be at all surprising to find close correlation between activism and McClelland's need-achievement.

opment similar to that of Japan has occurred in Thailand.[15] To this day, the exhortations, encouragement and direct participation in production by the Thai government have produced meager results. The Thai government has organized cooperatives, credit facilities, and industries, sent students abroad, invited foreign advisers, and otherwise followed rather closely the Japanese Meiji pattern. While some progress can be noticed, it is a far cry from the Japanese experience of even as far back as the Meiji period. The most noticeable difference is the almost complete absence of Thai entrepreneurs in all fields and at all levels (except, of course, traditional rice-farming, government bureaucracy, and some petty village trading). Available, albeit partly impressionistic, information leaves little doubt that much of the modest progress that has taken place in Thailand is due to ethnic Chinese and their descendants. An examination of the Thai value system will make clear the reasons for this state of affairs.[16]

In contrast with the Japanese multiplicity of organized religio-ethical groups, Thailand presented a highly simplified and uniform picture.[17] In many important respects, the Thai value system is inseparable from the Thai version of Theravada Buddhism, and one can learn a lot about the value system from its teachings. Practically every village had its Buddhist temple and priests, and the cycle of life of all status groups in society turned around activities directly or indirectly connected with Buddhism. It should be pointed out that we are interested in the Thai value system and not Buddhism as such. Thus, one could probably find in the value systems of non-Buddhist countries some aspects that bear close resemblance to those of the Thai. What is interesting in Thailand, however, is that the Buddhist teachings fit the value system hand and glove.

The Thai value system centers around personal values as opposed to the Japanese emphasis on political values. It requires very little in terms of obligation or commitment to other individuals or institutions. This is in complete accord with Buddhist teachings regarding the responsibility of the individual in working out his own *karma*. Thus, self-reliance and the avoidance of attachment, involvement, or emotional commitment are at the same time an essential part of the Thai value system and of Buddhist ethical teachings. The congruence between Buddhism and the Thai value system is much broader, of course. One Thai writer assesses the effect of Buddhism on Thai behavior in somewhat idealistic terms: "They are

[15] Much of the following still applies today, hence the frequent use of the present tense. Systematic research of Thai society and culture is of recent origin. However, statements made here have been checked with available material from the nineteenth century. Walter F. Vella's *Siam Under Rama III, 1824–1851* (Locust Valley, N.Y.: J. J. Augustin, 1957) and his sources were consulted for the historical background leading to the period under discussion.

[16] The value system studied here is that of the Thai, not the resident Chinese. What we are looking for is the reason why the over-all development of Thailand was so slow, *in spite* of the presence of a large number of active Chinese in the country.

[17] The mere existence of a multiplicity of sects in Japan and their absence in Thailand is quite significant in itself, since it indicates intellectual restlessness. The only (partial) exception in Thailand was the small Thammayut reform movement started by King Mongkut while he was a priest.

easily satisfied with what they earn; they rarely oppose authority. They work rather for their happiness than for material gain."[18] More light will be shed on these and related features as we examine the Thai value system more closely.

Practically all Thai believe in reincarnation and in *karma*, the Buddhist (originally Hindu) law of causation. On the behavioral level, this is reflected in the preoccupation of all Thai (including present-day Western-educated Thai) with merit-making, so as to improve their *karma*. This point cannot be overemphasized, since many activities of the Thai, from the cradle to the grave, are intimately connected with merit-making. Although what the majority of the Thai expect in return for merit-making is not the Buddhist Nirvana but rather more concrete rewards, such as to be reborn with higher worldly status in the next incarnation or perhaps to achieve higher status in this one, this does not affect either the form or the intensity of merit-making. The highest form of merit-making is to become a monk for life, with all the worldly deprivations that this involves. Next in line is to become a monk for a limited period. All able-bodied men aspired to do so in the period under discussion (second half of the nineteenth century), generally for three months during the monsoon period. The other, more common, forms of merit-making are helping others to become monks, feeding the monks on their daily rounds, building of temples and other religious structures, and so on. It is also considered meritorious to engage in ceremonies connected with Buddhist and other special occasions, such as the initiation of a novice or monk, cremation, and the like. The fact that the rituals are sometimes tinged with animistic, Brahministic, and other non-Buddhist practices does not diminish their meritorious significance. It should be pointed out that merit-making is the personal concern of each individual and is not a duty to an authority, either secular or divine.

An important point in connection with merit-making is that, in spite of the fact that one's accumulated merit is considered to be "measured" by the absolute and not relative size of the contribution, this does not provide an incentive for increasing wealth through capital accumulation. The reasoning is rather the reverse—it is the already accumulated merit that *explains* one's present wealth (and other good fortune). The possession of this wealth helps one to devote more to merit-making, which brings more wealth, and so on, a sort of cumulative process. Following this reasoning, the poorer you are, the *more* you should spend on merit-making to catch up. Thus, merit-making is rather "regressive" from a welfare point of view. As for capital accumulation, this reasoning requires that one spend existing assets for meritorious purposes rather than for investments since, as Ingersoll puts it, "merit-making *is* a sort of capital investment."[19]

[18] Luang Suriyabongs, *Buddhism in the Light of Modern Scientific Ideas* (Bangkok: 1954), p. 180.

[19] David E. Pfanner and Jasper Ingersoll, "Theravada Buddhism and Village Economic Behavior, A Burmese and Thai Comparison," *Journal of Asian Studies*, XXI, No. 3 (May, 1962), 356.

Another manifestation of the embodiment of Buddhist values in the Thai society is the model of the ideal personality which is inculcated in the home, school, and adult society and reinforced by the Thai socialization process. The four major qualities constituting the ethical component of the ideal self were formalized in the Buddhist *Brahem Vihara* (the four sublime states of consciousness). The Pali names for these qualities (and their approximate English equivalents) are: *karuna* (compassion), *metta* (loving kindness), *mudita* (empathic joy), and *uppekkha* (equanimity that involves impartiality and nonattachment).[20] Studies made by Mosel, Schular, and Thamavit[21] show that, even today, these traits are very highly valued by the Thai and that, in general, they perceive themselves as an ethnic group possessing these desirable attributes. These values are shared by Westernized government officials; the higher a person's status, the more completely is he supposed to display these qualities.[22]

These Buddhist values find their expression in the daily behavior of the people. Two of the most common and pervasive will be mentioned here: *choei* and *sanuk*. *Choei* is a secular equivalent of *uppekkha* and means, in essence, noninvolvement and keeping cool under all circumstances. This is intimately connected with the extreme tolerance the Thai show for deviant behavior, nonconformity, failure to live up to expectations, and the like. *Sanuk* is roughly translatable as "enjoyment." Everything the Thai does has to be *sanuk*, including religious activities. Thus, the Thai view life as something to be enjoyed here and now, with very little thought about future complications. The only possible exception is the concern about one's *karma*, but since the means employed are made as *sanuk* as possible, it is not really an exception. The Thai would stay away from activities (even meritorious ones) that are not *sanuk*, and most economic activities are hardly *sanuk*.

The third major aspect of the Thai value system that, as seen above, also bears a strong relationship to Buddhism, is the extreme Thai individualism. At this point a digression into the unique Thai social structure is called for. Throughout the relevant period, Thai society was composed of farmers, a few artisans, and government officials. The slaves (either debt slaves or war prisoners) who existed at the middle of the nineteenth century were subsequently freed and became freemen farmers. There were few class boundaries and certainly no castes with ascribed roles. The only partial exception was the existence of hereditary princes (sons of the king), who had a better chance than others to secure high posts in government, although this was by no means automatic. Moreover, even the special privilege of this group was mitigated by the rule that each succeeding generation of princes lost part of its "princehood," with the fifth generation reverting to the status of commoner.

[20] See Dr. Luang Suriyabongs, *Buddhism in Thailand* (Bangkok: Prae Bhittaya Co. Ltd., 1954).

[21] As recorded in James N. Mosel, "Communications Patterns in Transitional Thailand," unpublished manuscript, 1961.

[22] Often there is, of course, some divergence between these ideal qualities and actual behavior. But they clearly serve as guiding principles.

The only concrete organized social structures in the country were the government bureaucracy and the loosely organized Buddhist "church," which never possessed political or economic power. No other organizations, such as parties, pressure groups, clubs, or the like were to be found.[23] This absence of group structure went down as far as the family. Not only were there no extended families, but even the nuclear family was a rather loose affair.

In seeming contradiction to the almost anarchistic individualism of the Thai, one finds that Thai society has a very definite status hierarchy. Besides age and birth in the case of royalty, one's status was (and is) an achieved status that was almost invariably synonymous with one's position in government bureaucracy. These positions, and the equivalent statuses, depended on the judgment of the king or his close subordinates. According to this system, called *sakdi-na*, every position was given a numerical value (which in ancient times involved the granting of land by the king) and this indicated clearly one's position in the society *at the particular time*. These positions were not given for life and were not transmitted to offspring. Although it is quite likely that children of high officials had a better chance (on account of connections and better opportunities for education), there were no formal barriers to status mobility, and, from available evidence, there was a fair amount of mobility both up and down the status ladder.[24]

Thus, Thai society was (and is) built on a superior-subordinate relationship that was fixed in terms of status levels but fluid in terms of the individuals occupying them. In the eyes of most Thai, the fact that someone had achieved a higher status simply meant that his *karma* was better and, therefore, he deserved the higher position.

We can now return to the connection between Buddhist ethics and individualism in Thailand. The Buddhist equivalent of "salvation" is the responsibility of the individual. According to the Buddhist *Dhammapada*: "By oneself is evil done; By oneself one suffers; By oneself evil is left undone; By oneself one is purified."[25] Thus, it is a private affair. One is punished or rewarded according to one's own needs, thoughts, and cravings. This is probably the strongest conviction held by the Thai. In daily parlance, it is phrased: "Do good, receive good; do evil, receive evil."

While it is not clear to what extent we should consider Buddhism to be causal, the Buddhist emphasis on the individual is perfectly consistent with the fact that the Thai seldom have shown a sense of obligation, solidarity, ideological commitment, and possibly even loyalty, to anything beyond

[23] It was suggested by Wilson that this lack of need for affiliation, which has largely persisted to this day, is one of the main reasons for the small attraction of Marxism to the Thai. See David A. Wilson, "Thailand and Marxism," in Frank N. Trager, ed., *Marxism in Southeast Asia* (Stanford, Calif.: Stanford University Press, 1959), for this and some other points in the same vein.

[24] This seems to be true today also. See Lauriston Sharp, ed., *Thailand*, Subcontractor's Monograph (New Haven: Human Relations Area Files, Inc., 1958). There is, however, evidence of increasing economic class differentiation in present-day Thailand.

[25] English version by Dr. Luang Suriyabongs, *Buddhism in Thailand*, p. 20.

personal values. Research done by Phillips in the village of Bang Chan demonstrates that this situation has continued to this day. He concludes with the following characterization of the personal values of the villagers: "In a very real sense, Bang Chan is comprised of 1,701 individualists whose major goals in life are to obtain sufficient land to support themselves, their growing children, and their religion, free from physical insecurities and unencumbered by entangling social obligations."[26] Little local initiative for community projects has been demonstrated, even for such essential requirements as the clearing or deepening of irrigation canals. The villagers expected the government to see to it that such projects were carried out.[27]

We might summarize the available information on Thailand as follows: The Thai *Weltanschauung* was, by and large, represented by Theravada Buddhism. It emphasized the primacy of personal values and thus fortified individualism. Few commitments or obligations for the furtherance of social goals were expected or provided for. While one's status was determined by achievement rather than through ascriptive norms, it was the manipulation of other human beings rather than creativity that counted. *Choei* and *sanuk* militated against the extreme commitment and the sustained hard (and often unpleasant) work required for the establishment and operation of modern industrial undertakings. The Thai value highly those who are quick to take advantage of opportunities when these present themselves, but seldom would they take the trouble to create such opportunities, or cooperate with others in such an endeavor. The role of merit-making as a kind of investment reduced the incentive for economically productive investments. As for political motivation to action, the Thai feeling of loyalty to the government, in contrast with that of the Japanese, was more in the nature of passive obedience than of active loyalty.

If we attempt to relate these values to the economic propensities essential for economic development—to accumulate capital, to cooperate, and to apply oneself to systematic hard work—we have to conclude that these were hardly present. As for the propensity to innovate, there is little to suggest that the Thai value system opposes absorption of new ideas. At the same time, it does not provide the incentives to seek them. In our terminology, propensity for "secondary innovation" was largely absent and that for "acceptance of innovation" was in a rather dormant form. This highlights one of the most significant differences between Thailand and Japan—the great emphasis on activism in Japan and its complete absence in Thailand. The primacy of personal values over political values reinforced Thai non-

---

[26] Herbert Phillips, "Relationships Between Personality and Social Structure in a Siamese Peasant Community," *Human Organization*, XXII (Summer, 1963), 105–8.

[27] Studies made in the north of Thailand show that not in all cases does Thai individualism go to these extremes. For example, Konrad Kingshill has found, in the village he studied, somewhat more communal participation and initiative than our text would imply. But even in these cases, the major attraction was the fun involved in being in the group rather than the performance of the task. (See Konrad Kingshill, *Ku Daeng—The Red Tomb* [Chiengmai: The Prince Royal's College, 1960], especially p. 9). This applies also to most other group activities, even the building of a temple.

activism, since the Thai were deprived thereby of a compelling goal requiring cooperative action.

From the evidence supplied above, there is no doubt about the sharp contrasts between the Thai value system and the Japanese value system, especially in features relevant to the economic propensities. It is equally clear that these contrasts are consistent with the proposition that the appropriate value system is a necessary condition for economic development.

While the important question of how a change in values can be brought about is beyond the scope of the present paper, it does indicate some policy conclusions. The most obvious one is that development programs that do not entail changes in values, when such are required, are bound to be frustrated. To put it differently—the value system is a major component of the so-called "development potential" of a country and, therefore, should loom large in development projections and plans.

One does not have to look far for evidence supporting this contention. The annals of recent history are full of projects that were "good on paper" but ended in failure. An equally long list could be made of political and legal institutions that ended the same way. The constitutions and administrative structures of the central banks in some of the Latin American republics, as well as their political constitutions, are models of perfection, yet the realities in these countries are far from what these institutions were designed to achieve. Similar observations can be made about changes involved in "wars of independence" (Indonesia) and "revolutions" (Thailand). Even today, thirty years after the 1932 revolution in Thailand (which followed the Japanese experience as its model), there is as yet no sign that anything will be forthcoming like the rash of entrepreneurs that typified Japan.[28]

[28] While preparing this paper for publication, I ran across the following paragraph in William W. Lockwood, "The State and Economic Enterprise in Modern Japan," in Simon Kuznets, ed., *Economic Growth: Brazil, India, Japan* (Durham, N.C.: Duke University Press, 1955), p. 591:

The foregoing remarks all cast doubt on the thesis, even in the case of Japan, that the state was "the chief element in economic development" or the statesmen "the chief actors." Much of the same opinion may be ventured with regard to the Zaibatsu, especially in those undertakings which required continued patronage from the Government, because they were never able really to stand on their own feet. The energies, the skills, and the ambitions which provided the real motor force for Japanese industrialization were much too pervasive and too diverse to be compressed into any such formula. They found expression through the activities of millions of small industrialists, tradesmen, technicians, farmers, and workers, as well as in the superstructure of big business. The economic modernization of Japan cannot be explained by "laws" of economic determinism, in which new modes of production follow one another in an inexorable sequence. But equally it went far beyond the activities of a few bold pioneers and organizers, whether statesmen, industrial magnates, or scientists. Also involved were hosts of small, unknown entrepreneurs who introduced and spread the new learning, and still larger numbers of humble workers who provided the growing pool of modern technological skills. This, too, called for initiative and adaptability.

39

KINSHIP AND COMMERCE IN A
THAI-LUE VILLAGE*

MICHAEL MOERMAN[1]

This paper explicates two concepts whose names and specific referents are peculiar to Ban Ping, a Lue village in northern Thailand. More generally, my purpose is to suggest that the concepts and their relationships are quite common; that their coexistence presents a problem that characterizes peasant societies; and that Ban Ping's solution to this problem illustrates a common form of change in custom.

The first concept, which most of us would call "economic," is that of *xo mi laxa*, literally "things with a price." Since these are supposed to be transacted commercially, in terms of supply and demand, I use the English word "commodity" as my gloss for *xo mi laxa*.

The second concept, which most of us would call "social," is that of

* Reprinted by permission of the author and the publisher from *Ethnology*, V (October, 1966), 360–64.

[1] This paper is based on fourteen months of field work in the Lue village of Ban Ping in northern Thailand. The field research and some subsequent analysis were supported by a Foreign Area Training Fellowship from the Ford Foundation, which I acknowledge gratefully. The paper was presented in slightly different form at the November, 1963, meetings of the American Anthropological Association.

pinawng, literally "senior-junior" but more meaningfully translated as "kinsman." In Ban Ping, however, as everywhere in Thailand, genealogy does not suffice for predicting whom an individual will term and treat as *pinawng*. Although the English words "kinsman" and "kinship" are my glosses for *pinawng*, its actual referents do not coincide with a purely genealogical standard. To call someone a *pinawng* means that our relationship, in the present situation, is somehow more intimate, more demanding of fellowship and special privilege, than we would accord to others. Close residence, shared experience, proximate age, and potential profit can all, like genealogical proximity, serve to admit some of one's many acquaintances as *pinawng*, "kinsmen."

On the surface, the relationship between things called "commodities" and persons called "kinsmen" seems quite straightforward. Although "commodities" should always be sold at their market price, one should not deal with "kinsmen" *mën laek mën ka* (as in barter or business). More specifically, the closer the social ties of fellowship between two individuals, the less should economic transactions between them have the appearance of commerce. Ban Ping thus recognizes both a category of things which should be transacted commercially and a category of persons with whom it is improper to have commercial relationships. Clearly, this presents the villagers with a dilemma, for "things with a price" must sometimes be transacted with "kinsmen." Before outlining how the dilemma is resolved, I should like to indicate why it is probably not peculiar to Ban Ping.

The founders of Ban Ping came from a Thai principality in Yunnan about 100 years ago. Not until 1903 did the village come under direct Siamese administration. Not until 1930 was the main road sufficiently good to permit the passage of oxcarts, and, until 1950, there were no trucks. Despite this isolation, there have always been traders in the community. From the founding of Ban Ping until recent times, village traders would load surplus rice on pack oxen and go south toward Phrae, some 100 miles away, to return with salt or imported goods. Yunnanese Muslims came every year, with metal goods to sell. Villagers went annually with dried fish and sweetmeats to exchange for cotton in northern Laos. Adventurous young men often went on long trading expeditions to southern Laos, Chiengmai, and Burma with gold, water buffaloes, horses, and elephants. All these items were "things with a price," whose profits could buy land, animals, houses, and petty luxuries. The inventory and routes of trade are typical of northern Thailand, but trade itself, more specifically, the consigning of some local goods and services to be sold for money with which to buy the goods and services of others, is probably characteristic of all Thai, of every sedentary village in Southeast Asia, and, indeed, of all peasants.

In recent years, imported cups and clothing, trucks and tractors have suddenly come to Ban Ping. Yet this must not blind us to the fact that the village, like all communities that are "part-societies with part-cultures,"[2]

---

[2] Alfred L. Kroeber, *Anthropology* (New York: Harcourt, Brace and World, 1948), p. 284.

has never been completely self-sufficient. In order to buy what, by definition, it needs from others, the peasant community must sell some of what
it has. In order to do this, it permits some of its members to accumulate
sufficient goods and retain sufficient profits to make commerce worthwhile.
In Ban Ping, items for which there is a market, items that must be bought
or that may be sold, are called "things with a price." Though the phrase
may be local, I suggest that the existence of commodities that are bought,
sold, rented, or borrowed with interest is a universal feature of peasant
economies.

The economy of Ban Ping differs from our own modern one in that
there is a wider range of "kinsmen" with whom it is improper to transact
goods commercially. I suggest that this, too, is a feature general to those we
call peasants, for if there is to be a community, clan, kith, or kindred, then
its members must be distinguished from outsiders. One of the major distinctions is likely to be the way in which valued goods are transacted. Dependent incompleteness is the central meaning of "peasant," as Redfield,
Firth, and others use the word.[3] This meaning implies the universal coexistence of commerce and fellowship and thereby implies the universality
of Ban Ping's problem: How can "something with a price" be transacted
with a "kinsman"?

The villagers of Ban Ping claim that they transact an item in accordance
with its value. To quote a reliable and conservative informant: "Even in
the old days, the Lue said that things with a price should be sold at that
price. Land, animals, and similar goods should be sold to kinsmen at the
same price they would fetch elsewhere. It's good to make gifts of minor
items like food, vegetables, and meat, but things with a price should be
sold at that price." Although this ideal helps us to understand how Ban
Ping accommodates kinship to commerce, actual village behavior indicates
that value is not the sole distinction between things sold and things
given away. Villagers pay attention to the source and purpose of an item
as well as to its price. Moreover, one cannot predict the form of a transaction merely from the item transacted. Land and animals are sometimes
given away; food and vegetables are sometimes sold. I observed three
features, in addition to price, that influence the way in which an item is
transacted.

First, even the cheapest unprocessed items are rarely given away if they
have been obtained by purchase. Minor items, such as tobacco, sugar, or
salt, are given freely only to dependents, to the temple, and to the very old,
with the justification that "they cannot provide for themselves." Not the
item itself but the fact that it has been purchased makes it a commodity.
This can be seen from the various ways in which raw meat is transacted. In
the numerous instances when meat was bought in the market or from pass-

[3] Robert Redfield, *Peasant Society and Culture* (Chicago: University of Chicago
Press, 1956); Raymond Firth, *Elements of Social Organization* (Boston: Beacon Press,
1963).

ing vendors, none was ever given away. When a villager butchers an animal in order to sell its meat, he makes small gifts to close "kinsmen." When an animal dies a natural death, its owner distributes large amounts of meat generally through the village.

Second, even minor goods and services are paid for if they have been obtained for commercial purposes.[4] Before an old trader packed rice on the backs of oxen, female relatives milled it for him. These relatives were paid for the work, even if they happened to be members of the trader's household who milled subsistence rice daily for no charge. In contemporary Ban Ping, where fresh and dried fish are often given by one kinsman to another, those who want fish for trading must buy them even from their closest relatives.

Third, anything may be sold by someone who needs the money. Prepared foods and fruits are rarely sold within the village. Every household regularly sends a gift of some special stew to a few of its closest "kinsmen." Sweetmeats are exchanged far more widely, and one can obtain fruit merely by asking for it. Yet even bananas are sold by some poor households, and a relatively prosperous woman, temporarily short of cash while her husband was away, prepared sweets and sold them to her own sister. If the need is real and the behavior infrequent, no one criticizes such transactions.

From these three features, we can see that price alone does not determine whether an item will be sold. Nevertheless, it is extremely influential, and there is a delicate and shifting balance between the price of an item and the closeness of those with whom one transacts it. Since this balance can help us to understand Ban Ping's changing relations with other communities, I shall consider it in some detail.

Consider, for example, intravillage transactions in land, Ban Ping's most valuable possession. Land is sold to siblings and to strangers with complete freedom and at the same prices. Yet it is also possible to give land away. Irrigated land, which costs about ฿1000 per *rai*,[5] is given away only by extremely old men, who sometimes distribute their estate to its heirs before they die. However, able-bodied men occasionally give their children a gift of tractor-plowed land, which costs only ฿300 per *rai*. Land of even less value, worth about ฿100 per *rai*, is commonly given by older brothers to their juniors.

This pattern is repeated in transactions which involve usufruct rather than title. Everyone who farms irrigated land owned by someone else pays a rental to the landlord. Sons who farm their father's land, tenants who rent in order to help the landlord, and strangers who must rent irrigated land in order to support themselves all pay a share of the crop to the owner

---

[4] Quantity is also involved here, for large amounts are usually transacted only for commercial purposes. However, purpose seems to be the governing feature, for even small amounts are sold if their recipient openly intends to use the goods commercially.

[5] One *rai* equals .4 acre. During the period of field work, one *baht* (฿) was worth about 5 U.S. cents.

of the land.[6] Yet sons are given free use of rainfall fields, worth only ฿250 per *rai*. A friend may be given free use of a small parcel as a seedbed, and anyone can request permission to cultivate a fellow villager's garden land. For land, and for every commodity, the lower its market price, the larger is the circle of "kinsmen" who may receive it without paying that price.

This means that some get for nothing what others have to buy. A townsman pays for the condiments that a fellow villager can pluck. Someone from another village may be charged for the bananas for which a fellow villager has merely to ask. A distant "kinsman" must at least offer to pay for the fish that one gives away to close relatives and nearby neighbors. A sibling or first cousin can freely borrow rice for which others have to pay interest.

This relationship between market price and social intimacy introduces a dynamic principle into Ban Ping's accommodation of kinship to commerce. Prices vary seasonally, and, as one would expect, similar items are transacted differently as the year progresses. During April, when there are numerous ceremonies for which sweetmeats are used, the price of coconuts rises sharply, and a woman may sell some to a close "kinsman" with whom fruits and even stews are usually exchanged as gifts. During the dry hot season, when food is scarce, a housewife may buy a jackfruit from a "kinsman" who freely gives her such items at other times of the year.

A more important aspect of this dynamism arises from Ban Ping's ever deeper involvement in the national and the world market. Shortly after their arrival in 1903, the Siamese built a marketplace for the convenience of officials and of the Chinese merchants who followed them. With this event, reports an old informant, vegetables became "things with a price," and their free circulation became somewhat curtailed. With the introduction of trucks, mills, and tractors, the rice market became insatiable, and "rice became a thing with a price." Today it is common to charge 100 per cent interest on loans of rice, but informants over middle age agree that this is an innovation. Formerly, when rice was largely a subsistence good, no interest was charged; it would have been "bad" (*baw di*) and "calculating" (*khit ti*) to do so. There was a belief, for which scriptural authority is adduced, that those who charged interest for rice would be punished with an excruciating and incurable itch. Now, only a few old men refer to this

---

[6] Villagers do not like to admit that prices are sometimes lower for close "kinsmen," but the following table of rentals paid for irrigated land in 1960 indicates that such concessions are made and also shows which degrees of "kinship" are significant for rentals of the most valuable type of land.

	Proportion of Crop Paid as Rent			
Renter	One-Third	Two-Fifths	One-Half	Other or Unknown
Genealogically close fellow villager	5	3	0	2
Genealogically distant fellow villager	0	2	0	0
Nonvillager	0	1	15	4

belief, and even they charge interest for rice loaned to all but the closest "kinsmen."

The village economy has not moved from barter to sale, from status to contract. The change is more subtle because old institutions and old rhetoric have persisted. Most villagers still permit even somewhat distant "kinsmen" to borrow cash without charge. Yet the one man who collects interest from his mother can conceal his innovation by saying, quite correctly, that "money has always had a price," has always been a commodity.

In the past, a man could use little more rice than he could eat; today its market is infinite. In the past, a household could grow only as much rice as the strength of its men and its water buffalo allowed. Now tractors can be hired, and, in broadcast farming at least, cash is the sole limit on production. More and more goods are becoming commodities, more and more persons are being treated as customers. As more things come to "have a price," fewer "kinsmen" get things unless they pay for them.

There have been great changes in the actual things, persons, and activities referred to by the traditional concepts of "commodity" and "kinsman." But the concepts themselves and the relationships between them have persisted. This has permitted Ban Ping to retain the illusion of continuity, to camouflage commercialization, and so to make an amicable adjustment to the modern economic world.

I have suggested that the complementary concepts of kinship and commerce found in Ban Ping follow from the dependent incompleteness by which we define peasantry. I would also suggest that Ban Ping's process of camouflaging may also be a common reaction to compelling new circumstances, since people presumably find it less troublesome and threatening to re-sort the elementary forms[7] than to reformulate the defining features of their cathectic concepts.

[7] Ward H. Goodenough, *Cooperation in Change* (New York: Russell Sage Foundation, 1963).

40

ECONOMIC PROGRESS IN SOUTHEAST ASIA*

DOUGLAS S. PAAUW

Since the end of World War II, Southeast Asian economies have grown at widely diverging rates. Consistent and relatively rapid growth has occurred only in the Philippines; in that country, rehabilitation from World War II was completed relatively early, and the economy has gone on to provide gains in per capita real income,† though at a falling rate. In Thailand and Malaya, rehabilitation and growth have occurred, but progress has been unsteady. In Burma, Indonesia, and the Indochinese countries of Laos, Cambodia, and Vietnam, progress has taken the form primarily of restoring prewar levels of per capita production; it is unlikely that gains above prewar levels have been achieved.

Most of Southeast Asia's 215 million people—about 70 per cent—appear to share approximately the same low levels of per capita real income and consumption that were their lot prior to World War II, when the area was

* Reprinted by permission of the author and the publisher from *The Journal of Asian Studies*, XXIII (November, 1963), 69–92.
† For this and other economic terms, see the editor's glossary at the end of this chapter.

predominantly under colonial control, producing widening gaps between expectations and achievements. In the Southeast Asian countries, new aspirations have led to an emphasis on economic progress to improve general welfare, and national-development plans have been pursued with growing vigor. Yet, Southeast Asia's share of world income has fallen; it has lost ground in both industrial production and raw-material exports to more rapidly growing regions. Between 1938 and 1961, Asia's share of the world's income fell from 17.3 to 13.1 per cent, although its share of the world's population grew from 53.2 to 56.9 per cent.[1] In spite of rapid industrial expansion in Japan, non-Communist Asia's share in the free world's mining and industrial output fell from 7.4 per cent in 1938 to 6.6 per cent in 1958.[2] Moreover, Southeast Asia's share of non-Communist Asia's mining and industrial production fell from 15.4 to 13.1 per cent.[3] Even in its traditional forte, export of primary products, Southeast Asia—along with its neighbors in the Economic Commission for Asia and the Far East (ECAFE)—lost ground to industrial and other primary producing countries.[4] Similarly, Southeast Asia as a region has shown low rates of income growth and structural change, compared to other underdeveloped areas.

The lagging growth of the Southeast Asian region as a whole is primarily a matter of delayed rehabilitation from the setbacks of the 1940's in several of the region's important countries. This paper attempts to examine important differences in the performance of Southeast Asian countries, first in terms of restoration of prewar levels of output and rates of new expansion, and then in terms of a few variables that are strategic in the process of economic growth.

REHABILITATION VERSUS NEW GROWTH

Distinction between economic rehabilitation and development is essential for comparative evaluation of the performance of Southeast Asian economies. With the exception of Thailand, these countries have shared the major transition from colonialism to independence, a transition that has had pervasive effects on their economies. In some cases, independence was achieved only after prolonged political and military struggles; and in most newly independent countries in the area, the transfer of sovereignty from colonial to indigenous governments led to political instability. Communist insurrections have occurred in the Philippines, Malaya, and the Indochinese countries; civil strife marred the transition in Burma and Indonesia. Following the devastation of World War II, these added difficulties delayed the restoration of prewar levels of aggregate and per capita income, and differences in their severity are clearly reflected in the rapidity

[1] Phyllis Deane, "The Long Term Trends in World Economic Growth," *The Malayan Economic Review*, VI (October, 1961), Table I, 17.

[2] United Nations, *Patterns of Industrial Growth, 1938–1958* (New York: United Nations, 1960), Table 12, p. 116. All data show value added in 1948 U.S. dollars.

[3] *Ibid*. Calculated from Table 15, p. 126.

[4] Economic Commission for Asia and the Far East, "Foreign Trade of ECAFE Primary Exporting Countries," *Economic Survey of Asia and the Far East, 1959*, p. 55 and pp. 58–65.

with which Southeast Asian economies were rehabilitated. Southeast Asian countries have not been content to restore their economies along prewar colonial patterns. Revamping of colonial-type, export-oriented economies has become a major goal throughout the area, although countries have differed on the methods by which this goal is pursued. Colonial policies for promoting the growth of primary products for export, while minimizing domestic economic expansion, have been abandoned in favor of over-all development programs. This has been accompanied by attempts to transfer ownership and operation of modern export sectors from foreigners and minority groups to indigenous ethnic groups. There has been a frontal attack on the problem of distribution of gains from the relatively profitable export industries; public policies have been designed to shift gains from foreign to domestic factors of production. Economic rehabilitation, therefore, has become mixed with other major economic goals, reflecting the transition from a dependent to an independent status.

These pervasive changes raise problems for defining and measuring economic rehabilitation. Some Southeast Asian countries have pressed the development of new lines of output before prewar levels of traditional patterns of output were restored. Others have tended to rehabilitate output sector by sector before initiating major changes in the composition of output. In all Southeast Asian countries, the share of output contributed by government services has risen, and there has been a marked tendency toward expansion of the relative size of other service sectors as well. The implications of these changes are examined below, in the section concerned with structural change.

Evidence indicates that capital requirements for restoring previous levels of aggregate output are much lower than for new growth. Incremental capital-output ratios have been found to be low where rehabilitation consists of putting back into operation productive facilities that once existed.[5] Reclaiming fallow agricultural land, rebuilding or repairing idle factories, reviving once-operative financial and distribution systems are examples of rehabilitative activities that may not be costly in terms of providing the "external economies" required for relatively full and efficient utilization. Managers, labor skills, and markets are likely to exist to allow rapid revival of relatively efficient levels of output. In newly independent countries, however, the problem of rehabilitation may be complicated by a shift from foreign factors of production to domestic factors—particularly in the capital-intensive, export sector of the economy. To the extent that simple rehabilitation of previous patterns of output is mixed with attempts to alter the structure of output and to shift from foreign to domestic factors of production, the process more closely resembles development. Where the emphasis is on structural and institutional change prior to restoration of previously achieved aggregate output levels, problems that create rising incremental capital-output ratios are likely to appear before rehabilitation of real income has been completed. Domestic cadres of managers and skilled labor

[5] Benjamin Higgins, *Economic Development: Problems, Principles and Policies* (New York: Norton, 1959), pp. 648–52.

for operation of the capital-intensive industries have proved costly substitutes for foreign factors, and their rate of substitution has tended to impair efficient operation of productive capacity in countries pressing for rapid de-alienization of their economies. On the other hand, the capital and human investment costs associated with rehabilitation obviously vary with the extent of damage to capital stock as well as with the length of the hiatus between damage and rehabilitation. Both of these factors have some significance in explaining varying rates of rehabilitation in Southeast Asian countries.

Viewed with this distinction in mind, Southeast Asian economies fall into two fairly definite categories. Prewar levels of aggregate and per capita output were restored soon after World War II in Thailand, the Philippines, and Malaya, and progress during the 1950's represented additions to previously achieved levels. Elsewhere economic progress has proceeded at a much slower rate, and the decade of the 1950's was devoted to restoring prewar levels of output. Individual countries in the latter group, including Burma, Indonesia, South Vietnam, Laos, and Cambodia, have shown intermittent periods of relatively rapid expansion of output, so that it cannot be said that their economies have been persistently stagnant. In general, however, political stability was not adequate in these latter countries to permit rapid rehabilitation after World War II, and recurrent political traumas prevented private and public entrepreneurs from restoring and adding to productive capabilities to insure steady growth. In Burma and Indonesia, moreover, emphasis on rapid institutional change and replacement of foreign factors have compounded the difficulties; and, in Burma, the extent of wartime damage appears to have been particularly severe compared to that in other countries.

Data showing rehabilitation dates and postwar growth rates are presented in Tables 6 and 7. Average rates of growth of real product have been computed for periods of rehabilitation and postrehabilitation. Restoration of the prewar levels of *aggregate* output is taken as the criterion of rehabilitation. Table 6 demonstrates, however, that there is considerable discrepancy in some cases between restoration of prewar aggregate real product and real product per capita. For Burma, aggregate real product is estimated to have been restored to the prewar level by the end of 1957 (representing the most delayed recovery), but per capita real product had not yet been restored by 1960. Indonesian recovery also proceeded slowly, with aggregate real product restored in 1953 and per capita real product in 1957. Real-product data are not available for estimating postwar recovery in Malaya, but other evidence suggests that aggregate output was returned to prewar levels by 1947–48.[6] In the absence of a consistent real-product series, no data are suggested for restoring per capita real product, but the rapid growth of output after 1949, demonstrated by evidence collected by the International Bank for Reconstruction and Development mission, supports the presumption that Malayan per capita real product was restored

[6] See Appendix I.

shortly after aggregate real product.[7] Recovery in the Philippines appears to have been roughly parallel to that in Malaya. Goodstein's results suggest that aggregate real product in 1948 was about 11 per cent above 1938,[8] and taking into account population growth, per capita real product was clearly restored to the prewar level by 1950. The most rapid rehabilitation record was achieved in Thailand, where, if the real-product indicators are accurate, both aggregate and per capita real product were returned to pre-war levels by 1947. It is likely, however, that wartime damage to Thailand's productive capacity was less severe than in other Southeast Asian countries, a conclusion deducible from the data in Table 7. Aggregate output expanded as rapidly as 30–50 per cent per year in countries where prewar levels were reached soon after the end of World War II. In the slowly rehabilitating economies, on the other hand, output was restored sporadically, with years of significant recovery followed by serious reversals. In Burma, for example, the official national-income estimates show real gross domestic product in 1946–47 at 40 per cent below the 1938–39 level. In 1947–48, real product expanded by 18 per cent, but this achievement was followed by reverses of 10 per cent in 1948–49 and 5 per cent in 1949–50.[9] The 1947–48 level was not achieved until 1951–52.[10]

TABLE 6

Estimated Dates of Restoring Prewar Output Levels*

	Aggregate	Per Capita
Burma	1957	—[11]
Indonesia	1953	1957
Malaya	1947–48	N.A.
Philippines	1948	1950
Thailand	1947	1947

* For sources and explanatory notes, see Appendix I.

These differences among Southeast Asian countries emphasize the importance of distinguishing between rates of growth during the rehabilitation and postrehabilitation periods. Computing average growth rates for the decade of the 1950's, as some have done, obscures the significant differences in performance among Southeast Asian economies. Data from

[7] International Bank for Reconstruction and Development, *The Economic Development of Malaya* (Baltimore, Md.: 1955), chapter 2, especially pp. 20–22.

[8] Marvin E. Goodstein, *The Pace and Pattern of Philippine Economic Growth, 1938, 1948 and 1956* (Ithaca, N.Y.: 1962), Table I–1, p. 8.

[9] Data are taken from Ministry of National Planning and Religious Affairs, *The National Income of Burma* (Rangoon: August, 1954), p. 16.

[10] U Nu attributes this record to "insurrection." See "Premier Reports to the People," Appendix I in Louis J. Walinsky, *Economic Development in Burma, 1951–1960* (New York: Twentieth Century Fund, 1962), p. 63.

[11] Official Burmese Statistics show per capita real income in 1959–60 as 16 per cent below the immediate prewar level.

TABLE 7
Southeast Asia: Estimated Annual Rates of Growth of Real Product*

	REHABILITATION		POSTREHABILITATION		
	Average Growth Rate			*Average Growth Rate*	
Country	Period	Aggregate Product	Period	Aggregate Product	Per Capita[15] Product
Burma	1946–57	5.0	1957–60	3.5	1.7
Indonesia	1946–53	6.9[12]	1953–59	3.2	.7
Malaya	1946–48	N.A.	1949–53[13]	4.7	1.7
			1955–60[14]	3.8	.8
Philippines	1946–48	50.0	1948–60	6.0	3.0
Thailand	1946–47	30.0	1947–50	15.3	
			1951–60	5.1	2.1

* For sources, see Appendix II.

Kuznets' studies, for example, show relatively uniform annual growth rates (aggregate real gross domestic product, 1951–57) for two Southeast Asian countries: Burma, 6.01 per cent per year, and the Philippines, 6.81 per cent.[16] Similarly, United Nations estimates show average annual real-product growth rates during the 1950's for four Southeast Asian countries as follows: Burma, 5.7 per cent (1950–59); Indonesia, 3.6 per cent (1951–59); Philippines, 5.6 per cent (1950–59); and Thailand, 4.9 per cent (1952–59).[17] The discrepancies obscured by short-run averaging did not, however, escape the attention of the authors of an excellent review of economic growth in the ECAFE area, recently published by the Economic Commission for Asia and the Far East.[18] Although their estimates of growth rates for the 1950's (presented in Table 8) fail to distinguish between rehabilitation and subsequent expansion, the evaluation accompanying the data brings out the essential points clearly:

> Finally, in the case of ECAFE countries, the starting point itself has been a significant determinant of the rate of progress achieved. Countries such as China (mainland and Taiwan), Japan and the Philippines, which were

[12] 1951–53 only, Muljatno's data.
[13] Federation of Malaya and Singapore.
[14] Federation of Malaya only.
[15] Population growth rates are based on terminal census data for the Philippines (1948 and 1960) and Thailand (1947 and 1960), on United Nations estimates and the 1961 census for Indonesia, and on United Nations and ECAFE estimates for Burma and Malaya. A comparison of Burmese and United Nations population estimates for Burma is given in Arthur A. Wickmann, *Review of Economics and Statistics*, XLIV (August, 1962), 327.
[16] Simon Kuznets, "Quantitative Aspects of the Growth of Nations, Part V, Capital Formation Proportions: International Comparisons for Recent Years," *Economic Development and Cultural Change*, VIII, part II (July, 1960), 86.
[17] United Nations, *Yearbook of Nation Accounts Statistics 1960* (New York: United Nations, 1961), pp. 265–69.
[18] ECAFE, *Economic Survey of Asia and the Far East, 1961* (Bangkok: 1962), part I.

recovering from war damage when the 'fifties opened, showed a fast initial rate of growth and went on to break new ground during the rest of the decade. Burma, on the other hand, had just completed and Indonesia was still in the process of making good wartime damage when the 'fifties ended, although in both countries, attempts were simultaneously made to effect structural changes required for economic growth. India and Pakistan, although severely strained, were not damaged by the war, and their period of growth began with the 'fifties; hence part of the explanation for the rate of their aggregate growth being lower than that of Burma or Indonesia lies in the basic difference between the processes of net expansion and rehabilitation.[19]

TABLE 8

ECAFE Estimates of Average Annual Rates of Growth in Real
Aggregate and Per Capita Product, 1950–59*: ECAFE Countries

| | Growth Rate Per Cent Per Annum | |
| | Aggregate | Per Capita |
Country	Product	Product
Burma	5.1	3.9
Cambodia	4.0	1.3
Ceylon	3.9	1.4
China: Taiwan	7.9	4.2
India	3.1	1.1
Indonesia	3.6	1.6
Japan	9.1	7.9
Korea, South	5.0	2.1
Pakistan	2.6	0.4
Philippines	6.0	2.7
Thailand	5.0	1.9

* The period begins with 1951 for Burma, Cambodia, China: Taiwan, Indonesia and Thailand, and with 1953 for South Korea. Source: ECAFE, *Economic Survey of Asia and the Far East*, Table I–2, p. 11.

To recapitulate, a review of the available aggregate data suggests that aggregate real product was restored to prewar levels prior to 1950 in Malaya, the Philippines, and Thailand, and that these countries went on to raise both aggregate and per capita real product, although at varying rates, during the 1950 decade. Burma and Indonesia lagged behind these and most other ECAFE countries in rehabilitating their economies from wartime damage,[20] and their rates of economic growth, after aggregate real

[19] ECAFE, *Economic Survey*, p. 12.

[20] South Vietnam also appears to have been slow to restore output to prewar levels, although real-product estimates are not available to support this presumption. Evidence based on the behavior of other economic indicators may be found in Ton That Thien, "Economic Development in South Vietnam, 1954–1960," *The Malayan Economic Review*, VI (April, 1961), 55–80; see also Davy H. McCall, *The Effects of Independence on the Economy of Vietnam*, unpublished Ph.D. Thesis, Harvard University, 1961, *passim*, especially p. 119 and pp. 277–81.

product was restored to prewar levels, are well below those reported for Southeast Asian countries where rehabilitation was more rapid.

The distinction between rehabilitation of prewar productive capacity and new expansion as the critical variable for comparing rates of progress among Southeast Asian economies may now be put in more quantitative terms. If we view the postwar years 1946–60 as a period of both rehabilitation and new growth in all Southeast Asian countries, the real question concerns the relationship between the two. By employing our estimates of rehabilitation dates as the base year for measuring growth of new productive capacity, we can devise a measure of the ratio of new growth to rehabilitation of prewar aggregate real product during the fourteen-year period, 1946–60. Table 9 shows ratios for Southeast Asian countries, and it also indicates the estimated number of years devoted to rehabilitation and new growth. Comparing the two extreme cases, this measure indicates that Indonesia raised aggregate real product by only 11 per cent above the prewar level during seven years of new growth, while new growth in the Philippines occurred over a twelve-year period, slightly more than doubling the prewar level of aggregate real product. Burma's performance over the entire postwar period yields results similar to those in Indonesia, but because rehabilitation was delayed in Burma, only three years were devoted to new growth. It is important to observe, however, that even in the more rapidly growing economies, growth of real product slowed down after a lag of several years, following restoration of aggregate output to prewar levels. Between 1948 and 1954, aggregate real product in the Philippines grew at an average annual rate of 7 per cent, compared to 5 per cent from 1954 to 1960. Thailand's average rate of growth fell from 6.6 per cent for the years 1951 to 1955 to 3.9 per cent from 1955 to 1960.[21]

OTHER INDICATORS OF ECONOMIC PROGRESS

There is additional evidence, of varying quality, to support our general conclusions about economic rehabilitation and growth in Southeast Asia. It would be useful to compare rates of growth by major sectors over the entire period 1938–60, but reasonably reliable production indices by sector are not available. It is possible to examine growth of sectoral outputs only in terms of shares contributed by major sectors to total product, and this is done below in the section concerned with structural change. Of the many other variables germane to the study of comparative economic growth, two are singled out for brief attention here—capital formation and exports. The data on capital formation in Southeast Asia are inconclusive, while export data tend to confirm the conclusions derived from real-product indicators of growth and development.

Capital Formation

Two aspects of capital formation have been widely discussed in economic-development literature, the importance of raising the rate of capital forma-

[21] All averages are geometric means of annual rates of change in real product from the sources given in Appendix II.

TABLE 9

Ratio of New Growth to Rehabilitation, 1946–60

		Number of Years	
Country	Ratio	Rehabili- tation	New Growth
Burma	1.11	11	3
Indonesia	1.11	7	7
Malaya	1.64	2	12
Philippines	2.01	2	12
Thailand	1.91	1	13

Notes and Sources: All data are taken from sources given for Tables 6 and 7 without adjustment for Burma and the Philippines. For Indonesia, the growth ratio is based on evidence that new growth occurred only between 1953 and 1955, and that aggregate real product in 1960 had fallen to its 1955 level.[22] The length of the rehabilitation period is estimated from the source given in Table 6. For Malaya, the new growth ratio is estimated by averaging the rates of growth shown in Table 9 and applying the average to the entire new growth period, 1948–60. For Thailand, the rate of growth shown in Table 7 for the period of 1951–60 is employed for the entire new growth period 1947–60, on the assumption that the more recent domestic-product estimates are more accurate than the initial estimate for the period 1947–50.

tion (the share of total product devoted to creation of productive capital) and the relationship between the growth of capital and the growth of output (the incremental capital-output ratio). In general, economic development is a process of raising the productivity of labor by providing more capital per laborer and by shifting labor from less to more capital-intensive occupations. The rate at which labor can be shifted depends on many factors, economic as well as noneconomic. Among the important economic determinants are the rate at which the stock of capital can be expanded and capital intensity raised in the new labor-absorbing industries, the latter being reflected in the incremental capital-output ratio. Capital-output ratios vary considerably among industries, and societies that concentrate new investment in capital-intensive industries early in their development are likely to confront relatively high over-all incremental capital-output ratios.

Official capital formation estimates for Southeast Asian countries, presented in Table 10, do not yield much in the way of empirical support for conclusions on either aspect of capital formation. The striking feature of these data is the range of disparities among countries. Estimated gross fixed capital formation rates[23] vary from 6–7 per cent for Indonesia and the Philippines to 17 per cent for Burma. Further investigation suggests that the apparent discrepancies are more statistical in nature than real. There is

[22] Douglas S. Paauw, "From Colonial to Guided Economy," in Ruth T. McVey, ed., *Indonesia* (New York: Taplinger, 1963).

[23] Gross fixed capital formation rates show the ratio of fixed capital formation to gross domestic product; depreciation is not deducted from the total, and changes in inventories are excluded. Gross capital formation rates are used, since Southeast Asian countries do not employ uniform and reliable methods of estimating capital consumption allowances to obtain net capital formation.

general agreement that the estimated Burmese rate (17.1) is much too high, while the reverse is true for the Philippine estimate.[24] The evidence suggesting underestimation of gross investment in the Philippines is corroborated by a recent study that estimated gross domestic savings to have averaged 12.9 per cent of gross domestic product from 1951 to 1960 and 15 per cent from 1956 to 1960.[25] Since net foreign savings were positive, the savings data suggest that gross investment was somewhat above these rates. The Indonesian estimate suffers from uncorrected biases associated with measuring capital formation from import statistics under a multiple exchange-rate system[26] and incomplete coverage, yielding an estimated rate that appears to be much too low. It is highly probable, therefore, that gross (fixed) capital formation rates for all Southeast Asian countries would fall into the 10–15 per cent range if the statistical biases in the official estimates were removed.[27] It follows that attempts to estimate incremental capital-output ratios from existing capital formation and real-product data are likely to be misleading. In presenting such estimates in their recent study of ECAFE growth,[28] the Economic Commission for Asia and the Far East points out that the erratic values shown for several countries reflect basic deficiencies in the data. It appears obvious that no sound basis exists for speculating about nonstatistical causes of differences in incremental capital-output ratios among Southeast Asian countries.

All Southeast Asian economies for which data are available appear to have raised their gross capital formation rates during the 1950 decade—

[24] The Economic Commission for Asia and the Far East suggests that the Burmese fixed capital formation rate may, in fact, have been in the neighborhood of 11 per cent while "a more valid appraisal for the 'Philippine' rate would put it over 10 per cent." (*Economic Survey of Asia and the Far East*, 1961, p. 24.) Both Filipino and foreign observers concur with the ECAFE viewpoint on the Philippine rate. Reuben F. Trinidad, after studying Filipino capital formation for 1956–57, concludes that official estimates are 40 per cent too low. (Reuben F. Trinidad, "The Measurement of Gross Domestic Investment in Underdeveloped Countries with Special Reference to the Philippines," *Economic Research Journal* [Manila], VII [June 1960], 37–44.) For foreign evaluations see Benjamin Higgins, *Economic Development: Principles, Problems and Policies*, p. 650, and "Economic Growth in the Philippines: A Preliminary Report prepared by the Staff of the IBRD," January, 1962, published as Appendix II to the *Five-Year Integrated Socio-Economic Program of the Philippines*, p. 9.

[25] Averages computed from annual data in "Saving in the Philippine Economy," *Economic Bulletin for Asia and the Far East*, XIII (September, 1962), Table 17, 21.

[26] Imported capital goods and hence the estimate for Indonesian capital formation are valued at the overvalued official rupiah rate, while gross-product estimates reflect higher rupiah prices for imported goods generally and continuous price inflation for the domestic component.

[27] This would roughly place Southeast Asian gross fixed capital formation rates in the range found by Kuznets for underdeveloped countries in comparable per capita income groups. Kuznets' data covering the years 1951–57 yield an average gross fixed capital formation rate of 13.1 for countries in his groups VI and VII. (Simon Kuznets, *op. cit.*, Appendix, Table I, 77–79.) Although Kuznets' data do not correct for biases, it is likely that his sample is large enough to reduce the effect of opposite biases. For example, the arithmetic average of the uncorrected data for Southeast Asian countries would yield an average gross fixed capital formation rate of 11 per cent.

[28] The following values for crude incremental capital-output ratios are given for Southeast Asian countries, 1950–59: Burma, 3.4; Indonesia, 1.7; Philippines, 1.2; Thailand, 2.6. ECAFE, *Economic Survey of Asia and the Far East*, 1961, Table I–14, p. 24.

TABLE 10

Estimated Average Rates of Gross Fixed Capital
Formation, 1950 Decade*

Burma (1951–59)	17.1
Indonesia (1951–59)	6.2
Malaya (1954–58)	10.5
Philippines (1950–59)	7.0
Thailand (1952–59)	14.4

* Average of annual ratios of gross fixed capital formation to gross domestic product. Malayan capital formation data includes changes in rubber stocks.

Sources: For all countries except Malaya, ECAFE, *Economic Survey of Asia and the Far East*, 1961, Table I–14, p. 24. Malayan estimate refers to Federation of Malaya; capital formation data from "Saving of the Federation of Malaya, 1954–1958: A Preliminary Estimate," *Economic Bulletin for Asia and the Far East*, XIII (June, 1960), Table 4.5, 32. Gross domestic product estimates from United Nations, *Yearbook of National Accounts Statistics*, 1961, p. 89.

with the exception of Indonesia.[29] In the latter country, imported capital goods, the basic component of estimated capital formation, fell substantially in the last half of the decade. Excepting Indonesia, we again find that there is little correlation with growth rates. ECAFE data show that Burma raised its gross capital formation rate by 4.8 per cent (to 20.5 per cent) over the decade, while the increases were only 1.6 per cent for the Philippines and 1.2 per cent for Thailand. Since direction and relative magnitudes of change in capital formation rates appear to be more accurate than the estimated level, there is some significance in contrasting these changes with relative growth performance. Despite what appears to be a more rapid increase in the growth of capital stock in Burma, the expansion of aggregate real product continued to lag behind the Philippine and Thai growth rates during the last half of the 1950 decade.

If the presumption that capital formation rates did not vary significantly among Southeast Asian countries is correct, the divergent rates of rehabilitation and growth are to be explained largely in terms of differences in allocation and productivity of capital, rather than its volume. There is a sharp contrast between Burma, where rehabilitation and growth have lagged, and the more rapidly progressing economies of the Philippines and Thailand. In Burma, the government has encouraged the allocation of an increasingly large share of the economy's investment resources to capital-intensive investment projects. The growth of physical productive capacity in the capital-intensive sector has outpaced supplies of complementary organizational and technical skills, producing low rates of new capacity and yielding poor output results from capital increments.[30] In the more free-enterprise Philippine economy, where direct government allocation of resources has de-

[29] ECAFE, *Economic Survey of Asia and the Far East*, 1961, p. 23. As pointed out in this paragraph, there is a fairly high probability that trends are more accurately reflected in capital formation estimates than in the ratio of capital formation to gross product.

[30] Louis J. Walinsky, *op. cit., passim*.

creased over the decade, private entrepreneurs have channeled investment resources predominantly to manufacturing industries, where import replacement has provided strong inducements to expansion. New productive capacity in this rapidly growing sector has generally been intensively and effectively employed. Walinsky maintains that misallocation of investment resources in Burma has resulted from withholding resources from the potentially dynamic private sector, as well as from the government's propensity to undertake large and spectacular capital-intensive projects.[31] In the Philippines, a shift from public to private enterprise and policies, to encourage the growth of private investment, emerged with growing force during the 1950's.[32] Golay believes that this emphasis was based on recognition of the superior organizational and management capabilities of private over public enterprise.[33]

Exports

The relationship between exports and economic development is both strategic and complex. Few will dispute the assertion that "the expansion and diversification of exports is of paramount importance to primary producing countries seeking to develop their economies."[34] Domestic capital formation in developing economies tends to have a high import component, and economic development raises demand for imports through income effects. As investment and real income rise, changes in the structure of demand tend to outstrip changes in the structure of domestic output, and a part of the burden of accommodating these shifts—to allow continued growth—falls upon the foreign trade sector.

Export earnings are the basic source of foreign exchange to provide for the expansion of imports during this transitional stage of growth. With few exceptions, foreign savings cannot be relied on to cushion a major part of these foreign exchange strains. In global terms, foreign investment and foreign aid continue to meet only a small part of the foreign exchange requirements of developing countries, and prospects for large increases are not bright. During the decade of the 1950's, the inflow of foreign saving averaged between .1 per cent and 1.8 per cent of gross national product in four Southeast Asian countries, while the Federation of Malaya engaged in net lending abroad.[35]

The newly independent country pursuing development goals is likely to find that there are serious limitations to unequivocal adoption of policies to promote maximum growth of exports. In countries where colonial pat-

[31] *Ibid.*, pp. 299–317, 336–49, 380–81.

[32] Frank H. Golay, *The Philippines: Public Policy and National Economic Development* (Ithaca, N.Y.: Cornell University Press, 1961), pp. 242–65.

[33] *Ibid.*, pp. 243–45.

[34] Gertrud Lovasy, "Inflation and Exports in Primary Producing Countries," *International Monetary Fund Staff Papers*, IX (March, 1962), 38.

[35] Average percentages of foreign saving to gross national product for the decade were: Burma, 0.1; Indonesia, 0.4; Philippines, 1.6; Thailand, 1.8; Federation of Malaya (1955–59), −10.2. Significant changes were those in Burma from −7.0 in the early 1950's to 4.0 in 1957–59, in the Philippines from 0.7 to 1.9 and in Thailand from 2.1 to 2.9. ECAFE, *Economic Survey of Asia and the Far East*, 1961, pp. 43–48.

terns of trade and investment created specialization in export of primary products, representing a relatively large share of total product and yielding high returns to foreign factors of production, political independence has produced nationalistic reactions seeking to alter the built-in "export-bias." Specialization in primary products for export is alleged to have exposed the economy to fluctuating world market conditions and deteriorating long-run terms of trade with industrial countries. Diversification of output through industrialization and expansion of domestic sectors at the expense of exports may be embraced as nationalistic objectives, raising the danger of conflict with goals of increasing output. Golay believes that this conflict is becoming consciously recognized in the Philippines.[36]

Southeast Asia provides an interesting laboratory for the study of differing patterns of response to the dilemma presented to the newly independent export economy. In the immediate prewar period, all countries in the region showed a high ratio of exports to total product,[37] and there has been a general tendency for the new postwar governments to attempt to harness the export sector to programs related to domestic progress and welfare. Throughout the area, there have been efforts to shift the distribution of gains from trade in favor of domestic factors of production at the expense of foreign factors and, in some cases, against minority groups specialized in foreign trading roles. Where redistribution has been pressed to the point of seriously disrupting trading institutions, exports have been threatened by the lack of organizational competence. In other cases, export and import controls, multiple exchange-rate policies, and other devices to reach export profits have discouraged export activities. Inflation has produced similar problems in some countries, particularly Indonesia.

Quite apart from the internal obstacles to the growth of exports, it has been argued that primary producing countries have faced an uphill battle for export markets.[38] There is no evidence, however, that external demand factors are significant in explaining different rates of growth of exports from Southeast Asian countries. These countries are specialized in roughly similar tropical export products, and the same export products have fared quite differently in the various Southeast Asian countries. Discrepancies in export performance appear to be related to conditions affecting supply incentives and capabilities, roughly the same set of determinants that have to do with discrepancies in over-all economic progress.

There is one version of the supply deficiency hypothesis that is quite clearly contradicted by Southeast Asian experience. There is no evidence

[36] "Filipinos have been vocal in deploring their colonial-type specialization in primary production for exports. On the other hand, recent years have brought home the fact that lack of foreign exchange is the principal restraint on economic growth. It is not unlikely that the groping for a foreign investment policy will ultimately lead to more, rather than less, functional specialization of foreign investment and the strong demand conditions of industrial countries. It would be ironical if the much depreciated colonial specialization should emerge as conscious Philippine policy after a brief period of independence." Golay, *op. cit.*, pp. 264–65.

[37] Ratios of exports to total product in 1938 were: Burma, 33; Indochina, 29; Indonesia, 24; Philippines, 20; and Thailand, 19. See Table 11.

[38] A. Maizels, "The Effects of Industrialization on Exports of Primary Producing Countries," *Kyklos*, XIV (Fasc. 1, 1961), 18–46.

that industrialization per se has interfered with the capacity to supply exports of primary products. The data presented below suggest that export stagnation has been associated with slow growth of real product, while the reverse has been true for the more rapidly industrializing countries.

TABLE 11

Ratio of Exports to Gross Domestic Product, 1938 and 1957–59

	1938	Average 1957–59
Burma	33	19
Indonesia	24	5
Malaya	46[a]	42[b]
Philippines	20[c]	9
Thailand	19[d]	16

[a] Average, 1947–49 ratio of exports to gross national product, Singapore and Federation.

[b] Federation of Malaya only.

[c] Gross national product.

[d] Gross geographical product.

Sources: Gross product data are taken from sources for Tables 6 and 7. Export data refer to merchandise exports only and are taken from United Nations, *Yearbook of International Trade Statistics*, various issues.

Data relating the value of exports to gross domestic product, presented in Table 11, suggest that there have been large changes in the relative size of the export sector in Burma, Indonesia, and the Philippines during the two decades after 1938. Aggregative data are not available for prewar Malaya, but there is a presumption that the high ratio of the value of exports to total product found in both the late 1940's and late 1950's did not represent a significant departure from prewar experience.[39] Similarly, the evidence points to little change in Thailand's ratio between 1938 and 1957–59.

It is likely that these apparent differences in variations in the size of the export sector are partly a result of statistical factors. For both the Philippines and Indonesia, the magnitude of the decline in the export ratios is clearly exaggerated by the official data. In both, exports at the official exchange rate have been undervalued relative to the domestic components of total product for the postwar years. Moreover, the Philippine product estimate for the prewar period somewhat overstates the export ratio for 1938.[40] If more realistic exchange-rate valuation were used for the Philip-

[39] It should be noted that the Malayan data in Table 11 refer to Singapore and the Federation for the period 1947–49 and to the Federation only for 1957–59. The high Malayan ratio is partly explained by the large entrepôt component in Malayan exports, approximately one-half of the total during the period 1949–53. This estimate is based on data from International Bank for Reconstruction and Development, *The Economic Development of Malaya*, pp. 676 and 690.

[40] The prewar Philippine product estimate has serious downward biases compared to later estimates, thus overstating the prewar export ratio. The prewar product bias is discussed in ECAFE, "Analysis of National Income in Selected Asian Countries," *Economic Bulletin for Asia and the Far East*, III (January–June, 1952), 16.

pines and Indonesia, the resulting ratio of exports to total product in the late 1950's would appear to be in the neighborhood of 14 per cent for both countries,[41] and the magnitude of decline from the prewar ratio considerably smaller than official data suggest.

The differing rates of change are so great, however, that there is fairly high probability that they reflect real as well as statistical factors. The two Southeast Asian economies showing least change in the ratio of exports to total product, Malaya and Thailand, were those with the highest and lowest ratios in the earlier years, suggesting that initial size, per se, had little to do with an eventually falling ratio. One explanation for unchanging export ratios in these countries might run in terms of the relative absence of revolt against colonial economic institutions.[42] Thailand did not experience a formal break from a colonial political and economic relationship, and the Federation of Malaya became independent in 1957, roughly a decade later than other Southeast Asian countries. Moreover, the new Federation's foreign trade and investment policies have tended to be more moderate than those of other Southeast Asian countries.

For the countries for which the data indicate a real decline in the size of the export sector, the forces producing this change appear to be quite different in stagnating and growing economies. In the Philippines, the ratio of exports to total product has fallen, despite a substantial rise in the volume of exports over prewar. Domestic product has grown more rapidly than exports relative to the prewar period, while in Burma, and presumably in Indonesia as well, the ratio has fallen because prewar volumes and diversity of export products have not been restored. This conclusion emerges from indexes of export volumes presented in Table 12. It is important to emphasize the limitations of the export volume data pertaining to Indonesia. The Indonesian quantum index refers to only four major products (petroleum, rubber, tin, and copra), while the real decline in Indonesia's export capacity is reflected in reduced volumes from a wide variety of minor exports. The Philippines are unique in showing a continuing high rate of growth of exports during the decade of the 1950's when, according to our assessment, new expansion of productive capacity was occurring. Export volumes grew less rapidly during the decade in the other Southeast Asian countries, showing little variation between countries with differing rates of rehabilitation and growth.[43] The more significant comparison, however, relates averages for the late 1950's to the immediate prewar volume. Lagging rehabilitation and growth are clearly reflected in Burma's regaining only 48 per cent of her prewar export volume. Indonesia's export volumes were 21 per cent above prewar, but the improvement has been the result of greatly expanded

[41] This result assumes the more realistic export rate of 3 pesos to U.S. $1.00 (rather than 2 pesos to U.S. $1.00) for the Philippines, and the effective export rate of 30.4 rupiah to U.S. $1.00 (rather than the official 11.4 rupiah to U.S. $1.00) for Indonesia.

[42] There is evidence that foreign-trade ratios are higher in dependent than in sovereign countries. See Karl W. Deutsch et al., "Population, Sovereignty and the Share of Foreign Trade," *Economic Development and Cultural Change*, X (July, 1962), 363.

[43] Between 1950–52 and 1958–60, the volume of exports increased 10 per cent in Burma, 9 per cent in Malaya, 3 per cent in Indonesia, and 4 per cent in Thailand, compared to 49 per cent in the Philippines. See Table 12 for basic data.

TABLE 12

Indexes of Export Volumes (1953 = 100)

	Burma	Malaya	Indonesia	Philippines	Thailand
1937[a]	299	78	80	88	76
1948	117	95	50	62	69
1950–52	100	119	94	96	109
1958–60	110	130	97	143	113
1958–60 as percentage of 1937:	48	167	121	163	149

[a] 1938 for Malaya.

Sources: Derived from International Monetary Fund, *International Financial Statistics*, various issues, for all countries except Malaya. Malayan data from ECAFE, *Economic Bulletin for Asia and the Far East*, various issues.

petroleum exports (provided largely by foreign enterprises) while other categories of exports remain below prewar volumes.[44] In the more rapidly rehabilitating and growing economies of the Philippines, Malaya, and

Figure 7
Growth and Export Volumes

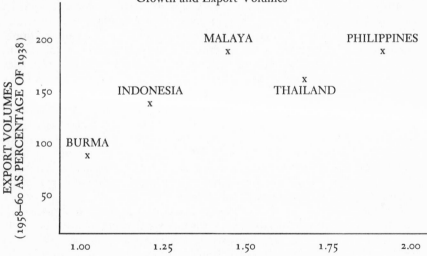

RATIO OF NEW GROWTH TO REHABILITATION (1946–60)

[44] Conditions affecting petroleum exports are predominantly external to the Indonesian economy; foreign factors of production continue to be dominant in this unique sector of the economy, and, under a combination of high profit rates, strong market demand, and partial exemption from Indonesian foreign-exchange controls, expansion of foreign investment, output, and exports have continued. Behavior of nonpetroleum export volumes, therefore, appears to be more indicative of the internal dynamics affecting growth of real product. The 1957–59 unweighted average of nonpetroleum exports was 45 per cent of the 1938 volume, while the average for the decade 1950–59 was 52 per cent. Percentages are computed from export-volume data published in annual editions of the *Report of the Bank of Indonesia*.

Thailand, export volumes in the late 1950's were substantially above prewar—63 per cent, 67 per cent, and 49 per cent respectively.

The relationship between the real-product indicators and export volumes is shown with greater precision in Figure 7. Employing our measure of the ratio of new growth to rehabilitation (see Table 9), we find a significant relationship between values of this ratio and volumes of exports in the late 1950's as a percentage of immediate prewar volumes. Indonesia departs from the almost linear relationship shown for the other countries, but the nature of the data and the special position of petroleum appear to explain this erratic case.[45] The capacity of Southeast Asian export economies to raise export volumes above prewar levels has varied considerably, but export performance has been closely related to the rapidity of rehabilitation and rates of new expansion of productive capacities throughout the economy.

Structural Change

Economists have believed for some time that economic growth produces shifts in the occupational distribution of labor from primary to secondary and tertiary production, essentially from agricultural and related activities to industrial and service employments. More recently the argument has been restated in the form of hypotheses associating growth of real product in some orderly and predictable way with changes in relative product shares by major sectors of the economy. In its most procrustean formulation, the argument has attempted to relate increases in per capita real income and rising shares of the industrial sector (falling shares of primary production). Using data from forty countries covering the early part of the 1950's, Hollis Chenery finds that the principal feature of the contemporary pattern of growth "is the rise in the share of industrial output from 17 per cent (12 per cent for manufacturing alone) at an income level of $100 to 38 per cent (33 per cent for manufacturing alone) at a level of $1000. The share of transportation and communication also doubles over this range, while primary production declines from 45 to 15 per cent."[46] It should be noted that Chenery does not trace these relationships in the growth of individual economies. His statistical analysis is based on the "cross-section" method, that is, a comparison of sector shares for countries at different per capita income levels at one point in time.

Generalizing from his study of a mass of empirical data, Simon Kuznets also finds a "marked association between industrial structure and per capita income."[47] Kuznets places emphasis on the expansion of the M+ sector (mining, manufacturing, construction, transportation, and communication), and his data show the share of this broad industrial grouping in gross domestic product varying from almost 60 per cent for countries with the

---

[45] Indonesian export-volume indexes published by the International Monetary Fund include only four major products that have contributed a growing share of total exports. Among these products, petroleum exports have grown most rapidly, and these are relatively unaffected by internal economic conditions (see above footnote).

[46] Hollis B. Chenery, "Patterns of Industrial Growth," *American Economic Review*, I (September, 1960), 635.

[47] Simon Kuznets, *op. cit.*, p. 8.

highest per capita incomes to 17–20 per cent for the lowest.[48] In an earlier paper, Kuznets explicitly relates rates of growth and rates of structural change: "One may argue that, in general, if real income per capita is growing rapidly, the accompanying changes in the industrial structure of the labor force or of total product, or of some aspects of both, should also be large; whereas moderate changes in per capita product should be accompanied by relatively moderate shifts in industrial structure."[49]

A study of the relevant data for Southeast Asian countries suggests that growth of real product produces unmistakable changes in the composition of product among major sectors, but that cross-section methods are likely to give a misleading impression of the historical process of structural change in newly independent countries. Caution in interpreting the data is essential, however, for a number of reasons. First, the data cover a limited period of time and during the short period under survey, growth of real product has been a mixture of rehabilitation and new growth. Second, the data are not adequate for a careful evaluation of the rates of growth of output by sector. The definition of sectors varies among the countries under review and, with one or two exceptions, censuses of industries have not been undertaken to provide value-added data in the industrial sector.

It may be useful to re-emphasize the distinction between rehabilitation and new growth to stress the implications of this distinction for relating structural change to economic growth in Southeast Asian countries. There is some evidence suggesting that war and political instability reduced output and capacity in the capital-intensive, industrial sectors more than in the labor-intensive, agricultural and related sectors. Independence followed the war in most Southeast Asian countries, and in the new situation of national sovereignty, foreign participation in the capital-intensive sector became subject to new restrictions. It was almost inevitable that the climate for foreign investment and entrepreneurship should change, and in the process of revamping conditions under which foreign enterprise operated in these economies, Southeast Asian countries confronted foreign factors with a combination of new redistribution policies and uncertainty as to their future status. These conditions tended to discourage rapid rehabilitation of the industrial sector by foreign factors, while domestic entrepreneurs and their governments were less capable of mobilizing the required supplies of capital and special skills. In some countries, rehabilitation was delayed by domestic policy struggles over the status and role of foreign enterprise. In others, the new governments were reluctant or unable to tackle the problem of restoring capital-intensive industries as long as major political issues stemming from independence remained unresolved, or actual security problems persisted.

Underlying these factors is an even more basic force, the pursuit of structural change within the capital-intensive sector as a major social goal. As in other emerging countries, Southeast Asian governments have sought to

[48] *Ibid*. Table 2, p. 9.
[49] Simon Kuznets, "Quantitative Aspects of the Economic Growth of Nations: II. Industrial Distribution of National Product and Labor Force," *Economic Development and Cultural Change*, supplement to Vol. V (July, 1957), 54.

convert capital-intensive production from predominantly export-processing operations to activities more oriented to the domestic market. Rehabilitation of the industrial sector, therefore, came to be not so much a matter of restoring prewar plants but rather of replacing export-processing and export-supporting facilities with import-replacing firms, or at least of encouraging production for the domestic market at the expense of export processing. In addition to its effects on growth of exports as reflected in the declining ratios of exports to aggregate product, this force tended to delay the return of Southeast Asian economies to colonial, prewar output patterns with relatively high industrial shares. Hence, relative shares of the capital-intensive industries in total product have not been restored to their prewar size, unless considerable new growth occurred after independence.

There is limited and rather shaky evidence suggesting retrogression and delayed rehabilitation of the capital-intensive sector. Estimates of prewar aggregate product by industry exist for the Philippines and Indonesia, and attempts have been made to compare the prewar estimates with postwar accounts. The Indonesian comparison shows a definite shift toward larger shares of the labor-intensive sectors between 1939 and 1952; national product data in current prices allocated between the capital-intensive and labor-intensive sectors indicated that 76 per cent of national product originated in the labor-intensive sector in 1952, compared to 68 per cent in 1939.[50] The share of manufacturing fell from 15 to 8 per cent during the period, and contributions from mining, agricultural plantations, and other components of the capital-intensive sector suffered similar setbacks.

Goodstein's study of the Philippines shows somewhat parallel changes in the sectoral composition of aggregate product in constant prices between 1938 and 1948. Value added in manufacturing in 1948 had recovered to only 80 per cent of its 1938 value, although aggregate real product had recovered to 111 per cent. Recovery of mining output proceeded even more slowly; by 1948, only 30 per cent of its prewar value had been restored. On the other hand, construction, transportation, utilities, and services were substantially above their prewar value, while the real value of agricultural output was estimated to be at the same level in 1948 as in 1938.[51] As a result, the ratio of manufacturing to total output fell from 17 per cent in 1938 to 12 per cent in 1948 and mining from 3 to 1 per cent. Much of the slack was taken up in the services sector, particularly government, however, rather than in agriculture; agriculture's share fell slightly over the period. By 1956, however, the pattern of aggregate real product by industrial origin was remarkably similar to 1938, and Goodstein comments on the stability of the relative shares of agriculture, manufacturing, and services.[52] In the

[50] Douglas S. Paauw, *Financing Economic Development: The Indonesian Case* (Glencoe, Ill.: The Free Press, 1960), p. 209.

[51] All data are taken from Marvin E. Goodstein, *op. cit.*, especially Table I–1, pp. 8–22, and Table I–2, p. 26. The results are approximately the same in Goodstein's calculations using 1938, 1948, and 1956 prices alternatively.

[52] Relative shares reported by Goodstein were as follows: Agriculture, 1938: 29.3 per cent, 1956: 30.5 per cent; Manufacturing, 1938: 16.7 per cent, 1956: 17.4 per cent; Services, 1938: 15.6 per cent, 1956: 17.5 per cent; Commerce, 1938: 15.5 per cent,

Philippine case, therefore, substantial growth of real product per capita between 1938 and 1956 apparently failed to induce structural change in the sense suggested by Chenery's and Kuznets' cross-section analysis, although import-substitution and foreign-trade changes were proceeding apace. When we view in the more limited perspective of the decade of the 1950's and use aggregate product in current prices for a comparison of changes in sector shares in several Southeast Asian countries, however, somewhat different conclusions emerge.

The data for Southeast Asia allow comparison for four countries (Burma, Indonesia, Philippines, Thailand) for a period that roughly coincides with the 1950 decade.[53] Structural change over this period is measured by the change in the contributions of three sectors to total product, agriculture, manufacturing, and industry.[54] Total product in *current prices* is employed, since usable data in constant prices are available only for the Philippines and Thailand. Three-year averages are used to estimate sector shares to reduce the effect of short-run influences, yielding a comparison between average sector shares during the early and latter parts of the 1950 decade. The results are presented in graphic form in Figure 8. A semilogarithmic graph is used, with percentage contributions by sectors measured on the vertical axis and time on the horizontal axis. Equal percentage changes in the sizes of sectors are shown by equal vertical distances. Changes in the three sectors—agriculture, industry, and manufacturing, as a subcategory of industry—are shown for Burma, the Philippines, and Thailand, while for Indonesia, only agriculture and manufacturing are shown.

Figure 8 demonstrates rather striking differences between the Philippines and Thailand on the one hand and Burma and Indonesia on the other.[55]

1956: 15.5 per cent. The share of commerce was assumed constant because "lack of data permits no alternative." Goodstein believes that it probably declined in fact. Using Kuznets' M+ sector, a calculation from Goodstein's results suggests a slight decline from 31.1 per cent in 1938 to 29.3 per cent in 1956. Goodstein, *op. cit.* Table I–2, p. 26.

[53] Data for Malaya are available for the latter half of the decade only, and that country is excluded from this comparison.

[54] The term "industry" is used to denote roughly the capital-intensive sector as a whole. It is used here in a sense close to that used by Chenery, *op. cit.*, and Kuznets' concept of the M+ sector. In the standard United Nations account, industrial origin of net product (which is used here) industry includes mining, manufacturing, construction, electricity, gas and water, and transportation, storage, and communication.

[55] A comparison of sector shares relative to total product in constant and current prices for the Philippines and Thailand suggests that the current price series tends to show greater changes in sector shares than the constant price series. This result raises the danger that measurement of structural change from sector contributions to total product in current prices may overstate the growth of manufacturing and industry. Relative price changes occur as development proceeds, and where tariff and exchange policies are tightened to protect domestic industry, prices of manufactures and related outputs tend to rise relative to agricultural prices. In general, this appears to have occurred during the 1950's in all Southeast Asian countries. Hence, it is likely that the data for all Southeast Asian countries are subject to the same bias, and comparisons in constant prices would probably not show significant differences by country, in the relative rates of changes in sector shares from those exhibited in Figure 8.

Figure 8. SECTORAL SHARES, 1950–52 to 1958–60

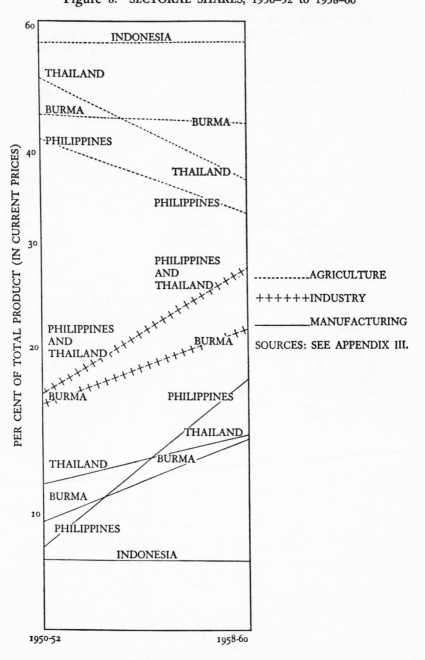

In Indonesia, sector shares apparently remained relatively constant between the early and late years of the 1950 decade,[56] while in Burma, the decline of agriculture and the expansion of the industrial sector were considerably less than in the Philippines and Thailand. The percentage rise in the share of Burmese manufacturing was greater than in Thailand, but at the end of the decade, manufacturing contributed slightly more to total product in Thailand than in Burma. Structural change in the Philippines appears to have outpaced that in the other countries; the share of agriculture was reduced to 34 per cent by 1958–60, compared to 37 for Thailand, although the rate of decline in Thailand was somewhat greater. The rise in the share of manufacturing was more rapid in the Philippines than elsewhere, roughly doubling from 9 to 18 per cent, while industry as a whole expanded at the same rate in the Philippines and Thailand.

The evidence from sector shares in current prices, therefore, appears to corroborate the hypotheses associating growth of real product with structural change. Moreover, Southeast Asian data suggest that the rapidity of rehabilitation has some relationship to structural change. In the Philippines and Thailand, the decade of the 1950's was essentially a period of new growth, although a closer study of the data suggests that, in the Philippines at least, a part of the momentum in the early years of the decade consisted in the rapid restoration of industrial sectors to their prewar shares, even though aggregate real product had been restored earlier. This suggests the hypothesis that growth of capital-intensive sectors tends to lag somewhat during rehabilitation, but if the momentum of rehabilitation continues, shares from capital-intensive sectors will eventually be restored and raised to higher levels consistent with new growth.

The constancy of sector shares in Indonesia over the 1950 decade and the decline of capital-intensive industries from the colonial period appear to confirm this hypothesis. Aggregate real product was expanded during the decade, but prewar output levels were restored so slowly that little momentum was developed to launch new growth, to rebuild fully, or to replace the prewar colonial capital-intensive sector. On the other hand, moderate structural change occurred in Burma during the 1950's, despite the slow recovery of aggregate output. Given the heavy emphasis on structural change and the pursuit of planned industrial development in Burma, however, Burmese experience may also be construed as evidence of the importance of rapid rehabilitation of devastated economies as a precondition for new growth and structural change. From this point of view, there is significance in the sluggishness of structural change in an economy where planning efforts were concentrated on expanding the capital-intensive sector over most of the decade.[57] There is fragmentary evidence pointing to

[56] Indonesian domestic product series show a slight tendency toward a decline of agriculture's share and rising industrial shares during the mid-1950's. Reversal of these trends during the last few years of the decade, suggested by domestic-product estimates, might be explained by a series of external shocks to the economy after 1957.

[57] In Burma, where public investment is estimated to have represented 47 per cent of the total fixed investment during the late 1950's (compared to 28 per cent

the conclusion that structural retrogression (in the sense of declining contributions from capital-intensive industries to total product) occurred in
the Burmese economy between the immediate prewar period and the late
1950's. It appears that the relative shares from mining and manufacturing
combined fell over this period,[58] and, given the lagging growth of primary
production as well,[59] there has been a pronounced increase in contributions
from services sectors to total product.[60]

It is likely that a part of the growth of services or certain subsectors in
this catch-all category tends to be overstated in most systems of national
income accounting used by developing countries. As population moves out
of the agricultural sector, promoting rapid urbanization (a phenomenon
associated with postwar conditions in all Southeast Asian countries), the
disguised unemployed tend to move from agriculture to fringe occupations
in the urban sector.[61] In part, this process represents a shift of factors of
production from relatively unproductive occupations in the rural sector to

---

in the Philippines and 24 per cent in Thailand), the capital-intensive sector received
much higher allocation percentages than in other Southeast Asian countries. ECAFE,
Economic Survey of Asia and the Far East, 1961, p. 27 and p. 36. The ECAFE _Survey_
criticizes this emphasis in Burma: "In the eight-year (1953–1960) plan of Burma, for
instance, transport, communications and power were to have absorbed 43 per cent of
total government expenditures or 77 per cent of public investment. This has been
considered excessive in an economy which has barely recovered prewar levels of production especially in agriculture, and where more attention needs to be given to augmenting
direct production" (p. 27).

[58] Walinsky, _op. cit._, p. 44 and p. 45, estimates the prewar contribution of mining at
5.5 per cent of total product, of manufacturing at 11–12 per cent. During the late
1950's, their combined contribution averaged about 15 per cent of total product, compared to the Walinsky estimate that would result in a combined prewar contribution of
about 17 per cent. It should be emphasized, however, that this phenomenon in Burma's
case is partly explained by the decline in petroleum mining, caused by approaching exhaustion of known oil reserves.

[59] Burma is unique among Southeast Asian countries for which data are published
in not having restored prewar agricultural output levels by the mid-1950's. In 1954–55,
Burma's index of production of all agricultural commodities (on a 1934–38 base equal
to 100) was 88, compared to 122 for Indonesia, 131 for Malaya, 137 for the Philippines,
and 152 for Thailand. Data are taken from ECAFE, _Economic Survey of Asia and the
Far East_, 1955, p. 195. It should be noted, however, that there is general agreement that
the value of agricultural output is underestimated in Burmese national accounts.

[60] It is difficult to demonstrate this conclusion statistically because Burmese domestic
product accounts by industrial origin lump together manufacturing and other industries
with services, and contributions from these sectors have not been separated from the
prewar period. Employing the Walinsky estimate of manufacturing's share for the prewar period, however, a comparison between 1939 and the late 1950's would show a
rise in services from roughly 25 per cent of gross domestic product in 1939 to about
38 per cent, with government services (public administration and defense) growing
from 7 to 11 per cent. Sector shares are based on official Burmese domestic product
data published in Ministry of National Planning, _The National Income of Burma_, annual editions, and the refined breakdown published in the United Nations, _Yearbook of
National Accounts Statistics_ for the postwar period.

[61] This point is made in Surinder K. Mehta, "A Comparative Analysis of the Urban
Labor Force of Burma and the United States," _Economic Development and Cultural
Change_, IX (January, 1961), 164–79.

equally unproductive activities in the urban sector. The problem is that unproductive activities tend to escape measurement in the rural sector but to be included in the more monetized urban sector. The accommodation of this shift by expansion of government expenditures to support make-work activities, for example, is reflected as an increase in product and income which is difficult to justify on economic grounds.

This study has attempted to establish the rough dimensions of economic growth in Southeast Asian countries from aggregative and supporting data. It has been argued that fairly clear differences in performance emerge if the data are interpreted in the context of important historical factors that have affected Southeast Asian countries over the past two-and-a-half decades. Viewed over this entire period, some countries have failed to raise per capita real product, while others have shown significant gains. These important differences have been obscured by published measures of growth rates during the 1950's, primarily because the time pattern of growth and rehabilitation has varied considerably among Southeast Asian countries. This result raises the question of the extent to which commonly held views about postwar growth and structural change in underdeveloped countries generally are based on data that fail to distinguish between rehabilitation and new expansion. Cross-section studies among countries at different per capita income levels during the 1950's are particularly suspect. Structural change found in such studies may merely reflect rapid rehabilitation of previous patterns of output during the course of recovering from severe external shocks to the economy.

This study suggests caution in other respects as well. Data for estimating capital formation rates are probably no worse in Southeast Asia than in many other underdeveloped areas, yet scrutiny of the existing estimates points to large margins of error. This suggests that there is potential danger in ready acceptance of the present estimates for planning purposes. To employ the official Philippine estimates for projecting capital requirements for achieving specific growth objectives. for example, would yield a development program too modest to achieve the specified objectives, while the reverse would be true for Burma.

Southeast Asia shares with other underdeveloped areas problems of statistical reliability of aggregative economic data. Difficulties in measuring and comparing dimensions of growth are compounded by unresolved conceptual problems. It is believed, however, that the data for evaluating growth in Southeast Asia are adequate to support conclusions pointing to the growing magnitude of the development problem. In particular, one can hardly view with equanimity the rising rate of population growth in both growing and stagnant economies. Confronted with this drag on raising per capita real income, no Southeast Asian country has succeeded in raising the rate of growth of aggregate real product over the course of the postwar period. On the contrary, it appears that there has been a perceptible retardation of growth rates in all Southeast Asian countries, and where new growth has occurred, it appears that incremental capital-output ratios have

risen sharply. In short, there has been a tendency for the slow-growth economies to become stagnant and for the growing economies to grow less
rapidly—both in terms of aggregate and per capita product. As the task of
rehabilitation has been completed in some countries or prolonged in others,
the growth momentum originally provided from output gains in the sectors
most responsive to mere restoration of political and social stability has
petered out. The mushrooming of economic plans throughout the area and
the conscious application of public policy to promote growth have failed
to reverse the trend toward a narrowing gap between growth of output and
growth of population. The question should at least be raised as to whether
these economies may not be tending to revert toward the underdeveloped
state where the equilibrium growth rate is zero, after experiencing a period
of growth induced by favorable external stimuli during the immediate
postwar period.[62] There is little to support the view that requisite internal
changes have been made to perpetuate the growth momentum that appeared to be general in Southeast Asia during the expansionary period of
the first half of the 1950 decade.

Appendix I: Sources and Notes to Table 6

Burma: Official Burmese domestic income and product estimates (Ministry
of National Planning, the National Income of Burma) show aggregate
real product restored to the 1938–39 level in 1956–57. Population data suggest that population had grown by approximately 22 per cent during this
eighteen-year period. In 1959–60, aggregate real product was only 11 per
cent above the prewar level although population is estimated to have
grown by 27 per cent. Population data are based on United Nations, Department of Economic and Social Affairs, Population Studies No. 31, *The
Population of Asia and the Far East, 1950–1980* (New York: United Nations, 1959), and the data published by ECAFE in *Economic Survey of
Asia and the Far East.*

Thailand: Joseph S. Gould, *Preliminary Estimates of the Gross Geographical Product and Domestic National Income of Thailand, 1938–1939, 1946–
1950*, shows real gross geographical product (in 1948 dollars) in 1947 at 15
per cent above the 1938–39 level, real *national* income 18 per cent above.
Population estimates, based on the 1937 and 1947 censuses, indicate a rise
in population of approximately 16 per cent between 1939 and 1947.

Philippines: The estimate for aggregate output is based on Marvin E.
Goodstein, *The Pace and Pattern of Philippine Economic Growth, 1938,
1948, and 1956* (Ithaca, N.Y.: 1962), and supported by data from the
"Bell Mission" report (Economic Survey Mission to the Philippines, *Report to the President of the United States* [Washington, D.C., 1950]). The

[62] This view of the developing and underdeveloped states has been put forth by
Hyman P. Minsky in "Indicators of the Development Status of an Economy," *Economic Development and Cultural Change*, VII (January, 1959), 151–72.

estimate for per capita real product is based on the above source and real-product figures presented in Bernardino G. Bantegui, "Composition and Growth of National Income in the Philippines," *Economic Research Journal*, VI (March, 1960), Tables 1 and 2, p. 241, adjusted for population growth from data taken from United Nations, *Population Growth and Manpower in the Philippines* (New York: United Nations, 1960). These data suggest that aggregate real product in 1948 was 10–11 per cent above the prewar (1938) level, while population had grown by 22.2 per cent. By 1950, aggregate real product exceeded the 1938 level by 25 per cent, while population had grown by 26.2 per cent.

Indonesia: Muljatno, "Perhitungan Pendapatan Nasional Indonesia Untuk 1953 dan 1954," *Ekonomi dan Keuangan Indonesia*, XIII (March–April, 1960), 162–216, represents the only published comparison of prewar and postwar real product. This estimate shows aggregate real product restored to the 1938 level in 1953, but per capita real product still slightly below the 1938 level in 1955. The 1961 census reveals that Muljatno's estimates for population growth in the intervening years are low. Muljatno's results show aggregate real product in 1955 at 15 per cent above the 1938 level, while the 1961 census suggests that 1955 population was approximately 20 per cent above the 1938 figure. Proceeding from this base and employing the population growth rate for the 1950's suggested by the population (2.5 per cent per year) and the official data on real product (published by both ECAFE and the United Nations) for the period 1955–57, per capita real income is estimated to have been restored to the 1938 level in 1957. Discussion in the text suggests, however, that this result probably overstates Indonesian growth performance.

Malaya: In the absence of aggregative data for the prewar period, no comparison using real product and population data is possible. There is agreement among observers, however, that recovery and rehabilitation from wartime damage proceeded relatively rapidly. In the words of the International Bank for Reconstruction and Development Mission: "By 1947 and 1948 the foundations of the economy had in large measure been restored; rubber and rice production exceeded the prewar output; tin production was nearly back to the average of the 1930's; shipping was again at about prewar levels; and the effects of the war on production and commerce generally were rapidly disappearing. Despite the outbreak of the emergency in 1948, . . . economic recovery continued and by 1950 Malaya was able to turn from its preoccupation with reconstruction to the problems of further economic expansion." International Bank for Reconstruction and Development, *The Economic Development of Malaya* (Baltimore, Md.: Johns Hopkins Press, 1955), p. 19. Similar conclusions emerge from data presented in John Paul Meek, *Malaya: A Study of Governmental Response to the Korean Boom* (Ithaca, N.Y.: 1955), pp. 4–10.

APPENDIX II: SOURCES TO TABLE 7

Burma: Ministry of National Planning, *The National Income of Burma,* annual issues.

Indonesia: Rehabilitation: Muljatno, "Perhitungan Pendapatan Nasional Indonesia Untuk 1953 dan 1954," *Ekonomi dan Keuangan Indonesia,* XIII (March–April, 1960), 184. Postrehabilitation: United Nations, *Yearbook of National Accounts Statistics, 1960* (New York: United Nations, 1961), p. 114.

Malaya: 1949–53: International Bank for Reconstruction and Development, *The Economic Development of Malaya,* p. 21. Rough estimates only. 1955–60: United Nations, Statistical Office.

Philippines: Rehabilitation: Bernardino G. Bantegui, "Composition and Growth of National Income in the Philippines," *Economic Research Journal,* VI (March, 1960), 241. Postrehabilitation: United Nations, *Yearbook of National Accounts Statistics, 1961* (New York: United Nations, 1962), p. 213, and data provided by the United Nations Statistical Office.

Thailand: Rehabilitation: Joseph S. Gould, *Preliminary Estimates of the Gross Geographical Product and Domestic National Income of Thailand, 1938–1939, 1946–1950,* p. 16. Postrehabilitation: 1947–50, Gould, *op. cit.,* p. 16. 1951–60, United Nations, *Yearbook of National Accounts Statistics, 1961,* p. 254 and data provided by the United Nations Statistical Office.

APPENDIX III: SECTORAL SHARES, 1950–52 TO 1958–60,
NOTE TO FIGURE 8

Sector shares as percentage of total product in current prices are computed as averages for three-year periods. The details of the years used and sources by country are as follows:

Burma: The two periods refer to 1951–53 and 1958–60. Data for calculations are taken from official estimates of Industrial Origin of Gross Domestic Product published by the Ministry of National Planning and also reproduced in annual editions of the United Nations, *Yearbook of National Accounts Statistics.*

Indonesia: The two periods refer to 1951–53 and 1957–59. Data for calculations are taken from official estimates of Industrial Origin of Net Domestic Product published in annual editions of ECAFE, *Economic Survey of Asia and the Far East* and also reproduced in annual editions of the United Nations, *Yearbook of National Accounts Statistics.*

Thailand: The two periods refer to 1950–52 and 1958–60. Data for calculations are taken from official estimates of Industrial Origin of Gross Domestic Product (new series). Estimates for the years 1954–60 are published in United Nations, *Yearbook of National Accounts Statistics, 1961.* Estimates for the years 1950–52 have been provided by the United Nations Statistical Office.

Philippines: The two periods refer to 1950–52 and 1958–60. Data for calculations are taken from official estimates of Industrial Origin of Net National Product, published in annual editions of United Nations, *Yearbook of National Accounts Statistics.*

A Glossary of Economic Terms*

Capital: man-made material wealth, usually expressed in terms of its money value, used in the production of goods and services. Often used to mean capital goods. *Capital consumption:* the depletion without replacement of existing capital stock through wear-and-tear (depreciation), diminishing inventory levels, obsolescence, and so on. *Capital formation:* the creation of capital goods, such as plant, equipment, and inventories used in the production of other goods. *Fixed capital:* permanent capital goods, such as plant and equipment, as opposed to circulating capital as is invested in inventories, wage funds, and the cost of raw materials and intermediate goods. *Fixed capital formation:* the creation of permanent capital goods. *Gross capital formation:* total new creation of capital goods before deductions are made for replacement of capital consumed through depreciation, scrapping of obsolescent equipment, which would give net capital formation. *Capital-intensive:* using more capital than labor or land in production. *Capital-output ratio:* the amount of capital required to produce an additional unit of output; capital investment divided by its output. *Capital stock:* existing capital goods available for productive use.

External economies: as used here, refers to the conditions created by government and other activities that reduce the cost of business activities. Examples are improved transportation, communications, financial institutions, etc.

Geographical product: includes output attributed to foreign factors of production (capital and labor) at work within a nation's borders but excludes nationally owned factors at work abroad.

Gross domestic product: total domestic production of goods and services before deductions are made for replacement, repair, and maintenance of existing capital stock, which would give net domestic product.

Gross investment: gross capital formation.

Growth ratio: as used here, refers to the relationship between new growth and postwar rehabilitation as expressed in Table IV (that is, aggregate real product of 1960 divided by the prewar aggregate real product).

Income effects: changes in an economic variable caused by a rise or fall in income; for example, as real incomes rise, the demand for imports may increase at an even faster rate.

* Prepared by the Editor.

Labor-intensive: using relatively more labor than capital or land in production.

National product: includes output attributed to domestic factors of production (capital and labor) within a nation's borders and income earned by national capital and labor abroad, but excludes the earnings of foreign investment and labor within the nation.

Ratio: as used in Tables 10 and 11, means percentage. In Table 10, it is gross fixed capital formation divided by gross domestic product. In Table 11, it is exports divided by gross domestic product.

Real income: income in terms of goods and services.

Real product: output of goods and services. *Real-product indicators:* as used here, refers to the deflated money figures used as estimates of real product.

Terms of trade: the relative amounts of domestic resources required to produce goods and services that will exchange for a particular bundle of foreign goods, at going exchange rates.

Value-added: generally refers to the value added to a particular commodity by a particular economic activity, such as a manufacturing or processing plant, that is, the price of a product minus the cost of raw material and intermediate goods inputs.

APPENDIX A

A STATISTICAL SUMMARY OF
CONTEMPORARY SOUTHEAST ASIA

Tables 13–17 are intended to provide the reader with a handy reference to the general statistical configurations of contemporary Southeast Asia. A warning must be voiced, however. Statistical reporting from Southeast Asia is often unreliable, and these tables should therefore be employed with some realistic caution.

TABLE 13

Southeast Asia: Area and Population, 1966*

	Estimated Mid-1966 Population (millions)	Annual Increase (per cent)	Area (square miles)	Density of Population (per square mile)
Burma	25.2	2.0	261,610	96
Cambodia	6.3	2.6	69,884	91
Indonesia	107.0	2.3	735,286	146
Laos	2.7	2.5	89,343	29
Malaysia				
Sabah	0.6	3.5	29,387	18
Sarawak	0.9	2.5	47,071	18
Malaya	8.3	3.1	50,686	164
Philippines	33.5	3.3	115,600	292
Singapore	1.9	3.0	225	8560
Thailand	31.5	3.0	200,148	158
Vietnam, North	19.5	3.3	60,278	252
Vietnam, South	16.5	3.1	65,970	63
Brunei	0.1	4.0	2,225	47
Portuguese Timor	0.6	1.5	5,751	99

* Based on data contained in United Nations, *Demographic Yearbook*, 1966 (New York: United Nations, 1967).

TABLE 14
Asia: Rank Ordering by Ten Indexes of Development*

	1	2	3	4	5	6	7	8	9	10	Average Scores	Rank by Average Scores
Japan	2	1	1	1	1	1	1	1	1	1	1.1	1
Singapore	1	2	—	5	2	2	—	—	—	2	2.3	2
Malaysia	4	3	2	6	4	3	2	2	5	3	3.4	3
Philippines	3	4	3	2	3	6	3	3	3.5	4	3.45	4
Thailand	8	7	6	3	5.5	8	5	5	3.5	6	5.7	5
China (CPR)	—	—	4.5	—	5.5	5	7	6	8	—	6.0	6
South Vietnam	—	9	8	—	7	4	4	4	—	7	6.1	7
Indonesia	5	6	9	7	10	8	6	7	10	11	7.9	8
Cambodia	—	11	—	8	9	11	8	8	6	5	8.2	9
India	6	5	4.5	9	11	13	9	9	7	10	8.35	10
Burma	—	10	—	4	8	10	11	11	2	12	8.5	11
Pakistan	7	8	7	10	12	12	10	10	9	9	9.4	12
Laos	—	12	—	—	13	8	12	12	—	8	10.8	13

* Rank orders have been tabulated from data appearing in Robert E. Ward, *Japan's Political System* (Englewood Cliffs, N.J.: Prentice-Hall, 1967), pp. 115–23. Ward unfortunately excluded Taiwan. While ample Taiwan data are available, for reasons of uniformity it seemed advisable not to seek other sources. Given the wide variation often found in aggregate economic data among various sources, to include Taiwan would have sacrificed comparability for the sake of comprehensiveness.

The ten indexes of development numbered above are as follows:
1. Percentage of labor force *not* in primary industry
2. Per capita energy consumption
3. Per capita steel consumption
4. Literacy
5. Ratio of school enrollment to school-age children
6. Daily newspapers per 1,000 population
7. "Money" per capita GNP
8. "Real" per capita GNP
9. Origin of Gross Domestic Product *not* from primary industry
10. Per capita Gross Domestic Product

Note: Dashes indicate that the necessary data are not available. Underlined figures indicate ties in rank-ordering. Rank-ordering is based on the actual number of entries in each column; thus, index 1, for example, has only eight possible ranks. In view of the problem of missing data and the frequent disagreement among statistical sources, these rankings should be regarded only as suggestive, not as definitive.

TABLE 15

Southeast Asia: Summary of Economic Data, 1966–67*

	Per Capita Income, est., 1967 (U.S.$)	Total GNP (billion U.S.$)	Growth in Per Capita GNP, est., 1966	Growth in Per Capita GNP, est., 1967
Burma	68	1.7	0[a]	NA
Cambodia	120	0.7[b]	NA	NA
Indonesia	85	8.9	NA	NA
Laos	65	NA	NA	NA
Malaysia	300	3.0	5.7[c]	0.0
Philippines	163	5.5[b]	2.0[be]	2.3[d]
Singapore	555	1.0	6.0[d]	NA
Thailand	128	4.2	6.0[d]	3.0[d]
Vietnam, South	119	1.9[b]	2.3[ae]	NA

* Unless otherwise indicated, these figures have been derived from information contained in the annual economic survey of Southeast Asia; *New York Times*, January 19, 1968.

[a] 1960–64 average

[b] 1965

[c] 1960–66 average

[d] Calculated on basis of total GNP growth less estimated population growth.

[e] Derived from United Nations, *Statistical Yearbook*, 1966 (New York: United Nations, 1967).

Note: NA means not available.

TABLE 16
Southeast Asia: Education Summary*

	Number of Schools	Number of Staff Members	Number of Students
Brunei (1965)			
Pre-school	11	24	858
Primary	167	1,129	28,336
Secondary	17	242	3,917
Teacher-training	1	16	331
Burma (1964)			
Primary	13,721	43,025	1,887,490
Secondary	1,625	15,631	497,275
Technical	38	99	2,846
Teacher-training	8	145	3,138
Higher	17	1,764	20,515
Cambodia (1964)			
Primary	4,011	14,622	691,131
Secondary	184	2,230	81,619
Technical	42	477	6,000
Teacher-training	3	126	1,949
Higher	37	430	4,763
Indonesia (1961)			
Pre-school	2,030	4,192	119,006
Primary	39,982	241,574	9,642,886
Secondary	5,452	35,156	754,434
Technical	768	5,132	90,822
Teacher-training	537	2,245	38,593
Higher	101	3,940	65,535
Specialized	22	115	1,774
Laos (1964)			
Pre-school	7	14	324
Primary	2,570	3,853	145,543
Secondary	8	133	4,140
Technical	3	57	674
Teacher-training	4	102	1,496
Higher	2	5	129

* Derived from United Nations, *Statistical Yearbook*, 1966 (New York: United Nations, 1967). Dashes indicate no data available.

TABLE 16   (continued)

	Number of Schools	Number of Staff Members	Number of Students
Malaysia (West Malaya only, 1964)			
Pre-school	412	—	14,345
Primary	4,785	44,238	1,182,527
Secondary	713	10,201	276,512
Technical	53	299	9,966
Higher	25	719	8,818
Specialized	28	21	391
Philippines (1963)			
Pre-school	283	637	28,996
Primary	34,100	155,413	5,233,611
Secondary	1,638	—	823,065
Technical	280	—	112,911
Higher	—	—	359,465
Specialized	3	60	371
Singapore (1964)			
Pre-school	15	184	5,455
Primary	469	11,420	348,167
Secondary	88	3,360	89,924
Technical	14	474	9,668
Higher	6	926	16,228
Specialized	6	39	424
Thailand (1964)			
Pre-school			65,627
Primary	27,600	150,658	4,500,207
Secondary			311,664
Technical	202 ⎫	7,076	38,228
Teacher-training	29 ⎭		14,612
Higher	35	1,767	52,037
Specialized	4	38	553
Vietnam, South (1964)			
Pre-school ⎫	34	609	30,002
Primary ⎬	5,762	26,786	1,563,756
Secondary ⎭	592	10,065	329,229
Technical	28	783	7,989
Teacher-training	5	97	2,251
Higher	23	745	23,437
Specialized	2	8	59

TABLE 17
Overseas Chinese in Southeast Asia
(100,000)

	Ch'iao Wu Wei Yuan Hui[1]	Skinner[2]	Kahin[3]	Purcell[4]
Burma	4.2[e]	4.0[f]	5.0	3.5
Cambodia	2.6[a]	4.4	3.5	3.5
Indonesia	25.5[e]	27.5	25.0	26.9
Laos	0.2[e]	0.5	0.4	0.4
Malaysia	28.0	33.2	29.3	28.9
Sabah	1.0[c]	1.2	1.0	1.0[h]
Sarawak	2.3[d]	2.8	2.3	2.4[h]
Malaya	24.6[e]	29.2	26.0	25.5
Philippines	1.5[e]	4.5	2.5	1.8[h]
Singapore	13.0[e]	14.0	12.3	12.3
Thailand	38.0[e]	26.0	23.2	26.7
Vietnam, North	1.0[b]	1.9[g]	—	0.6
Vietnam, South	9.3[b]	8.6	8.5	8.0
Brunei	0.2[e]	0.3	0.2	0.2[h]
Southeast Asia—Total	123.5	124.6	109.9	112.8

[1] Overseas Chinese Affairs Commission (Taipei, Taiwan), data drawn from individual country studies and from the summary volume, *Hua Ch'iao Chih Tsung Chih—Overseas Chinese Register* (Taipei: Overseas Chinese Affairs Commission, 1964), Table 1. Note varying dates of estimates.

[2] Lea E. Williams, *The Future of the Overseas Chinese in Southeast Asia*, 1966, p. 11. The figures were compiled by G. William Skinner in mid-1965 from the following sources:

I. *Chung-hua min-kuo nien-chien—Republic of China Yearbook* (Taipei: Chung-hua min-kuo nien-chien she, 1961), pp. 327–28.

II. *Chugoku nokeizai-kensetu no Kakyo—China's Economic Development and the Overseas Chinese* (Tokyo: Ajiya Keizai-kensysuho, 1960), p. 8.

III. *Malaysia in Brief* (Kuala Lumpur: Department of Information, 1963), p. 8.

IV. Statistical Office of the United Nations, Department of Economic and Social Affairs, *Demographic Yearbook*, 1963 (15th ed.; New York: United Nations, 1964), *passim*.

V. Statistical Office of the United Nations, "Population and Vital Statistics Report," *Statistical Papers*, Series A, v. 16, no. 3 (1964), *passim*.

VI. *The New York Times*, October 21, 1964.

[3] Derived from estimates made by each of the authors of the country studies in George McT. Kahin, ed., *Governments and Politics of Southeast Asia* (2d ed.; Ithaca, N.Y.: Cornell University Press, 1964). Dates of these estimates vary greatly. For consistency, lower figures were used where a general range was indicated.

[4] Victor Purcell, *The Chinese in Southeast Asia* (2d ed.; New York: Oxford University Press, 1965), p. 3.

[a] 1955
[b] 1959
[c] 1960
[d] 1961
[e] 1962

[f] Williams notes "As an untallied but presumably substantial number of Chinese have illegally crossed the border into Burma figures for that country are especially incertain."

[g] Williams again, "United Nations figures indicate that this many *Hoa* people are in North Vietnam. As no 'Chinese' are listed and as *Hoa* is a Vietnamese term for Chinese, Skinner has concluded that the Chinese population of the country is 190,000. This is an unusually high figure."

[h] These are census figures; the others are estimates.

APPENDIX B

MAPS

The maps reprinted in this section were prepared by students of cartography and graphics at the University of South Florida and were published originally in Robert H. Fuson, ed., *Southeast Asia: A Cartographic Analysis* (Tampa: University of South Florida, 1965). I am indebted to Professor Fuson, to his students, and to the University of South Florida for permission to reprint them here.

592

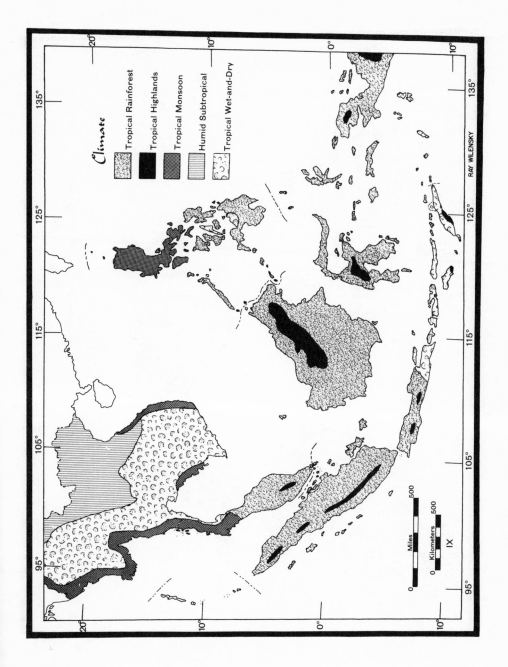

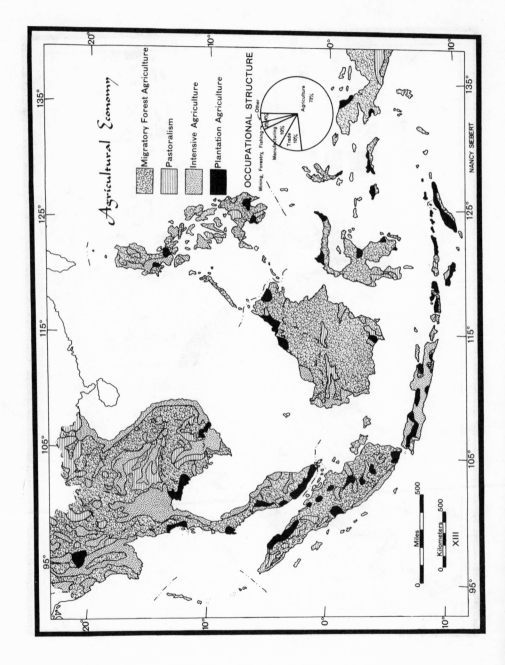

Agricultural Economy

Migratory Forest Agriculture

Pastoralism

Intensive Agriculture

Plantation Agriculture

OCCUPATIONAL STRUCTURE

Agriculture 73%

Trade 10%

Manufacturing 10%

Mining, Forestry, Fishing 3%

Other 4%

Miles

Kilometers

XIII

NANCY SIEBERT

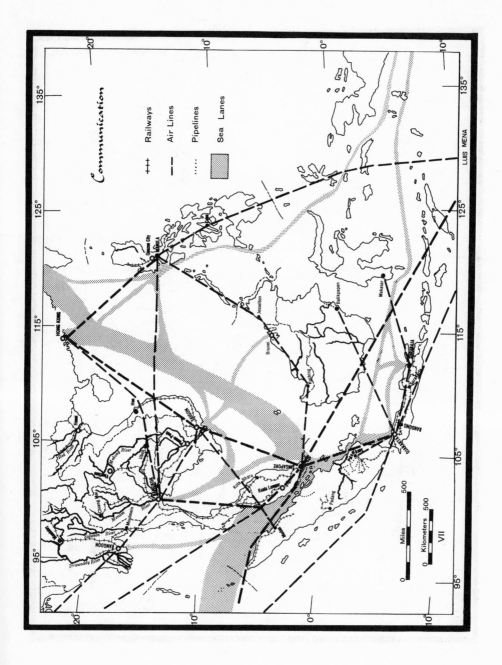

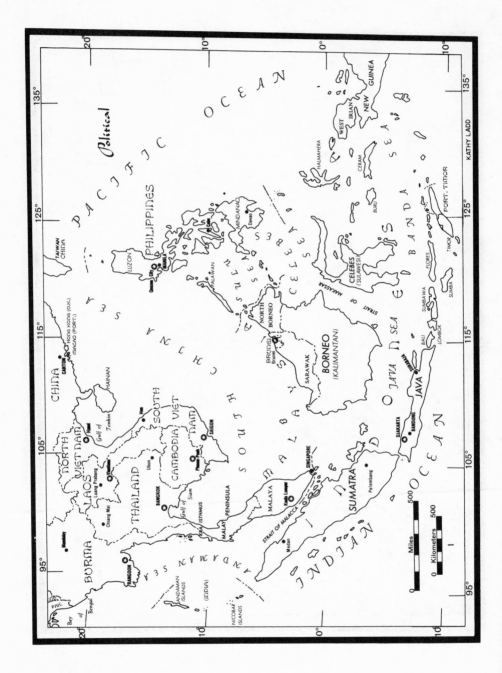

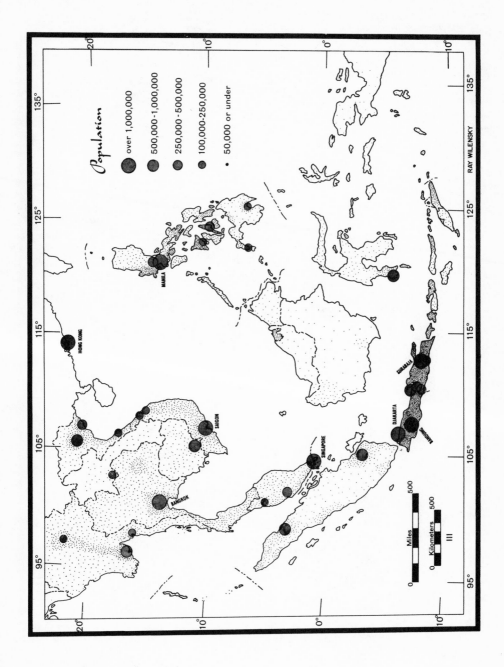

CONTEMPORARY SOUTHEAST ASIA:
AN INTRODUCTORY BIBLIOGRAPHICAL GUIDE

BOOKS

I. General

No attempt has been made to compile a comprehensive bibliography of modern Southeast Asia. Rather, I have attempted here to provide two kinds of bibliographical assistance. Part A suggests some of the basic monographic works dealing with contemporary Southeast Asia. Part B provides additional periodical references to literature concerned with some of the problems discussed in readings in this volume and is organized in a similar manner. For additional references, the reader is directed to the annual bibliographical issues of *The Journal of Asian Studies.*

In part because of its diversity, and in part because of the recent origins of much of the social science literature on Southeast Asia, there is not an abundance of good general studies dealing with the area as a whole. Some disciplines, of course, have almost none, due to the very nature of the subject. Anthropological studies, for example, are almost nonexistent, because anthropologists are usually concerned with micro-analysis, though their studies often yield generalizations that are probably more widely applicable than anthropologists themselves choose to claim. Moreover, even where disciplines have produced studies encompassing more than a single country, these perforce are more often a series of parallel descriptions (at best) or unconnected random observations (at worst) by one or several authors dealing, hopefully, with a single subject, problem, or cluster of problems. Some of these are very informative and useful; some are not. Some of the more recent studies likely to be of value to the neophyte to Southeast Asia's problems are suggested in this section.

In the field of modern history, and the modern period is our only concern here, several conveniently available and very recently published volumes deserve mention. Harry J. Benda and John Bastin, *The Modern History of Southeast Asia** (Englewood Cliffs, N.J.: Prentice Hall, 1969), provides an excellent brief introduction for the beginning student and a clear and reliable one-book summary for the interested layman. A companion volume of selected historical readings, somewhat more extensive in historical scope, is available in Harry J. Benda and John A. Larkin, eds., *The World of Southeast Asia** (New York: Harper and Row, 1967). With its explanatory introductions and careful organization, it might serve as interesting reading for the concerned layman or supplementary reading for the more serious student. Nicholas Tarling's *A Concise History of Southeast Asia** (New York: Frederick A. Praeger, 1966) is also very useful and emphasizes the period after 1760, though not to the extent of the Benda and Bastin history. Although there are other general histories available by well-recognized scholars, such as D. G. E. Hall, John F. Cady, Brian Harrison, and so on, most of these are less specifically oriented toward the modern period.

Geographical studies of Southeast Asia have generally tended to be parallel country descriptions of man and his relation to his environment undertaken by a single scholar. Most are fairly traditional in organization, provide rather unexciting reading for all but the more professionally committed students of geography, and almost invariably contain essential reference information. For most purposes, then, the usefulness of a geography book must be judged by its table of contents and index as well as by the comprehensiveness and accuracy of its text. One of the most recent volumes that measures up well on both standards is C. A. Fisher, *Southeast Asia: A Social, Economic, and Political Geography* (2d ed.; New York: Dutton, 1966). There will be few geographical facts that readers will not be able to find in Fisher's 831 pages, and, unlike many such texts, he will probably be delighted to discover that much of Fisher's material even makes enjoyable reading.

In the related field of ethnography, the best general study—again more a reference work—is unhappily limited to mainland Southeast Asia (including the peninsula of Malaya). Nevertheless, Frank M. LeBar, *et al.*, *Ethnic Groups of Mainland Southeast Asia* (New Haven, Conn.: Human Relations Area Files, 1964), is an indispensible reference source for all social scientists, and the map included in the back pocket considerably enhances the value of the volume. It dramatically and colorfully illustrates the fundamental diversity of mainland Southeast Asia.

Unfortunately, it requires considerable detective work to find precisely the map of Southeast Asia most useful for a particular purpose. The standard world atlases, of course, contain good maps of the area, but, for more specialized use, these are often inadequate. Djambatan Uitgeversbedrijf, *Atlas of Southeast Asia*, with an introduction by D. G. E. Hall, is useful but disappointing. Each geography book on Southeast Asia, and, indeed, almost every book dealing with any aspect of the area, contains maps, but these are often in black and white (the diversity of Southeast Asia cannot be adequately described by cross-hatching) and are seldom of outstanding quality. The Army Map Service and other government agencies (particularly the CIA) have produced some excel-

* Asterisks are used throughout to indicate that a paperback edition was available at the time of writing.

lent unclassified maps of Southeast Asia as a whole and of single Southeast Asian countries, but it usually requires considerable research to discover what is available, and how it may be obtained. Cecil Hobbs, in his *Southeast Asia: An Annotated Bibliography of Selected Reference Sources in Western Languages** (rev. ed.; Washington, D.C.: U.S. Government Printing Office, 1964), has included an index entry on the various kinds of maps found in the volumes selected for annotation, but this was not, of course, one of his primary aims, and the volume itself is now dated. A map inventory and index would be a most welcome addition to the bibliographical literature on Southeast Asia.

In the field of politics, the volume edited by George McT. Kahin—*Governments and Politics of Southeast Asia* (2d ed.; Ithaca, N.Y.: Cornell University Press, 1964)—stands out as one of the most useful general studies available, though it admittedly has some defects. On the debit side, it is really a series of parallel descriptions, each with a pronounced historical bias, and there is no compensating general introduction or conclusion that attempt to point out some of the more striking parallels and contrasts. Nevertheless, the authors of the individual country studies are solid scholars; the editor has done a good job of encouraging them to address themselves to similar problems in a consistent format; and the bibliographical suggestions following each country section (and the final brief "General Reading List") all together make this an important volume for many different purposes. A companion volume of documentation is being prepared and will be available soon. In marked contrast to the detailed country-by-country presentation and the reluctance of the editor to generalize, which together characterize this collection, stands the brief paperback by Lucian W. Pye—*Southeast Asia's Political Systems** (Englewood Cliffs, N.J.: Prentice-Hall, 1967). This particular essay was originally part of a larger hardback volume dealing with the political systems of Asia, but the publisher broke the collection into individual paperbacks, in this case, with little apparent change in the original. Pye's book is really only an essay on the subject (82 pages), but it does serve as a good summary introduction for the incoming student, and this was apparently what both the author and the publisher intended it to be.

In the field of international politics and foreign policy, several works deserve mention. Russell J. Fifield's *Southeast Asia in American Foreign Policy** (New York: Frederick A. Praeger, 1963) has now been dated by the events of the 1960's, but it is still an important work. Bernard K. Gordon's *The Dimensions of Conflict in Southeast Asia** (Englewood Cliffs, N.J.: Prentice-Hall, 1966) has been superseded by his *Toward Disengagement in Asia: A Strategy for American Foreign Policy** (Englewood Cliffs, N.J.: Prentice-Hall, 1969), though for the Southeast Asia specialist with particular interest in Malaysian-Indonesian-Philippine relations, this is still a useful volume. Finally, for a somewhat disorganized but always interesting and often insightful study of some of the social and emotional roots of domestic and international disputes in Southeast Asia (with emphasis on insular Southeast Asia and with particular attention to Malaysia), Guy Hunter's *Southeast Asia: Race, Culture, and Nation** (New York: Oxford University Press, 1966) is highly recommended.

II. Mainland Southeast Asia

The countries of mainland Southeast Asia are Laos, Cambodia, Vietnam (grouped together here under the no longer correct but still convenient heading "Indochina"), Thailand, and Burma. Malaysia is both mainland and insular, but will be grouped in the latter category, as is the common practice.

INDOCHINA (CAMBODIA, LAOS, NORTH VIETNAM, SOUTH VIETNAM)

Given the information explosion triggered by French and American involvement in Indochina following World War II, and given the fact that much of this material is not without bias, it is difficult to know where to begin. This is particularly true in the case of Vietnam. It would probably be most profitable to begin with some of the work of the late Bernard B. Fall, a French-born, American-educated journalist-scholar long resident in the United States. Fall was killed not far from Colonial Route 1, which had earlier been christened by the French soldiers "la rue sans joie," a description Fall himself had used for the title of his fascinating human account of the earlier phases of the war, *Street Without Joy: Insurgency in Indochina, 1946–63* (rev. ed.; Harrisburg, Pa.: The Stackpole Co., 1963). Fall is probably best known for his *The Two Viet-Nams* (2d rev. ed.; New York: Frederick A. Praeger, 1967), which is more scholarly but less sensitively written. Finally, his meticulously detailed account of the battle of Dien Bien Phu, *Hell in a Very Small Place* (Philadelphia: J. B. Lippincott, 1967), will remain for many years the standard reference source on the battle that marked the demise of French colonialism, but the book's very detail makes it difficult reading for all but the most dedicated military strategist.

For the French-speaking reader, Paul Mus, *Viet-Nam: Sociologie d'une Guerre* (Paris: Éditions du Seuil, 1952), will provide some brilliant insights into the psychology and sociology of French-Vietnamese relations, and, happily, a partial translation of this important study will soon be available in an English-language edition, translated, revised, and expanded by John T. McAlister under the title, *Revolution in Viet Nam: The Politics of the War*. McAlister's *Viet-Nam: The Origins of Revolution* (New York: Alfred A. Knopf, 1969) deals with the development of Vietnamese nationalism and should also have considerable impact.

As might well be expected, studies of politics and economics in this area are often colored by implicit or explicit ideological commitments. The *Area Handbooks*, prepared by American University, with separate volumes on the North and the South (Washington, D.C.: U.S. Government Printing Office, 1967), are convenient and useful sources of data, though the neat, clean, crisp format often disguises the unreliability of much of the data on Vietnam. For South Vietnam prior to the fall of Ngo Dinh Diem in 1963, Robert Scigliano's *South Vietnam: Nation Under Stress** (Boston: Houghton Mifflin Co., 1963) provides an excellent introduction. Scigliano's postscript on Diem's demise (*Asian Survey*, January, 1964) was slipped into the paperbound copies by the publisher, but it was written too close to the event to add much to Scigliano's perceptive treatment of earlier events. For North Vietnam, in addition to the works by Fall, there are several books by one of the leading British authorities on Vietnam, P. J. Honey. Although now dated, his *North Vietnam Today* (New York: Frederick A. Praeger, 1962) and *Communism in North Vietnam* (Cambridge, Mass.: M.I.T. Press, 1963) remain useful.

Journalistic accounts of international politics focusing on Vietnam are in great abundance today, but many are not very reliable. Among the better ones are Jean Lacouture, *Vietnam: Between Two Truces** (New York: Random House, 1966), which was translated from the original French for the American edition; David Schoenbrun's *Vietnam: How We Got In and How to Get Out** (New York: Atheneum, 1968); and Harrison E. Salisbury's *Behind the Lines— Hanoi, December 23, 1966—January 7, 1967** (New York: Harper and Row,

1967). A volume that falls somewhere between scholarship and journalism is George McT. Kahin and John Wilson Lewis, *The United States and Vietnam** (New York: Dell Publishing Co., 1967). Both Kahin and Lewis are highly respected scholars in their own fields (Indonesia and China, respectively), but in this particular volume their emotional involvement in contemporary American politics is apparent.

Finally, in dealing with Vietnam, mention must be made of the growing number of military experts prescribing solutions for America's first antiguerrilla war. Many of these unfortunately draw on the British experience in Malaya (1948–60), which appears comparable only when the military aspect of the war is abstracted from the total political context. One of the more readable of these accounts, which still overemphasizes the role of the military, is Sir Robert G. K. Thompson, *Defeating Communist Insurgency; The Lessons of Malaya and Vietnam* (New York: Frederick A. Praeger, 1966). Thompson, a veteran of both wars, gives a good account of the military side of each.

For the remainder of Indochina, there is comparatively little material available in English. Arthur Dommen's *Conflict in Laos: The Politics of Neutralization* (New York: Frederick A. Praeger, 1964) is a carefully researched journalistic account of political cleavages in contemporary Laos that does a good job of linking these to the historic splits of a country that is more a geographic expression than a state. Similarly, Joel Halpern's two short monographs provide valuable insights for understanding the centrifugal forces of present-day Laos. Although Halpern's *Government, Politics, and Social Structure in Laos** (New Haven, Conn.: Yale University Southeast Asia Studies, 1964) is more oriented toward questions overtly political, his *Economy and Society in Laos: A Brief Survey** (New Haven, Conn.: Yale University Southeast Asia Studies, 1964) is almost equally valuable for understanding the social bases of political fragmentation. There are two handbooks dealing with Laos. American University's *Area Handbook for Laos* (rev. ed.; Washington, D.C.: U.S. Government Printing Office, 1967) contains the more recent data, but Frank M. LeBar and Adrienne V. Suddard, eds., *Laos: Its People, Its Society, Its Culture* (New Haven, Conn.: Human Relations Area Files, 1960), is better organized, more reliable, and more readable.

Cambodia is receiving increasing attention in English-language publications, but there is still no profusion of material available. For the newcomer to the study of the country, a useful historical introduction is Martin F. Herz, *A Short History of Cambodia from the Days of Angkor to the Present* (New York: Frederick A. Praeger, 1958). In the field of international politics, Michael Leifer's *Cambodia: The Search for Security* (New York: Frederick A. Praeger, 1967) is a recent and reliable interpretation of Sihanouk's attempts to guarantee the continuing existence of a country that is sandwiched between larger and historically hostile neighbors. Roger M. Smith's *Cambodia's Foreign Policy* (Ithaca, N.Y.: Cornell University Press, 1965) is not as recent, but Smith's analysis of the rationale underlying Cambodian foreign policy deserves close attention. Finally, since Cambodian independence, the leading figure of the country has been the versatile Norodom Sihanouk—statesman, politician, actor, musician, playwright, author, journalist, producer, and so on. Unfortunately, there is no good English-language biography of this remarkable man, and, for the time being, we shall have to turn to the uncritical study by John P. Armstrong, *Sihanouk Speaks* (New York: Walker, 1964), which also contains some interesting, but poorly selected and edited, speeches of the Prince.

THAILAND

Two volumes can provide the unfamiliar student of Thailand with at least an entering wedge into the life of the country. Both of these tend to be heavy on description and light on analysis, which, regardless of the shortcomings, is their intent. Wendell Blanchard, *Thailand: Its People, Its Society, Its Culture** (New Haven, Conn.: Human Relations Area Files, 1966), is the standard HRAF country handbook, which grew out of the 1956 HRAF edition prepared by Lauriston Sharp. Unfortunately, the 1966 edition was not a major revision, and the volume is therefore seriously dated. Somewhat more analytical, better integrated, and more recent is D. Insor's *Thailand: A Political, Social, and Economic Analysis* (New York: Frederick A. Praeger, 1963).

The standard study of Thai politics is David A. Wilson, *Politics in Thailand** (Ithaca, N.Y.: Cornell University Press, 1962), which unhappily does not cover the period after the death of Marshal Sarit in 1963, even in the 1966 reprinting. However, with the exception of this deficiency, Wilson's treatment of coups, countercoups, mini-coups, and near-coups in Thai political history is the best available. Thailand after Sarit has not taken any marked departures from the military pattern of government under Sarit, so Wilson's study is not seriously dated. Another important study of Thai politics, which also seeks to explain rather than merely to describe Thai political history, is Fred W. Riggs, *Thailand: The Modernization of a Bureaucratic Polity* (Honolulu: East-West Center Press, 1966). Although the reader unfamiliar with Rigg's previous work may get bogged down in Riggsian English, his readers have been spared the terminological excesses of some of his previous writings, and this monograph is well worth the reader's efforts. For a study that focuses more explicitly on the development of the modern Thai bureaucracy—the lifeline of the Thai state since the bureaucratic reforms instituted by the great King Chulalongkorn in the nineteenth century—there is nothing more recent or better than William J. Siffin, *The Thai Bureaucracy: Institutional Change and Development* (Honolulu: East-West Center Press, 1966). Siffin is a long-time student of Thai administration, and, in many ways, this study represents a culmination of his research to date.

Although anthropological studies of Thailand are numerous today, several monographs deserve particular mention. Herbert Phillips' *Thai Peasant Personality* (Berkeley, Calif.: University of California Press, 1965) has successfully interwoven substantive material on the personality traits of Central Plain Thai peasants with methodological guidelines for future psycho-cultural research. Phillips has even provided a road map through the volume for the reader interested in one aspect but not in the other (p. viii). The foremost authority on the Overseas Chinese in Thailand is the anthropologist G. William Skinner. His *Chinese Society in Thailand: An Analytical History* (Ithaca, N.Y.: Cornell University Press, 1957) is precisely what the subtitle purports it to be. Students in the social sciences will probably find Skinner's *Leadership and Power in the Chinese Community of Thailand* (Ithaca, N.Y.: Cornell University Press, 1958) somewhat more useful. This is a meticulously documented, carefully analyzed, and cogently presented sociological and anthropological study of the Bangkok Chinese community. Students with a poor grasp of statistics need not be frightened by Skinner's statistical sections, for he carries statisticians and nonstatisticians alike through his complex web of analysis, with practically no loss of information.

Thailand's involvement in world affairs has unfortunately produced its share of polemical writing, the most outspoken being Louis E. Lomax, *Thailand: The War That Is, The War That Will Be** (New York: Random House, 1967). Lomax's thesis, his research, and his style leave much to be desired, but his book has had a considerable impact in Thailand, and for this reason alone is worth reading. Moreover, it is exciting and even worthwhile, provided one takes it with a grain of salt. Far more balanced and scholarly, but not entirely devoid of ideological overtones, is Donald E. Nuechterlein, *Thailand and the Struggle for Southeast Asia* (Ithaca, N.Y.: Cornell University Press, 1965). Frank C. Darling, *Thailand and the United States* (Washington, D.C.: Public Affairs Press, 1965), places Thai–United States relations in the broader context of domestic Thai politics and the involvement of the major powers in Southeast Asia. Darling concludes with some useful prescriptive advice and warnings to both Thailand and the United States.

BURMA

Although Burma has remained virtually closed to Western scholarly research for the past half-decade, considerable documentation is still available today. For the reader unfamiliar with the country, there are at least two good introductory works. The most recent is Frank N. Trager, *Burma—from Kingdom to Republic: A Historical and Political Analysis* (New York: Frederick A. Praeger, 1966), which covers events well beyond the second Ne Win coup against U Nu on March 2, 1962, and Maung Htin Aung, *A History of Burma* (New York: Columbia University Press, 1967). Both authors are regarded by many critics as not without their biases—Trager's being the less apparent of the two—but both are useful. A more journalistic introduction, slightly more dated than its year of publication implies, is provided in Hugh Tinker, *The Union of Burma* (London and New York: Oxford University Press, 1957).

After the assassination of Aung San and most of the leading Burmese nationalist elite on July 19, 1947, the mantle of leadership fell on the well-intentioned but often ineffectual U Nu, who in turn was twice deposed by the Burmese military. For a careful and sympathetic political portrait of the enigmatic and retiring U Nu, the best source is Richard Butwell, *U Nu of Burma* (Stanford, Calif.: Stanford University Press, 1963). There is no straightforward, book-length study of modern Burmese politics, but for a controversial, fascinating, neo-Freudian analysis of the political manifestations of the Burmese elite personality, which draws heavily on the theoretical work of Erik Erikson, the reader should consult Lucian W. Pye, *Politics, Personality, and Nation Building: Burma's Search for Identity** (New Haven, Conn.: Yale University Press, 1962). The most complete treatment of Burmese foreign policy is William C. Johnstone, *Burma's Foreign Policy: A Study in Neutralism* (Cambridge, Mass.: Harvard University Press, 1963). Although somewhat dated now, it remains an interesting (though not universally accepted) interpretation.

It has proved increasingly difficult through the years to gather data in Burma, and, of all the fields of investigation, economics has probably suffered the most. The most recent book-length study is Louis J. Walinsky, *Economic Development in Burma, 1951–1960* (New York: Twentieth Century Fund, 1962). This account tends to be somewhat personalistic, however, and the data are almost a decade old. Fortunately, Walinsky and others have published a number of more recent articles, one of the most important of which has been reprinted in this collection of readings.

Three studies of various aspects of the impact of religion and social customs on Burmese life should be cited. On the macro-level are two volumes of importance. Donald E. Smith, *Religion and Politics in Burma* (Princeton, N.J.: Princeton University Press, 1965), provides a solid, if somewhat formalistic, account of the interaction of Buddhism and politics, both under the British and after independence. More historical, more difficult for the lay reader, but more rewarding in the end is the scholarly study by Emanuel Sarkisyanz, *Buddhist Backgrounds of the Burmese Revolution* (The Hague: M. Nijhoff, 1965). At the micro-level, Manning Nash's *The Golden Road to Modernity: Village Life in Contemporary Burma* (New York: John Wiley, 1965) provides a fascinating worm's-eye view of social change in the villages of Upper Burma and suggests some useful insights into similar problems elsewhere. Finally, because of its impact on the field, attention must be directed to the study by Edmund Leach, *Political Systems of Highland Burma** (London: G. Bell and Sons, 1954), which has been accepted as the standard work on Kachin social and political organization.

III. Insular Southeast Asia

MALAYSIA AND SINGAPORE

The Malaysian-Singapore union was very brief (September 16, 1963–August 9, 1965), but because of their geographic proximity, economic interdependence, and unequal size, the two are still frequently considered together in scholarly and journalistic works. For many years, "British Malaya and Borneo" (the accepted prewar terminology) lay outside the American sphere of academic influence, and little American scholarship dealt with this area. At the same time, British writings tended to be more anecdotal and to consist chiefly of personal memoirs. There were some notable exceptions, but most of the better British scholarship tended to focus on the larger and intrinsically more interesting Indian subcontinent. In recent years, the nature of British writing has changed, and American scholarship has "discovered" Malaysia, but there is still no plethora of published scholarly research in the social sciences.

There are several standard reference handbooks, which are useful to keep on one's shelf but hardly make exciting reading for even the most serious student. The most recent is American University, *Area Handbook for Malaysia and Singapore** (Washington, D.C.: U.S. Government Printing Office, 1966), but where information on the peninsula alone is needed, the older Norton S. Ginsburg and Chester F. Roberts, *Malaya* (Seattle, Wash.: University of Washington Press, 1958) may prove more useful. Introductory narratives are available in J. M. Gullick, *Malaya* (rev. ed.; New York: Frederick A. Praeger, 1964), and in the lengthy collection of original essays presented in Wang Gungwu, ed., *Malaysia: A Survey* (New York: Frederick A. Praeger, 1964). The latter volume contains twenty-six essays dealing with everything Malaysian (including Singapore), from flora and fauna to the elite structure, though the limitations of space imposed on the authors and the uneven quality of their contributions make the volume less valuable than it might have been. Gullick's book is more integrated but less comprehensive and does not deal with Bornean Malaysia at all.

The most comprehensive introductory treatment of Malaysian politics is R. S. Milne, *Government and Politics in Malaysia** (Boston: Houghton Mifflin Co., 1967). To pursue further some of the subjects that Milne summarizes so well, the reader is directed to the following: K. J. Ratnam, *Communalism and the Political Process in Malaya* (Kuala Lumpur: University of Malaya Press, 1965); R. O. Tilman, *Bureaucratic Transition in Malaya* (Durham, N.C.:

Duke University Press, 1964); Gordon P. Means, "Malayan Government and Politics in Transition" (Seattle: University of Washington Ph.D. thesis, 1960); Gayl D. Ness, *Bureaucracy and Rural Development in Malaya* (Berkeley, Calif.: University of California Press, 1967); and Harry E. Groves, *The Constitution of Malaysia* (Singapore: Malaysia Publishing House, 1964). More recent works than Milne's general study include R. O. Tilman, "Malaysian Foreign Policy: The Dilemmas of a Committed Neutral," in John D. Montgomery and Albert O. Hirschman, eds., *Public Policy* (Cambridge, Mass.: Harvard University Press, 1967), and James C. Scott's very perceptive *Political Ideology in Malaysia* (New Haven, Conn.: Yale University Press, 1968). K. J. Ratnam and R. S. Milne's *The Malaysian Parliamentary Election of 1964* (Singapore: University of Malaya Press, 1967) also appeared after the completion of Milne's earlier book. Finally, two recently completed dissertations are worth mentioning. Thomas J. Bellows, "The Singapore Party System" (New Haven, Conn.: Yale University Ph.D. thesis, 1968), is the first full study of Singapore politics. John A. MacDougall, "Shared Burdens" (Cambridge, Mass.: Harvard University Ph.D. thesis, 1968), provides an excellent study of communalism in Malaysian politics, which goes far beyond the usual institutional analysis. Both of these will probably be published in the near future.

The most complete study of the Malaysian economy, unfortunately dated almost immediately by the unexpected withdrawal of Singapore from Malaysia, is the multivolume collection prepared by the Development Planning Unit of the National Planning Association (Washington, D.C.) during 1964–65. Although these volumes were not given wide distribution, an important part of the study was published by its author in Pierre Crosson, *Economic Growth in Malaysia* (Jerusalem: Israel Program for Scientific Translations, 1966). The International Bank for Reconstruction and Development study, which was prepared shortly before Malayan independence in 1957, *The Economic Development of Malaya* (Baltimore: Johns Hopkins Press, 1956), is still useful. A frequently controversial, but provocative and useful, treatment is James J. Puthucheary, *Ownership and Control in the Malayan Economy* (Singapore: Donald Moore, 1960).

There is a paucity of good anthropological writing on Malaysia, though recent work by Robert Jay and Manning Nash's current study of the northeast will soon be available. William Newell's *Treacherous River* (Kuala Lumpur: University of Malaya Press, 1962) is a fascinating and informative study of a Teochew (Chinese) village, despite the almost nonexistent methodological framework. Malaysia's Chinese population has been discussed by many but carefully examined by few. The best work has been done by Maurice Freedman in anthropology and the late Victor Purcell in history. Of particular interest are Freedman's *Chinese Family and Marriage in Singapore* (London: Her Majesty's Stationery Office, 1957) and his numerous articles and published lectures and Purcell's compendium, *The Chinese in South East Asia* (2d ed.; London: Oxford University Press, 1965). This work contains a lengthy section on Malaya, which, given Purcell's long acquaintance with the subject, is by far the best in the book. His *The Chinese in Malaya* (2d ed.; London: Oxford University Press, 1967) is similar to this section in the larger volume. T'ien Jukang's brief monograph, *The Chinese of Sarawak** (London: London School of Economics, 1953), is still of great value despite its age. Many of T'ien's significant observations are equally valid today.

Finally, some mention must be made of the various monographs dealing with the Communist guerrilla war (1948–60), already mentioned in the section on Vietnam in this bibliography. One of the first serious scholarly attempts to understand the psychology of the Chinese who joined the guerrillas was Lucian W. Pye, *Guerrilla Communism in Malaya: Its Social and Political Meaning* (Princeton, N.J.: Princeton University Press, 1956). Later volumes have concentrated more on the military aspects of the operation. One of the better ones, despite some oversimplification is Edgar O'Ballance, *Malaya: The Communist Insurgent War, 1948–1960* (London: Faber and Faber, 1966).

INDONESIA

One of the best introductions and also a reliable reference work is Ruth T. McVey, ed., *Indonesia* (Yale University Human Relations Area Files; New York: Taplinger, 1963). The valuable essays in this collection were written especially for the volume by a number of well-established scholars, whose published research on Indonesia during the past decade is the source of much of our knowledge of the country today. Appended to each essay is an annotated bibliography.

As an introduction to the contemporary period, the student must first have a good grasp of the Japanese occupation, the demise of Dutch colonialism following World War II, and the early attempts of Indonesia to establish a liberal democratic system of government. Although Harry J. Benda's *The Crescent and the Rising Sun* (The Hague and Bandung: W. van Hoeve, 1958) is more concerned with Indonesian Islam under the Japanese occupation, it also provides a good description and analysis of the Japanese interregnum. Any student with more than a passing interest in Indonesia must read the highly sympathetic and perceptive account of the anti-Dutch revolution written by the leading American political scientist concerned with Indonesia, George McT. Kahin. Kahin's *Nationalism and Revolution in Indonesia* (Ithaca, N.Y.: Cornell University Press, 1952) is a standard work that will not be supplanted for many years. For a view of much the same period from a different perspective, see Alastair M. Taylor, *Indonesian Independence and the United Nations* (Ithaca, N.Y.: Cornell University Press, 1960). Herbert Feith, an Australian scholar trained in the United States, in his *The Decline of Constitutional Democracy in Indonesia* (Ithaca, N.Y.: Cornell University Press, 1962) has provided an excellent sequel to Kahin's work on the earlier period. As yet, there is nothing comparable for the period of Sukarno's Guided Democracy, though Daniel S. Lev, *The Transition to Guided Democracy** (Ithaca, N.Y.: Cornell University Modern Indonesia Project, 1966), and Feith's essay, "Dynamics of Guided Democracy," in the McVey collection mentioned above are both of great value. Feith is presently at work on a comprehensive study of this period, and, when available, this can be expected to be the standard treatment.

The fascinating political personality of the Indonesian nationalist period, Sukarno, has been much discussed, but the biographical accounts of him in English are very weak. Sukarno, *Sukarno: An Autobiography As Told to Cindy Adams* (Indianapolis, Ind.: Bobbs, Merrill, 1965), probably throws as much light on the wife of the well-known comedian as on Sukarno himself. One of the long-time Sukarno-watchers, Willard A. Hanna, has drawn a narrative sketch of Sukarno in his *Eight Nation Makers* (New York: St. Martin's Press, 1964) that is entertaining reading and often reveals considerable insight. Its major weakness is that Hanna sometimes permits his prose to become even more colorful than his subject. Bernhard Dahm's *Soekarno en der Strijdem Indonesie's Onafhankelijkheim* (Meppel, Netherlands: J. A. Boom, 1964) is soon to be published in an English-language edition by Cornell University Press and should fill a major void.

Sukarno was an important figure in Indonesian politics until 1965, but he was only one side of a complex triangle. The Partai Komunis Indonesia (PKI or Communist Party of Indonesia) and the army were the other two sides, and during 1959–65, regardless of appearances, the three were so intimately related that an action by one produced instantaneous and equal reactions from the other two. Before it ran into trouble in 1965, the PKI was the largest Communist Party in a non-Communist state, a fact that in itself makes the organization worthy of study. Ruth T. McVey, *The Rise of Indonesian Communism* (Ithaca, N.Y.: Cornell University Press, 1965), examines the beginnings and early development of the Party (1914–27), and subsequent volumes now in progress will bring the development of the Party up to the present time. Justus M. van der Kroef's *The Communist Party of Indonesia* (Vancouver, B.C.: University of British Columbia Press, 1965) is a more general study of the PKI's historical development and political strategy written by an ideologically committed but perceptive and well-informed scholar who has written extensively on Indonesian politics. Donald Hindley, *The Communist Party of Indonesia, 1951–1963* (Berkeley, Calif.: University of California Press, 1964), is a detailed organizational analysis of the Party during the period when it moved from near oblivion to unprecedented strength under the leadership of D. N. Aidit. Unfortunately, all of these studies were published before the PKI made its third attempt to commit suicide in 1965 (previous attempts were made in 1927 and 1948), but each of these authors has written articles on this subject, and presumably this later period will be covered in future books.

The army has been less intensively studied, and there is no major book-length study of this important subject. A highly perceptive essay by Guy J. Pauker for The RAND Corporation has become one of the standard references on the subject. Fortunately, this paper "The Role of the Military in Indonesia," has been reprinted in J. J. Johnson, ed., *The Role of the Military in Underdeveloped Countries* (Princeton, N.J.: Princeton University Press, 1963). Unfortunately, the circulation of other important studies by Pauker has been restricted, but presumably some of these will eventually be published.

The best social history of modern Indonesia, regrettably somewhat befogged by the author's pronounced ideological leanings, is W. F. Wertheim, *Indonesian Society in Transition* (The Hague: W. van Hoeve, 1956). Wertheim is one of the leading Southeast Asia scholars in the Netherlands today, though his Marxian interpretations of history are likely to disturb some readers and obscure the genuine brilliance of his scholarship. Clifford Geertz is America's leading anthropologist dealing with Indonesia, and no even moderately serious student of Southeast Asia should fail to read his *The Religion of Java** (Glencoe, Ill.: The Free Press, 1960), which has quickly become the definitive study of the basic cleavages of Javanese society. There are a number of significant anthropological studies that grew out of the M.I.T. study group at "Modjokuto" (of which Geertz's is the most important), and some work has been done on Sumatra and elsewhere. One of the better and most accessible collections is G. William Skinner, ed., *Local, Ethnic, and National Loyalties in Village Indonesia: A Symposium** (New Haven, Conn.: Yale University Southeast Asia Studies, 1959). There have been several historical studies of the overseas Chinese minority but very few social and political analyses. One of the better is the brief but informative essay by G. William Skinner, "The Chinese Minority," in Ruth T. McVey, *Indonesia.*

The Indonesian economy has changed so rapidly over the years that any study is dated before it comes off the press. The very best statement of its time was Douglas S. Paauw, *Financing Economic Development: The Indonesian Case* (Glencoe, Ill.: The Free Press, 1960), and, though dated, it is still important for its statement of some of the basic problems. John O. Sutter, *Indonesiansasi: Politics in a Changing Economy, 1940–1955** (Ithaca, N.Y.: Cornell University Southeast Asia Program, Data Paper 36, 1959), is encyclopedic in nature, and this in itself has made the volume more viable than many Indonesian economic studies. The United States Economy Survey Team to Indonesia (Don D. Humphrey, *et al.*), *Report to the President: Perspectives and Proposals for United States Economic Aid** (New Haven, Conn.: Yale University Southeast Asia Studies, 1963), is useful for sober reflection now that we enjoy more perspective on the Sukarno period, but it is not likely to become a standard reference source.

THE PHILIPPINES

Despite intimate Philippine-American contacts for more than half a century, there is not a wealth of social-science material dealing with this former colonial territory of the United States. The best brief historical introduction for the period up to the end of World War II is David Bernstein, *The Philippine Story* (New York: Farrar, Straus, 1947). Two later sources provide a convenient and scholarly introduction to more recent Philippine history. The American Assembly (Frank H. Golay, ed.), *The United States and the Philippines** (Englewood Cliffs, N.J.: Prentice Hall for The American Assembly, 1966), is a collection of essays prepared by some of the most competent American and Philippine scholars for the 1966 meeting of The American Assembly. The second volume is Frederick L. Wernsted and J. E. Spencer, *The Philippine Island World* (Berkeley, Calif.: University of California Press, 1967).

There are three general studies of Philippine politics. For the lay reader, the best of these is O. D. Corpuz, *The Philippines** (Englewood Cliffs, N.J.: Prentice Hall, 1965), which was written by a highly competent Philippine political scientist with a historical orientation. The second is Jean Grossholtz, *Politics in the Philippines** (Boston: Little, Brown, 1964). The latter, a series of uneven but generally good essays on various aspects of politics, follows the format originally presented in Gabriel A. Almond and James S. Coleman, eds., *Politics of the Developing Areas* (Princeton, N.J.: Princeton University Press, 1960). Finally, Carl Landé's "Politics in the Philippines" (Cambridge, Mass.: Harvard University Ph.D. thesis, 1958) is an excellent study that analyzes the subject within a framework constructed on theoretical foundations borrowed from elsewhere in the social sciences. Landé's thesis has not been published, but his major arguments are presented in his *Leaders, Factions, and Parties: The Structure of Philippine Politics** (New Haven, Conn.: Yale University Southeast Asia Studies, 1965), a significant portion of which has been reprinted in this collection. For a careful study of the qualitative change that took place in Philippine politics with the 1953 election of Ramon Magsaysay, as well as some penetrating analysis of land-reform legislation, see Frances L. Starner, *Magsaysay and the Philippine Peasantry* (Berkeley, Calif.: University of California Press, 1961). The *Reports* of Albert Ravenholt, the Philippines' correspondent for the American Universities Field Service, provide some of the most perceptive in-depth commentaries on contemporary events in the islands. Ravenholt is a long-time observer of the Philippines, with close personal contacts both in and out of government.

Three economic studies dealing with the Philippines are of interest. The standard work is Frank H. Golay, *The Philippines: Public Policy and National Economic Development* (Ithaca, N.Y.: Cornell University Press, 1961). Thomas R. McHale's unpublished dissertation, "An Econological Approach to Economic Development: The Philippines" (Cambridge, Mass.: Harvard University Ph.D. thesis, 1959), is of note for both the data and the approach. John J. Carroll, S.J., *The Philippine Manufacturing Entrepreneur* (Ithaca, N.Y.: Cornell University Press, 1965), is an important study of the social origins of some 100 Filipino businessmen. As the author is well aware, this is not the definitive study of the making of the Filipino entrepreneural class, but it is a significant beginning.

ESSAYS AND PERIODICAL LITERATURE

I. The Setting

BENDA, HARRY J. "Decolonization in Indonesia: The Problem of Continuity and Change," *American Historical Review*, LXX (July, 1965), 1058–73.

———. "Democracy in Indonesia" [a review of Herbert Feith, *The Decline of Constitutional Democracy in Indonesia*], *The Journal of Asian Studies*, XXIII (May, 1964), 449–56 (read in conjunction with Feith, below).

ELAHI, M. K. "Agriculture in South East Asia," *Pakistan Geographical Review*, 14 (1959), [76]–92.

FEITH, HERBERT. "History, Theory, and Indonesian Politics: A Reply to Harry J. Benda," *The Journal of Asian Studies*, XXIV (February, 1965), 305–12 (read in conjunction with Benda's review of Feith's book, above).

HEINE-GELDERN, ROBERT. "Conceptions of State and Kingship in Southeast Asia," *Data Paper*, No. 18 (Ithaca, N.Y.: Southeast Asia Program, Cornell University, 1956), 13 pp.

LE BAR, FRANK M. "The Ethnography of Mainland Southeast Asia: A Bibliographic Survey," *Behavior Science Notes*, 1 (1966), 14–40.

LENT, JOHN A. "The Press of the Philippines: Its History and Problems," *Journalism Quarterly*, 43 (Winter 1966), 739–52.

PELZER, KARL J. "Land Utilization in the Humid Tropics: Agriculture," *Proceedings of the 9th Pacific Science Congress*, 20 (1958), 124–43.

———. "Man's Role in Changing the Landscape of Southeast Asia," *The Journal of Asian Studies*, XXVII (February, 1968), 269–79.

SENDUT, HAMZAH. "City Size Distribution of Southeast Asia," *Asian Studies*, 4 (August, 1966), 268–80.

II. Tradition, Modernity, and Social Change

ALZONA, ENCARNACION. "Our Sense of History and Its Implications for Philippine Education," *Education Quarterly*, 7 (October, 1959), 67–79.

BROHM, JOHN. "Buddhism and Animism in a Burmese Village," *The Journal of Asian Studies*, XXII (February, 1963), 155–67.

BUXBAUM, DAVID C. "Chinese Family Law in a Common Law Setting: A Note on the Institutional Environment and the Substantive Family Law of the Chinese in Singapore and Malaysia," *The Journal of Asian Studies*, XXV (August, 1966), 621–44.

CADIÈRE, L. "La famille et la religion au Viêt-Nam," *France-Asie*, 13 (1958), 260–71.

CUNNINGHAM, CLARK E. "Order and Change in an Atoni Diarchy," *Southwestern Journal of Anthropology*, 21 (Winter 1965), 359–82.

EBIHARA, MAY. "Interrelations Between Buddhism and Social Systems in Cambodian Peasant Culture," in *Anthropological Studies in Theravada Buddhism* (New Haven, Conn.: Southeast Asia Studies, Yale University, 1966), 175–96.

FISCHER, JOSEPH. "Universities and the Political Process in Southeast Asia," *Pacific Affairs*, 36 (Spring 1963), 3–15.

FRANKE, W. "Problems of Chinese Education in Singapore and Malaya," *Malaysian Journal of Education*, 2 (December, 1965), 182–91.

FREEDMAN, MAURICE. "Religion et adaptation sociale chez les Chinois de Singapore," *Archives de Sociologie de Religions*, 4 (January/June, 1959), 89–104.

GALLAGHER, CHARLES F. "Contemporary Islam: A Frontier of Communalism; Aspects of Islam in Malaysia," *American Universities Field Staff Reports Service, Southeast Asia Series*, 14, No. 10 (1966), 1–24.

———. "Islam in Politics: Southeast Asia," *Muslim World*, 56 (October, 1966), 257–62.

HICKEY, GERALD C. "Problems of Social Change in Vietnam," *Société des Études Indonchinoises*, 33 (1958), 407–18.

INGERSOLL, JASPER. "Fatalism in Village Thailand," *Anthropological Quarterly*, 39 (July, 1966), 200–25.

LANDÉ, CARL H. "The Philippines," in James S. Coleman, *Education and Political Development* (Princeton, N.J.: Princeton University Press, 1965), 313–49.

LEV, DANIEL S. "The Lady and the Banyan Tree: Civil Law Change in Indonesia," *American Journal of Comparative Law*, 14 (Spring 1965), 282–307.

MENDELSON, E. MICHAEL. "Buddhism and the Burmese Establishment," *Archives de Sociologie des Religions*, No. 17 (1964), 85–95.

MODESTO, SALVADOR TRANI. "The Inglesia ni Kristo," *Unitas*, 31 (October/December, 1958), 625–718.

MYA MAUNG. "The Elephant Catching Cooperative Society of Burma: A Case Study on the Effect of Planned Socio-economic Change," *Asian Survey*, 6 (June, 1966), 327–37.

PIKE, EDGAR N. "Public and Private Education in Vietnam," *Asian Culture*, 2 (April/June, 1960), 79–116.

PRINS, J. "Some Notes About Islam and Politics in Indonesia," *Welt des Islams*, 6 (1959), 117–29.

SILVERSTEIN, JOSEF and WOHL, JULIAN. "University Students and Politics in Burma," *Pacific Affairs*, 37 (Spring 1964), 50–65.

VAN DER KROEF, JUSTUS M. "Javanese Messianic Expectations: Their Origins and Cultural Context," *Comparative Studies in Society and History*, 1 (June, 1959), 299–323.

———. "Nanyang University and the Dilemmas of Overseas Chinese Education," *The China Quarterly*, No. 20 (October/December, 1964), 96–127.

———. "Religious and Economic Factors in Indonesia," *Southwestern Social Science Quarterly*, 39 (December, 1958), 187–202.

WILLNER, A. R. "Social Change in Javanese Town-Village Life," *Economic Development and Cultural Change*, 6 (1958), 299–342.

III. Politics: Ideology, Identity, and Political Organization

ABUEVA, JOSÉ V. "Bridging the Gap Between the Elite and the People in the Philippines," *Philippine Journal of Public Administration*, VIII (October, 1964), 325–47.

APPLETON, SHELDON. "Communism and the Chinese in the Philippines," *Pacific Affairs*, 32 (1959), 376–91.

BELLOWS, THOMAS J. "The Singapore Party System," *Journal of Southeast Asian History*, 8 (March, 1967), 122–38.

BIGELOW, LEE S. "The 1960 Election in Burma," *Far Eastern Survey*, 20 (May, 1960), 70–74.

BUTWELL, RICHARD, and VON DER MEHDEN, FRED. "The 1960 Election in Burma," *Pacific Affairs*, 33 (June, 1960), 144–57.

CADY, JOHN F. "Burma's Military Regime," *Current History*, 38 (1960), 75–81.

CONCEPCION, M. V. "Nationalism and Filipino First Policy," *Comment*, No. 10 (1960), 30–44.

DARLING, FRANK C. "Marshal Sarit and Absolutist Rule in Thailand," *Pacific Affairs*, 33 (December, 1960), 347–60.

DEVILLERS, PHILIPPE. "Les circonstances et la signification de l'affaire du 30 Septembre, 1965 en Indonésie," *Politique étrangère*, 31 (1966), 425–50.

DOMMEN, ARTHUR J. "The Attempted Coup in Indonesia," *The China Quarterly*, No. 25 (January/March, 1966), 144–70.

DUPUY, TREVOR NEVITT. "Burma and Its Army: A Contrast in Motivation and Characteristics," *Antioch Review*, 20 (Winter 1960/61), 428–40.

EVERS, HANS-DIETER. "The Formation of Social Class Structure: Urbanization, Bureaucratization and Social Mobility in Thailand," *American Sociological Review*, 31 (August, 1966), 480–88.

FALL, BERNARD B. "The Political-Religious Sects of Viet-Nam," *Pacific Affairs*, XXVIII (September, 1955), 235–53.

FISCHER, JOSEPH. "Indonesia" in James S. Coleman, *Education and Political Development* (Princeton, N.J.: Princeton University Press, 1965), 92–122.

JUMPER, ROY. "Sects and Communism in South Vietnam," *Orbis*, 3 (Spring 1959), 85–96.

LANDÉ, CARL H. "The Philippine Political Party System," *Journal of Southeast Asian History*, 8 (March, 1967), 19–39.

———. "Political Attitudes and Behavior in the Philippines," *Philippine Journal of Public Administration*, 3 (July, 1959), 341–65.

LEIFER, MICHAEL. "Politics in Singapore: The First Term of the People's Action Party 1959–1963," *Journal of Commonwealth Political Studies*, 2 (May, 1964), 102–19.

———. "Sihanouk: A Prince Among Neutrals," *The Australian Quarterly*, 34 (December, 1962), 38–49.

LEV, DANIEL S. "Political Parties in Indonesia," *Journal of Southeast Asian History*, 8 (March, 1967), 52–67.

LOCKHARD, CRAIG A. "Parties, Personalities, and Crisis Politics in Sarawak," *Journal of Southeast Asian History*, 8 (March, 1967), 111–21.

MARYANOV, GERALD S. "Political Parties in Mainland Malaya," *Journal of Southeast Asian History*, 8 (March, 1967), 99–110.

MILNE, R. S. "Political Parties in Sarawak and Sabah," *Journal of Southeast Asian History*, 6 (September, 1965), 104–17.

MOSEL, JAMES N. "Fatalism in Thai Bureaucratic Decision-making," *Anthropological Quarterly*, 39 (July, 1966), 191–99.

NORMAND, MARJORIE WEINER. "The Party System in North Vietnam," *Journal of Southeast Asian History*, 8 (March, 1967), 68–82.

PHILLIPS, HERBERT P. "The Election Ritual in a Thai Village," *Journal of Social Issues*, 14 (1958), 36–50.

REY, LUCIEN. "Dossier of the Indonesian Drama," *New Left Review*, No. 36 (March/April, 1966), 26–40.

ROBERTS, ADAM. "Buddhism and Politics in South Vietnam," *The World To-day*, 21 (June, 1965), 240–50.

SCHMEITS, ERIC. "The 'September 30th Affair' in Indonesia," *France-Asie*, 20 (1965/1966), 209–38.

SCIGLIANO, R. G. and SNYDER, W. W. "Political Parties in South Vietnam Under the Republic," *Pacific Affairs*, 33 (December, 1960), 327–46.

SILVERSTEIN, JOSEF. "The Burma Socialist Program Party and Its Rivals: A One-Plus Party System," *Journal of Southeast Asian History*, 8 (March, 1967), 8–18.

SUTTER, JOHN O. "Two Faces of Konfrontasi: 'Crush Malaysia' and the Gestapu," *Asian Survey*, 11 (October, 1966), 523–46.

VAN DER KROEF, JUSTUS M. "Communism and Chinese Communalism in Sarawak," *The China Quarterly*, No. 20 (October/December, 1964), 38–66.

———. "Role of Islam in Indonesian Nationalism and Politics," *Western Political Quarterly*, 11 (March, 1958), 33–54.

———. "Sukarno's Fall," *Orbis*, 11 (Summer 1967), 491–531.

VASIL, R. K. "The 1964 General Elections in Malaya," *International Studies*, 7 (July, 1965), 20–65.

WEATHERBEE, DONALD E. "Traditional Values in Modernizing Ideologies: Indonesian Example," *Journal of Developing Areas*, 1 (October, 1966), 41–53.

WERTHEIM, W. F. "Indonesia Before and After the Untung Coup," *Pacific Affairs*, 29 (1966), 115–27.

IV. Internal and International Integration

CARROLL, JOHN J. "Philippine Social Organization and National Development," *Philippine Studies*, 14 (October, 1966), 575–90.

CONDOMINAS, GEORGES. "Aspects of a Minority Problem in Indochina," *Pacific Affairs*, 24 (March, 1951), 77–82.

DARTFORD, GERALD PERCY. "Malaya: Problems of a Polyglot Society," *Current History*, 34 (June, 1958), 346–51.

DONG, KHUE. "The Vietnamese of Khmer Origin," *Vietnam*, 3 (1958), 71–89.

FALL, BERNARD B. "Viet-Nam's Chinese Problems," *Far Eastern Survey*, 27 (April, 1958), 65–72.

FREEDMAN, MAURICE. "The Growth of a Plural Society in Malaya," *Pacific Affairs*, 33 (June, 1960), 158–60.

FREYN, HUBERT. "The Chinese in Thailand," *Far Eastern Economic Review*, 30 (December 29, 1960), 657–60.

GOLAY, FRANK H. "The Nature of Philippine Economic Nationalism," *Asia*, No. 1 (Spring, 1964), 13–30.

GOWING, PETER G. "Kris and Crescent: Dar Islam in the Philippines," *Studies in Islam*, 3 (January, 1966), 1–18.

HUMBARACI, ARSLAN. "Anti-Chinese Feelings in Indonesia," *Far Eastern Economic Review*, 27 (September 10, 1959), 389–91.

KEYES, CHARLES F. "Ethnic Identity and Loyalty of Villagers in Northeastern Thailand," *Asian Survey*, 6 (July, 1966), 362–69.

NEVILLE, WARWICK. "Singapore: Ethnic Diversity and Its Implications," Association of American Geographers, *Annals*, 56 (June, 1966), 236–53.

PRESCHEZ, PHILIPPE. "Le conflit Khmero-Thailandais," *Revue Française des Sciences Politiques*, 16 (April, 1966), 332–48.

SILVERSTEIN, JOSEF. "The Federal Dilemma in Burma," *Far Eastern Survey*, 28 (July, 1959), 97–105.
———. "Politics in the Shan State: the Question of Secession from the Union of Burma," *The Journal of Asian Studies*, XVIII (November, 1958), 43–57.
SKINNER, G. WILLIAM. "Chinese Assimilation and Thai Politics," *Guardian*, 4 (August, 1957), 11–14.
———. "Overseas Chinese in Southeast Asia," *The Annals of the American Academy of Social and Political Science*, 321 (January, 1959), 136–47.
———. "The Thailand Chinese: Assimilation in a Changing Society," *Asia*, No. 2 (Autumn, 1964), 80–92.
SMYTHE, HUGH H. "The Myth of Thailand's Unity," *United Asia*, XVI (May/ June, 1964), 195–98.
THE, SIAUW GIAP. "Group Conflict in a Plural Society," *Revue du Sud-est Asiatique*, No. 1 (1966), 1–31.
———. "Group Conflict in a Plural Society," *Revue du Sud-est Asiatique*, No. 2 (1966), 185–217.
UCHIDA, NAOSAKU, "Overseas Chinese Problems in Southeast Asian Nations," *Asian Affairs*, 5 (October, 1960), 71–81.
VAN DER KROEF, JUSTUS M. "Eurasian Dilemma in Indonesia," *The Journal of Asian Studies*, 20 (November, 1960), 45–60.
———. "Sources of Indonesian Disunity," *Orbis*, 2 (1958), 478–91.
WAY, TSUNG-TO. "Overseas Chinese in Vietnam," *Far Eastern Economic Review*, 24 (January 2, 1958), 20–22.
WERTHEIM, W. F. "Sociological Aspects of Inter-Island Migration in Indonesia," *Population Studies*, 12 (1959), 184–201.

V. *The Quest for Economic Progress*

APPLETON, SHELDON. "Overseas Chinese and Economic Nationalization in the Philippines," *The Journal of Asian Studies*, XIX (February, 1960), 151–61.
AYAL, ELIEZER B. "Private Enterprise and Economic Progress in Thailand," *The Journal of Asian Studies*, 26 (November, 1966), 5–14.
BOURRIÈRES, PAUL. "The Mekong Valley Project," *Impact of Science on Society*, 14 (1964), 263–79.
BURANASIRI, PRAYAD, and UNAKUL, SNOH. "Obstacles to Effective Planning Encountered in the Thai Planning Experience," *The Philippine Economic Journal*, 4 (Second Semester, 1965), 327–40.
CROSSON, PIERRE R. "Planning Data and Information Flows in Malaysia," *The Philippine Economic Journal*, 4 (Second Semester, 1965), 226–48.
FABELLA, ARMAND. "Problems of Plan Implementation," *The Philippine Economic Journal*, 4 (Second Semester, 1965), 341–54.
GOLAY, FRANK H. "The Environment of Philippine Economic Planning," *The Philippine Economic Journal*, 4 (Second Semester, 1965), 284–309.
HARA, KAHUTEN. "Trade Instability and Imbalance in Southeast Asian Nations," *Asian Affairs*, 4 (March, 1960), 25–38.
HAWKINS, EVERETT D. "Job Inflation in Indonesia," *Asian Survey*, 6 (May, 1966), 264–75.
HIGGINS, BENJAMIN H. "Dominant Problems in Southeast Asian Planning: A Western View," *The Philippine Economic Journal*, 4 (Second Semester, 1965), 424–47.
———. "Economic Development in Indonesia and the Philippines: A Comparative Study," *United Asia*, 10 (1958), 32–43.

————. "Western Enterprise and the Economic Development of Southeast Asia," *Pacific Affairs*, 31 (March, 1958), 74–87.

LIM, JOO-JOCK. "Tradition and Peasant Agriculture in Malaya," *Malayan Journal of Tropical Geography*, III (October, 1954), 44–47.

LONG, MILLARD F. "Economic Development in Northeast Thailand: Problems and Prospects," *Asian Survey*, 6 (July, 1966), 355–61.

LOUKA, KATHYRN T. "The Role of Population in the Development of Southeast Asia," (Washington: Population Research Project, George Washington University, 1960), 50 pp.

MA, RONALD, and YOH, POH SENG. "The Economic Characteristics of the Population of the Federation of Malaya 1957," *Malayan Economic Review*, 5 (October, 1960), 10–45.

MCPHELIN, MICHAEL. "The 'Filipino First' Policy and Economic Growth," *Philippine Studies*, 8 (April, 1960), 271–91.

MORGAN, THEODORE, "Economic Planning—Points of Success and Failure," *The Philippine Economic Journal*, 4 (Second Semester, 1965), 403–23.

NESS, GAYL D. "Subdivision of Estates in Malaya 1951–1960: A Methodological Critique," *Malayan Economic Review*, 9 (April, 1964), 55–62.

NG, KAY FONG, TAN CHU LIAN, and WIKKRAMATILEKE, R. "Three Farmers of Singapore: An Example of the Mechanics of Specialised Food Production in an Urban Unit," *Pacific Viewpoint*, 7 (September, 1966), 169–97.

OSHIMA, HARRY T. "Improving the Statistics of National Accounts for Development Planning with Special Emphasis on Southeast Asia," *The Philippine Economic Journal*, 4 (Second Semester, 1965), 249–83.

PAAUW, DOUGLAS S. "Economic Planning in Southeast Asia: Introduction," *The Philippine Economic Journal*, 4 (Second Semester, 1965), 147–50.

PAAUW, DOUGLAS S., and FEI, JOHN C. H. "Development Strategies and Planning Issues in Southeast Asian Type Economies," *The Philippine Economic Journal*, 4 (Second Semester, 1965), 200–25.

PAL, AGATON P. "Barrio Institutions and Economic Change," *Philippine Sociological Review*, 7 (January/April, 1959), 51–63.

RODRIGUEZ, FILEMON C. "Status of the Philippine Economy," *Philippine Economy Bulletin*, 4 (March/April, 1966), 5–17.

ROSS, ANTHONY CLUNIES, "The Philippine Economic Challenge," *Australia's Neighbours*, 4 (September/October, 1966), 1–8.

————. "Politics and Economics in Philipino [*sic*] Growth," *Dissent*, No. 18 (Spring 1966), 16–21.

ROXAS, SIXTO K. "Lessons from Philippine Experience in Development Planning," *The Philippine Economic Journal*, 4 (Second Semester, 1965), 355–402.

SADLI, MOHAMMAD. "National Goals and Development Strategy: The Role of Economists," *The Philippine Economic Journal*, 4 (Second Semester, 1965), 173–99.

SEWELL, W. R. DERRICK, and WHITE, GILBERT F. "The Lower Mekong: An Experiment in International River Development," *International Conciliation*, No. 558 (May, 1966), 63 pp.

TAEUBER, IRENE B. "Population: Dilemma of Modernization in Southeast Asia," *Asia*, No. 1 (Spring 1964), 51–61.

TAN, ELIZABETH R. "The Nationalization of the Retail Business in the Philippines," *Philippine International Law Journal*, 4 (January/June, 1965), 152–86.

Vu, Quoc-Thuc. "The Influence of Western Civilization on the Economic Behavior of the Vietnamese," *Asian Culture,* 1 (1958), 42–53.

Wharton, Clifton R., Jr. "Non-economic Factors in Southeast Asian Agricultural Development," *International Development Review,* 4 (December, 1963), 15–18.

Wolf, Charles. "National Priorities and Development Strategies in Southeast Asia," *The Philippine Economic Journal,* 4 (Second Semester, 1965), 156–72.

Yap, Santiago. "Chinese Influence on the Socio-Economic Life of the Filipinos," *Philippine Economic Review,* 4 (May, 1958), 14–15.

Yoh, Poh Seng. "The Population Growth of Singapore," *Malayan Economic Review,* 4 (1959), 56–59.

INDEX

A-*lhu*, 530
Abangan, 116, 123
Abduh, Muhammad, 119, 204
Abdulgani, Ruslan, 193, 404
Abdullah, Muljadi, 125*n*.
Abidhamma, 104
Achin, 31, 41
Achin War, 33
Adams, Cindy, 409*n*.
Adjie, Brigadier General, 300
Adjitorop, Jusuf, 312*n*.
Adloff, Richard, 252*n*.
Afro-Asian Conference, Bandung (1955), 507
Agriculture, Faculty of, Indonesia, 189
Agung, Anak Agung Gde, 123
Ahlus-sunnah wal jama'ah, 118
Ahmad, Jamil-ud-din, 218*n*.
Aidit, Dipa N., 183, 296*n*., 303–13
Akutho, 104

Al-Afghani, Jamaluddin, 119
Al-Baghawi, 119
Al-Ghassali, 205
Alatas, Syed Hussein, 32*n*.
Albar, Syed Ja'afar, 504*n*.
Aligarh Muslim University, India, 189
Allahabad, 191
Allahabad University, 189
Allen, G. C., 537*n*.
Alliance Party, Malaya, 355*n*.
Alliance Party, Malaysia, 491*n*., 502, 505
Alliance Party, Sabah, 13
Alliance Party, Sarawak, 13
Ambonese people, 67
Anderson, C. Arnold, 217*n*.
Andhra University, India, 189
Andrzejewski, Stanislaw, 287*n*.
Aneiska, doka, anatta, 106
Angkor, 25, 29–30, 32, 60

Angkor Wat, 251
Anglo-Dutch treaty (1824), 9
Anglo-French agreement (1896), 9
Anglopayan sect, 7
Annam, 37; Sinicization of, 24, 60–61
Annamite Cordillera, 60
Annamites, 60–61
Anshary, Isa, 123
Anti-Fascist People's Freedom League (AFPFL), Burma, 340, 341–43
Anwar, Rosihan, 32n., 100
Aphyo, 110
Arakan, 454
Arakan Yoma, 57
Armstrong, R. C., 542n.
Arthaud, Jacques, 30n.
Asian Development Bank, 521
Asian Relations Conference (1948), 507
Asoka, King, 30
Association of Southeast Asia (ASA), 9, 507–13
Association of Southeast Asian Nations (ASEAN), 9, 507, 512–20
Atjeh, Indonesia, 121, 474n.
Aung Gyi, 341, 344, 345, 346
Aung San, 188, 252
Aung Shwe, 345, 346
Austroasiatic ethnolinguistic group, 6
Awgatha, 106
Awsa, 113
Ayal, Eliezar, 524
Ayuthia, Thailand, 75
Azad, Maulana Kalam, 119n.

Ba Swe, U, 345
Babas, 436, 440
Badan Kerdja-Sama (BKS), 290
Badan Pendukung Sukarnoisme (BPS; Body to Support Sukarnoism), 306
Badgley, John H., 220n.
Bahasa Indonesia language, 68–69
Bali, Hinduism in, 68
Balkan War (1912), 57
Banaras, 191
Banaras Hindu University, 189
Bandung Conference (1955), 507
Bangkok, 72, 73, 74, 75, 76, 77, 79, 82, 83, 87, 443; population of, 85
Bangkok dynasty, Thailand, 327
Bantegui, Bernardino, G., 581, 582
Banten, 31
Bao Dai, Emperor, 251, 422
BAPERKI, 314n., 443
Basri, Hasan, 129
Bastin, John, 34n.
Batak people, 67, 473, 474, 475
Batavia, 70, 75, 76, 77, 78; Europeans in, 86; population of, 84

Baw Maw, 244, 252
Bellah, Robert N., 201n., 221n., 541n.
Benda, Harry J., 20, 40n., 244, 404
Benedenstad (old Batavia), 76
Benedict, Ruth, 542n.
Berdirkari, 308
Berval, René de, 28n.
Beureueh, Daub, 121, 474, 478, 479
Blackmer, Donald L. M., 229n.
Blalock, Hubert M., Jr., 225n.
Blanchard, Wendell, 483n.
Bodha batha, 105
Bogor, Indonesia, 78, 189
Bombay University, 189
Bomoh, 138
Borneo (*see also* Indonesia), 9, 70, 88–97
Bose, Subhas Chandra, 188
Bowman, Mary Jean, 217n.
Boworadet Rebellion, Thailand, 338
Bowordet, Prince, 329
Bowring Treaty (1855), 537
Brahem Vihara, 546
Brahmanism, 26, 27
Braibanti, Ralph, 213n., 216n., 218n.
Briggs, Lawrence Palmer, 30n.
British Malaya, 490n.
British North Borneo, 12, 490n., 509
Brown, W. Norman, 45
Brunei, 12 (*see also* Malaysia)
Buddhism, 26, 27, 28, 29, 30, 31, 33, 39, 68, 399, 540, 544–48; in Burma, 103–14, 528–31; and monks, 107, 108, 111, 483–85; in Thailand, 483–85
Buitenzorg, Indonesia, 78
Burchett, W., 388n.
Burger, D. H., 40n.
Burma, 4, 9, 12, 39, 58, 59, 67, 68, 72, 245, 257, 268; army of, 219–21; Buddhism in, 68, 103–14, 528–31; civil service in, 213–22; civilian rule in, 345–46; cultural value in, 527–34; economic progress in, 527–34, 556, 557, 559, 560, 561, 562, 563, 564, 565, 566, 567, 569, 570, 571, 575, 576, 578, 580, 582; education in, 212–27; Eurasians in, 67; exports of, 65; geography of, 4; independence movement in, 11; and Israel, 342; Japanese occupation in, 42; military caretaker government in, 343–45; military role in development planning in, 340–50; nationalism in, 71; Oriental despotism in, 37; overseas Chinese in, 67, 435; overseas Indians in, 67, 452, 454–58, 464–65; population of, 457n.; revolutionary military government in, 346–50; universities in, 189, 190, 191, 192, 197, 198, 200; university students in, 188

Burma Economic Development Corporation, 345–46
Burman people, 68
Burmese language, 69
"Burmese Way to Socialism, The," 527, 533
Bushido, 541
Bymmas, 106

Cadière, Leopold, 28n.
Calcutta, 191
Calcutta, University of, 189
Cambodia, 4, 8, 12, 14, 25, 59, 60, 64, 67, 70, 266, 393–402; economic progress in, 556, 559, 562; independence movement in, 11–12; overseas Chinese in, 435; religions in, 7
Cambodian people, 70
Caskel, W., 205
Cebu City, 75
Celebes (Sulawesi) (*see also* Indonesia), 52n., 121, 467–68, 474n.
Ceylon, 4, 53n; Buddhism in, 30; economic progress in, 562; Indianization of, 24; overseas Indians in, 452; university students in, 188, 191, 192, 197–98
Ceylon, University of, 189, 190, 192
Cham people, 52n.
Champa, 58, 61
Ch'en Yi, 306, 311n.
Chenery, Hollis B., 572n.
Chesneaux, Jean, 28n., 73
Chettiars, 458–59
Cheverny, Julien, 382n.
Chiang Kai-shek, 64, 250, 254, 260, 262, 266
Chiengkham, Thailand, 148
Chin people, 340, 346, 347
China, 53n.; Communist, in Southeast Asia, 16; cultural continuity in, 45–46; Nationalist, economic progress in, 562
China's Destiny (Chiang Kai-shek), 266
Choei, 546
Cholon, 75, 79, 80, 83; overseas Chinese in, 85
Chou En-lai, 307
Christian, J. L., 528
Chulalongkorn, King, 79, 483
Chulalongkorn University, Thailand, 189, 190
Co-Prosperity Sphere, 62
Cochinchina, 75, 79; Oriental despotism in, 37; overseas Chinese in, 85
Coedès, George, 30n.
Coen, Jan Pieterszoon, 75
Coleman, James S., 214n., 217n.
Colombo Plan, 507

Committees of Resistance and Administration (CRA), North Vietnam, 387, 390
Communist Labor Federation (SOBSI), Indonesia, 308
Communist Party of Indonesia (PKI), 116, 117, 121, 125, 127, 183, 290, 291, 292, 294, 296, 298, 301, 303–25, 407
Conference of Southeast Asian Ministers of Education, 9
Confucianism, 26, 254, 540
Consultative Body for Indonesian Citizenship (BAPERKI), 314n., 443
Conze, Edward, 104n.
Coughlin, Richard J., 446, 448
Credner, Wilhelm, 73
Crissman, Lawrence W., 449
Cuisinier, Jeanne, 24n.
Cumpston, I. M., 452n.
Cu'u Quoc (national salvation) groups, North Vietnam, 387
Cyr, Ann Crown, 9

Dacca University, India, 189, 191
Daendels, Governor General, 78
Dahlan, K. Mohammed, 131, 515n.
Dahm, Bernhard, 404n.
Dahna, 530
Damrong, Prince, 156
Dang Lao-Dong (Workers Party), North Vietnam (*see* Lao Dong)
Dang Xuan Khu (*see* Truong Chinh)
Darul Islam, 121, 254, 300, 473, 474, 475, 477, 478n.
Da'wah Islamiyah, 124
Dayak people, 88–97
Deane, Phyllis, 557n.
Defense Services Institute, Burma, 342, 344, 345
Dekker, E. F. E., 407
Delhi University, India, 189
Democratic Alliance, Philippines, 380
Democratic Islamic Indonesian Party (PDII), 130
Democratic Party, Cambodia, 395
Democratic Republic of Vietnam, 11 (*see also* North Vietnam)
Demokrasi Pantja Sila, 131
Dennis, Charles M., 212n.
Deutero-Malay people, 58, 66
Deutsch, Karl W., 229n., 240, 255n., 451n., 491n.
Deva, 106
Devendra, D. T., 29n.
Devillers, Philippe, 42n.
DeVos, George A., 221n.
Dhammayon, 106
Dhani, Omar, 312, 316n., 323
Dien Bien Phu, 11, 64

Djajadiningrat, Hoesein, 118
Djakarta, 70, 72, 73, 74, 75, 77, 79, 80,
    81, 82, 84, 189; overseas Chinese in,
    86; population of, 84
Djakarta Charter, 120, 122
Djambek, Dahlan, 470n., 473, 474
Djambi, 474n., 475
Djatinagara, Indonesia, 79
Djayabaya, Prince, 182, 183
Djuanda, Prime Minister, 122, 290, 294
Dobby, E. H. G., 80n.
Dong Duong Cong San Dang (see Indo-
    chinese Communist Party)
Dongson period, 51
Dongson Rock Fortress Mountain in Yun-
    nan, 53
Drewes, G. W. J., 33n.
Dupuy, Trevor N., 220n.
Dutch East India Company, 31, 75
Duverger, Maurice, 363
Duy-Tan, Emperor, 416

Early Southeast Asian Neolithic, 49, 50
East Pakistan, 191
East Sumatra, 474n.
Eberhard, Wolfram, 46
Eisenstadt, S. N., 25n., 28n.
Emergency Military Government, Indone-
    sia, 478
Emerson, Rupert, 13, 37n., 240
English East India Company, 229–30
Evers, Hans-Dieter, 12n.

Fairbank, John K., 46n.
Fall, Bernard, 14, 245
Fan Ch'o, 51n.
Farrell, R. Barry, 451n.
Federated Malay States, 230
Federation of Malaya Agreement, 355
Feith, Herbert, 122n., 288n., 291n., 292n.,
    428
Fikh, 119
Finer, S. E., 220n.
Firth, Raymond, 552n.
Fischer, Joseph, 100, 212n., 216n.
Fisher, Charles A., 5n., 20
Foster, Philip J., 217n.
France in Southeast Asia, 9, 11, 12, 16,
    42, 63
Fraser, Thomas M., Jr., 158n.
Freedman, Maurice, 428
Fryer, D. W., 5n., 20
Funan, 58
Furnivall, John S., 217, 462n.

Gadjah Mada University, Indonesia, 192,
    194, 199

Gaings, 108
Gandhi, Mohandas K., 250, 252, 254, 266
Garcia, Carlos, 373
Gasbiindo, 129
Gatotkatja, 183
Gaw Si Kang, 83
Geddes, W. R., 20–21, 88n.
Geertz, Clifford, 7, 39n., 100, 116, 209n.,
    229n., 451n., 535n.
General Council of Buddhist Associations,
    Burma, 528
Geneva Conference (1954), 11, 64
Gerakan Mahasiswa Indonesia (GER-
    MINDO; Indonesian Student Move-
    ment), 322n.
Gerakan Mahasiswa Nasional Indonesia
    (GMNI; National Indonesian Students
    Movement), 322n.
Gerakan Pemuda Ansor (GPA; Ansor
    youth group), Indonesia, 315
GERWANI (Communist Party women's
    front), Indonesia, 308
GESTAPU (Gerakan September Tiga
    Puluh; Thirty September Movement),
    Indonesia, 303–25
Gibb, H. A. R., 206
Gifis, Steven, 212n.
Glamann, Kristof, 34n.
Glasenapp, Helmuth von, 27n.
Golay, Frank H., 567
Gon, 113
Gondangdia, Indonesia, 79
Goodenough, Ward H., 555n.
Goodstein, Marvin E., 560, 574, 580
Gordon, Bernard K., 8n., 9n., 429, 508n.
Gould, Joseph S., 580, 582
Government of Burma Act (1935), 455
Government of India Emigration Act
    (1922), 453
Gracey, Douglas, 10
Graham, Walter A., 328
Grand Palace, Bangkok, 76
Great Britain in Southeast Asia, 9, 11, 16,
    63, 423, 454
Great Tradition, 52
Groslier, Bernard, 30n.
Grossholtz, Jean, 229n.
Grunebaum, G. E. von, 33n., 205n.
Guided Democracy, 13, 118, 122, 123,
    183, 288, 291, 469
Gullick, J. M., 40n., 448
Gungwu, Wang, 233n., 448
Gupta period, 46
Gutteridge, William F., 220n.
Guyot, James, 100, 213n.
Gyi, 108

Hagen, E. E., 214n., 533n., 536n., 543n.

Hall, D. G. E., 30*n*., 34*n*., 407
Halpern, Joel M., 277*n*.
Ham-Nghi, Emperor, 414
Han period, 46
Hanks, L. M., Jr., 334
Hannah, Willard A., 499*n*.
Hanoi, 79
Harahap, Burhanuddin, 123, 129, 470*n*., 473, 475
Harappa period, 46
Harbison, Frederick H., 216*n*.
Harrison, Brian, 23
Hartshorne, Richard, 66
Haryono, Anwar, 129
Hasan, Salihin, 126*n*.
Hasjim, Kiaji Wachid, 120
Hatley, Ronald, 428
Hatta, Mohammed, 120, 129–30, 252, 266, 321, 324, 471
Hayden, Joseph Ralston, 249*n*.
Hayes, Samuel P., 535*n*.
Heine-Geldern, Robert von, 30, 51*n*.
Hickey, Gerald C., 6*n*.
Higgins, Benjamin, 558*n*., 565*n*.
Himpunan Mahasiswa Islam (HMI; Muslim Student Association), Indonesia, 307
Hinayana Buddhism (*see* Theravada Buddhism)
Hinden R., 462*n*.
Hindley, D., 292*n*., 310*n*.
Hindu Mahasaba, 254
Hinduism, 26, 68
Hiok, Lee Boon, 212*n*.
Hirschman, A. O., 531
Hla Myint, 190*n*., 531*n*.
Ho Chi Minh, 11, 14, 64, 244, 246, 265, 267, 383–84, 385, 386, 389, 412–25
Hoabinhian remains, 49
Holmes, Robert A., 458*n*.
Hoselitz, Bert F., 163*n*., 533*n*.
Hotoku movement, Japan, 542
Htamin che gaung, 111
Hué, University of, 190
Hunter, Guy, 450*n*.
Huntington, S. P., 287*n*., 289
Hurgronje, C. Snouck, 210
Husein, Colonel, 292, 470, 474, 475, 476, 478

Idjtihad, 119
Iglesia-ni-Kristo sect, 7, 375
Imam mahdi, 182
Independence of Malaya Party (IMP), 355
India, 4, 53*n*., 62; Buddhism in, 27; cul-
tural continuity in, 45–46; economic progress in, 562; university students in, 188, 191, 192, 198
Indian Independence League (IIL), 456–57, 460
Indochina, 9, 63; geography of, 4; independence movement in, 11
Indochina, Federation of, 63
Indochina War (1946), 386
Indochinese Communist Party (ICP), 384, 386, 388
Indonesia, 4, 8, 9, 12, 13, 15, 16, 33, 34, 62, 63, 69, 244, 245, 249, 268, 403–11, 507; Association of Southeast Asian Nations (ASEAN) and, 513–18; Christians in, 68; economic progress in, 556, 557, 559, 560, 561, 562, 563, 564, 566, 569, 571, 574, 575, 576, 581, 582; Eurasians in, 67; exports of, 65; GESTAPU (*Gerakan September Tiga Puluh*; Thirty September Movement) in, 303–25; higher education in, 189, 190; independence movement in, 10; Islam in, 29, 68, 115–31; Islamization of, 32; Japanese occupation in, 42; military role in politics of, 287–301; modernization in, 201–11; mysticism in politics of, 179–86; nationalism in, 71; overseas Chinese in, 67, 69, 435, 440–43; politics in, 115–31; rebellion in (1958–61), 467–80; religions in, 7, 39; university students in, 188, 189, 190, 191, 192, 197 (*see also* Borneo, Celebes, Java, Sumatra)
Indonesian Federal Republic (RPI), 474
Indonesian Islamic Association Party (PSII), 118, 121, 125, 128
Indonesian Lawyers' Association, 127
Indonesian Nationalist Party (*see* PNI)
Indonesian Workers, Federation of, 129
Ingersoll, Jasper C., 152*n*., 545*n*.
Ingram, James C., 145
Intramuros, Manila, 76, 77
Iqbal, 119*n*.
Iran, 188
Irrawaddy River, 59, 61
Islam, 28, 29, 31, 32, 33, 39, 68, 353, 357–60, 473; in Indonesia, 115–31, 201–11
Islam, University of, Indonesia, 190
Islam-statistik, 116
Islamic Education Party (Perti), 119, 125
Islamic State of Atjeh, 474*n*.
Islamic Students Association (Organization of Indonesian Islamic Students; Peladjar Islam Indonesia; PII), 115, 129
Itagaki, Yoichi, 41*n*.

Jackson, Barbara Ward, 133
Jackson, R. N., 459n.
Jacob, Phillip E., 491n.
Jacoby, Erich H., 39n.
Jain, Ravindra K., 460n.
Jani, Major General, 288n., 292, 296, 477n.
Janowitz, Morris, 220n.
Japan, 266, 267; economic development in, 535–49, 557, 562; in Southeast Asia, 9, 10; university students in, 188, 198; value systems in, 535–49
Jataka tales, 107, 108
Java, 25, 27, 32, 34, 57n., 59, 62, 69, 72, 181; early factory system in, 164–65; exports of, 65; Japanese occupation in, 42; management and authority in, 162–78; Oriental despotism in, 37; overseas Chinese in, 69, 440–43; population density of, 5; supervision in, 165–66 (*see also* Indonesia)
Java War, 32
Jay, Robert, 116
Jefferson, Mark, 72
Jessy, Joginder Singh, 457n.
Jinnah, Mohammed Ali, 218n., 252
Jogjakarta, 75, 190
Johns, Anthony, 29n.
Johnson, J. J., 287n., 326n.
Johore, 230n.
Jumsai, M. L. Manich, 155n.
Jumud, 119

Kachin people, 340, 346, 347
Kahar, Jusuf, 479
Kahin, George McT., 288n., 327n., 395n.
Kalijogo, Sunan, 183
Kan, 104, 105, 112, 528
Kan ami, 105
Kan makambu, 105
Kanaphi, 105
Kaplan, Bert, 223n., 334n.
Karen people, 59, 67, 68, 341, 346, 347
Karma, 528, 529, 545
Kartosuwirjo, S. M., 121, 478n.
Kashani, Ayatallah, 254
Kasim, 305n.
Katain, 111
Kawilarang, Colonel, 476, 477, 478
Kedah, 230n.
Kelantan, 230n.
Kendall, Willmore, 370, 371
Keppel Harbor, Singapore, 82
Kertapati, Sidik, 312n.
Key, V. O., Jr., 363n.
Keyes, Charles, 483n.
Khin, Maung Kyi, U, 213n., 221

Khmer people, 14, 52n.
Kijaji, 119, 205
Kinabalu, Mount, Sabah, 4
King, Seth S., 300n.
King Edward College of Medicine, Malaya, 232
Kingshill, Konrad, 548n.
Kirsch, A. Thomas, 428
Klong Toi, Thailand, 83
Komando Aksi Mahasiswa Indonesia (KAMI), 322, 324
Komando Ganjang Malaysia (KOGAM; Crush Malaysia Command), Indonesia, 324
Kondapi, C., 452n.
Koyin, 108
Kroeber, Alfred L., 50n., 551n.
Kuala Lumpur, 70, 81
Kunhi, M. K. Muhammad, 453n.
Kunstadter, Peter, 8n.
Kusalasaya, Karuma, 29n.
Kutho, 104, 105
Kux, Ernst, 383
Kuznets, Simon, 561, 573n.
Kyaung, 107
Kyaw Nyein, U, 215, 345

Lafont, Pierre-Bernard, 29n.
Land Nationalization Act of 1953 (Burma), 458
Landé, Carl, 245, 362n.
Landon, Kenneth P., 331n.
Lao-Dong (Workers Party), North Vietnam, 388, 389
Lao people, 70
Lao Soong people, 482
Laos, 4, 12, 59, 64; agrarian economy of, 5–6; economic progress in, 556, 559; independence movement in, 11–12; nationalism in, 277–86; overseas Chinese in, 435; religions in, 7
Lasker, Harry, 223n.
Lasswell, Harold, 244
Late Southeast Asian Neolithic, 50, 51, 52, 53
Latif, A., 313, 314n., 317
Le Duan, 389
Le Hong Phong, 385
Le Page, R. B., 448
Le Thanh Khoi, 26n.
League for Revolution and Independence, North Vietnam (*see* Vietminh), 387
League for the National Union of Vietnam (*see* Lien-Viet)
League of Upholders of Indonesian Independence (IPKI), 294, 295
LeBar, Frank M., 6n., 482n.
Lee, Douglas H. K., 538n.

Lee Kuan Yew, 13, 491*n.*, 499, 500, 503, 504, 505
Leimena, Johannes, 314
Lenin, Nikolai, 261
Lerner, Daniel, 16
Lesser Sundas, 52*n.*
Leur, J. C. van, 25*n.*, 33, 34, 35, 53, 54*n.*
Lev, Daniel S., 122*n.*, 245, 292*n.*, 428
Lévy, Roger, 64*n.*
Lewis, W. A., 528
Li Hsueh-feng, 307
Liberal Party, Philippines, 13, 379
Lien-Viet (League for the National Union of Vietnam), 387, 388
Lim Yew Hock, 499
Lingat, Robert, 24*n.*
Lipset, Seymour Martin, 15
Lissak, Moshe, 220*n.*
Literature, Faculty of, Indonesia, 189
Little Tradition, 38, 39, 52
Lockwood, William W., 549*n.*
Lokas, 106
Lon Nol, 401
Lopez, Fernando, 379
Lovasy, Gertrud, 567*n.*
Luang Pradit, 252
Luang Suriyabongs, 545*n.*, 546*n.*
Lubis, Mochtar, 100
Lubis, Zulkifli, 288, 292, 478
Lubyo, 110
Lucknow, 191
Lucknow University, 189
Lukman, M. H., 312*n.*
Lyautey Louis H. G., 64
Lyde, L. W., 57*n.*

Macapagal, Diosdado, 373, 509
Macaulay, Thomas Babington, 230*n.*
McCall, Davy H., 562*n.*
McClelland, David C., 216*n.*, 221, 543*n.*
McVey, Ruth T., 40*n.*, 291*n.*, 408*n.*, 448, 564*n.*
Madjelis Mahasiswa Indonesia (MMI; Indonesian Students Council), 322*n.*
Madras University, India, 189
Madrasah, 205, 206, 207, 208
Magsaysay, Ramon, 373, 380
Mahābhārata epic, 181, 183
Mahajani, Usha, 455*n.*
Mahayana Buddhism, 26, 28, 30
Mai Tho Truyen, 28*n.*
Maine, Sir Henry, 228*n.*
Maizels, A., 558*n.*
Majapahit kingdom, 26, 59, 60, 68
Malacca, 9, 31, 34, 76, 230*n.*, 423, 459, 490*n.*; overseas Chinese in, 436
Malay Administrative Service, 231*n.*, 232

Malay College, Kuala Kangsar, Malaysia, 230, 231, 232
Malay language, 68, 242
Malay Peninsula: culture of, 134–41; medicine in, 132–44; overseas Chinese in, 435
Malay people, 70
Malay States, 490*n.*
Malay States, Unfederated, 230*n.*
Malaya, 9, 33, 37, 41, 62, 63, 67, 70, 72, 229, 257, 266, 267, 491; economic progress in, 557, 559, 560, 561, 564, 566, 569, 570, 571, 575*n.*, 581, 582; Eurasians in, 67; exports of, 65; independence movement in, 11; overseas Chinese in, 67, 435–36, 439–40; overseas Indians in, 67, 452, 465; politics in, 351–61; religion in, 351–61 (*see also* Malaysia)
Malaya, Federation of, 63, 68, 69, 81, 490*n.*; overseas Chinese in, 67; overseas Indians in, 67
Malaya, University of, 233
Malayan Chinese Association (MCA), 355, 357, 491*n.*
Malayan Civil Service, 232
Malayan Communist Party, 235
Malayan Indian Congress (MIC), 355, 464, 491*n.*
Malayan Races Liberation Army, 241
Malayan Union, 230*n.*, 354, 355, 490*n.*, 503–4
Malayo-Polynesian ethnolinguistic group, 6
Malaysia, 4, 8, 9, 12, 13, 14, 15, 63, 245, 301, 305, 404–5, 490–505, 507; colonialism in, 241; education in, 228–42; industrialization in, 5; languages in, 6; literacy in, 242; overseas Chinese in, 233–42, 435, 439–40, 501; overseas Indians in, 458–62, 464, 501; parliamentary system in, 502*n.*; political development in, 228–42; population of, 500*n.*; university students in, 192, 200 (*see also* Brunei, Malaya, Sarawak, Singapore)
Malaysia, Federation of, 12, 63*n.*, 233, 490–505; air traffic in, 494; conflicts in, 499–505; postal services in, 494; press in, 493–94; radio and television in, 494–99; trade in, 491–93
Malaysia/Singapore Airways, 494
Malaysia Solidarity Convention, 503
Malaysian Airways, 494
Malaysian Alliance; 13, 491*n.*
Malik, Adam, 324, 514, 515, 518
Man Shu (Fan Ch'o), 51*n.*
Manahan, Manuel, 380
Mandailing Batak people, 473

Mandalay, 191
Mandalay, University of, 190
Mangakurat I, King, 32
Mangkusamito, Prawoto, 123, 127, 128, 129
MANIKEBU (*Manifes Kebudajaan*), 306
Manila, 72, 73, 74, 76, 77–78, 81, 82, 84, 194; overseas Chinese in, 85–86; population of, 84–85
Mano, *Phraya*, 330
Mao Tse-tung, 261, 262, 263, 265
MAPHILINDO, 513, 516, 517
Marcos, Ferdinand, 379, 509, 517n.
Marshall, David, 499
Mashab of Sjafi'i, 118
Masjumi Party, Indonesia, 117, 118, 119, 121, 122, 127, 128, 129, 130, 131, 294n., 295, 306, 324, 468, 472, 473
Mason, Philip (Woodruff), 220n.
Matak, Prince Sisowath Sirik, 401
Mataram, 25, 26, 31, 32, 34
Maung Maung, 345, 346
Mauritius, 452
Maurya period, 46
Medan, Indonesia, 190
Medicine, Faculty of, Indonesia, 189
Meek, John Paul, 581
Meester Cornelis, Indonesia, 78, 79
Mehta, 112
Mehta, Surinder K., 578n.
Mekong Development Committee, 519
Mekong River, 59, 61
Menam River, 59, 62
Menteng, Indonesia, 79
Mentu Tapuh, Sarawak, 88–97
Merdeka Indonesia, 271–76
Merton, Robert K., 150n.
Mesolithic period, 49
Metteyya, Bhikkhu Ananda, 528n.
Middleton, Drew, 458n.
Military Bank (Thanakan Thahan), Thailand, 336
Millikan, Max F., 229n.
Milne, R. S., 356n.
Minahasan people, 473, 475
Minangkabau people, 473
Mingala Thok, 106
Mitra, R. C., 27n.
Moerman, Michael, 100, 524, 535n.
Moluccas, 67, 68, 474n.
Mon kingdom, 58
Mon people, 66, 68
Mongkut, King, 544n.
Monireth, Prince Sisowath, 401
Monivong, King Sisowath, 395
Monks, Buddhist, 107, 108, 111, 483–85
Montagu-Chelmsford Reforms (India), 454

Morgan, Theodore, 530n.
Morse, Chandler, 535n.
Mosel, James N., 535n., 546
Mossman, James, 472n.
Moutet, Marius, 423
Muballigh, 124
Mudadalam, Jusuf, 183
Muhammadiyah, 116, 119, 125, 128, 129, 209n.
MUKER, 184
Mulder, D. C., 124n.
Muljatno, 581, 582
Murba (Proletarian) Party, Indonesia, 127, 306, 468
Murray, Douglas P., 237n., 448
Mus, Paul, 31n., 423, 424
Musgrave, John K., 6n.
Muslims (*see* Islam)
Muzakir, Kahar, 121, 478
Mya Maung, 524
Myers, C. A., 216n.
Myinmodaung, 106
Mysore University, India, 189

Nacionalista Party, Philippines, 13, 379
Nāgarakĕrtāgama, 407
Nagpur University, India, 189
Nahdatul Ulama (NU), 116, 117, 118, 119, 121, 122, 125, 128, 209n., 131, 295, 298, 306
Namier, L. B., 366n.
Nan-yang, 422, 423, 447
Nan Yüeh, 60
Nanyang University, Singapore, 438
Naradipo, Prince Norodom, 401n.
NASAKOM, 122, 123, 183, 404
Nash, June C., 103n.
Nash, Manning, 100, 222
Nasution, A. H., 288, 289, 290, 292, 293, 294, 295, 296, 297, 300, 301, 306, 315, 317, 324, 469, 470, 475, 476, 479–80
National Assembly, Thailand, 327, 332
National Education Council, Thailand, 190
National Front, Indonesia, 291, 298–99
National Front for the Liberation of West Irian (FNPIB), 290, 291
National Indonesian Party (*see* PNI)
Nationalist Party of Indonesia (*see* PNI)
Nats, 110
Natsir, Mohammed, 123, 473, 475
Ne Win, 12, 188, 340, 343, 344, 345, 346, 458
Negara Islam, 120
Negri Sembilan, 230n.
Negrito people, 67
Nehru, Jawaharlal, 218–19, 250, 252, 254, 266

Netherlands, in Southeast Asia, 9, 16, 33, 62, 63, 65, 69, 423
Netto, George, 453*n*.
New Guinea, 9
Ngo Dinh Diem, 14
Nguyen Ai-Quoc (*see also* Ho Chi Minh), 383
Nhiek Tioulong, 401
Nibban, 105, 530
Nirvana, 105, 530, 545
Njono, 304*n*., 312, 313, 316*n*.
Nommensen Lutheran University, Indonesia, 190
Nong Son, Thailand, 482
North Celebes, 474*n*.
North Vietnam, 8*n*., 11, 12, 14, 63, 64, 382–92 (*see also* Vietnam)
Northrop, F. S. C., 254*n*.
Nu, U, 12, 188, 215, 252, 340, 345, 346, 350, 528, 560*n*.

Obelsky, Alvan J., 535*n*.
Oey, G. P., 51*n*.
Ohkawa, Kazushi, 537*n*.
Onn, Dato', 355
Organization of Indonesian Islamic Students (Islamic Students Association; Peladjar Islam Indonesia; PII), 115*n*., 129
Organski, A. F. K., 228*n*.
Oriental despotisms, 34, 37
Oriental Lower and Middle Paleolithic, 48
Osmeña, Sergio, 252, 380

Paauw, Douglas S., 214*n*., 525, 564*n*., 574*n*.
Padri War, 32
Pahang, 230*n*.
Pai thiaw, 487–89
Pakistan, 4, 191, 268; economic progress in, 562; university students in, 188, 197, 198
Palembang, 58
Paleolithic period, 49
Pan-Malayan Islamic Party (PMIP), 353, 354, 356, 357, 358, 359, 360, 361, 501, 504*n*.
Pannikar, K. M., 34*n*.
Pantja Sila, 120, 122, 123, 125, 271–76, 294, 324, 474
Papuan people, 67
Parākramabāhu, King, 29
Pararaton, 407
Parmer, J. Norman, 453*n*.
Party Negara, Malaya, 355*n*.
Patna, India, 191
Pauker, G., 288*n*., 310*n*.
Pearn, B. R., 454

Peladjar Islam Indonesia (PII; Islamic Students Association; Organization of Indonesian Islamic Students), 115*n*., 129
Pelaez, Emmanuel, 380
Pemerintah Darurat Militer (Emergency Military Government, Indonesia), 478
Pemerintah Revolusioner Republik Indonesia (PRRI; *see* Revolutionary Government of the Republic of Indonesia)
Pemuda Muhammadiyah, 129
Penang, 230*n*., 423, 490*n*.
Penang Free School, 229
Pendidikan Nasional Indonesia, 130
People's Action Party (PAP), Singapore, 13, 491*n*., 492, 499, 502, 503, 504, 505
People's Consultative Congress, Indonesia (MPRS), 128
People's Socialist Community, Cambodia (*see* Sangkum)
Peradeniya, Ceylon, 191
Peradeniya, University of, 190
Perak, 230*n*.
Peranakans, 440–43
Perang Gerilja (Nasution), 294*n*.
Perlis, 230*n*.
PERMESTA, 471*n*.
Persatuan Ummat Islam, 128
Pesantren, 119, 205, 206, 207, 208
Pfanner, David E., 545*n*.
Pham Van Dong, 384*n*., 418, 419
Phan Khoi, 392
Phan Thao, 392
Phanomyong, Pridi, 330, 331
Phao, General, 333
Phelan, John L., 24*n*.
Philippines, 4, 9, 12, 13, 14, 33, 41, 57*n*., 62, 63, 70–71, 245, 249, 266, 267, 507, 508; democracy in, 368–77; distribution of influence in, 376–77; economic progress in, 557, 560, 561, 562, 563, 564, 565, 566, 567, 569, 570, 571, 574, 575, 576, 580–81, 582, 583; Hispanization of, 28–29, 37; independence movement in, 11; Indianization of, 24; industrialization in, 5; Islam in, 28, 60; Japanese occupation in, 42; overseas Chinese in, 67, 69, 435; party government in, 370–74, 377–81; politics in, 362–81; public participation in government of, 374–76; religions in, 7, 260; universities in, 190; university students in, 191, 194, 198, 200
Phillips, Herbert P., 334, 487, 535*n*., 548
Phonphayuhasena, Phahon, 329, 330
Phu Thai people, 481–89
Piagam Djakarta, 120
Piekaar, A. J., 41*n*.
Platenius, Hans, 481*n*.

Pleistocene, 48
PNI (Nationalist Party of Indonesia), 116, 117, 295, 298, 306, 320, 322, 407
Polk, W. R., 206n.
Pon, 108, 109, 113
Pongyi, 31, 43, 104, 108
Portugal, in Southeast Asia, 9, 33
Potsdam Agreement (1945), 10
Prasangsit, W. J., 329n.
Prawiranegara, Sjafruddin, 123, 470, 471, 473, 474, 475, 478
Preschez, Philippe, 395n.
Presthus, Robert V., 216n.
Primbon, 205
Progressive Party of the Philippines (PPP), 380
Proto-Malay people, 58, 67
PRRI (*see* Revolutionary Government of the Republic of Indonesia)
Purcell, Victor, 447
Pusat Perhimpunan Mahasiswa Indonesia (PPMI; Central Indonesian Student Organization), 322n.
Puspojudo, Wilujo, 299n.
Pwes, 108, 111
Pye, Lucian W., 214n., 216, 229n., 450n., 451n.
Pyidaungsu Party, Burma, 345

Qiyas, 119
Quezon, Manuel, 244, 249, 252
Quezon City, 78
Quirino, Elpidio, 379

Raffles, Sir Thomas Stamford, 76, 80
Raffles College, Malaya, 232–33
Raffles Institute, Singapore, 229
Rahman, Tunku Abdul, 244, 404, 499, 507, 508, 512, 517
RAKER, 184
Rama III, King, 482
Ramayana epic, 181
Ramos, Narciso, 515, 517n.
Rangoon, 191, 455, 456, 457n.
Rangoon, University of, 188, 189, 190, 191, 192, 194, 196
Ranney, Austin, 370, 371
Ratnam, K. J., 245, 356n., 461n.
Ratzel, F., 66n.
Razak, Tun Abdul, 232
Redfield, Robert, 25, 228n., 552n.
Reischauer, A. K., 541n.
Reischauer, Edwin O., 46n.
Rekosamudro, Pranato, 321
Republik Persatuan Indonesia (RPI; Indonesian Federal Republic), 474
Revolutionary Council, Burma, 220
Revolutionary Government of the Repub-

lic of Indonesia (PRRI), 121–23, 468, 470–80
Rewang, 312n.
Rey, Lucien, 314n.
Rhee, Syngman, 188
Riau, 474n., 475
Rice technology, 50
Riggs, Fred, 228n.
Rocher, Ludo, 27n.
Roem, Mohammed, 123
Roff, William R., 39n., 237n.
Rootselaar, F. J. van, 476n.
Rosjadi, Imron, 291n.
Rosovsky, Henry, 537n.
Roxas, Manuel, 379
Royal City, Bangkok, 76
Russo-Japanese War, 253

Sabah, 4, 13, 63n., 490n., 491, 509; independence movement in, 12; languages in, 6; overseas Chinese in, 435; population density of, 5 (*see also* Malaysia)
Saerang, Laurens, 477
Saigon, 72, 73, 74, 75, 76, 77, 79, 80, 82, 83
Saigon-Cholon, 75; overseas Chinese in, 85; population of, 84
Sailendra dynasty, 26n.
Sainu, Ahmed, 304n.
Saipradit, Kulab, 329n.
Sajidiman, Major, 300n.
Sakirman, 312n., 316n.
Salim, Hadji Agus, 120
Salween River, 59
Samsara, 528, 530
Samurai, 541, 542, 543
Sangha, 108
Sangkum (People's Socialist Community, Cambodia), 396, 397, 400
Santo Tomas, University of, Philippines, 190
Santri, 116, 205, 206, 208
Sanuk, 546
Sanusi, Ir., 116n.
Sarawak, 13, 63n., 88–97, 490n., 491; independence of, 12; languages in, 6; overseas Chinese in, 435; population density of, 5 (*see also* Malaysia)
Sarekat Islam, 39, 116, 117, 118
Sarekat Islam Merah, 117
Sarit, Thanarat, 190
Sastroamidjojo, Ali, 289, 468, 470n.
Sastrosatomo, Subadio, 123
Saya San revolt, Burma, 39
Sayadaw, 108
Sayadaw, Ledi, 528n.
Scalapino, Robert A., 310n.
Schrieke, B. J. O., 32

Schular, 546
Scott, J. G., 529
Seidenfaden, Erik, 482n.
Sejarah Melaju, 407
Sekolah Islam, 208
Selangor, 230n.
Seni, Anwar, 518
Serat Tjentini, 205
Shakyamuni, 105
Shan people, 59, 66, 68, 70, 346, 347
Shang period, 46
Sharp, Lauriston, 20, 47n., 50n., 158, 547n.
Shaw, S. J., 206n.
Shils, E., 287n.
Shinbyus, 108, 110
Shingaku, 541
Shintoism, 540, 541
Siam, 35, 58, 59, 61
Sieu Heng, 388
Siffin, William, 228n.
Sigit, Agus, 313, 318
Sihanouk, Prince Norodom, 11, 14, 244, 246, 393–402, 518n.
Simatupang, T. B., 288
Simbolon, Colonel, 289, 292, 470n., 473, 474, 475, 476, 478
Sinai, I. R., 214n.
Singapore, 4, 6, 9, 12, 13, 14, 63, 65, 67, 68, 70, 72, 73, 74, 76, 77, 80, 81, 82, 83, 84, 229, 230n., 423, 490–505, 507; independence of, 12; overseas Chinese in, 85, 435, 437–38; overseas Indians in, 86, 458–62; population density of, 5; population of, 85; press in, 493–94 (*see also* Malaysia)
Singapore, University of, 233
Sino-Tibetan ethnolinguistic group, 6
Siva-Buddhism, 26
Siyanon, Phin Chunhawan-Phao, 333
Sjahrir, Soetan, 252
Sjari'at, 120
Sjarifuddin, Amir, 121
Sjarir, Sutan, 123
Skinner, G. William, 442, 444, 448
Slater, R. L., 529n.
Smail, John R. W., 54n., 64
Smith, Roger M., 395n.
Smith, W., 202n.
Socialist Labor Federation, Indonesia, 306
Socialist Party of Indonesia (PSI), 122, 294, 295, 468, 472
Soedjatmoko, 210n.
Sokowati, Brigadier General, 300n.
Somers, Mary F., 448
Son Sann, 401
Song Ca Delta, 57n., 61
Songkhram, Phibun, 330, 331, 333, 336

Sontoku, Ninomya, 542n.
Souphanouvong, Prince, 388
South Celebes, 474n.
South Korea: economic progress in, 562; university students in, 188
South Moluccas, 474n.
South Sumatra, 474n.
South Vietnam, 12, 14; economic progress in, 559, 562n.; exports of, 65; overseas Chinese in, 67, 69; university students in, 191 (*see also* Vietnam)
Southeast Asia: agrarian nature of, 5; Balkanization of, 55–71; boundaries of, 7–9; cities in, 72–87; classical era of, 23–28; colonialism in, 9–10, 35–40; Communism in, 259–69; continuity and change in, 55–71; countryside of, 88–97; cultural continuities and discontinuities in, 45–54; definition of, 3; democratic regimes in, 12, 13; demography of, 4–6; early European involvement in, 33–34; economic progress in, 15–16, 556–83; geography of, 4–6; history of, 23–44; independence era in, 44; independence movements in, 10–12; Indianization of, 23, 26, 27, 29, 59, 60; industrial development in, 83–84; Islamization of, 31–33; Japanese occupation of, 40–44, 62; jungle of, 88–97; languages in, 6; military regimes in, 12–13; national integration in, 14–15; nationalism in, 38, 42, 62, 71, 247–58; overseas Chinese in, 67, 84, 431–49; overseas Indians in, 450–66; politics in, 9–14; population densities in, 5, 57; port cities in, 81–83; postclassical era in, 28–33; races in, 6; regionalism in, 506–22; religions in, 6–7, 26–28, 38–40; Sinicization of, 23, 27–28; strong-man rule in, 12, 13; university students in, 187–200; urban populations in, 84–86
Southeast Asia Command (SEAC), 3n.
Southeast Asia Treaty Organization (SEATO), 507
Southeast Asian Association for Regional Cooperation (SEAARC), 514, 515–18
Southeast Asian Conferences on Education and Transport, 519
Spain in Southeast Asia, 9
Spanish-American War (1898), 9
Spencer, J. E., 73n.
Spiro, Melford E., 104n.
Srivijaya, 25, 26n., 27, 58
Stalin, Joseph, 260
State Agricultural Bank, Burma, 344
Steiner, H. Arthur, 218n.
Stockdale, J. J., 76n.
Straits Settlements, 230n., 423, 459, 490n.

Subandrio, 183, 310, 311n., 316, 320, 322, 323n., 324, 516
Sufism, 29, 32
Suharto, 13, 127, 128, 131, 318, 321, 324, 325, 518n.
Suherman, Colonel, 313
Sujono, Major, 314n., 316n.
Sukarno, 13, 15, 68, 117, 118, 120, 122, 123, 128, 179, 180, 181, 182, 183, 188, 244, 246, 248n., 252, 266, 271–76, 288, 289, 290, 291–98, 303–25, 403–11, 468–71, 477, 479, 480, 514, 515n.
Sukiman, 120
Sulawesi (see Celebes)
Sultan Idris Training College, Malaya, 237
Sumardjo, 323, 324
Sumatra, 32, 52n., 62, 67, 121, 467–68; exports of, 65 (see also Indonesia)
Sumitro, 470n., 476, 478
Sumual, Colonel, 289, 292, 478
Sun Yat-sen, 64, 250, 252, 254, 266
Sunjwes, 108, 111
Sunni Islam, 204
Surakarta, 70
Suramit, King Norodom, 396
Suryadarma, Mrs. Utami, 314n.
Suryadarma, Utami, 312
Suwirjo, 470n.
Swaraj Movement, in India, 62

Ta Quang Buu, 388
Taik, 108
Taiwan, 4, 52n.
Takari, 183
Tan Malaka, 406
Tandjung Priok, Djakarta, 82
T'ang period, 46
Tantric Buddhism, 27
Tanwir, 129
Taoism, 26
Tapanuli, 474n.
Taqlid, 119
Tat, Oei Tjoe, 311n.
Tathagata, 105
Technical Institute, Bandung, 189
Tenasserim, 454
Tep Phan, 401
Teune, Henry, 491n.
Textor, Robert B., 24n.
Thai-Kadai ethnolinguistic group, 6
Thai people, 58, 70
Thailand, 4, 8, 9, 12, 35, 37n., 41, 70, 75, 245, 266, 267, 507, 508; bureaucracy in, 485–86; economic progress in, 535–49, 560, 561, 562, 564, 566, 569, 570, 571, 572, 575, 576, 580, 582; education in, 155–59, 486–87; exports of, 65; geography of, 4; industrialization in, 5; kin-

ship in, 550–55; military role in politics of, 326–39; overseas Chinese in, 67, 69, 435, 443–46; Phu Thai people of, 481–89; religions in, 7; universities in, 190; university students in, 192, 197, 200; value systems in, 535–49; village commerce in, 550–55; and Western culture, 145–61
Thajeb, Sjarif, 304n.
Thamavit, 546
Thammasat University, Thailand, 189, 190
Thanakan Thahan (Military Bank), Thailand, 336
Thanarat, Sarit, 333, 334
Thanat Khoman, 509, 514, 515, 516, 517
Thanthayah, 528
The Siauw Giap, 449
Thera, Narada, 530n.
Theravada Buddhism, 29, 30, 31, 33, 39, 540, 544
Thittila, U Bhikkhu, 104n.
Thok, 104
Thompson, Victor, 216n.
Thompson, Virginia, 252n.
Thonburi, Thailand, 75, 85n.
Tibeto-Burman people, 52n.
Tilman, Robert O., 100, 233n.
Timor, 9, 12, 70
Tito, 261
Tjhan, Siauw Giok, 314n.
Tjokroaminoto, Hadji Oemar Said, 116
Toba Batak people, 473, 474, 475
Tönnies, Ferdinand, 228
Ton Duc Thang, 388
Ton That Thien, 562n.
Tonkin, Sinicization of, 24
Tonle Sap River, 59
Toscano, James V., 491n.
Totoks, 441–43
Trager, Frank N., 547n.
Tran Huy Lieu, 385n.
Tran-Phu, 385
Tran Van Giau, 422
Trengganu, 230n.
Trinidad, Reuben F., 565n.
Tripitaka, 104
Triple jewel, 106
Truong Chinh, 385, 386, 388, 389
Tun Sein, 346
Turkey, 188
Tydings-McDuffie Act (1934), 11

Ubazein, 107
Uboneh, 105
Uchuwah Islamiyah, 125, 128
Ulama, 31, 32, 34, 43, 119, 206
Ummat, 115

Ummat Adam Ma'rifat Indonesia, 182
Union of Soviet Socialist Republics, in Southeast Asia, 16
United Malays National Organization (UMNO), 354, 355, 356, 357, 358, 359, 360, 491*n.*, 502, 503, 504, 505
United Nations Economic Commission for Asia and the Far East (ECAFE), 507
United Nations in Southeast Asia, 16
United Republic of Indonesia (RPI), 121
United States in Southeast Asia, 9, 11, 16, 62, 476
University College, Burma, 189
University of the East, Philippines, 190
University of the Far East, Philippines, 190
Untung, 313, 314*n.*, 318
Uppekkha, 546
USDEK, 294
Usman, Fahik, 129, 130
Utomo, Bambang, 407
Utrecht, E., 290*n.*

Van der Kroef, Justus, 33*n.*, 245, 305*n.*, 306*n.*, 323*n.*
Vandenbosch, Amry, 81*n.*
Vella, Walter F., 145, 544*n.*
Verba, Sidney, 450*n.*
Verenigde Oost Indische Compagnie (V.O.C.; United East India Company), 32, 34, 35
Vientiane, 277
Viet people, 52*n.*, 70
Vietminh (League for Revolution and Independence), 64, 387, 388
Vietnam, 4, 8, 10–11, 33, 42, 48, 51, 70; Buddhism in, 26; economic progress in, 556, 559; higher education in, 190; independence movement in, 10; nationalism in, 63–64; overseas Chinese in, 435; partition of, 64; religions in, 7, 28

(*see also* North Vietnam, South Vietnam)
Vlekke, B. H. M., 75*n.*
Vo Nguyen Giap, 385
Vredenbregt, J., 204*n.*

Wadah politik Islam, 125, 126
Wahhabism, 33, 39
Walcott, Robert, Jr., 364, 365, 366, 367, 368
Walinsky, Louis J., 214*n.*, 560*n.*, 567
Waliyul Amri Da-ruri, 183
Warouw, 470*n.*, 473
Weatherbee, Donald E., 404
Weber, Max, 25*n.*, 27*n.*, 221, 228*n.*
Weltevreden, Indonesia, 78, 79
Wertheim, W. F., 25*n.*, 39*n.*, 449
West Irian, 16
West Sumatra, 474*n.*, 475
Western New Guinea, 63, 69, 70
Wickberg, Edgar, 449
Wilkinson, R. J., 231, 237
Williams, Lea E., 448
Willmott, Donald E., 448
Willmott, E. W., 449
Willner, Ann Ruth, 100
Willner, Dorothy, 163*n.*
Wilson, David A., 245, 547*n.*
Wilson, Peter J., 460*n.*
Winstedt, R. O., 238
Wittfogel, Karl A., 25, 27, 28
Wolff, Robert, 100
Wright, Arthur F., 26*n.*

Yani, Ahmad, 306
Young Men's Buddhist Association, Burma, 39, 528
Yunnan, 51, 53

Zengakuren, 188
Zinkin, Maurice, 257*n.*

CONTRIBUTORS

ROSIHAN ANWAR, a well-known Indonesian journalist born in West Sumatra, has written widely on Islam and modernization in Indonesia. He served as editor of *Pedoman*, a socialist daily published in Djakarta, from 1948 to 1961, and he is a frequent contributor to many Indonesian publications.

ELIEZER B. AYAL was educated at Hebrew University in Jerusalem and Cornell University, where he received his Ph.D. degree in Economics in 1961. He is the author of a number of essays dealing with economic development and theory and is co-author of *Economic Nationalism in Southeast Asia* (1969). Dr. Ayal has served as a senior economist of the National Planning Association, Washington, D.C., since 1965.

HARRY J. BENDA, a native of Czechoslovakia, was educated in Europe and New Zealand before acquiring his Ph.D. degree at Cornell University in 1954. He served as an assistant professor of history at the State University of New York, Buffalo, before joining the faculty at Yale University in 1959. He is presently professor of history at Yale. Dr. Benda is the author of *The Crescent and the Rising Sun* (1958), and many articles and collections of readings dealing with modern Indonesian and Southeast Asian history.

BERNHARD DAHM, a native of Germany, received his Ph.D. degree from Christian-Albrechts-Universität, in Kiel, in 1964. He served as an assistant there before coming to Yale University as a post-doctoral fellow and lecturer in history in 1967. Dr. Dahm is the author of a number of studies in German, his major contribution being *Sukarnos Kampf Um Indonesiens Unabhängigkeit* (1966), which will appear in English shortly.

RUPERT EMERSON, professor of government at Harvard University, received his Ph.D. degree from the London School of Economics in 1927. His *Malaysia: A Study in Direct and Indirect Rule* (1937) was a pioneering English-language study. This was followed by numerous other important works including *Representative Government in Southeast Asia* (1955) and *From Empire to Nation* (1960).

BERNARD B. FALL, a Vienna-born French citizen, received his M.A. and Ph.D. degrees from the University of Syracuse. Professor of International Relations at Howard University, he was a distinguished journalist and scholar. Among his books are *Street Without Joy, Viet-Nam Witness* and *The Two Viet-Nams*. In 1966, he won the George Polk Memorial award for "outstanding interpretive reporting" of the Vietnamese war. In 1967, during his seventh visit to Vietnam, he was killed by a Viet-Cong mine near Hue.

HERBERT FEITH, an Australian, received his Ph.D. degree in political science from Cornell University in 1961. He joined the faculty at Monash University in 1962 and became chairman of the political-science department in 1969. His best-known work is *The Decline of Constitutional Democracy in Indonesia* (1962), and he has contributed many significant essays to learned journals and symposia volumes.

JOSEPH FISCHER, the author of *Universities of Southeast Asia* (1964), received his Ph.D. degree from the University of Chicago in 1958; he has taught at Rangoon University in Burma, Gadjah Mada University in Indonesia, and the University of California, Berkeley, where he is presently a research associate at the Center for Southeast Asian Studies.

CHARLES A. FISHER, British by birth, was educated at Cambridge, and he has served as professor of geography at the University of London since 1964. His *Southeast Asia: A Social, Economic and Political Geography* was published first in 1964 and in a second edition in 1966. In addition, he has made many significant shorter contributions to the field.

MAURICE FREEDMAN, a native of London, was educated at the University of London, where he presently serves as professor of anthropology at the London School of Economics. His work encompasses both East and Southeast Asia. Mr. Freedman's *Chinese Family and Marriage in Singapore* was published in 1957, and his *Chinese Lineage and Society: Fukien and Kwang Tung*, in 1966. His present research concerns China and the overseas Chinese and social organization in the New Territories of Hong Kong.

D. W. FRYER, also a London native, received his Ph.D. degree from the University of London in 1948, and he is now a member of the faculty of the Department of Geography of the University of Hawaii. Dr. Fryer is the author of *World Economic Development* (1965), and his *Growth and Stagnation: The Changing World of Southeast Asia* will be published in 1969.

W. R. GEDDES is an Australian born in New Zealand who obtained his Ph.D. degree at the London School of Economics in 1948, in anthropology. Dr. Geddes has worked in government and U.N. service in Sarawak and Thailand and has taught at the University of Auckland before moving to his present post of professor of social anthropology at the University of Sydney in 1959. Mr. Geddes has written anthropological studies on the Land Dayaks of Sarawak and hill-tribe problems in Thailand, in addition to his *Nine Dayak Nights*, from which a selection in this volume has been taken.

CLIFFORD GEERTZ received his Ph.D. degree in anthropology from Harvard University in 1956 and was associated with MIT, Harvard, and the University of California, Berkeley, before joining the faculty of the University of Chicago, where he now serves as professor of anthropology. His most significant monographs include *The Religion of Java* (1960), *Agricultural Involution* (1963), and *Islam Observed* (1968). Mr. Geertz is presently doing field work in Morocco.

BERNARD K. GORDON obtained his Ph.D. degree in international politics in 1959, at the University of Chicago, and taught at Vanderbilt University before becoming adjunct professor of political science at George Washington University and project director, Southeast Asia Studies, Research Analysis Corporation. His book *The Dimensions of Conflict in Southeast Asia* was published in 1966, and his volume *Toward Disengagement in Asia: A Strategy for American Foreign Policy* appeared in 1969.

JAMES F. GUYOT received his Ph.D. degree from Yale University in 1961 and has taught at the University of Rangoon, the University of Malaya, and the University of California at Los Angeles. He is now associate professor of government at Columbia University. His work on education and bureaucracy in Southeast Asia has appeared in several collections of essays.

JOEL M. HALPERN received his Ph.D. degree in anthropology from Columbia University in 1956 and taught at the University of California at Los Angeles and Brandeis University before moving, in 1967, to the University of Massachusetts, where he is presently associate professor of anthropology. His published monographs include *Economy and Society of Laos: A Brief Survey* (1964), in addition to the work on Laos from which the selection in this volume was taken.

R. HATLEY is a Ph.D. candidate in political science at Yale University who studied at Washington State University and the University of Ceylon before coming to Yale to enter the Southeast Asia M.A. program in 1965. He is presently undertaking field work in Indonesia.

A. THOMAS KIRSCH, who obtained his Ph.D. degree in anthropology at Harvard University in 1967, is now an assistant professor of anthropology at Princeton University. Several of his articles are already in print, and his monograph on "Religious Syncretism in Thailand" will be published soon.

CARL H. LANDÉ, born in Tübingen, Germany, received his Ph.D. degree in political science at Harvard University in 1958. He has undertaken extensive field research in the Philippines on three occasions since 1954, and he is presently at work on a historical study of urban politics in the Southern Tagalog region. Mr. Landé is the author of numerous essays, in addition to his *Leaders, Factions, and Parties: The Structure of Philippine Politics*, a portion of which is reprinted in this collection.

DANIEL S. LEV, who obtained his Ph.D. degree in political science at Cornell University in 1964, is presently an assistant professor of political science at the University of California, Berkeley. His study *The Transition to Guided Democracy in Indonesia* was published in 1965. Dr. Lev is presently at work on a study of the politics and sociology of legal change in Indonesia.

MOCHTAR LUBIS, who was educated in Sumatra, is one of Indonesia's most articulate intellectuals. He served as the editor and publisher of the influential *Indonesian Raya* from its creation in 1949 until the paper was closed by the government in 1958. He was imprisoned for short periods in 1956–57, placed under house arrest thereafter, released briefly in early 1961, and re-arrested and placed in prison later in 1961. His imprisonment lasted until Sukarno was ousted in the aftermath of the abortive coup attempt in 1965. Mr. Lubis is the author of *Twilight in Djakarta*, translated by Clare Holt (1963), and many newspaper and journal articles.

MYA MAUNG, a native of Burma, received his Ph.D. degree in economics at Catholic University in 1961 and served as the head of the Department of Economics of the Defense Services Academy, Maymyo, Burma, before moving to the United States in 1963. In 1966, he joined the Finance Department of Boston College, where he now holds the rank of associate professor. Mya Maung has written extensively on the impact of cultural forces on Burmese economic development, and he is presently completing a comparative study of the development experiences of Burma and Pakistan.

MICHAEL MOERMAN, who received his Ph.D. degree in anthropology from Yale University in 1964, has served as assistant professor of anthropology at the University of California at Los Angeles since that time. His *Agricultural Change and Peasant Choice in a Thai Village* was published in 1968, and he is presently working on an analysis of natural conversation in Thailand.

MANNING NASH received his Ph.D. degree in anthropology from the University of Chicago in 1955, and he has taught at that institution since 1957. He is presently professor of anthropology. *The Golden Road to Modernity: Village Life in Contemporary Burma* was published in 1965, and his study of social and economic modernization in northeastern Malaya will appear soon.

DOUGLAS S. PAAUW, director of the Center for Development Planning of the National Planning Association, received his Ph.D. degree in Economics from Harvard University in 1950 and taught at Nommensen University (Medan, Sumatra) and Yale University before joining the National Planning Association in 1963. His major works include *Financing Economic Development: The Indonesian Case* (1966) and *Development Planning in Asia* (1965).

K. J. RATNAM, a Malaysian citizen, received his Ph.D. degree at the London School of Economics and Political Science in 1960 and joined the faculty of the University of Singapore in the same year. He is presently professor of political science, head of the department, and dean of the Faculty of Social Sciences. His major monographs include *Communalism and the Political Process in Malaya* (1965) and *The Malaysian Parliamentary Elections of 1964* (with R. S. Milne, 1967).

LAURISTON SHARP, a former president of the Association for Asian Studies, obtained his Ph.D. degree in anthropology at Harvard University in 1937 after doing graduate work at the University of Vienna. He is presently professor of anthropology and Asian studies at Cornell University, where he was director of the Southeast Asian program. His work on rice farmers and hill tribes in Thailand has appeared in several monographs, and he co-authored the Human Relations Area Files' *Handbook on Thailand* (1956).

ROGER M. SMITH received his Ph.D. degree from Cornell University in 1964 and taught at Cornell, the University of Washington, and the University of Michigan before joining The Ford Foundation in 1969. Dr. Smith's *Cambodia's Foreign Policy* was published in 1965, and he is presently involved in a study of conflict and cooperation among Burma, Cambodia, Laos, Thailand, and North and South Vietnam.

ROBERT O. TILMAN received his Ph.D. degree in political science from Duke University in 1961 and served as an assistant professor of political science at

Tulane University before moving in 1965 to Yale University, where he is presently associate professor of political science. His publications include *Bureaucratic Transition in Malaya* (1964) and numerous essays in learned journals.

JUSTUS M. VAN DER KROEF, who was born in Djakarta, acquired his university education in the United States, receiving his Ph.D. degree at Columbia University in 1953. Dr. Van der Kroef has taught at Nanyang University, Singapore, and the University of the Philippines, and he is presently professor and chairman of the Department of Political Science of the University of Bridgeport. Of his many monographs, *The Communist Party of Indonesia: Its History, Program and Tactics* (1965) and *Communism in Malaya and Singapore: A Contemporary Survey* (1967) are the most recent.

LOUIS J. WALINSKY was born in London and educated at Cornell University and the New School for Social Research. Since 1949, he has served as a senior economist with Robert R. Nathan Associates. Mr. Walinsky was chief of an advisory mission to Burma during 1953–58. His publications include *Economic Development in Burma 1951–60* (1962) and other monographs and essays.

ANN RUTH WILLNER received her Ph.D. degree in international relations from the University of Chicago in 1961 and taught at the State University of New York, Binghamton, before serving as research associate at the Center for International Studies, Princeton University. She is presently associate professor of political science at the University of Kansas. Dr. Willner is the author of *The Neotraditional Accommodation to Political Independence: The Case of Indonesia* (1966) and *Charismatic Political Leadership: A Theory* (1968), in addition to other publications.

DAVID A. WILSON is an associate professor of political science at the University of California, Los Angeles, where he joined the faculty after he received his Ph.D. degree from Cornell University in 1960. Dr. Wilson's *Politics in Thailand* was published in 1962, and a second edition appeared in 1966.

ROBERT J. WOLFF was born in Surinam and did graduate work at the University of Michigan, where he was awarded a Ph.D. degree in social psychology in 1953. He is presently an associate professor of public health at the University of Hawaii. Dr. Wolff has published extensively on the social-psychological aspects of medicine and diet in changing societies.